LIFE AS THEATER

LIFE AS THEATER
a dramaturgical sourcebook

Dennis Brissett
The University of Minnesota
Duluth

Charles Edgley
Oklahoma State University
Stillwater

ALDINE PUBLISHING COMPANY   chicago

ABOUT THE EDITORS

Dennis Brissett is Associate Professor and Head of the Department of Behavioral Science, University of Minnesota School of Medicine at Duluth. He received his Ph.D. at the University of Minnesota and has been affiliated with State University of New York at Buffalo and Portland State University.

Charles Edgley received his Ph.D. at State University of New York at Buffalo. He is Associate Professor of Sociology at Oklahoma State University and Associate Professor of Sociology at Oklahoma Baptist University.

Copyright © 1975 by Aldine Publishing Company

All rights reserved. No part of this publication may be
reproduced or transmitted in any form or by any means,
electronic or mechanical, including photocopy, recording,
or any information storage and retrieval system,
without permission in writing from the publisher.

First published 1974 by
Aldine Publishing Company
529 South Wabash Avenue
Chicago, Illinois 60605

ISBN   0-202-30277-6   clothbound edition
       0-202-30278-4   paperbound edition

Library of Congress Catalog Number 74-82604

Printed in the United States of America

to
Ernest Becker

CONTENTS

FOREWORD

This book is about social psychology. It is a collection of articles written by a number of persons who appear to think in much the same manner about the nature of man and society. The contributors to this book, while they may differ in terms of research interests, methodological techniques and even academic disciplines, appear to approach the world with a common, albeit vaguely defined, perspective. We have sought to label this common frame of reference "dramaturgical" and this book is clearly an attempt to define and elucidate the nature of dramaturgical social psychology.

However, we feel that the book is much more than a simple delineation and illustration of a "way of thinking" in social psychology. It is, as well, an anthology of some awfully good pieces of social psychology. We have included only those writings in which the authors really appear "to swing" with their ideas. To us, the selections share an enthusiasm that is all too often lacking in the scholarship of social psychology: The contributors to this volume seem to enjoy the business of social psychology.

The book is organized around seven substantive issues in social psychology. As with all books of readings, this one is not an exhaustive treatment of these matters. Rather, we are hopeful that an exposure to these writings will stimulate the reader's interest in pursuing a larger understanding of the issues and, as well enhance his critical assessment of the current understanding. An attempt has been made in each section to provide a balance of theoretical discussion and empirical observation. We also have included in each section, readings of varying levels of difficulty. Consequently, some of the selections are much more challenging, and hopefully, more provocative, than others.

The appendix of materials by Kenneth Burke is included for persons who wish to delve into the development of the dramaturgical perspective in some depth. For those who wish to utilize the book principally as a general survey of readings in social psychology, the material in the appendix probably will be superfluous.

We, of course, want to express our appreciation to the authors whose works are reprinted here. As well, Charles Bolton and Ronny Turner contributed valuable input, both in terms of the concept and substance of this volume. We are also thankful for the valuable assistance of Lynn Furlong and Donna Purifry.

LIFE AS THEATER

INTRODUCTION

To someone encountering the field of social psychology for the first time, it must appear that being a social psychologist demands an unnerving commitment to ambiguity. For one thing, the definitional boundaries of the field are unclear, ranging from a grand eclectic fusion of sociology and psychology, on the one hand, to the rather narrow experimental study of interpersonal processes on the other. Furthermore, the content of these studies seems endless. Social psychologists study attitudes, motives, selves, stresses, perceptions, identities, leadership, anxiety, conformity—in fact, just about anything people do, or experience. Even the subjects of inquiry are various social psychologists have investigated the behavior of rats, dogs, chickens, apes, cats, ants, and fish as well as human beings.

To many people, however, the most bewildering aspect of the field stems from the great many theoretical orientations encompassed by the term, "social psychology." Owing much to the interdisciplinary character of the field, theoretical orientations have proliferated. Social psychology has become a "no-man's land" in which scholars from sociology, psychology, anthropology, and elsewhere have tried their hands at constructing their own unique version of reality. As a result, the student is confronted with a rather remarkable range of "truth." Too often it appears that a valid explanation by one social psychologist is dismissed as irrelevant trivia by another.

Within this spectrum of definitions, subject matter, and theoretical orientations is a body of social psychological thought and research that

1

has maintained a position of prominence over the years. Although more popular in sociology than psychology, it has served as a solid influence throughout the entire field. It is the basis for the branch of social psychology referred to as "symbolic interactionism." Originating in the early 1900's, symbolic interactionism rapidly became one of the dominant schools of thought in U. S. social psychology. With its growth in popularity came inevitable specialization; subtypes emerged, all sharing the same theoretical underpinnings but each providing its own peculiar emphasis and elaboration. One of these subtypes, dramaturgical theory, provides the focus for this book.

The historical development of dramaturgical social psychology is rather obscure and we will not attempt to describe its emergence in detail. However, its origins are usually traced to the writings of literary critic Kenneth Burke. In his early work, in the 1930's, Burke sketched the beginnings of what he came to develop as a "dramatistic model" of human behavior. According to Burke, human behavior is in the realm of action and purpose and, therefore, is most directly analyzable by terms that begin in theories of *action* rather than in theories of *knowledge*. For Burke, attempts to explain human action in terms of either the internal needs of the organism or the external conditioning of the environment tell us precious little about *human* interaction. Since people are not simply animals or machines, human interaction, Burke argues, is analyzed best in terms of drama. In other words, in order to achieve distinctively human satisfactions, people relate to each other as if they were actors playing roles.

Burke's model served as a springboard for many different types of concerns. Students of language and the arts, students of society, poets—all found his thinking provocative. His ideas found their way into social psychology largely through the efforts of Hugh Duncan. They were elaborated and given social psychological substance primarily in the work of Nelson Foote, Gregory Stone, and Erving Goffman. By working within a symbolic interactionist framework, these scholars were able to integrate the "dramatistic model" of Burke with many of the theoretical principles of social psychology. What began to emerge was a dramaturgical social psychology.

The Dramaturgical Perspective

Essentially, dramaturgical social psychology is the study of meaningful behavior. Meaning in this sense emerges out of the behavioral consensus between human actors. It is a consequence of at least two individuals responding in the same (or similar) ways to people and objects in their environment. The meaning of the wide range of behavior that constitutes an individual's social world is established only through human interaction. In this sense, meaning is not an inherent characteristic of one's world. Rather, a person builds up meaning through day-to-day activities with other people. What is crucial here is that meaning is not a stable, dependable thing. It is problematic. Take a simple, well-known, flat, white object. Write on it and it becomes a page of manuscript. Fold it up with wings and it's an airplane. Crush it and it's a ball. Throw it at somebody and it's a weapon. In each of these cases, the meaning of the object is established by how it is acted upon. In a fundamental sense, the meaning of anything is continually being established and reestablished by behavior toward that something. Meaning is not a given; people create it.

The nature of meaning can be illustrated by briefly examining the manner in which dramaturgists describe a person's individuality. Like most sociologically based social psychologists, dramaturgists utilize the term, "self," rather than personality, when speaking of individuality. Unlike most social psychologists, dramaturgists describe "self" as simply the meaning of the human organism. In dramaturgical analysis the meaning of a human organism is established by its activity and the activity of others with respect to it. The self is not something that, once formed, is inherent in the individual. A person's individuality is a shared, interactive phenomenon. Likewise, one's self is not an artifact that is carried from situation to situation. Nor is it internal to the organism and reflected in one's behavior. There is no "ghost in the machine" that makes people act in certain ways. Selves are outcomes, not antecedents of human interaction. What you do establishes who you are, not the other way around.

This emphasis on the problematic-interactive nature of human meaning provides the dramaturgical approach with a unique basis for handling many of the traditional concerns of social psychology. For instance, socialization has long been understood to be a social process in which the human being is molded in accordance with a particular culture. That is, the socialization process is said to define the various meanings of a person's world through a kind of "social inheritance." Dramaturgists would prefer, on the other hand, to think of socialization as a process whereby a person is provided with basic resources that enable him to act meaningfully, not in narrowly prescribed ways but in terms of the whole range of human possibilities. In this sense, the socialized individual is not most usefully understood as a repository of cultural meanings and values. Rather, the individual is viewed as one who is capable of creating new meanings or, at the very least, helping to reestablish the old. Victims of the socialization process (e.g., those persons who come to be labeled mentally ill) should be viewed as ignorant of cultural resources and human alternatives, not as having developed inadequate personalities or psychological disturbances that are allegedly reflected by their behavior.

In fact, dramaturgists shy away from construing one's society and one's self as distinct entities. Socialization, then, is not something society does to the individuals within it. The reality of society, and of the socialization process itself, is to be found only in the interaction between individuals. Therefore the terms generally used to refer to individuals and societies are noticeably absent from dramaturgical analysis; notions of needs, desires, drives, cognitions, etc., often used to describe individuals, are not a part of the dramaturgical lexicon. Likewise, ideas of social organization and social structure are viewed, for the most part, as describing only the very general framework within which human activity occurs.

This fusion of the individual and society and the insistence that human activity be examined within the framework of interaction is buttressed by an epistemological stance that impugns any form of classic determinism. The focus of dramaturgical social psychology is not to discover or impute to human behavior causal relationships, whether of a cultural-social or individualistic nature. Likewise, dramaturgical understanding of human behavior does not involve explaining the causal relations between individual characteristics and elements of the culture or society. Rather, the concern is simply to describe the process of human behaving. This involves a prospective analysis of the possible consequences of ongoing activity and does not lead to a retrospective search for the antecedents of this activity. For instance, dramaturgists claim that the most useful understanding of a person's current difficulties (e.g., depression) lies in terms of the possible (future) behavioral responses of the person and others to these difficulties. A documentation of the series of historical antecedents that allegedly produced the difficulties does little to illuminate how to deal with one's current problems.

The sequences and patterns of behavior discussed by dramaturgists are expressed in very conditional terms. The conditions, moreover, are invariably considered to be of a necessary but not a sufficient cast. That is, although certain behavior may be construed as a necessary condition for future activities (e.g., the consumption of ethanol is a necessary condition for becoming an alcoholic), in no way should present activity be viewed as sufficient to guarantee an inevitable future (e.g., consuming ethanol does not guarantee that one will ever be an alcoholic). Dramaturgy provides the basis for a formalistic analysis of the processes of man's interaction. Descriptive understanding, not explanation, is the goal of this analysis.

This general indeterminancy of dramaturgical understanding carries with it a stance of extreme relativity. Even more than most other social psychologists, dramaturgists construe human activity as related to particular temporal and spatial arrangements. That human behavior is relative to the broad outlines of culture has been established beyond doubt by sociologists and anthropologists. People, however, do not act in the culture-at-large but rather in terms of immediate personal circumstances. Thus people's behavior is not only relative to the culture in which they live but also to the situation that they help to create. An understanding of individual behavior necessarily involves a sensitive analysis of individual circumstances.

The emphasis on the active-doing nature of human beings has, in fact, led dramaturgists to reevaluate what is meant by "situational behavior." The conventional understanding of the relation between a person's behavior and their social situation has been that individuals come to situations, define them, and then (and only then) act in them. The "definition of the situation" is construed as essentially mentalistic; it is an interpretation people make of their environment. The human being is said to act only after the environment has been identified and conceptualized.

In contrast to this, the dramaturgical view is that people act, and it is in the process of their activity that situations come to be defined. Definitions of situations are themselves activities, not mentalistic tracings; rather than residing in the heads of social actors, they are located squarely in interaction. In fact, a considerable part of every individual's activity involves influencing (not necessarily intentionally) the "definition of the situation" of others. Using the imagery of the theater, dramaturgists claim that social actors manipulate such elements of the situation as stage props and equipment. The character of this manipulation gives others a certain impression of the actor and his circumstance. This is not to say that definitions of situations are interpretations made on the basis of staging and associated activity; rather, they *are* the staging and associated activity. The actors' appearances and stagings and the audiences' responses, all of which are activities, are said to define situations. The very process of defining is therefore interactional.

Underlying the dramaturgical conception of the social world are the general assumptions that human beings are symbol users and that their symbols take on meaning in the course of interaction. In fact, symbols are said to be the most important resource one acquires through socialization. In a sense, dramaturgical theory is simply an attempt to describe the process whereby the symbolic productions of human beings become meaningful. However, the focus on the variety of ways in which people establish meaning has forced the dramaturgists to consider a wider spectrum of communication than that which is traditionally labeled symbolic. Most social psychological attempts to understand human communication have been concerned almost exclusively with verbal (denotative) behavior. The dramaturgical view, on the other hand, emphasizes also the significance of nonverbal (connotative) forms of communication. People are said not only to create impressions through verbalizations but also to give them off by means of an enormous variety of nonverbal behavior. *How* individuals go about "saying" and "doing" becomes as important a consideration as *what* they say and do. Implicit as well as explicit communication is recognized as a salient context for human interaction.

The general nature of the dramaturgical perspective may be illustrated in terms of how it deals with human motivation. Taking as a point of departure John Dewey's dictum that all people are characteristically active, dramaturgical analysis does not involve any speculation as to why this activity originates. Rather, it is an attempt to identify the directions action takes. Consequently, motives are not viewed as forces that stir people to act. Rather, motives are communications, verbal and nonverbal, that are utilized in certain encounters to justify or rationalize the conduct of the actors in that encounter. Motives enable certain interactions to persist; their absence may make the interaction tenuous. In this sense, motives are understood as elements in situations, not as phenomena that reside in individuals, societies, or cultures.

This conception of motivation points to an extremely important relationship between motives and the self that is not ordinarily emphasized in social psychology. Previously we discussed self as the meaning of the organism and argued that this meaning is established in social interaction between an actor and a validating audience. Motives play an important part in this process, for they "turn on" understanding in problematic situations by linking the question of who one is with the question of what one is doing. This linkage provides us with a way of understanding how the various identities that comprise self are created, whether those identities be routine as "mother" or "father" or deviant as "mentally ill" or "criminal." To know the identity of a person is to know that person's motives, for the identities into which a person is cast assume the motives which are to be imputed to that person. As a matter of fact, we very often answer questions about our motives by simply stating who we are. To be motivated then, is not to be energized by internal or external forces. Rather, it is simply to be in communication with others about the sense of one's potentially questionable behavior.

This dramaturgical conception of motivation implies a final assertion about the nature of human beings. In many theories of motivation, an individual who is motivated is generally viewed as being conscious: of oneself (and others), of one's behavior, and of the relation between oneself and one's behavior. The motivated activity of a person is generally construed as rational, at least in terms of consciousness of self and others. Within the dramaturgical frame of reference, however, this is not necessarily so. People are not considered as rational; they are rationalizing. Only when an individual's activity is interrupted does one become conscious of oneself, and then in a rationalizing manner. As paraphrased in much the same context elsewhere, it is not so much a matter of something believed to be true being true in its consequences (a traditional notion in social psychology); rather, something believed to be true is true *only* in its consequences. Motivation, similar to all that is true of human life, is again defined in terms of a basic human faculty: meaningful communication.

The nature of the dramaturgical perspective can be summarized by a delineation of its nine principal characteristics:

1. It is the study of meaningful behavior; meaning is viewed as problematic, arising in and through interaction.
2. It views one's sense of individuality (one's self) as established, not reflected, in interaction.
3. It views socialization as a process that furnishes the resources for situational variation, not as one that produces mechanisms for insuring cultural uniformity.
4. It rejects classic determinism; its method is prospective rather than retrospective.
5. It is situationally, as well as culturally, relativistic.
6. It views situations as defined interactionally, not mentalistically.
7. It views the human being as fundamentally a communicator.
8. It views interaction and situations, not individuals, as the locus of motivation.
9. It views human beings as consciously rationalizing, not consciously rational.

SUGGESTED READINGS

Blumer, Herbert. *Symbolic Interactionism* (Englewood Cliffs: Prentice-Hall, 1969).

Burke, Kenneth. *Permanence and Change* (New York: Bobbs-Merrill Co., Inc., 1965).

Burns, Elizabeth. *Theatricality* (New York: Harper and Row, 1972).

Dewey, John. "On Motive," from Dewey, J., *Human Nature and Conduct* (New York: Holt, Rinehart and Winston, 1922), pp. 119-120.

Dewey, Richard. "The Theoretical Analogy Reconsidered," *American Sociologist* (November, 1969), pp. 307-311.

Duncan, Hugh. *Communication and the Social Order* (New York: Bedminster Press, 1962).

Goffman, Erving. *Relations In Public* (New York: Basic Books, 1971).

Hall, Edward. *The Hidden Dimension* (Garden City, N. Y.: Doubleday and Company, Inc., 1966).

Kuhn, Manford. "Major Trends in Symbolic Interaction Theory in the Past Twenty-Five Years," *Sociological Quarterly* V (Winter, 1964) pp. 61-84.

Lofland, J., "Morals Are The Message: The Work of Erving Goffman," *Psychiatry and Social Science Review*, Vol. 4, No. 9 (July, 1970) pp. 17-19.

Lyman, Sanford and Marvin Scott. *A Sociology of the Absurd* (New York: Appleton-Century-Crofts, 1970).

Stone, Gregory and Harvey Farberman. *Social Psychology Through Symbolic Interaction* (Waltham, Mass.: Ginn-Blaisdell, 1970).

Tiryakiran, A., "Existential Phenomenology and the Sociological Tradition," *American Sociological Review*, Vol. 34, No. 6, pp. 922-934.

Zicklin, G., "A Conversation Concerning Face-To-Face Interaction," *Psychiatry* Vol. 31, No. 3 (August, 1968) pp. 236-249.

I. THE NATURE OF SOCIAL LIFE

One recurring—some would say dominant—theme in the history of social psychology has been an attempt to describe and analyze the nature of the social bond. Whether cast in the language of group cohesion, consciousness of kind, herd instinct, or reward and punishment, most social psychologists have wrestled with the question of "How is it that people cooperate with each other?" The task has been to account for the relations between seemingly discrete individuals that make for social solidarity.

Dramaturgists, too, have turned their attention to this problem but have asked a slightly different question. They are not so much concerned with social consensus as such, but rather with the ways in which people both facilitate and interfere with the ongoing behavior of others. The metaphor used here to explore this concern is the theater, the emphasis being on the interactive nature of the social bond. Cooperation, hostility, solidarity, conflict—these are all viewed as among the possibilities of social life. They are human possibilities, which is to say they are created and sustained only through human interaction.

In the readings that follow, we hope you will see the unique view of social life that emerges out of this intense focus on the interactive process. The readings deal with different dimensions of social life, but each of the four authors informs his discussion with the question: what difference does "it" make in interaction? And this indeed is *the* dramaturgical question.

The selection by Peter Berger is an excerpt from a larger work in which

9

Berger squarely confronts the question of human freedom. The context of his dramatic image of social life is his larger argument against the more deterministic views of human existence. Although recognizing that many conventional approaches of social science exclude freedom as a human possibility, Berger argues that neither the internal nor external controls on human beings may be as infallible as alleged. People exercise control themselves, inasmuch as they are definers of social situations. All situations and indeed all social structures are built up by people and therefore can be modified by them.

> No social structure, however massive it may appear in the present, existed in this massivity from the dawn of time. Somewhere along the line each of its salient features was concocted by human beings, whether they were charismatic visionaries, clever crooks, conquering heroes or just individuals in positions of power who hit on what seemed to them a better way of running the show. Since all social systems were created by men, it follows that men can also change them.[1]

It follows also that if the control systems in a society are to persist, they must be supported by the individuals in that society. They are in constant need of confirmation and reconfirmation by the very persons they are meant to control. People can withhold this confirmation in three possible ways: through *transformation, detachment,* and *manipulation.* It is on the possibility of manipulation that Berger builds his dramaturgical image of social life.

The key to Berger's dramaturgical perspective is that in manipulation people do not attempt to change the social structure, nor do they detach themselves from it. Rather, they choose to make deliberate use of the structure in accordance with their own purposes.[2] Here the individual can capture a sense of freedom, can experience a sense of personal control. It is, in fact, in the change of consciousness occasioned by manipulation that Berger locates the focus of the dramaturgical view of social life. This consciousness he exemplifies in two principal concepts, *role distance* and *ecstasy. Role distance* pertains to those situations in which an individual is truly playing-with-a-role. The individual is playing a social part with full consciousness and thereby has the choice of either modifying the part or ceasing to play it altogether. *Ecstasy* seems almost a necessary concomitant to persistent role distance. It refers to standing or stepping outside the taken-for-granted world of everyday life. *Ecstasy* changes one's awareness of social life. It obliterates the absolutes; the things people do, and the things people believe, all be-

---

1. Berger, Peter, *Invitation to Sociology* (New York: Anchor Books, 1963), p. 128.
2. On this point dramaturgists are often criticized for building an image of man as conniving, deceitful, and even anti-social. However, it is clear that man can have many types of purposes, some honorable, some not. Therefore, it seems somewhat Hobbesian on the part of the critics to argue that the clever use of the social structure inevitably has all of the negative chracteristics they ascribe to it.

come relative to particular events and situations. In Berger's words, "ecstasy transforms one's awareness of society in such a way that *givenness* becomes *possibility*."

Within this frame of reference, Berger presents what is probably the clearest characterization of the dramaturgical view of society. He concludes by analyzing the "reality" of freedom. His discussion of human choice and liberty does much to embellish and extend the dramaturgical image of human existence.

The selection by Nelson Foote attempts to apply the dramatistic analysis of Kenneth Burke to the social psychology of human development. Foote takes as his starting point not some *a priori* set of stages through which humans are alleged to develop but rather the analysis of episodes of interaction. The understanding of human development is construed as the understanding of how episodes of interaction condition each other. In his words, "development occurs as the cumulative product of successive outcomes of episodes of interaction."

Although Foote dwells a bit more on the connections between episodes than is consistent with a truly dramaturgical perspective, he beautifully explores the essentially episodic and situational character of social life. His argument evolves around four principal assertions: (1) episodic organization is characteristic of human behavior; (2) there are no hiatuses in behavior, and one episode begins where the other ends; (3) there is an implicit compulsion to finish an episode once begun; and (4) episodes have a "story" quality. Foote's discussion of the substance and implication of these assertions is richly dramaturgical. Running through his characterization of developmental trends is the basic observation that situations, people, and behavior are all revealed in episodes. Human interaction is depicted as a precarious, exploratory, and ambiguous undertaking whose every outcome is uncertain.

In the selection by Messinger *et al.*, the authors dwell on the relation of people to their everyday interactions. Although they espouse a rather arbitrary (and consequently, debatable) distinction between "being on" and "being natural," the authors deal very well with the fact that certain persons become conscious of their "playing-at-roles" and that this consciousness is sometimes disturbing. However, their generalization regarding the abnormality of "being on" should be tempered by the realization (which we will examine in Part VI) that whatever else mentally ill people may be, they are most assuredly "bad actors." Finally, the authors clarify a very important element of dramaturgical analysis: that dramaturgy does not attempt to present a model of the actor's consciousness. Rather, the theatrical model serves as a metaphor for focusing attention on the consequences of human interaction. In this context, consciousness of self and others is simply another variable, albeit an important one.

In the selection by Orrin Klapp, the nature of modern society is described in terms of the resources (or lack of them) that are available for human interaction. Klapp's general thesis is that many persons in modern society suffer from a lack of identity and that this stems from faults in the nature of social life. With remarkable insight, Klapp traces the interactive consequences of the vast accumulation of impersonal, objective knowledge at the expense of knowledge that has personal connection; the modernization process, whereby place is transformed into space; mobility, wherein person becomes category; and the decline of identifying ritual and ceremony.

SUGGESTED READINGS

Becker, Ernest. The Birth and Death of Meaning, (Glencoe: The Free Press, 1962).

Berger, Peter and Thomas Luckmann. The Social Construction of Reality, (New York: Anchor Paperbacks, 1967).

Burke, Kenneth. Language as Symbolic Action, (Berkeley: University of California Press, 1966).

Birenbaum, Arnold and Edward Sagarin. People In Places, (New York: Praeger Publishers, 1973).

Farberman, Harvey and William Goode. Social Reality, (Englewood Cliffs, N. J.: Prentice-Hall, 1973).

Glasser, William. The Identity Society, (New York: Harper and Row, 1972).

Goffman, Erving. Behavior in Public Places, (New York: The Free Press, 1963).

Henry, Jules. On Sham, Vulnerability, and Other Forms of Self-Destruction, (New York: Vintage Books, 1973).

Ichheiser, Gustav. Appearances and Realities, (San Francisco: Jossey-Bass, Inc., 1970).

Laing, R. D. The Politics of Experience, (New York: Pantheon Books, 1967).

McCall, George (ed.). Social Relationships, (Chicago: Aldine Publishing Co., 1970).

Roszak, Theodore. Where The Wasteland Ends, (Garden City, N. Y.: Doubleday and Co., Inc., 1972).

1. SOCIOLOGICAL PERSPECTIVES— SOCIETY AS DRAMA

Reprinted from *Invitation to Sociology*, copyright © 1963 by Peter L. Berger. Reprinted by permission of Doubleday & Company, Inc. Peter Berger is Professor of Sociology at Rutgers University. He is the author of *The Social Construction of Reality* (with Thomas Luckmann), and numerous articles and books dealing with the sociology of religion.

The discussion of the art of "ploying" has already brought us close to the third major way of escaping the tyranny of society, that of manipulation. Here the individual does not try to transform the social structures nor does he detach himself from them. Rather he makes deliberate use of them in ways unforeseen by their legitimate guardians, cutting a path through the social jungle in accordance with his own purposes. Erving Goffman, in his analysis of the world of "inmates" (be it of mental hospitals or prisons or other coercive institutions), has given us vivid examples of how it is possible to "work the system," that is, to utilize it in ways not provided for in the official operating procedures. The convict who works in the prison laundry and uses its machinery to wash his own socks, the patient who gets access to the staff communications system to transmit personal messages, the soldier who manages to transport his girl friends in military vehicles—all these are "working the system," thereby proclaiming their own relative independence of its tyrannical demands. It would be rash to dismiss such manipulations too quickly as pathetic and ineffective efforts at rebellion. There have been instructive cases in which motor-pool sergeants successfully ran call-girl rings and hospital patients used the official message center as a bookie joint, such operations going on in subterranean fashion for long periods of time. And industrial sociology is full of examples of how workers can employ the official organization of a factory for purposes deviant from and sometimes contradictory to the intentions of management.

The ingenuity human beings are capable of in circumventing and subverting even the most elaborate control system is a refreshing antidote to sociologistic depression. It is as relief from social determinism that we would explain the sympathy that we frequently feel for the swindler, the impostor or the charlatan (as long, at any rate, as it is not ourselves who are being swindled). These figures symbolize a social Machiavellianism that understands society thoroughly and then, untrammeled by illusions, finds a way of manipulating society for its own ends. In literature there are characters such as Andre' Gide's Lafcadio or Thomas Mann's Felix Krull that illustrate this fascination. In real life we could point to a man like Ferdinand Waldo Demara, Jr., who bamboozled a long line of eminent specialists in various fields into accepting him as a colleague, successfully impersonating such respected social identities as college professor, military officer, penologist and even surgeon. Inevitably, in watching the swindler take on various roles of respectable society, we are pushed towards the uncomfortable impression that those who hold these roles "legitimately" may have attained their status by procedures not so drastically different from the ones employed by him. And if one knows the bamboozling, bunkum and (to use Potter's term) "one-up-manship" that go into, say, a professorial career one may even come dangerously close to the conclusion that society is a swindle to begin with. In one way or another, we are all impostors. The ignoramus impersonates erudition, the crook honesty, the skeptic conviction—and any normal university could not exist without the first confidence trick, no business organization without the second and no church without the third.

Another concept elaborated by Goffman is helpful in this connection—the one he calls "role distance." By this Goffman means the playing of a role tongue-in-cheek, without really meaning it and with an ulterior purpose. Every strongly coercive situation will produce this phenomenon. The "native" underling plays up to the pukka sahib in the expected way while planning the day on which all white throats will be cut. The Negro domestic plays the role of self-depreciating [sic] clown, and the enlisted man that of spick-and-span military fanatic, both with hindthoughts that are diametrically contrary to the mythology within which their roles have a meaning they inwardly reject. As Goffman points out, this kind of duplicity is the only way by which human dignity can be maintained within the self-awareness of people in such situations. But Goffman's concept could be applied more widely to all cases where a role is played deliberately without inner identification, in other words, where the actor has established an inner distance between his consciousness and his role-playing. Such cases are of paramount importance for sociological perspective because they depart from the normal pattern. This, as we have been at pains to point out, is that roles are played without reflection, in immediate and al-most automatic response to the expectations of the situation. Here this fog of unconsciousness is suddenly dispelled. In many instances this may not affect the visible course of events, yet it constitutes a qualitatively different form of existence in society. "Role distance" marks the point at which the marionette clown becomes Bajaccio —the puppet theater is transformed into a living stage. Of course, there is still a script, a stage management and a repertoire that includes one's own role. But one is now playing the part in question with full consciousness. As soon as this happens, there is the ominous possibility that Bajaccio may jump out of his role and start playing the tragic hero—or that Hamlet may begin to do somersaults and sing dirty ditties. Let us repeat our previous assertion that all revolutions begin in transformations of consciousness.

A useful concept to introduce in this connection is that of "ecstasy." By this we refer not to some abnormal heightening of consciousness in a mystic sense, but rather, quite literally, to the act of standing or stepping outside (literally, ekstasis) the taken-for-granted routines of society. In our discussion of "alternation" we have already touched upon a very important form of "ecstasy" in our sense, namely, the one that takes place when an individual is enabled to jump from world to world in his social existence. However, even without such an exchange of universes it is possible to achieve distance and detachment vis-à-vis one's own world. As soon as a given role is played without inner commitment, deliberately and deceptively, the actor is in an ecstatic state with regard to his "world-taken-for-granted." What others regard as fate, he looks upon as a set of factors to reckon with in his operations. What others assume to be essential identity, he handles as a convenient disguise. In other words, "ecstasy" transforms one's awareness of society in such a way that *givenness* becomes *possibility*. While this begins as a state of consciousness, it should be evident that sooner or later there are bound to be significant consequences in terms of action. From the point of view of the official guardians of order, it is dangerous to have too many individuals around playing the social game with inner reservations.

The consideration of "role distance" and "ecstasy" as possible elements of social existence raises an interesting sociology-of-knowledge question, namely, whether there are social contexts or groups that particularly facilitate such consciousness. Karl Mannheim, who greatly favored such a development on ethical and political grounds (a position that some might want to debate), spent a good deal of time looking for its possible social ground. His view of the "freely suspended intelligentsia" (that is, of a stratum of intellectuals with minimal involvement in the vested interests of society) as the best carriers of this sort of liberated consciousness may be disputed. At the same time, there can be little doubt that certain kinds of intellectual training and activity are capable of leading to "ecstasy," as we indicated in our discussion of the forms of detachment.

Other tentative generalizations can be made. "Ecstasy" is more likely to take place in urban than in rural cultures (*vide* the classic role of cities as places of political freedom and liberality in thought), among groups that are marginal to society than among those at its center (*vide* the historic relationship of European Jews to various liberating intellectual movements— or, in a very different way, take the example of the itinerant Bulgarian journeymen carrying the Manichaean heresy all the way across Europe into Provence), as it is also more likely in groups that are insecure in their social position than among those that are secure (*vide* the production of debunking ideologies among rising classes that have to fight against an established order, the rising French bourgeoisie in the seventeenth and eighteenth centuries providing us with a prime example). Such social location of the phenomenon reminds us once more that not even total rebellion takes place in a social vacuum without predefinitions. Even nihilism is predefined in terms of the structures it is driven to negate—before one can have atheism, for instance, there must be an idea of God. In other words, every liberation from social roles takes place within limits that are social themselves. Nevertheless, our consideration of the various forms of "ecstasy" has taken us some way from the deterministic corner into which our previous argument had chased us.

We thus arrive at a third picture of society, after those of the prison and the puppet theater, namely that of society as a stage populated with living actors. This third picture does not obliterate the previous two, but it is more adequate in terms of the additional social phenomena we have considered. That is, the dramatic model of society at which we have arrived now does not deny that the actors on the stage are constrained by all the external controls set up by the impresario and the internal ones of the role itself. All the same, they have options—of playing their parts enthusiastically or sullenly, of playing with inner conviction or with "distance," and, sometimes, of refusing to play at all. Looking at society through the medium of this dramatic model greatly changes our general sociological perspective. Social reality now seems to be precariously perched on the cooperation of many individual actors—or perhaps a better simile would be that of acrobats engaged in perilous balancing acts, holding up between them the swaying structure of the social world.

Stage, theater, circus and even carnival—here we have the imagery of our dramatic model, with a conception of society as precarious, uncertain, often unpredictable. The institutions of society, while they do in fact constrain and coerce us, appear at the same time as dramatic conventions, even fictions. They have been invented by past impresarios, and future ones may cast them back into the nothingness whence they emerged. Acting out the social drama we keep pretending that these precarious conventions are eternal verities. We act *as if* there were no other way of being a man, a political subject, a religious devotee or one who exercises a certain profession—yet at times the thought passes through the minds of even the dimmest among us that we could do very, very different things. If social reality is dramatically created, it must also be dramatically malleable. In this way, the dramatic model opens up a passage out of the rigid determinism into which sociological thought originally led us.

Before we leave behind us our narrower sociological argument we would like to point to a classical contribution that is very relevant to the points just made—the theory of sociability of the German sociologist Georg Simmel, a contemporary of Weber's whose approach to sociology differed considerably from the latter's. Simmel argued that sociability (in the usual meaning of this word) is the play-form of social interaction. At a party people "play society," that is, they engage in many forms of social interaction, but

without their usual sting of seriousness. Sociability changes serious communication to noncommittal conversation, *eros* to coquetry, ethics to manners, aesthetics to taste. As Simmel shows, the world of sociability is a precarious and artificial creation that can be shattered at any moment by someone who refuses to play the game. The man who engages in passionate debate at a party spoils the game, as does the one who carries flirtation to the point of open seduction (a party is *not* an orgy) or the one who openly promotes business interests under the guise of harmless chitchat (party conversation must at least pretend to be disinterested). Those who participate in a situation of pure sociability temporarily leave behind their "serious" identities and move into a transitory world of make-believe, which consists among other things of the playful pretense that those concerned have been freed from the weights of position, property and passions normally attached to them. Anyone who brings in the gravity (in both senses of the word) of "serious" outside interests immediately shatters this fragile artifice of make-believe. This, incidentally, is why pure sociability is rarely possible except among social equals, since otherwise the pretense is too strenuous to maintain—as every office party shows painfully.

We are not particularly interested in the phenomenon of sociability for its own sake, but we can now relate what Simmel maintains about it to our earlier consideration of Mead's notion that social roles are learned through play. We contend that sociability could not exist at all as the artifice it is if society at large did not have a similarly artificial character. In other words, sociability is a special case of "playing society," more consciously fictitious, less tied up with the urgent ambitions of one's career—but yet of one piece with a much larger social fabric that one can also play with. It is precisely through such play, as we have seen, that the child learns to take on his "serious" roles. In sociability we return for some moments to the masquerading of childhood—hence perhaps the pleasure of it.

But it is assuming too much to think that the masks of the "serious" world are terribly different from those of this world of play. One plays the masterful *raconteur* at the party and the man of firm will at the office. Party tact has a way of being translated into political finesse, shrewdness in business into the adroit handling of etiquette for purposes of sociability. Or, if you like, there is a nexus between "social graces" and social skills in general. In this fact lies the sociological justification of the "social" training of diplomats as well as of debutantes. By "playing society" one learns how to be a social actor anywhere. And this is possible only because society as a whole has the character of a play. As the Dutch historian Johan Huizinga has brilliantly shown in his book *Homo ludens*, it is impossible to grasp human culture at all unless we look at it *sub specie ludi*—under the aspect of play and playfulness. . . .

As we remarked before, only an intellectual barbarian is likely to maintain that reality is only that which can be grasped by scientific methods. Since, hopefully, we have tried to stay out of this category, our sociologizing has been carried on in the foreground of another view of human existence that is not itself sociological or even scientific. Nor is this view particularly eccentric, but rather the common (if very differently elaborated) anthropology of those who credit man with the capacity for freedom. Obviously, a philosophical discussion of such an anthropology would utterly break the framework of this book and would, for that matter, lie beyond the competence of its writer. But while no attempt will be made here to provide a philosophical introduction to the question of human freedom, it is necessary to our argument that at least some indications be given of how it is possible to think sociologically without abandoning this notion of freedom, and, more than that, in what way a view of man that includes the idea of freedom may take cognizance of the social dimension. We contend that here is an important area of dialogue between philosophy and the social sciences that still contains vast tracts of virgin territory. We point to the work of Alfred Schuetz and to the contemporary efforts of Maurice Natanson as indicating the direction in which this dialogue could move. Our own remarks in the following pages will, of necessity, be exceedingly sketchy. But it is hoped that they will suffice to indicate to the reader that sociological thought need not necessarily end in a positivistic swamp.

We shall now begin with the postulate that men are free and from this new starting point return to the same problem of social existence. In doing this, we shall find helpful some concepts developed by existentialist philosophers (though we shall use these without any doctrinaire intentions). Herewith the reader is invited to undertake an epistemological *salto mortale*—and this behind him, to return to the matter at hand.

Let us now retrace our steps to the point where we looked at Gehlen's theory of institutions. The latter, we will recall, are interpreted in this theory as channeling human conduct

very much along the lines that instincts channel the behavior of animals. When we considered this theory,
we made the remark that there is, however, one crucial difference between
the two kinds of channeling: The animal, if it reflected on the matter of following its instincts, would say, "I have
no choice." Men, explaining why they
obey their institutional imperatives,
say the same. The difference is that the
animal would be saying the truth; the
men are deceiving themselves. Why?
Because, in fact, they can say "no" to
society, and often have done so. There
may be very unpleasant consequences
if they take this course. They may not
even think about it as a possibility, because they take their own obedience
for granted. Their institutional character may be the only identity they can
imagine having, with the alternative
seeming to them as a jump into madness. This does not change the fact that
the statement "I must" is a deceptive
one in almost every social situation.

From our new vantage point, within
an anthropological frame of reference
that recognizes man as free, we can
usefully apply to this problem what
Jean-Paul Sartre has called "bad faith."
To put it very simply, "bad faith" is to
pretend something is necessary that in
fact is voluntary. "Bad faith" is thus a
flight from freedom, a dishonest eva-
sion of the "agony of choice." "Bad
faith" expresses itself in innumerable
human situations from the most commonplace to the most catastrophic.
The waiter shuffling through his appointed rounds in a cafe is in "bad
faith" insofar as he pretends to himself
that the waiter role constitutes his real
existence, that, if only for the hours he
is hired, he is the waiter. The woman
who lets her body be seduced step by
step while continuing to carry on an
innocent conversation is in "bad

faith," insofar as she pretends that
what is happening to her body is not
under her control. The terrorist who
kills and excuses himself by saying
that he had no choice because the party
ordered him to kill is in "bad faith,"
because he pretends that his existence
is necessarily linked with the party,
while in fact this linkage is the consequence of his own choice. It can easily
be seen that "bad faith" covers society
like a film of lies. The very possibility
of "bad faith," however, shows us the
reality of freedom. Man can be in "bad
faith" only because he is free and does
not wish to face his freedom. "Bad
faith" is the shadow of human liberty.
Its attempt to escape that liberty is
doomed to defeat. For, as Sartre has
famously put it, we are "condemned to
freedom."

If we apply this concept to our
sociological perspective, we will suddenly be faced with a startling conclusion. The complex of roles within
which we exist in society now appears
to us as an immense apparatus of "bad
faith." Each role carries with it the
possibility of "bad faith." Every man
who says "I have no choice" in referring to what his social role demands of
him is engaged in "bad faith." Now,
we can easily imagine circumstances
in which this confession will be true
to the extent that there is no choice
within that particular role. Nevertheless, the individual has the choice
of stepping outside the role. It is true
that, given certain circumstances,
a businessman has "no choice" but
brutally to destroy a competitor, unless he is to go bankrupt himself, but it
is he who chooses brutality over bank-
ruptcy. It is true that a man has "no
choice" but to betray a homosexual attachment if he is to retain his position
in respectable society, but he is the one
making the choice between respecta-

bility and loyalty to that attachment. It is true that in some cases a judge has "no choice" but to sentence a man to death, but in doing so he chooses to remain a judge, an occupation chosen by him in the knowledge that it might lead to this, and he chooses not to resign instead when faced with the prospect of this duty. Men are responsible for their actions. They are in "bad faith" when they attribute to iron necessity what they themselves are choosing to do. Even the law itself, that master fortress of "bad faith," has begun to take cognizance of this fact in its dealings with Nazi war criminals.

.... Since society exists as a network of social roles, each one of which can become a chronic or a momentary alibi from taking responsibility for its bearer, we can say that deception and self-deception are at the very heart of social reality. Nor is this an accidental quality that could somehow be eradicated by some moral reformation or other. The deception inherent in social structures is a functional imperative. Society can maintain itself only if its fictions (its "as if" character, to use Hans Vaihinger's term) are accorded ontological status by at least some of its members some of the time—or, let us say, society as we have so far known it in human history.

Society provides for the individual a gigantic mechanism by which he can hide from himself his own freedom. Yet this character of society as an immense conspiracy in "bad faith" is, just as in the case of the individual, but an expression of the possibility of freedom that exists by virtue of society. We are social beings and our existence is bound to specific social locations. The same social situations that can become traps of "bad faith" can also be occasions for freedom. Every social role can be played knowingly or

blindly. And insofar as it is played knowingly, it can become a vehicle of our own decisions. Every social institution can be an alibi, an instrument of alienation from our freedom. But at least some institutions can become protective shields for the actions of free men. In this way, an understanding of "bad faith" does not necessarily lead us to a view of society as the universal realm of illusion, but rather illuminates more clearly the paradoxical and infinitely precarious character of social existence.

Another concept of existentialist philosophy useful for our argument is what Martin Heidegger has called *das Man*. The German word is untranslatable literally into English. It is used in German in the same way that "one" is used in English in such a sentence as "One does not do that" ("*Man tut das nicht*"). The French word *on* conveys the same meaning, and José Ortega y Gasset has caught Heidegger's intention well in Spanish with his concept of *lo que se hace*. In other words, *Man* refers to a deliberately vague generality of human beings. It is not this man who will not do this, nor that man, nor you nor I—it is, in some way, all men, but so generally that it may just as well be nobody. It is in this vague sense that a child is told "one does not pick one's nose in public." The concrete child, with his concretely irritating nose, is subsumed under an anonymous generality that has no face—and yet bears down powerfully on the child's conduct. In fact (and this ought to give us a long pause), Heidegger's *Man* bears an uncanny resemblance to what Mead has called the "generalized other."

In Heidegger's system of thought the concept of the *Man* is related to his discussion of authenticity and inauthenticity. To exist authentically is to live in full awareness of the unique,

authenticity

irreplaceable and incomparable quality of one's individuality. By contrast, inauthentic existence is to lose oneself in the anonymity of the *Man*, surrendering one's uniqueness to the socially constituted abstractions. This is especially important in the way one faces death. The truth of the matter is that it is always one single, solitary individual who dies. But society comforts the bereaved and those who are to die themselves by subsuming each death under general categories that appear to assuage its horror. A man dies, and we say "Well, we all have to go someday." This "we all" is an exact rendition of the *Man*—it is everybody and thus nobody, and by putting ourselves under its generality we hide from ourselves the inevitable fact that we too shall die, singly and solitarily. Heidegger himself has referred to Tolstoi's story *The Death of Ivan Ilyitch* as the best literary expression of inauthenticity in the facing of death. As an illustration of authenticity to the point of torment we would submit Federico García Lorca's unforgettable poem about the death of a bullfighter, *Lament for Ignacio Sánchez Mejías*.

Heidegger's concept of *Man* is relevant for our view of society not so much in its normative as in its cognitive aspects. Under the aspect of "bad faith" we have seen society as a mechanism to provide alibis from freedom. Under the aspect of the *Man* we see society as a defense against terror. Society provides us with taken-for-granted structures (we could also speak here of the "okay world") within which, as long as we follow the rules, we are shielded from the naked terrors of our condition. The "okay world" provides routines and rituals through which these terrors are organized in such a way that we can face them with a measure of calm.

All rites of passage illustrate this function. The miracle of birth, the mystery of desire, the horror of death—all these are carefully camouflaged as we are led gently over one threshold after another, apparently in a natural and self-evident sequence; we all are born, lust and must die, and thus every one of us can be protected against the unthinkable wonder of these events. The *Man* enables us to live inauthentically by sealing up the metaphysical questions that our existence poses. We are surrounded by darkness on all sides as we rush through our brief span of life toward inevitable death. The agonized question, "Why?" that almost every man feels at some moment or other as he becomes conscious of his condition is quickly stifled by the cliché answers that society has available. Society provides us with religious systems and social rituals, ready-made, that relieve us of such questioning. The "world-taken-for-granted," the social world that tells us that everything is quite okay, is the location of our inauthenticity.

Let us take a man who wakes up at night from one of those nightmares in which one loses all sense of identity and location. Even in the moment of waking, the reality of one's own being and of one's world appears as a dream-like phantasmagorion that could vanish or be metamorphosed in the twinkling of an eye. One lies in bed in a sort of metaphysical paralysis, feeling oneself but one step removed from that annihilation that had loomed over one in the nightmare just passed. For a few moments of painfully clear consciousness one is at the point of almost smelling the slow approach of death and, with it, of nothingness. And then one gropes for a cigarette and, as the saying goes, "comes back to reality." One reminds oneself of one's name, address and occupation, of one's plans for the next day. One walks about one's house, full of proofs of past and present identity. One listens to the noises of the city. Perhaps one wakes up wife or children and is reassured by their annoyed protests. Soon one can laughingly dismiss the foolishness of what has just transpired, raid the refrigerator for a bite or the liquor closet for a nightcap, and go to sleep with the determination to dream of one's next promotion.

So far, so good. But what exactly is the "reality" to which one has just returned? It is the "reality" of one's socially constructed world, that "okay world" in which metaphysical questions are always laughable unless they have been captured and castrated in taken-for-granted religious ritualism. The truth is that this "reality" is a very precarious one indeed. Names, addresses, occupations and wives have a way of disappearing. All plans end in extinction. All houses eventually become empty. And even if we live all our lives without having to face the agonizing contingency of all we are and do, in the end, we must return to that nightmare moment when we feel ourselves stripped of all names and all identities. What is more, we know this—which makes for the inauthenticity of our scurrying for shelter. Society gives us names to shield us from nothingness. It builds a world for us to live in and thus protects us from the chaos that surrounds us on all sides. It provides us with a language and with meanings that make this world believable. And it supplies a steady chorus of voices that confirm our belief and still our dormant doubts.

Again we would repeat in this slightly altered context what we have said before about "bad faith." It is cor-

rect that society, in its aspect of *Man*, is a conspiracy to bring about inauthentic existence. The walls of society are a Potemkin village erected in front of the abyss of being. They function to protect us from terror to organize for us a cosmos of meaning within which our lives make sense. But it is also true that authentic existence can take place only within society. All meanings are transmitted in social processes. One cannot be human, authentically or inauthentically, except in society. And the very avenues that lead to a wondering contemplation of being, be they religious or philosophical or aesthetic, have social locations. Just as society can be a flight from freedom or an occasion for it, society can bury our metaphysical quest or provide forms in which it can be pursued. We come up once more on the persistently Janus-faced paradox of our social existence. All the same, there can be but little doubt that society functions as alibi and as Potemkin village for more people than it functions for as an avenue of liberation. If we maintain that authenticity in society is possible, we are not thereby maintaining that most men are indeed making use of this possibility. Wherever we ourselves may be socially located, one look around us will tell us otherwise.

With these observations we have come once more to the edge of ethical considerations that we want to postpone for another moment. We would stress at this point, however, that "ecstasy," as we have defined it, has metaphysical as well as sociological significance. Only by stepping out of the taken-for-granted routines of society is it possible for us to confront the human condition without comforting mystifications. This does not mean that only the marginal man or the rebel can be authentic. It does mean that freedom presupposes a certain liberation of consciousness. Whatever possibilities of freedom we may have, they cannot be realized if we continue to assume that the "okay world" of society is the only world there is. Society provides us with warm, reasonably comfortable caves, in which we can huddle with our fellows, beating on the drums that drown out the howling hyenas of the surrounding darkness. "Ecstasy" is the act of stepping outside the caves, alone, to face the night.

2. CONCEPT AND METHOD IN THE STUDY OF HUMAN DEVELOPMENT

NELSON N. FOOTE

Reprinted from M. Sherif and M. C. Wilson, *Emerging Problems in Social Psychology* (Norman: University of Oklahoma Press, 1957) excerpts from pp. 29-40 and p. 49, by permission of the author and the University of Oklahoma Press. Copyright 1957 by University of Oklahoma Press. Nelson Foote is Professor of Sociology at the Graduate School of the City University of New York. In a long and productive career, Prof. Foote has been the author of many ground-breaking statements written from the Symbolic Interactionist viewpoint.

The study of human development is chronically beguiled by analogies and antinomies which obscure and distort realistic analysis of the phenomena it selects to observe. Human development may be taken to include all aspects of personal change from the growth of infants to the cultural history of world society. As a synthetic discipline emerging from the social sciences, however, it has barely differentiated itself clearly as yet from its ancestry in child psychology and educational theory. Although the term is recognized to cover behavioral change throughout the life cycle, it has thus had—to illustrate—a hard and slippery climb to escape from the limiting connotations of "growth" and "maturity."

As biological concepts, growth and maturity are legitimate, exact and useful. But as means for designating the processes by which behavior of human beings gets organized into patterns which distinguish them as persons, the same terms are misleading organic analogies which hinder more than they help. Wittingly to reinstate the discredited though persistent body-mind dualism would not be a satisfactory solution, since behavior is not classifiable into two neat kinds, physical and social. At best a dim line—and getting dimmer—can be drawn analytically between those aspects of behavior which seem biologically given and those which are potentially modifiable through experience. In the study of aging, as an example, while holding rigorously to the aim of generalizing in terms of identifiable sequences of personal change, we recognize that the behavioral variation possible within almost any given biological limits remains infinite. If we are to understand the way in which adults come to label each other as "mature" and "immature," therefore, we are not likely to get far by taking these epithets at face value. We need a set of methods and concepts adapted for referring precisely to a wide range of common research problems, for identifying and ordering the sequences of development observable in personality, family, society and history at large.[1]

The contention here is that the only vocabulary clearly appropriate for the study of human development in a scientific manner is not, by the nature of the subject matter, biological or physical, but dramatistic, as proposed by Kenneth Burke.[2] As a literary critic, Burke has never been misled into recognizing as science the unconfessed poetry of those partisans of biologese who liken social actions to homeostasis, genotypy, organic evolution,

23

plant ecology, contagion, blood circulation, or health and disease. Fondness for organic analogy in some writers seems to occur at the expense of genuine interest in the actual physiological substrates of interpersonal transactions.[3] Neither has Burke found it as plausible as the sycophants of physics to reduce some baffling human complex like Communist Party membership to entropy, equilibrium, cybernetics, valence, warmth, molding, freezing, or the hydraulic and visual analogies so dear to psychoanalysts and gestaltists. Poor old Isaac Newton would blush in his grave if he knew how his outworn intellectual garments get refurbished for stylish wear in the social sciences. These inappropriate metaphors are so tempting, however, that considerable literature is devoted solely to justifying their continued indulgence as "models." Eventually all this debris must be swept out of social psychology, as was done, for example, with the idea of personal magnetism (still hiding out in sociology as *charisma*).

Meanwhile, on the constructive side, it must be faced that Burke has the defects of his virtue as a literary critic. He has not gone forward to elaborate an adequate glossary of concept and method based on his dramatistic premise. His five key terms of scene, agent, act, agency and purpose are only a common-sense beginning. In the research and thinking by several colleagues of the Committee on Human Development, effort has produced some rudimentary additions, which can be reported here as suggestive of the ultimate task confronting all social psychologists who study human development in its many phases and forms.

If space permitted, it would be worthwhile to outline the similarity in pitfalls to thinking among theories of societal and personal development.[4]

Grandiose efforts in the past to divide history into three or more vast stages have led more recently to strong reactions against even much less sweeping attempts to impose some kind of order upon the mass of human experience. The extreme has been to deny the existence of any connected sequences at all, or at most only those of an addictive or repetitive sort. In dealing with individual life histories, for example, these have been generalized statistically in terms of chronological norms.[5] Whether applied to the life of one man or the history of mankind, however, both the speculative and the rigidly empirical approaches seem to start from a kind of all-or-nothing assumption—either a series of stages full-blown *a priori* or a merely statistical association of behavioral development with growth. Neither gets down to cases in the close examination of how transformation occurs.

This antinomy of a complete schedule of inevitable and necessary stages *versus* the denial of order in developmental sequences is dispelled when limited segments of behavior are scrutinized with a view to discerning relationships among their antecedent, intermediate and consequent elements. No doubt the sophisticated seven- and eight-stage schemes of Sullivan and Erickson[6] are superior to the crude three-stage schemes of Freud and Piaget,[7] in the same way that Teggart and Toynbee seem more realistic than Comte and Spencer, but scientifically it appears premature to leap aboard any scheme of stages so far proposed. Significantly, neither goes beyond the beginnings of adulthood. The ingenuity exhibited in devising stage theories might better be reserved for coming to grips with the smaller units of human development concretely and analytically, and then moving toward their combination in longer sequences of the total career.

The basic unit that seems most appropriate for study is the *episode of interaction*. Certainly this is the unit of observation most suitable for social as against individual psychology. The problem of how development occurs can then be construed essentially as requiring investigation of *how one episode of interaction conditions another*.

In the use of sociodrama, it is common to structure a problematic situation in which subjects are assigned statuses as actors and told to play appropriate roles spontaneously as the situation indicates. Invariably the episode of role-playing—unless interfered with by an outside person —terminates itself; the participants recognize when the problem implicit in the situation has been resolved. This observation does not imply uniformly happy endings (any more than progress or decline in history has to be inevitable). Even the Mead-Dewey concept of the consummatory phase of the social act may connote too much the desirability of the outcome from the standpoint of any or all the actors.[8] Indeed the term resolution may itself be too strong, because some problems turn out to be so refractory or insoluble that the frustration becomes unbearable. As the episode proceeds, the frustration of an actor may cause him to terminate the scene abruptly and arbitrarily by walking out on the others, silencing them, or changing the target of attention, perhaps by jocularity. The episode is thus undeniably terminated, and in a way that developed out of the intermediate interaction, but not by a consummation or resolution that will be evaluated by the frustrated actor as successful. Conversely, an episode frequently appears to near a resolution in the view of the participants, only to be reproblematized and lengthened by the introduction of some complicating element or resis-

tance by one of the actors, which may or may not get worked into an integrated outcome. . . .

Now the episodic organization of behavior so conspicuous in sociodrama (or in theater drama) is just as characteristic of so-called real life, though usually the action is not quite so condensed. In real life, each episode is imbedded among other episodes —an inconvenience to the researcher which will require much technical ingenuity to overcome. The consecutive series of episodes in the life of each actor intersects with but necessarily differs from the series of other actors. And a series of episodes connecting some persons in interaction may form contributing segments of overarching episodes involving whole groups, as in war-time separations of families. To employ a figure of speech more apt than physical or biological analogies, living gets organized like conversation into sentences, paragraphs and whole stories, of diverse length, complexity and intercontingency. Nonetheless the interpersonal episode remains the prototypical unit of organization.

Research can isolate episodes of interaction from this intricate context through the use of sociodrama and through a variety of other devices now being invented.[9] The main problem of distinguishing and characterizing episodes, however, is not technical but conceptual. Criteria for distinguishing where one episode ends and another begins in real life need refinement and elaboration, though in ordinary instances their disjunction may be inescapable.

In observing the transition from one episode to the next in real life, a second characteristic of human behavior stands out: there are no hiatuses; one episode begins where the other ends. It might be reasonably postulated, as by equilibrium theorists and John Dewey himself, that most of living is routine, only intermittently disturbed by the intrusion of novel problems. But this postulate may serve more to obscure than to illuminate what actually happens. Empirically—if we take the sequential organization of behavior as our theoretical problem—it appears both more valid in observation and more useful in analysis to put an opposite construction upon routine. It is a fertile assumption to include the givens within the problems, and not the problems, within the givens.

Routines—cultural traits, rules, forms, habits, folkways—are imbedded as elements within episodes which proceed to resolution; their use is not self-evident, but varied and selected as if materials of which a pattern or plot is constructed. The given elements in the problematic situation which evokes an episode of interaction may—and usually do—have familiar uses. But the specific use to which each will be put—the unique combination of these elements in the particular episode—is not necessary, predetermined or certain.

Insufficient weight is given in the literature of social interaction to the uncertainty of every outcome, to the degree that actual human behavior is exploratory, formulative, creative in every observable episode. As persons develop, they acquire access to a choice of routines, an enlarging repertoire accumulated through experience and loosely bundled in familiar roles. They may be adept or inept in utilizing these repertoires. Their competence in resolving episodes satisfactorily may itself be exhibited in handling problematic situations through individually distinctive routines. But the given conditions only set the scene and furnish the resources or agencies available to deal with a problem. The definition of the problem tends to de-termine the ensuing structure of the full episode, but even the defining of the situation is itself an act of construction—a not-given, and, as Mead insists[10], visualization of later phases influences earlier. The episode of interaction, therefore, includes generically all behavior of persons in situations.

A third noticeable feature of all episodes of interaction is that, once begun, there is an implicit but usually definitely-felt compulsion to finish them. Each actor, moreover, exerts some compulsion toward every other actor in the situation to stay with the episode until it is resolved, even if the detectable sign of such compulsion be no more than keeping his eyes on another while hearing the last of a sentence. This principle of "unfinished business" has to be analyzed in its social dimension, which goes considerably beyond the concept of closure found in gestaltist theory, though it appears to be involved in the recall of interrupted tasks—the famous Zeigarnik effect.[11] It is compounded of a progression of involvement, identification, obligation, discipline and expectations of positive and negative evaluations of outcomes by significant audiences, present or imagined. These influences add inducements more compelling than the appreciable esthetic or physiological appeal of completing the overt operations of the task in hand. In fact, in the ordinary interpersonal situation, the problem is far more often that of knitting several competing possibilities into a harmonious plan, i.e. getting a unified decision, than of performing any visible instrumental task.[12]

It might be useful to insert here a criticism of the currently diffusing concept of role. Role ought to specify an actual, observable sequence of behavior appropriate to the status of an actor in a situation—or, more accurately, his part in an episode, the remainder of which consists of the roles of the others involved. The social anthropologists have abstracted the role into a standard set of performances which are associated with a given status, i.e. a kind of modal performance by an individual in highly recurrent situations, or else an ideal type, approached but never realized in action, and hence never observed at all. Newcomb has tried to get away from such a static conception by suggesting the phrase "role behavior," to stand for what a person actually does in a specific situation that is recognizable by others as functionally related to their behavior.[13] Role behavior thus pertains to an individual's performance, but nonetheless it still remains abstracted from the reciprocal performances of the other(s) which account for its concrete shape and appropriateness in the actual situation. One cannot predict very well from the early portions of a "role behavior" what the later portions will be, unless he can ascertain the concomitant responses and assertions of the other(s). Moreover, it is vital to the study of behavioral development to recognize that *at the conclusion of any episode of interaction, the position of the participants vis-a-vis each other is always and necessarily different from what it was at its commencement.* Structural-functional abstraction obscures this all-important feature of social action.

The re-structuring of relationships is what human action is all about. A mother feeds a hungry child, whereupon the statuses of hungry child and nurturant mother are no more. The child may then go to sleep, run outdoors, or start a fight with her little brother. In each case, the role relationships at the commencement of the next episode are redefined in accordance

with the nature of the new problem which obtrudes upon attention. These are the reasons why—although the concept of role will remain very useful despite its slipperiness—it is not as precise or clarifying as the concept of episode to form the foundation unit for social-psychological analysis.

Microscopic scrutiny of many, many episodes of interaction—with all the drudgery that implies—will go on a long time before the precision attained reaches diminishing returns. Some of that work is going forward and will be mentioned below, since it deals with elements and processes within and between episodes. But there is finally another salient and regularly present characteristic of episodes as wholes which should be mentioned here: their story feature.

As already hinted, by the story feature of an episode is meant primarily the interest of participants in the more or less unforeseeable outcome toward which the intervening item events contribute. The "problematicness" of the presenting situation furnishes much but far from all the uncertainty as to outcome. The involvement of participants, for instance, is a function of the degree of risk involved. The importance of the values at stake may vary widely, from person to person and time to time. A door blows open and has to be closed to keep out noise; this episode is neither as problematic nor as important as when its blowing open exposes a naked person to others. In the former instance, the analyst might even be inclined to treat the item as a scenic detail within some encompassing episode, rather than as an episode in its own right.

The utility of including the uses of the givens within the problematic deserves further stress here, because it is quite in contrast with the outlook of those theorists who conceive human action as the overt expression of given values in repetitive situations; these in turn constituting a single, enveloping social system whose functioning is quite regular except for more or less remediable strains and deviations from within or interferences from without.[14] As we would conceive of values, they arise immediately in situations, in terms of estimated alternative outcomes, and they are recurrently verified or modified by actual outcomes ("I was mistaken; I'll never try that again.")[15]

To be sure, such outcomes have to be categorized in some vocabulary of motive and value. Such vocabularies of motive and value are derived from experience in previous episodes and are available for application to new episodes; as concepts, they are instrumental and even influential in defining situations or evaluating outcomes. But the terms should never be confused with their referents, even when the seemingly least-referential terms seem the most evocative of identification, emotion and action. As put in one of Mannheim's pregnant sentences:

"That is why unambiguousness, too great clarity is not an unqualified social value; productive misunderstanding is often a condition of continuing life."[16]

Almost by definition, if a person does not get involved in the problem which launches the episode—does not define it as a problem *to him*, being who he takes himself to be—its outcome has no real value to him, or mobilizing effect, regardless of the beautifully scalable hierarchy of attitudes which he might express verbally in response to questions about hypothetical situations. Conversely a person may become vicariously so identified with an actor in some vast political drama as to weep over a bit of news announced on the radio. Fully to analyze and understand the participation of any person

in an episode of interaction, account must be taken of what was authentically at stake for him in that situation, how he estimated such alternative outcomes as occurred to him erstwhile or emerged meanwhile, in terms of their relative chances of realization.

Chance in human behavior takes multiple forms. Much of the uncertainty—all too much, the anxious say—is engendered by the vague or conflicting expectations and intentions of others; some degree of ignorance and mistake in the assessment of these is almost the only certainty. Much effort therefore goes not only into predicting but into controlling the behavior of others—which means reciprocally into conformance with the rules and sanctions imposed by others. Yet the leeway and discrepancy remain as conspicuous as the consensus. One can marvel at both how few and how many of the cars which rush toward each other on the highways ever collide.

Uncertainty of outcome—surprise and danger—should by no means be conceived as evils toward extinguishing which all human effort is directed. We move as often toward increasing it as toward diminishing it; that is how we grow in capacity; without hazard, social life would be as stale as a jail sentence. We court the peril of overreaching ourselves. We attempt the as yet unachieved. The forms of gambling—euphemized as risk-taking—are legion. Disaster and destruction fascinate us; our highest drama is the fall of heroes. None of us are beyond enjoyment of bluff and deception in dealing with others; in small children its appearance is the index of full self-consciousness (the child has then reached the age of reason, as the theologians say). We profess to despise credulity yet continue to delight in illusion, mystery and magic. Although research and invention are defended in the name of greater control over nature, the pursuit of novelty and propagation of change break up traditional securities and introduce modern demons. In our culture, the explorer is as honored as the prophet elsewhere. How far can the analogy to entropy or equilibrium go toward explaining the frequently fatal aspirations to jump quicker, dive deeper, climb higher or travel faster than anyone else? Consider even the meaning of the traditional appeal to Divine Providence.

Who plays it safe may not develop, at least not in the optimal sense. Human development occurs as the cumulative product of successive outcomes of episodes of interaction. The thinkers who are contributing much to insight into this cumulative gain or loss from episode are Sullivan (through posthumous publication) and Erikson, as they struggle to deal with the question of transition from one to another of their putative stages. In this respect at least, the effort to derive stages indubitably has heuristic value. Cameron, who abjures stages, has derived the horrendous phrase "progressive reaction-sensitization" to stand for this cumulative feature of development, but his view leaves out the emphasis upon coping and mastery stressed among the neo-Freudians.[17] Further elaboration, however, will probably come as much from those who treat optimal development through play and education as from the psychopathologists, since any full concept of cumulation specifies that benevolent as well as vicious "circles" occur continually.[18]

In education, for instance, one of the most suggestive contributions has been the concept of *developmental tasks*. Without positing regular stages, Havighurst points out that in normal development there is a customary succession of challenging problems put to the person throughout his life-history, which are ordered timewise, and, more conspicuously during the earlier years, in terms of ascending difficulty.[19] Success in mastering each task when it becomes appropriate to do so contributes to competence and success in encountering the next. Failure contributes to further failure, with arrest or retrogression likely to follow. Like the graded school system, this scheme may be too over-generalized to take account of specific processes of differentiation, but it is a useful guide for further research and experimentation. . . .

The classic case of the vicious downward spiral in development is the paranoid trend. The initially suspicious person projects upon a problematic new encounter a definition of the other as unfriendly, and reacts to that image by a defensive response which is as logical as it is unrealistic. His defensiveness is apprehended by the other as unprovoked aggressiveness, and equally logically evokes from him the appropriate response. This virtually automatic retaliation or reply-in-kind serves to confirm the suspicious one in his previous apprehension, and he is thus more predisposed than before to project the same paranoid definition upon the next situation. After a certain repetition and intensification of this sequence, only the utmost effort can prevent complete distortion of clearcut signs of friendliness put forth by the other. Mobilization to halt threatened downward movement and disintegration can as effectively arrest development as can fear of challenge to higher performance, e.g. the rigidity (and fragility) of some reformed alcoholics. Unfortunately some downward spirals are not arrested, and some upward spirals do reach plateaus.

The general principle of cumulation by which some privileged few seem to enjoy charmed careers is no different from the process by which paranoid or schizoid trends get intensified through the unwitting "cooperation" of others. The youngest child in a family sometimes gets off to a highly beneficent start. As the baby he may get unusual attention and responsiveness from others, including the imputation of ideal characteristics to him even before he can talk. He expects well of later people as a result of his family experience, and often enough the world accepts him at his own evaluation as worthy of its approval. As the saying goes, things come easy to him. He has the support of an alert and friendly audience which rejoices as he resolves each developmental task set before him, but does not demand more of him than he is ready to perform at any given point. In experimental groups we watch the rapid emergence of leadership from week to week through successive ventures of initiative and responsibility.[20] The joint episodes of group development are concomitantly episodes in personal development. It cannot be underlined too heavily that every developmental trend is—figuratively speaking—gestated if not conceived by the implicit conspiracy of others.

It would obviously be incorrect to insist that the outcome of every episode of interpersonal interaction is equally influential in shaping the character of future episodes, but it is fruitful of a whole range of research hypotheses to assume that every episode contributes something— however little or much—to defining the curve of future development. The contrary assumption—that most behavior is purely repetitive or cyclical—is apt for those who enjoy constructing abstract closed systems, but its usefulness in research is limited. A large share of the important theoretical questions derive from practical interest in the direction of de-

velopment. Even though one day in general is much like the previous one, it is the small difference that makes all the difference. If this paper were revised tomorrow, 98 per cent of it might remain the same, but it would be the 2 per cent which would foretell where this kind of thinking is headed. . . .

. . . We can repeat with added meaning the observation that the development of society and the development of persons are joint problems. The study of human development therefore is the study of the organization of behavior in sequences that exhibit order interactionally, i.e. from both personal and social points of view. Unless we project upon society the lockstep image of the reformatory, however, we must conclude that the order it achieves arises through personal autonomy and its necessary reciprocal—social slack, freedom, play in the systems of relationship, loose rather than tight scheduling. Personal integrity and self-conscious scheduling as reciprocals mean social planning based on voluntary participation. The sterile antinomy of freedom and order is based on a static view. It is resolved when identity is recognized to originate and transform itself in the successive episodes of social interaction. In the free society of the future, every man must become his own social psychologist.

In this developmental view, both society and personality dissolve as static structures and merge in an open-ended progression or procession of re-identifications, accomplished through shared competence for nonlogical thematic organization. For this broad task our subjects' own dramatic analogues will remain more appropriate than the physical and biological shibboleths still treasured among the reputed professionals of social psychology.

NOTES

1. Herbert Blumer, "Psychological Import of the Human Group," M. Sherif and M. C. Wilson, (eds.) *Group Relations at the Crossroads* (New York: Harper and Bros., 1953), pp. 185-202.

2. Kenneth Burke, *A Grammar of Motives* (New York: Prentice-Hall, Inc., 1945).

3. L. S. Cottrell and Nelson N. Foote, "Sullivan's Contributions to Social Psychology," P. Mullahy (ed.), *The Contributions of Harry Stack Sullivan—A Symposium* (New York: Hermitage House, 1952), chap. vi.

4. The Summer Seminar on Family Research, sponsored by the Social Science Research Council at Boulder, Colorado in 1952, traversed most of the problems touched upon in this paper, and its members—Oscar Lewis, Daniel Miller, Edward Rose, Melford Spiro, Anselm Strauss, and Guy Swanson—were helpful in its formulation. Edward Rose systematically presented some correspondence between theories of individual and societal development which deserve publication.

5. Arnold Gesell and Frances L. Ilg, *Infant and Child in the Culture of Today* (New York: Harper and Bros., 1943).

6. Harry S. Sullivan, *The Interpersonal Theory of Psychiatry* (New York: W. W. Norton and Co., 1953).

Erik H. Erikson, *Childhood and Society* (New York: W. W. Norton and Co., 1950).

7. Sigmund Freud, "Three Contributions to the Theory of Sex," in *Basic Writings of Sigmund Freud* (New York: Random House, Inc., 1938).

Jean Piaget, *The Moral Judgment of the Child* (Glencoe: The Free Press, 1948).

8. George H. Mead, *The Philosophy of the Act* (Chicago: University of Chicago Press, 1938, Essay xxii "Value and the Consummatory Phase of the Act," pp. 445-453.

9. E.g. Fred L. Strodtbeck, "The Family as a Three-Person Group," *American Sociological Review*, XIX, No. 1 (February, 1954), pp. 23-29.

10. George H. Mead, *Mind, Self and Society* (Chicago: University of Chicago Press, 1934).

11. Murray Horwitz, "The Recall of Interrupted Group Tasks: An Experimental Study of Individual Motivation in Relation to Group Goals," in Dorwin Cartwright and Alvin Zander, (eds.), *Group Dynamics* (Evanston: Row, Peterson and Co., 1953), pp. 361-385.

12. Frank H. Knight, *Freedom and Reform* (New York: Harper and Bros., 1947), Chap. xiv "The Planful Act: The Possibilities and Limitations of Collective Rationality," pp. 335-369.

13. Theodore M. Newcomb, *Social Psychology* (New York: The Dryden Press, 1950), pp. 328-334.

14. Talcott Parsons, *The Social System* (Glencoe: The Free Press, 1951), chap. vii, "Deviant Behavior and the Mechanisms of Social Control," pp. 249-325.

15. Nelson N. Foote, "Identification as the Basis for a Theory of Motivation," *American Sociological Review*, XVI, No. 1 (February, 1951), pp. 14-21.

16. Karl Mannheim, *Essays on the Sociology of Knowledge* (London: Routledge and Kegan Paul, Ltd., 1952), p. 305.

17. Norman Cameron, *The Psychology of Behavior Disorders: A Biosocial Interpretation* (Boston: Houghton Mifflin Company, 1947), pp. 68-77.

Karen Horney, *Neurosis and Human Growth* (New York: W. W. Norton and Co., 1950).

18. Gunnar Myrdal, *An American Dilemma* (New York: Harper and Bros., 1944), appendix 3, "A Methodological Note on the Principle of Cumulation," pp. 1065-1070.

19. Robert J. Havighurst, *Developmental Tasks and Education* (2nd ed.; New York: Longmans Green and Co., 1952), pp. 1-100.

20. George Theodorson, "Elements in the Progressive Development of Small Groups," *Social Forces*, XXXI, No. 4 (May, 1953), pp. 311-320.

...S THEATER:
... NOTES ON THE
...RAMATURGIC APPROACH
TO SOCIAL REALITY

SHELDON E. MESSINGER,
HAROLD SAMPSON, AND ROBERT D. TOWNE

Reprinted from Sheldon Messinger, Harold Sampson, and Robert D. Towne, in *Sociometry*, XXV (September, 1962), pp. 98-110. Reprinted by permission of the American Sociological Association and the authors. Sheldon Messinger is the Dean of the School of Criminology at the University of California in Berkeley. Harold Sampson and Robert D. Towne were part of the Bay Area Health Study, a research project supported by the California Department of Mental Hygiene and the National Institute of Mental Health when this article was written.

The aim of this paper is to raise some questions about the uses of the "dramaturgic approach"[1] to social experience, a mode of analysis finding increasing use in social-psychological circles. In particular, we wish to inquire into and comment upon the nature of the actor's[2] perspective in everyday life, as this is sometimes assumed to appear to the dramaturgic analyst.

To this end, we shall describe a perspective on the world and the self within it, a perspective that renders life a kind of "theater" in which a "show" is "staged." Someone viewing self and world from within this perspective will be said to be "on." In order to show the incompatibility of this perspective with the view that persons in everyday life seem to consider "natural," we shall present some observations by and about mental patients taken from a recently completed study.[3] Finally, we shall suggest that the perspective of persons who are "on" is akin or identical to the view seemingly attributed by the dramaturgic analyst to his subjects, that is, to persons plying their routine rounds of daily activities. We shall hold that this seeming attribution is a misreading of

dramaturgic analysis, if a misreading against which the dramaturgic analyst has not sufficiently guarded.

I

A reported comment by Sammy Davis, Jr. first suggested our usage of the term "to be on." Remarking on the hazards of fame, he said, "As soon as I go out the front door of my house in the morning, I'm on, Daddy, I'm on."[4] And further, "But when I'm with the group I can relax. We trust each other" (12). Drawing on his experience in the theater, Davis seems to be saying that there are times when, although "off-stage," he feels "on-stage." He contrasts this perspective on self and other with another associated with "relaxation" and "trust."

Seeing that someone who has been "on-stage" may find the same experience in everyday life, we can appreciate that those who have never crossed the boards may attain the same perspective, even though they may have no consistent name for it. Thus Bernard Wolfe tells us that, seldom out of sight of a white audience, "Negroes in our culture spend most of their lives 'on'. . . . Every Negro is to some extent a performer." At other times, "relaxing among themselves," Negroes will "mock the 'type' personalities they are obliged to assume when they're 'on' " (11, p. 202). We may expect, perhaps, that the members of any oppressed group will have similar experiences.

But there seems no reason to confine these experiences to the oppressed. It would seem that adolescents at graduation ceremonies, as well as buying drinks at bars, and clerks taken for store owners, as well as those mistaken for customers, share with Norman Mailer's "hip" the need to "come on strong" (8). And we can see that a person may be rendered "on" when he has no prior reason to believe that this will be his fate. Thus, the plight of one "put on" by joking of sadistic friends, and the person suddenly made aware of a *gaffe* by another's inability to be tactful (3,5).

All of these situations point up the fact that under some circumstances in everyday life the actor becomes, is, or is made *aware* of an actual or potential discrepancy between his "real" and his "projected" selves, between his "self" and his "character."[5] He may greet this sensed discrepancy with joy or anxiety; presumably he usually finds himself somewhere between these affective poles. However this may be, insofar as he *consciously* orients himself to narrow, sustain, or widen this discrepancy and thereby achieves a sense of "playing the role" or "managing a character," he is "on" in the sense intended here. It may be inferred that it is during such periods, if his projection is a joint enterprise, that the actor *experiences* the constraints of "dramaturgic loyalty," "discipline," and "circumspection" (6, pp. 212-222); although, as we shall try to make clear later, it may *not* be inferred that when the actor fails to

experience these constraints they have ceased to operate. It is at these other times, however, when the actor is not "on," that we shall refer to his perspective as "natural." At these other times persons tell us that their conduct appears to them as "spontaneous."

II

We may be better able to appreciate the difference between being "on" and being "natural"—and the difference this difference makes—if we turn to the experiences of a class of persons who must cope with it for a relatively long period of time. Entertainers would seem to be such a class, as Davis' statement suggests. Davis' statement also suggests, however, that a relatively well supported hiatus exists for entertainers between occasions of being "on" and "natural." There are those before whom one is "on," like the "public," and those with whom one is "natural," like the "group." These worlds may on occasion touch or even overlap, but presumably the boundaries usually remain clear.[6] What we seek is a class of persons who have difficulty creating or sustaining such a hiatus. For them, presumably, the incompatibilities of being "on" and being "natural," should such incompatibilities exist, will be magnified. Mental patients are such a class of persons.

There can be little doubt that mental patients are in a situation productive of being "on." Bereft of membership in the group of reasonable men, they are forced to address the task of restoring their "character," of becoming "sane persons" again. It does not take mental patients long to discover that, as they lost their "sanity" in the eyes of others through what they did and said, so may they regain it. Under these conditions, we might expect mental patients to be "on" without reserve, that for them, truly, life becomes a theater.[7] There is some truth in this: mental patients are "on" at times and feel under pressure to be "on" even more often. But, given their motives to be "on" and the pressure they are under, it is perhaps more remarkable that mental patients cannot sustain this perspective without experiencing severe anxiety and discomfort. From this, as from other experiences of mental patients, we may learn something of importance about everyday life.[8]

We can get at this experience by considering more closely some aspects of the perspective of being "on." Let us consider that, when one is "on," activities come to be regarded as "performances," other persons as an "audience," and the world around as a series of "scenes" and "props." Let us also consider how this view conflicts with what mental patients consider "natural."

Like others who are "on," the mental patient comes to regard his own activities as potential "performances," as potential means of creating and sustaining a "character" for the benefit of others. At times, he uses them this way. Unlike some who are "on," however, the mental patient faces a dilemma. The "show" he experiences himself as "staging" concerns a fundamental matter, a matter that, as he sees it, should not and should not need to be "staged"; namely, his "normality." This is not only an aspect of self that he wants others to again take for granted. This he might indeed accomplish through a judicious "performance." More important, "normality" is an aspect of self the mental patient himself profoundly desires to take for granted again. And regarding his activities as "performances" interferes with this crucial aim.

Thus, a patient may enact a "normal character," succeed in "taking in" the audience, and retrospectively discover that he has, in the process, left himself more unconvinced than ever about the "reality" of his "normality."

Mr. Yale[9] told the interviewer that a nurse had remarked to him that his wife was much "improved." As a mark of "improvement" the nurse cited the fact that Mrs. Yale was playing "Scrabble" (a word game) a great deal. The next day, after some hesitance about confidentiality, Mrs. Yale confided to the interviewer that she and her friends had recently taken to playing "Scrabble" as a means of impressing the staff with their ability to think clearly and be sociable. During the balance of the interview, Mrs. Yale expressed a great deal of concern over whether she was "really" better or had merely misled personnel.

Or, anticipating this sort of conflict, a patient may pointedly avoid "performing."

Mrs. White said that, if she decided to, she could easily get out of the hospital: she realized that she had come to learn what one was "supposed to say and do" to accomplish this. However, she added, to do these things was to deny one's "own self" and what "one felt."

Finally, what the patient has been saying and doing may be defined by an authoritative other as "performing," thereby provoking the conflict.

Mrs. Quinn said that when Dr. X suggested that she was "painting the picture too rosy," she realized that she had been trying to impress hospital staff just to get out of the hospital, and this frightened her.

We are led to see, then, that the mental patient is not satisfied to appear "normal," he strives to be "normal." Paradoxically, this means, in part, that he wants to "appear normal" to himself. Striving to "appear normal" for others—"putting on a show of normality"—interferes with this objective.

It may also be noted that the mental patient addresses others as a potential "audience." The hospital, self-defined as a place of "observation," is obviously conducive to this effect. Others, the patient learns, are "witnesses" of as well as "participants" in his activities. With this a matter of awareness—and, moreover, assumed by the patient to be a matter of awareness for the other—it becomes difficult for a patient to have a relationship in which the impression the other receives of his "illness" or lack of it is not relevant.

During hospitalization patients tend to construe all situations as, potentially, "test" situations in which their "sanity" is being assessed. Thus, many patients make a particular point of knowing the day, month, year, and season, anticipating that "requests for information" will in fact be "orientation examinations." And others, not appreciating how seldom hospital personnel have a chance to become familiar with "the record," consider what are in fact requests for information (like, "how many children do you have?") as further tests. The perspective, in a few cases, tends to become omnipresent: thus, Mrs. Karr believed throughout her hospitalization that several of the "patients" were "spies" who collected information for the hospital and were only feigning illness. And, of course, there is little reason to believe that regarding others as an "audience" ends with release from the hospital. So for a time during the post-hospital period several patients responded to the greeting "How are you?" by launching a description of their mental health or by inquiring into the interviewers' motives for asking such a "question." Information received from patients' relatives suggests that this kind of response was not confined to the interview situation.

These kinds of responses suggest that, within his perspective, the patient consciously follows a kind of "script" in which his primary appearance is that of a "suspect person." In part, it is the others who have these "suspicions" and the patient must disabuse them of these. This is to be accomplished by "watching" one's own "reactions" and by fitting them to the model of a "normal person," also included in the "script." As well, the patient attempts to restrict the actions of others toward him to those which may appropriately be directed to a "normal person."

But, again, the patient's appearance before others is only part of a weighty problem. Not only must he fashion a "normal character" for others and attempt to induce them to provide the social conditions under which he can carry this off, he must do these things while remaining the most critical "audience" of his own "show." Viewing his own activities from "inside," the mental patient finds that he must work with "reactions" which *he* perceives as contrived and controlled. And, for him, as for his other "audiences," a critical aspect of "normality" is that "reactions" are just that: they appear "spontaneous." More is at stake, then, than "putting on" a creditable "performance" for an "audience"; indeed, doing so would seem to undermine the most important "show" of all.

Finally, let us note that the mental patient tends to view things as potential "props." That is, "things," including persons and places ("scenes"), tend to be appreciated directly for the information they potentially and actually convey about the self, for their communicative value in creating, sustaining, or disrupting a "character."

Thus some patients, as well as some sociologists, recognize that the limited expressive materials afforded by the hospital insure that many activities will almost certainly "look crazy." And patients feel under constant pressure to remain aware of the communicative value of their own affective expressions.

Mrs. Vick said, "Life is a pretense. I have to pretend every day that I'm here. That I'm gay and happy in order to stay out of the isolation ward. So I laugh and pretend to be gay."

Other persons, too, may be regarded as "props" to be maneuvered in the interests of the "show" at hand. Thus patients frequently demand that relatives visibly express affection and need for them on the ward. Such expressions were correctly perceived by patients as important to personnel in establishing the patients' "return to normality."

The problem with this view of "things" is that the patient reinforces his own uncertainty as to what is "real" and what is "mere appearance." Thus, the effort to appear "gay" seems to make patients wonder if all "gayness" isn't "mere appearance"; and prearrangements with relatives seem to make patients more uncertain about just what their relatives "really" feel toward them, as well as how they "really" feel toward their relatives. Indeed, this seems to be the core problem with being "on" in regard to fundamental matters: not only can the patient no longer trust others but, most devastating of all, he can no longer trust himself. He is, for a while, anxiously uncertain as to whether the "normal character" he projects is his "self." And the more he appears to himself as "acting"—the more single-mindedly he strives for "effect"—the more uncertain he seems to become.

The foregoing may be summarized in this way. The mental patient is under pressure to experience the world, with his self at its center, in a "technical" way. Like the stage actor contemplating the cloak-over-self he will don for his audience, so the

mental patient comes to address his own character. Instead of a "natural" phenomenon, flowing from and reflecting the self, the mental patient's character comes to appear to him as a "constructed object,"[10] as a "function" of manipulated activities and contrived scenes, of the assessments of an audience and the standards they invoke, and of the nature and availability of props.[11] The connection between self and character becomes a questionable, undependable matter. Or, to use another figure, this connection becomes a matter of wit and stagecraft, of the contingencies of "staging a show." An intrinsic link is shattered.

III

We have said that, for a while, the mental patient is "on." It remains to note that this perspective bears a remarkable resemblance to the perspective that the dramaturgic analyst seems to attribute to the individual in everyday life, whatever the mental status of the latter. Thus, the dramaturgic analyst conceives the individual as a "performer" whose activities function to create the "appearance" of a "self"-a "character"—for an "audience." In the process of maintaining or changing his "character" for others, the individual manipulates things as "props." Others are related to the individual in terms of their "parts" in putting a "show" together, of witnessing it, of sustaining it, or of disrupting it. Places become "scenes" which are fitted or unfitted for the creation of "character" at hand. The outcome of interest to the analyst is the "effective" creation of a "character" which, by "taking in" the "audience" or failing to do so, will permit the individual to continue a rewarding line of activity or to avoid an unrewarding one, or which will result in his being "discredited."

Finally, the dramaturgic analyst seems to make mental patients of us all, for he conceives the individual as "staging" *fundamental* qualities: aspects of self taken for granted *with* intimate others.[12]

This vision of the world is for a time, as we have tried to show, a core aspect of the mental patient's perspective. Finding himself in the eyes of others either a doubtful person or a thoroughly discredited one, he may consciously undertake to fashion an image of "normality." Insofar as this is the case, he will "act" with full awareness; he will see himself as "acting"; he will be "on."

Now we must ask, is the dramaturgic analyst asserting that individuals are "on" in everyday life, routinely and as a matter of course? Is he suggesting that ordinarily, say among family and friends, the individual views "life as theater?" If so, what shall we make of the fact that the mental patient experiences being "on" as an *interruption* of his "normal" perspective and as a source of anxiety and alienation? How shall we account for the patient's intense desire to get "off?"

We wish to suggest that no paradox is involved. In viewing "life as theater," the dramaturgic analyst does not present us with a model of the actor's consciousness; *he is not suggesting that this is the way his subjects understand the world.* Instead, the dramaturgic analyst invokes the theatrical model as a device, a tool, to permit *him* to focus attention on the consequences of the actor's activities for others' perceptions of the actor. The dramaturgic analyst finds this important because, according to *his* theory of social stability and change, others' "impressions" determine the ways they will act toward the actor. Thus, whether the actor self-consciously takes account of these "impressions" or not, whether or not he is even aware that he is creating

an "impression," such "impressions" are demonstrably relevant to the fate of such interaction as the actor enters.

In one sense, then, the actor's "perspective," that is, the actor's view of what he is doing, is not relevant to the dramaturgic analyst. For whatever the actor believes he is doing, so long as he is engaged in interaction, the analyst finds and focuses on the "impression" the actor is making on others. The analyst's "frame of reference," his rules for converting the actor's motions into conduct (1), are given by the theatrical simile. This frame of reference, these rules, may be quite different than those used by the actor to understand his own behavior.[13] This feature of dramaturgic analysis seems to be frequently misunderstood, even by its appreciators.[14] At least in part, this seems to be due to a lack of explicitness, if not a lack of clarity,[15] on the part of those using the dramaturgic framework.

In another sense, however, the actor's perspective is quite relevant to the dramaturgic analyst. As a social-psychologist, the dramaturgic analyst is little interested in documenting what "everybody knows." Instead he wants to get at *how* everybody knows what they know, at "hidden" effects or *latent* functions of interaction. The theatrical simile, like any of the similes invoked by the dramaturgic analyst, is revealing precisely insofar as it clarifies a latent function. Moreover, it seems to do so only when the actor is "unconscious" of the "impressive" effects of his activities, that is, only insofar as the actor "takes for granted" or "takes notice of without seeing" these effects. This may be appreciated by considering what a dramaturgic analysis of a theatrical performance might be.

A dramaturgic analysis of a theatrical performance would presumably *not* focus on how stage actors manage to bring a play "to life" for an audience. An analysis in these terms would be merely a technical analysis of the business at hand as the principles and the audience define this business. It would produce a manual of stage directions. In order to produce an account of interest to the dramaturgic analyst, what would have to be considered is how stage actors manage to keep the audience continually convinced that the play they are witnessing *is a play*. Such an analysis might point out, for example, that, by altering the segments of time within which events can "really" be accomplished, actors provide the audience with a sense of "play" as distinguished from "reality." It might document the gestures actors employ on stage which *interrupt* the audience member's sense of emerging character, which remind the audience that "character" and actor are not the same. It might note that returning for bows after the curtain has fallen not only services actors' egos, but also functions to remind the audience that there *is* someone "behind" the "appearance" they have been attending, for example, that the "appearance" of the dead man was "merely an appearance." Such an analysis might inquire as to which members of the audience, children under certain ages, for example, cannot retain the sense of the play *as a play*. And more. In general, a dramaturgic analysis of a theatrical performance would ask, what are the relations between the world in which the attitude of "play acting" prevails and that in which the attitude of "daily life" or "fundamental reality" obtains? What are the social devices whereby these worlds are kept distinct, and under what circumstances does this distinction collapse?

It should be noted that, insofar as the above is correct, the dramaturgic analyst seeks to describe the ways in which "impressions" are created, sustained, and ruptured under the condition that the actor is "unconscious" or only dimly "conscious" that this is a part of the business he is in. The other "models" used by the dramaturgic analyst reveal the same feature. Thus, the "con man" instructs us how, in everyday life, without being explicitly aware of it, those who do not conceive themselves as "con men" may sustain another's conception of themselves as "trustworthy" in the face of events which might lead him to conceive them quite differently. And persons who attach television aerials to their houses but do not own sets, those who put exotic travel labels on luggage that gets no further than the front door, in brief, those who *intentionally* misrepresent their qualities, thereby taking on a "character" for the audience to which they feel they have no "real" claim, are interesting to the dramaturgic analyst, not in themselves, but as persons who furnish "clear-cut evidence of the impressive function of presumably instrumental objects" and acts (6, p. 67).

Indeed, it does not seem too much to say that the power of dramaturgic analysis lies *in* the discrepancy between the perspective of the actor and that of the analyst. It is through this discrepancy that the analyst is able to elucidate matters that are beyond the immediate awareness of his subjects. It is when this discrepancy exists, when, for example, the actor provides "impressions" without being aware that he is doing so, that the theatrical simile is most revealing. What it reveals is this: the ways in which interactants *manage*, that is, *produce through their own activities*, that which they "take for granted" is "out there, really." Since the dramaturgic analyst aims to explore the conditions of constancy and change in others' impressions of actors as "being" what they claim, the theatrical simile seems exquisitely suited to his purpose. It focuses attention on that *aspect* of interaction of central interest to the analyst; affecting others' perceptions is the principal business of those in the theater. In the theater, creating appearances is regarded as a *task*; thus the analyst can more easily consider what individuals in everyday life *do* to create and sustain the realities they honor, even though they are not entirely aware of their doings. In the theater, the "expressive" and "impressive" functions of activity are *separated*; therefore, the analyst can consider in isolation that function of interaction so central to his theory of social stability and change.

All this adds up to pointing out some of the ways in which the theatrical simile is a simile, not a homology. It is a simile, a frame of reference, invoked by the analyst to segregate and permit him to analyze one of the multiple functions of interaction: its "impressive" function. The purpose is facilitated *because* this function is segregated in the theater; in daily life, this function is a concretely inextricable part of a larger complex.

It is also worth noting that this frame of reference enables the analyst to himself abandon, if only for a while, the perspective of everyday life; it enables or forces him to *stop* taking for granted what his subjects *do* take for granted, thereby permitting him to talk *about* these matters. In this way, the perspective stands ready, as does the anthropologist's "tribe," to furnish a lens through which "what everybody knows" can be rendered problematic. We may then ask what we do that stabilizes Grand Central Station as a place for people with destinations, and not a place to live, subway cars as objects for travel, not for sleeping, a hotel

lounge as a place to meet people in, a library for reading, a fire escape for survival, and more (7, p. 182).

But, as with any model, so the theatrical one has limits which, if not observed, pose dangers to analysis. The analyst and his readers run the risk of considering the dramaturgic framework to represent his subjects' model of the world. Because "impression management" is critical in the *analyst's* scheme of things, because in any situation it is this dimension that *he* attends to, he may leave the impression that this is the way things "are" as his subjects see things—or at least that, if they could be brought to be honest for a bit, they would see and admit that this is the case. There is, of course, no justification for this. Indeed, within the dramaturgic framework one must address in all seriousness the subjects' view of self and world; this is, after all, the topic of analysis. On the other hand, there is no justification for overlooking the impressive function of daily activities in an analysis of human conduct. Adding the dramaturgic perspective to the social-psychological tool kit should go some way toward preventing this.

Second, if we are correct in asserting that the dramaturgic analyst does not present "life as theater" as his subjects' view of the world, then we must ask after the relation between his subjects' view and "life as theater." The dramaturgic analyst does not claim that the actor is aware of the impressive functions of his activities; indeed, he seems to claim that, to the extent that the actor is aware of these functions, he becomes alienated from interaction and, moreover, from himself (5). We concur with this view and have presented some observations by and about mental patients to help warrant it. But, although in the dramaturgic vision the actor does not attend to the impressive effects of his activities *as* impressive effects, he nonetheless exhibits a remarkable ability to produce the right effect at just the right time, or, short of this, to correct for the errors he and his teammates may make. How is this accomplished? More pointedly, what is the relation between the *actor's* model of the world and the *dramaturgic analyst's* model? Is the actor merely the outcome of a dynamicized set of "organizational principles" which shove and haul him about without his awareness? Anyone committed to an understanding of everyday life and of the "actor's world" must cope with such a question. The dramaturgic analyst is self-admittedly so committed.

Finally, the theatrical simile may encourage the analyst to forget another important aspect of any everyday actor's communications: the actor is communicating *about* himself, and this constrains the attitude he may take toward the qualities he projects.

The stage actor's obligations do not ordinarily include a belief that the character he projects be a "presentation of self." It is an "Anybody" that the stage actor presents, if a particular one: an other-than-himself. His task, as usually defined, is to employ whatever means will facilitate the "coming alive" of the character for the audience. This leaves the actor free, or relatively so, to select an attitude toward the character he plays. He may, for example, conceive that getting "inside" the character will aid the accomplishment of his task; he may conceive that this is not necessary, taking a "classical" stance rather than a "method" one. So long as he convinces the audience that the character he portrays is a plausible one, his obligations are fulfilled. It is presumably only "method" actors, however, who succeed in experiencing the characters they are projecting as their selves, however temporarily.

The everyday actor's obligations, at least so far as fundamental qualities are concerned, do not leave him free to select an attitude toward the character he communicates. He does not, finally, experience life as theater. He does not expect the curtain to ring down, returning what came before to the realm of make-believe. He is constrained to *be* what he claims, and mental patients suggest that these constraints operate "inside" the individual as well as "on" him. Indeed, his need to believe in himself seems even stronger than his need to be certain that others entertain a particular view of him. He is in the grip of an ethic, and he violates this ethic so long as he is "on."

The basic task joined by mental patients would seem to be the locating and fixing of the reality of themselves. In this, they differ from stage actors; they cannot remain "on" with impunity. And in this, mental patients represent us all.

NOTES

1. This phrase is used by Erving Goffman in (4). Reference (6) is a revised and enlarged edition of the same work. Our criticism, as well as appreciation, of the "dramaturgic approach" are directed primarily at Goffman's work as its foremost exponent.

2. When used in an unqualified way, we intend the term "actor" to refer to that "Anybody" whose "action" is the subject of the dramaturgic analyst's analytic efforts. "Anybody" need not be a stage actor.

3. The study was carried out by the California Department of Mental Hygiene and partially supported by Grant 3M-9124 from the National Institute of Mental Health. The study, carried out by the authors and others, consisted in observing

and frequently interviewing the members of 17 families in which the wife was hospitalized for "schizophrenia." A description of the study group and of study procedures may be found in (10).

4. The context of his remarks is Davis' discussion of a group of intimates of which he is a member—known as the "Clan" by some, the "Rat Pack" by others—and the relations between this group and the "public."

5. Perhaps the best description of the variety of these situations is found in Goffman (5).

6. Jonathan Winters, an entertainer, provides us with an example of the breakdown of these boundaries. Of a period in his life when he experienced a "crack-up" he says, "I was 'on' all the time, always playing the part—in parks, restaurants, whenever [sic] I went—and I couldn't get 'off.' Well, I got 'off.' I look around now and think how much I have to be thankful for. And there's no use throwing myself on the floor because once in a while something bugs me" (13, p. 32). Stories about stage actors who carry their "parts" home, as well as audience members who take "character" for "reality," are common, if the events they point to infrequent.

7. Goffman has something like this in mind when he remarks that the mental patient "can learn, at least for a time, to practice before all groups the amoral arts of shamelessness" (7, "The Moral Career of the Mental Patient," p. 169). . . .

8. The whole remarkable series of papers by Goffman on mental patients and their keepers provides an example of what we may learn about everyday life from them (7).

9. This, as the other patients' and relatives' names we have used, is fictitious. We have, however, consistently used the same names for identical patients and relatives throughout the several papers we have published or are publishing.

10. Harold Garfinkel has used this term —and "assembled object"—in a similar way, but in another connection, in his unpublished work.

11. Compare Goffman's view of the "self" in (6), especially pp. 252-253, in (2), "The Moral Career . . . ," pp. 168-169, and in (3), p. 271.

12. Consider Goffman's statement to the effect that "when we observe a young American middle-class girl playing dumb for the benefit of her boy friend, we are ready to point to items of guile and contrivance in her behavior. But like herself and her boy friend, we accept as an unperformed fact that this performer *is* a young American middle-class girl. But surely here we neglect the greater part of the performance. . . . The unthinking ease with which performers consistently carry off such standard-maintaining routines does not deny that a performance has occurred, merely that the participants have been aware of it" (6, pp. 74-75).

13. In this respect, if in no other, the dramaturgic analyst's approach resembles that of the psychoanalytic psychiatrist. The psychoanalyst, too, is professionally engaged in attributing meanings to the behavior of individuals which are variant from the individuals' understandings of their own behavior.

14. For example, Don Martindale (9, pp. 61-72) discusses Goffman's work as if it were a representation of the growing amorality of urban individuals. We are explicitly disagreeing with this interpretation and would hold that the dramaturgic approach is applicable to the analysis of moral conduct in any age. We agree with Martindale, however, that the growing amorality of urban individuals may help account for the emergence of the dramaturgic perspective.

15. Surely it does little to clarify matters to suggest that "the *object* of a performer is to sustain a particular definition of the situation, this representing, as it were, his claim as to what reality is" (6, p. 85, italics added). "Performer" here refers to a person in everyday life carrying out his routine projects of action, *not* to someone who is "on."

BIBLIOGRAPHY

1. Burke, K. *A Grammar of Motives.* Englewood Cliffs, N. J.: Prentice-Hall, 1952.
2. Goffman, E. "Cooling the Mark Out: Some Aspects of Adaptation to Failure," *Psychiatry*, 1952, 25, 451-463.
3. Goffman, E.. "Embarrassment and Social Organization," *The American*

Journal of Sociology, 1956, 62, 264-271.

4. Goffman, E. *The Presentation of Self in Everyday Life.* Edinburgh: University of Edinburgh Social Sciences Research Center, 1956.

5. Goffman, E. "Alienation from Interaction," *Human Relations,* 1957, 10, 47-60.

6. Goffman, E. *The Presentation of Self in Everyday Life.* Garden City, New York: Doubleday, 1959.

7. Goffman, E. *Asylums.* New York: Doubleday, 1961.

8. Mailer, N. *Advertisements for Myself.* New York: The New American Library of World Literature, 1960.

9. Martindale, D. *American Society.* New York: D. Van Nostrand, 1960.

10. Sampson, H., S. L. Messinger, and R. D. Towne, "The Mental Hospital and Marital Family Ties," *Social Problems,* 1961, 9, 141-155.

11. Wolfe, B. "Ecstatic in Blackface: The Negro as a Song-and-Dance Man," *Modern Review,* 1950, 111, 196-208.

12. *Life Magazine,* December 22, 1958, 45, p. 116.

13. *San Francisco Chronicle.* January 24, 1961, p. 32.

4. SOURCES OF IDENTITY PROBLEMS

ORRIN KLAPP

Reprinted from *Collective Search for Identity* by Orrin E. Klapp. Copyright © 1969 by Holt, Rinehart and Winston, Inc. Reprinted by permission of Holt Rinehart and Winston, Inc. Orrin Klapp is currently Professor of Sociology at the University of Western Ontario. Since receiving his Ph.D. from the University of Chicago in 1948 he has contributed regularly to the development of the study of collective behavior and popular culture. He is the author of *Heroes, Villains, and Fools* as well as several other books and articles.

LACK OF IDENTITY IN ACCUMULATING INFORMATION

A leading "rock" group, "The Rolling Stones," complain in one of their best known songs about the deluge of irrelevant information—that a man comes on the radio telling one more and more, which gives no satisfaction because it does not drive one's imagination. Thus they express, in terms eloquent for teenagers, what many of us feel about public communication, whether advertising, news or education. The paradox we have already noted is that with increasing knowledge modern societies have not gained in self-knowledge and assurance, that the knowledge explosion of modern times is associated with an increase in identity problems. By ordinary reasoning, as knowledge of the world and the past increases, man should know himself better, and feel more a part of the world he knows. But this does not seem to be the case. As the number of potential reference points has multiplied, the ability to refer oneself to these points has declined. The knowledge explosion of modern life has not been accompanied by a self-knowledge implosion. On the contrary, as with Faust, when man knows the most he begins to suffer an identity problem.

History provides one example, offering the paradox that as historical knowledge accumulates, a sense of familiarity with the past lessens. When we feel the obvious pride the English take in battles like Waterloo or in the defeat of the Spanish Armada—or the Americans in the Boston Tea Party, or the Greeks in "Okhi Day"—we see that history is a series of events which can greatly intensify a people's sense of who they are. The formation of the state of Israel was a tremendous shot-in-the-arm to the Jewish identity. Yet, in spite of this obvious function that historical knowledge can have for identity, people today are getting out of touch with *their* past. Our society is becoming, in a real sense, traditionless and history-less; history and tradition are becoming less relevant to what we do as a people. There is a break with the past at precisely the time when books of history, as of other kinds of information, are being published by the hundreds. There seems to be less reference to the past of the kind that can identify one with the past.

The key is in the distinction between knowledge as information and knowledge which identifies. It seems at first glance nonsense to say that any people could be free from their own history, unless we bear in mind that a people's behavior is not just the effect of causes in the past but also the effect of continual reference to the past which makes them more or less traditional, more or less characteristic as a people, and more or less predictable. On the one hand, it would be absurd to deny that causation chains ever stopped, that there is any discontinuity in the causations of time. All the causes operating in any historical period are carried into the next, and in this sense, nothing ever escapes from the past. But, on the other hand, people can lose culture and knowledge of the past; for example, the Mayan Indians of Yucatan today, although they speak the Mayan language, are unable to recall anything of the grandeur of the culture they once had, and cannot even explain the architecture and artistic ruins found in the jungle. In this sense, it is a very real possibility to lose the past.

But this isn't the problem in a civilization with a vast amount of printed and broadcast information. It is, rather, that very little of this information can be claimed as "mine" or "ours." It lacks personal connection. One uses it to describe what happens to "some people," not to "my people." The knowledge of today is information *about*, not knowledge which *identifies*, which creates a sense of union. Objective knowledge is neutral, it excludes the subject and his feelings, it is factual rather than poetic. By contrast, knowledge which identifies creates a sense of union, takes a person into the subject; it may not be factual at all. For example, a movie we call a "tear jerker" takes a person into an experience. So does a letter from home, which is more than knowledge about certain people. Empathic knowledge involves you, heightens the sense of "I" and "we." But it seems plain that today most information is impersonal: even the history of one's country or region, even the description of the community in which one was born lacks that "hometown" feeling. Further, most empathic experiences are with strangers, with whom one can feel no personal bond.

This is the reason, it seems to me,

that we can have today the paradox of accumulating history and decline of tradition. I define tradition as the sense of living continuity with the past, the feeling of ownership that goes along with ideas from the past, normally the record we call history is part of tradition; but it is possible to lose tradition and still gain history. History, when it is not tradition, becomes a dead record of the ages and generations which we do not feel as ours. It is remote, irrelevant; our ancestors might as well be some other people. Yet traditionless history is, I think, taught today both at the high school and the university level. Debunking great men and criticizing the legendary aspects of history merely add to the alienation. Did Betsy Ross make the first flag? Did Dame Frietchie do what Whittier said she did? Was Lincoln an idealist? "No" to such questions means that another warm link with the past has been sundered. Traditionless history poses a problem of teaching history and making it come alive. But how can you make history come alive in a society that assumes the past is dead, antique, mythical, or irrelevant? If the past becomes dehumanized, impersonal, and irrelevant, even though we know about it, there is still a general loss of touch with the past as a source of we-feeling, ancestral pride, as roots of identity for the collectivity and the person.

What I am saying applies, of course, not only to history but to sociology, psychology, biology, and the other, less human, sciences. In short, the creators of objective knowledge (and to a great extent this is true also of art) are producing a body of information with which *no one can identify* in a personal way—not even (final irony!) the author himself. Such a mass of impersonal information is incapable of being forefather, father, mother, brother, comrade, friend—let alone God. So knowledge explodes beyond the mind, but not into the heart of man. Always we are outside, and even when we enter such knowledge we do so as strangers. Obviously the pursuit of mystiques—Yoga union, LSD "trips," group catharsis—counteracts such knowledge and represents an effort to get to the heart of things.

Traditionless history and inhuman knowledge illustrate the fact that it is possible for society to accumulate knowledge and things in such a way that they do not help people to establish identity—and may even stand in the way of it. The question is one of symbolic reference points; whether our society is supplying enough reference points for people to identify themselves, or whether it is erasing them too rapidly. Identity—the answer to the question, Who am I?—depends upon symbolic reference points which enable a person to remember who he is. For example, a diary—you go back to a diary to find out how you felt and how you thought in past days. It is a symbolic reference point for you. But what is happening to the symbolic reference points of modern life? Are we losing them in our knowledge of the past and our relations with people?

MODERNISM: PLACE INTO SPACE

Those who are optimistic about modernization, such as Daniel Lerner, think of it as bringing an increased freedom to imagine oneself as a kind of person (or in a situation) different from what is. But the other side of the question is whether, in gaining such freedom, people lose symbolic ties with the meaning of their lives. For example, anthropologists note that corn is not just a utilitarian economic good among American Indians but a means of worshipping the gods. When we

teach them to shift to other kinds of cash crops, we may give them more income but deprive them of a meaningful area of their lives. Here is a similar example that applies to more Americans. It is a statement by a Connecticut dairy farmer about what happened to the meaning of his life. One might call it a sentimental essay in favor of rootedness. He speculates on why few people who live where they were born commit suicide:

Too many of their ancestors are watching as they load the gun or mix the poison. Natives of a place feel themselves in the presence of a continuing life force larger than they are. Someone cares. Surrounded by sights, sounds, and people totally familiar to him, the man who lives where he was born is rarely alone. No matter what a failure he may be—and everyone broods on failure as he measures himself against what he once hoped to accomplish—no matter how wasted his life may have been, it is difficult for the man who lives where he was born, be it city, town, or tiny village, not to derive pleasure from something each day of his life. A tree he saw planted—now sixty feet tall—the first patch of grass that sets green early in the spring, a bunch of boys playing baseball in the same lot where he once played baseball.

The town or village native knows many secrets. He knows, for instance, who lived in what is now a funeral parlor. He knows where the old road went before the new one was built. Let the air be filled with the smell of sewage, he will tell you whose septic tank is overflowing. He can also tell you when it's going to rain. Considered one by one, these secrets have little value. Taken as a whole, however, they can be as priceless as life itself. Furthermore, the man who lives where he was born, when he hears a train whistle or a church bell or the voices of children as they are let out of school, can in the merest of instants, relive his entire life. Sounds that are inaudible to most ears can make him young again. He possesses an indestructible immortal contentment.

People need the familiar just as they need food. Most people would truly rather see the same places, the same things, the people every day of their lives than be exposed to the new and different.

In my New England city, one of our more prominent citizens was persuaded by his family to take a round the world cruise. He saw London, Paris, Rome, the Near East, the Far East, all the oceans, and most of the wonders produced by man. Home at last and having appeared at his club where for forty years he had sat at the same table and eaten the same lunch being served by the same waiter, he was asked how he had enjoyed his trip. "Oh," he said, with an obvious lack of enthusiasm, "it was okay, I guess, except all I could think about was all the fun I was missing at home."

What should we feel for this citizen? Contempt for his provincialism? Should we scorn him because he prefers his own house to the Taj Mahal? Or should we instead envy him his contentment? Hamlin Garland describes his emotions as he returned to the prairy home of his boyhood. He was depressed to find how much everything had changed at the hands of even so few enterprising settlers. The prairy, trackless and wild when he was a boy, had been tamed and plowed. Where there had been only crossroads, there were now towns, and towns had become cities. It took him a full day of searching to discover even a small patch of virgin prairy sod. But if progress was unsettling to an absentee Garland, one may well imagine how distressing these same changes are to the man who remains in his birthplace and who, therefore, sees them happen. This being the era of the bulldozer, if a patch of prairy sod or any sod at all is to be preserved, it must be declared a national monument.

However, just as it is impossible for almost any man to live where he was born and be totally miserable, so it is impossible for him to be totally happy. He lives in a state of constant outrage against those who are confining his childhood memories in concrete pipes all in the name of flood control. He resents the miles of plywood he sees snaking over the land. "Where are the trees on which I carved my initials?" he asks. As he looks about his birthplace, he feels the bulldozers crush him as well. He feels himself being engulfed by the inexorable tide of men and machinery. The man who lives where he was born prefers things that have not changed to those which have. It may now take him only eight minutes to reach the center of the city instead of thirty-five, but he prefers to remember what was under the new road. He sees growing numbers of people as a skin disease. Secretly, he longs for a plague to stop every bulldozer dead in its tracks. Only his ever dwindling supply of secrets sustains him. Perhaps it would

have been better if he had moved. Every day on his way to work, the man who lives where he was born passes the grave of his ancestors and their aspirations, noble or ignoble, by some osmosis become part of his own. He is a sentimentalist and an increasingly frustrated one. Of course, all those who live where they were born are, like philosophers, without immediate honor in their own community. We still have in our city, for instance, a native son who may shortly become the president of one of the richer corporations in the world. Only 45, but already a director of a score of companies, the father of four children and the owner of a yacht, the recipient of a dozen national awards in his chosen profession, he has everything that it is possible for a generous providence to bestow—except the respect of those who went to school with him, because he cried, he *cried* on his graduation day when he failed to win the good posture prize. He should, of course, have moved away and triumphed elsewhere, because just as others who live where born know many secrets about you, you also know many secrets about them.[1]

This New Englander's complaint about the destruction of the scene of his boyhood illustrates what I mean about the loss of the symboblic reference points of identity. What is one to say about his complaint? Why doesn't he welcome the bulldozer? Is it mere sentimentality, a fear of the newfangled, a wish to hold up progress and turn the clock back? I think it is a mistake to put this issue in terms of progress versus antiprogress. If we do so, we shall miss the real issue. It seems to me he has a legitimate complaint. He is expressing an injury to his integrity which came from wiping away the symbols that made *his* environment meaningful and *his* kind of identity possible. He has, in a sense, been robbed of identity—a loss which to some extent applies to practically everyone in the United States. This injury to integrity comes not from progress, but from a too rapid and indiscriminate sweeping away of symbols. In the accumulation of new things, it is possible for society to pass the optimum point in the ratio between the new and the old: between piling up information and material wealth on the one hand and old things which have merely souvenir value; between innovation and acculturation on the one hand and tradition on the other. Beyond this optimum point, where a society is roused to creativity by introduction of new elements, is a danger point where consensus and integrity of the person break down. At such a point, too many symbols lose their meaning and there begin to be questions about whether life is meaningful, life styles become unstable and confused, there is excessive faddism and a general loss of touch with the past and the present as a source of we-feeling. Much of this comes not from progress per se, but from insufficient recognition of the symbolic problem: that symbols are important, and cannot be replaced by mere things. The only intelligent way to replace a symbol is to build another symbol. Who worries about this?

We suffer in America from rampant, dogmatic modernism; we look with complacency, if not pleasure, at the fact that we are a country of vanishing traditions—with perhaps the fewest traditions in the world. One aspect of this is faddism; the rate of change in American styles is too fast to be good even for a modernist. We find, for example, the curious phenomenon of the old learning from the young. Passing a dancing school in Santa Monica, California, I looked in to see a number of men and women of 40 to 60 dancing with young instructors and instructresses. A person not born in America could not help but think it strange that there is a reversal of the usual socialization pattern, in which we find the old turning to the young for knowhow, if not wisdom—with style change among the young so rapid that the old

feel out of date and can get "with it" only by turning to the young for guidance. I thought no more about this until I went to a party and found the hostess, who was well over 50 years in age, announcing that they were going to do some of the new dances; and the lady had, in fact, brought in three teenagers to teach the new steps. This phenomenon of the old looking to youth for guidance raises questions about the dignity and integrity of identity in America, and whether the optimum ratio of change has not been passed. Not only is the rate of change too fast for persons over 40, but there is a melange of styles borrowed from almost everywhere—for example, in popular music—which makes it hard to identify a national style even of the moment. With such a style melange, the natural question for the person is, Which style identifies me? Which identities my class? My people? In the light of such ambiguity, we see a nostalgia for tradition in the fad of folk singing, which has the ability to transport a person momentarily back to the frontiers, to the cotton fields, to a Mississippi River boat, to the feeling of a lonely cowboy or a Civil War campfire—to a sense of the living past to which one belongs. But pseudofolk singing is only a pseudosymbol and creates only a pseudopast.

Modernism acting upon the American scene is symbolized by the bulldozer and the ever-changing faces of billboards. The call to bring in the bulldozer is linked with slogans like "live modern, smoke a _____." This modernism rides roughshod over every consideration that is not economically and politically organized. Aside from a few antiquarian and historical interests, there is no voice, no pressure group, for symbols as such. Bulldozers wipe away every scene and the reference points that make local identity possible. It is commonplace that the wide-open spaces are disappearing in the United States (that even camping is coming to have an uncomfortable resemblance to apartment-house dwelling). It is not yet so keenly realized, however, that *places* are disappearing even faster than space in the United States.

What is a place? A place is a space with a sense of locality and identity. It is a recognized territory of symbols: my old neighborhood, Plymouth Rock, Canterbury Cathedral where Becket was murdered. Stepping over the battlefield at Vicksburg, one is aware one is in a place. Obviously, bulldozers, as they clear spaces for tract housing, high-rise apartments, and parking lots, for hordes of strangers moving in, destroy places because they destroy the symbols and sense of familiarity with the territory. As America becomes one vast suburbia, high-rise center, and parking lot, it will cease to be a place and become a modernized space. Even Hilton Hotels, grand as they are, seem more space than place. Space is *in* human geography (just as history can be traditionless). A geographer, Philip Wagner, remarked, "I wonder if geography is not working at cross purposes with history?" By this he meant that the tendency of geography to treat places in an indifferent way, like other places, deprives them of their identity.

In this sense, much of Los Angeles is a space, not a place. Some slums are not much to look at, but they have the distinction, at least, of being places. Disneyland, though fun to go to, a children's mecca perhaps, might be called a pseudoplace, really more space than place—a lot of ingeniously arranged concrete that creates the illusion of somewhere one has been. My point is that space—perhaps even pseudoplace—robs identity. Place, on the other hand, nurtures it, tells you

who you are—either "I belong" or "This is foreign to me, I am an outsider"—and one achieves identity by differentiation. Will the trend from place into space continue? Will the future world become a modernized space rather than a place? One sees already phenomena such as Aswan Dam drowning historic monuments in Egypt. A traveler may wake up some morning and not know where he is —Egypt, South Africa, Japan or Los Angeles. In the light of these considerations, I cannot see a gain for identity in modernization as a destroyer of place. It still is an open question whether new human symbols can be devised which will replace local sense of place.

MOBILITY: PERSON INTO CATEGORY

The conversion of place into space is, of course, closely associated with the well-known mobility and "rootlessness" of Americans. And this mobility is associated with an ambiguity of the person, which may not be such a crisis to Americans as it is to foreigners in America because we natives are used to it. Daniel Boorstin calls it the "ideal of the undifferentiated man"; it is not a shock to find a judge shoeing a horse, the boss playing baseball with employees, the housewife who is also a business executive. We do not expect people to maintain differences, be status-conscious, hold themselves apart. (By contrast, Kurt Lewin noted that a German customs official in a bathing suit is still a customs official.) You cannot place a man by where he comes from, his antecedents, even the status symbols he displays. It is entirely up to him. "Prove yourself. Who are you?"

But ambiguity is perhaps a terrible burden for a social system to bear. I wish to analyze here how it is a problem for the reference points and feedback which identity needs. Mobility, of which American society provides such good examples, is one of the favorite concepts of the sociologist. He distinguishes physical mobility as movement in space from social mobility as contact with different groups, classes, and kinds of people (including what I would call places). To take a familiar example, a society doctor meeting charity cases at the county hospital is contacting classes of people different from himself and is highly mobile socially. The history of our country is a kind of story of physical and social mobility, of the immigration of pilgrims and other settlers, the movement westward, the escape into the frontier, the success story of Babbitt, the status revolutions of new classes rising into power—*nouveaux riches* overthrowing Tories, Whigs, and Mugwumps; the rise of bureaucrats, technicians, and managers; the overthrow of society by "publiciety" as described by Cleveland Amory. There are also what might be called the convection currents of population —such as the drift from land to the towns, the flight from the central cities to the suburbs, the movement of migratory workers, the daily motions of commuters, even grandma and grandpa on wheels in their retirement. I have asked my sociology classes whether they intend to follow their parents' occupation. The answer, as you may expect, is almost unanimously No. Ask them how many changes of residence they have had since they were born, and the median is sometimes ten or eleven moves.

Now the centrally significant psychological fact about social mobility of any kind is that you can't move without leaving a place, therefore losing a place; and you can't make new

contacts without in some way lessening or disrupting old relationships. Thus mobility pulls roots, and *makes particular persons less important* in their relationships with one another. In very mobile societies, there is a feeling of "Bye bye, I won't see you long." It can be illustrated by the experience of changing schools: the student makes friends all over again—are his new friends the same as the friends he left in his previous school? Or it is illustrated by a series of love affairs and marriages: Is the first the same as the fifth and the tenth?

We have the general effect of numbers in similar relationships as pointed out by sociologists. As long as only one person is in a relationship, he is "somebody special"; if others can share it or replace him, it is a class of relationship. If you have a hundred or a thousand people in the same relationship, you begin to have a mass. As greater numbers are encountered in a category, there is a dilution of attention and concern which results in impersonality and mass-likeness of human relations. So the students become just one in a class of a hundred, and a patient becomes just case number fifteen in a ward. But this mass-likeness, as we well know, is not just found in large groups, but also in America has entered friendly and personal relationships. If you are lucky enough still to be living with the twenty or so people that you were raised with, you probably still feel you are "somebody special," but the majority of people are not living and working with lifelong friends, but merely with acquaintances.

Indeed, it is becoming characteristic of our society that nobody really knows anybody. The "friendship" is only a role, a categorical relationship. People with hundreds of "friends" suddenly discover that they didn't know one of their "friends" had been ill or separated, or alcoholic, or psychotic; or they find to their discomfort that after they had been away for months they had not been missed (unless their role had been called for). Worse, yet, is the discovery that one's category—to which he may have given his life—can be so easily filled by someone else. Now this awareness that "friendship" is only a role played on certain occasions and the feeling that "they can get along without me" lead to a sense of insignificance. A categorical, refillable status is incapable of giving a person the feeling of being "somebody special"—indeed, even really there as a person. And the more easily refillable the status, the more this is so. Americans live and try to maintain identities in such shallowness of relationship[2] in which even "intimates" are transitory—like telephone operators replaceable at either end of the line. Facile and enthusiastic playing of the role is the limit of commitment and "sincerity," which easily leads to the feeling that one cannot get through to people, can't reach the "real man"—only facades and masks are presented. The frustration of excessive mobility (in dating) is well expressed by this statement of a television actress:

You can go out every night with a different guy, but after a while you're bound to get tired of it, because all the running around you're doing is in a circle. Really, you don't get anything. You don't get to learn anything about people. You'll find six months of it is a very long time. After that, you're asking yourself, "What's going on? What's it all about?"[3]

In such mobility, people cannot answer their emotional questions; they find their insight into others dulled rather than deepened. Finally, in frustration, people seek group therapy or to "tune in" with LSD. Such shallowness, based on skillful (and impenetrable) role-playing, combined with

mobility converting a person into a category, is a milieu in which identity easily perishes from lack of the assurance of being somebody special that everyone needs.

Aggravating, rather than helping, this is the furious pursuit of status and ego symbols which, past a certain point, becomes a vicious circle. It is now true, in our land of ambiguous identity, that anyone may adopt almost any status symbol which he can afford. He may have his Cadillac, the new look of fashion, the fashionable address, the fancy letterhead. He announces and maintains any identity that he can get away with. But to consider the ultimate effect of free adoption of symbols on identity itself, we might imagine a play in which the actors were free to costume themselves as they pleased. Would it not soon become impossible to tell who was really who? Would not the action become, instead of a meaningful play, a confusing masquerade? The changeability of symbols makes life like a masquerade. That employee I intend to hire, that person I want to marry, that friend —who is he really? Life acquires a Fred Demara-like quality of pose. When everybody is adopting symbols, how does one tell who one really is? The paradox seems to be that when anybody can be anybody, nobody can be "somebody."

Another detrimental influence on identity from mobility in a pluralistic setting is inconsistency and unreliability of signals. From the conflict of subcultures, confusion of styles, rapidity of changes, diversity of viewpoints, shifting of positions, and difficulty of sorting out poses, a person has a hard time feeling he is right—whether he follows or rejects a certain position. He has trouble, first, in deciding which persons, styles, and authorities are right and true among the poses, pretexts, and rationalizations of those playing "games." Secondly, when he takes a position, he doesn't know whether the expressions of opinion and concern of others are sincere, so he doesn't know whether he will be really supported or whether he is "going out on a limb." An undetermined number of people with whom he deals in a mobile society are "phonies" (inauthentic role-players)[4]—he cannot be sure which—and their responses do not help him become authentic by sincere revelation or, ordinarily, by challenging encounter. Like the polite applause that does not tell an entertainer how good his act is, such signals do not tell a person what he needs to know. Seeking adequate signals from others, he becomes other-directed, anxious about what people think but not, even when comforming, having assurances he is really right; he is gullible to tastemakers and opinion pundits, but their advice does not help him build sound judgment or know his own position at all—or where his real comrades are among the poseurs.

This is like putting one's foot into the soft mud of a lake bottom seeking a firm place to stand—and not finding it. Since, in such a milieu, one doesn't really know where people stand, one cannot say what "people think"—cannot, in the terminology of George Herbert Mead, build a realistic generalized other. One builds instead a pragmatic concept of roles which get by; and a concept of oneself as a conforming performer (expert role-player) who is "making it" socially but has not had a chance to check his real feelings against what people really think, let alone infer from their deceptive responses what is right to think. The whole thing means weakness and fragmentation of the generalized other (which Mead said is the basis of some rather important qualities such as objectivity, truth, morality, and justice).

Excessive mobility also makes family relations fragile which, of course, strikes at the heart of identity. Divorce, serial marriage, desertion of children, alienation of youth from parents, dispersion of kin, insecurity of old people deprive a person of the ability to define himself by relations which should be most reliable, intimate, and meaningful. Even when kinship structure is not destroyed, mobility brings in the whole problem of "adjustment"—of mate to mate, parent to child, neighbor to neighbor, man to work (relationships which in stable societies are simply taken for granted; you don't adjust to Uncle Henry or the person you marry or the baby you have because it is simply in the order of things to get along with them—anyway, you have lived with that kind of person all your life). As mobility increases, it becomes a problem to make relationships work which a person ought to be able to count on and not worry about. He has a need for "contacts," role-playing—the Dale Carnegie problem. We do not dwell here on those disturbances of parent-child and sibling relationships which produce the severest identity problems—neuroses and psychoses —about which psychologists have written so much, because our focus is on those general societal conditions which affect "normal" people (sufficiently ordinary to be a mass), the meaning of life and happiness of almost anyone. Doubtless such conditions as loss of tradition, shallowness of relationships, inadequacy of feedback, which make normal people unhappy, are crises with which it may be impossible to cope for those who were cheated in their first relationship.

LACK OF IDENTIFYING RITUAL

Modern society also fails to give a person an adequate conception of himself through a lack of identifying ritual. The average person today is unlikely to experience many ceremonies which intensify his awareness of shared mystiques or his awareness of himself as a person. Most of our participations in art, drama, mass entertainment, and other "language of the emotions" are as strange and "outside" as impersonal information. Even when they are emotionally moving and involving, one gets little sense of belonging to something from them, and even less sense of being somebody. And many of the ceremonies which are supposed to increase our sense of identification with groups (for example, church and patriotic) are . . . formalistic and boring, or otherwise lacking in significance. Though church attendance is high, there is a general decline of significant rites of passage; people are denied adequate "rebirth" rituals by a society that is largely secular-minded and anti-ceremonial. Mircea Eliade says:

Modern man no longer has any initiation of the traditional type . . . a ritual death followed by resurrection or a new birth. . . . For archaic thought . . . man is made—he does not make himself all by himself. It is the old initiates, the spiritual masters, who make him. But these masters apply what was revealed to them at the beginning of time by the supernatural beings . . . this birth requires rites instituted by the supernatural beings; hence it is a divine work . . . the puberty initiation represents, above all, the revelation of the sacred . . . the new man is no longer a "natural man."[5]

Of course, modern man does not hanker for primitive initiation rites; but what many people seem to be striving for in strenuous and dangerous play—not to say sex and other things

not usually thought of as sports—is some kind of ritual by which to prove themselves, some test which requires a person to extend his whole self, not merely play a role. This test element is the mystique of many sports, perhaps even of some crimes. But, on the whole, though modern American society offers many models by which a person can try to make himself as he pleases—with the help of such peer groups as will accept him—relatively few of these have initiatory or rebirth rites. The majority of roles a man takes are "grown into" or contracted for without his ever having a clear impression of himself as having "made it," or having been created, remade, reborn—without, in other words, a distinct experience: "I am a new man."

Such factors as I have mentioned —lack of identity in accumulating information, modernism changing place into space, mobility changing person into category and supplying unreliable signals, and lack of ritual—work toward a kind of emotional emptiness in America, a situation in which nobody "counts." I have tried to point to some of the most obvious things that defeat identity in America—deficiencies in interaction and symbols, which mean insufficient feedback for personal integrity and emotional well-being. As I said before, I am not concerned with deficiencies of interaction which would result in severe personal and mental disorder, but only with those which stand in the way of the ordinary man's having a satisfyingly meaningful life.

NOTES

1. Roger Eddy, "On Staying Put," *Mademoiselle*, May, 1966, pp. 108-110. Another writer, Harvey Cox, comments on the destruction of "sacral space" (religiously significant place) by secularization, and recommends emphasis on "humanly significant space" to replace this loss. Harvey Cox, "The Restoration of a Sense of

Place: A Theological Reflection on the Visual Environment," *Religious Education*, Jan. 11, 1966; reprinted in *Ekistics* (Athens, Greece), Vol. 25, 151, June, 1968, pp. 422-424.

2. Shallowness of relationships ranks high among the images of Americans reported by foreign students at the University of California, Los Angeles. Richard T. Morris, *The Two Way Mirror, National Status in Foreign Students' Adjustment* (Minneapolis: University of Minnesota Press, 1960), pp. 120-125.

3. "The Pleasures and Pains of the Single Life," *Time*, Sept. 15, 1967, pg. 37.

4. Seeman discusses the problem of au-thenticity. I have referred to lack of authenticity in roles as pseudointegration in *Heroes, Villains and Fools*, (Englewood Cliffs: Prentice-Hall, 1963) pp. 110-116.

5. *Birth and Rebirth, The Religious Meanings of Initiation in Human Culture* (New York: Harper & Row, 1958), pp. XII, XIV, 3. Fred Davis and Virginia Oleson relate the identity stresses of student nurses to an absence of rite of initiation to minimize "the sense of discontinuity with a former identity, the mourning for a lost self." "Initiation in a Woman's Profession: Identity Problems in the Status Transition of Coed to Student Nurse," *Sociometry*, Vol 26, March, 1963, pp. 98-99.

II. THE NATURE OF SELF

In the first section we explored the dramaturgical view of social life as interaction. In this section we focus on the sense of individuality that a person acquires through interacting with others. Traditionally, when the question of individuality has been broached by social psychologists, two concepts have been most prominently utilized: personality and self.[1] Dramaturgists, like most other sociologically anchored social psychologists, have preferred the concept "self" in order to avoid certain assumptions inherent in personality theory. This semantic preference for self avoids construing (1) individuality as an internal psychobiological entity consisting of conscious and unconscious elements; (2) individuality as a structure of attitudes, values, traits and needs; and (3) individuality as the mainspring for or motivation of a person's consistent behavior.[2]

In contrast to personality theorists, dramaturgists view individuality as basically a social and not a psychological phenomenon. This means that a person's individuality is shared with others. To use Harry Stack Sullivan's terminology, a person's self emerges and is maintained through a process of "consensual validation." The self of the human organism is established by the action of that organism and the action of others with respect to it. That society labels as delusional those indi-

1. For a cogent discussion of the pros and cons of these two concepts, see Stone, G. and Farberman, H., *Social Psychology Through Symbolic Interaction* (Waltham, Mass.: Ginn Blaisdell, 1970).
2. Turner, Ronny E., "Who Am I?" The Absurd Question," *The Sociological Focus: The Utah State University Journal of Sociology*, Vol. 3, No. 1, June, 1972, pp. 1-13.

viduals who cling to an image of themselves that is in no way validated by others—speaks to the social reality of individuality.

The self is social not only in the larger connotation of the word but also in the idea that a person's sense of individuality is situationally specific. Different situations occasion the establishment of different selves. In this context, a person's sense of individuality is plural, not singular. A person's self (in the singular) is not carried from situation to situation. Rather, individuality is fashioned in terms of the resources and audiences available in the immediate situation in which the individual is acting.

The observation that many people's selves appear to be the same from situation to situation does not deny the necessity of establishing themselves anew in each situation. It speaks only to the fact that an increasing number of situations in society have become standardized; consequently the selves that are established in these situations share a certain similarity. Yet there still appears to be a good deal more behavioral variation between the same person in different situations than among different persons in the same situation. This reaffirms the contention that a person's individuality is not something that is brought to interaction. People do not have selves that are activated or reflected in social situations. Individuality, like all other features of life, is built up in human interaction. Kenneth Burke aptly and succinctly characterizes the dramaturgical view of self: *doing is being.*

In the first selection, Ernest Becker delves into the symbolic conditions for individuality. To Becker, the self is basically a system of language and ideas that is in a constant state of modification as a person interacts with others. In his thinking, the presentation of an infallible self is a presentation of a self that has unshakeable control over words. Manipulation is the key to individuality. Life is a continuously staged social ceremony whose purpose is to create and sustain meaning for its participants. So one's sense of individuality is the measure of one's power of participation in this ceremony. Becker speaks also of the very tenuous nature of an individual's self, "the utter fragility of his delicately constituted fiction." According to Becker, people need to be most skilled performers to emerge from an interaction better than they came in. Consequently, there is a creative but also a threatening aspect to every social encounter.

The relationship between the dramaturgical view of human interaction and individuality is probably best expressed in Erving Goffman's essay. Goffman's premise is that when individuals appear in front of others, they have many reasons for attempting to control the impression the others will receive. Since people require information about each other in order to interact, each person acts so as to *express* himself, and the other people in the situation in turn are *impressed* in some way by that person. Herein lies Goffman's major theme of impression management. To manage people's impressions of you and the situation in which you are interacting is to control the conduct of others. It is in this control and manipulation that individuality is fashioned. Goffman also speaks of the moral imperatives in interaction. In so doing, he touches upon what some dramaturgists feel is the basis of the social bond: the moral obligation of persons to be impressed by the performances of others.

Gregory Stone fashions what is perhaps the most careful dramaturgical analysis of self. Beginning with the assumption that appearance as well as discourse establishes social reality, Stone develops the notion that individuality often resides in the meaning of one's appearance. In his view, interaction is basically a process of identification. This process is said to entail two dimensions: identification *of* and identification *with*. Identification *of* has to be made before identification *with* can occur. In other words, a person has to know who the other is before engaging in further interaction with that other. These identifications *of* one another are made, for the most part, on the basis of appearance. Apparent symbols such as body idiom, clothing, facial expressions, and the like therefore serve as means of establishing one's self. Drawing upon the tradition of symbolic interaction, Stone goes on to analyze the self in terms of four researchable components: identity, value, mood, and attitude, all of which are seen as situationally emergent.

In the final selection, Richard Travisano utilizes Stone's notion of identity in an attempt to understand the changes of self that occur during the usual lifetime. Although Travisano's empirical focus is on changes in religious affiliation, his theoretical exposition has broad relevance for understanding the ubiquity of identity changes in modern society. His careful analysis of alternation and conversion nicely underscores the dramaturgical image of the human being as a performing artist.

SUGGESTED READINGS

Becker, Howard and Anselm Strauss. "Careers, Personality, and Adult Socialization," *American Journal of Sociology*, Vol. 62 (1957) pp. 253-263.

Cooley, Charles H. *Human Nature and the Social Order*, (New York: Scribner's, 1922).

DeLevita, D. H. *The Concept of Identity*, (New York: Harper & Row, 1967).

Goffman, Erving. *Interaction Ritual*, (New York: Anchor Books, 1967).

Goffman, Erving. *The Presentation of Self In Everyday Life*, (New York: Anchor Books, 1959).

Gordon, Chad and Kenneth Gergen. *The Self In Social Interaction*, (New York: John Wiley and Sons, Inc., 1968).

Lynd, Helen. *On Shame and the Search For Identity*, (New York: Science Editions, 1958).

McCall, George and J. L. Simmons. *Identities and Interaction*, (New York: The Free Press, 1966).

Mead, George Herbert. *Mind, Self, and Society*, (Chicago: University of Chicago Press, 1934).

Ruitenbeek, H. *The Individual and the Crowd*, (New York: New American Library, 1965).

Smith, M. Brewster, "Competence and Socialization," in John Clausen (ed.), *Socialization and Society* (Boston: Little, Brown and Company, 1968).

Strauss, Anselm. *Mirrors and Masks*, (Glencoe, Ill.: The Free Press, 1959).

Sullivan, Harry S. "The Illusion of Personal Individuality," in H. S. Sullivan, *The Fusion of Psychiatry and Social Science* (New York: W. W. Norton and Co., Inc., 1964).

5. THE SELF AS A LOCUS OF LINGUISTIC CAUSALITY

ERNEST BECKER

Reprinted from Ernest Becker, *The Birth and Death of Meaning* (Glencoe: The Free Press, 1962), pp. 101-115, by permission of the author and The Free Press. Ernest Becker, until his untimely death in the spring of 1974, was Professor in the Department of Political Science, Sociology, and Anthropology at Simon Fraser University in Canada. He is the author of eight books including *The Birth and Death of Meaning* and *The Revolution in Psychiatry*. His last book, *The Denial of Death*, won a Pulitzer Prize for non-fiction.

Fundamental to social ceremonial is the proper use of the words; the actor must be able to deliver the lines correctly. The conventions which facilitate social action are largely verbal. But what is the self if not an identifiable locus of communication? What we term "personality" is largely a locus of word possibilities. When we expose our self-esteem to possible undermining by others in a social situation, we are exposing a linguistic identity to other loci of linguistic causality. We have no idea what words are going to spout forth from another's self-system. The self-system in this sense is an ideational linguistic device, in a continual state of modification and creation. We sit comfortably in our armchairs pouring forth conventional symbolic abstractions. In this shadowy monotone, we exercise and modify our fragile selves, while our pet cat sits purringly by, convinced probably that we are only purring too.

After the child has fashioned a transactable self his work has hardly begun. He must then learn to use the ritual rules for social interaction. Children are notoriously termed "cruel"—the only way we find of expressing the idea that they have not yet learned to use the face-preserving social conventions. Probably the reason for the child's blustering early encounters is that he still basks in the parental omnipotence, and has no need to protect *himself* in the social situation, and therefore no thought to handling others gently. "Cripple!" "Fatty!" "Four-Eyes!" He can see the selves of others as something to be overcome, but not yet to be appeased in his own interest. His self-esteem is still dependent upon ministrations from the adult and not yet from society at large. Socialization can be deemed successful when he has learned to interact outside the family. The early peer group contacts are crucial in learning to transact with others, to protect their selves and to maintain one's own. "If you keep calling my doll ugly, I won't come play over at your house tomorrow." This is not a threat, but a plea for gentle handling, an enjoinder to exercise mutuality.

Sociologists insist on the importance of early training in role-playing. The child plays at various adult roles and learns the proper lines for each part—husband, wife, policeman, robber. By the time he grows up, he is already skilled at assuming the identity of some of the major figures in the cultural plot. But there is a more subtle side to early role-playing. The child learns to put forth and sustain a self and learns to modify the demands of that self, as well as to evaluate the performance of his peers. *He learns that there are certain reactions to his cues that he can discount.* We all remember, hopefully, at least one person with whom we could compare our performance favorably in early peer interaction, and feel properly social at a very early age. There was always one "sore loser" who filled us with a sense of social self-righteousness. "Ya, ya, you're a sore loser!" The child learns thereby to sustain his own valued self in the face of negative responses: there are those, he finds, whose evaluation he can ignore, who use improperly personal gambits in the social situation. He learns that there exists a privatization of the social context: an unwarranted handling by someone else of the child's own properly presented self. "Wasn't *I* right?" is a plea for reassurance that one is sustaining the social plot with proper mastery. To fail to learn this simple fact, as many schizophrenics do, is to remain a center of error in a constantly correct world. Paranoia begins as a private rather than a public way of justifying oneself.

If the self is primarily a linguistic device, and the identity of the self primarily the experience of control over one's powers, one fundamental conclusion is inescapable. To present an infallible self is to present one which has unshakable control over words. It is amazing how little we realize this even after Dale Carnegie's unambiguous message: "It matters not what you *mean*: you and those around you become according to what you *say*." This simple and crucial fact for understanding human behavior stares us so disarmingly in the face that we pass on to more involved and less important things. The proper word or phrase, properly delivered, is the highest attainment of human interpersonal power. The easy handling of the verbal context of action gives the only possibility of direct exercise of control over others.

How does this come about? Psychoanalysis traces the beginning of word power to the magical world of the child. The word, a mere sound, miraculously obliges the adult to do one's bidding; it brings food and warmth, and closeness. The word which pleases the angry adult transforms him before one's eyes into a newly appreciative protector. The adult retains in prayer some of this early proof of the full efficacy of words; and in his reluctance (or eagerness) to curse, a conviction of how delicately everything in the universe hangs on the proper sound. Obsessive-compulsives carry over a preoccupation with just the right utterance, and a perpetual uneasiness over a potential slip in control. Primitives too, it is thought, derive their beliefs about the magical efficacy of words from this childhood awe at the power of sound. A word can take form and kill; it enters the air and becomes embodied into the evil wish it expresses. When we use a four-letter word for copulation, we recapture some of this concretization: the word takes on the immediacy of the act itself. In military life where nothing in one's fate is in his own control, continual cursing may become a substitute form of decisiveness.

Sullivan ... understood the self-system as primarily a linguistic device which is fashioned by the child to conciliate his environment. The efficacy of words is at the very basis of our adaptation to anxiety. This is the background to that marvelous feeling of power that comes with the simplest utterance: "I'm *terribly* sorry," "Good show!" "*Good* to see you!" With these simple phrases we frame the context for interaction. It is now up to our interlocutor to sustain our sincerity, to put forth the proper answer, to maintain the rhythm of the lines. The parents' early enjoinder "Say 'thank you' to the man" is not an inculcation of obsequiousness. It is an exercise in control: it is now up to "the man" to frame an appropriate response or to end the social situation gracefully. Words are the only tools we have for confident manipulation of the interpersonal situation. By verbally setting the tone for action by the proper ceremonial formula, we permit complementary action by our interlocutor. Not only do we permit it; we *compel* it, if he is to sustain his face. By properly delivering our lines we fulfill our end of the social bargain, and oblige the other to fulfill his in turn.

It is surprising how many people never learn confidently to manipulate the verbal context for action. The young schizophrenic often provides the best example of failure to handle even the simple greeting. With a self-esteem brittle to the core, the threat of an encounter can be overwhelming. One schizophrenic, beginning his army career, quickly signaled his "queerness" to the other soldiers. He learned that a simple greeting used by all never failed to elicit a friendly response, and he followed others around, even to the latrine, repeating the greeting again and again. Another learned, perhaps for the first time, a sure ritual of presentation, a reliable way to engage another in social intercourse without eliciting a hostile response: one had only to offer a cigarette. But even this act has its appropriateness, and the others quickly became embarrassed by his incessant offerings of handfuls of cigarettes, often at inappropriate times.

We are uncomfortable in strange groups and subcultures largely because we cannot frame the appropriate verbal context for sustaining the action or the ceremonial. We do not hear cues familiar to us, nor can we easily give those that make for smooth transitions in conversation. The English invariably discomfort Americans because they seem to be saying just the right thing at the right time, and they confidently terminate an interaction with a "Cheers" that is unfamiliar to the American and leaves him uneasy. We may venture into a strange subgroup and hear exotic words like the psychologist's "tachistoscopically" —warm cues to the ears of this group but foreign to our own. We feel left on our own goal line with no team members in sight—the game cannot be sustained.

Take the fascination of youth for the theater. Goethe considered acting in one's youth an indispensable preparation for adult life. Theatrical acting is a vicarious freedom of *acting control* of a situation. It demonstrates perfectly how control can be gained merely by properly saying the right things. Perfect acting is a unique exercise in omnipotence, gained simply by infallible command of the script. By impeccable wielding of deference and demeanor the actor is at the same time undisputed director of his destiny. It is impossible to be undermined when one properly controls the verbal context of action. Learning a foreign tongue sometimes conveys the experiencing of the sheer power-control aspects of language. The individual finds that he is capable of utterances which usher others into appropriate complementary action, but which utterances, because they are new (and in a foreign tongue) he at first experiences as unreal and ego-alien. It is then that he can best "watch himself perform," and see and feel in action the power aspects of language.

A kindred experience occurs in psychotherapy where the patient, getting no answer to his accustomed automatic usage of verbal ritual, sees crystallized his whole style of attempted verbal conciliation and manipulation of others. In the "transference" the patient relates to the therapists as he did to significant people in his past. "Transference" is simply another word for rule-following ability as it is constricted within a narrow stylistic range. The artificial crystallization of this stylistic range is what takes place in psychoanalytic therapy. By bringing it into full view the analyst hopes to permit performance over a broader range: he presents the patient with the possibility of a greater number of choices.[1]

By using word ceremonial properly the individual can navigate without fear in a threatening social world. He can even ignore the true attitudes of others, as long as he can get by them with the proper ritual formulas of salutation, sustaining conversation, farewells, and so on. The actor has only to be sure of the face-saving ritual rules for interaction. Everyone is permitted the stolid self-assurance that comes with minute observation of unchallengeable rules—we can all become social bureaucrats.

However, there is a more subtle aspect to this mutual protection of fragile self-esteem. We have already touched on it: not only do words enable us to protect ourselves by confidently manipulating the interpersonal situation; also, by verbally setting the tone for action by the proper ritual formula, we permit complementary action by our interlocutor. That is, the ability to use formulas with facility actually implies the power to manipulate others indirectly, by providing the symbolic context for their action.[2] I remember an audacious beggar who, approaching an obviously potentially lucrative handout, said, "How're you, Colonel?" The "Colonel" had to manufacture the appropriate lines. "Fine" would have left the interaction open and, after acknowledging this expression of interest in his health, would have made a handout unavoidable. He chose to end the interaction by responding, "Better."

We cannot wonder that a newly liberated slave may be reluctant to relinquish his lifelong pattern of obsequious formulas of deference, tested means for engaging others in a manner appropriate to his status. But this does not mean that he has a "degenerate character." Rather, the ingratiating and respectful expressions for engaging others in anxiety-free fashion are his only tools for manipulating the interpersonal situation. They are proved methods of control for which substitutes cannot easily be learned. What is more, by doing his part in permitting the action to continue he actually calls the tune for his superior, even from his inferior position. Thus, an army officer may exclaim to his sergeant, "Stop 'sirring' me!" It is a protest against being manipulated by an overly constrictive social definition of one's identity. One is too easily being put in another's box. The delight with which young recruits learn all the military jargon testifies to the pervasive feeling of power that accompanies proper definition of the situation for action: "Private Johnson reporting, sir!" not only creates the context for action, but at the same time *provides the motivation to act.* We sustain one another with properly placed verbal formulas.

. . . The fundamental task of culture is to constitute the individual as an object of primary value in a world of meaning. Without this, he cannot act. Now, the proper exercise of ritual formulas provides just this. The actor can feel himself an object of primary value, motivated to act in a mutually meaningful situation. "Private Johnson reporting, sir!" affirms the self, the proper motivation, and the life meaning which for ever is. And when we permit our interlocutor as well as ourself [sic] to act in a fabric of shared meaning, we provide him with the possibility of self-validation. As we act meaningfully in pursuit of agreed goals we exercise our self-powers as only they can be exercised. This is vitally important. It is easy to see the reverse side of this same coin: namely, that if we bungle the verbal context for action, if we deliver the wrong lines at the wrong time, we frustrate the possibility of meaningful action and unquestioned motivation. "P-P-P-P-Private Johnson reporting, s-s-s-sir!" not only arrests all movement on stage but also undermines word power where it is most useful: in its expediency. Directness is self-convincing.[3] Unflinching mastery of the lines actually serves to *create* meaning by providing an unequivocal context for action. The leader who, after a short whispered outline plan of attack, shouts, "Let's go men!" with proper gravity and conviction, says much more than simply that. He implies that of all times and all places, this is the situation that man should want most to be in; and that "to go" into the attack is unquestionably the greatest, most meaningful act that one could hope to perform. Thus, the word not only sustains us by outlining a context of action in which we can be meaningfully motivated. It also "creates" us, in a sense, by infusing our action with meaning. That is, as we act meaningfully we exercise our powers and create our identity. Self-validation is only possible through meaningful action in a social context.

The self, after all, is in a continued process of creation. It is a linguistic, ideational system in a constant state of modification. There is another side to the social credo "Let us all protect each other so that we can carry on the business of living." Man is a social creator as well as a social creature. By the social exercise of linguistic power man creates his own identity and reinforces that of others. In this sense, identity is simply the measure of power and participation of the individual in the joint cultural staging of self-enhancing ceremony.[4] Only by proper performance in a social context does the individual fashion and renew himself by purposeful action in a world of shared meaning. Loneliness is not only a suspension in self-acquaintance. It is a suspension in the very fashioning of identity; cut off from one's fellows, one cannot add his power to the enhancing of cultural meaning or derive his just share of it. Social ceremonial is a joint theatrical staging whose purpose it is to sustain and create meaning for all its members. It is the vital drama in which socialization schools the infant to act.

THE FICTIONAL NATURE OF HUMAN MEANING: A REVIEW

The remarkable convergence of twentieth-century thinkers ... is the elaboration of the idea that human meaning is arbitrary. As the self-reflexive animal learns symbols, he constructs an action world which permits anxiety-free functioning (and skews perceptions at the same time). The child orients to himself, to person-objects and thing-objects, to space and time. He learns worthwhile strivings from worthless ones, right choices from wrong. The linguistic self-system spins itself like a web, wondrously suspended in space. It feeds on sound and ideation, and just enough other experience to make peace with the exigencies of physiology and survival.

The world of human aspiration is fundamentally fictitious. If we do not understand this, we understand nothing about man. It is a purely symbolic creation, by an ego-controlled animal, that permits action in a psychological world; a behavioral world removed from the tyranny of the present moment, of immediate stimuli which enslave all lower organisms. Man's freedom is a fabricated freedom from boundness to here and now. But the price he pays for this loftiness is not only a confinement of his perceptions to the world view he has learned. It is the *utter fragility of his delicately constituted fiction.* That is why we can speak of "joint theatrical staging," "ritual formulas for social ceremonial," and "enhancing of cultural meaning," with utmost seriousness. There is no cynicism implied here, no derision, or any pity. We must realize simply that this is how *this* animal must act if he is to function as *this* animal. If an arbitrarily constructed psychological world is our *modus vivendi,* so be it. We may even find some so-called "human dignity" in this state of affairs—which is often no more than an indirect way of expressing self-pity at our psychological burden.

It is really one of the most remarkable achievements of thought that anxiety-prone man could come to see *through himself,* to discover the fictional nature of his action world. It is all the more remarkable, really, because all our efforts are directed to sustaining and enhancing the cultural fiction. All the time. Sociologists like Simmel, Cooley and, more recently, Goffman, have detailed with great intricacy the qualities of players and performance which infuse social life with meaning, and sustain the fiction thereby. Social life is a staging of performance, and part of the basic training of the players is an inordinate sensitivity to cues. We want to know that everyone is playing correctly. Goffman says:

As members of an audience it is natural for us to feel that the impression the performer seeks to give may be true or false . . . valid or 'phony.' So common is this doubt that . . . we often give special attention *to features of the performance that cannot be readily manipulated.*[5]

When we discover that someone with whom we have dealings is an impostor and out-and-out fraud, we are discovering that he did not have the right to play the part he played, that he was not an accredited member of the relevant status.[6]

Status, remember, is a social technique for facilitating action. It divides our social environment into a behavioral map, and by living according to the positional cues, our actions take on the only meaning they can have. Our alertness to the performance of others, therefore, is an expression of our concern over sustaining the underlying meaning of the plot:

. . . Paradoxically, the more closely the impostor's performance approximates the real thing, the more intensely we may be threatened, for a competent performance by someone who proves to be an impostor may weaken in our minds the moral connection between legitimate authorization . . . and capacity to play.[7]

In other words, we must feel that the performer *deserves* his status, and if he didn't deserve it he wouldn't be able convincingly to play it. Goffman observes that skilled mimics who admit that their intentions are not serious may provide one way to work through our anxieties in this delicate area. We want to know that the performance represents the real thing when it is supposed to. Also, of course, when we see a mimic of, say, Jack Benny, it establishes another connection in our mind: if there is a false Jack Benny, then there must be a real one—the true Jack Benny is undoubtedly true if we see the false one. Illegitimacy implies above all that legitimacy exists.

We touch here upon a subtle area of human interaction that sociologists and social psychologists have richly mined. The child, we saw, was trained as a performer primarily to fulfill a basic social function: to protect his self-esteem and that of others in social interaction. He learns to put forth a self that is dependable, that can be transacted with, without threatening others in their self-esteem. He learns the proper ceremonial for another reason: he has to be counted on to give a convincing performance *that enhances the culturally meaningful action.* Each actor contributes not only his own reliability as a transactable self: he must also bring to the social scene his own special dramatic talent, whereby the quality of the performance is enriched. It would be impossible to overinsist on the importance of this talent for social life. It is probably the most subtle and most important area of social creativity—a creativity in which everyone takes part, and in which there are the widest differences in skill.[8] Part of our talent in this creativeness is our inordinate sensitivity to cues, both verbal and nonverbal, kinesic and unconscious. The inferences upon which our lines are based must be gathered from as many cues as possible, if we are to judge accurately and perform creatively in a given part.

Anselm Strauss points out that each person has to assess three things about another. He must be alert to a myriad of cues to determine:

1. The other's general intent in the situation.

2. The other's response toward *himself.*

3. The other's response or feelings toward me, the recipient or observer of his action.[9]

This interweaving, observes Strauss, of signs of intent, of self-feeling, and of feeling toward the other, must be exceedingly complex in any situation. Why is the assessment of these three things so important? Simply because this trilogy allows one to fulfill his

"social human nature"—it allows him to exercise those unique capacities into which he has been schooled. The adept performer should be able to:

1. Save his own face (protect his fragile self-esteem) against unwarranted attack or privatization.

2. Prepare the appropriate lines that may be necessary to protect the other's self-esteem, if the other inadvertently makes a *gaffe.* Part of one's social obligation is to protect the other person as well as oneself, against undermining in the social context.

3. Frame creative and convincing lines that carry the interaction along in the most meaningful, life-enhancing fashion.[10]

A person's response toward himself, his self-alert, critical eye, is a transaction with what Sullivan called his "fantastic auditor." Other psychoanalysts call it the "observing ego." Now and again, we slip out of the alert censorship of our "fantastic auditor," as when we explode into a mass of uncontrolled nonsense. When we watch another perform we think that we can see how he feels about himself. Actually, we don't see this at all; we can have little idea how he "feels about himself." What we do see is how smoothly the individual is staging himself, controlling his performance. We do not like to see another who is too absorbed in his own staging at the expense of convincing delivery of the lines. This kind of stage ineptitude is like performance in a high-school play, where self-conscious actors deliver stilted, halting, unconvincing lines, or overly fluent ones. When we talk about someone who is "phony," we mean that his staging of himself is overly obvious. He is unconvincing because he allows us to see his efforts at delivering the right lines.

Continual, keen scrutiny of the performance of others is the life preoccupation of an animal trained to be on-stage. Many of us have probably had the experience of joyfully meeting a friend in a crowded public place. As we take leave of him smilingly we plunge back into our own daily cares, and quickly efface the smile as soon as our head turns away. If someone is watching us at that moment we redden with embarrassment at our quick change in mood. From then on we make a studied effort to "keep" the smile upon parting from all friends in public places—we may even hold onto it musingly for some distance. Performance has to be convincing, meaningful, genuine, or we fall down on our part of the social bargain—cultural meaning must be sustained by the individual actors.

The adolescent may see in the courtesy of manners a certain deceit. But the whole question of feigned politeness is integral to good performance. "Hypocrisy" is merely a shorthand expression for an adaptation to a social situation despite our own feelings. We mask our private thoughts and sentiments to allow action to go forward. If these thoughts are inappropriate, masking them performs a vital social function: it allows the objective elements of the situation to hold sway. Instead of submerging the social context with our own private perceptions, we facilitate it by responding to its exigencies as cleanly as possible. Again, this is what Goethe meant when he said that there was a courtesy of the heart which is akin to love, and that the overt expression of manners flowed from this.

Of course, the masking of inappropriate elements is never clear-cut. This is because, if we put our self-esteem on the block in society, we also need society to add to that self-esteem. Our identity can only be validated in the social encounter. As we enhance cultural meaning, we also seek to enhance ourselves. Every social encounter is a potential life source for self-aggradizement. The eternal question "Who am I?" can only be answered, as Cooley and Mead insisted, by the society in which one is mirrored. It is natural, therefore, that part of the delicately subtle creativity of social encounter is its potential for increasing the value of the self in one's own eyes. This is what the social psychologists call "status-forcing." But one needs to be a most skillful performer to come out of an interaction better than he came in. He needs to have an acute sensitivity to the manifold cues, deliver the proper lines necessary to sustain his image and that of others; he must enhance the cultural meaning as well as the personal meaning of all the selves concerned. We see a clear example of inept performance, and of constant attempts to force status, in the phenomenon called "riding." "Riding" is simply clumsy acting, a grotesque attempt to heighten one's self-esteem by denigrating another. It is a continuous preoccupation of close in-groups temporarily thrown together in distasteful occupations, like waiters and counter-men and counter-girls. "Riding" makes a mockery of the delicate skill of cue-sensitive performance.

We would expect this where people are thrown together without rigid ceremonial rules for protecting against privatization. A similar phenomenon occurs when a "line" is used: to employ a "line" usually means trying to get something out of an interaction that is grossly at the other person's expense. In traditional society there is less of this because cues are more dependable, and the situation tightly structured. There is very little "line" that one can employ on a date that is chaperoned, for instance. "Line" is a probing for advantage in the absence of standardized prescriptions for behavior, an attempt to emerge from the fluid interaction much better than one came in. Of course, every interaction, as we saw, has this creative element, the possibility of emerging from it somewhat enhanced in one's feeling of warmth about oneself.

This enhancement need not derive solely from success in forcing one's status in an encounter. Every performance has another creative element: by presenting uniquely creative lines the actor obliges his interlocutor to cope with the unexpected, also in a creative fashion. Each individual presents his own unique version of cultural meaning, as it is reworked and fashioned in his linguistic self-system. By constantly fabricating the unexpected, we edge our egos to new assimilative mastery. After all, the individual who can be counted on to give us exactly that ceremonial proper to each situation is the one we call a crashing bore. He doesn't inspire us to grow by coping with the unexpected.

Thus there is a creative as well as a primarily threatening aspect of social encounter. It may be difficult to extricate the two. A Balinese mother meeting a high-status stranger on the road flawlessly executed the proper greeting with smiling, impassive face. The only clue to her pounding heart was the loud wail her baby put up—he received the more direct communication. One of the impetuses to the fragmentation of society into subgroups is that they provide some respite from the continual strain on creative alertness of the self-system. In the subgroup, conversation is familiar, automatic, untaxing for the most part. In some primitive societies "joking relationships" are established between certain individuals. These people, when they meet, engage in an unashamed mockery, teasing, and joking that is denied to others. Joking relationships seem to be established at points of tension in the social system—among inlaws, for example—and relieve the individuals of the strain of meeting these encounters, and the necessity of facilitating them creatively. Joking carries the encounter along automatically, and also provides for release of tension. One of the reasons marriage often loses its stimulating color is that it provides a ready refuge from the challenge to ego-mastery of other social encounters. It may even degenerate into a relaxedness in which the merest privatizations are indulged: "Do you notice, dear, how the nail on my big toe seems to be growing at an angle?"

NOTES

1. By "choices" I mean, obviously, *other verbal formulas*. The therapist educates the patient to new performance vocabularies to replace the constrictive old vocabularies, learned in childhood—but which no longer fit complex, contemporary situations to which the patient strives to adapt. The patient must come *to dissociate his feeling of self-value from the old vocabularies* learned from the parents. When he learns new words with which to dress his action he acquires new motives for that action. *For a symbolic animal motives are words.* Words facilitate action; words dress action in meaning; words convey an image of the self. The individual discovers himself in the social performance part; therefore, he discovers himself in words. Our whole discussion in this chapter is based on the idea of the primary derivation of meaning from words alone. Cf. Kenneth Burke, *A Grammer of Motives* (New York: Braziller, 1955) and *A Rhetoric of Motives* (New York: Braziller, 1955). C. Wright Mills was the first, I think, to make explicit the implications for sociological analysis, of Burke's elaboration of motives as merely words. See "Situated Actions and Vocabularies of

Motive," *American Sociological Review*, Vol. 5 (1940), pp. 904-913; see also H. Gerth and C. W. Mills, *Character and Social Structure* (New York: Harcourt, Brace and World, 1953).

Admittedly, this view is difficult to accept because it makes individual action seem guided by mere whims of the moment, or by the changing demands of each different situation. It makes human character seem a mere will-o'-the-wisp. Thus, Martindale takes issue with Gerth and Mills' view of motives as words (Don Martindale, *The Nature and Types of Sociological Theory* [Boston: Houghton Mifflin, 1960], pp. 373-374.) He reasons that this reduces motives to mere social strategies, and says: "Presumably for this purpose one might find such handbooks as Dale Carnegie's *How to Win Friends and Influence People* extremely helpful." But of course, this is it exactly! In ordinary social interaction, man will use anything to facilitate his performance part, and dress his action in socially agreed meaning. And, by performing according to standards of which others approve, he earns an identity. It is only when he has previously committed his self-esteem to other vocabularies of motive that the situational motives may not be satisfactory.

2. Furthermore, we are well aware of this, at least subconsciously. We need only reflect on the inordinate amount of time we spend in anguished self-recrimination over having failed merely to say the right thing at a given point in a conversation. Self-torture for having let power slip from one's grasp is pitiless: "If only I'd said *that*! Oh, if *only* I'd said that!"

3. This follows from the idea that motives are words. I am using stuttering as merely a shorthand, graphic example of how inappropriateness of language frustrates conduct. The power of words lies in the fact that they dress our action with meaning—frosting on the cake, so to speak. For energy-converting organisms action and forward momentum are primary. Meaning does not need language. Possibilities for the forward momentum of action exist *in nature*. Action gives experience which provides meaning because it commands attention and leads to further action. Language merely makes action more meaningful for a symbolic animal.

But, since we have grown up learning verbal meaning and hence motivation for all our acts, something novel occurs: for man there is no cake if the frosting is missing. We are paralyzed to act unless there is a verbal prescription for the situation. Man, in other words, loses very early the capacity to "act in nature," as it were. His simplest act has to take on meaning, has to point to something beyond itself, exist in a wider referential context. . . .

4. Compare Searles' apt observation on the schizophrenic: He needs to find something in himself *that contributes to the growth and enrichment of his fellow man*. H. F. Searles, "Anxiety Concerning Change, as Seen in the Psychotherapy of Schizophrenic Patients—with Particular Reference to the Sense of Personal Identity," *International Journal of Psychoanalysis*, Vol. 42 (January-April, 1961), pp. 74-85.

5. *The Presentation of Self in Everyday Life*, (Garden City, NY: Doubleday Anchor Books, 1959), p. 58, his italics.

6. *Ibid.*

7. *Ibid.*

8. . . . Each individual's personality represents a unique style of maintaining self-esteem. Each social act, therefore, serves a private as well as a social motive. When the private motive upsets meaningful performance and joggles the self-esteem of others, we call it privatization. "Social skill" merely refers to a palatable balance of private self-enhancement and social self-enhancement, in one's performance style. To be socially creative, therefore, requires some degree of privatization. The person who merely fawningly facilitates the social situation is usually avoided. It seems that when we play a game we want to know that the other players have stakes—in this case a feeling of self-value that is placed "on the line."

9. *Mirrors and Masks, The Search for Identity* (New York : The Free Press of Glencoe, 1959), p. 59.

10. We assume for purposes of the example that this would be the most common general intent. He might, of course, seek to get out of the interaction at the other's expense. Again, see Goffman for a full detailing of the subtleties involved in interpersonal encounters.

6. THE PRESENTATION OF SELF

ERVING GOFFMAN

Reprinted from "The Presentation of Self in Everyday Life", copyright © 1959 by Erving Goffman from the book *The Presentation of Self in Everyday Life.* Reprinted by permission of Doubleday & Company, Inc. Erving Goffman is Benjamin Franklin Professor of Anthropology at the University of Pennsylvania where he is editor of a series of publications on conduct and communication. He was the first scholar to apply the dramaturgical framework to the traditional concerns of social psychology in his now-classic *The Presentation of Self in Everyday Life,* from which the following selection is drawn.

When an individual enters the presence of others, they commonly seek to acquire information about him or to bring into play information about him already possessed. They will be interested in his general socio-economic status, his conception of self, his attitude toward them, his competence, his trustworthiness, etc. Although some of this information seems to be sought almost as an end in itself, there are usually quite practical reasons for acquiring it. Information about the individual helps to define the situation, enabling others to know in advance what he will expect of them and what they may expect of him. Informed in these ways, the others will know how best to act in order to call forth a desired response from him.

For those present, many sources of information become accessible and many carriers (or "sign-vehicles") become available for conveying this information. If unacquainted with the individual, observers can glean clues from his conduct and appearance which allow them to apply their previous experience with individuals roughly similar to the one before them or, more important, to apply untested stereotypes to him. They can also assume from past experience that only individuals of a particular kind are likely to be found in a given social setting. They can rely on what the individual says about himself or on documentary evidence he provides as to who and what he is. If they know, or know of, the individual by virtue of experience prior to the interaction, they can rely on assumptions as to the persistence and generality of psychological traits as a means of predicting his present and future behavior.

However, during the period in which the individual is in the immediate presence of the others, few events may occur which directly provide the others with the conclusive information they will need if they are to direct wisely their own activity. Many crucial facts lie beyond the time and place of interaction or lie concealed within it. For example, the "true" or "real" attitudes, beliefs, and emotions of the individual can be ascertained only indirectly, through his avowals or through what appears to be involuntary expressive behavior. Similarly, if the individual offers the others a product or service, they will often find that during the interaction there will be no time and place immediately available for eating the pudding that the proof can be found in. They will be forced to accept some events as conventional or natural signs of something not directly available to the senses. In Ichheiser's terms,[1] the individual will have to act so that he intentionally or unintentionally *expresses* himself, and the others will in turn have to be *impressed* in some way by him.

The expressiveness of the individual (and therefore his capacity to give impressions) appears to involve two radically different kinds of sign activity: the expression that he *gives*, and the expression that he *gives off*. The first involves verbal symbols or their substitutes which he uses admittedly and solely to convey the information that he and the others are known to attach to these symbols. This is communication in the traditional and narrow sense. The second involves a wide range of action that others can treat as symptomatic of the actor, the expectation being that the action was performed for reasons other than the information conveyed in this way. As we shall have to see, this distinction has an only initial validity. The individual does of course intentionally convey misinformation by means of both of these types of communication, the first involving deceit, the second feigning.

Taking communication in both its narrow and broad sense, one finds that when the individual is in the immediate presence of others, his acitivity will have a promissory character. The others are likely to find that they must accept the individual on faith, offering him a just return while he is present before them in exchange for something whose true value will not be established until after he has left their presence. (Of course, the others also live by inference in their dealings with the physical world, but it is only the world of social interaction that the objects about which they make inferences will purposely facilitate and hinder this inferential process.) The security that they justifiably feel in making inferences about the individual will vary, of course, depending on such factors as the amount of information they already possess about him, but no amount of such past evidence can entirely obviate the necessity of acting on the basis of inferences. As William I. Thomas suggested:

It is also highly important for us to realize that we do not as a matter of fact lead our lives, make our decisions, and reach our goals in everyday life either statistically or scientifically. We live by inference. I am, let us say, your guest. You do not know, you cannot determine scientifically, that I will not steal your money or your spoons. But inferentially I will not, and inferentially you have me as a guest.[2]

Let us now turn from the others to the point of view of the individual who presents himself before them. He may wish them to think highly of him, or to think that he thinks highly of them, or to perceive how in fact he feels toward them, or to obtain no clear-cut impression; he may wish to ensure sufficient harmony so that the interaction can be sustained, or to defraud, get rid of, confuse, mislead, antagonize, or insult them. Regardless of the praticular objective which the individual has in mind and of his motive for having this objective, it will be in his interests to control the conduct of the others, especially their responsive treatment of him.[3] This control is achieved largely by influencing the definition of the situation which the others come to formulate, and he can influence this definition by expressing himself in such a way as to give them the kind of impression that will lead them to act voluntarily in accordance with his own plan. Thus, when an individual appears in the presence of others, there will usually be some reason for him to mobilize his activity so that it will convey an impression to others which it is in his interests to convey. Since a girl's dormitory mates will glean evidence of her popularity from the calls she receives on the phone, we can suspect that some girls will arrange for calls to be made, and Willard Waller's finding can be anticipated:

It has been reported by many observers that a girl who is called to the telephone in the dormitories will often allow herself to be called several times, in order to give all the other girls ample opportunity to hear her paged.[4]

Of the two kinds of communication—expressions given and expressions given off—this report will be primarily concerned with the latter, with the more theatrical and contextual kind, the non-verbal, presumably unintentional kind, whether this communication be purposely engineered or not. As an example of what we must try to examine, I would like to cite at length a novelistic incident in which Preedy, a vacationing Englishman, makes his first appearance on the beach of his summer hotel in Spain:

But in any case he took care to avoid catching anyone's eye. First of all, he had to make it clear to those potential companions of his holiday that they were of no concern to him whatsoever. He stared through them, round them, over them—eyes lost in space. The beach might have been empty. If by chance a ball was thrown his way, he looked surprised; then let a smile of amusement lighten his face (Kindly Preedy), looked round dazed to see that there *were* people on the beach, tossed it back with a smile to himself and not a smile *at* the people, and then resumed carelessly his nonchalant survey of space.

But it was time to institute a little parade, the parade of the Ideal Preedy. By devious handlings he gave any who wanted to look a chance to see the title of his book—a Spanish translation of Homer, classic thus, but not daring, cosmopolitan too—and then gathered together his beach-wrap and bag into a neat sand-resistant pile (Methodical and Sensible Preedy), rose slowly to stretch at ease his huge frame (Big-Cat Preedy), and tossed aside his sandals (Carefree Preedy, after all).

The marriage of Preedy and the sea! There were alternative rituals. The first involved the stroll that turns into a run and a dive straight into the water, thereafter smoothing into a strong splashless crawl towards the horizon. But of course not really to the horizon. Quite suddenly he would turn on to his back and thrash great white splashes with his legs, somehow thus showing that he could have swum further had he wanted to, and then would stand up a quarter out of water for all to see who it was.

The alternative course was simpler, it avoided the cold-water shock and it avoided the risk of appearing too high-spirited. The point was to appear to be so used to the sea, the Mediterranean, and this particular beach, that one might as well be in the sea as out of it. It involved a slow stroll down and into the edge of the water—not even noticing his toes were wet, land and water all the same to *him!*—with his eyes up at the sky gravely surveying portents, invisible to others, of the weather (Local Fisherman Preedy).[5]

The novelist means us to see that Preedy is improperly concerned with the extensive impressions he feels his sheer bodily action is giving off to those around him. We can malign Preedy further by assuming that he has acted merely in order to give a particular impression, that this is a false impression, and that the others present receive either no impression at all, or, worse still, the impression that Preedy is affectedly trying to cause them to receive this particular impression. But the important point for us here is that the kind of impression Preedy thinks he is making is in fact the kind of impression that others correctly and incorrectly glean from someone in their midst.

I have said that when an individual appears before others his actions will influence the definition of the situation which they come to have. Sometimes the individual will act in a thoroughly calculating manner, expressing himself in a given way solely in order to give the kind of impression to others that is likely to evoke from them a specific response he is concerned to obtain. Sometimes the individual will be calculating in his activity but be relatively unaware that this is the case. Sometimes, he will intentionally and consciously express himself in a particular way, but chiefly because the tradition of his group or social status require this kind of expression and not because of any particular response (other than vague acceptance or approval) that is likely to be evoked from those impressed by the expression. Sometimes the traditions of an individual's role will lead him to give a well-designed impression of a particular kind and yet he may be neither consciously nor unconsciously disposed to create such an impression. The others, in their turn, may be suitably impressed by the individual's efforts to convey something, or may misunderstand the situation and come to conclusions that are warranted neither by the individual's intent nor by the facts. In any case, in so far as the others act *as if* the individual had conveyed a particular impression, we may take a functional or pragmatic view and say that the individual has "effectively" projected a given definition of the situation and "effectively" fostered the understanding that a given state of affairs obtains.

There is one aspect of the others' response that bears special comment here. Knowing that the individual is likely to present himself in a light that is favorable to him, the others may divide what they witness into two parts; a part that is relatively easy for the individual to manipulate at will, being chiefly his verbal assertions, and a part in regard to which he seems to have little concern or control, being chiefly derived from the expressions he gives off. The others may then use what are considered to be the ungovernable aspects of his expressive behavior as a check upon the validity of what is conveyed by the governable aspects. In this a fundamental asymmetry is demonstrated in the communication process, the individual presumably being aware of only one stream of his communication, the witnesses of this stream and one other. For example, in Shetland Isle one crofter's wife, in serving native dishes to a visitor from

the mainland of Britain, would listen with a polite smile to his polite claims of liking what he was eating; at the same time she would take note of the rapidity with which the visitor lifted his fork or spoon to his mouth, the eagerness with which he passed food into his mouth, and the gusto expressed in chewing the food, using these signs as a check on the stated feelings of the eater. The same woman, in order to discover what one acquaintance (A) "actually" thought of another acquaintance (B), would wait until B was in the presence of A but engaged in conversation with still another person (C). She would then covertly examine the facial expressions of A as he regarded B in conversation with C. Not being in conversation with B, and not being directly observed by him, A would sometimes relax usual constraints and tactful deceptions, and freely express what he was "actually" feeling about B. This Shetlander, in short, would observe the unobserved observer.

Now given the fact that others are likely to check up on the more controllable aspects of behavior by means of the less controllable, one can expect that sometimes the individual will try to exploit this very possibility, guiding the impression he makes through behavior felt to be reliably informing.[6] For example, in gaining admission to a tight social circle, the participant observer may not only wear an accepting look while listening to an informant, but may also be careful to wear the same look when observing the informant talking to others; observers of the observer will then not as easily discover where he actually stands. A specific illustration may be cited from Shetland Isle. When a neighbor dropped in to have a cup of tea, he would ordinarily wear at least a hint of an expectant warm smile as he passed through the door into the cottage. Since lack of physical obstructions outside the cottage and lack of light within it usually made it possible to observe the visitor unobserved as he approached the house, islanders sometimes took pleasure in watching the visitor drop whatever expression he was manifesting and replace it with a sociable one just before reaching the door. However, some visitors, in appreciating that this examination was occurring, would blindly adopt a social face a long distance from the house, thus ensuring the projection of a constant image.

This kind of control upon the part of the individual reinstates the symmetry of the communication process, and sets the stage for a kind of information game—a potentially infinite cycle of concealment, discovery, false revelation, and rediscovery. It should be added that since the others are likely to be relatively unsuspicious of the presumably unguided aspect of the individual's conduct, he can gain much by controlling it. The others of course may sense that the individual is manipulating the presumably spontaneous aspects of his behavior, and seek in this very act of manipulation some shading of conduct that the individual has not managed to control. This again provides a check upon the individual's behavior, this time his presumably uncalculated behavior, thus re-establishing the asymmetry of the communication process. Here I would like only to add the suggestion that the arts of piercing an individual's effort at calculated unintentionality seem better developed than our capacity to manipulate our own behavior, so that regardless of how many steps have occurred in the information game, the witness is likely to have the advantage over the actor, and the initial asymmetry of the communication process is likely to be retained.

When we allow that the individual projects a definition of the situation when he appears before others, we must also see that the others, however passive their role may seem to be, will themselves effectively project a definition of the situation by virtue of their response to the individual and by virtue of any lines of action they initiate to him. Ordinarily the definitions of the situation projected by the several different participants are sufficiently attuned to one another so that open contradiction will not occur. I do not mean that there will be the kind of consensus that arises when each individual present candidly expresses what he really feels and honestly agrees with the expressed feelings of the others present. This kind of harmony is an optimistic ideal and in any case not necessary for the smooth working of society. Rather, each participant is expected to suppress his immediate heartfelt feelings, conveying a view of the situation which he feels the others will be able to find at least temporarily acceptable. The maintenance of this surface of agreement, this veneer of consensus, is facilitated by each participant concealing his own wants behind statements which assert values to which everyone present feels obliged to give lip service. Further, there is usually a kind of division of definitional labor. Each participant is allowed to establish the tentative official ruling regarding matters which are vital to him but not immediately important to others, e.g., the rationalizations and justifications by which he accounts for his past activity. In exchange for this courtesy he remains silent or non-committal on matters important to others but not immediately important to him. We have then a kind of interactional *modus vivendi*. Together the participants contribute to a single over-all definition of the situation which involves not so much a real agreement as to what exists but rather a real agreement as to whose claims concerning what issues will be temporarily honored. Real agreement will also exist concerning the desirability of avoiding an open conflict of definitions of the situation.[7] I will refer to this level of agreement as a "working consensus." It is to be understood that the working consensus established in one interaction setting will be quite different in content from the working consensus established in a different type of setting. Thus, between two friends at lunch, a reciprocal show of affection, respect, and concern for the other is maintained. In service occupations, on the other hand, the specialist often maintains an image of disinterested involvement in the problem of the client, while the client responds with a show of respect for the competence and integrity of the specialist. Regardless of such differences in content, however, the general form of these working arrangements is the same.

In noting the tendency for a participant to accept the definitional claims made by the others present, we can appreciate the crucial importance of the information that the individual *initially* possesses or acquires concerning his fellow participants, for it is on the basis of this initial information that the individual starts to define the situation and starts to build up lines of responsive action. The individual's initial projection commits him to what he is proposing to be and requires him to drop all pretenses of being other things. As the interaction among the participants progresses, additions and modifications in this initial informational state will of course occur, but it is essential that these later developments be related without contradictions to, and even built up from, the initial positions taken by the several participants. It would seem that an in-

dividual can more easily make a choice as to what line of treatment to demand from and extend to the others present at the beginning of an encounter than he can alter the line of treatment that is being pursued once the interaction is underway.

In everyday life, of course, there is a clear understanding that first impressions are important. Thus, the work adjustment of those in service occupations will often hinge upon a capacity to seize and hold the initiative in the service relation, a capacity that will require subtle aggressiveness on the part of the server when he is of lower socio-economic status than his client. W. F. Whyte suggests the waitress as an example:

The first point that stands out is that the waitress who bears up under pressure does not simply respond to her customers. She acts with some skill to control their behavior. The first question to ask when we look at the customer relationship is, "Does the waitress get the jump on the customer, or does the customer get the jump on the waitress?" The skilled waitress realizes the crucial nature of this question. . . .

The skilled waitress tackles the customer with confidence and without hesitation. For example, she may find that a new customer has seated himself before she could clear off the dirty dishes and change the cloth. He is now leaning on the table studying the menu. She greets him, says, "May I change the cover, please?" and, without waiting for an answer, takes his menu away from him so that he moves back from the table, and she goes about her work. The relationship is handled politely but firmly, and there is never any question as to who is in charge.[8]

When the interaction that is initiated by "first impressions" is itself the initial interaction in an extended series of interactions involving the same participants, we speak of "getting off on the right foot" and feel that it is crucial that we do so. Thus, one learns that some teachers take the following view:

You can't ever let them get the upper hand on you or you're through. So I start out tough. The first day I get a new class in, I let them know who's boss . . . You've got to start off tough, then you can ease up as you go along. If you start out easy-going, when you try to get tough, they'll just look at you and laugh.[9]

Similarly, attendants in mental institutions may feel that if the new patient is sharply put in his place the first day on the ward and made to see who is boss, much future difficulty will be prevented.[10]

Given the fact that the individual effectively projects a definition of the situation when he enters the presence of others, we can assume that events may occur within the interaction which contradict, discredit, or otherwise throw doubt upon this projection. When these disruptive events occur, the interaction itself may come to a confused and embarrassed halt. Some of the assumptions upon which the responses of the participants had been predicated become untenable, and the participants find themselves lodged in an interaction for which the situation has been wrongly defined and is now no longer defined. At such moments the individual whose presentation has been discredited may feel ashamed while the others present may feel hostile, and all the participants may come to feel ill at ease, nonplussed, out of countenance, embarrassed, experiencing the kind of anomy that is generated when the minute social system of face-to-face interaction breaks down.

In stressing the fact that the initial definition of the situation projected by an individual tends to provide a plan for the co-operative activity that follows—in stressing this action point of view—we must not overlook the crucial fact that any projected definition of the situation also has a distinctive moral character. It is this moral character of projections that will chiefly concern us in this report. Soci-

ety is organized on the principle that any individual who possesses certain social characteristics has a moral right to expect that others will value and treat him in an appropriate way. Connected with this principle is a second, namely that an individual who implicitly or explicitly signifies that he has certain social characteristics ought in fact to be what he claims he is. In consequence, when an individual projects a definition of the situation and thereby makes an implicit or explicit claim to be a person of a particular kind, he automatically exerts a moral demand upon the others, obliging them to value and treat him in the manner that persons of his kind have a right to expect. He also implicitly forgos all claims to be things he does not appear to be[11] and hence forgos the treatment that would be appropriate for such individuals. The others find, then, that the individual has informed them as to what is and as to what they ought to see as the "is."

One cannot judge the importance of definitional disruptions by the frequency with which they occur, for apparently they would occur more frequently were not constant precautions taken. We find that preventive practices are constantly employed to avoid these embarrassments and that corrective practices are constantly employed to compensate for discrediting occurrences that have not been successfully avoided. When the individual employs these strategies and tactics to protect his own projections, we may refer to them as "defensive practices"; when a participant employs them to save the definition of the situation projected by another, we speak of "protective practices" or "tact." Together, defensive and protective practices comprise the techniques employed to safeguard the impression fostered by an individual during his presence before others. It should be added that while we may be ready to see that no fostered impression would survive if defensive practices were not employed, we are less ready perhaps to see that few impressions could survive if those who received the impression did not exert tact in their reception of it.

In addition to the fact that precautions are taken to prevent disruption of projected definitions, we may also note that an intense interest in these disruptions comes to play a significant role in the social life of the group. Practical jokes and social games are played in which embarrassments which are to be taken unseriously are purposely engineered.[12] Fantasies are created in which devastating exposures occur. Anecdotes from the past—real, embroidered, or fictitious—are told and retold, detailing disruptions which occurred, almost occurred, or occurred and were admirably resolved. There seems to be no grouping which does not have a ready supply of these games, reveries, and cautionary tales, to be used as a source of humor, a catharsis for anxieties, and a sanction for inducing individuals to be modest in their claims and reasonable in their projected expectations. The individual may tell himself through dreams of getting into impossible positions. Families tell of the time a guest got his dates mixed and arrived when neither the house nor anyone in it was ready for him. Journalists tell of times when an all-too-meaningful misprint occurred, and the paper's assumption of objectivity or decorum was humorously discredited. Public servants tell of times a client ridiculously misunderstood form instructions, giving answers which implied an unanticipated and bizarre definition of the situation.[13] Seamen, whose home away from home is rigorously he-man, tell

stories of coming back home and inadvertently asking mother to "pass the fucking butter."[14] Diplomats tell of the time a near-sighted queen asked a republican ambassador about the health of his king.[15]

To summarize, then, I assume that when an individual appears before others he will have many motives for trying to control the impression they receive of the situation. This report is concerned with some of the common techniques that persons employ to sustain such impressions and with some of the common contingencies associated with the employment of these techniques. The specific content of any activity presented by the individual participant, or the role it plays in the interdependent activities of an on-going social system, will not be at issue; I shall be concerned only with the participant's dramaturgical problems of presenting the activity before others. The issues dealt with by stagecraft and stage management are sometimes trivial but they are quite general; they seem to occur everywhere in social life, providing a clear-cut dimension for formal sociological analysis.

It will be convenient to end . . . with some definitions that are implied in what has gone before . . . . For the purpose of this report, interaction (that is, face-to-face interaction) may be roughly defined as the reciprocal influence of individuals upon one another's actions when in one another's immediate physical presence. An interaction may be defined as all the interaction which occurs throughout any one occasion when a given set of individuals are in one another's continuous presence; the term "an encounter" would do as well. A "performance" may be defined as all the activity of a given participant on a given occasion which serves to influence in any way any of the other participants. Taking a particular participant and his performance as a basic point of reference, we may refer to those who contribute the other performances as the audience, observers, or co-participants. The pre-established pattern of action which is unfolded during a performance and which may be presented or played through on other occasions may be called a "part" or "routine."[16] These situational terms can easily be related to conventional structural ones. When an individual or

performer plays the same part to the same audience on different occasions, a social relationship is likely to arise. Defining social role as the enactment of rights and duties attached to a given status, we can say that a social role will involve one or more parts and that each of these different parts may be presented by the performer on a series of occasions to the same kinds of audience or to an audience of the same persons.

NOTES

1. Gustav Ichheiser, "Misunderstandings in Human Relations," Supplement to *The American Journal of Sociology*, LV (September, 1949), pp. 6-7.

2. Quoted in E. H. Volkart, editor, *Social Behavior and Personality*, Contributions of W. I. Thomas to Theory and Social Research (New York: Social Science Research Council, 1951), p. 5.

3. Here I owe much to an unpublished paper by Tom Burns of the University of Edinburgh. He presents the argument that in all interaction a basic underlying theme is the desire of each participant to guide and control the responses made by the others present. A similar argument has been advanced by Jay Haley in a recent unpublished paper, but in regard to a special kind of control, that having to do with defining the nature of the relationship of those involved in the interaction.

4. Willard Waller, "The Rating and Dating Complex," *American Sociological Review*, II, p. 730.

5. William Sansom, *A Contest of Ladies* (London: Hogarth, 1956), pp. 230-32.

6. The widely read and rather sound writings of Stephen Potter are concerned in part with signs that can be engineered to give a shrewd observer the apparently incidental cues he needs to discover concealed virtues the gamesman does not in fact possess.

7. An interaction can be purposely set up as a time and place for voicing differences in opinion, but in such cases participants must be careful to agree not to disagree on the proper tone of voice, vocabulary, and degree of seriousness in which all arguments are to be phrased, and upon the mutual respect which disagreeing partici-

pants must carefully continue to express toward one another. This debaters' or academic definition of the situation may also be invoked suddenly and judiciously as a way of translating a serious conflict of views into one that can be handled within a framework acceptable to all present.

8. W. F. Whyte, "When Workers and Customers Meet," Chap. VII, *Industry and Society*, ed., W. F. Whyte (New York: McGraw-Hill, 1946), pp. 132-133.

9. Teacher interview quoted by Howard S. Becker, "Social Class Variations in the Teacher-Pupil Relationship," *Journal of Educational Sociology*, XXV, p. 459.

10. Harold Taxel, "Authority Structure in a Mental Hospital Ward" (unpublished Master's thesis, Department of Sociology, University of Chicago, 1953).

11. This role of the witness in limiting what it is the individual can be has been stressed by Existentialists, who see it as a basic threat to individual freedom. See Jean-Paul Sartre, *Being and Nothingness*, trans. by Hazel E. Barnes (New York: Philosophical Library, 1956), p. 365 ff.

12. E. Goffman, . . . ["Communication Conduct in an Island Community" (unpublished Ph.D. dissertation, Department of Sociology, University of Chicago, 1953).], pp. 319-27.

13. Peter Blau, "Dynamics of Bureaucracy" (Ph.D. dissertation, Department of Sociology, Columbia University, forthcoming, University of Chicago Press), pp. 127-29.

14. Walter M. Beattie, Jr., "The Merchant Seaman" (unpublished M.A. Report, Department of Sociology, University of Chicago, 1950), p. 35.

15. Sir Frederick Ponsonby, *Recollec-*

)

tions of Three Reigns (New York: Dutton, 1952), p. 46.

16. For comments on the importance of distinguishing between a routine of interaction and any particular instance when this routine is played through, see John von Neumann and Oskar Morgenstern, *The Theory of Games and Economic Behaviour* (2nd ed.; Princeton: Princeton University Press, 1947), p. 49.

7. APPEARANCE AND THE SELF

GREGORY P. STONE

Reprinted from A. Rose (ed.), *Human Behavior and Social Processes* (Boston: Houghton-Mifflin Publishing Co., 1962), pp. 86-118, with permission of the author and Houghton-Mifflin Publishing Company. Gregory Stone has been one of the most persistent spokesmen for the dramaturgical point of view. He is Professor of Sociology at the University of Minnesota. He received his Ph.D. in 1959 from the University of Chicago with a dissertation on the interactional significance of clothing in social relationships, and he is presently engaged in research on the sociology of sports.

A primary tenet of all symbolic interaction theory holds that the self is established, maintained, and altered in and through communication. Seeking to probe this tenet, most investigations have emphasized discourse—or, somewhat inexactly, verbal communication—and have shown that language exerts a very great influence indeed upon the structure and process of the self. The present essay attempts to widen the perspective of symbolic interaction studies by isolating a dimension of communication that has received relatively little attention by sociologists and social psychologists—appearance. Except for psychoanalysts, some psychiatrists, and a few anthropologists, one finds almost no scholars willing to bend their efforts to the study of appearance.[1]

This paper seeks to demonstrate that the perspective of symbolic interaction, as it has been formulated by George H. Mead, requires (indeed, *demands*) a consideration of appearance for the adequate interpretation of social transactions as well as the careers of selves in such transactions. Mead's analysis of communication, it is suggested, suffers from what might be called a "discursive bias."[2] Consequently, there are crucial unanswered questions posed by his analysis of communication that can only be answered by extending and refining his perspective. This requires a demonstration that: (1) every social transaction must be broken down into at least two analytic components or processes —appearance and discourse; (2) appearance is at least as important for the establishment and maintenance of the self as is discourse; (3) the study of appearance provides a powerful lever for the formulation of a conception of self capable of embracing the contributions of Cooley and Sullivan as well as Mead; and (4) appearance is of major importance at every stage of the early development of the self. These assertions are all empirically grounded in the author's long-term study of dress as an apparent symbol (16).

APPEARANCE, DISCOURSE, AND MEANING

According to Mead, meaning is established only when the response elicited by some symbol is the "same" for the one who produces the symbol as for the one who receives it.[3] "Same" appears here in quotation marks, because the responses are *really* never the "same." This is an integral feature of Mead's perspective and calls for some elaboration. The fundamental implication is that *meaning is always a variable.*

We can trace this variable nature of meaning to Mead's conception of the self as process and structure, subject and object, or "I" and "me." The "I" imbues the self with a certain tentativeness—a "certain uncertainty."

78

As a consequence, any future line of action (for example, one's response to one's own symbolic productions) can never be fully anticipated. Mead put it this way:

So the "I" really appears experientially as a part of the "me." But on the basis of this experience we distinguish that individual who is doing something from the "me" who puts the problem up to him. The response enters into his experience only when it takes place. If he says he knows what he is going to do, even there he may be mistaken. He starts out to do something and something happens to interfere. The resulting action is always a little different from anything which he could anticipate. . . . The action of the "I" is something the nature of which we cannot tell in advance (14, p. 177).

But the meaning of a symbol, as we have said, is premised upon the notion that the response called out in the other is the *same* as the response called out in the one who produces the symbol—*always a little different from anything which he could anticipate.* Moreover, the other's response has the same characteristically unanticipatable quality.

Meaning, then, is always a variable, ranging between non-sense, on the one hand—the total absence of coincident responses—and what might be called boredom on the other—the total coincidence of such responses. Neither of these terminals can be approached very often in the duration of a transaction, for either can mean its end. It is seldom that we continue to talk non-sense with others, and boredom encourages us to depart from their presence. Thus, meaning is present in communication when the responses that are symbolically mobilized only *more or less* coincide.

This raises the question of *guarantees* for the meaningfulness of social transactions. How can the transaction be prevented from spilling over into non-sense or atrophying into boredom? Because the self is in part an "I"— unpredictable—the risks of boredom are minimized; but, for Mead, the guarantee against non-sense in the transaction is "role-taking," or, more accurately, placing one's self in the attitude of the other. By placing one's self in the attitude or incipient action of the other and representing one's own symbolic production to oneself from that attitude, one guarantees that one's own response will be rather more than less coincident with the response of the other, since the other's incipient actions have become incorporated in the actions of the one producing the symbol. It is here, however, that a gap in Mead's analysis occurs, for a further question arises, and that question was not systematically considered by Mead: if role-taking is the guarantee of meaning, how then is role-taking possible? Obviously, one must apprehend the other's role, the other's attitude—indeed, the other's self—before one can take the other's role or incorporate the other's attitude.

At this point a shift in terminology is required to expedite the analysis of meaning and to provide initial answers to the questions that have been raised. Let us suggest that the guarantee against non-sense in the social transaction is heuristically better conceptualized as *identification*,[4] not role-taking or taking the other's attitude—at best a very partial explanation of how meaning is established in social transactions. The term "identification" subsumes at least two processes: *identification of* and *identification with*. Role-taking is but one variant of the latter process, which must also include sympathy,[5] and there may well be other variants.[6] Nevertheless, the point to be made is this: identifications *with* one another, in whatever mode, cannot be made without identifications *of* one another.

Above all, identifications of one another are ordinarily facilitated by appearance and are often accomplished silently or non-verbally. This can be made crystal clear by observing the necessity for and process of establishing gender in social transactions. Everywhere we find vocabularies sexually distinguished: there are languages for males only, languages for females only, and languages employed to communicate across the barriers of gender. Obviously, identifications of the other's gender must be established before the appropriate language can be selected for the upcoming discourse. Seldom, upon encountering another, do we inquire concerning the other's gender. Indeed, to do so would be to impugn the very gender that must be established. The knowing of the other's gender is known silently, established by appearances.

Appearance, then, is that phase of the social transaction which establishes identifications of the participants. As such, it may be distinguished from *discourse,* which we conceptualize as the text of the transaction—*what* the parties are discussing. Appearance and discourse are two distinct dimensions of the social transaction. The former seems the more basic. It sets the stage for, permits, sustains, and delimits the possibilities of discourse by underwriting the possibilities of meaningful discussion.

Ordinarily appearance is communicated by such non-verbal symbols as gestures, grooming, clothing, location, and the like; discourse, by verbal symbolism. Yet the relationship between the kinds of symbolism and the dimension of the transaction is not at all invariant. Gestures and other non-verbal symbols may be used to talk about things and events, and words may have purely apparent signifi-

cance. In fact, appearances are often discussed, while discussions often "appear"—that is, serve only to establish the identities of the discussants. In the latter case, the person may seem to be talking about matters other than identifications of self or other, but may actually be speaking only about himself. "Name-dropping" serves as an example. In the former case, which we will term *apparent discourse,* whole transactions may be given over to the discussion of appearances, and this occurs most often when some new turn has been taken by the transaction requiring re-identification of the parties. Indeed, apparent discourse is often *news* and vice versa.

Appearance and discourse are in fact dialectic processes going on whenever people converse or correspond. They work back and forth on one another, at times shifting, at other times maintaining the direction of the transaction. When the direction of the transaction shifts, appearance is likely to emerge into the discursive phases of the transaction; when the direction is maintained over a relatively long period of time and is uninterrupted, discourse is likely to be submerged in appearances. In all cases, however, discourse is impossible without appearance which permits the requisite identifications with one another by the discussants. One may, nevertheless, appear without entering the discourse. As Veblen suggested, we may escape our discursive obligations, but not our clothed appearances (19, p. 167).

APPEARANCE AND THE SELF

Appearance *means* identification of one another,[7] but the question arises whether such identifications follow any ordered pattern. Mead's perspective insists that we look for the meaning of appearance in the responses that appearances mobilize, and we have examined more than 8,000 such responses supplied by interview materials to discern whether they are consistently patterned. Many responses are, of course, gestural in nature. One's appearance commands the gaze of the audience. An eyebrow is lifted. There is a smile or a frown, an approach or withdrawal. One blushes with shame for the shamelessness of the other's appearance or with embarrassment at one's own. The nature of our data precluded the study of such gestural responses unless they were recorded by the interviewer. Consequently apparent discourse was examined for the most part—talk about appearance aroused, in particular, by clothing. Over 200 married men and women living in a Midwestern community of 10,000 population supplied the talk. Of the many statements these people made about dress, only statements referring to those who wore the clothing in question were scrutinized. These were construed as identifications of the wearer. Here we shall be concerned for simplicity's sake with only two modes of such responses: (1) responses made about the wearer of clothes by others who, we shall say, *review* his clothing; and (2) responses made about the wearer by the wearer—we shall call these responses *programs*. A third mode of response is relevant, but will not be considered here—the wearer's imagination of others' responses to his dress.

When programs and reviews tend to coincide, the self of the one who appears (the one whose clothing has elicited such responses) is validated or established; when such responses tend toward disparity, the self of the one who appears is challenged, and conduct may be expected to move in the direction of some redefinition of the challenged self. Challenges and vali-

dations of the self, therefore, may be regarded as aroused by personal appearance. As a matter of fact, the dimensions of the self emphasized by Mead, Cooley, and Sullivan effectively embrace the content of the responses to clothing we examined in our quest for the meaning of appearance. In response to his clothes, the wearer was cast as a social object—a "me"—or, as we shall say, given some identity. A person's dress also imbued him with attitudes by arousing others' anticipations of his conduct as well as assisting the mobilization of his own activity. In Mead's terms, then, the self as object and attitude is established by appearance. However, the most frequent response to dress was the assignment of value-words to the wearer. One's clothes impart value to the wearer, both in the wearer's own eyes and in the eyes of others. Both Sullivan and Cooley underscore the relevance of value for any adequate conceptualization of the self; Sullivan, by referring to the self as comprised by the "reflected *appraisals* of others," Cooley, by emphasizing "imagined *judgments* of appearance." Finally, Cooley's emphasis upon self-*feeling* or the self as *sentiment* was provided with empirical support by this analysis. A person's clothing often served to establish a mood for himself capable of eliciting validation in the reviews aroused from others. The meaning of appearance, therefore, is the establishment of identity, value, mood, and attitude for the one who appears by the coincident programs and reviews awakened by his appearance. These terms require further discussion.

IDENTITY

It is almost enough to demonstrate the significance of the concept "identity" by referring to the rapidity with which it has caught on in social science. Recently re-introduced to the social sciences by Erik Erikson, the term has provided many new social-psychological insights. Specifically, fruitful inquiries into the sociological implications of the ego have been made possible by releasing the investigator from the commitment to argument and partisanship that alternative concepts such as "personality" demand. Identity, as a concept, is without any history of polemics. However, the impetus to discovery afforded by the term has been so great that its meaning threatens to spill over the bounds of analytic utility. Before its meaning becomes totally lost by awakening every conceivable response in every conceivable investigator (like the term "personality"), the concept must be salvaged.

Almost all writers using the term imply that identity establishes *what* and *where* the person is in social terms. It is not a substitute word for "self." Instead, when one has identity, he is *situated*—that is, cast in the shape of a social object by the acknowledgment of his participation or membership in social relations. One's identity is established when others *place* him as a social object by assigning him the same words of identity that he appropriates for himself or *announces*. It is in the coincidence of placements and announcements that identity becomes a meaning of the self, and often such placements and announcements are aroused by apparent symbols such as uniforms. The policeman's uniform, for example, is an announcement of his identity as policeman and validated by other's placements of him as policeman.

Such a conception of identity is, indeed, close to Mead's conception of the "me," the self as object related to

and differentiated from others. To situate the person by establishing some identity for him is, in a sense, to give him position, and a pun permits further elucidation of the concept: identity is established as a consequence of two processes, apposition and opposition, a bringing together and setting apart. To situate the person as a social object is to bring him together with other objects so situated, and, at the same time to set him apart from still other objects. *Identity is intrinsically associated with all the joinings and departures of social life.* To have an identity is to join with some and depart from others, to enter and leave social relations at once.

In fact, the varieties of identity are isomorphic with the varieties of social relations. At least four different types of words were used to place and announce the identities communicated by clothing: (1) universal words designating one's humanity, such as age, gender, and community (we call these "universal" words because people everywhere make such distinctions); (2) names and nicknames; (3) titles, such as occupational and marital titles; (4) "relational categories," such as customer, movie-goer, jazz fan, and the like. Social relations, viewed as on-going transactions, can be classified according to the identities which must be placed and announced to permit entry into the transaction. Thus, *human relations* are those requiring the placement and announcement of such universal identities as age, gender, or community membership. *Interpersonal relations* are those that may only be entered by an exchange of names or nicknames,[8] while *structural relations* are those that may only be entered by exchanging a name for a title. Finally, we may speak of *masses* as social relations that may be anonymously entered.

The distinction between interpersonal and structural relations seems, at this point, to have the greatest analytical utility. Since one's name ordinarily outlasts one's titles, interpersonal relations probably provide an important social basis for the continuity of identity. Structural relations, on the other hand, are more discontinuous and changing.

We can note how one's name is established by dress if we imagine Teddy Roosevelt without the pince-nez, F.D.R. without the cigarette holder, or Thomas Dewey without the moustache. One of our informants, a small-time real estate operator, was well aware of the significance of clothing in his attempts to personalize his occupational identity. Asked, "What do your fellow workers say and think when you wear something new for the first time on the job?" he replied:

Well, I always have a new hat, and I suppose my clientele talks about it. But, you know, I always buy cheap ones and put my name in them. I leave them around in restaurants and places like that intentionally. It has advertising value.

The interviewer asked later, "Would you rather wear a greater variety or a smaller variety of clothes on the job?" and the informant replied:

A smaller variety so you will look the same everyday. So people will identify you. They look for the same old landmark.

In response to the same question, a working man who had recently opened a small business said:

A smaller variety for both sales and shop. I think if a person dresses about the same continually, people will get to know you. Even if they don't know your name, you're easier to describe. I knew an insurance man once who used a wheel chair. Everyone knew him because of that chair. It's the same with clothes.

Distinctive, persistent dress may replace the name as well as establish it!

On the other hand, one's career within the structural relation is marked by changes of title, and the change of title demands a change of dress. All of the men in this study were presented with the following story:

John had an excellent record as foreman in an automobile factory. Eventually, he and two other foremen were promoted to the position of division head. John was happy to get the job, because of the increase in pay. However, he continued to wear his old foreman's vest and work clothes to the office. This went on for several months until the division heads he had been promoted with began to avoid him at lunch and various social gatherings. They had dressed from the beginning in business suits and had mingled more and more with older managerial employees. John found himself without friends in the office.

When asked, "What finally happened to John?" about 80 per cent of the men interviewed predicted termination, demotion, or no further promotion (5, pp. 47-51). One informant, interviewed by the writer, quite seriously suggested that John was a potential suicide.

Appearances, then, are interrupted in social structures as identities are set apart; appearances, so to speak, endure in interpersonal relations where identities are brought into closer proximity. Yet we find that, in the context of structural relations, identities are given a somewhat different cast than in interpersonal relations. In the former, identities are qualified along the axis of value; in the latter, more usually along the axis of mood.

QUALIFICATIONS OF IDENTITY: VALUE AND MOOD

To engage meaningfully in some transactions it is enough to know merely "what" the parties are—to know their identities. This would seem often to be the case in the anonymous transactions of the masses.

As Louis Wirth used to tell his students in his elaborations of the "massive" character of urban life, "You go to a bootblack to have your shoes shined; not to save your soul." The implication is, I think, that, when we become concerned with the bootblack's moods or his larger worth in terms of some scheme of value, our relations with him will lose their anonymous character. By so doing, we have, perhaps, disadvantaged ourselves of the freedom the city offers. Ordinarily, however, if transactions persistently engage the same persons or seem likely to continue into an ill-defined future, it is not enough merely to establish identities in the guarantee of meaningful discourse. Thus, when we are introduced to strangers who may become acquaintances or possibly friends, we *express* our pleasure with the introductions, and such expressions are ordinarily *appreciated* by those we have met. Or, meeting an acquaintance on the street, we inquire how he *feels* before the discourse is initiated. In a certain sense, interpersonal relations demand that the *moods* of the participants be established (as well as their names or nicknames) prior to the initiation of discursive phases in the transaction: that "Joe" or "Jane" is mad or sad will have definite consequences for the talk with "Jim" or "Joan."

Ordinarily, also, before a title is bestowed upon us or before we are invested with office, our identities must undergo qualifying scrutiny. In such cases, the qualification does not usually get accomplished in terms of our anger or sadness, but in terms of some assessment of our former careers and future prospects with reference to their *worth*. The tendency is to assess worth in terms of a relatively objective set of standards that can transcend the whim of the assessing one and the whimsy of the one assessed. Upon the initiation of what we have called structural relations, the *values* of the participating persons (as well as their titles) must be established.

Value and mood provide two fundamental axes along which the qualifications of identity are accomplished in *appraising* and *appreciative* response to appearance. This seems obvious on the face of it: that a teacher is competent has different consequences for faculty-student transactions than that a teacher is a teacher; and that a teacher is temperamental or easygoing presents the possibility of a still different set of consequences for upcoming discussions. The differences between value and mood are suggested by the distinction that Park has made between interests and sentiments, that Helen Lynd has made between guilt and shame, or that Kenneth Burke has made between poetry and pathos (*poiema* and *pathema*). It is the difference between virtue and happiness, and, as we know full well, the virtuous man is not necessarily happy nor the happy man necessarily virtuous. The problem arises when we observe that happiness may be a virtue in some social circles or that one may be happy because he is virtuous (cynics might say "smug"). Value and mood, so patently distinguishable in discourse, merge together inextricably in experience. Can we conceive of feelings of pride without reference to a set of values? I think not, although it does seem possible to conceive of merit without feeling. Yet, in situations that are totally value-relevant, totally given over to matters of appraisal—the courtroom, the examination, the military review—the very constriction of feeling and mood, their suppression, may saturate the situation with a grim somberness that can transform dispassion into passion—as the austerity of the courtroom has provided a curiously fitting context for the impassioned plea; the silence of the examination room is interrupted by nervous laughter; the ordered rhythm of the march engenders song.

As Helen Lynd has written of guilt and shame, so we conceive value and mood:

They are in no sense polar opposites. Both the guilt axis and the shame axis enter into the attitudes and behavior of most people, and often into the same situation. But there are for different persons different balances and stresses between the two, and it does matter whether one lives more in terms of one or the other (11, p. 208).

And we would add that one differentiating condition is the type of social relation that regularly mobilizes the time and attention of the person. Thus, we have found that value has a greater saliency for most men in their conceptions of self and others, while, for most women, mood has a greater saliency. This finding is ascribed in part to the American male's more frequent participation and absorption in the structure of work relations, in comparison with the American woman's more frequent preoccupation with the interpersonal relations she carries on with friends and acquaintances.

It is much more difficult to characterize value and mood than it has been to characterize identity. However, the responses to dress that were classified as words of value manifested the following references: (1) to *consensual goals*, such as wealth, prestige, or power; (2) to *achievement standards*, universalistic criteria applied to the assessment of one's proximity to or remoteness from such goals; (3) *norms* or rules regulating the pursuit of consensual goals; and (4) *moral precepts* stipulating valued behavior often em-

TABLE 1
VALUE AND MOOD AS AXES ALONG WHICH QUALIFICATIONS
OF IDENTITY ARE ESTABLISHED

PHASES	*VALUE AXIS*	*MOOD AXIS*
Relational Basis	Structural relations	Interpersonal relations
Criteria	Universalistic Abstract Objective Detachment Poetic (Pious) Neutrality Scalar	Particularistic Concrete Subjective Attachment Pathetic Affectivity Absolute
Establishment	Rationalized Investment Conformity-deviation with respect to universal rules or a social code Future reference Legitimated by appeals to the appraisals of others	Spontaneously communicated Preoccupation or rapture Ease-dis-ease with respect to engagement in social transactions Present reference Legitimated by appeals to the expression of the self
Relational Consequences	Stratification	Rapport

ployed in the assessment of character (e.g., cleanliness, politeness, thriftiness, and the like). Responses classified as mood-words were even more difficult to order, including references to ease and lack of ease in social transactions, liking, disliking, fearing, and dreading. Anxiety, monotony, rapture, and surprise also were included in the category, as were references to that ill-defined state which the informants called morale.

It may be helpful to borrow again from Helen Lynd, using her technique for contrasting guilt and shame to contrast value and mood. Table 1 attempts to state the social relations for which value and mood *ordinarily* have the greatest saliency, the nature of the criteria which are applied in the establishment of value and mood, the processes by which these qualifications of identity are established, and finally the consequences for the social relationship when identities are qualified along one or the other axis. I wish to emphasize that the summary presentation in Table 1 is in no way meant to be definitive, and that the axes which are characterized as value and mood, although they are set down in a contrasting manner, are not meant to be established as polar opposites. In particular, *sentiments* represent a convergence of the two axes in the qualification of identity. Sentiments are valued feelings or felt values, as for example in Cooley's "looking-glass self"—the sentiments of pride or mortification are *expressive* responses to the judgments or *appraisals* of others.

ACTIVATIONS OF IDENTITY: ATTITUDE

In a brilliant discussion, Kenneth Burke has established the essential ambiguity of the term "attitude": an attitude can be looked upon as a substitute for an act—the "truncated act" of John Dewey—or as an incipient act—a "beginning" from the standpoint of George H. Mead (2, pp. 235-247). The establishment of identity, value, and mood by appearances represents the person as *there, stratified* or assigned a particular distance, and *rapt* or engrossed. There remains the matter of his activation, the assessment of the path along which he has traveled, the path he is traveling, and where he is about to go. These aspects of the person—that he has acted, is acting, and will act further—are also established by appearance. We refer to them as *attitudes*.[9] Attitudes are *anticipated* by the reviewers of an appearance, *proposed* by the one who appears.

Appearance *substitutes* for past and present action and, at the same time, conveys an *incipience* permitting others to anticipate what is about to occur. Specifically, clothing represents our action, past, present, and future, as it is established by the proposals and anticipations that occur in every social transaction. Without further elaboration, I think that this can be clearly seen in the doffing of dress, signaling that an act is done (and another act about to begin), the donning of dress, signaling the initiation of a new act, and the wearing of dress, signaling that action is going on.

APPEARANCE AND THE SELF

The meaning of appearance, therefore, can be studied by examining the responses mobilized by clothes. Such responses take on at least four forms: identities are placed, values appraised, moods appreciated, and attitudes anticipated. Appearance provides the identities, values, moods, and attitudes of the person-in-communication, since it arouses in others the assignment of words embodying these dimensions to the one who appears. As we have noted earlier, this is only one part of the total picture.

Cooley, Mead, and Harry Stack Sullivan have reminded us often that such responses are reflexive in character, reverberating back upon the one who produces them and the one toward whom they are directed. In short, identifications of others are always complemented by identifications of the self, in this case, responses to one's own appearance. In a variety of ways, as a matter of fact, reviews of a person's appearances are intricately linked with the responses he makes to his own appearance. We have called the process of making identifications of the one who appears by that one a *program*. Programmatic responses parallel the responses that have been called reviews. One appears, reflects upon that appearance, and appropriates words of identity, value, mood, or attitude for himself in response to that appearance. By appearing, the person *announces* his identity, *shows* his value, *expresses* his mood, or *proposes* his attitude. If the meaning of appearance is "supplied" by the reviews others make of one's appearance, it is established or consensually validated, as Sullivan would have said, by the relative coincidence of such reviews with the program of the one who appears. In other words, when one's dress calls out in others the "same" identifications of the wearer as it calls

out in the wearer, we may speak of the appearance as meaningful. It turns out, in fact, that this is the self, and this may be diagrammed as in Table 2.

In appearances, then, selves are established and mobilized. As the self is dressed, it is simultaneously addressed, for, whenever we clothe ourselves, we dress "toward" or address some audience whose validating responses are essential to the establishment of our self. Such responses may, of course, also be challenges, in which case a new program is aroused. This intimate linkage of the self and clothing was masterfully caricatured by a forty-year-old carpenter's wife who was herself working in a local factory. Our guess is that a few bottles of beer were conducive to the spontaneous flow of words, but their import is none the less striking. The woman had interpreted a modified TAT scene as a religious depiction, and the interviewer asked her, after the completion of the stories, which card she liked best:

[*Interviewer:* Of those three, which did you like best? . . .]
Oh, that is kinda hard for me to do. I like them all. This one here is good, and that one is good, and that one is good. I think, of course, religion should come first, but I still think this is first right here—of her trying to help this girl. [Note: the card depicts a well-dressed woman talking with another woman in rather drab masculine dress.] Looks to me like she is just telling her what

TABLE 2

SCHEMATIC REPRESENTATION OF THE MEANING OF APPEARANCE, EMPHASIZING THE VALIDATION OF PERSONAL APPEARANCE

PROGRAM OF APPEARANCE	REVIEW OF APPEARANCE			
	Placement	*Appraisal*	*Appreciation*	*Anticipation*
Announcement	Identity			
Show		Value		
Expression			Mood	
Proposal				Attitude

she should do and how she should dress. Don't look very nice. I think that has a lot to do with a person's life afterwards. If they can get straightened out on their personal appearance, they can get straightened out in their religion a lot quicker. You take personal appearance; goes with their minds. Their mind has to work to go with that. They get that straightened out; I think they can go back to religion and get that straightened out. I don't go to church now, but I used to be, and I am still, and always will be, regardless of what it is I ever do. I smoke a cigarette, drink a bottle of beer. I'm not Catholic. I'm Protestant. Church is my first thing. But this [informant hits the picture] comes first, before church. I don't care what anybody says. Clothes, our personal appearance, and getting our minds settled is how we should do. Some people don't believe that, but I do, 'cause you can go into a church and worship but that ain't all that makes a go of this world. You have got to have something beside that. I don't care how much you worship. People can laugh at you. When you go into a church, they laugh at a girl dressed like this girl is or this woman is. They'll think she is not all there. But, if she gets herself fixed up, and looks nice, and goes to church like this picture here, they'll think she knows what she's talking about. I've seen too much of that. In other words, *clothes, personal appearance, can make one's life.* [Said slowly, deliberately, with much emphasis.] There is something about it that gives you courage. Some people would call it false courage, but I wouldn't. . . . I think anyone has to have a certain amount of clothes to give them courage. It ain't false courage either or false pride. It's just it. . . . Suppose it was just like it was when I went to that banquet tonight. Everybody told me how nice I looked, but I didn't think so. I had to feel right. . . . when I get the dress I feel right in, I feel like a million dollars. It makes an altogether different person out of me. That's an awful thing to say, but that's true for me.

Similar, but less dramatic, remarks abound in our interview materials. All point to the undeniable and intimate linkage of self and appearance. As a matter of fact, the analysis we have made permits a suggested modification of perhaps the best definition of the self in the social-psychological literature. Lindesmith and Strauss

. . . think of the self as: (1) a set of more or less consistent and stable responses on a conceptual level, which (2) exercise a regulatory function over other responses of the same organism at lower levels (10, p. 416).

Dispensing with the motion of levels of behavior, which seems unnecessarily misleading (surely the self exercises a regulatory function over discourse—a set of conceptual responses!), we suggest the following definition: *the self is any validated program which exercises a regulatory function over other responses of the same organism, including the formulation of other programs.* What this definition does is spell out the regulatory responses—that is, one's announcements, shows, expressions, or proposals—while linking their consistency to the consensual validations of others. Such selves are established in significant appearances which provide the foundations of significant discourse and which, of course, may be played back upon and altered as the discourse transpires.

NOTES

1. Erving Goffman (7) must be exempted from the indictment. Recently, he has pushed sociological or social psychological analysis far beyond the conventional limits of a perspective that has restricted the study of social transactions to their linguistic characteristics, conditions, and consequences.

2. Of course, the gesture is considered at length, and gestures may often be employed to establish appearances, as we shall see. However, Mead views the gesture as incipient discourse, more typical of communication in its rudimentary phases. The aptness of the vocal gesture for explaining the emergence of meaning in sub-social

communication may be an important source of Mead's discursive bias. Even more than discourse, appearance presupposes an on-going social process for its meaning. Apparent symbols are often silent and are best intercepted by mirrors, while one's own ear always intercepts one's own vocal gesture about as it is intercepted by others. But mirrors are not always handy; so it happens that the silent appearance, even more than the vocal utterance, comes to require an audience which can serve as a mirror, reflecting one's appearance back upon himself.

3. "Response" is usually the production of other symbols. The term is distinguished from "symbol" merely to permit the observer to shift his view as he analyzes what is going on in the social transaction. Actually, all that distinguishes a "response" from any symbol in question is its occurrence later in time. I am indebted to my colleague, Keith Miller, for this clarification.

4. The precedent has been incisively established by Nelson N. Foote (4).

5. Mead himself distinguishes sympathy as a particular mode of "attitude-taking" in a seldom cited article (13); but for the empirical utility of the distinction, see Sheldon Stryker (17).

6. An imposing taxonomy has been erected in Howard Becker (1).

7. The question of how the meaning of appearance is guaranteed is germane and recognized, but will not be treated here. Aside from the "team work" analyzed so carefully by Goffman in his *Presentation of Self in Everyday Life* (7), other guarantees are suggested in his "Symbols of Class Status." (6)

8. This characterization of interpersonal relations is not reversible. The exchange of names does not guarantee that an interpersonal relationship will always be established.

9. Of course, the concept "attitude" is of central significance for the social psychology of George Herbert Mead, but, in some ways, it is the least satisfying of the terms we have characterized here. All the meanings of dress or appearance have an attitudinal or "activated" character. In particular, programs and reviews may be conceived as incipient, truncated, or on-going acts. It may be, in fact, that the concept "attitude" is of a different order from the concepts "identity," "value," and "mood," asking the observer to inquire not into the content or structure of the events under scrutiny, but rather to seize those events in their full-blown capacity as processes.

REFERENCES

1. Becker, Howard. "Empathy, Sympathy, and Scheler," *International Journal of Sociometry*, Vol. 1 (September, 1956), pp. 15-22.
2. Burke, Kenneth. *A Grammar of Motives*. Englewood Cliffs, N. J.: Prentice-Hall, Inc., 1945.
3. Cooley, Charles H. *Human Nature and the Social Order*. New York: Charles Scribner's Sons, 1902.
4. Foote, Nelson N. "Identification as a Basis for a Theory of Motivation," *American Sociological Review*, Vol. 16 (February 1951), pp. 14-21.
5. Form, William H., and Gregory P. Stone. *The Social Significance of Clothing in Occupational Life*. East Lansing, Mich.: Michigan State University Agricultural Experiment Station Technical Bulletin 262 (November 1957).
6. Goffman, Erving. "Symbols of Class Status," *British Journal of Sociology*, Vol. 2 (December 1951), pp. 294-304.
7. Goffman, Erving. *The Presentation of Self in Everyday Life*. Edinburgh: University of Edinburgh Social Science Research Centre Monograph, No. 2, 1956.
8. Gorer, Geoffrey. *The American People*. New York: W. W. Norton & Company, Inc., 1948.
9. Huizinga, Jan. *Homo Ludens: A Study of the Play-Element in Culture*. London: Routledge & Kegan Paul, Ltd., 1949.
10. Lindesmith, Alfred R., and Anselm L. Strauss. *Social Psychology*. New York: The Dryden Press, 1956.
11. Lynd, Helen Merrell. *On Shame and the Search for Identity*. New York: Harcourt, Brace and Co., 1958.
12. Markey, John F. *The Symbolic Process and Its Integration in Children*. London: Kegan Paul, Trench, Trübner and Co., Ltd., 1928.
13. Mead, George H. "Philanthropy from the Point of View of Ethics," in Ellsworth Faris, Ferris Laune, and Arthur J. Todd (eds.), *Intelligent Philan-*

thropy. Chicago: The University of Chicago Press, 1930, pp. 133-148.

14. Mead, George H. *Mind, Self, and Society*, ed. by Charles W. Morris. Chicago: The University of Chicago Press, 1934.

15. Piaget, Jean. *The Language and Thought of the Child*. New York: Meridian Books, 1955.

16. Stone, Gregory P. "Clothing and Social Relations: A Study of Appearance in the Context of Community Life." Unpublished Ph.D. dissertation, Department of Sociology, University of Chicago, 1959.

17. Stryker, Sheldon. "Relationships of Married Offspring and Parent: A Test of Mead's Theory," *American Journal of Sociology*, Vol. 62 (November 1956), pp. 308-319.

18. Sullivan, Harry Stack. *The Psychiatric Interview*. New York: W. W. Norton & Company, Inc., 1954.

19. Veblen, Thorstein. *The Theory of the Leisure Class*. New York: Modern Library, Inc., 1934.

8. ALTERNATION AND CONVERSION AS QUALITATIVELY DIFFERENT TRANSFORMATIONS

RICHARD V. TRAVISANO

Reprinted from G. P. Stone and H. Farberman, *Social Psychology Through Symbolic Interaction* (Waltham, Mass.: Ginn Blaisdell, 1970) pp. 594-606, with permission of the author and Ginn Blaisdell. Richard Travisano wrote the following selection while a student at the University of Minnesota from which he received his Ph.D. in 1973. He is currently Associate Professor of Sociology at the University of Rhode Island and is working on a book about motives.

Kenneth Burke has suggested that every man is a poet. Peter Berger suggests an artist. Ernest Becker suggests a dramatist. They each are concerned with how the individual rationalizes his life; rationalizes, not in the psychological sense of propaganda to conceal "real" motives, but in Weber's sense of legitimizing behavior. Legitimation socializes behavior, and proceeds by labeling behavior with socially understandable categories. This view of human conduct argues that what a man does often has little meaning, rhyme, or reason, until the individual gets busy making autobiographical use of his already completed actions. As Berger has pointed out, we constantly remake our own biographies, and our interpretations and revisions are rarely integrated and consistent:[1]

... Most of us do not set out deliberately to paint a grand portrait of ourselves. Rather we stumble like drunkards over the sprawling canvas of our self-conception, throwing a little paint here, erasing some lines there, never really stopping to obtain a view of the likeness we have produced. ...

This perspective, then, sees man as an artist who more or less blunders into his biographical materials and then must work them into his story one way or another. From this perspective we wish to distinguish two different kinds of personal transformation.

CONSTANCY AND CHANGE

Certainly, as Anselm Strauss has said, "The awareness of constancy of identity ... is in the eye of the beholder rather than 'in' the behavior itself."[2] The corollary of this statement is that *change* in identity is also in the eye of the beholder. But who *is* this beholder? He is the self-reflective actor, the actor's others, the generalized others, the sociological observer. As identities are retained, discarded, transformed, or assumed, one or more of these observers will note that a change has, or is, taking place. It is they who say how great that change is. Strauss, then, is saying that such permanence as our personal histories have is defined through the give and take of interaction within shared universes of discourse.[3] We add that, as permanence is rationalized into the confusion of contrary actions and meaning that make up a life, so also is change. Our task, then, as Nelson Foote has put it, is to apprehend the categories of identity and motive employed by the persons we study.[4]

Peter Berger has succinctly portrayed the flux of life and the ubiquity of personal transformations in it. For him values have become "relativized" in modern society. "Traditional societies assign definite and permanent

91

identities to their members," whereas "In modern society identity itself is uncertain and in flux."[5] He argues that our unprecedented rates of geographical mobility and travel, along with the enormous amount of information available through our mass media "imply at least potentially the awareness that one's own culture, including its basic values, is relative in space and time."[6]

To continue in Berger's words:[7]

Social mobility . . . augments this relativizing effect. Wherever industrialism occurs, a new dynamism is injected into the social system. Masses of people begin to change their social position, in groups or as individuals. And usually this change is in an "upward" direction. With this movement an individual's biography often involves a considerable journey not only through a variety of social groups but through the intellectual universes that are, so to speak, attached to these groups. Thus the Baptist mail clerk who used to read the *Reader's Digest* becomes an Episcopalian junior executive who reads *The New Yorker*, or the faculty wife whose husband becomes department chairman may graduate from the bestseller list to Proust or Kafka.

Berger then points out that each viewpoint available to modern man carries with it its own slant on some aspect of reality and that,[8]

. . . the more fully elaborated meaning systems [such as Freudianism or Communism] . . . can provide a total interpretation of reality, within which will be included an interpretation of the alternate systems and of the ways of passing from one system to another.

In reference to these "fully elaborated meaning systems," Berger states:[9]

Instead of speaking of conversion (a term with religiously charged connotations) we would prefer to use the more neutral term of "alternation" to describe this phenomenon. The intellectual situation just described brings with it the possibility that an individual may alternate back and forth between logically contradictory meaning systems. Each time, the meaning system he enters provides him with an interpretation of his existence and of his world, including

in this interpretation an explanation of the meaning system he has abandoned.

It is plain enough that Berger is offering a broad sociological explanation for the prevalence of identity changes in our times (i.e., our society assigns us no definite permanent identity while at the same time exposing us to many alternative universes of discourse). Also, he prefers the term "alternation" to the term "conversion." There are, however, certain points to be considered if we are to get at the nature of these transformations.

To begin with, when Berger talks about alternation to "fully elaborated meaning systems" he is referring to what is called conversion in the narrowest everyday sense. These are the most radically reorganizing changes of everyday life: Christian college students become atheists; Jews become fundamental Christians; communists become Catholics. Berger claims that ". . . an individual may alternate back and forth between contradictory meaning systems." This does not seem true. There are contradictions throughout our meanings, but it is the socially recognized and sanctioned contradictions that are central in what we recognize as antithetic universes of discourse. In addition, adoption of antithetic universes of discourse involves a complete reinterpretation and reorganization of life or autobiography. Kenneth Burke insists that conversion involves a change in the "informing aspect" of character.[10] That a person could change quickly back and forth in this respect seems quite unlikely. Experience does leave its mark. As Strauss writes, "one . . . misconception about conversion is that when a person becomes partly converted and then is 'lost' he returns to his previous identity. . . ."[11] Surely the point holds for complete conversion as well as for partial conversion. *One can't go home again.* The black sheep who return to the fold are somehow different from those who never left. Do not the angels rejoice more when one sinner repents? This is not to say that less than totally disruptive transformations do not occur. Middle-class youth, after all, will have their fling before they settle down into the world of meaning in which they were raised. While the break with middle-class respectability may be a conversion for such people, settling back into it is no conversion backwards. It is simply "learning the ropes." The fact is that genuine change back and forth between antithetic total universes of discourse is a rare possibility.

In his definition of alternation, Berger ignores many identity changes which do not involve total universes of discourse. Thus he neglects his own example of the Baptist mail clerk who used to read the *Reader's Digest*, who becomes an Episcopalian junior executive who reads *The New Yorker*. What of this fellow? Do all Baptist organization men undergo total and disruptive reorientations of their lives in becoming Episcopalians? Do they all make the difficult move from one total universe of discourse to another? Certainly not! But surely such a move is a change in perspective, in identity, and in situation. Berger has discussed different kinds of changes, but has grouped them all together under the general term "alternation." We will propose that important and useful distinctions between transformations can and should be made.

ALTERNATION AND CONVERSION AS DIFFERENT IDENTITY CHANGES

IDENTITY

To discuss and distinguish transformations we shall utilize the concept of identity. It seems best, moreover, to limit our notion of identity by a con-

cise behaviorally objectified definition. Thus, we may follow Stone, who writes:[12]

Almost all writers using the term imply that identity establishes *what* and *where* the person is in social terms. It is not a substitute word for "self." Instead, when one has identity, he is *situated*—that is, cast in the shape of a social object by the acknowledgement of his participation or membership in social relations. One's identity is established when others *place* him as a social object by assigning him the same words of identity that he appropriates for himself or *announces*. . . .

Identity, then, is a placed or validated announcement. One announces that he is some particular social object; others read his cue and respond in kind, saying by their behavior, that he indeed is what he claims. This "coincidence of placements and announcements" gives one the feeling that he embodies what he has announced himself as, that is, gives him an experiential sense of felt identity. But note Stone's phrase: "when one has identity, he is situated . . ." This acknowledges the fact that people must establish identities for *both* themselves *and* others if an interaction is to proceed in any meaningful manner.

ROLE

Every social interaction proceeds in terms of some definition of the situation, and placing people in identities is an important part of that definition.[13] The importance of identities in this regard indicates the crucial nature of the concept. "Role" is a conceptualization of social probabilities. It is impossible to delineate a role completely because a single role demands many different actions in different situations. But "identity" *is* a signal *in interaction* for the mobilization of specific role expectations. Identities are, so to speak, the labels or names on the scripts of various situationally specified programs of behavior which make up the abstract totalities we call roles. Identities tell people what to do and expect during a given interaction. We use the plural because the specified behavior that an identity mobilizes usually depends on the identities of the others in the interaction. A sociologist acts like a sociologist. But what this means depends on where he is interacting—in the classroom, in the office, at home, or wherever else the identity might be relevant.[14] This is nothing new, but it is important because it emphasizes the interactional specificity of role as compared to identity, and the experiential reality of being a thing (say a sociologist) in a specific interaction, as compared to the non-experiential contemplation of being the same thing in general. Identities alone, of course, do not define situations. But we shall bypass, perhaps arbitrarily, a full consideration of the elements and process of situation definition, and simply state that the establishment of identities is usually an important part of the process.[15]

All this clearly has implications for our discussion of transformation. In the flux of life, it is the changes which get named that are dwelled upon, and the changes dwelled upon that get named. What, then, is the import of these considerations for an analysis of identity change? To establish a new identity, a new announcement must be recurrently made and validated.[16] But one does not take on only an abstract property called an identity, one takes on new definitions of situations and new situated behavior. This may be relatively easy (as when a husband becomes a father) or difficult (as when a wife becomes a divorcee). This relative ease or difficulty depends on how far afield one goes; that is, on whether a new identity is irrelevant, related, or opposed to old ones; on whether old relationships are unchanged, trans-. formed, or destroyed. And it is on the interactional contingencies which make for relative ease or difficulty that our distinction between conversion and alternation rests. Complete disruption signals conversion while anything less signals alternation. Summary statements from the research which led to this paper will exemplify the differences in these transformation processes.

HEBREW CHRISTIANS AND JEWISH UNITARIANS: CONVERTS AND ALTERNATORS

The differences between a Jew becoming a fundamental Christian (a process of conversion) and a Jew becoming a member of a Unitarian Society (a process of alternation) are simply enormous. The "average" Hebrew Christian (the subjects' term for themselves) is about 23 years old at the time of his conversion. He is likely to be unsettled in occupation and life style. He very likely had a usual Jewish upbringing, religiously and "culturally," but he is quite unlikely to be a synagogue member at the time of his conversion. If he does hold membership, it will be dropped. His conversion causes serious consternation among his relatives and friends. He is viewed as an apostate, a traitor, and heavy pressure is brought to bear against him. His change changes his life as his conversion and new identity become his central concern. He is quite likely to become a missionary worker by vocation or, at least, to adopt proselytizing as a very serious avocation. He loves to tell the story of his salvation and is, by this and other means, constantly trying to weave together the broken threads of his biography. The

Hebrew Christian very definitely identifies himself as a Jew. He has not
abandoned his Jewish identity but has
transformed it into a Hebrew Christian
one. This affords continuity from the
past to the demanding new role of
"born-again-believer," and it also affords an argument to meet the multitude of challenges that such a drastic
change elicits. After all, who can argue
with the basic logic of a statement
made by one of my respondents:

I was born a Jew, and now I have accepted
the promised Messiah of Israel who came in
fulfillment of the Scriptures. Christ came to
the Jews. The first Christians were Jews. As
a Hebrew Christian I am a completed Jew.

But the focus of the Hebrew Christian
identity is fundamental Christianity.
The Hebrew Christian is, so to speak,
more Christian than Jewish. He probably knows, and spends time with,
other Hebrew Christians,[17] but he attends a gentile Christian church and
has mostly gentile Christian friends
and associates. The Hebrew Christian
identity is viable enough, but only in
the limited circle of fundamental
Christianity.[18] The wider world rejects
the Hebrew Christian as logically impossible, or regards him with a suspicious eye. Against the position of
this wider world, his old others, and
his old self, the Hebrew Christian is
always arguing.

The "average" Jewish Unitarian is
about 32 years old at the time of his
alternation. He is settled in occupation
and life style. He is likely to have had
the usual Jewish upbringing, religiously and "culturally," and there is
about a 50 per cent chance that he is a
member of a synagogue. If he is a
member, he is most likely to retain
membership concurrently with Unitarian Society membership. The Jew
who joins a Unitarian Society does not
feel he has made any significant
change. He does not think of himself as

a "Jewish Unitarian," and he may not
even think of himself as a "Unitarian."
One may just be a member of a Unitarian Society, one does not have to
accept a new label as definitive of self,
and most Jewish Unitarians do not.[19]
The Jewish Unitarian usually encounters little or no resistance from family
or friends. His change does not change
his life but actually can be understood
as one of the possibilities in an already
established and settled life style or
program. Being solid middle- or up-
per-middle class, "liberal," "humanistic," and usually limited in formal
ties to the Jewish community, he finds
out about the Unitarian Society from
friends or some other source; investi-
gates; and joins. He may attend meetings (they are usually not called
"services") regularly, or he may
never attend, simply giving monetary
support to what he feels is a good organization with good aims. If you ask
whether he still considers himself a
Jew, he will answer, "Yes, of course,"
but will consider your question
strange and unnecessary. If pressed on
this matter, he will suspect you are
defining him as an apostate and will
greatly resent your labeling his Unitarian Society membership in a way
which neither he nor any of his associates, old or new, do. An example
from an interview will serve well here.
After a series of questions, which
began with the phrase, "Since you became a Unitarian," a subject ex-
claimed:

One thing that bothers me is your phrases. I
would say I'm Jewish, and you keep identifying me as a Unitarian. I'm Jewish. There
is a Unitarian Society in [another city]
where they have candles and robes and crap
like that. If that were the case here, you
wouldn't be interviewing me.

Clearly, we have in these examples,
very different kinds of change. The
Hebrew Christian has broken with his

past, the Jewish Unitarian has not. The Hebrew Christian has completely reorganized his life, the Jewish Unitarian has not. In short, the Hebrew Christian has a new principle of organization for his action and autobiography, while the Jewish Unitarian has simply extended his old programs in one of many permissible directions. Symptomatically, the Jewish Unitarian identity is seldom or never central to an interaction, while the Hebrew Christian identity is very often central, and, when it is not, it is usually threatening. We propose to call these distinctly different kinds of change *conversion* and *alternation*.

CONVERSION AND ALTERNATION
DISTINGUISHED

Conversions are drastic changes in life. Such changes require a change in the "informing aspect" of one's life or biography. Moreover, there must be a negation (often specifically forbidden) of some former identity. Conversion is signaled by a radical reorganization of identity, meaning, and life. The convert is recognizable by his piety. As William James observed, "To say a man is 'converted' means . . . that religious ideas, previously peripheral in his consciousness, now take a central place, and that religious aims form the habitual centre of his energy."[20] James unnecessarily limited his statement to religious transformations. Of course it is more widely applicable. Kenneth Burke purposely chose an unusual non-religious example in discussing piety:

. . . If a man who is a criminal lets the criminal trait in him serve as the informing aspect of his character, piously taking unto him all other traits and habits that he feels should go with his criminality, the criminal deterioration which the moralist with another point of view might discover in him is the very opposite of deterioration as

regards the tests of piety. It is *integration*, guided by a scrupulous sense of the appropriate which, once we dismiss our personal locus of judgment, would seem to bear the marks of great conscientiousness.[21]

Conversion, then, involves a change in *informing aspect*. Given the social basis of meanings, such a change implies a change of allegiance from one source of authority to another.[22] Translating into symbolic interactionist terms, we may say that a conversion involves the adoption of a pervasive identity[23] which rests on a change (at least in emphasis) from one universe of discourse to another. Such universes of discourse are, of course, the properties of social groups or authorities. (After all, what is an authority, if not a legislator and guardian of meanings?) We may also note that conversion often involves a period of emotional upset and indecision during which the individual may become severely depressed or confused and may experience emotionally induced somatic upsets. As for the convert's former associates, they are usually disturbed by the convert's new identity and allegiances and may well treat him as a traitor.

Finally, we must defend our use of the term "conversion" for this kind of transformation. It is, of course, the traditional term, but Berger suggests "alternation" to escape the religious connotations of "conversion." Yet, given the nature of conversion as distinguished from other changes, the religious connotation is just what is needed. By applying the "religious" word to secular areas (examples are communism, psychoanalysis, and science as an enterprise), social thinkers have gained insight into activities in these areas. Such elucidation through juxtaposition of meanings foreign to each other Kenneth Burke has called "perspective by incongruity." in fact,

Burke quite correctly sees conversion itself as a process of perspective by incongruity.[24] "Conversion," then, is an apt word for these changes.

As we saw in our Jewish Unitarian example, there are identity changes which are not so drastic as those we have called conversions. These we propose to call "alternations." These are relatively easily accomplished changes of life which do not involve a radical change in universe of discourse and informing aspect, but which are a part of or grow out of existing programs of behavior. A Baptist mail clerk becomes an Episcopalian junior executive; a high school student becomes a college boy; a husband becomes a father; a professor becomes department chairman. To say such changes are easily accomplished, of course, does not mean that everyone makes them with no trouble whatsoever. Adjustments to college or to fatherhood, for example, are often quite painful and pervasive. But these changes and their attendant problems are provided for in established universes of discourse. The actor is only learning well a new part of a world he was always committed to, with the help of his established others. In conversion, a whole new world is entered, and the old world is transformed through reinterpretation. The father sees his bachelorhood as youthful fun; the convert sees his as debauchery.

Alternations and conversions, then, are different kinds of identity change. Alternations are transitions to identities which are prescribed or at least permitted within the person's established universes of discourse. Conversions are transitions to identities which are proscribed within the person's established universes of discourse, and which exist in universes of discourse that negate these formerly established ones. The ideal typical

conversion can be thought of as the embracing of a negative identity.[25] The person becomes something which was specifically prohibited. Thus we might think of a continuum (but infinite gradations are neither implied nor denied at this point). On one side we have the most easily accomplished alternations. One joins a conservation club or perhaps frequents a different bar. Little change is noticed by most of the person's others.[26] There is no trauma. There is little reflection on the part of the actor either before or after. There is no important change in universe of discourse. On the other side we have the most radical of conversions. The person goes through a period of intense "inner struggle." There is great trauma. The actor reflects at great length on his change. The actor and all his others see his change as monumental and he is identified by himself and others as a new or different person. The actor has a new universe of discourse which negates the values and meanings of his old ones by exposing the "fallacies" of their assumptions and reasoning. The actor has great involvement with his new identity and perspective.[27] This ideal is approached and reached in Jews who become fundamental Christians, in young intellectuals who become communists, in communists who become monks, and in psychoanalysis.[28]

IDENTITIES AND ALTERNATIONS

In this paper we have delimited conversion much more closely than alternation. But since we have designated alternations as the usual changes in life and since we have posited that our lives are riddled with change, the reader might well expect that alternations bear much closer attention than we have given them so far.

This indeed is true, and in this final section we shall address some of the problems that will face future thinking and research in what, as shall be seen, is a very difficult area.

We used as examples of alternation: a Baptist mail clerk becoming an Episcopalian junior executive; a high school student becoming a college boy; a husband becoming a father; and a professor becoming a department chairman. Our first two examples involve identities which negate old ones in a fully anticipated way. One identity grows "naturally" out of another. Such changes cause little disruption in the lives of those involved. We may call such linked identities *identity sequences*.[29] Such sequences may involve changes which are somewhat compulsory (graduate student to Ph.D. or "flunkie") or are a matter of choice or fate (high school student to college boy). Our last two examples, husband to father and professor to department chairman, involve identities which do not replace, but rather are added to, established identities. Again, this happens in an expected way with one identity arising "naturally" out of the other. And again such changes are easily accomplished. We may call these related identities *cumulative identity sequences*. As with non-cumulative identity sequences, changes may be somewhat compulsory (expectant father to husband) or open to choice or chance (spouse to parent). We should also note that some identity sequences are more casual and less insistent than these we have considered. "Liberal," "humanitarian" Jews become Unitarians; nature lovers become conservationists or birdwatchers. These changes are logical; they are extensions or addenda to formerly established programs; they are cumulative identity sequences. But they *are* casual and almost strictly a matter of choice

or chance. Relative insistence in identity sequences seems to be *at least in part* dependent on the fact that some sequences (like husband-to-father) are related to formal structure and thus carry relatively binding commitments. For example, a young man may become a casual or frequent dater, a girl-chaser, or an out-and-out rake. He can maintain such an identity for some time. But, once engaged, he is caught in the fiancé-to-spouse (noncumulative) sequence; and, once married, the spouse-to-parent cumulative sequence begins to press. One senses the difference in commitment between the fiancé-to-spouse and spouse-to-parent sequences; the difference between proposing membership in a legally established structure and actually holding membership. When one is betrothed, one is a long way down a "betrayal funnel,"[30] yet it clearly is easier to break off an engagement than, once married, to decide against having children.

Having attempted some delineation of the identity linkages that alternation gets people involved in, we may turn to a consideration of the pervasiveness of different identities and identity linkages in interaction.

Identities can be pervasive in two ways: they can be relevant in many situations, and they can be central to interaction. As we have noted, identity is trans-situational while role is situationally specified, and these situationally specific expectations of course mean that the meaning of an identity varies with situation. Some identities are relevant to more situations than others. By relevant we mean that the identity is an important part of the situation. One can be a father at home or at a PTA meeting, but one can't be a father at a faculty meeting. One can leave a faculty meeting early because one is a father who must take a child to the dentist, but in this case the identity is invoked as a motive to legitimate the termination of interaction.[31]

The centrality of an identity is a question of how many situations it can be dominant in. What we need, then, is some classifications of identities according to how they usually operate in interaction. Banton has suggested a classification of roles, in terms of their currency in interaction, which is useful to our purpose here.[32] In a review of Banton's work, Stone has suggested that identity, not role, was the concept needed, as it is identities, not roles, that persist across situations. Bearing identity in mind, then, let us quote from Stone:[33]

... Banton asks us to distinguish at least three different kinds of role, classified, one might say, in terms of their "stickiness"—the number of situations with reference to which their performance is expected. *Basic roles*, like sex, are usually ascribed and seldom "shaken off." *General roles*, like priest, are not ascribed, but nevertheless, extend through a variety of situations. *Independent roles*, like golfer, are relatively easy to take up or put down.

We may follow Stone's suggestion and change these concepts to basic, general, and independent identities. Now, as Banton realizes, these distinctions are not hard and fast; but they are at least modal, and they are based on the way identities function in interaction. Basic identities, like sex and age, function most often to help set the ground rules for interaction in terms of language and demeanor. "Basic," then, is an apt description. They are neither central nor secondary to an interaction, rather they are woven throughout it generally without much ado. General and independent identities are more difficult to distinguish. The identity, golfer, certainly is easier to take up and put down than the identity, priest, but it does extend through a variety of situations. One can be a

golfer not only on the course, but in the clubhouse, at business luncheons, at cocktail parties, in sporting goods shops, etc. The difference between golfer and priest, however, is the insistence of the priestly identity. Others expect this identity to inform the whole man—he wears a uniform—and so it takes on the quality of a basic identity, i.e., it determines the language and demeanor trans-situationally. It is not a basic identity, however, because it tends to be central to interaction; it is the identity around which the interaction turns. Still, the distinction between general and independent identities is basically sound, and we can see a connection with our concept of identity sequence. Insistent identity sequences, like fiance-to-husband-to-father, are usually general identities. More casual identity sequences, like nature-lover-to-conservationist-to-birdwatcher, are usually independent identities. Changes in independent identities cause little disruption and are alternations. Changes in general identities can cause much more disruption (one thinks of divorce or of leaving the priesthood) but these also are usually alternations.[34] Changes in basic identities are, of course, seldom made.[35]

Thus far, we have distinguished differences in how identities are linked and differences in how identities pervade interaction, and we have noted that adoptions of the kinds of identities we have been speaking of are usually alternations. More careful delineation of these issues awaits future work and research. But where, finally, do conversions come in?

CONVERSION AND UBIQUITY

Conversion means a change in informing aspect. When a person converts, his new identity has, from his new perspective, fantastic generality.

Converts, as is well known, make their new identity central to almost all interactions. Actually, a conversion may not be merely a *change* in informing aspect but a *discovery* of one. This is the lure of a total universe of discourse. In a life of multiple alternations demanding constant autobiographical revision, most of us, as Berger notes, "do not set out deliberately to paint a grand portrait of ourselves."[36] Yet this is precisely what converts do. Total universes of discourse offer nothing less than the possibility of organizing and explaining an entire life on a single principle. Conversion, then, involves the ubiquitous utilization of an identity.[37]

Now, the adoption of even independent identities often looks something like conversion. We all know zealous golfers, fishermen, or whatever. Every alternation has the incipience of conversion,[38] which is to say that identities can be insisted upon in situations where they are irrelevant. But independent identities lack the total universe of discourse which would make them ubiquitous. This is why they are independent. They don't threaten to spill into, and flood out every interaction. And this is what our middle class society prefers. We don't like identity without moderation. We don't like identities to be too general. Outside of ethnic communities, one sees no widow's weeds.

Ours, then, is an age of alternation, but not an age of conversion. Although we complain about the lack of focus and direction in our lives (a lack of informing aspect), we are very suspect of converts, who are people with just such focus and direction. While work (in the face of a consumption society) continues to be our most important focus, we insist that the job be left at the office. We insist that the work identity not be too general. The few people we allow informing aspects and ubiquitous identities to are those closely circumscribed by structure (like priests) or by exclusion (like artists). And we are upset when they are too rabid,[39] like Oral Roberts, or when they aren't devout enough, like the Dutch Catholic hierarchy. The clergy seem to be our official "true believers," and we want no others.[40] We look askance at the many who flock to Oral Roberts, who listen religiously to right wing radio programs, who follow the gospel of Timothy Leary. And we simply do not believe Muhammad Ali. But our dislike for converts does not mean that we don't need them. As Kai Erickson has shown, to know "what one is," one needs examples of "what one isn't" handy for comparison.[41]

NOTES

1. Peter L. Berger, *Invitation to Sociology* (Garden City, N. Y.: Anchor Doubleday, 1963), p. 61.

2. Anselm Strauss, *Mirrors and Masks* (Glencoe, Ill.: The Free Press, 1959), p. 147.

3. "Universe of discourse" is used in Mead's sense of "a system of common or social meanings." It "is constituted by a group of individuals carrying on and participating in a common social process of experience." See George Herbert Mead, *Mind, Self and Society* (Chicago, Ill.: University of Chicago Press, 1934), pp. 89-90.

Peter Berger uses the term "meaning system" to denote the same idea. (See Berger, *op. cit.*) We shall use "universe of discourse" for two reasons: first, the word "system" implies integration and universes of discourse contain inconsistencies; second, the term "universe of discourse" emphasizes that meanings are established and exist in symbolic interaction.

4. Nelson Foote, "Identification as the Basis for a Theory of Motivation," *American Sociological Review*, XVL (1951), p. 18. . . .

5. Berger, *op. cit.*, p. 48.

6. *Ibid.*, p. 49.

7. *Ibid.*, pp. 49-50.

8. *Ibid.*, p. 51. The writer prefers the term "total (i.e., closed and all explaining) universes of discourse" to Berger's "fully elaborated meaning systems." Also see footnote 3 above.

9. *Ibid.*, pp. 51-52.

10. Kenneth Burke, *Permanence and Change* (rev. ed.; Los Altos, Cal.: Hermes Publications, 1954), p. 77.

11. Strauss, *op. cit.*, p. 123.

12. Gregory P. Stone, "Appearance and the Self" in Arnold Rose (ed.), *Human Behavior and Social Processes* (Boston: Houghton Mifflin Co., 1962), p. 93. . . . We might add that even in the best available study of identity, the author, for some mysterious reason, refuses to define the central concept. See Strauss, *op. cit.*, p. 13.

13. On this point see Foote, *op. cit.*, p. 18. Also Strauss, *op. cit.*, p. 43; Erving Goffman, *The Presentation of Self in Everyday Life* (Garden City, N. Y.: Doubleday Anchor, 1959), p. 13; and the plays of Luigi Pirandello, especially *Enrico IV* and *Six Characters in Search of an Author*.

14. Identities vary in relevance. Practically anyone, six years old or older, could validate the identity "president of the United States." But a six year old could not validate the identity, "stock broker," as the child has no notion of what a stock broker is, and, more importantly, because the identity, "stock broker," cannot be a meaningful part of the interaction between the man and the child.

15. Although identities usually play an important part in defining situations, situations often indicate identities, or at least severely limit the range of identities, that can be utilized. When one takes the rostrum before an assembly of dutifully registered students, one has to be a professor.

16. Of course, the establishing of identities does not always follow the sequence we have indicated. Sometimes a person will be placed before, or differently, than he announces. He may then acknowledge the placement, or he may deny or ignore it and announce another identity. Such placement before or without announcement sometimes results in identity forcing, i.e., a person is forced to take on an identity which is strange to him or which he would rather avoid. Such identity forcing is much utilized by evangelists of all kinds, from students of Stephen Potter to emulators of Elmer Gantry.

17. Glick reports a small sect of Hebrew Christians who had organized their own Hebrew Christian Church and who defined themselves as separate and different from gentile Christians. There was no similar phenomenon where the writer conducted his study. See Ira O. Glick, "The Hebrew Christians: A Marginal Religious Group," in Marshall Sklare (ed.), *The Jews* (Glencoe, Ill.: The Free Press, 1958), pp. 415-431.

18. Gentile fundamental Christians, it should be noted, are very sensitive to a "holier than thou" attitude in the Hebrew Christian's much-voiced claim that the first Christians were Jews. They often complain about it.

19. In personal conversation Gladys Stone reports a similar finding among Japanese-Americans. They are Buddhist and Christian concurrently, but don't think of either identity as definitive of self.

20. William James, *The Varieties of Religious Experiences* (New York: Modern Library, 1929), p. 193. Since James talks about ideas "previously peripheral," we should note that some changes which are called conversions in everyday interaction are not conversions in our sense. Many religious "conversions" do not meet our criterion of a change in universe of discourse. While individuals who "get religion," or "get filled with the Spirit," may experience a period of intense emotional upset and indecision, they are not switching to a new authority or universe of discourse when that "religion" or "Spirit" belongs to their established universe of discourse. Such adoption of the 'true believer" identity, whether it is for the first time in an individual's life or is a "regeneration" after a period of "backsliding," is not a conversion in our terminology. On this very point see Kurt and Gladys Engel Lang, *Collective Dynamics* (New York: Thomas Y. Crowell Co., 1961), pp. 154-155.

21. Burke, *op. cit.*, p. 77.

22. On the point that conversion involves a change in allegiance, see Lang and Lang, *op. cit.*, p. 157, and Strauss, *op. cit.*, p. 123.

23. By "pervasive identity" we mean an identity which is made central to many, if not most, interactions.

24. Burke, *op. cit.*, pp. 69-163, especially pp. 69-70 and p. 154.

25. The concept of negative identity is found in Erik H. Erickson's "The Problem of Ego Identity," *Journal of the American Psychoanalytic Association*, IV, No. 1 (1956), pp. 58-121. Essentially the same idea is expressed in the concept of "anti-model" as found in Roy G. Francis, "The

Anti-Model as a Theoretical Concept," *The Sociological Quarterly*, IV (Fall, 1963), pp. 197-205.

26. We are assuming that the person is already a conservationist, or that the person is not a bar "regular." We say *most* of the person's others notice little change because the breaking of even very casual relationships can stir comment from those involved. A friend reports that ending an eighteen-month absence from a bar he had formerly frequented brought him warm welcomes from old associates and the feeling that he was "home." He adds that his return gives these associates the feeling that things are "right," a conviction which they apparently lacked because of his absence.

27. Accuracy is sacrificed here for a simple definition. The actor does not always consider what is happening to him. Especially where new identities grow out of old ones (i.e., husband to father), the person may well find himself in a new identity before he knows it, and then may grieve for his former situation and identity.

28. For a delightful fictional account of a career from intellectual-to-communist-to-monk see Nigel Dennis, *Cards of Identity* (New York: Meridian Books, 1960), pp. 255-285. For an equally excellent explication of psychoanalysis as a conversion process see Burke, *op. cit.*, pp. 125-129.

29. I am indebted to Gregory P. Stone for the concept "identity sequence." Stone also makes some useful distinctions between what he calls "identity sets," categorizing relationships between identities as *formal*, *modal*, and *contingent*. Formal sets include identities which are formally or legally linked—the president of the United States must be thirty-five years old and must be an American citizen. Modal sets are not formally or legally linked, but if a person has one identity in such a set there is a high probability that he will have others—the president is most probably a man. In contingent sets, given one identity, it is neither probable nor required that a person have the other identities involved; but one must be cognizant of them to understand the person's behavior—John F. Kennedy was a Catholic, Muhammad Ali is a Muslim. The terms, "identity set" and "identity sequence" will remind the reader of Merton's terms, "status-set" and "status-sequence." Stone prefers his own terms to Merton's because, while every status is an identity, every identity is not a status (e.g., most nicknames).

We may note that Merton also distinguished "role-sets." What this term indicates, in Merton's own terms, is that a person has many different roles to play within a given status. His example is the medical student, who is a student to his teachers, but something else to fellow students, nurses, medical technicians, etc. Actually, the student is a student in all these situations. It is the behavior and meaning of the identity "medical student" which varies situationally. The identity mobilizes different situationally specified role behavior in different situations. As mentioned earlier in this paper the term "role" rests on the conceptualization of all these possible behaviors. Perhaps "role-set" might be a useful term to adopt since the word "set" reminds one of the situationally specific character of behavior in a way that the word "role" does not. See Robert K. Merton, *Social Theory and Social Structure* (Glencoe, Ill.: The Free Press, 1957), pp. 368-371.

30. On "betrayal funnels" see Erving Goffman, *Asylums* (Garden City, N. Y.; Doubleday Anchor, 1961), p. 140.

31. Stone has discussed how value and mood are differentially relevant to structural and interpersonal interaction respectively. We can see a similar relationship in the case of identities. A secretary is expected to be a worker first and a woman second. But if, when under fire, she bursts into tears, she is making her womanhood foremost in the interaction. If her boss buys this, he is reduced to being a "man helping a woman in distress" and will sheepishly offer her a tissue. See Stone, *op. cit.*, pp. 96-100.

32. Michael Banton, *Roles: An Introduction to the Study of Social Relations*, (New York: Basic Books, 1965).

33. Gregory P. Stone, Review of *Roles: An Introduction to the Study of Social Relations*, by Michael Banton, *American Sociological Review*, XXXI (December, 1966), p. 899.

34. We say changes in general identities are "usually" alternations because such changes can be conversions. Of course, identity alone does not explain conversion. The keystone of conversion, as we have noted, is a change in "informing aspect." Sometimes (as with monks, nuns, and Black Muslims) converts take a new name to lead their new life with. Just as often, however, converts retain their old identity (as the Hebrew Christian retains the identity "Jew") but build new roles around it. Any transformation, of course, involves continuity, as the paradox of permanence and change is the key to personal life.

35. Stone, in his review of Banton,

points out that modern society has a whole technology (e.g., cosmetics) for changing age. But there are obvious limits to this technology. Besides, one always knows what his age really is, and others are always trying to find out. Where basic identities are really changed, as in sex change operations, society and social psychology are faced with interesting, but perplexing, problems. For a most informative report on the social psychological issues attending a sex change see Harold Garfinkel, *Studies in Ethnomethodology* (Englewood Cliffs, N. J.: Prentice-Hall, 1967), pp. 116-187.

36. Berger, *op. cit.*, p. 61.

37. This ubiquity, of course, lies in the total universe of discourse in whose terms the identity is defined. It is the total universe of discourse which enables the convert to define almost every situation in his own terms, make every event part of one grand portrait of life. The identities involved in conversions are usually *general* in Banton's terms. They are sometimes *basic* and this raises some very special problems, as changes are called for in what are unquestioned and supposedly unchangeable grounds of interaction. Garfinkel has dealt with this issue insightfully (see footnote 35). The aforementioned Hebrew Christians had, in these terms, taken the general identity "Jew" and transformed it by becoming "completed Jews" who accepted the promised Messiah of Israel. Thus they entered an evangelical (total) universe of discourse which enabled them to utilize ubiquitously their now transformed Jewishness. Being Jewish is a problem in this society. One has to come to terms with it as others can never leave it alone. Some Jews will claim that being Jewish makes no difference one way or the other and some gentiles will agree. But this claim is belied by the frequency of the question, "By the way, are you Jewish?" The Hebrew Christians have come to terms in the most logical way possible in this Christian society. The bother for them is that only other fundamental Christians appreciate their position.

38. I am indebted to Gregory Stone for this insightful observation. We should note here that while every alternation has the incipience of conversion, the reverse is not true. Conversions cannot be played as alternations in interaction. An example will serve well. One of the writer's informants proved to be a case of what might be called "incomplete conversion." Living far from home with a gentile husband, this subject went along with her husband's suggestion that she become a Christian for the sake of their children. She met a Hebrew Christian woman and attended some social meetings at a nearby mission. In less than a year she joined her husband's church and was baptized. Her story is that simple, and because of the simplicity she was caught in the tensions of trying to maintain conflicting identities. Having embraced Christianity without any "soul-searching" she did not feel certain that she was a Christian, or that she wanted to be one. She feels she may have made a mistake. She knows the line, "The Hebrew Christian is the true complete Jew who has accepted the promised Messiah of Israel," but it means nothing to her. Her family berates her displays of Jewishness and so the only identity she really knows goes unvalidated. One of her final statements to the writer was a display of her Jewishness through an explanation of her predicament in terms of fate or chance, which stands in contradistinction to the fundamental Christian belief in God's direction of His peoples' lives. She said, with a sad smile, "I don't know. Nothing seems to be right for me. I guess I haven't got the mahzel, that's luck in Jewish." This is the outcome of making a change with little thought as if it were an alternation, and finding that the change is socially defined as a drastic one and thus demands a conversion to make it workable.

39. We must note the word "rabid." Anyone who is greatly enthused about something, be it God, birds, or baseball, we label a mad dog.

40. Perhaps symptomatically for an age of alternation, the Catholic clergy seems to be defecting in greater numbers of late, or at least such defections are getting better press.

41. Kai T. Erickson, *Wayward Puritans* (New York: John Wiley and Sons, 1966).

III. THE NATURE OF SOCIAL ROLES

"Role" is undoubtedly the most belabored term in the language of social psychology. As early as 1951, Neiman and Hughes[1] commented upon the myriad definitions of the term, and definitions have proliferated since that time. "Role" is, in fact, one of the few concepts that seems to have captured the imagination of social psychologists in both psychology and sociology. To psychologists, the concept encompasses the social component in those types of behavior considered essentially psychological. To sociologists, on the other hand, "role" hints at the psychological aspect of essentially sociological matters. In this sense, the concept has provided theoretical closure for those schemes in both psychology and sociology that attempt to provide an "eclectic" understanding of human behavior by labeling those phenomena for which neither a purely psychological nor sociological explanation can account. For this reason, the term "role" has served, historically, as a link between psychology and sociology.

At the same time, there has been little consensus on the part of social psychologists as to what the term specifically means. Although there appears to be wide agreement that "role" refers to an organization, pattern, or structure of some sort, it is not clear what the content of this configuration is. In some instances "role" is used to refer to an organization of rights and privileges associated with a position in society. In other instances "role" designates a consistent pattern of behavior or a structure of attitudes and expectations.

1. Neiman, L. J. and Hughes, J. W., "The Problem of the Concept of Role—A Resurvey of the Literature," *Social Forces* 30 (1951) pp. 141-49.

In the face of this lack of agreement, and perhaps because of it, social psychologists have employed the term in discussing nearly every facet of social life. Indeed, if one takes seriously the idea of sexual roles in marriage, it can be said that the human organism encounters a jungle of roles from the moment of conception to some time after death. According to social psychologists, the shadows cast by roles are visible throughout the life cycle—one's parents, one's friends, one's spouse, one's children, one's lover, one's failure, one's occupation, and one's own selves are but a few of the roles with which a person is said to deal during a lifetime. Add to this the burden of having roles "ascribed" to oneself, "achieving" roles, "taking" roles, "playing" roles and, in cases of misfortune, experiencing "role conflict" and "role stress," and we have a formidable array of role-related activities for each individual.

One of the consequences of so wide a use of the term "role" in social psychological analysis has been that many accounts of social life have emphasized what is typical, consistent, constant, and by implication, immutable, about human behavior. There has evolved a kind of "role perspective" in social psychology in which what is deemed important to study and understand about people is what they are and do in common with other people. The patterns, organizations, and structure of human life have been emphasized at the expense of the process of human interaction. To the queries of those who ask whether they are simply the roles they play, social psychologists may calmly reply, "Of course not." However, given the dominance of the role perspective, social psychologists are hard pressed to account for how individuals are different from their roles, and in fact, the answer is too often reduced to simplistic biological and psychological terms.

As will become clear in this section, the culprit is of course not the term "role" itself; it is rather the use to which the term has been put in social psychological analysis. In the dramaturgical sense of things, the "role perspective" has tended to obscure the variety and richness of human interaction. It also has led in some instances to needless reductionism and, in general, has betrayed a preoccupation with conformity. Dramaturgists agree, as Ralph Turner argues in the first selection, that a more useful view of human behavior is to see roles not as series of expectations or norms to which people conform, but rather as outcomes of human interaction. Turner observes that people act as if there were roles, so that roles are "created" (or in Turner's words, "made") in the process of interaction. To him, role-taking does not involve following a prescribed role but rather devising one's performance on the basis of a role one "makes" and attributes to others. Role-taking crucially involves preparedness, not expectation.

In the second essay, Erving Goffman extends and elaborates Turner's rather voluntaristic conception of role behavior. Here Goffman speaks of peoples' ability to separate themselves from their roles, or at least from what the roles imply about them. This "role distance" is not a denial of role, for as Turner and Goffman agree, human beings continually create roles for themselves and others in order to facilitate interaction. What "role distance" constitutes is a claim by the individual that one is not "just the role" in which one has been cast. It is a demonstration that the role is not playing the individual but that the individual is "playing with the role." It is an affirmation of personal worth.

Goffman illustrates this conception of role distance by discussing the ways in which children and adults on merry-go-rounds, psychoanalysts in their offices, and surgeons in the operating room use the very trappings of their roles to point out who they are not, or are not merely. "Role distance" becomes a sociological means of dealing with what people are, above and beyond their roles.

In his article on jazz musicians, Robert Stebbins clarifies some of Goffman's notions regarding role distance. Stebbins distinguishes between "role distance" as a conception and "role distance behavior," which is the actual performance of the individual that expresses the role distance conception. Stebbins examines the nature and types of role distance behavior among jazz musicians and clearly articulates one of the primary functions of role distance; that is, to promote "identification of" other poeple. In Stebbins' case, the boundaries between the "square" world and the world of the jazz musician were tightly drawn by the use of role distance behavior. In general, it may well be that people learn more about others by attending to their "role distance behavior" than by observing the roles they play.

In the final essay in this section, Fred Davis depicts the unique role cabdrivers create when dealing with their customers. Faced with a heterogeneous aggregate of clients, unknown to each other and over whom he has little control, the cabdriver develops a heightened preoccupation with the purely instrumental aspects of the relationship. Tipping becomes the focus of attention and consequently a high degree of ambiguity and uncertainty is an important contingency of the driver's occupation. The ways in which cabdrivers reduce the ambiguity by "making roles" for their clients and themselves parallels beautifully Turner's discussion of the process of role-taking. Davis' conclusion about the relative ineffectiveness of the cabdriver's role-making in reducing ambiguity speaks also to the general theme of dramaturgical analysis. Ambiguity, not closure, is the dominant experience in social life.

SUGGESTED READINGS

Banton, Michael. *Roles: An Introduction to the Study of Social Relations*, (New York: Basic Books, 1965).

Biddle, B. J. and Thomas, E. J. *Role Theory:* *Concepts and Research*, (New York: John Wiley and Sons, Inc., 1966).

Burns, Tom. "Friends, Enemies, and the Polite Fiction," in *American Sociological*

Review, Vol. 18, (1953) pp. 654-662.

Coser, Rose. "Role Distance, Ambivalence, and Transition Status," in *American Journal of Sociology*, Vol. 72, No. 2, (1966), pp. 173-187.

Coutu, Walter. "Role-Playing Versus Role-Taking: An Appeal for Clarification," in *American Sociological Review*, Vol. 16, (1951), pp. 180-184.

Cressey, Donald. "Role Theory, Differential Association and Compulsive Crimes," in A. Rose (ed.), *Human Behavior and Social Processes* (Boston: Houghton-Mifflin, 1962) pp. 443-462.

Stone, Gregory and Gross, Edward. "Embarrassment and the Analysis of Role Requirements," in *American Journal of Sociology*, LXX (July, 1964) pp. 1-15.

Turner, Ralph. "Role-Taking, Role Standpoint, and Reference Group Behaviour," in *American Journal of Sociology*, Vol. 61 (January, 1956), pp. 316-328.

9. ROLE-TAKING:
PROCESS VERSUS CONFORMITY

RALPH H. TURNER

Reprinted from A. Rose (ed.), *Human Behavior and Social Processes* (Boston: Houghton-Mifflin Co., 1962), pp. 20-40, with permission of the author and Houghton-Mifflin Company. Ralph Turner has written a number of books and articles dealing with social psychology, role theory and collective behavior. He is Professor of Sociology at the University of California in Los Angeles, and is a past president of the American Sociological Association.

Only a cursory glance at sociological journals is necessary to document both the great importance and the divers applications of "role theory" in current thought and research. First gaining currency as G. H. Mead's (17) "taking the role of the other," and adopted by psychologists reflecting Kurt Lewin's Gestalt approach (22), role theory was made to serve rather different purposes by three popular developments. Ralph Linton (16, pp. 113-131) employed the concept "role" to allow for variability within culture; Jacob Moreno (20) made staged "role-playing" the basis of psychodramatic therapy and research; and investigators bent on uncovering strains in organizational functioning chose "role conflict" as their orienting concept.

Simultaneously, several important criticisms have emerged. The charge has been made that the referents for the term "role" are so heterogeneous as to defy rigorous study and coherent theory formation. Some critics have minimized the importance of roles, suggesting that they are superficially adopted and abandoned without important implications for the actor's personality (14). Role theory has been repudiated as a system of rigid cultural and mechanical determinism (1, pp. 81-82). Role theory often appears to be entirely negative, to consist of elaborate generalizations about the mal-

functioning of roles in role conflict, role strain, and so on, but to lack any theory of how roles function normally. Finally, role theory is sometimes redundant, merely substituting the term "role" for "social norm" or "culture" without introducing any novel dynamic principle.

All of these criticisms have some merit, but we believe that their validity arises from the dominance of the Linton concept of role and the employment of an oversimplified model of role functioning in many current organizational studies. Role-conflict theory should be firmly grounded in a sophisticated conception of normal role-playing and role-taking as processes. Such a conception is found or implied in the earlier Meadian theory. This essay will call attention to some pertinent aspects of the theory in order to show that there is more to it than simply an extension of normative or cultural deterministic theory and that the concept of role does add novel elements to the conception of social interaction.

BASIC ELEMENTS IN ROLE-TAKING

THE ROLE-MAKING PROCESS

An initial distinction must be made between taking the existence of distinct and identifiable roles as the starting point in role theory, and postulating a tendency to create and modify conceptions of self- and other-roles as the orienting process in interactive behavior. The latter approach has less interest in determining the exact roles in a group and the specific content of each role than in observing the basic tendency for actors to behave *as if* there were roles. Role in the latter sense is a sort of ideal conception which constrains people to render any action situation into more or less explicit collections of interacting roles. But the relation of the actor to the roles which he comfortably assumes may be like that of the naive debater to the set of assumptions from which he confidently assumes that his explicit arguments are deducible, but which he can neither specify nor defend fully when challenged. Roles "exist" in varying degrees of concreteness and consistency, while the individual confidently frames his behavior as if they had unequivocal existence and clarity. The result is that in attempting from time to time to make aspects of the roles explicit he is creating and modifying roles as well as merely bringing them to light; the process is not only role-taking but *role-making*.

Military and bureaucratic behavior had best be viewed not as the ideal-typical case for role theory, but as a distorted instance of the broader class of role-taking phenomena. The formal regulation system restricts the free operation of the role-making process, limiting its repertoire and making role boundaries rigid. As the context approaches one in which behavior is completely prescribed and all misperformance is institutionally punished, the process of role-taking-role-making becomes increasingly an inconsequential part of the interaction that occurs.

Free from formal regulation, the self- and other-role perspective in any situation may occasionally shift. Roles resemble poles on axes, each axis constituting a dimension in space. In factor analysis, an infinite number of placements of the axes will meet equally well the logical requirements of the data. Similarly, from the point of view of the role-making process an actor has an infinite number of definitions of the boundaries between roles which will serve equally well the logical requirements of role-taking. But the placement of any one of these boundaries, whether for a fleeting instant or for a longer period, limits or determines the identification of other roles. It is this tendency to shape the phenomenal world into roles which is the key to role-taking as a core process in interaction.

"SELF-ROLES" AND "OTHER-ROLES"

Within the ideal framework which guides the role-taking process, every role is a way of relating to other-roles in a situation. A role cannot exist without one or more relevant other-roles toward which it is oriented. The role of "father" makes no sense without the role of child; it can be defined as a pattern of behavior only in relation to the pattern of behavior of a child. The role of the compromiser can exist only to the extent that others in a group are playing the role of antagonists. The role of hero is distinguished from the role of the foolhardy only by the role of the actor's real or imaginary audience.

This principle of role reciprocity provides a generalized explanation for changed behavior. A change in one's own role reflects a changed assessment or perception of the role of relevant others. Interaction is always a *tentative* process, a process of continuously testing the conception one has of the role of the other. The response of the other serves to reinforce or to challenge this conception. The product of the testing process is the stabilization or the modification of one's own role.

The idea of role-taking shifts emphasis away from the simple process of enacting a prescribed role to devising a performance on the basis of an imputed other-role. The actor is not the occupant of a position for which there is a neat set of rules—a culture or set of norms—but a person who must act in the perspective supplied in part by his relationship to others whose actions reflect roles that he must identify. Since the role of alter can only be inferred rather than directly known by ego, testing inferences about the role of alter is a continuing element in interaction. Hence the tentative character of the individual's own role definition and performance is never wholly suspended.

Linton's famous statement of status and role probably established the conception of role as a cultural given in contrast to Mead's treatment of role chiefly as the perspective or vantage point of the relevant other. Linton moved the emphasis from taking the role of the other to enacting the role prescribed for the self. In so doing, he disregarded the peculiar conception of interaction which revolves about the improvising character of the "I," the more rigid social categorization of the "me" than of the "I," and the continuing dialectic between "I" and "me" (17).

ROLES AS MEANINGFUL GROUPINGS OF BEHAVIOR

Role-taking and role-making always constitute the grouping of behavior into units. The isolated action becomes a datum for role analysis only when it is interpreted as the manifestation of a configuration. The individual acts as if he were expressing some role

through his behavior and may assign a higher degree of reality to the assumed role than to his specific actions. The role becomes the point of reference for placing interpretations on specific actions, for anticipating that one line of action will follow upon another, and for making evaluations of individual actions. For example, the lie which is an expression of the role of friend is an altogether different thing from the same lie taken as a manifestation of the role of confidence man. Different actions may be viewed as the same or equivalent; identical actions may be viewed as quite different: placement of the actions in a role context determines such judgments.

The grouping aspect of role-taking is perhaps most clearly indicated in the judgments people make of the *consistency* of one another's behavior. Such judgments often violate logical criteria for consistency. But the folk basis for these judgments is the subsumability of a person's behavior under a single role. The parent who on one occasion treats his child with gentleness and on another spanks him is unlikely to be adjudged inconsistent because both types of behavior, under appropriate circumstances, are supposed to be reasonable manifestations of the same parental role. A more devastating extension of the judgment of inconsistency is that the behavior doesn't make sense, that it is unintelligible. Behavior is said to make sense when a series of actions is interpretable as indicating that the actor has in mind some role which guides his behavior.

The socially structured world of experience has many dimensions of classification. The role dimension refers to types of actors. It is the nature of the role that it is capable of being enacted by different actors, but remains recognizable in spite of individual idiosyncrasies. While people tend to be given stable classification according to the major roles they play, the specific referent for the term "role" is a type of actor rather than a type of person. Such a distinction allows for the contingency that one individual may adopt even conflicting roles on occasion, and that otherwise quite different people may play the same role.

There is a kind of structure represented in this conception of role —and implied, we believe, in the work of G. H. Mead—that falls between the rigidity of role as a set of prescriptions inherent in a position and Kingsley Davis' view of role as the actual behavior of the occupant of a status (8, pp. 89-91). Role refers to a pattern which can be regarded as the consistent behavior of a single type of actor. The behavior of the occupant of a given status is a unique constellation, its components tied together only by their emanation from a single individual who is oriented to a single status during the period of his action. But the folk judgment of consistency requires that some more general principle be invoked. The principle must either be one which is already recognized in the group or one which is capable of representation to a relevant group. The unique behavior of the occupant of a given position may or may not constitute a role, either to him or to relevant others, depending upon whether a principle is employed in light of which the behavior seems consistent.

A point of view in important respects similar to this one but also in important respects dissimilar is represented in Merton's statement on role-sets (18). The occupant of an organizational position is said to have a distinct role for each type of relevant other with whom he interacts in that position. The cluster of roles which he assumes by virtue of occupying the position is his "role-set." The key importance of self-other interaction in role theory is thus acknowledged. But limitation of the concept "role" to a single reciprocity provides less scope for what we regard as the other important feature of the role-taking process, namely, the process of discovering and creating "consistent" wholes out of behavior. The problem of the school teacher-mother which arises out of the need to compromise two roles because of simultaneous involvement in both is in important respects different from that of the school teacher who must devise and enact her role in simultaneous relationship to students, parents, and principal. In the latter instance there is no question of abandoning one relationship, and the essence of the role is devising a pattern which will cope effectively with the different types of relevant others while at the same time meeting some recognizable criteria of consistency. Except in special instances, these are not experienced as separate roles by their enactors or those to whom they are relevant other-roles.

Role-taking as a process of devising and discovering consistent patterns of action which can be identified with types of actors suggests a theorem regarding role-conflict situations which should be worthy of empirical test. Whenever the social structure is such that many individuals characteristically act from the perspective of two given roles simultaneously, there tends to emerge a single role which encompasses the action. The single role may result from a merger process, each role absorbing the other, or from the development and recognition of a third role which is specifically the pattern viewed as consistent when both roles might be applicable. The parent and spouse roles illustrate the former tendency. In popular usage the sharp distinctions are not ordinarily made between parent and spouse behavior that sociologists invoke in the name of logical, as distinct from folk, consistency. The politician role exemplifies the second tendency, providing a distinct perspective from which the individual may act who otherwise would be acting simultaneously as a party functionary and as a government official. What would constitute a role conflict from the latter point of view is susceptible of treatment as a consistent pattern from the point of view of the politician role.

THE CHARACTER OF ROLES AS UNITS

Two lines of further clarification are required in order to give substance to the view enunciated here. First, the character of the reciprocities among roles must be specified in greater detail. How do self and other interact? How does the role of alter affect that of ego? Second, the character of the grouping principle that creates boundaries between roles requires further exploration. There is an apparent paradox in saying on the one hand that a fixed set of roles does not exist and on the other hand that people make judgments of consistency and inconsistency on the basis of their success in bringing a succession of actions into the sphere of a single role. Since the second area of elaboration concerns the relation of role-taking as process to the kind of investigation which centers on social structure rather than the individual actor, we shall examine it first.

ROLES IN ORGANIZATION AND CULTURE

The normal role-taking process, as we have suggested, is a tentative process in which roles are identified and given content on shifting axes as interaction proceeds. Both the identification of the roles and their content undergo cumulative revision, becoming relatively fixed for a period of time only as they provide a stable framework for interaction. The usual procedures of formal organization lessen the tentative character of interaction, making each functionary's performance less dependent upon his conception of the roles of relevant others, and minimizing the Gestalt-making process by substituting role prescriptions. The effort is normally only partially successful, as indicated by the abundant literature on informal organization within formal structures.

Studies of informal groups suggest that role differentiation develops around the axes of group functioning, such as the axes of securing agreement, acceptance of responsibility, guarding of group norms, etc. (3). Interaction in such a context permits role-taking in its "purest" form to occur. Interaction involving organizational or status roles is more complex, producing a compromise between the role-taking process and the simple conformity behavior demanded by organizational prescriptions.

The manner in which formal designations "cramp" role-taking can perhaps best be seen in relation to the reciprocity of self-other roles. In actual interaction the identification of a role is not merely a function of the behavior of the actor but of the manifested other-role. The role of leader, for example, incorporates a complex of actions which are supposed to be reflections of certain competencies and sentiments. But if the relevant others fail to reciprocate, or if they are already reciprocating to another person in the role of leader, the identical behavior serves to label the actor as "dissenter" and "trouble-maker" rather than "leader." Such labeling by the relevant others eventually forces redefinition on the would-be leader, who must then either continue in the dissenter role or change his behavior. Organizational definitions, however, seek to attach the informal leader-follower roles to specific positions whose occupants can be formally named. Part of the formalization procedure is the specification of ritual forms of behavior by which each participant acknowledges the nature of the reciprocity. The formalization is supposed to keep the officially designated followers adhering to the follower role, even when the leader fails to enact his leader role, and similarly to prohibit erosion of the leader role in case of non-reciprocation.

The effectiveness of such formalization efforts in limiting the normal range of role-taking adjustments is quite varied. The parent may maintain the exemplar role in the face of his child's non-reciprocation, or he may abandon it to enact a role on the axis of his child's pattern of behavior. The corporation official may continue to act with dignity as if his orders were being obeyed, or he may abandon responsibility and adopt a comprehensive pattern attuned to impotency. But the formal role itself, considered apart from the effective incorporation of the informal role, is merely a skeleton consisting of rules which are intended to invoke the appropriate informal roles. The formalized roles are to the full roles as detonators to explosives—merely devices to set them in motion.

THE FRAMEWORK OF ROLE DIFFERENTIATION

The unity of a role cannot consist simply in the bracketing of a set of specific behaviors, since the same behavior can be indicative of different roles under different circumstances. The unifying element is to be found in some assignment of purpose or sentiment to the actor. Various actions by an individual are classified as intentional and unintentional on the basis of a role designation. The administrator, for example, must make decisions which necessarily help some and hurt others. But the hurt done to some is defined as inadvertent insofar as the role is viewed as that of the impartial or responsible administrator. The individual who plays a nurturant, comfort-giving role necessarily establishes a relationship in which he is superordinated to the comfort-receiver, but the superordination is inadvertent. Since the role definition itself directs perception selectively, the superordination or the administrative harm may not be noticed by the actor or by relevant others. Role-taking involves selective perception of the actions of another and a great deal of selective emphasis, organized about some purpose or sentiment attributed to the other.

Not all combinations of behavior are susceptible of being classed into a single role. Since, as we indicated at the start, the role-taker acts as if roles were real and objective entities, there must be criteria by which the actor assures himself that what he has in mind is truly a role. Such verification derives from two sources, the "internal" validation of the interaction itself, and the external validation supplied by what G. H. Mead called "the generalized other."

Internal validation lies in the successful anticipation of the behavior of relevant others within the range necessary for the enactment of one's own role. This in turn depends upon the existence of roles which provide a pattern for interacting with an individual exhibiting the peculiar selection of behavior whose coherency as a role is subject to verification. The internal criterion means that a given constellation of behavior is judged to constitute a role on the basis of its relation to other roles.

The internal criterion can easily suggest that we have let a system of fixed roles in through the back door unless two important observations are made. First, there is not just one role which enables an individual to interact in what is adjudged a consistent way with any given other-role. Roles are often comprehensive alternative ways of dealing with a given other-role. The range of possibilities is further enhanced by the fact that normal interaction is to a large extent limited in intimacy, intensity, and duration, so that only a small segment of each role is activated. We propose as a reasonable hypothesis that the narrower the segment of a role activated the wider the range of other-roles with which it may deal and which may deal with it.

Second, in light of our statement that role-making is a Gestalt-making process, what cannot be conceived as constituting a role when related to a single relevant other-role may be so conceived when viewed as interacting with two or more different other-roles. The total role of the school superintendent in the study by Gross and associates (12) would not produce the requisite predictability in the responding teacher role, and therefore would have to be treated as incoherent behavior when viewed from its relation to the teacher role alone. But when seen as a way of maximizing predictability simultaneously in the relevant other-roles of school board member, teacher, and parent, the behavior becomes increasingly susceptible of in-

terpretation as the manifestation of a single role. What is inconsistent behavior viewed in relation to only a single type of relevant other is perfectly coherent in relation to a system of others.

The internal criterion insures that there is constant modification of the content of specific roles, occasional rejection of the identification of a role, and sometimes the "discovery" or creation of a new role. Such modification takes place in the continued interplay between the somewhat vague and always incomplete ideal conceptions of roles and the experience of their overt enactment by self and other. Since each interaction is in some respects unique, each interaction incorporates some improvisation on the theme supplied by self-role and other-role. The very act of expressing a role in a novel item of role behavior enables the actor to see the role in a slightly different light. Similarly, the uniqueness in alter's behavior and the unique situation in which alter's behavior must be anticipated or interpreted serve to cast his role slightly differently. Internal testing includes experiencing in varying degrees the sentiments or purposes which provide the role's coherence. Differing degrees of involvement in the role at the time of its enactment, and differing relations vis-à-vis alter, allow the role to be understood in different ways, and each such experience leaves its residual effect upon the self- and other-role conceptions of the participants.

What we have called the *external validation* of a role is based upon ascertaining whether the behavior is judged to constitute a role by others whose judgments are felt to have some claim to correctness or legitimacy. The simplest form of such a criterion is discovery of a name in common use for the role. If the pattern of behavior can be readily assigned a name, it acquires *ipso facto* the exteriority and constraint of Durkheim's "collective representations" (9). Naming does not assure that there will be agreement on the content of the role; it merely insures that people will do their disagreeing as if there were something real about which to disagree.

Major norms and values serve as criteria of role coherency since they are ordinarily applied with the implicit assumption that no person can really both support and disparage any major norm or value. There is probably considerable popular agreement on the existence and character of a role of murderer, which incorporates a much more comprehensive pattern of behavior than just the act of killing or actions which are functionally connected with murder. The role is a more or less imaginary constellation of actions and sentiments and goals which describe an actor whose relation to the major sacred norms of society is consistent in the simplest way—by being comprehensively negative. Because most individuals have no opportunity to test their conception of the role of murderer by internal criteria, such roles remain relatively impervious to the lack of empirical confirmation, and can serve as sufficient other-roles for the highly segmented self-roles which the ordinary citizen has an opportunity to enact in relation to the murderer.

Role validation is also anchored in the membership of recognized groups and the occupancy of formalized positions. People easily form conceptions of the American Legionnaire, the Jew, the Oriental, etc., incorporating the sentiment and goals distinctively ascribed to members of the group. The greater tangibility of formal statuses and organizational positions as compared with informal roles means

further that there is a tendency to merge the latter with the former. Informal roles are often named by borrowing from formal statuses with which they are associated, as in references to a "fatherly" role or a "judicious" role.

Finally, external verification includes a sense of what goes together and what does not, based upon experience in seeing given sets of attitudes, goals, and specific actions carried out by the same individuals. The sense derives on the one hand from what has actually been rendered customary by the prevailing social structure and on the other from the example of key individuals whom the individual takes as role models. Some of the divisions of task and sentiment imposed by the culture follow lines which increase efficiency in society, but others arise from accidental circumstances or perpetuate divisions which no longer have functional implications. Acceptance of the role behavior of an individual model as a standard may lead to the inclusion of much otherwise extraneous behavior within a role and to the judgment that kinds of actions which, by other criteria are contradictory, are actually not inconsistent.

Each of the several criteria, both internal and external, must operate in relation to the others. Under conditions of perfect harmony, the various criteria converge to identify the same units as roles and to identify their content similarly. But under the normal loose operation of society various criteria are partially consistent and partially at odds. Since working human motivations do not divide as neatly as society's major norms would have them, there is often a penumbra on the boundaries of those roles which are oriented to the mores when both the external normative and the internal interactive criteria are brought into play. The formal rules which are invoked when roles are named from organizational positions and statuses do not necessarily fit entirely the sentiment which is experienced when the role is played or taken in actual interaction. These discrepancies which arise from the operation of multiple criteria for role units insure that the framework of roles will operate as a hazily conceived ideal framework for behavior rather than as an unequivocal set of formulas. In a sense, role conceptions are creative compromises, and an important phase of role theory should concern itself with how they are achieved.

THE NATURE OF ROLE INTERACTION

Two facets of the role-taking process have been stressed in this statement, namely, the process of grouping behavior into "consistent" units which correspond to generalizable types of actors, and the process of organizing behavior vis-à-vis relevant others. We have elaborated somewhat the character and bases for the Gestalt-forming aspect of role-taking. There remains for further clarification the nature of relationships between self- and other-roles.

DYNAMICS OF SELF AND OTHER

The customary use of the concept of role in sociological and related literature today depicts the dynamic relationships between roles as primarily *conformity*. There are three key terms in this popular model, namely, *conformity, expectation*, and *approval*. A component of each role is a set of expectations regarding the behavior of individuals in relevant other-roles. When ego takes the role of alter the aspect of alter's role to which he is crucially sensitive is the set of expectations with respect to his (ego's) role. Ego takes the role of alter in order to conform to alter's expectations. Lack of conformity must be explained by erroneous role-taking, or by deficiencies in empathic ability or opportunities to perceive and judge the role of the other. The confirmation that role-taking and role-playing have proceeded correctly according to the conformity principle is the registration of approval.

We suggest that the foregoing model is not in itself incorrect; it is merely of insufficient generality. It describes only one of several ways in which the role-taking and role-playing process may occur, only one of several kinds of dynamic relations which may exist between self- and other-roles. Instead, we propose that the relations between self- and other-roles are interactive in a full sense, the dynamic principles being of several sorts, depending upon the objectives of the role-players and upon the character of their relationships with one another. Furthermore, the enactment of a given role often involves the simultaneous role-taking relationship with several different other-roles, and the dynamic relationship between each self- and other-role may be of a different sort.

In some athletic events such as the game of baseball the roles are highly standardized and the allowance for improvisation is at a minimum, so that the assumption that each role incorporates clear expectations for each other-role is quite valid. But in most situations what the role-player expects from the relevant other on the basis of the latter's role is not likely to be a specific action but some behavior which will be susceptible to interpretation as directed toward the ends associated with the other-role, expressive of the sentiment which dominates the role in question, or as consistent with the values attached to the role. A group torn by internal dissension may turn to someone who it is hoped will enact the role of compromiser. In doing so they have an expectation which identifies the general purpose and sentiment which will guide his actions and some general conception of the kind of behavior which will contribute to the achievement of compromise and which will not. But they do not have any exact notion of what the specific steps will be.

The articulation of behavior between roles may be described better by the term "preparedness" than by the term "expectation." The crucial consideration is that ego's role *prepares* him for a loosely definable *range* of responses from alter on the basis of the latter's role. The potential responses of alter, then, divide into those which are readily interpretable upon the basis of the assumed self- and other-roles and those which seem not to make sense from this vantage point. A response which fell outside of the preparedness range would be one of two kinds. It might be a response which was initially perceived as irrelevant, that is, not interpretable as the expression of any role in the context of the present focus of interaction. Or it might be a response which seemed to indicate a different role from that which had been attributed to alter.

The more or less definite expectations for ego's role which are part of alter's role, the preferences, the conceptions of legitimate and illegitimate behavior, and the evaluations, all directed toward ego's role, are a part but not the whole of alter's role. Role-taking may or may not concentrate on these aspects, and when it does it has been referred to as reflexive role-taking (25). Role-taking is always incomplete, with differential sensitivity to various aspects of the other-role. Only under special circumstances is the sensitization likely to be exclusively to the reflexive aspect. Such sensitization goes along with a conformity relationship, but not necessarily with approval in the simple sense.

The most general purpose associated with sensitization to the reflexive aspects of the other-role is to validate a self-image. The object is to present the self in a fashion which will conform to the relevant other's conception of the role by which the actor seeks to be identified. The role may, however, be one of which the relevant other approves or disapproves or toward which he is neutral. The young "tough" may be unsure that he has sufficiently exemplified the desired self-image until he provokes a vigorous condemnation from the teacher. The individualist may be dissatisfied until he provokes disagreement from a conventional person.

Elsewhere the kinds of dynamic relationship between roles have been discussed under the headings of role standpoint and reflexive versus non-reflexive role-taking (25). But the most general form of self-other relationship is that in which the relationship is a means to the accomplishment of either some shared goal or separate individual goals. Under such circumstances, the role relationship will be pragmatic, the two roles (or the same role enacted by two interacting individuals) being viewed as an efficient division of labor. In role-taking the salient aspects of the other-role will be their instrumental features, and the self-role will be enacted in such a fashion as to combine effectively with the instrumental features of the other-role to accomplish the intended purpose. Conformity to alter's expectations may enter as a partial determinant in this truly interactive relation but principally because it is an adjunct to the efficient accomplishment of the objective. The conformity principle may also come to be dominant because the effects of the role interaction in the promotion of the group goal are not readily apparent, as in a standby military organization or in an educational organization where no real tests of the effectiveness of the educational process are available. But conformity remains a special instance of the more general interactive principle rather than the general principle itself.

THE NORMATIVE COMPONENT OF ROLE-TAKING

Roles are often identified as sets of norms applicable to an actor playing a recognizable part. Since norms are at least partially equatable with expectations, such a conception may convey the same simple conformity formula with which we have just dealt. However, there is an essentially normative element in the concept of role which derives from the fact that a minimum of predictability is the precondition of interaction. This interdependency has been well described by Waller and Hill (28, pp. 328-332) by reference to the "interlocking habit systems" which develop between marriage partners. To the extent to which one member patterns his behavior to fit with the past regularities of behavior in the other, the former's behavior becomes inappropriate when the latter makes unanticipated alterations in his behavior. The inappropriateness invokes indignation against the innovator and the charge that he had no right to alter his behavior. Thus, although no norm originally existed and no explicit commitment had been made, a norm has in fact developed because of the damage which one person's unpredictable behavior does to the other.

The prediction is of two sorts, prediction of the role to be played and prediction that behavior will continue to exemplify the same role once it is established in interaction. It is the latter which is most fundamental. The basic normative element in role-taking-and-playing is the requirement that the actor be consistent—that his behavior remain within the confines of a single role. So long as it remains within the role, the other will be generally prepared to cope with the behavior, whether he approves of it or not.

In institutional contexts, the additional normative element that designates a priori what role each individual must play is introduced to insure the required division of labor and to minimize the costs of exploratory role-setting behavior. But the norm of consistency is the more fundamental since it applies to role-taking in both informal and formalized settings, while the norm which assigns roles to persons applies chiefly in the latter.

The norm of consistency is mitigated in operation by an implicit presumption that actors are adhering to the norm. Indications that an actor is from an out-group, special symbols of deviant identity, or glaring evidences of "inconsistency," cause the assumption to be questioned. But in the absence of such cues, the initial presumption that each actor must be adhering to *some* role creates a strong bias in favor of finding a set of interpretations of his behavior which will allow it to be seen as pertaining to a single role. The bias may go as far as the synthesizing of a partially new role for one of the actors. Once the actor's role has been identified, either on the basis of indications of his position, placing oneself in his situation, or bits of his behavior, there is a further presumption that his subsequent behavior represents the same role. The flexibility with which most actions can be interpreted, emphasized, and de-emphasized, affords considerable scope for the role-taker to find confirmation of his preconceptions.

The normative principle of consistency, then, works both in the direction of enforcing a pattern onto behavior and in the direction of allowing a range of actions to be subsumed under a given role. The following hypotheses are suggested. The restricting impact of the consistency norm on behavior tends to be greater under conditions of dominance, whether authoritarian or instrumental, when participants are sensitized to interpret deviations from standard roles as symbolic denials of the dominance-submission relationship. The restricting effect tends to be greater when there is relatively little basis for faith in the role enactor's possession of the appropriate role sentiment. Such faith in turn arises out of prior experience with the other's role performance or out of esteem accorded the other by persons whose judgments are respected.

Many studies of role conflict proceed as if the dynamics of adjustment lie primarily in a choice of which set of expectations to honor in the face of an urgent desire to adhere to two or more incompatible sets. If the view is accepted that conformity is but one type of working adjustment to the other-role, then role conflict should be seen in the light of attempts to establish some kind of working relationship with the roles of relevant others. In its most general sense, role conflict exists when there is no immediately apparent way of simultaneously coping effectively with two different relevant other-roles, whether coping is by conformity to expectation or by some other type of response. The problem of

a man whose friend has committed a serious crime need not be primarily or exclusively how to conform to the expectations both of his friend and of the police. The problem is to cope with the roles of each, conformity to expectation being but one of the alternatives before him. The definition of modern woman's problem as primarily how to conform simultaneously to the conflicting expectations of those with traditional and egalitarian views of her role reveals the same limited conception. The problem is more fundamentally how to engage in effective interaction with men, some of whom have modern and some traditional and some mixed conceptions of the masculine role, and with women who may have the same or different conceptions of the feminine role.

SUMMARY AND IMPLICATIONS

Role theory, originally depicting a tentative and creative interaction process, has come increasingly to be employed as a refinement of conformity theory. In consequence, the theory has become relatively sterile except with respect to the consequences of role conflict and other forms of deviation from the conventional model of role behavior. Role taking, however, suggests a process whereby actors attempt to organize their interaction so that the behavior of each can be viewed as the expression of a consistent orientation which takes its meaning (or consistency) from its character as a way of coping with one or more other actors enacting similarly consistent orientations. Conformity to perceived expectations is but one special way in which an actor's role-playing may be related to the role of relevant others. From this viewpoint, role behavior in formal organizations becomes a working compromise between the formalized role prescriptions and the more flexible operation of the role-taking process. Role conflict is the attempt to devise an orientation from which the actor can cope effectively with multiple other-roles which apparently cannot be dealt with in a "consistent" fashion.

The conception of role relations as fully interactive rather than merely conforming harmonizes with current trends in sociology and anthropology to subordinate normative to functional processes in accounting for societal integration. Emphasis on the binding power of the mores and folkways or on the blind adherence to custom corresponds with a society populated by people playing roles principally as sets of expectations with which they must comply. On the other hand, a functional view emphasizes the interdependence of activities in accounting for cultural persistence and social stability. The interactive consequence of role relationships provides the social-psychological mechanism through which the functional principle of social stability operates.

References

1. Allport, Gordon. *Becoming*. New Haven: Yale University Press, 1955.
2. Bates, Frederick L. "Position, Role, and Status: A Reformulation of Concepts," *Social Forces*, Vol. 34 (May 1956), pp. 313-321.
3. Benne, Kenneth D., and Paul Sheats. "Functional Roles of Group Members," *Journal of Social Issues*, Vol. 4 (May 1948), pp. 41-49.
4. Blumer, Herbert. "Psychological Import of the Human Group," in Muzafer Sherif and M. O. Wilson (eds.), *Group Relations at the Crossroads*. New York: Harper & Brothers, 1953, pp. 185-202.
5. Brim, Orville G., Jr. "Family Structure and Sex-Role Learning by Children," *Sociometry*, Vol. 21 (March 1958), pp. 1-18.
6. Cottrell, Leonard S., Jr. "The Analysis of Situational Fields in Social Psychology," *American Sociological Review*, Vol. 7 (June 1942), pp. 370-382.
7. Coutu, Walter. *Emergent Human Nature*. New York: Alfred A. Knopf, 1949.
8. Davis, Kingsley. *Human Society*. New York: The Macmillan Company, 1948.
9. Durkheim, Émile. *Sociology and Philosophy*. London: Cohen and West, 1953.
10. Faris, Ellsworth. *The Nature of Human Nature*. New York: McGraw-Hill Book Company, Inc., 1937.
11. Faris, Robert E. L. *Social Psychology*. New York: The Ronald Press Company, 1952.
12. Gross, Neal, Ward S. Mason, and Alexander W. McEachern. *Explorations in Role Analysis*. New York: John Wiley & Sons, 1958.
13. Kirkpatrick, Clifford. "The Measurement of Ethical Consistency in Marriage," *International Journal of Ethics*, Vol. 46 (July 1936), pp. 444-460.
14. Kluckhohn, Clyde, and Henry A. Murray. "Personality Formation: The Determinants," in Clyde Kluckhohn, Henry A. Murray, and David Schneider (eds.), *Personality in Nature, Society, and Culture*. New York: Alfred A. Knopf, 1953, pp. 53-67.
15. Lindesmith, Alfred R., and Anselm L. Strauss. *Social Psychology*. New York: The Dryden Press, 1956.
16. Linton, Ralph. *The Study of Man*. New York: Appleton-Century Co., 1936.
17. Mead, George H. *Mind, Self, and Society*, ed. by Charles W. Morris. Chicago: The University of Chicago Press, 1935.
18. Merton, Robert K. "Role Set: Problems in Sociological Theory," *British Journal of Sociology*, Vol. 8 (June 1957), pp. 106-120.
19. Miyamoto, S. Frank, and Sanford M. Dornbusch. "A Test of Interactionist Hypotheses of Self-Conception," *American Journal of Sociology*, Vol. 61 (March 1956), pp. 399-403.
20. Moreno, Jacob. *Who Shall Survive?* Washington, D. C.: Nervous and Mental Disease Monograph, No. 58, 1934.
21. Neiman, Lionel J., and James W. Hughes. "The Problem of the Concept of Role: A Resurvey of the Literature,"

122 / THE NATURE OF SOCIAL ROLES

Social Forces, Vol. 30 (December 1951), pp. 141-149.

22. Newcomb, Theodore. *Social Psychology.* New York: The Dryden Press, 1950.

23. Parsons, Talcott, Robert F. Bales, and others. *Family, Socialization and Interaction Process.* Glencoe, Ill.: The Free Press, 1955.

24. Sarbin, Theodore R. "Role Theory," in Gardner Lindzey (ed.), *Handbook of Social Psychology,* Vol. I. Reading, Mass.: Addison-Wesley Publishing Company, Inc., 1954, pp. 223-258.

25. Turner, Ralph H. "Role Taking, Role Standpoint, and Reference Group Behavior," *American Journal of Sociology,* Vol. 61 (January 1956), pp. 316-328.

26. Videbeck, Richard. "Dynamic Properties of the Concept Role," *Midwest Sociologist,* Vol. 20 (May 1958), pp. 104-108.

27. Videbeck, Richard, and Alan P. Bates. "An Experimental Study of Conformity to Role Expectations," *Sociometry,* Vol. 22 (March 1959), pp. 1-11.

28. Waller, Willard, and Reuben Hill. *The Family: A Dynamic Interpretation.* New York: The Dryden Press, 1951.

10. ROLE DISTANCE

ERVING GOFFMAN

Reprinted from *Encounters* by Erving Goffman, copyright © 1961, by the Bobbs-Merrill Company, Inc., by permission of the publisher. Erving Goffman prepared the following selection as part of a series of advanced studies in sociology. It was first published in a book called *Encounters* in 1961.

A merry-go-round horse is a thing of some size, some height, and some movement; and while the track is never wet, it can be very noisy. American middle-class two-year-olds often find the prospect too much for them. They fight their parents at the last moment to avoid being strapped into a context in which it had been hoped they would prove to be little men. Sometimes they become frantic halfway through the ride, and the machine must be stopped so that they can be removed.

Here we have one of the classic possibilities of life. Participation in any circuit of face-to-face activity requires the participant to keep command of himself, both as a person capable of executing physical movements and as one capable of receiving and transmitting communications. A flustered failure to maintain either kind of role poise makes the system as a whole suffer. Every participant, therefore, has the function of maintaining his own poise, and one or more participants are likely to have the specialized function of modulating activity so as to safeguard the poise of the others. In many situated systems, of course, all contingencies are managed without such threats arising. However, there is no such system in which these troubles might not occur, and some systems, such as those in a surgery ward, presumably provide an especially good opportunity to study these contingencies.

Just as a rider may be disqualified during the ride because he proves to be unable to handle riding, so a rider will be removed from his saddle at the very beginning of the ride because he does not have a ticket or because, in the absence of his parents, he makes management fear for his safety. There is an obvious distinction, then, between qualifications required for permission to attempt a role and attributes required for performing suitably once the role has been acquired.

At three and four, the task of riding a wooden horse is still a challenge, but apparently a manageable one, inflating the rider to his full extent with demonstrations of capacity. Parents need no longer ride alongside to protect their youngsters. The rider throws himself into the role in a serious way, playing it with verve and an admitted engagement of all his faculties. Passing his parents at each turn, the rider carefully lets go one of his hands and grimly waves a smile or a kiss—this, incidentally, being an example of an act that is a typical part of the role but hardly an obligatory feature of it. Here, then, doing is being, and what was designated as a "playing at" is stamped with serious realization.

Just as "flustering" is a classic possibility in all situated systems, so also is the earnest way these youngsters of three or four ride their horses. Three matters seem to be involved: an admitted or expressed attachment to the role; a demonstration of qualifications and capacities for performing it; an active *engagement* or spontaneous involvement in the role activity at hand, that is, a visible investment of attention and muscular effort. Where these three features are present, I will use the term *embracement*. To embrace a role is to disappear completely into the virtual self available in the situation, to be fully seen in terms of the image, and to confirm expressively one's acceptance of it. To embrace a role is to be embraced by it. Particularly good illustrations of full embracement can be seen in persons in certain occupations: team managers during baseball games; traffic policemen at intersections during rush hours; landing signal officers who wave in planes landing on the decks of aircraft carriers; in fact, any one occupying a directing role where the performer must guide others by means of gestural signs.[1]

An individual may affect the embracing of a role in order to conceal a lack of attachment to it, just as he may affect a visible disdain for a role, thrice refusing the kingly crown, in order to defend himself against the psychological dangers of his actual attachment to it. Certainly an individual may be attached to a role and fail to be able to embrace it, as when a child proves to have no ticket or to be unable to hang on.

Returning to the merry-go-round, we see that at five years of age the situation is transformed, especially for boys. To be a merry-go-round horse rider is now apparently not enough, and this fact must be demonstrated out of dutiful regard for one's own character. Parents are not likely to be allowed to ride along, and the strap for preventing falls is often disdained. One rider may keep time to the music by clapping his feet or a hand against the horse, an early sign of utter control. Another may make a wary stab at

standing on the saddle or changing horses without touching the platform. Still another may hold on to the post with one hand and lean back as far as possible while looking up to the sky in a challenge to dizziness. Irreverence begins, and the horse may be held on to by his wooden ear or his tail. The child says by his actions: "Whatever I am, I'm not just someone who can barely manage to stay on a wooden horse." Note that what the rider is apologizing for is not some minor untoward event that has cropped up during the interaction, but the whole role. The image of him that is generated for him by the routine entailed in his mere participation—his virtual self in the context—is an image from which he apparently withdraws by *actively* manipulating the situation. Whether this skittish behavior is intentional or unintentional, sincere or affected, correctly appreciated by others present or not, it does constitute a wedge between the individual and his role, between doing and being. This "effectively" expressed pointed separateness between the individual and his putative role I shall call *role distance*. A shorthand is involved here: the individual is actually denying not the role but the virtual self that is implied in the role for all accepting performers.

In any case, the term role distance is not meant to refer to all behavior that does not directly contribute to the task core of a given role but only to those behaviors that are seen by someone present as relevant to assessing the actor's attachment to his particular role and relevant in such a way as to suggest that the actor possibly has some measure of disaffection from, and resistance against, the role. Thus, for example, a four-year-old halfway through a triumphant performance as a merry-go-round rider may sometimes go out of play, dropping from his face and manner any confirmation of his virtual self, yet may indulge in this break in role without apparent intent, the lapse reflecting more on his capacity to sustain any role than on his feelings about the present one. Nor can it be called role distance if the child rebels and totally rejects the role, stomping off in a huff, for the special facts about self that can be conveyed by holding a role off a little are precisely the ones that cannot be conveyed by throwing the role over.

At seven and eight, the child not only dissociates himself self-consciously from the kind of horseman a merry-go-round allows him to be but also finds that many of the devices that younger people use for this are now beneath him. He rides no-hands, gleefully chooses a tiger or a frog for a steed, clasps hands with a mounted friend across the aisle. He tests limits, and his antics may bring negative sanction from the adult in charge of the machine. And he is still young enough to show distance by handling the task with bored, nonchalant competence, a candy bar languidly held in one hand.

At eleven and twelve, maleness for boys has become a real responsibility, and no easy means of role distance seems to be available on merry-go-rounds. It is necessary to stay away or to exert creative acts of distancy, as when a boy jokingly treats his wooden horse as if it were a racing one: he jogs himself up and down, leans far over the neck of the horse, drives his heels mercilessly into its flanks, and uses the reins for a lash to get more speed, brutally reining in the horse when the ride is over. He is just old enough to achieve role distance by defining the whole undertaking as a lark, a situation for mockery.

Adults who choose to ride a merry-go-round display adult techniques of role distance. One adult rider makes a

joke of tightening the safety belt around him; another crosses his arms, giving popcorn with his left hand to the person on his right and a coke with his right hand to the person on his left. A young lady riding sidesaddle tinkles out, "It's cold," and calls to her watching boy friend's boy friend, "Come on, don't be chicken." A dating couple riding adjacent horses holds hands to bring sentiment, not daring, to the situation. Two doubledating couples employ their own techniques: the male in front sits backwards and takes a picture of the other male rider taking a picture of him. And, of course, some adults, riding close by their threatened two-and-a-half-year-old, wear a face that carefully demonstrates that they do not perceive the ride as an event in itself, their only present interest being their child.

And finally there is the adult who runs the machine and takes the tickets. Here, often, can be found a fine flowering of role distance. Not only does he show that the ride itself is not—as a ride—an event to him, but he also gets off and on and around the moving platform with a grace and ease that can only be displayed by safely taking what for children and even adults would be chances.

Some general points can be made about merry-go-round role distance. First, while the management of a merry-go-round horse in our culture soon ceases to be a challenging "developmental task," the task of expressing that it is not continues for a long time to be a challenge and remains a felt necessity. A full twist must be made in the iron law of etiquette: the act through which one can afford to try to fit into the situation is an act that can be styled to show that one is somewhat out of place. One enters the situation to the degree that one can demonstrate that one does not belong.

A second general point about role distance is that immediate audiences figure very directly in the display of role distance. Merry-go-round horsemen are very ingenuous and may frankly wait for each time they pass their waiting friends before playing through their gestures of role distance. Moreover, if persons above the age of twelve or so are to trust themselves to making a lark of it, they almost need to have a friend along on the next horse, since persons who are "together" seem to be able to hold off the socially defining force of the environment much more than a person alone.

A final point: two different means of establishing role distance seem to be found. In one case the individual tries to isolate himself as much as possible from the contamination of the situation, as when an adult riding along to guard his child makes an effort to be completely stiff, affectless, and preoccupied. In the other case the individual cooperatively projects a childish self, meeting the situation more than halfway, but then withdraws from this castoff self by a little gesture signifying that the joking has gone far enough. In either case the individual can slip the skin the situation would clothe him in. . . .

ROLE DISTANCE AND SERIOUS ACTIVITY

The role of merry-go-round rider can be regularly performed at any amusement park but hardly by a regular performer. After a few years each of us "outgrows" the role and can only perform it as an occasional thing and as an occasion for the display of much role distance. As an example, then, merry-go-round riding is not a very serious one; furthermore, it is somewhat misleading, since it implies that role distance is displayed in connection with roles no adult can take seriously.

Actually, we deal with a more general phenomenon, with roles that categories of individuals find it unwise to embrace. Even a short step away from merry-go-rounds shows this. Take, for example, six lower-middle-class high-school girls, not of the horsy set, taking a vacation in a national park and deciding to "do" horseback riding on one of their mornings. As long as they come to the riding stable in self-supporting numbers, they can nicely illustrate distance from a role that persons of another social class and region might take seriously all their lives. The six I observed came in clothing patently not designed as a consolidation of the horsewoman role: pedal pushers, cotton leotards, ballet-type flats, frilly blouses. One girl, having been allotted the tallest horse, made a mock scene of declining to get on because of the height, demanding to be allowed to go home. When she did get on, she called her horse "Daddy-O," diverting her conversation from her friends to her horse. During the ride, one girl pretended to post while the horse walked, partly in mockery of a person not in their party who was posting. Another girl leaned over the neck of her horse and shouted racing cries, again while the horse was locked in a walking file of other horses. She also slipped her right foot out of the stirrup and brought it over the saddle, making a joke of her affectation of riding sidesaddle and expressing that both positions were much alike to her—both equally unfamiliar and uncongenial; at the same time she tested the limits of the wrangler's permissiveness. Passing under low branches, the girls made a point of making a point of this by pulling off branches, waving them like flags, then feeding them to their horses. Evidences of the excretory capacities of the steeds were greeted with merriment and loud respect. During the latter part of the two-hour ride, two of the girls became visibly bored, dropped the reins over the saddlehorn, let their hands fall limply to their sides, and gave up all pretense at being in role.

Again we can detect some general facts about role distance. We can see that a role that some persons take seriously most of their lives may be one that others will never take seriously at any age. We see that participation with a group of one's similars can lend strength to the show of role distance and to one's willingness to express it. In the presence of age-peers elegantly attired for riding and skilled at it, the girls I observed might falter in displaying role distance, feeling hostile, resentful, and unconfident. Presumably, if one of these girls were alone with thoroughgoing horsewomen she would be even less prone to flourish this kind of distance. We can suspect, then, that role distance will have defensive functions. By manifesting role distance, the girls give themselves some elbow room in which to maneuver. "We are not to be judged by this incompetence," they say. Should they make a bad showing, they are in a position to dodge the reflection it could cast on them. Whatever their showing, they avoid having to be humbled before those who are socially placed to make a much better showing. By exposing themselves in a guise to which they have no serious claim, they leave themselves in full control of shortcomings they take seriously.

While horse trails and children's playgrounds provide fine places for studying repertoires of role distance, we need not look to situations that are so close to being unserious, situations where it is difficult to distinguish role playing from playing at. We know, for example, that tasks that might be embraced by a housewife or maid may be tackled by the man of the house with carefully expressed clumsiness and with self-mockery. Perhaps it should be noted that similar out-of-character situations can easily be created experimentally by asking subjects to perform tasks that are inappropriate to persons of their kind.

The published literature on some of our occupational byways provides serious material on role distance. Psychoanalysts, for example, who have told us so much about the contingencies of a particular trade (even when not telling us all we might want to know about their patients), provide interesting data on role distance in connection with "resistance" on the part of the patient. Resistance here takes the form of the patient refusing to provide relevant associations or refusing to allow the therapist to function solely as a "therapist." From the therapist's view of the patient's motivation, then, resistance expresses some rejection of the constraints of one's role as patient:

Up to this point I found myself, as the doctor, comfortably installed in my explicit instrumental role; the role assignment given me by the patient appeared to be concerned with her "problem." The system of roles was complementary and apparently well integrated. The next moment, however, the patient initiated a new role assignment. She asked me if I had seen a recent performance of "Don Juan in Hell" from *Man and Superman*. The question seemed a simple enough request for information regarding my playgoing habits. But since I did not know what role I was being invited to take, and because I suspected that behind whatever explicit role this might turn out to be there lurked a more important implicit one, I did not answer the question. The patient paused for a moment, and then, perceiving that I would not answer the question, she continued. . . .

In continuing after the pause, the patient delivered a highly perceptive account of Shaw's intention in the Don Juan interlude, of the actors' interpretations, and of her reactions. The account was so long that I finally interrupted to ask if she knew why she wanted to tell all this. At the point of interruption I had become aware that my new role was an expressive one—to play the appreciative audience to her role as a gifted art and drama critic.[2]

The therapist then goes on to explain that had he merely fallen in with the patient's maneuver to keep herself at a distance from the role of patient he would have had to pass up "the opportunity to get more information regarding the hidden, implicit role buried in this transaction and thus to learn more about her motivation for shifting out of her initial instrumental role in which she had started the interview."[3] The therapist could have added that to ask the patient why she felt it necessary to run on so is a classic therapist's ploy to put the patient in her place, back in role.

Situated roles that place an individual in an occupational setting he feels is beneath him are bound to give rise to much role distance. A good example is provided by Isaac Rosenfeld in a reminiscence about a summer job as a barker at Coney Island. The writer begins his description by telling of his return after many years, seeing someone else handling his old job:

He was sneering, just as I used to do in the old days, and no doubt for the same reason: because the summer was hot, and the work hard, sweaty and irritating, stretching over long hours for poor pay. It was absolutely indispensable, now as it was then, to separate oneself from the job—one had to have a little ledge to stand on all to himself; otherwise perish. I used to pitch this ledge very high. The higher I stood, the greater my contempt, and the more precious the moments of freedom I won for myself by this trick of balancing above the crowd. I remembered how I used to mix T. S. Eliot with my spiel (in those days there was hardly anyone in Freshman English who did not know a good deal of *The Waste Land* by heart): "Step right up ladies and gentlemen mingling memory with desire

for the greatest thrill show on earth only a dime the tenth part of a dollar will bring you to Carthage then I come burning burning burning burning O Lord thou pluckest me out ten cents!"[4]

Some of the most appealing data on role distance come from situations where a subordinate must take orders or suggestions and must go along with the situation as defined by superordinates. At such times, we often find that although the subordinate is careful not to threaten those who are, in a sense, in charge of the situation, he may be just as careful to inject some expression to show, for any who care to see, that he is not capitulating completely to the work arrangement in which he finds himself.[5] Sullenness, muttering, irony, joking, and sarcasm may all allow one to show that something of oneself lies outside the constraints of the moment and outside the role within whose jurisdiction the moment occurs.

Given these various examples of role distance, I want to go on to argue that this conduct is something that falls between role obligations on one hand and actual role performance on the other. This gap has always caused trouble for sociologists. Often, they try to ignore it. Faced with it, they sometimes despair and turn from their own direction of analysis; they look to the biography of the performer and try to find in his history some particularistic explanation of events, or they rely on psychology, alluding to the fact that in addition to playing the formal themes of his role, the individual always behaves personally and spontaneously, phrasing the standard obligations in a way that has a special psychological fit for him.

The concept of role distance provides a *sociological* means of dealing with one type of divergence between obligation and actual performance.

First, we know that often distance is not introduced on an individual basis but can be predicted on the grounds of the performers' gross age-sex characteristics. Role distance is a part (but, of course, only one part) of *typical* role, and this routinized sociological feature should not escape us merely because role distance is not part of the normative framework of role. Secondly, that which one is careful to point out one is not, or not merely, necessarily has a directing and intimate influence on one's conduct, especially since the means for expressing this disaffection must be carved out of the standard materials available in the situation.

We arrive, then, at a broadened sociological way of looking at the trappings of a social role. A set of visible qualifications and known certifications along with a social setting well designed as a showplace, provides the individual with something more than an opportunity to play his role self to the hilt, for this scene is just what he needs to create a clear impression of what he chooses not to lay claim to. The more extensive the trappings of a role, the more opportunity to display role distance. Personal front and social setting provide precisely the field an individual needs to cut a figure in—a figure that romps, sulks, glides, or is indifferent. . . .

SURGERY AS AN ACTIVITY SYSTEM

I have suggested some cases where the scene of activity generates for the individual a self which he is apparently loath to accept openly for himself, since his conduct suggests that some disaffiliation exists between himself and his role. But a peek into some odd corners of social life provides no basis, perhaps, for generalizing about social life. As a test, then, of the notion of role distance (and role), let us take a scene in which activity generates a self for the individual that appears to be a most likely one for self-attachment. Let us take, for example, the activity system sustained during a surgical operation. The components consist of verbal and physical acts and the changing state of the organism undergoing the operation. Here, if anywhere in our society, we should find performers flushed with a feeling of the weight and dignity of their action. A Hollywood ideal is involved: the white-coated chief surgeon strides into the operating theater after the patient has been anesthetized and opened by assistants. A place is automatically made for him. He grunts a few abbreviated preliminaries, then deftly, almost silently, gets to work, serious, grim, competently living up to the image he and his team have of him, yet in a context where momentary failure to exhibit competence might permanently jeopardize the relation he is allowed to have to his role. Once the critical phase of the operation is quite over, he steps back and, with a special compound of tiredness, strength, and disdain, rips off his gloves; he thus contaminates himself and abdicates his role, but at a time when his own labors put the others in a position to "close up." While he may be a father, a husband, or a baseball fan at home, he is here one and only one thing, a surgeon, and being a surgeon provides a fully rounded impression of the man. If the role perspective works, then, surely it works here, for in our society the surgeon, if anyone, is allowed and obliged to put himself into his work and get a self out of it.[6]

As a contrast, then, to the insubstantial life of horses-for-ride, I want to report briefly on some observations of activity in surgery wards.[7]

If we start with the situation of the lesser medical personnel, the intern and the junior resident, the test will not be fair, for here, apparently, is a situation much like the ones previously mentioned. The tasks these juniors are given to do—such as passing hemostats, holding retractors, cutting small tied-off veins, swabbing the operating area before the operation, and perhaps suturing or closing at the end—are not large enough to support much of a surgical role. Furthermore, the junior person may find that he performs even these lowly tasks inadequately, and that the scrub nurse as well as the chief surgeon tells him so. And when the drama is over and the star performer has dropped his gloves and gown and walked out, the nurses may underline the intern's marginal position by lightly demanding his help in moving the body from the fixed table to the movable one, while automatically granting him a taste of the atmosphere they maintain when real doctors are absent. As for the intern himself, surgery is very likely not to be his chosen specialty; the three-month internship is a course requirement and he will shortly see the last of it. The intern may confirm all this ambivalence to his work on occasions away from the surgery floor, when he scathingly describes surgery as a plumber's craft exercised by mechanics who are told what to look for by internists.

The surgical junior, especially the intern, has, then, a humbling position during surgery. Whether as a protection against this condition or not, the medical·juniors I observed, like overage merry-go-round riders, analysands, and carnival pitchmen, were not prepared to embrace their role fully; elaborate displays of role dis-

tance occurred.[8] A careful, bemused look on the face is sometimes found, implying, "This is not the real me." Sometimes the individual will allow himself to go "away," dropping off into a brown study that removes him from the continuity of events, increases the likelihood that his next contributory act will not quite fit into the flow of action, and effectively gives the appearance of occupational disaffection; brought back into play, he may be careful to evince little sign of chagrin. He may rest himself by leaning on the patient or by putting a foot on an inverted bucket but in a manner too contrived to allow the others to feel it is a matter of mere resting. Interestingly enough, he sometimes takes on the function of the jester, endangering his reputation with antics that temporarily place him in a doubtful and special position, yet through this providing the others present with a reminder of less exalted worlds:

Chief Surgeon Jones (in this case a senior resident): A small Richardson please.
Scrub Nurse: Don't have one.
Dr. Jones: O.K., then give me an Army and Navy.
Scrub Nurse: It looks like we don't have one.
Dr. Jones (lightly joking): No Army or Navy man here.
Intern (dryly): No one in the armed forces, but Dr. Jones here is in the Boy Scouts.

Scrub Nurse: Will there be more than three [sutures] more? We're running out of sutures.
Chief Surgeon: I don't know.
Intern: We can finish up with Scotch tape.

Intern (looking for towel clamps around body): Where in the world . . . ?
Scrub Nurse: Underneath the towel.
(Intern turns to the nurse and in slow measure makes a full cold bow to her.)
Scrub Nurse (to intern): Watch it, you're close to my table! [A Mayo stand containing instruments whose asepsis she must guard and guarantee.] (Intern performs a mock gasp and clownishly draws back.)

As I have suggested, just as we cannot use a child over four riding a merry-go-round as an exhibition of how to embrace an activity role, so also we cannot use the junior medical people on a surgical team. But surely the chief surgeon, at least, will demonstrate the embracing of a role. What we find, of course, is that even this central figure expresses considerable role distance.

Some examples may be cited. One can be found in medical etiquette. This body of custom requires that the surgeon, on leaving the operation, turn and thank his assistant, his anesthetist, and ordinarily his nurses as well. Where a team has worked together for a long time and where the members are of the same age-grade, the surgeon may guy this act, issuing the thanks in what he expects will be taken as an ironical and farcical tone of voice: "Miss Westly, you've done a simply wonderful job here." Similarly, there is a formal rule that in preparing a requested injection the nurse show the shelved vial to the surgeon before its sealed top is cracked off so that he can check its named contents and thereby take the responsibility on himself. If the surgeons are very busy at the time, this checking may be requested but not given. At other times, however, the checking may be guyed.

Circulating Nurse: Dr. James, would you check this?

Dr. James (in a loud ministerial voice, reading the label): Three cubic centimeters of heparin at ten-milligram strength, put up by Invenex and held by Nurse Jackson at a forty-five-degree angle. That is right, Nurse Jackson.

Instead of employing technical terms at all times, he may tease the nurses by using homey appellations: "Give me the small knife, we'll get in just below the belly button"; and he may call the electric cauterizer by the apt name of "sizzler," ordering the assistant surgeon to "sizzle here, and here." Similarly, when a nurse allows her nonsterile undergown to be exposed a little, a surgeon may say in a pontifical and formal tone, "Nurse Bevan, can I call your attention to the anterior portion of your gown. It is exposing you. I trust you will correct this condition," thereby instituting social control, reference to the nurse's non-nursing attributes, and satire of the profession, all with one stroke. So, too, a nurse, returning to the operating room with a question, "Dr. Williams?" may be answered by a phrase of self-satirization: "In person," or, "This is Dr. Williams." And a well-qualified surgeon, in taking the situated role of assistant surgeon for the duration of a particular operation, may tell the nurses, when they have been informed by the chief surgeon that two electric cauterizers will be employed, "I'm going to get one too, just like the big doctors, that's what I like to hear." A chief surgeon, then, may certainly express role distance. Why he does so, and with what effect, are clearly additional questions, and ought to be considered.

NOTES

1. Here, as elsewhere, I am indebted to Gregory Stone.

2. J. P. Spiegel, "The Social Roles of Doctor and Patient in Psychoanalysis and Psychotherapy," *Psychiatry*, 17 (1954), pp. 372-373.

3. *Ibid.*, p. 373.

4. Isaac Rosenfeld, "Coney Island Revisited," in *Modern Writing*, eds. William Phillips and Philip Rahv (New York: Avon Publications, 1953), p. 219.

5. Some excellent illustrations of this

may be found in Tom Burns, "Friends, Enemies and the Polite Fiction," *American Sociological Review*, 18 (1953), pp. 654-662, a paper to which I am very much indebted. A good illustration from army life is provided in William Styron's story, *The Long March* (New York: Modern Library, 1952), in connection with a captain's minor remonstrances against orders issued by his colonel.

6. Much the same conceit has already been employed by Temple Burling in *Essays on Human Aspects of Administration*, Bulletin 25 (August, 1953) of the New York State School of Industrial and Labor Relations, Cornell University, pp. 9-10. The fullest published accounts of conduct in the operating room that I know of are to be found in T. Burling, E. Lentz and R. Wilson, *The Give and Take in Hospitals* (New York: Putnam, 1956), Chap. 17, pp. 260-283, and R. Wilson, "Teamwork in the Operating Room," *Human Organization*, 12 (1954), pp. 9-14.

7. My own material on interaction during surgery, from which all staff practices and verbal responses cited in this paper are drawn, derives from brief observations in the medical building of a mental hospital and the operating rooms of a suburban community hospital. Not deriving from the most formal hospitals, these data load the facts a little in my favor.

I am grateful to Dr. Otis R. Farley, and his staff in the Medical and Surgical Branch of St. Elizabeths Hospital, Washington, D. C., and to John F. Wight, Administrative Director, and Lenore Jones, Head Surgical Nurse, of Herrick Memorial Hospital, Berkeley, California, for full research freedom and great courtesy.

8. Some of the interns I observed had plans to take a psychiatric residency and, apparently because of this, were doing their stint of surgical internship in the medical building of a mental hospital; they therefore had wider institutional support for their lack of interest in physical techniques.

11. ROLE DISTANCE, ROLE DISTANCE BEHAVIOR AND JAZZ MUSICIANS*

ROBERT STEBBINS

Reprinted from *The British Journal of Sociology*, Vol. XX, No. 4 (December, 1969), pp. 406-415, with permission of the author and *The British Journal of Sociology*. Robert Stebbins is Associate Professor of Sociology and Anthropology at Memorial University of Newfoundland. He received his Ph.D. in 1964 from the University of Minnesota and has written extensively on deviant careers. His latest work is a book entitled *Commitment to Deviance*.

It has been seven years since Erving Goffman published his essay on role distance in *Encounters*.[1] Perhaps one of his most original and insightful contributions to sociology and social psychology, there has been during this period a surprisingly small amount of empirical research on this subject, although some sporadic discussion of it has occurred.[2] There are at least two reasons for this lack of interest: (1) Goffman's own formulation is logically vague and ambiguous and (2) the nature of role distance makes investigation of it difficult. Our objectives here are to resolve as much of this vagueness and ambiguity as is possible and desirable at this stage of theoretical development and to suggest ways in which research might be carried out on this phenomenon. Observations on role distance and role distance behaviour among jazz musicians will be used to illustrate our points.

The very definition of role distance which is presented by Goffman in the course of ten pages, often by means of the liberal use of example, is the principal source of confusion.[3] Yet, upon careful perusal of this section of his essay it becomes clear that the defining elements of this idea are present, need-

ing only to be collected into a more coherent statement. Role distance develops in connection with a particular status or identity and, more specifically, in connection with all or part of its associated role expectations. Role distance which is part of the individual's interpretation of these expectations reflects a desire to dissociate himself from them, the reason for this being traceable to their threat to his self-conception.[4] The inclination to engage in role distance behaviour is stimulated by the presence of a certain 'audience' or special other persons in the ongoing situation who will denigrate the role player for enacting the expectations. However, such behaviour should not be conceived as a refusal to play out those expectations. Rather it is best seen as an adaptive strategy, whereby the performer can more or less fulfil his role obligations while maintaining his self-respect.

The idea of role distance is not so abstract and complex as to preclude a more formal definition of it. Indeed such is required in order to bring together the essential elements which make up this concept and to minimize ambiguity and confusion. Thus, role distance can be defined as an attitude of dislike toward all or part of a set of role expectations which, when enacted, bring the threat of a loss of respect and at least momentary lack of

*The author wishes to express his gratitude to Professor John W. Prehn whose comments and suggestions have added much of value to this paper.

support for one's self-conception from certain reference others present in the situation.[5] The role distance attitude is to be distinguished from the actual performance expressing this predisposition which we shall call *role-distance behaviour* or *taking role distance*.

That Goffman's presentation of the defining qualities of role distance has spawned confusion is evident in the few papers which have followed his. Levitin never does grasp the fact that role distance is expressed in behaviour before an audience of reference others and not, as he thinks, before sub-categories of customers whom the puller[6] is trying to convince to enter the store to make a purchase. It is doubtful that any of his examples are instances of taking role distance since the customers are clearly not reference others to the puller, and he certainly does not need to convince himself that specific expectations in his occupational role threaten his self-esteem. If there is an audience of reference others, it is either the salesmen within the store or other pullers down the street. But they are not mentioned in this capacity.[7]

Elsewhere, the author has discussed in greater detail the significance of the threat of enacting certain expectations to the actor's self-conception. This theme is present, though rather dimly, in Goffman's essay. Its relative obscurity there seems to have led Rose Coser to overlook this important aspect of role distance in her attempt to relate it to sociological ambivalence and transitional status systems.[8]

The shortcomings in the treatment of role distance by Ford, Young, and Box can also be attributed to the inadequacies of Goffman's initial statement. However, before we consider their ideas it will facilitate our aims if we draw some new distinctions. First of all, we can differentiate 'major role distance' from 'minor role distance'. The former refers to the attitude which develops toward highly threatening expectations. They are usually perceived in this way because they are associated with an identity *high* in the person's salience hierarchy. The latter refers to the attitude toward moderate or only slightly threatening expectations. These expectations relate to an identity *low* in the salience hierarchy; or regardless of the position of the identity, their enactment makes a person appear oddly different from the reference others in some more or less trivial way. One might appear trivially different from others by being identified as liking expectations generally defined as boring, difficult, or physically uncomfortable. The salience hierarchy is the situational rearrangement of the actor's overall prominence or importance hierarchy of his total set of identities or statuses.[9]

A distinction between kinds of role-distance behaviour will also prove beneficial. We shall use the term "true role-distance behaviour' to refer to actions which are an expression of a genuine role-distance attitude (major or minor). The expectations are genuinely disliked, and the actor does not wish the reference others present to get the impression that he likes them. 'False role-distance behaviour' shall designate actions which are *not* an expression of a genuine role-distance attitude. Instead the actor tries to create the impression that he holds this attitude while, in fact, he is actually attracted to the expectations.

Getting back to the paper by Ford and her associates, we are told that role distance is not possible to any significant degree among lower-class people because they lack the skills necessary to step outside their roles, because they 'receive' rather than 'interpret' their norms (they are bound by 'rule-fulness'), and because they have 'total' friendships with each other.[10] These assertions can be challenged on the following grounds, most of which are misunderstandings of the nature of role distance. Thus, if taking role distance is impossible because of total interpersonal relationships, then this can only pertain to false role-distance behaviour rather than to the true variety. The high level of intimate knowledge characteristic of such relationships is a barrier only to dissimulative behaviour. True role-distance behaviour expresses a genuinely held attitude.

Moreover, though not mentioned explicitly by Goffman, it seems to this author that there is usually the requirement—very much a part of the set of role expectations of an identity—that one will hold a role-distance attitude toward certain other expectations and behave accordingly. If those in the lower-classes are bound by rulefulness, they must also be bound by this rule. By way of caveat it should be noted that it is not true as Coser believes that role distance is itself part of the normative framework; it is part of the interpretation of that framework, although an interpretation which is expected by the reference others.[11] This feature will be evident in our observations on jazz musicians to be presented shortly. Finally, if lower-class people are expected to hold role-distance attitudes towards certain role requirements, then it is not unreasonable to assume that in the course of their socialization, they will also learn the techniques for expressing these dispositions just as they learned the expectation that they should have them in the first place.

So far we have been engaged in identifying and attempting to resolve some of the confusion created by Goffman's presentation of the fundamentals of role distance. One other factor was also cited as inhibiting research on this subject: namely, the difficulties involved in studying empirically such a subjective phenomena. It is obvious that the modes of expression of role distance will vary widely from community to community and from subculture to subculture within any one community. Consequently, the researcher is forced to gain an intimate knowledge of the group under study before he can make any meaningful statements about when role distance occurs and how it is externalized for the benefit of reference others. An extensive amount of participant observation is clearly a prerequisite for empirical investigation of role distance anywhere except in circles well known to the social scientist. Furthermore, since instances of role-distance behaviour are probably only a small proportion of the total number of acts performed by an individual, observational research conducted expressly for the purpose of studying role distance may be relatively unrewarding because the return is so low. Indeed, it is probably better to include this interest in a larger investigation, such as some sort of participant observer form of community study.

The observations on jazz musicians reported below do not wholly comply with these suggestions. They are based upon the author's participation in jazz music over a period of ten years in two communities in which a close acquaintance was developed with the associated sub-culture.[12] But, gathering data on role distance and role-distance behaviour was never part of a larger study design, so that the observations recorded here are somewhat less systematic than is desirable. Still, the historical nature of jazz musical life in the two cities lends a good measure of confidence to the generality of the observations even though we may be unable to give much precision to the frequency of the occurrence of role-distance behaviour.[13]

ROLE DISTANCE AMONG JAZZ MUSICIANS

At least six general modes of role-distance behaviour can be identified:

1. Presence of special vocal behaviour: e.g., grunts, speech, laughs, etc.
2. Absence of ordinary vocal behaviour
3. Presence of special gestures: e.g., face, hands, body movements, etc.
4. Absence of ordinary gestures
5. Presence of special deeds
6. Absence of ordinary deeds

By the phrase 'presence of special vocal behaviour' (gestures or deeds) is meant simply that these expressions are manifestations of a role-distance attitude toward certain expectations salient at the moment. Because it is 'special' behaviour should not lead one to lose sight of the fact that some meaningful mode of taking role distance is expected by the reference others. Also, the phrase 'absence of ordinary vocal behaviour' (gestures or deeds) merely refers to the withholding of certain usual practices as an expression of role distance. Again such withholding behaviour is expected by the reference others. Lastly, it should be apparent that modes 1 and 2, 3 and 4, 5 and 6 are not in any way dichotomous. The use of these modes by jazz musicians is evident in the following description of two major role-distance attitudes which are expected of them at certain times during musical performances.

One of these attitudes lies behind the jazz musician's reaction to the expectation that he play the 'tunes' or songs requested by the listening audience. This is not an objectionable requirement as long as the requests are recognized as appropriate jazz fare. But in an unknown but distressingly large proportion of such instances this is not the case. Non-jazz numbers are requested which are referred to as 'square tunes' or some uncomplimentary equivalent (e.g., old-time waltzes and polkas, folk songs, many popular songs, rock and roll hits, etc.), and are regarded with great scorn by the true artist. Under these circumstances the individual jazz musician is expected by other jazz musicians present, whether they are in the band or in the audience, to exhibit role-distance behaviour.

The vocal behaviour mode of expression is widely used. The choice of words and the tone of voice used in communication among those in the band convey their disgust as they pass the news of the loathed request to each other, commenting upon it as they do so. Even the speech and tone of voice of the band leader in conversation with the requester may be freighted with externalizations of role distance directed less at the requester himself than at reference others present. Equally prominent and usually accompanying vocal behaviour are certain hand and facial gestures, such as a thumbs down motion, a frown, and expression denoting an odious gustatory taste, and the like. During the actual playing of the maligned tune, members of the band may take further role distance by displaying complete disinterest (e.g., placid face, eyes shut as if asleep), or, if possible, engage in other activities with their spare hands, such as drinking beer, smoking a cigarette, toying with one's clothing, or even scratching parts of the body. These obvious signs of disinterest are simultaneously an example of the absence of gestures, since in the performance of a jazz tune there is considerable evidence of concentration and outright enjoyment, if not ecstasy.

On occasion certain deeds may be employed to express this role-distance attitude. Hence, one or more of the musicians may intentionally 'jazz up' the square tune even though this makes for poor jazz itself. That jazz musicians and knowledgeable buffs present recognize the significance of this action is evident by the round of laughter and chuckles from those in the room who are 'hip' or aware of the intended meaning. The very stalling of the playing of the requested square tune can be seen as the absence of an expected deed full of in-group significance. The musicians may also demonstrate their disinterest during the performance by talking to one another, not infrequently telling jokes or some colourful anecdote about mutual musical acquaintances.

Somewhat less regular in occurrence but often even more disliked, is the request by some member of the audience to 'sit-in' for two or three numbers and sing with the band. If, in fact, the singer is good this is heartily welcomed, but usually the capable singers in a community are known and if present they will be invited to sing. When the singer is reputed to be poor or the state of his talent is unknown, jazz musicians fear the worst and react accordingly. These reactions include most if not all of the expressions employed in playing square tunes.[14] In addition, there will usually be a noticeable absence of such vocal behaviour as compliments (unless the singer is young and is perceived as working to improve) and any mention of further opportunities to sing with the band. If the person who asks to sit-in is a musician instead of a singer but is still defined as square, a member of the band may express role distance by suggesting a square tune to play while he is performing with them. This is doubly significant since jazz musicians who sit-in are conventionally allowed to select the tune themselves because they are in the role of honoured guest instead of intruder. An amusing but more idiosyncratic practice of expressing role distance when such intruders appear was used by a piano player known to the author who delighted in signalling the exit of such people from the bandstand by playing the song 'Fine and Dandy' at a fast tempo—a rendition of a tune traditionally employed by musicians providing the exit music for stripteasers at the end of their performance.

Although there may be others these are the two most prevalent major role-distance attitudes of the jazz musician in his capacity as musical performer. The repugnancies of square music and square musicians are both social-psychological manifestations of the omnipresent problem of the tension between art and commercialism which characterizes the jazz life.[15]

MINOR ROLE DISTANCE AND ROLE-DISTANCE BEHAVIOR

Several minor role-distance attitudes develop out of the occupational life of jazz musicians. Many of these are connected with the working conditions of the jazz job where, for instance, one is expected to be ready to play at a certain time in the evening (punctuality) and to be in such physical condition as to finish in good form four to six hours later. This often includes employment under considerably less than ideal circumstances, like being expected to perform on undersized bandstands, on dilapidated and out-of-tune pianos, in excessive heat and cigarette smoke, with faulty electronic equipment, and so forth.[16] Jazz musicians generally do not care for many or all of these requirements of their work. But, even if one should take pride in his punctuality or show such unusual exuberance for the music that he is not even ready to quit six hours later, his reference others do not take this as evidence of a major blemish in his character. He is simply regarded as a bit different ('somewhat of a nut') in a world characterized by extensive tolerance for unusual personalities.[17]

Additionally, jazz musicians typically show a dislike for individual practice on their musical instruments, an attitude which probably exists in many other categories of musicians as well. When talk about practising comes up, one is expected to take role distance, and it is this author's observation that many do.

The fact that some of the serious, hard-working jazz musicisns do not object to but often enjoy their individual practice sessions leads to instances of false role-distance behaviour. They do not usually do a very good job of dissembling, however, for their occasional weak expressions of supposed role distance are more than overbalanced by their insistence in conversation that practice is the key to success and by their rather steady improvement. There is in fact a certain amount of ambivalence about individual practice in jazz communities; the one who does this extensively is regarded as different in a strange but admirable way. The respected musician is a competent musician, and he arrives at this position through no other route than by constant hard work on his instrument. It is also this person

who commands the greatest influence in local jazz circles.[18]

Another occasion for false role-distance behaviour is found in the situation where the jazz musician is involved in playing 'legit' music or that which he must read instead of improvise. Because a large proportion of jazz musicians are poor readers[19] they often scorn music made in this manner and consequently scorn those who enjoy playing it. Yet, a smaller percentage of jazz musicians are able readers and they find pleasure in successfully playing music which is difficult from this point of view. Nonetheless, they often discover that they must feign role-distance behaviour here in order to avoid a certain amount of loss of respect. It is true that some types of reading are more undesirable than others because the expectation that the jazz musician will play only improvised music is roughly related to the degree of commercialism involved. It is wonderful if the musician can read the musical scores written for big jazz bands or even for small combos (both of which involve some improvisation as well). It is less so if he shows an interest in the classical side of music, and it is heresy if he likes reading polka music (which is very challenging) or something else designed for mass consumption.

In these cases of minor role distance and false role-distance behaviour, the variety in the modes of expression is considerably less than in major role distance. Theoretically, this is to be expected from the fact that there is much less of a threat here for the individual's self-conception. From our jazz observations, attitudes of minor role distance appear to be weak, partly because they are not congruent with other attitudes of similar strength. Therefore, ambivalence may be characteristic of a person's orientation toward certain role expectations leading him to take role distance at some points and to avoid such behaviour at others. One does not greatly elaborate the externalizations of his role distance under such conditions since he is not sure of his own sentiments toward the expectations.

SUMMARY AND CONCLUSIONS

In response to the observation that the current state of theoretical and descriptive development of the concept of role distance has led to a paucity of research and to an abundance of confusion, the following aims were pursued: to try to resolve some of the vagueness and ambiguity inherent in Goffman's initial definition and explanation and to suggest a few ways in which research can be carried out on this phenomenon. A concise definition of role distance was presented and differentiated from role-distance behaviour. Additional distinctions were made between kinds of role distance (major and minor) and between types of role-distance behaviour (false and true). Research in this area is hampered by the time consuming necessity of gaining an intimate knowledge of the culture or subculture where role distance is to be studied and by the fact that the occurrence of role distance is probably relatively infrequent. It was suggested that the best strategy to meet these obstacles was to incorporate this research interest as part of a larger participant observer study. By way of illustration some observations on role distance among jazz musicians were presented within the framework of six modes of role-distance behaviour. They were found to hold both major and minor role-distance attitudes and to make true and false role distance on various occasions.

The importance of role distance and role-distance behaviour for the man of modern mass society is put most picturesquely by Peter Berger. Role distance, properly expressed, promotes 'ecstasy' or 'the act of standing or stepping outside [literally, *ekstasis*] the taken-for-granted routines of society', and ecstasy in turn leads to a transformation of our awareness of everyday life.[20] Not only do we gain a new perspective, but we have exercised our will in the process, thereby informing ourselves that we are not completely the automatons that so much of life seems to suggest.

Contrary to the views of Ford, Young, and Box the arguments advanced in this paper seem to retain something of the voluntarist flavour both for lower-class men and for symbolic interactionist theory.[21] True it is not a totally voluntaristic view; few responsible social scientists would take such a position today. But rather it is a 'soft determinism', to borrow David Matza's phrase, where man is neither completely free nor wholly determined.[22] Our ecstatic man taking role distance is exercising his limited choice by selecting between the perspectives offered him by his various reference groups and by expressing himself through those modes of role-distance behaviour which are personally most appropriate. When two reference-group perspectives clash, and that is often in modern life even among a substantial proportion of the lower classes, he has no alternative but to act in harmony with one or the other or to improvise some sort of intermediate stand. The reference others in the audience will have a significant effect upon his choice. But, in electing to take role distance in order to maintain their support of his self-image, he has simultaneously stepped out of part or all of the other role and rejected the perspective of its reference group.

NOTES

1. Erving Goffman, *Encounters*, Indianapolis, Ind., The Bobbs-Merrill Co., 1961, pp. 85-152.

2. To this author's knowledge, there is only one empirical investigation of role distance: that of Levitin, a case study of a single clothing store 'puller' in Chicago. See T. E. Levitin, 'Role Performance and Role Distance in a Low Status Occupation: The Puller', *Sociological Quarterly*, vol. 5, no. 3 (1964), pp. 251-60. Discursive articles have been produced by Rose Coser, 'Role Distance, Sociological Ambivalence, and Transitional Status Systems', *Amer. J. Sociol.*, vol. 72 (1966), pp. 173-187; Robert A. Stebbins, 'A Note on the Concept of Role Distance', *Amer. J. Sociol.*, vol. 73, no. 2 (1967), pp. 247-250; Julienne Ford, Douglas Young, and Steven Box, 'Functional Autonomy, Role Distance, and Social Class', *Brit. J. Sociol.*, vol. 18, no. 4 (1967), pp. 370-81.

3. Goffman, op. cit., pp. 105-15.

4. As part of the interpretation of role expectations, role distance is an aspect of what Pugh calls the 'role conception'. See Derek Pugh, 'Role Activation Conflict: A Study of Industrial Inspection', *Amer. Sociol. Rev.*, vol. 31, no. 6 (1966), p. 836.

5. Coser introduced the idea of reference group to the role-distance framework (op. cit., p. 174). Stebbins contributed the idea that role distance is really an attitude toward role expectations (op. cit., p. 250).

6. Levitin describes a puller as 'a salesman who stations himself outside the store for which he works, selects potential customers from passing individuals, and persuades them to enter the store, where other salesmen assist them in selecting merchandise' (op. cit., p. 251).

7. Ibid., *passim*. Supporting the contention that Goffman's formulation of role distance is vague and ambiguous, is the observation that a committee of sociologists selected this paper for First Prize in the Manford H. Kuhn Memorial Essay Contest for students held each year by the Midwest Sociological Society in the United States.

8. Stebbins, op. cit.; Coser, op. cit.

9. We rank our identities by their significance to us in general, but in specific ongoing settings we may modify this ranking to some extent as a result of the influences of others present. For a further discussion of these ideas, see George J. McCall and J. L. Simmons, *Identities and Interactions*, New York, The Free Press, 1966, pp. 76-87.

10. Ford, *et al.*, op. cit.

11. Possibly it is true that individual members of lower-class groups receive far more than they interpret rules. What is being suggested here is that they also receive an interpretation of rules which may be quite different from that held by other segments of the community or by other reference groups of which they are members. This, of course, also pertains to the person who is socially mobile; he is receiving interpretations from the group he aspires to join.

12. Roughly four of the ten years were spent performing on a regular professional basis in the historically significant Minneapolis jazz community.

13. The observations made on role distance in Minneapolis are supported by subsequent observations made in St. John's, Newfoundland. Jazz and jazz musicians in this latter city have a very diversified background, developing largely around musicians in a United States Air Force Band stationed there during and after the Second World War. Since these musicians were recruited from all parts of the United States, role distance among today's jazz musicians in St. John's can be said to have a wide base.

14. When the singer is unknown jazz musicians may delay their role-distance behaviour until he shows his talent. A number of cues are used to predict how he will perform, and they influence whether or not a musician takes role distance immediately or waits with guarded suspicion.

15. For a discussion of art versus commercialism in jazz, see Howard S. Becker, 'The Professional Dance Musician and His Audience', *Amer. J. Sociol.*, vol. 57 (1951), pp. 140-1; Robert A. Stebbins, 'The Conflict Between Musical and Commercial Values in the Minneapolis Jazz Community', *Proc. Minnesota Acad. Sci.*, vol. 30, no. 1 (1962), pp. 75-9; William Bruce Cameron, 'Sociological Notes on the Jam Session', *Social Forces*, vol. 33 (1954), p. 182.

16. These expectations are first of all those of nightclub management; but jazz musicians, knowing the state of the market, also expect their colleagues not to be overly fastidious in this respect.

17. Cameron, Merriam and Mack, and Stebbins all express this theme of the greater tolerance for unusual personalities and behaviour found within the jazz community as compared to the larger urban milieu. See Cameron, op. cit., p. 181; A. P.

Merriam and R. W. Mack, 'The Jazz Community', *Social Forces*, vol. 38 (1960), p. 218; Robert A. Stebbins, 'Class, Status, and Power among Jazz and Commercial Musicians', *Sociological Quarterly*, vol. 7, no. 2 (1966), p. 206.

18. Stebbins, 'Class, Status, and Power among Jazz and Commercial Musicians', op. cit., pp. 208-9; Robert A. Stebbins, 'A Theory of the Jazz Community', *Sociological Quarterly*, vol. 9, no. 3 (1968), p. 328.

19. Although this is less true today than at any time in the past, a majority are still to be considered bad readers.

20. Peter L. Berger, *An Invitation to Sociology*, Garden City, N.Y., Doubleday & Co., 1963, pp. 135-7.

21. Ford, *et al.*, op. cit., pp. 377-8.

22. David Matza, *Delinquency and Drift*, New York, John Wiley & Sons, 1964, ch. 1. See also Arnold M. Rose's eight qualifications to cultural determinism in *Human Behavior and Social Processes*, Boston, Houghton Mifflin Co., 1962, pp. 14-15.

12. THE CABDRIVER AND HIS FARE: FACETS OF A FLEETING RELATIONSHIP[1]

FRED DAVIS

Reprinted from *American Journal of Sociology*, Vol. 65 (September, 1959), pp. 158-165, with permission of the author and the *American Journal of Sociology*. Fred Davis is a senior member of the medical sociology program at the University of California, San Francisco. He has written widely in the areas of social psychology, medical sociology, and on youth culture in American society. The selection which follows is based on extensive participant observation while Davis worked for a taxicab company in Chicago.

Even in an urban and highly secularized society such as ours, most service relationships, be they between a professional and his client or a menial and his patron, are characterized by certain constraints on too crass a rendering and consuming of the service.[2] That is to say, in the transaction, numerous interests besides that of simply effecting an economic exchange are customarily attended to and dealt with. The moral reputation of the parties,[3] their respective social standing, and the skill and art with which the service is performed[4] are but a few of the non-instrumental values which are usually incorporated into the whole act.

Tenuous though such constraints may become at times, particularly in large cities where anonymous roles only, segmentally related, occur in great profusion, it is at once evident that for them to exist at all something approximating a community must be present. Practitioners and clients must be sufficiently in communication for any untoward behavior to stand a reasonable chance of becoming known, remarked upon, remembered, and, in extreme cases, made public. And, whereas the exercise of sanctions does not necessarily depend on a community network[5] that is closely integrated (or one in which there is a total identity of values and interests), it does depend on there being some continuity and stability in the relationships that make up the network, so that, at minimum, participants may in the natural course of events be able to identify actions and actors to one another.[6]

It is mainly, though not wholly, from this vantage point that big-city cabdriving as an occupation is here discussed, particularly the relationship between cabdriver and fare and its consequences for the occupational culture.[7] Approximating in certain respects a provincial's caricature of the broad arc of social relations in the metropolis, this relationship affords an extreme instance of the weakening and attenuation of many of the constraints customary in other client-and-patron-oriented services in our society. As such, its analysis can perhaps point up by implication certain of the rarely considered preconditions for practitioner-client relations found in other, more firmly structured, services and professions.

In a large city like Chicago the hiring of a cab by a passenger may be conceived of in much the same way as the random collision of particles in an atomic field. True, there are some sectors of the field in which particles come into more frequent collision than others, for example, downtown at railroad depots, and at the larger neighborhood shopping centers. But this kind of differential activity within the field as a whole provides little basis for predicting the coupling of any two specific particles.

To a much more pronounced degree than is the case in other client-and-patron-oriented services, the occupation of cabdriver provides its practitioners with few, if any, regularities by which to come upon, build up, and maintain a steady clientele. The doctor has his patients, the schoolteacher her pupils, the janitor his tenants, the waitress her regular diners; and in each case server and served remain generally in some continuing or renewable relationship. By contrast, the cabdriver's day consists of a long series of brief contacts with unrelated persons of whom he has no foreknowledge, just as they have none of him, and whom he is not likely to encounter again.

Furthermore, by virtue of the differential spatial, social, and organizational arrangements of the community, it is also likely that the clients of these other practitioners will, in some manner at least, know one another and be related to one another in ways that often transcend the simple circumstance of sharing the same services: they may also be friends, kin, neighbors, or colleagues. For this reason the clientele of most practitioners is something more than an aggregate of discrete individuals; it is, as well, a rudimentary social universe and forum to which the practitioner must address himself in other than purely individual terms.[8]

The cabdriver, by comparison, has no such clientele. He has no fixed business address, and his contacts with

passengers are highly random and singular. To a striking degree he is a practitioner without reputation because those who ride in his cab do not comprise, except perhaps in the most abstract sense, anything approximating a social group. They neither know nor come into contact with one another in other walks of life, and, even if by chance some do, they are unaware of their ever having shared the services of the same anonymous cabdriver. Even were the driver deliberately to set out to build up a small nucleus of steady and favored passengers, the time-space logistics of his job would quickly bring such a scheme to nought. Unable to plot his location in advance or to distribute time according to a schedule, he depends on remaining open to all comers wherever he finds himself. Much more so than other classes of service personnel, cabdrivers are both the fortuitous victims and the beneficiaries of random and highly impersonal market contingencies.

This set of circumstances—fleeting, onetime contact with a heterogeneous aggregate of clients, unknown to one another—exerts an interesting influence on the role of cabdriver.

Unable, either directly through choice or indirectly through location, to select clients, the cabdriver is deprived of even minimal controls. His trade therefore exposes him to a variety of hazards and exigencies which few others, excepting policemen, encounter as frequently; for example: stick-ups, belligerent drunks, women in labor, psychopaths, counterfeiters, and fare-jumpers. Unlike the policeman's, however, his control over them is more fragile.

Nor, incidentally, is the cabdriver's social status or level of occupational skill of much help in inducing constraint in fares. Patently, his status is low, in large part precisely because, unlike the professional and other practitioners commanding prestige, he can hardly be distinguished from his clients in task-relevant competence. Not only is the operation of a motor car a widely possessed skill, but a large proportion of fares have, for example, a very good idea of the best routes to their destination, the rules and practices of the road, and the charges for a trip. Though they are rarely as adept or sophisticated in these matters as the cabdriver, the discrepancy is so small that many think they know the driver's job as well as he does. Periodically, a cabdriver will boldly challenge a difficult and critical passenger to take over the wheel himself. Others, wishing to impress on the fare that theirs is a real service requiring special talent and skill, will resort to darting nimbly in and out of traffic, making neatly executed U-turns and leaping smartly ahead of other cars when the traffic light changes.

Goffman[9] speaks of a category of persons who in some social encounters are treated as if they were not present, whereas in fact they may be indispensable for sustaining the performance. He terms these "nonpersons" and gives as an example a servant at a social gathering. Although cabdrivers are not consistently approached in this way by fares, it happens often enough for it to become a significant theme of their work. Examples are legion. Maresca[10] tells of the chorus girl who made a complete change from street clothing into stage costume as he drove her to her theater. More prosaic instances include the man and wife who, managing to suppress their anger while on the street, launch into a bitter quarrel the moment they are inside the cab; or the well-groomed young couple who after a few minutes roll over on the back seat

to begin petting; or the businessman who loudly discusses details of a questionable business deal. Here the driver is expected to, and usually does, act as if he were merely an extension of the automobile he operates. In actuality, of course, he is acutely aware of what goes on in his cab, and, although his being treated as a non-person implies a degraded status, it also affords him a splendid vantage point from which to witness a rich variety of human schemes and entanglements.

The fleeting nature of the cabdriver's contact with the passenger at the same time also makes for his being approached as someone to whom intimacies can be revealed and opinions forthrightly expressed with little fear of rebuttal, retaliation, or disparagement. And though this status as an accessible person is the product of little more than the turning inside-out of his non-person status—which situation implies neither equality nor respect for his opinion—it nevertheless does afford him glimpses of the private lives of individuals which few in our society, apart from psychiatrists and clergy, are privileged to note as often or in such great variety. It is probably not a mistaken everyday generalization that big-city cabdrivers, on their part, feel less compunction about discussing their own private lives, asking probing questions, and "sounding off" on a great many topics and issues than do others who regularly meet the public, but less fleetingly.[11]

In cabdriving, therefore, propriety, deference, and "face" are, in the nature of the case, weaker than is the case in most other service relationships. This absence contributes to a heightened preoccupation with and focusing on the purely instrumental aspect of the relationship which for the driver is the payment he receives for his services.

This perhaps would be less blatantly the case were it not for the gratuity or tip. For the non-cab-owning company driver, the sum collected in tips amounts roughly to 40 per cent of his earnings. Considering, for example, that in Chicago in the late forties a hard-working cabdriver, who worked for ten hours a day, six days a week, would on the average take home approximately seventy-five dollars a week including tips, the importance of tipping can readily be appreciated. For the family man who drives, tips usually represent the difference between a subsistence and a living wage. Also, tips are, apart from taxes, money "in the clear," in that the driver does not have to divide them with the company as he does his metered collections.[12] Sum for sum, therefore, tips represent greater gain for him than do metered charges.

It would probably be incorrect to hold that pecuniary considerations are the sole ones involved in the cab-driver's attitude toward the tip. Yet in such tip-sensitive occupations as cabdriving, waitering, and bellhopping to suggest[13] that the tip's primary significance is its symbolic value as a token of affection or appreciation for a service well performed would be even wider of the mark. Vindictive caricatures abound among cabdrivers, as they do among waiters, waitresses, and bellhops, of the "polite gentleman" or "kind lady" who with profuse thanks and flawless grace departs from the scene having "stiffed" (failed to tip) them. In occupations where the tip constitutes so large a fraction of the person's earnings, the cash nexus, while admittedly not the only basis upon which patrons are judged, is so important as to relegate other considerations to a secondary place. Will the fare tip or will he "stiff"? How much will he tip? The answers remain in

nearly every instance problematic to the end. Not only is there no sure way of predicting the outcome, but in a culture where the practice of tipping is neither as widespread nor as standardized as in many Continental countries, for example, the driver cannot in many cases even make a guess.

No regular scheme of work can easily tolerate so high a degree of ambiguity and uncertainty in a key contingency. Invariably, attempts are made to fashion ways and means of greater predictability and control; or, failing that, of devising formulas and imagery to bring order and reason in otherwise inscrutable and capricious events. In the course of a long history a rich body of stereotypes, beliefs, and practices[14] has grown up whose function is that of reducing uncertainty, increasing calculability, and providing coherent explanations.

A basic dichotomy running through the cabdriver's concept of his client world is of regular cab users and of non-cab users, the latter referred to as "jerks," "slobs," "yokels," "public transportation types," and a host of other derogatory terms. The former class, though viewed as quite heterogeneous within itself, includes all who customarily choose cabs in preference to other forms of local transportation, are conversant with the cab-passenger role, and, most of all, accept, if only begrudgingly, the practice of tipping. By comparison, the class of non-cab users includes that vast aggregate of persons who resort to cabs only in emergencies or on special occasions, and are prone too often to view the hiring of a cab as simply a more expensive mode of transportation.

Take, for example, the familiar street scene following a sudden downpour or unexpected breakdown in bus service, when a group of individuals cluster about a bus stop, several of whom dart from the curb now and then in hope of hailing a cab. Such persons are almost by definition non-cab users or they would not be found at a bus stop in the rain; nor would they be keeping an eye out for a possible bus. A potential fare in this predicament is to the cabdriver a foul-weather friend, and drivers are on occasion known to hurdle by in spiteful glee, leaving the supplicant standing.

He who hires a cab only on special occasions, frequently to impress others or, perhaps, himself alone, is another familiar kind of non-cab user. Writing of his experiences as a London cabdriver, Hodge relates a by no means uncommon encounter:

But tonight is different. Perhaps the Pools have come up for once. Anyhow, he's got money. He signals me with exaggerated casualness from the cinema entrance. . . . She steps in daintily, the perfect lady, particularly where she puts her feet. As soon as she's safely inside, he whispers the address . . . and adds, as one man of the world to another, "No hurry, driver." Then he dives in with such utter *savoire faire, comme il faut*, and what not, that he trips over the mat and lands face first on the back seat.[15]

Perhaps the most obvious kind of nonuser is the person who, after hailing a cab, will ask the driver some such question as, "How much will it cost to take me to 500 Elm Street?" By this simple inquiry this person stands revealed as one who takes a narrow view of cab travel and from whom not much, if anything, can be expected by way of tip. On the other hand, regular cab users demonstrate in a variety of ways that for them this is a customary and familiar mode of travel. The manner in which they hail a cab, when and how they announce their destination, the ease with which they enter and exit, how they sit—these, and more, though difficult to describe in precise detail, comprise the Gestalt.

There exists among drivers an extensive typology of cab users, the attributes imputed to each type having a certain predictive value, particularly as regards tipping. Some of the more common and sharply delineated types are:

The Sport.—The cabdriver's image of this type combines in one person those attributes of character which he views as ideal. While the Sport's vocation may be any one of many, his status derives more from his extra-vocational activities, e.g., at the race track, prize fights, ball games, popular restaurants, and bars. He is the perennial "young man on the town." Gentlemanly without being aloof, interested without becoming familiar, he also is, of course, never petty. Most of all, his tips are generous, and even on very short rides he will seldom tip less than a quarter. A favorite success story among cabdrivers describes at length and in fine detail the handsome treatment accorded the driver on an all-night tour with a Sport.[16]

The Blowhard.—The Blowhard is a false Sport. While often wearing the outer mantle of the Sport, he lacks the real Sport's casualness, assured manners, and comfortable style. Given to loquaciousness, he boasts and indiscriminately fabricates tales of track winnings, sexual exploits, and the important people he knows. Often holding out the promise of much by way of tip, he seldom lives up to his words.

The Businessman.—These are the staple of the cab trade, particularly for drivers who work by day. Not only are they the most frequently encountered; their habits and preferences are more uniform than those of any other type: the brisk efficiency with which they engage a cab, their purposefulness and disinclination to partake of small talk. Though not often big tippers, they are thought fair. Thus they serve as something of a standard by which the generosity or stinginess of others is judged.

The Lady Shopper.—Although almost as numerous as businessmen, Lady Shoppers are not nearly as well thought of by cabdrivers. The stereotype is a middle-aged woman, fashionably though unattractively dressed, sitting somewhat stiffly at the edge of her seat and wearing a fixed glare which bespeaks her conviction that she is being "taken for a ride." Her major delinquency, however, is undertipping; her preferred coin is a dime, no more or less, regardless of how long or arduous the trip. A forever repeated story is of the annoyed driver, who, after a grueling trip with a Lady Shopper, hands the coin back, telling her, "Lady, keep your lousy dime. You need it more than I do."[17]

Live Ones.[18]—Live Ones are a special category of fare usually encountered by the cabdriver who works by night. They are, as a rule, out-of-town conventioneers or other revelers who tour about in small groups in search of licentious forms of entertainment: cabarets, burlesques, strip-tease bars, pick-up joints, etc. As often as not, they have already had a good deal to drink when the cabdriver meets them, and, being out-of-towners they frequently turn to him for recommendations on where to go. In the late forties an arrangement existed in Chicago whereby some of the more popular Near North Side and West Madison Street "clip joints" rewarded cabdrivers for "steering" Live Ones to their establishments. Some places paid fifty cents "a head"; others a dollar "for the load." As do the many others who regularly cater to Live Ones—e.g., waitresses, bartenders, female bar companions (B-girls), night-club hosts and hostesses, entertainers, prostitutes—cabdrivers often view them as fair game. And while their opportunities for pecuniary exploitation are fewer and more limited than those open, for example, to B-girls and night-club proprietors, many drivers feel less inhibited about padding charges and finagling extras from Live Ones than they do from other fares. Often extravagant in their tips because of high spirits and drink, Live Ones are also frequently careless and forget to tip altogether. Knowing that Live Ones are out to "blow their money" anyway, many drivers believe they are justified in seeing to it that they are not deprived of a small portion.

Although the cab culture's typology of fares stems in a large part from the attempt to order experience, reduce uncertainty, and further calculability of the tip, it is questionable of course as to how accurate or efficient it is. For, as has often been remarked, stereotypes and typologies have a way of imparting a symmetry and regularity to behavior which are, at best, only crudely approximated in reality. Too often it happens, for example, that a fare

tabbed as a Sport turns out to be a Stiff (non-tipper), that a Blowhard matches his words with a generous tip, or that a Lady Shopper will give fifteen or even twenty cents. The persistence of the typology therefore has perhaps as much to do with the cabdriver's a posteriori reconstructions and rationalizations of fare behavior as it does with the typology's predictive efficiency.

To protect and insure themselves against an unfavorable outcome of tipping, many drivers will, depending upon circumstances, employ diverse tactics and stratagems (some more premeditated than others) to increase the amount of tip or to compensate for its loss should it not be forthcoming. Certain of these are listed below. It should be understood however, that in the ordinary instance the driver makes no attempt to manipulate the fare, believing resignedly that in the long run such means bears too little fruit for the effort and risk.

Making change.—Depending on the tariff and the amount handed him, the driver can fumble about in his pockets for change, or make change in such denominations as often to embarrass a fare into giving a larger tip than he had intended. The efficacy of this tactic depends naturally on the determination and staying power of the fare, qualities which many fares are averse to demonstrate, particularly when it comes to small change.

The hard-luck story.—This is usually reserved for young persons and others who, for whatever reason, evidence an insecure posture vis-a-vis the driver. Typically, the hard-luck story consists of a catalogue of economic woes, e.g., long and hard hours of work, poor pay, insulting and unappreciative passengers, etc. In "confiding" these to the fare, the driver pretends to esteem him as an exceptionally sympathetic and intelligent person who, unlike "the others," can appreciate his circumstances and act accordingly. Most drivers, however, view the hard-luck story as an unsavory form of extortion, beneath their dignity. Furthermore, while it may work in some cases, its potential for alienating tips is probably as great as its success at extracting them.

Fictitious charges.—The resort to fictitious and fraudulent charges occurs most commonly in those cases in which the driver feels that he has good reason to believe that the fare will, either through malice or ignorance, not tip and when the fare impresses him as being enough of a non-cab user as not to know when improper charges are being levied. Once, when I complained to a veteran cabdriver about having been "stiffed" by a young couple, newly arrived in Chicago, to whom I had extended such extra services as carrying luggage and opening doors, I was told: "Wise up kid! When you pick up one of these yokels at the Dearborn Station carrying a lot of cheap straw luggage on him, you can bet ninety-nine times out of a hundred that he isn't going to tip you. Not that he's a mean guy or anything, but where he comes from, they never heard of tipping. What I do with a yokel like that is to take him to where he's going, show him what the fare is on the meter, and tell him that it costs fifteen cents extra for each piece of luggage. Now, he doesn't know that there's no charge for hand luggage, but that way I'm sure of getting my tip out of him."

The "psychological" approach.—Possibly attributing more art to their trade than is the case, some drivers are of the opinion that a cab ride can be tailored to fit a passenger in much the same way as can a suit of clothes. One cabdriver, boasting of his success at getting tips, explained: "In this business you've got to use psychology. You've got to make the ride fit the person. Now, take a businessman. He's in a hurry to get someplace and he doesn't want a lot of bullshit and crapping around. With him you've got to keep moving. Do some fancy cutting in and out, give the cab a bit of a jerk when you take off from a light. Not reckless, mind you, but plenty of zip. He likes that.[19] With old people, it's just the opposite. They're more afraid than anyone of getting hurt or killed in a cab. Take it easy with them. Creep along, open doors for them, help them in and out, be real folksy. Call them 'Sir' and 'Ma'am' and they'll soon be calling you 'young man.' They're suckers for this stuff, and they'll loosen up their pocketbooks a little bit."

In the last analysis, neither the driver's typology of fares nor his stratagems further to any marked degree his control of the tip. Paradoxically, were these routinely successful in achieving predictability and control, they would at the same time divest the act of tipping of its most distinguishing characteristics—of its uncertainty, variability, and of the element of revelation in its consummation. It is these—essentially the problematic in human intercourse[20]—which distinguish the tip from the fixed service charge. And though another form of remuneration might in the end provide the cabdriver with a better wage and a more secure livelihood, the abrogation of tipping would also lessen the intellectual play which uncertainty stimulates and without which cabdriving would be for many nothing more than unrelieved drudgery.

That the practice of tipping, however, expressively befits only certain kinds of service relationships and may under slightly altered circumstances easily degenerate into corruption or extortion is demonstrated, ironically enough, by the predicament of some cabdrivers themselves. To give an example: In the garage out of which I worked, nearly everyone connected with maintenance and assignment of cabs expected tips from drivers for performing many of the routine tasks associated with their jobs, such as filling a tank with gas, changing a tire, or adjusting a carburetor. Although they resented it, drivers had little recourse but to tip. Otherwise, they would acquire reputations as "stiffs" and "cheapskates," be kept waiting interminably for repairs, and find that faulty and careless work had been done on their vehicles. Particularly with the dispatcher did the perversion of the tipping system reach extortionate proportions. His power derived from the assignment of cabs; to protect themselves from being assigned "pots" (cabs that would break down in the middle of the day), drivers tipped him fifty cents at the beginning of every week. Since nearly every driver tipped the dispatcher and since there were more drivers than good cabs, a certain number of drivers would still be assigned "pots." Some, wishing to insure doubly against this would then raise the bribe to a dollar and a half a week, causing the others to follow suit in a vicious spiral. If little else, this shows how the tip—as distinguished from the gift, honorarium, inducement, or bribe—depends for its expressive validity on there not being a too close, long sustained, or consequential relationship between the parties to a service transaction.

Among service relationships in our society, that between the big city cabdriver and his fare is, due to the way in which they come into contact with each other, especially subject to structural weakness. The relationship is random, fleeting, unrenewable, and largely devoid of socially integrative features which in other client and patron oriented services help sustain a wider range of constraints and controls between the parties to the transaction. (Much the same might be said of such service occupations as waitress, bellhop and hotel doorman, the chief difference being, however, that these operate from a spatially fixed establishment, which in itself permits of greater identifiability, renewability, and hence constraint in one's relation-

ship to them.) As a result, the tendency of the relationship is to gravitate sharply and in relatively overt fashion toward those few issues having to do with the basic instrumental terms of the exchange. The very fact of tipping, its economic centrality and the cab culture's preoccupation with mastering its many vagaries reflect in large part the regulative imbalance inherent in the relationship.

By inference, this analysis raises anew questions of how to account for the many more formidable and apparently more binding practitioner-client constraints found in other personal service fields, in particular the professions. To such matters as career socialization, colleague groups, socially legitimated skill monopolies, and professional secrecy there might be added a certain safe modicum of continuity, stability, and homogeneity of clientele.[21] For, given too great and random a circulation of clients among practitioners, as might occur for example under certain bureaucratic schemes for providing universal and comprehensive medical service, the danger is that informal social control networks would not come into being in the community, and, as in big-city cabdriving, relations between servers and served would become reputationless, anonymous, and narrowly calculative.

NOTES

1. This article is based largely on notes and observations made by me over a six-month period in 1948 when I worked as a cabdriver for one of the larger taxicab firms in Chicago. I am greatly indebted to Erving Goffman, Everett C. Hughes, and Howard S. Becker for their comments and criticisms.

2. Talcott Parsons, *The Social System* (Glencoe, Ill.: Free Press, 1951), pp. 48-56.

3. Erving Goffman, *The Presentation of Self in Everyday Life* (Edinburgh: University of Edinburgh Social Science Research Centre, 1956), pp. 160-62.

4. Everett C. Hughes, *Men and Their Work* (Glencoe, Ill.: Free Press, 1958), pp. 88-101.

5. Because it better delineates the boundaries and linkages of informal sanctioning groups found in large cities, the term "net-work" is used here to qualify the

more global concept of "community." See Elizabeth Bott, *Family and Social Network* (London: Tavistock, 1957), pp. 58-61.

6. Robert K. Merton, "The Role Set: Problems in Sociological Theory," *British Journal of Sociology*, VIII, No. 2 (June, 1957), 114.

7. Parallel studies of this aspect of occupational culture are: Hughes, *op. cit.*, pp. 42-55; Howard S. Becker, "The Professional Dance Musician and his Audience," *American Journal of Sociology*, LVII (September, 1951), 136-44; Ray Gold, "Janitors versus Tenants: A Status-Income Dilemma," *American Journal of Sociology*, LVII (March, 1952), 486-93.

8. Merton, *op. cit.*, pp. 110-12.

9. Goffman, *op. cit.*, p. 95.

10. James V. Maresca, *My Flag Is Down* (New York: E. P. Dutton & Co., 1945). Essentially the same incident is related by an unidentified cabdriver on the documentary recording of Tony Schwartz, *The New York Taxi Driver* (Columbia Records, ML5309, 1959).

11. Cf. Schwartz, *op. cit.* In fact, these characteristic qualities, with a work-adapted, bitter-sweet admixture of cynicism and sentimentality, comprise the core of the personality widely imputed to cabdrivers by the riding public. Cf. Hughes, *op. cit.*, pp. 23-41.

12. In Chicago in 1948 the company driver's share of the metered sum was 42½ per cent. Since that time the proportion has been increased slightly.

13. Cf. William F. Whyte, *Human Relations in the Restaurant Industry* (New York: McGraw-Hill Book Co., 1948), p. 100.

14. Cf. here and in the section to follow the pertinent remarks of Hughes on "guilty knowledge" developed by those in a service occupation with reference to their clientele. Hughes, *op. cit.*, pp. 81-82.

15. Herbert Hodge, "I Drive a Taxi," *Fact*, No. 22 (January, 1939), pp. 28-29.

16. As in the past, the Sport still serves as something of a hero figure in our culture, particularly among the working classes. A type midway between the Playboy and the Bohemian, his unique appeal rests perhaps on the ease and assurance with which he is pictured as moving between and among social strata, untainted by upper-class snobbishness, middle-class conventionality and lower-class vulgarity. In *The Great Gatsby*, Fitzgerald gives us a penetrative exposition of the myth of the Sport and its undoing at the hands of the class system.

17. The sterotype of women as poor tippers is widely shared by other tip-sensitive occupations. Cf. Frances Donovan, *The Woman Who Waits* (Boston: Badger, 1920).

18. The term "Live Ones" is employed in a variety of pursuits as apparently diverse as retail selling, night-club entertainment, traveling fairs, and panhandling. Generally, it designates persons who are "easy touches," eager to succumb to the oftentimes semifraudulent proposals of the operator. Cf. W. Jack Peterson and Milton A. Maxwell, "The Skid Row Wino," *Social Problems*, V (Spring, 1958), 312.

19. Cf. Hodge, *op. cit.*, p. 17.

20. Cf. Donovan, *op. cit.*, p. 262.

21. William J. Goode, "Community within a Community: The Professions," *American Sociological Review*, XXII, No. 2 (April, 1957), 198-200, and Eliot Freidson, "Varieties of Professional Practice," draft version of unpublished paper, 1959.

IV. THE NATURE OF MOTIVATION

One of social psychology's most vexing and persistent problems is the formulation of an adequate theory of motivation. Various schools of social psychological thought are distinguished by their varying treatments of this problem, and a considerable body of literature has been devoted to it. The dramaturgical orientation employed in this book is especially well-defined by its conceptualization of motivation, and the readings in this section should give the reader a feel for some of the sweeping implications this view holds for the study of human beings.

Traditionally, motives have been construed as internal or external forces that either push or pull action. Internal motivational schemes have viewed social life as pushed along by drives, instincts, or needs such as sex, hunger, self-interest, self-preservation, and some newer glosses such as self-actualization, all of which are presumed to be intrinsic to the human organism. Such "inside" views of motivation have been complemented by various "outside" interpretations. External motivational schemes are to be found in various environmental determinisms: Marxian economics, organizational and structural determinism, and the psychological behaviorism of such writers as B. F. Skinner. In fact, the departmental organization of any university is a veritable handbook of all types of motive schemes. Students attempting to work their ways through this morass are frequently confronted with bewildering arrays of motivational perspectives (often not billed as perspectives at all, but as absolute truth) as they go from biology to psychology to sociology.

All such conceptualizations of motivation, whether of an internal or an external cast, are based on a particular image of human beings. In the case of the conventional motive schemes named above, a human being is assumed to be a passive agent in a world of forces—a mere reactor, pushed or pulled to action by internal or external stimuli. By their assumption of human passivity, such points of view have had to deal with the nature of the agents or forces required to get people acting. Whether the focus is on the internal or external motivation of the actor, stress is placed on the "before-the-act" nature of motives. In other words, some motivational structure (mental, physical, etc.) makes action occur. In each instance, people are regarded as basically neutral, and the focus is on the causative agents responsible for the behavior in question. Such metaphors are likely to be highly deterministic.

Early work in symbolic interactionism stressed the inherent activity of human beings, an emphasis that seemed to negate the passive metaphors of traditional motivational analysis. Dewey, for example, described human beings in the following terms:

> In truth, man acts anyway, he can't help acting. In every fundamental sense, it is false that a man requires a motive to make him do something . . . While a man is awake he will do something, if only to build castles in the air . . . It is absurd to ask what induces a man to activity generally speaking. He is an active being and that is all there is to be said on that score.[1]

Following this emphasis, the dramaturgical orientation stresses not how activity originates but how it is directed. The question that guides most traditional motivational research—"Why do people act?"—must be rephrased if action is already present. Human beings, considered from a dramaturgical perspective, are rationalizers who engage in motive behavior during the course of their ongoing activities. They do so to make their conduct meaningful to those around them and to themselves, and typically they do so retrospectively.

Under what circumstances, then, do motives arise? The prototypical motive situation involves the interruption of some line of action. This interruption takes the form of one person challenging the behavior of another. A primary assumption in this line of analysis is that an individual's attention is typically directed outside oneself until activity is in some way frustrated or disrupted. It is then that the problem of motive arises and must be dealt with, for if challenges to conduct persist, the very basis on which concerted action rests is threatened.

The other side of the problem of motivation has to do with the removal of the challenge posed by the demand for a motive. Here a dramaturgy of motives stresses efficacy. Does the motive presented work? By "work," we mean, is it acted upon? When an audience accepts a motive statement, the challenge is removed and the interaction proceeds. The emphasis here is on dependability. In this sense, a dramaturgical perspec-

1. John Dewey, *Human Nature and Conduct* (New York: Holt, Rinehart & Winston, Inc., 1922) p. 119.

tive blurs the commonsense distinction between "real" or "true" motives and "untrue" or "false" ones. Any motive that is accepted (acted upon) by the audience is socially "real" in the sense that it becomes the basis for future action.

The first two readings that follow represent classic statements in the development of a dramaturgical conception of motivation. Alfred Lindesmith and Anselm Strauss boldly introduced the first in an early edition of their textbook on social psychology. In their view, the process of rationalization is in the forefront of human activities, not pejoratively as some kind of "defense mechanism" but as an essential feature of social life. Previous points of view tended to discount the interpretation of an act given by its participants in favor of motives built on another framework. As the authors suggest, the Freudian interpretation of motives tends to call any account of conduct given by a participant a "rationalization" and to ignore it in favor of a psychoanalytic vocabulary of unconscious motives that only the analyst knows.

As C. Wright Mills points out in the second selection, despite the beguiling temptation to search for the "deeper" reasons why a person does the things he does (a strategy that has brought economic prosperity to many a psychiatrist), there is nothing "deeper" we can infer from verbal phenomena. If language does not "represent" internal states, as Mills cogently argues, we cannot infer physiology from linguistics, for all we can ever hope to find are other linguistic forms.

Mills also introduces the concept of motive "vocabularies," and in fact much of the dramaturgical work done on motives has been stimulated by this ground-breaking article. Here he argues that motives are best understood as socially-approved vocabularies that function rhetorically in an encounter. The existence of various vocabularies makes it clear that one man's reasons are another man's rationalizations. What makes the difference is the relevant universe of discourse (language area) in which the motive is articulated. Biological motives (such as appeals to sickness) won't work if the audience refuses to accept them as adequate grounds for the conduct in question.

Marvin Scott and Stanford Lyman extend the dramaturgical view of motivation in their analysis of the giving and taking of what they refer to as "accounts." They are concerned primarily with categorizing the manner in which human beings utilize linguistic devices to build up, maintain, and sometimes repair social relationships. Excuses are those motive-accounts where an actor admits that the act in question is inappropriate but denies full responsibility for it. Justifications, on the other hand, are those accounts where an individual accepts responsibility for the act but denies the negative quality associated with it. The authors' attempt to catalog some of the more predominant vocabularies of motives and motive situations gives us many illustrations of the pervasiveness of motive appeals in social relationships.

Motives as social constructs differ from time to time and from place to place. In the final selection, Pauline Bart demonstrates in her research on admissions of women to mental hospitals, that whether or not a woman presents herself for psychiatric treatment to begin with, or is referred from a neurology service where she had gone on the assumption that she was physically ill, depends on whether she possesses a psychiatric vocabulary of motives with which to interpret her problems. Lower-class persons are much less likely to use such vocabularies, while middle- and upper-class persons may use them routinely (and in some cases almost exclusively) as ways of understanding their personal and interpersonal difficulties.

SUGGESTED READINGS

Austin, J. L., "A Plea for Excuses," in *Proceedings of the Aristotelian Society*, LVIII, 1956-57.

Burke, Kenneth. *A Grammar Of Motives and A Rhetoric Of Motives*, one-volume edition. (New York: Meridian Books, 1962).

Deutscher, Irwin. *What We Say/What We Do* (Glenview, Illinois: Scott, Foresman and Co., 1973).

Dewey, John. "On Motive," from Dewey, *Human Nature and Conduct* (New York: Holt, 1922), pp. 119-120.

Foote, Nelson. "Identification as the Basis for a Theory of Motivation," in *American Sociological Review*, Vol. 16 (February, 1951) pp. 14-21.

Gerth, Hans and Mills, C. Wright. *Character and Social Structure* (New York: Harcourt, Brace and World, 1953), pp. 112-129.

Louch, A. R., *Explanation and Human Action*, (Berkeley: University of California Press, 1966).

Peters, R. S. *The Concept of Motivation*, (London: Routledge and Kegan Paul, 1958).

Schutz, Alfred. "In-Order-To and Because Motives," in Schutz, *Collected Papers I: The Problem of Social Reality* (The Hague: Martinus Nijoff, 1967).

White, Alan R. *The Philosophy of Action*, (New York: Oxford Paperbacks, 1968).

13.   A SOCIOLOGICAL CONCEPTION OF MOTIVES

ALFRED LINDESMITH AND ANSELM STRAUSS

Reprinted from *Social Psychology*, Revised Edition, by Alfred R. Lindesmith and Anselm L. Strauss. Copyright 1949 © 1956 by Holt Rinehart and Winston, Inc. Reprinted by permission of Holt, Rinehart and Winston, Inc. Alfred Lindesmith is professor of sociology at Indiana University. He has applied symbolic interactionist and dramaturgical social psychology to a variety of practical areas such as deviant behavior, criminology and the social psychology of drug use, and has written one of the first social psychology texts to fully adopt the symbolic interactionist framework. Anselm Strauss is presently engaged in medical research and teaching at the University of California in San Francisco. Since graduating from the University of Chicago in 1945, Strauss has written widely on the sociology of medicine, occupations and professions and the social psychology of self and identity.

RATIONALIZATION AND INTERPRETATION

Both Freudians and Marxists regard as suspect the verbal accounts which individuals give of their own purposes. The Marxists often regard such accounts as a cover-up of real economic motives or as evidence of ignorance. Freudians call them "rationalizations" and heavily discount them. Although they admit that some statements of purpose of a rational and conscious sort are in accord with reality, they are mainly concerned with irrational and unconscious motivations.

A technical definition of rationalization is that it "is a common technique by which the ego keeps certain tendencies repressed. . . . Emphasis upon the acceptable motivation allows the ego to keep the unacceptable repressed, since the selected motives can sufficiently explain the act in question."[1] It should be stressed that the psychoanalytic concept of rationalization implies that when acceptable motives are substituted for unacceptable ones, the individual is actually unable to think of the latter: when he denies their existence he is not being dishonest or "kidding" himself. In popular discourse, the term "rationalization" is usually taken to mean "giving socially acceptable but 'phony' reasons instead of the socially unacceptable but 'real' reasons for one's acts." Thus, a woman quarrels with her husband in the morning and throughout the day deals harshly with her daughter on the grounds that she needs discipline. This conception implies that the real reasons for one's acts are usually known, and hence tends to equate rationalization with dishonest or deluded thinking. It is a common belief that honest people do not rationalize or that they do so infrequently.

Strictly speaking, dishonesty has nothing to do with rationalization, for if a person deliberately makes false statements he is not really rationalizing at all but merely lying. A genuine rationalization is a formulation which the individual himself believes to be true even though it may be labeled self-deception by outside observers. The concept is probably used so widely by the layman because it allows him to disregard or discredit the opinions of other people. As Burke has said:

Much deep sympathy is required to distinguish our reasoning from another's rationalizing. . . . As people tend to round out their orientations verbally, we sometimes show our approval of their verbalizations by the term reasoning and disapproval by the term rationalizing. Thus these words also serve as question begging words.[2]

The central idea of rationalization is that people interpret their behavior and the entire situation in which it occurs either before the act or after the act—or both. Such interpretations sometimes represent distortions, however subtle, of the facts, so that one's face or self-esteem is preserved. Concerning the interpretations that are made after the act, note that they may have to do mainly either with "purpose"—that is, motive—or with "the objective situation" in which the act occurred. For example, suppose that a man shows cowardice when he is attacked or threatened at a party by another man. He may avoid the implications of cowardice, either in his own eyes or those of others, by a rationalization in terms of motives ("I didn't fight because I wanted to wait until a better moment to answer him"); or he may rationalize by interpreting and perhaps distorting the objective situation ("He had a number of friends there and they would have helped him.") Whether the interpretation after the act is chiefly concerned with purpose (of the self or of others) or with the objective situation, distortion or inaccuracy may creep in because of the person's self-involvement. In order to obtain a true or correct interpretation of an event or situation, one thus attempts to rule out all bias stemming from personal involvement and to base interpretation upon genuine evidence, so that if possible all disinterested observers may agree on "the facts." Procedure in courts of law is the classic example of a formalized, if not always successful, attempt to accomplish this. No sharp line can be drawn between a rationalization about a situation and a description of it, for it is difficult to rule out the influence of all personal interest and bias.

In common experience many acts are interpreted more than once. Indeed, if the act is at all important, it may receive several interpretations, sometimes distributed over a number of years. The individual is sometimes aware of this reinterpretation, but more often he is not. . . . It should be apparent that a large proportion of the later interpretation is not at all concerned with the preservation of self-esteem—that is, it is not rationalization in the narrower sense of the word.

Interpretations of an act may also be made before the act takes place. Such preinterpretations include an estimate of the situation in which behavior is called for—including the possible actions, intentions, and expectations held by others—and some judgment of how and why one proposes to act with regard to the situation. The *how* and *why* of the individual's coming act has to do with his purposes; and if he should happen to phrase the matter aloud to someone else and explicitly to himself, he will generally use the word "because" when referring to these purposes. For example, someone is asked what he is going to do next summer and answers "Go to Europe"; when asked "Why?" or "Why next year?," he offers a statement that includes purpose: "Because I am getting to the age where I feel I can spend my savings and because I have never been there." The initial statement of purpose is likely to be somewhat condensed; if he is encouraged the person may present his reasons in more detail. "I have never been there" may be expanded to an explanation that he wants to go to Europe so that he too can talk about Paris when others speak of their experiences there. Purpose, as we are using the term, is synonymous with motive; and Mills[3] has called statements about purpose "motivational statements," whether offered to others or to self, since they are formulated, at least partially, in verbal terms. When others ask us to account for an act, either forthcoming or past, we usually give them a motivational statement so that they may understand the reasons or grounds for our act. The statement that we offer them may be quite false. We may couch it in terms that appear reasonable to them so as to "get by," or we may conceal our real motives for various other reasons.

MOTIVE AND CAUSE

"Motive," as we are using it, should not be confused with "cause." "Motive" has a forward reference in time. It is concerned with purpose and with the anticipated consequences of acts. Causation has a backward reference: it refers to antecedent conditions, i.e., those which immediately precede or accompany an event and which influence it decisively or determine it. Motives are in a sense personal and private, whereas causes are general and public. Causation applies to classes of events, and causal conditions are subject to public verification. The causation of human behavior is poorly understood, but it is known that much more than motives is involved.

Motives appear or are mobilized at the beginning of an act and indeed are a part of the act, since they persist throughout its course. They may, of course, change during the act by becoming more complicated or more simple, they may be joined by other motives, or they may even be replaced, particularly if the act has considerable duration. Hence, in describing any complicated event in a person's life, reference must be made to the purposes the individual had in mind. But in addition, a whole range of other conditions must be taken into account—namely, the motives of others and the material or objective situation. The individual himself is in

a sense the final authority on his own purposes, since he knows better than anyone else what he has in mind, even though the mechanisms of repression or rationalization may have operated to obscure it. With respect to the objective situation, on the other hand, the individual usually cannot be well informed, since it is impossible for anyone to be in possession of all the information concerning his own nervous system, physiological state, and past experiences which might be relevant to an explanation of why he performed a specific act exactly as he did at exactly the time he did.

Before an action is completed the purposes of the behavior are likely to loom large to the person engaged in it. After the action is completed, second thoughts often occur and he may then wonder whether his reasons were as simple as they seemed. When asked to account for past actions, persons often give common-sense, causal explanations rather than motivational ones. For example, a husband may scold his wife at the breakfast table, believing at the time that he is scolding her because she has spoiled the coffee. He may later explain the quarrel by saying that neither he nor his wife had had enough sleep the previous night.

Since motives appear at the beginning of acts or in preparation for action, and since each individual feels his own motives in a direct way, it is easy to understand how they have come to be viewed as causes of the behavior of which they are a part, and indeed as "forces" which "make" the behavior occur. It was a common practice in the earlier years of this century for sociologists to explain institutional and other cultural behavior in terms of the operation of wishes, desires, interests, needs, and other "social forces." However, the idea of causation no longer includes the conception of force in this sense at all. There are many different ideas of causation in the philosophy of science, but on this particular point there is rather general agreement.

The scientific concept of causation is, of course, a general feature of many scientific fields in which no problem of motivation exists. Indeed, in view of the instability and variability of human purposes, and in view of the fact that purposes are really part of behavior rather than mysterious forces lying behind it, motives are not so much explanations of behavior as they are behavioral problems, themselves requiring analysis and explanation. From this viewpoint, the problem of explaining such behavior as stealing, for example, includes the problem of accounting for the fact that people steal from so many different motives.

An example will help to clarify some of the points we have been making. Let us suppose that a company of American soldiers is ordered to advance in the face of strong enemy fire and that the order is obeyed. If we then try to answer the question of why the company advanced in terms of the motives of each soldier we become involved in a bewildering network. Perhaps no two soldiers have advanced for precisely the same reasons, and perhaps they may have advanced for almost opposite reasons. The problem of accounting for the fact that the company actually moves as a unit seems insoluble from this perspective.

From the standpoint of the Army general who issued the order which was passed on till it finally reached the company commander, the individual motives of the men are of little significance in the total picture and are ignored at the moment of action. As the only requirement is that troops obey the orders and fight effectively, it is sufficient for the commander to know that motivations to advance exist in

troops. It may be said of a reasonably well-organized and efficient army that it is ultimately the individual soldier's private and personal problem to seek and hold onto whatever rationalization he can find to help him do what he has to do in any case, although indoctrination procedures probably help him. Max Lerner made this point on the group level in a speech at the time of Hitler's rise when he asserted that the Balkan nations would surely have to surrender to the Nazis and that the only problem was what rationalization would be found for the surrender.

These examples point up the truism that people and groups may do the same things for different reasons and different things for the same reason. Since causal generalizations are based upon elements that are common to various instances of a given form of behavior, in problems like the above these generalizations cannot be stated in terms of motive. Psychoanalysts have attempted to meet this difficulty by looking for uniformity and common motivations on the unconscious level. What is suggested here is that the matter may be dealt with in another way, provided that one conceives of motive as something other than a specific determinant of behavior. It may be conceded that most significant human behavior is and must be motivated, but this is a far cry from contending that any given form of behavior must always be motivated in the same way.

The conception developed here may be further clarified by reemphasizing the fact that gross organic needs ordinarily do not lead to anything but random or restless behavior, and that they merely prepare the organism to respond when an appropriate situation appears and thus to learn rapidly. The ease with which the newly born infant is taught to nurse is a case in point. Organic needs do not automatically trigger behavioral responses which satisfy these needs. . . . Organic needs become motivational, as a rule, only after the organism has learned to interpret them in certain ways and to associate certain objects or modes of behavior with the satisfaction of the need. In other words, physiological states in human beings give rise to purposes when they are harnessed in conceptual schemes. When this has happened, the drive-satisfying behavior may vary with the intensity of the physiological need (as it does within limits in the case of hunger) and may thus appear to depend directly on it, although this may not be the case. A physiological state of disequilibrium without direction or goals is not a motive—it is merely a biological condition.

UNDERSTANDING AND EXPLANATION

Rejecting motives as an explanatory concept—that is, as causes—does not mean that it is unimportant to know the purposes which people have in mind. Knowledge of the motivation of other people and of ourselves is indeed . . . a constant necessity in all social intercourse. Through such knowledge we are enabled to acquire insight into the actions of others, to identify with them, and to put ourselves in their places imaginatively or to "take their roles". . . . An individual's motives are part of the way he thinks, and as such cannot be omitted from any adequate description of his behavior. Neither can a fruitful depiction of interaction between persons be given unless we take into account the purposes of the actors and their assessment of each other's purposes.

The scientific analysis of human conduct should begin by gathering information on motives, but it cannot end there. If grasp of motives provided a complete explanation of behavior, artists and creative writers would be the best social scientists: for it is they who teach us most about understanding those who differ greatly from us in conception of the world and in organization of life. "Understanding," in this context, means something other than scientific understanding. It refers to what happens when we read a great realistic novel, see an effective play or motion picture, or become intimately acquainted with another person. Through such understanding we learn to see through another's eyes, to appreciate another's values and motives, and to identify with him. Although we cannot explain the scientific "why" of the other's behavior on such a basis, through our intimate understanding of his background, experiences, knowledge, biases, and rationalizations we are able to anticipate, at least in general, how he will act. This sort of prediction of the actions of individuals is more or less intuitive in nature. The person who is asked to explain why he is so sure that his friend will respond to a given situation in a particular way, answers in terms of the intimacy of his acquaintance with him. "Acquaintance with," or understanding, and "knowledge about," or explanation, involve two different kinds of knowing, as William James has pointed out.

The explanation formulated on the basis of scientific analysis is of a special character. Ideally, a relationship between events or classes of events is described in some form such as this: If an event of Type A occurs under certain conditions—a,b,c,d, etc.—then, and only then, will an event of Type B occur. Thus, if a mosquito of a certain type bites a human being under certain specified conditions, then, and then only, will the bitten person contract malaria. To use an illustration in the field of human behavior: . . . [I]f a person takes or is given opiates regularly, experiences and recognizes the withdrawal distress that comes when he stops taking the drug, and uses the drug after this recognition, only then does he become a drug addict. Sequences such as this are causal sequences. It will be noted that popular motivational explanations do not take this form. If a hundred thieves are asked to give their motives for stealing, each will give a different account, so that no single statement can be made about the motives of all of them.

Purposes, or motives . . . are formulated. This means that they arise in communication and are either partially or fully stated in words. When thought of in this manner, motives do not exist in a mysterious nonverbal realm such as "the unconscious." As Mills says, "Motives are of no value apart from delimited societal situations for which they are appropriate vocabularies. They must be situated. . . . Motives vary in content and character with historical epochs and societal structures."[4]

SOCIAL SOURCES OF INDIVIDUAL MOTIVATION

An individual's motives generally appear to him as peculiarly personal and private, although many of them are in fact learned from others and are in a sense furnished him tailor-made by the society or the groups in which he lives.

When one joins a group of long standing, he finds that the proper codes of conduct, including the ends and means of group activity, have been spelled out in considerable detail. They may even be formalized and embodied in written documents such as the Hippocratic Oath, an oath of allegiance, or in constitutions, contracts, codes, and the like. When persons leave groups and join new ones, they must learn new motivations. As Weber has pointed out in connection with work, for instance, "The motives which induce people to work vary with different social classes. . . . When a man changes rank, he switches from one set of motives to another."[5] Even when persons live rather stable lives, changing their group memberships very little, some of their motives nevertheless change with advancing age according to prevailing social definitions. Although the physical processes of aging are much alike in all cultures, the motivational adaptations to them are endlessly varied.

An individual cannot express purposes or rationalize behavior in terms which he has not learned. One cannot motivate a man to act by using terms outside his comprehension: one must appeal to purposes which he understands and which make sense to him. Conversely, it is incorrect to impute rationalizations to an individual when these involve motivational terms which he does not possess. Nevertheless, such imputation is a common recourse when it is found to be impossible to assess behavior in one's own terms. There is almost always a tendency to explain other people's behavior in terms of one's own vocabulary of motives. This form of incorrect assessment is called "projection" and is seen in a crude form in most romantic historical novels. The characters, supposedly living a century or two ago, are made to rationalize their activities according to the symbols of the twentieth century. Likewise, in American movies, heroes and heroines dress in the clothes of other eras but act as if their incentives were those of twentieth-century Americans. But the projection of motives may take more subtle forms. The disgust we feel with Russians when they interpret a purely "philanthropic" move on our part as "imperialism," or vice versa when we impute motives of "nationalism" to them while they maintain that they are acting in the interests of the working class, are both instances of the projection of motives. The tendency for American radicals to suspect plots behind the acts of upper-class persons, and the attribution of purely selfish economic motives to labor-union leaders by employers, are parallel examples on the local American scene.

The fallacious common-sense imputation of motives has its academic counterpart. For example, psychoanalysts have reinterpreted the private lives of famous persons such as St. Augustine and Leonardo da Vinci in terms of twentieth-century sexual symbols. They thus ignore the fact that these historical characters viewed the conduct of others and themselves in very different terms than do people of our own era. Such scholarly interpretation is equivalent to translating other rationalizations into our own. Since human beings are interested in the lives of past generations, such translating is inevitable. The only corrective to a superficial handling of the past is an adequate understanding of the period under consideration through exhaustive examination of historical sources. The accuracy of the account should rest upon an understanding of the actual symbols available to the historical personages; it should not rest upon the degree to which their motives appear plausible to us in the light of our own motives at the present time.

NOTES

1. In F. Alexander and H. Ross (eds), *Dynamic Psychiatry*, University of Chicago Press, 1952, "Development of the Fundamental Concepts of Psychoanalysis," p. 13.

2. K. Burke, *Permanence and Change*, New York: New Republic, 1936, pp. 19-20.

3. C. W. Mills, "Situated Actions and Vocabularies of Motive," *Am. Soc. Rev.*, 5 (1940): 904-913.

4. *Ibid.*, p. 913.

5. M. Weber, paraphrased by K. Mannheim in *Ideolgoy and Utopia*, Harcourt, Brace, 1936, pp. 316-317.

14. SITUATED ACTIONS AND VOCABULARIES OF MOTIVE

C. WRIGHT MILLS

Reprinted from C. Wright Mills, in American Sociological Review, Vol. V. (December 1940), pp. 904-913, with permission of the author and the American Sociological Review. Before his premature death in 1962 at the age of 46, C. Wright Mills was one of the most prolific researchers and writers in American sociology. His early work dealt with attempts to link social psychology with broader structural and institutional concerns. During this period he wrote Character and Social Structure with Hans Gerth after having completed a doctoral dissertation on the relationship between sociology and pragmatism. His later work dealt primarily with power, ideology, and political sociology. He was one of the first to apply dramaturgical thinking to traditional sociological concerns.

The major reorientation of recent theory and observation in sociology of language emerged with the overthrow of the Wundtian notion that language has as its function the "expression" of prior elements within the individual. The postulate underlying modern study of language is the simple one that we must approach linguistic behavior, not by referring it to private states in individuals, but by observing its social function of coordinating diverse action. Rather than expressing something which is prior and in the person, language is taken by other persons as an indicator of future actions.[1]

Within this perspective there are suggestions concerning problems of motivation. It is the purpose of this paper to outline an analytic model for the explanation of motives which is based on a sociological theory of language and a sociological psychology.[2]

As over against the inferential conception of motives as subjective "springs" of action, motives may be considered as typical vocabularies having ascertainable functions in delimited societal situations. Human actors do vocalize and impute motives to themselves and to others. To explain behavior by referring it to an inferred and abstract "motive" is one thing. To analyze the observable lingual mechanisms of motive imputation and avowal as they function in conduct is

quite another. Rather than fixed elements "in" an individual, motives are the terms with which interpretation of conduct by social actors proceeds. This imputation and avowal of motives by actors are social phenomena to be explained. The differing reasons men give for their actions are not themselves without reasons.

First, we must demarcate the general conditions under which such motive imputation and avowal seem to occur.[3] Next, we must give a characterization of motive in denotable terms and an explanatory paradigm of why certain motives are verbalized rather than others. Then, we must indicate mechanisms of the linkage of vocabularies of motive to systems of action. What we want is an analysis of the integrating, controlling, and specifying function a certain type of speech fulfils in socially situated actions.

The generic situation in which imputation and avowal of motives arise involves, first the social conduct or the (stated) programs of languaged creatures, i.e., programs and actions oriented with reference to the actions and talk of others; second, the avowal and imputation of motives is concomitant with the speech form known as the "question." Situations back of questions typically involve alternative or unexpected programs or actions which phases analytically denote "crises."[4] The question is distinguished in that it usually elicits another *verbal* action, not a motor response. The question is an element in *conversation*. Conversation may be concerned with the factual features of a situation as they are seen or believed to be or it may seek to integrate and promote a set of diverse social actions with reference to the situation and its normative pattern of expectations. It is in this latter assent and dissent phase of conversation that persuasive and dissuasive speech and vocabulary arise. For men live in immediate acts of experience and their attentions are directed outside themselves until acts are in some way frustrated. It is then that awareness of self and of motive occur. The "question" is a lingual index of such conditions. The avowal and imputation of motives are features of such conversations as arise in "question" situations.

Motives are imputed or avowed as answers to questions interrupting acts or programs. Motives are words. Generically, to what do they refer? They do not denote any elements "in" individuals. They stand for anticipated situational consequences of questioned conduct. Intention or purpose (stated as a "program") *is* awareness of anticipated consequence; motives are names for consequential situations, and surrogates for actions leading to them. Behind questions are possible alternative actions with their terminal consequences. "Our introspective words for motives are rough, shorthand descriptions for certain typical patterns of discrepant and conflicting stimuli."[5]

The model of purposive conduct associated with Dewey's name may briefly be stated. Individuals confronted with "alternative acts" perform one or the other of them on the basis of the differential consequences which they anticipate. This nakedly utilitarian schema is inadequate because: (a) the "alternative acts" of *social* conduct "appear" most often in lingual form, as a question, stated by one's self or by another; (b) it is more adequate to say that individuals act in terms of anticipation of *named* consequences.

Among such names and in some technologically oriented lines of action there may appear such terms as "useful," "practical," "serviceable," etc., terms so "ultimate" to the pragmatists, and also to certain sectors of the American population in these delimited situations. However, there are other areas of population with different vocabularies of motives. The choice of lines of action is accompanied by representations, and selection among them, of their situational termini. Men discern situations with particular vocabularies, and it is in terms of some delimited vocabulary that they anticipate consequences of conduct.[6] Stable vocabularies of motives link anticipated consequences and specific actions. There is no need to invoke "psychological" terms like "desire" or "wish" as explanatory, since they themselves must be explained socially.[7] Anticipation is a subvocal or overt naming of terminal phases and/or social consequences of conduct. When an individual names consequences, he elicits the behaviors for which the name is a redintegrative cue. In a *societal* situation, implicit in the names of consequences is the social dimension of motives. Through such vocabularies, types of societal controls operate. Also, the terms in which the question is asked often will contain both alternatives: "Love or Duty?", "Business or Pleasure?" Institutionally different situations have different *vocabularies of motive* appropriate to their respective behaviors.

This sociological conception of motives as relatively stable lingual phases of delimited situations is quite consistent with Mead's program to approach conduct socially and from the outside. It keeps clearly in mind that "both motives and actions very often originate not from within but from the situation in which individuals find themselves. . . ."[8] It translates the question of "why"[9] into a "how" that is answerable in terms of a situation and its typical vocabulary of motives, i.e., those which conventionally accompany that type situation and function as cues and justifications for normative actions in it.

It has been indicated that the question is usually an index to the avowal and imputation of motives. Max Weber defines motive as a complex of meaning, which appears to the actor himself or to the observer to be an adequate ground for his conduct.[10] The aspect of motive which this conception grasps is its intrinsically social character. A satisfactory or adequate motive is one that satisfies the questioners of an act or program whether it be the other's or the actor's. As a word, *a motive tends to be one which is to the actor and to the other members of a situation an unquestioned answer to questions concerning social and lingual conduct.* A stable motive is an ultimate in justificatory conversation. The words which in a type situation will fulfil this function are circumscribed by the vocabulary of motives acceptable for such situations. Motives are accepted justifications for present, future, or past programs or acts.

To term them justification is *not* to deny their efficacy. Often anticipations of acceptable justifications will control conduct. ("If I did this, what could I say? What would they say?") Decisions may be, wholly or in part, delimited by answers to such queries.

A man may begin an act for one mo-

tive. In the course of it, he may adopt an ancillary motive. This does not mean that the second apologetic motive is inefficacious. The vocalized expectation of an act, its "reason," is not only a mediating condition of the act but it is a proximate and controlling condition for which the term "cause" is not inappropriate. It may strengthen the act of the actor. It may win new allies for his act.

When they appeal to others involved in one's act, motives are strategies of action. In many social actions, others must agree, tacitly or explicitly. Thus, acts often will be abandoned if no reason can be found that others will accept. Diplomacy in choice of motive often controls the diplomat. Diplomatic choice of motive is part of the attempt to motivate acts for other members in a situation. Such pronounced motives undo snarls and integrate social actions. Such diplomacy does not necessarily imply intentional lies. It merely indicates that an appropriate vocabulary of motives will be utilized—that they are conditions for certain lines of conduct.[11]

When an agent vocalizes or imputes motives, he is not trying to *describe* his experienced social action. He is not merely stating "reasons." He is influencing others—and himself. Often he is finding new "reasons" which will mediate action. Thus, we need not treat an action as discrepant from "its" verbalization, for in many cases, the verbalization is a new act. In such cases, there is not a discrepancy between an act and "its" verbalization, but a difference between two disparate actions, motor-social and verbal.[12] This additional (or *"ex post facto"*) lingualization may involve appeal to a vocabulary of motives associated with a norm with which both members of the situation are in agreement. As such, it is an integrative factor in *future* phases of the original social action or in other acts. By resolving conflicts, motives are efficacious. Often, if "reasons" were not given, an act would not occur, nor would diverse actions be integrated. Motives are common grounds for mediated behaviors.

Perry summarily states the Freudian view of motives "as the view that the real motives of conduct are those which we are ashamed to admit either to ourselves or to others."[13] One can cover the facts by merely saying that scruples (i.e., *moral* vocabularies of motive) are often afficacious and that men will alter and deter their acts in terms of such motives. One of the components of a "generalized other," as a mechanism of societal control, is vocabularies of acceptable motives. For example, a businessman joins the Rotary Club and proclaims its public-spirited vocabulary.[14] If this man cannot act out business conduct without so doing, it follows that this vocabulary of motives is an important factor in his behavior.[15] The long acting out of a role, with its appropriate motives, will often induce a man to become what at first he merely sought to appear. Shifts in the vocabularies of motive that are utilized later by an individual disclose an important aspect of various integrations of his actions with concomitantly various groups.

The motives actually used in justifying or criticizing an act definitely link it to situations, integrate one man's action with another's, and line up conduct with norms. The societally sustained motive-surrogates of situations are both constraints and inducements. It is a hypothesis worthy and capable of test that typal vocabularies of motives for different situations are significant determinants of conduct. As lingual segments of social action, motives orient actions by enabling discrimination between their objects. Adjectives such as "good," "pleasant," and "bad" promote action or deter it. When they constitute components of a vocabulary of motives, i.e., are typical and relatively unquestioned accompaniments of typal situations, such words often function as directives and incentives by virtue of their being the judgments of others as anticipated by the actor. In this sense motives are "social instruments, i.e., data by modifying which the agent will be able to influence [himself or others]."[16] The "control" of others is not usually direct but rather through manipulation of a field of objects. We influence a man by naming his acts or imputing motives to them—or to "him." The motives accompanying institutions of war, e.g., are not "the causes" of war, but they do promote continued integrated participation, and they vary from one war to the next. Working vocabularies of motive have careers that are woven through changing institutional fabrics.

Genetically, motives are imputed by others before they are avowed by self. The mother controls the child: "Do not do that, it is greedy." Not only does the child learn what to do, what not to do, but he is given standardized motives which promote prescribed actions and dissuade those proscribed. Along with rules and norms of action for various situations, we learn vocabularies of motives appropriate to them. These are the motives we shall use, since they are a part of our language and components of our behavior.

The quest for "real motives" supposititiously set against "mere rationalization" is often informed by a metaphysical view that the "real" motives are in some way biological. Accompanying such quests for something more real and back of rationalization is the view held by many sociologists that language is an external manifestation or concomitant of something prior, more genuine, and "deep" in the individual. "Real attitudes" versus "mere verbalization" or "opinion" implies that at best we only infer from his language what "really" is the individual's attitude or motive.

Now what *could we possibly* so infer? Of precisely *what* is verbalization symptomatic? We cannot *infer* physiological processes from lingual phenomena. All we can infer and empirically check[17] is another verbalization of the agent's which we believe was orienting and controlling behavior at the time the act was performed. The only social items that can "lie deeper" are other lingual forms.[18] The "Real Attitude or Motive" is not something different in kind from the verbalization or the "opinion." They turn out to be only relatively and temporally different.

The phrase "unconscious motive" is also unfortunate. All it can mean is that a motive is not explicitly vocalized, but there is no need to infer unconscious motives from such situations and then posit them in individuals as elements. The phrase is informed by persistence of the unnecessary and unsubstantiated notion that "all action has a motive," and it is promoted by the observation of gaps in the relatively frequent verbalization in everyday situations. The facts to which this phrase is supposedly addressed are covered by the statements that men do not always explicitly articulate motives, and that *all* actions do not pivot around language. I have already indicated the conditions under which motives are typically avowed and imputed.

Within the perspective under consideration, the verbalized motive is not used as an index of something in the individual but as a basis of inference for a typical vocabulary of motives of a situated action. When we ask for the "real attitude" rather than the "opinion," for the "real motive" rather than the "rationalization," all we can meaningfully be asking for is the controlling speech form which was incipiently or overtly presented in the performed act or series of acts. There is no way to plumb behind verbalization into an individual and directly check our motive-mongering, but there is an empirical way in which we can guide and limit, in given historical situations, investigations of motives. That is by the construction of typal vocabularies of motives that are extant in types of situations and actions. Imputation of motives may be controlled by reference to the typical constellation of motives which are observed to be societally linked with classes of situated actions. Some of the "real" motives that have been imputed to actors were not even known to them. As I see it, motives are circumscribed by the vocabulary of the actor. The only source for a terminology of motives is the vocabularies of motives actually and usually verbalized by actors in specific situations.

Individualistic, sexual, hedonistic, and pecuniary vocabularies of motives are apparently now dominant in many sectors of twentieth-century urban America. Under such an ethos, verbalization of alternative conduct in these terms is least likely to be challenged among dominant groups. In this milieu, individuals are skeptical of Rockefeller's avowed religious motives for his business conduct because such motives are not *now* terms of the vocabulary conventionally and prominently accompanying situations of business enterprise. A medieval monk writes that he gave food to a poor but pretty woman because it was "for the glory of God and the eternal salvation of his soul." Why do we tend to question him and impute sexual motives? Because sex is an influential and widespread motive in our society and time. Religious vocabularies of explanation and of motives are now on the wane. In a society in which religious motives have been debunked on a rather wide scale, certain thinkers are skeptical of those who ubiquitously proclaim them. Religious motives have lapsed from selected portions of modern populations and other motives have become "ultimate" and operative. But from the monasteries of medieval Europe we have no evidence that religious vocabularies were not operative in many situations.

A labor leader says he performs a certain act because he wants to get higher standards of living for the workers. A businessman says that this is rationalization, or a lie; that it is really because he wants more money for himself from the workers. A radical says a college professor will not engage in radical movements because he is afraid for his job, and besides, is a "reactionary." The college professor says it is because he just likes to find out how things work. What is reason for one man is rationalization for another. The variable is the accepted vocabulary of motives, the ultimates of discourse, of each man's dominant group about whose opinion he cares. *Determination of such groups, their location and character, would enable delimitation and methodological control of assignment of motives for specific acts.*

Stress on this idea will lead us to investigations of the compartmentalization of operative motives in personalities according to situation and the general types and conditions of vocabularies of motives in various types of societies. The motivational

structures of individuals and the patterns of their purposes are relative to societal frames. We might, e.g., study motives along stratified or occupational lines. Max Weber has observed:[19]

... that in a free society the motives which induce people to work vary with ... different social classes. ... There is normally a graduated scale of motives by which men from different social classes are driven to work. When a man changes ranks, he switches from one set of motives to another.

The lingual ties which hold them together react on persons to constitute frameworks of disposition and motive. Recently, Talcott Parsons has indicated, by reference to differences in actions in the professions and in business, that one cannot leap from "economic analysis to ultimate motivations; the institutional patterns *always* constitute one crucial element of the problem."[20] It is my suggestion that we may analyze, index, and gauge this element by focusing upon those specific verbal appendages of variant institutionalized actions which have been referred to as vocabularies of motive.

In folk societies, the constellations of motives connected with various sectors of behavior would tend to be typically stable and remain associated only with their sector. In typically primary, sacred, and rural societies, the motives of persons would be regularly compartmentalized. Vocabularies of motives ordered to different situations stabilize and guide behavior and expectation of the reactions of others. In their appropriate situations, verbalized motives are not typically questioned.[21] In secondary, secular, and urban structures, varying and competing vocabularies of motives operate coterminously and the situations to which they are appropriate are not clearly demarcated. Motives once unquestioned for defined situations are now questioned. Various motives can release similar acts in a given situation. Hence, variously situated persons are confused and guess which motive "activated" the person. Such questioning has resulted intellectually in such movements as psychoanalysis with its dogma of rationalization and its systematic motive-mongering. Such intellectual phenomena are underlaid by split and conflicting sections of an individuated society which is characterized by the existence of competing vocabularies of motive. Intricate constellations of motives, for example, are components of business enterprise in America. Such patterns have encroached on the old style vocabulary of the virtuous relation of men and women: duty, love, kindness. Among certain classes, the romantic, virtuous, and pecuniary motives are confused. The asking of the question: "Marriage for love or money?" is significant, for the pecuniary is now a constant and almost ubiquitous motive, a common denominator of many others.[22]

Back of "mixed motives" and "motivational conflicts" are competing or discrepant situational patterns and their respective vocabularies of motive. With shifting and interstitial situations, each of several alternatives may belong to disparate systems of action which have differing vocabularies of motives appropriate to them. Such conflicts manifest vocabulary patterns that have overlapped in a marginal individual and are not easily compartmentalized in clear-cut situations.

Besides giving promise of explaining an area of lingual and societal fact, a further advantage of this view of motives is that with it we should be able to give sociological accounts of other theories (terminologies) of motivation. This is a task for sociology of knowl-edge. Here I can refer only to a few theories. I have already referred to the Freudian terminology of motives. It is apparent that these motives are those of an upper bourgeois patriarchal group with strong sexual and individualistic orientation. When introspecting on the couches of Freud, patients used the only vocabulary of motives they knew; Freud got his hunch and guided further talk. Mittenzwey has dealt with similar points at length.[23] Widely diffused in a postwar epoch, psychoanalysis was never popular in France where control of sexual behavior is not puritanical.[24] To converted individuals who have become accustomed to the psychoanalytic terminology of motives, all others seem self-deceptive.[25]

In like manner, to many believers in Marxism's terminology of power, struggle, and economic motives, all others, including Freud's, are due to hypocrisy or ignorance. An individual who has assimilated thoroughly only business congeries of motives will attempt to apply these motives to all situations, home and wife included. It should be noted that the business terminology of motives has its intellectual articulation, even as psychoanalysis and Marxism have.

It is significant that since the Socratic period many "theories of motivation" have been linked with ethical and religious terminologies. Motive is that in man which leads him to do good or evil. Under the aegis of religious institutions, men use vocabularies of moral motives: they call acts and programs "good" and "bad," and impute these qualities to the soul. Such lingual behavior is part of the process of social control. Institutional practices and their vocabularies of motive exercise control over delimited ranges of possible situations. One could make a typal catalog of religious motives from widely read religious texts, and test its explanatory power in various denominations and sects.[26]

In many situations of contemporary America, conduct is controlled and integrated by *hedonistic* language. For large population sectors in certain situations, pleasure and pain are now unquestioned motives. For given periods and societies, these situations should be empirically determined. Pleasure and pain should not be reified and imputed to human nature as underlying principles of all action. Note that hedonism as a psychological and an ethical doctrine gained impetus in the modern world at about the time when older moral-religious motives were being debunked and simply discarded by "middle class' thinkers. Back of the hedonistic terminology lay an emergent social pattern and a new vocabulary of motives. The shift of unchallenged motives which gripped the communities of Europe was climaxed when, in reconciliation, the older religious and the hedonistic terminologies were identified: the "good" is the "pleasant." The conditioning situation was similar in the Hellenistic world with the hedonism of the Cyrenaics and Epicureans.

What is needed is to take all these terminologies of motive and locate them as *vocabularies* of motive in historic epochs and specified situations. Motives are of no value apart from the delimited societal situations for which they are the appropriate vocabularies. They must be situated. At best, socially unlocated *terminologies* of motives represent unfinished attempts to block out social areas of motive imputation and avowal. Motives vary in content and character with historical epochs and societal structures.

Rather than interpreting actions and language as external manifestations of subjective and deeper lying elements in individuals, the research task is the locating of particular types of action within typal frames of normative actions and socially situated clusters of motive. There is no explanatory value in subsuming various vocabularies of motives under some terminology or list. Such procedure merely confuses the task of explaining specific cases. The languages of situations as given must be considered a valuable portion of the data to be interpreted and related to their conditions. To simplify these vocabularies of motive into a socially abstracted terminology is to destroy the legitimate use of motive in the explanation of social actions.

NOTES

1. See C. Wright Mills, "Bibliographical Appendices," Section I, 4: "Sociology of Language" in *Contemporary Social Theory*, ed. by Barnes, Becker & Becker, New York, 1940.

2. See G. H. Mead, "Social Psychology as Counterpart of Physiological Psychology," *Psychol. Bul.*, VI: 401-408, 1909; Karl Mannheim, *Man and Society in an Age of Reconstruction*, New York, 1940; L. V. Wiese-Howard Becker, *Systematic Sociology*, part I, New York, 1932; J. Dewey, "All psychology is either biological or social psychology," *Psychol. Rev.*, vol. 24:276.

3. The importance of this initial task for research is clear. Most researches on the verbal level merely ask abstract questions of individuals, but if we can tentatively delimit the situations in which certain motives *may* be verbalized, we can use that delimitation in the construction of situational questions, and we shall be testing deductions from our theory.

4. On the "question" and "conversation," see G. A. DeLaguna, *Speech: Its Function and Development*, 37 (and index), New Haven, 1927. For motives in crises, see J. M. Williams, *The Foundations of Social Science*, 435 ff., New York, 1920.

5. K. Burke, *Permanence and Change*,

45, New York, 1936. I am indebted to this look for several leads which are systematized into the present statement.

6. See such experiments as C. N. Rexroad's "Verbalization in Multiple Choice Reactions," *Psychol. Rev.*, Vol. 33:458, 1926.

7. Cf. J. Dewey, "Theory of Valuation," *Int. Ency. of Unified Science*, New York, 1939.

8. K. Mannheim, *Man and Society*, 249, London, 1940.

9. Conventionally answerable by reference to "subjective factors" within individuals. R. M. MacIver, "The Modes of the Question Why," *J. of Soc. Phil.*, April, 1940. Cf. also his "The Imputation of Motives," *Amer. J. Sociol.*, July 1940.

10. *Wirtschaft und Gesellschaft*, 5, Tubingen, 1922, " 'Motiv' heisst ein Sinnzusammenhang, Welcher dem Handelnden selbst oder dem Beobachtenden als sinnhafter 'Grund' eines Verhaltens in dem Grade heissen, als die Beziehung seiner Bestandteile von uns nach den durchschnittlichen Denk- und Gefühlsegewohnheiten als typischer (wir pflegen in sagen: 'richtiger') Sinzusammenhang bejaht Wird."

11. Of course, since motives are communicated, they may be lies; but, this must be proved. Verbalizations are not lies merely because they are socially efficacious. I am here concerned more with the social function of pronounced motives, than with the sincerity of those pronouncing them.

12. See F. Znaniecki, *Social Actions*, 30, New York, 1936.

13. *General Theory of Value*, 292-93, New York, 1936.

14. *Ibid.*, 392.

15. The "profits motive" of classical economics may be treated as an ideal-typical vocabulary of motives for delimited economic situations and behaviors. For late phases of monopolistic and regulated capitalism, this type requires modification; the profit and commercial vocabularies have acquired other ingredients. See N. R. Danielian's AT & T, New York, 1940, for a suggestive account of the *noneconomic* behavior and motives of business bureaucrats.

16. *Social Actions*, 73.

17. Of course, we could infer or interpret constructs posited in the individual, but these are not easily checked and they are not explanatory.

18. Which is not to say that, physiologically, there may not be cramps in the stomach wall or adrenalin in the blood, etc., but the character of the "relation" of such items to social action is quite moot.

19. Paraphrased by K. Mannheim, *op. cit.*, 316-17.

20. "The Motivation of Economic Activities," 67, in C. W. M. Hart, *Essays in Sociology*, Toronto, 1940.

21. Among the ethnologists, Ruth Benedict has come up to the edge of a genuinely sociological view of motivation. Her view remains vague because she has not seen clearly the identity of differing "motivations" in differing cultures with the varied extant and approved vocabularies of motive. "The intelligent understanding of the relation of the individual to his society . . . involves always the understanding of the types of human motivations and capacities capitalized in his society . . ." "Configurations of Culture in North America," *Amer. Anthrop.*, 25, Jan.-Mar. 1932; see also: *Patterns of Culture*, 242-43, Boston, 1935. She turns this observation into a quest for the unique "genius" of each culture and stops her research by words like "Apollonian." If she would attempt constructively to observe the vocabularies of motives which precipitate acts to perform, implement programs, and furnish approved motives for them in circumscribed situations, she would be better able to state precise problems and to answer them by further observation.

22. Also motives acceptably imputed and avowed for one system of action may be diffused into other domains and gradually come to be accepted by some as a comprehensive portrait of the motive of men. This happened in the case of the economic man and his motives.

23. Kuno Mittenzwey, "Zur Sociologie der psychoanalystischer Erkenntnis," in Max Scheler, ed. *Versuche zu einer Sociologie des Wissens*, 365-375, Munich, 1924.

24. This fact is interpreted by some as supporting Freudian theories. Nevertheless, it can be just as adequately grasped in the scheme here outlined.

25. See K. Burke's acute discussion of Freud, *op. cit.*, Part I.

26. Moral vocabularies deserve a special statement. Within the viewpoint herein outlined many snarls concerning "value-judgments," etc., can be cleared up.

15. ACCOUNTS

MARVIN B. SCOTT AND STANFORD LYMAN

Reprinted from Marvin B. Scott and Stanford Lyman in *American Sociological Review*, Volume 33, No. 1 (1968) pp. 46-62, with permission of the authors and the *American Sociological Review*. Marvin Scott completed his Ph.D. at the University of California at Berkeley where he worked with Erving Goffman. He and Stanford Lyman have collaborated on a number of articles, many of which are collected in their book, *A Sociology of the Absurd*. In addition, Scott is the author of *The Racing Game*, and (with Lyman) *The Revolt of the Students*. Stanford Lyman also graduated from the University of California at Berkeley, and in addition to writing a number of articles with Marvin Scott, is the author of *The Oriental in North America*. His latest book is entitled *The Black American in Sociological Thought*.

From time to time sociologists might well pause from their ongoing pursuits to inquire whether their research interests contribute in any way to the fundamental question of sociology, namely, the Hobbesian question: How is society possible? Attempts to answer this question could serve to unite a discipline that may not yet have forgotten its founders, but may still have forgotten why it was founded.

Our purpose here is not to review the various answers to the Hobbesian question,[1] but rather to suggest that an answer to this macro-sociological problem might be fruitfully explored in the analysis of the slightest of interpersonal rituals and the very stuff of which most of those rituals are composed—talk.

Talk, we hold, is the fundamental material of human relations. And though sociologists have not entirely neglected the subject,[2] the sociology of talk has scarcely been developed. Our concern here is with one feature of talk: Its ability to shore up the timbers of fractured sociation, its ability to throw bridges between the promised and the performed, its ability to repair the broken and restore the estranged. This feature of talk involves the giving and receiving of what we shall call *accounts*.

An account is a linguistic device employed whenever an action is subjected to valuative inquiry.[3] Such devices are a crucial element in the social order since they prevent conflicts from arising by verbally bridging the gap between action and expectation.[4] Moreover, accounts are "situated" according to the statuses of the interactants, and are standardized within cultures so that certain accounts are terminologically stabilized and routinely expected when activity falls outside the domain of expectations.

By an account, then, we mean a statement made by a social actor to explain unanticipated or untoward behavior—whether that behavior is his own or that of others, and whether the proximate cause for the statement arises from the actor himself or from someone else.[5] An account is not called for when people engage in routine, common-sense behavior in a cultural environment that recognizes that behavior as such. Thus in American society we do not ordinarily ask why married people engage in sexual intercourse, or why they maintain a home with their children, although the latter question might well be asked if such behavior occurred among the Nayars of Malabar.[6] These questions are not asked because they have been settled in advance in our culture and are indicated by the language itself. We learn the meaning of a "married couple" by indicating that they are two people of opposite sex who have a legitimate right to engage in sexual intercourse and maintain their own children in their own household. When such taken-for-granted phenomena are called into question, the inquirer (if a member of the same culture group) is regarded as "just fooling around," or perhaps as being sick.[7]

To specify our concerns more sharply we should at this point distinguish accounts from the related phenomenon of "explanations." The latter refers to statements about events where untoward action is not an issue and does not have critical implications for relationship. Much of what is true about accounts will also hold for explanations, but our concern is primarily with linguistic forms that are offered for untoward action. With this qualification to our concern, we may now specify further the nature and types of accounts.

TYPES OF ACCOUNTS

There are in general two types of accounts: excuses and justifications.[8] Either or both are likely to be invoked when a person is accused of having done something that is "bad, wrong, inept, unwelcome, or in some other of the numerous possible ways, untoward."[9] Justifications are accounts in which one accepts responsibility for the act in question, but denies the pejorative quality associated with it. Thus a soldier in combat may admit that he has killed other men, but deny that he did an immoral act since those he killed were members of an enemy group and hence "deserved" their fate. Excuses are accounts in which one admits that the act in question is bad, wrong, or inappropriate but denies full responsibility. Thus our combat soldier could admit the wrongfulness of killing but claim that his acts are not entirely undertaken by volition: he is

"under orders" and must obey. With these introductory remarks, we now turn our focus to a more detailed examination of types of justifications and excuses.

Excuses are socially approved vocabularies for mitigating or relieving responsibility when conduct is questioned. We may distinguish initially four modal forms by which excuses are typically formulated:[10] appeal to accidents, appeal to defeasibilty, appeal to biological drives, and scapegoating.

Excuses claiming accident as the source of conduct or its consequences mitigate (if not relieve) responsibility by pointing to the generally recognized hazards in the environment, the understandable inefficiency of the body, and the human incapacity to control all motor responses. The excuse of accident is acceptable precisely because of the irregularity and infrequency of accidents occurring to any single actor. Thus while hazards are numerous and ubiquitous, a particular person is not expected ordinarily to experience the same accident often. In other words, social actors employ a lay version of statistical curves whereby they interpret certain acts as occurring or not occurring by chance alone. When a person conducts himself so that the same type of accident befalls him frequently, he is apt to earn a label—such as "clumsy"—which will operate to stigmatize him and to warn others not to put him and themselves or their property in jeopardy by creating the environment in which he regularly has accidents. When the excuse is rooted in an accident that is unobservable or unable to be investigated—such as blaming one's lateness to work on the heaviness of traffic—frequent pleas of it are likely to be discredited. Excuses based on accidents are thus most likely to be honored precisely because they do not

[margin note: can't be used often or become ineffective]

occur all the time or for the most part to the actor in question.[11]

Appeals to *defeasibility*[12] are available as a form of excuse because of the widespread agreement that all actions contain some "mental element." The components of the mental element are "knowledge" and "will." One defense against an accusation is that a person was not fully informed or that his "will" was not completely "free." Thus an individual might excuse himself from responsibility by claiming that certain information was not available to him, which, if it had been, would have altered his behavior. Further, an individual might claim to have acted in a certain way because of misinformation arising from intentional or innocent misrepresentation of the facts by others. An excuse based on interference with the "free will" of an individual might invoke duress or undue influence. Finally both will and knowledge can be impaired under certain conditions, the invocation of which ordinarily constitutes an adequate mitigation of responsibility—intoxication (whether from alcohol or drugs) and lunacy (whether temporary or permanent) being examples.

In ordinary affairs and in law a person's actions are usually distinguished according to their intent. Further, a person's intentions are distinguished from the consequences of his actions. Under a situation where an action is questioned an actor may claim a lack of intent or a failure to foresee the consequences of his act, or both. If the action in question involves a motor response—such as knocking over a vase—the situation is not very different from that subsumed under the term accident. When actions going beyond motor responses are at issue, the actor's intentions and foresight can be questioned. "Why did you make her cry?" asks the accuser. The presenta-

tional strategies in reply to this question allow several modes of defeating the central claim implied in the question, namely, that the actor intended with full knowledge to make the lady weep. The accused may simply deny any intention on his part to have caused the admittedly unfortunate consequence. However, men ordinarily impute to one another some measure of foresight for their actions so that a simple denial of intent may not be believed if it appears that the consequence of the action in question was indeed what another person might expect and therefore what the actor intended.

[margin note: denial of intent not accepted if outcome is felicitous to instigator]

In addition to his denial of intent an actor may also deny his knowledge of the consequence. The simplest denial is the cognitive disclaimer, "I did not *know* that I would make her cry by what I did." But this complete denial of cognition is often not honored, especially when the interactants know one another well and are expected to have a more complete imagery of the consequences of their acts to guide them. A more complex denial—the gravity disclaimer—includes admitting to the possibility of the outcome in question but suggesting that its probability was incalculable: "I knew matters were serious, but I did not know that telling her would make her weep."

Still another type of excuse invokes biological drives. This invocation is part of a larger category of "fatalistic" forces which in various cultures are deemed in greater or lesser degree to be controlling of some or all events. Cultures dominated by universalist-achievement orientations[13] tend to give scant and ambiguous support to fatalistic interpretations of events, but rarely disavow them entirely. To account for the whole of one's life in such terms, or to account for events which

[margin note: bio]

are conceived by others to be controlled by the actor's conscience, will, and abilities is to lay oneself open to the charge of mental illness or personality disorganization.[14] On the other hand, recent studies have emphasized the situational element in predisposing certain persons and groups in American society to what might be regarded as a "normalized" fatalistic view of their condition. Thus, for example, Negroes[15] and adolescent delinquents[16] are regarded and tend to regard themselves as less in control of the forces that shape their lives than Whites or middle-class adults.

Among the fatalistic items most likely to be invoked as an excuse are the biological drives. Despite the emphasis in Occidental culture since the late nineteenth century on personality and social environment as causal elements in human action, there is still a popular belief in and varied commitment to the efficacy of the body and biological factors in determining human behavior. Such commonplaces as "men are like that" are shorthand phrases invoking belief in sex-linked traits that allegedly govern behavior beyond the will of the actor. Precisely because the body and its biological behavior are always present but not always accounted for in science or society, invocation of the body and its processes is available as an excuse. The body and its inner workings enjoy something of the status of the sociological stranger as conceived by Simmel, namely, they are ever with us but mysterious. Hence, biological drives may be credited with influencing or causing at least some of the behavior for which actors wish to relieve themselves of full responsibility.

The invocation of biological drives is most commonly an appeal to natural but uncontrollable sexual appetite. Among first and second generation Italians in America the recognition and fear of biologically induced sexual intercourse serves men as both an excuse for pre- and extra-marital sexual relations and a justification for not being alone with women ineligible for coitus. Thus one student of Italian-American culture observes:

What the men fear is their own ability at self-control. This attitude, strongest among young unmarried people, often carries over into adulthood. The traditional Italian belief—that sexual intercourse is unavoidable when a man and a woman are by themselves—is maintained intact among second-generation Italians, and continues even when sexual interest itself is on the wane. For example, I was told of an older woman whose apartment was adjacent to that of an unmarried male relative. Although they had lived in the same building for almost twenty years and saw each other every day, she had never once been in his apartment because of this belief.[17]

Biological drive may be an expected excuse in some cultures, so that the failure to invoke it, and the use of some other excuse, constitutes an improper account when the appropriate one is available. Oscar Lewis provides such an example in his ethnography of a Mexican family. A cuckolded wife angrily rejects her wayward husband's explanation that the red stains on his shirt are due to paint rubbed off during the course of his work. She strongly suggests, in her retelling of the incident, that she would have accepted an excuse appealing to her husband's basic sex drives:[18]

And he had me almost believing it was red paint! It was not that I am jealous. I realize a man can never be satisfied with just one woman, but I cannot stand being made a fool of.

Homosexuals frequently account for their deviant sexual desires by invoking the principle of basic biological nature. As one homosexual put it:[19]

It's part of nature. You can't alter it, no matter how many injections and pills they give you.

Another of the biological elements that can be utilized as an excuse is the shape of the body itself. Body types are not only defined in purely anatomical terms, but also, and perhaps more importantly, in terms of their shared social meanings. Hence fat people can excuse their excessive laughter by appealing to the widely accepted proverb that fat men are jolly. Similarly persons bearing features considered to be stereotypically "criminal"[20] may be exonerated for their impoliteness or small larcenies on the grounds that their looks proved their intentions and thus their victims ought to have been on guard. The phrase, "he looks crooked to me," serves as a warning to others to carefully appraise the character and intentions of the person so designated, since his features bespeak an illegal intent.

The final type of excuse we shall mention is scapegoating. Scapegoating is derived from another form of fatalistic reasoning. Using this form a person will allege that his questioned behavior is a response to the behavior or attitudes of another. Certain psychological theory treats this phenomenon as indicative of personality disorder, and, if found in conjunction with certain other characteristic traits, a signal of authoritarian personality.[21] Our treatment bypasses such clinical and pathological concerns in order to deal with the "normal" situation in which individuals slough off the burden of responsibility for their actions and shift it on to another. In Mexican working-class society, for example, women hold a distinctly secondary position relative to men, marriage causes a loss of status to the latter, and sexual intercourse is regarded ambivalently as healthy and natural, but also as a necessary evil.[22] Such a set of orientations predisposes both men and women to attribute many of their

shortcomings to women. An example is found in the autobiography of a Mexican girl:[23]

I was always getting into fights because some girls are vipers; they get jealous, tell lies about each other, and start trouble.

Similarly, a Mexican youth who tried unsuccessfully to meet a girl by showing off on a bicycle explains:[24]

She got me into trouble with my father by lying about me. She said I tried to run her down with my bike and that all I did was hang around spying on her.

In another instance the same youth attributes his waywardness to the fact that the girl truly loved was his half-sister and thus unavailable to him for coitus or marriage:

So, because of Antonia, I began to stay away from home. It was one of the main reasons I started to go on the bum, looking for trouble.[25]

Like excuses, *justifications* are socially approved vocabularies that neutralize an act or its consequences when one or both are called into question. But here is the crucial difference: to *justify* an act is to assert its positive value in the face of a claim to the contrary. Justifications recognize a general sense in which the act in question is impermissible, but claim that the particular occasion permits or requires the very act. The laws governing the taking of life are a case in point. American and English jurisprudence are by no means united on definitions or even on the nature of the acts in question, but in general a man may justify taking the life of another by claiming that he acted in self-defense, in defense of others' lives or property, or in action against a declared enemy of the state.

For a tentative list of types of justifications we may turn to what has been called "techniques of neutralization."[26] Although these techniques have been discussed with respect to accounts offered by juvenile delinquents for untoward action, their wider use has yet to be explored. Relevant to our discussion of justification are the techniques of "denial of injury," "denial of victim," "condemnation of condemners," and "appeal to loyalties."[27]

In denial of injury the actor acknowledges that he did a particular act but asserts that it was permissible to do that act since no one was injured by it, or since no one about whom the community need be concerned with was involved, or finally since the act resulted in consequences that were trifling. Note that this justification device can be invoked with respect to both persons and objects. The denial of injury to persons suggests that they be viewed as "deserving" in a special sense: that they are oversupplied with the valued things of the world, or that they are "private" persons ("my friends," "my enemies") who have no standing to claim injury in the public, or to be noticed as injured. Denial of injury to objects involves redefining the act as not injurious to it but only using it, e.g., car "borrowing" is not theft.

In denial of the victim the actor expresses the position that the action was permissible since the victim deserved the injury. Four categories of persons are frequently perceived as deserving injury. First, there are proximate foes, i.e., those who have directly injured the actor; second, incumbents of normatively discrepant roles, e.g., homosexuals, whores, pimps; third, groups with tribal stigmas, e.g., racial and ethnic minorities; and finally, distant foes, that is, incumbents of roles held to be dubious or hurtful, e.g., "Whitey," the "Reds," "politicians." Besides categories of persons, there are categories of objects perceived as deserving of injury. To begin with, the property of any of the above mentioned categories of persons may become a focus of attack, especially if that property is symbolic of the attacked person's status. Thus the clothing of the whore is torn, the gavel of the politician is smashed, and so on. Secondly, there are objects that have a neutral or ambiguous identity with respect to ownership, e.g., a park bench. A final focus of attacked objects are those having a low or polluted value, e.g., junk, or kitsch.

Using the device of condemnation of the condemners, the actor admits performing an untoward act but asserts its irrelevancy because others commit these and worse acts, and these others are either not caught, not punished, not condemned, unnoticed, or even praised.

Still another neutralization technique is appeal to loyalties. Here the actor asserts that his action was permissible or even right since it served the interests of another to whom he owes an unbreakable allegiance or affection.[28]

Besides these "techniques of neutralization," two other sorts of justification may be mentioned: "sad tales," and "self-fulfillment." The sad tale is a selected (often distorted) arrangement of facts that highlight an extremely dismal past, and thus "explain" the individual's present state.[29] For example, a mental patient relates:[30]

I was going to night school to get an M.A. degree, and holding down a job in addition, and the load got too much for me.

And a homosexual accounts for his present deviance with this sad tale:[31]

I was in a very sophisticated queer circle at the university. It was queer in a sense that we all camped like mad with "my dear" at the beginning of every sentence, but there was practically no sex, and in my case there was none at all. The break came when I went to a party and flirted with a merchant seaman who took me seriously and cornered me in a bedroom. There was I, the great sophisticate, who, when it came to the point, was quite raw, completely inexperienced; and I might tell you that seaman gave me quite a shock. I can't say I enjoyed it very much but it wasn't long after before I started to dive into bed with anyone.

Finally we may mention a peculiarly modern type of justification, namely, *self*-fulfillment. Interviewing LSD users and homosexuals in the Haight-Ashbury district of San Francisco, we are struck by the prominence of self-fulfillment as the grounds for these activities. Thus, an "acid head" relates:[32]

The whole purpose in taking the stuff is self-development. Acid expands consciousness. Mine eyes have seen the glory—can you say that? I never knew what capacities I had until I went on acid.

And a Lesbian:[33]

Everyone has the right to happiness and love. I was married once. It was hell. But now I feel I have fulfilled myself as a person and as a woman.

We might also note that the drug users and homosexuals interviewed (in San Francisco) who invoked the justification of self-fulfillment did not appear to find anything "wrong" with their behavior. They indicated either a desire to be left alone or to enlighten what they considered to be the unenlightened establishment.

HONORING ACCOUNTS, AND BACKGROUND EXPECTATIONS

Accounts may be honored or not honored. If an account is honored, we may say that it was efficacious and equilibrium is thereby restored in a relationship. The most common situation in which accounts are routinely honored is encounters interrupted by "incidents"—slips, boners, or gaffes which introduce information deleterious to the otherwise smooth conduct of the interactants.[34] Often a simple excuse will suffice, or the other interactants will employ covering devices to restore the *status quo ante*. A related situation is that in which an individual senses that some incident or event has cast doubt on that image of himself which he seeks to present. "At such times," the authority on impression management writes, "the individual is likely to try to integrate the incongruous events by means of apologies, little excuses for self, and disclaimers; though the same acts, incidentally, he also tries to save his face."[35]

One variable governing the honoring of an account is the character of the social circle in which it is introduced. As we pointed out earlier, vocabularies of accounts are likely to be routinized within cultures, subcultures and groups, and some are likely to be exclusive to the circle in which they are employed. A drug addict may be able to justify his conduct to a bohemian world, but not to the courts. Similarly kin and friends may accept excuses in situations in which strangers would refuse to do so. Finally, while ignorance of the consequences of an act or of its prohibition may exculpate an individual in many different circles, the law explicitly rejects this notion: "Ignorance of the law excuses no man; not that all men know the law but because 'tis an excuse every man will plead, and no man can tell how to confute him."[36]

Both the account offered by *ego* and the honoring or nonhonoring of the account on the part of *alter* will ultimately depend on the *background expectancies* of the interactants. By background expectancies we refer to those sets of taken-for-granted ideas that permit the interactants to interpret remarks as accounts in the first place.[37] Asked why he is listless and depressed, a person may reply, "I have family troubles." The remark will be taken as an account, and indeed an account that will probably be honored, because "everyone knows" that "family problems" are a cause of depression.

This last illustration suggests that certain accounts can fit a variety of situations. Thus in response to a wide range of questions—why don't you get married? Why are you in a fit of depression? Why are you drinking so heavily?—the individual can respond with "I'm having family problems." The person offering such an account may not himself regard it as a true one, but invoking it has certain interactional payoffs: since people cannot say they don't understand it—they are accounts that are part of our socially distributed knowledge of what "everyone knows"—the inquiry can be cut short.

Clearly, then, a single account will stand for a wide collection of events, and the efficacy of such accounts depends upon a set of shared background expectations.

In interacting with others, the socialized person learns a repertoire of background expectations that are appropriate for a variety of others. Hence the "normal" individual will change his account for different role others. A wife may respond sympathetically to her depressed husband because his favorite football team lost a championship game, but such an account for depression will appear bizarre when offered to one's inquiring boss. Thus background expectancies are the means not only for the honoring, but also for the nonhonoring of accounts. When the millionaire accounts for his depression by saying he is a failure, others will be puzzled since "everyone knows" that millionaires are not failures. The incapacity to invoke situationally appropriate accounts, i.e.,

accounts that are anchored to the background expectations of the situation, will often be taken as a sign of mental illness.[38] There are grounds then for conceptualizing normal individuals as "not stupid" rather than "not ill."[39] The person who is labeled ill has been behaving "stupidly" in terms of his culture and society: he offers accounts not situationally appropriate according to culturally defined background expectations.[40]

Often an account can be discredited by the appearance of the person offering an account. When a girl accounts for her late return from a date by saying the movie was overlong—that no untoward event occurred and that she still retains virgin status—her mother may discredit the account by noting the daughter's flushed appearance. Since individuals are aware that appearances may serve to credit or discredit accounts, efforts are understandably made to control these appearances through a vast repertoire of "impression management" activities.[41]

When an account is not honored it will be regarded as either *illegitimate* or *unreasonable*. An account is treated as *illegitimate* when the gravity of the event exceeds that of the account or when it is offered in a circle where its vocabulary of motives is unacceptable. As illustration of the former we may note that accidentally allowing a pet turtle to drown may be forgiven, but accidentally allowing the baby to drown with the same degree of oversight may not so easily be excused. As illustration of the latter, male prostitutes may successfully demonstrate their masculinity within the subculture of persons who regularly resort to homosexual acts by insisting that they are never fellators, but such a defense is not likely in heterosexual circles to lift from them the label of "queer."[42]

An account is deemed <u>unreasonable</u> when the stated grounds for action cannot be "normalized" in terms of the background expectancies of what "everybody knows." Hence when a secretary explained that she placed her arm in a lighted oven because voices had commanded her to do so in punishment for her evil nature, the account was held to be grounds for commitment to an asylum.[43] In general those who persist in giving unreasonable accounts for questioned actions are likely to be labelled as mentally ill. Or, to put this point another way, unreasonable accounts are one of the sure indices by which the mentally ill are apprehended. Conversely, those persons labeled as mentally ill may relieve themselves of the worst consequences of that label by recognizing before their psychiatrists the truth value of the label, by reconstructing their past to explain how they came to deviate from normal patterns, and by gradually coming to give acceptable accounts for their behavior.[44]

Beyond illegitimacy and unreasonableness are special types of situations in which accounts may not be acceptable. One such type involves the incorrect invocation of "commitment" or "attachment"[45] in account situations where one or the other, but only the correct one, is permitted. By commitment we refer to that role orientation in which one has through investiture become liable and responsible for certain actions. By attachment we refer to the sense of vesting one's feelings and identity in a role. Certain statuses, especially those dealing with distasteful activities or acts that are condemned except when performed by licensed practitioners, are typically expected to invest their incumbents with only commitment and not with attachment. Hangmen who, when questioned about their occupation,

profess to be emotionally attracted to killing, are not likely to have their account honored. Indeed, distasteful tasks are often imputed to have a clandestine but impermissible allure, and so those who regularly perform them are often on their guard to assert their commitment, but not their attachment, to the task.

Organizations systematically provide accounts for their members in a variety of situations. The rules of bureaucracy, for instance, make available accounts for actions taken toward clients—actions which, from the viewpoint of the client, are untoward.[46] Again, these accounts "work" because of a set of background expectations. Thus when people say they must perform a particular action because it is a rule of the organization, the account is regarded as at least reasonable, since "everyone knows" that people follow rules. Of course, the gravity of the event may discredit such accounts, as the trials of Nazi war criminals dramatically illustrate.[47]

Under certain situations behavior that would ordinarily require an account is normalized without interruption or any call for an account. Typically such situations are social conversations in which the values to be obtained by the total encounter supersede those which would otherwise require excuses or justifications. Two values that may override the requirement of accounts are *sociability* and *information*.

In the case of sociability the desire that the interactional circle be uninterrupted by any event that might break it calls for each interactant to weigh carefully whether or not the calling for an account might disrupt the entire engagement. When the gathering is a convivial one not dedicated to significant matters—that is, matters that have a proactive life beyond the en-

avoid asking for account if it's too disruptive

gagement itself—the participants may overlook errors, inept statements, lies, or discrepancies in the statements of others. Parties often call for such behavior but are vulnerable to disruption by one who violates the unwritten rule of not questioning another too closely. In unserious situations in which strangers are privileged to interact as a primary group without future rights of similar interaction—such as in bars— the interactants may construct elaborate and self-contradictory biographies without fear of being called to account.[48]

In some engagements the interactants seek to obtain *information* from the speaker which is incidental to his main point but which might be withheld if any of the speaker's statements were called into account. Among the Japanese, for example, the significant item in a conversation may be circumscribed by a verbal wall of trivia and superfluous speech. To interrupt a speaker by calling for an account might halt the conversation altogether or detour the speaker away from disclosing the particularly valued pieces of information.[49] Among adolescent boys in American society engaged in a "bull session" it is usually inappropriate to challenge a speaker describing his sexual exploits since, no matter how embellished and exaggerated the account might be, it permits the hearers to glean knowledge about sex—ordinarily withheld from them in the regular channels of education —with impunity. Calling for an account in the midst of such disclosures, especially when the account would require a discussion of the speaker's morality, might cut off the hearers from obtaining precisely that kind of information which is in no other way available to them.[50]

So far we have discussed accounts in terms of their content, but it should be pointed out that accounts also differ in form or style. Indeed, as we will now suggest, the style of an account will have bearing on its honoring or dishonoring.

LINGUISTIC STYLES AND ACCOUNTS

We may distinguish five linguistic styles that frame the manner in which an account will be given and often indicate the social circle in which it will be most appropriately employed. These five styles, which in practice often shade into one another and are not unambiguously separated in ordinary life, are the *intimate, casual, consultative, formal,* and *frozen* styles.[51] These styles, as we shall see, are ordered on a scale of decreasing social intimacy.[52]

The *intimate* style is the socially sanctioned linguistic form employed among persons who share a deep, intense and personal relationship. The group within which it is employed is usually a dyad—lovers, a married pair, or very close friends. The group can be larger but not much larger, and when it reaches four or five it is strained to its limits. The verbal style employs single sounds or words, and jargon, to communicate whole ideas. An account given in this form may be illustrated by the situation in which a husband, lying beside his wife in bed, caresses her but receives no endearing response. His wife utters the single word, "pooped." By this term the husband understands that the account given in response to his unverbalized question, "Why don't you make love to me? After all I am your husband. You have wifely duties!" is "I realize that under ordinary circumstances I should and indeed would respond to your love making, but tonight I am too exhausted for that kind of activity. Do not take it to mean that I have lost affection for you, or that I take my wifely duties lightly."

The *casual* style is used among peers, in-group members and insiders. It is a style employed by those for whom the social distance is greater than that among intimates but is still within the boundaries of a primary relationship. Typically it employs ellipses, i.e., omissions, and slang. In casual style certain background information is taken for granted among the interactants and may be merely alluded to in order to give an account. Thus among those who are regular users of hallucinogenic drugs, the question "Why were you running about naked in the park?" might be answered, "I was 'on.' " The hearer will then know that the speaker was under the influence of a familiar drug and was engaged in an activity that is common in response to taking that drug.

While each style differs from that to which it is juxtaposed by degree, the difference between any two styles— skipping an interval on the aforementioned social intimacy scale— is one of kind. Thus intimate and casual styles differ only in degree from one another and suggest a slight but significant difference in social distance among the interactants, but the *consultative* style differs in kind from the intimate. Consultative style is that verbal form ordinarily employed when the amount of knowledge available to one of the interactants is unknown or problematic to the others. Typically in such an interaction the speaker supplies background information which he is unsure the hearer possesses, and the hearer continuously participates by means of linguistic signs and gestures which indicate that he under-stands what is said or that he requires

more background information. In offering accounts in this form there is a definite element of "objectivity," i.e., of non-subjective and technical terms. The individual giving an account relies on reference to things and ideas outside the intimate and personal realm. In response to the question, "Why are you smoking marijuana? Don't you know that it's dangerous?," the individual might reply, "I smoke marijuana because everybody who's read the LaGuardia Report knows that it's not habit-forming." But a casual response might be simply, "Don't be square."

Formal style is employed when the group is too large for informal co-participation to be a continuous part of the interaction. Typically it is suited to occasions when an actor addresses an audience greater than six. Listeners must then wait their turn to respond, or, if they interject comments, know that this will be an untoward event, requiring some kind of re-structuring of the situation. Speaker and audience are in an active and a passive role, respectively, and, if the group is large enough, may be obligated to speak or remain silent according to preestablished codes of procedure. Formal style may also be employed when speaker and auditor are in rigidly defined statuses. Such situations occur in bureaucratic organizations between persons in hierarchically differentiated statuses, or in the courtroom, in the interaction between judge and defendant.

Frozen style is an extreme form of formal style employed among those who are simultaneously required to interact and yet remain social strangers. Typically interaction in the frozen style occurs among those between whom an irremovable barrier exists. The barrier may be of a material or a social nature, or both. Thus pilots

how do nature of accounts change over group size?

communicate to air scanners in a control tower in the same lingual style as prisoners of war to their captors or telephone operators to angered clients. Often the frozen accounts offered are tutored, memorized or written down in advance, and they may be applicable to a variety of situations. Thus the prisoner of war reiterates his name, rank and serial number to all questions and refers his interrogators to the Geneva Convention. The pilot replies to questions about his aberrant flight pattern, coming from the anonymous control tower, with a smooth flow of technical jargon quoted from his handbook on flying. The telephone operator refuses to become flustered or angered by the outraged demands and accusations of the caller unable to reach his party, and quotes from memory the rules of telephone conduct required of the situation.

In summary, then, accounts are presented in a variety of idioms. The idiomatic form of an account is expected to be socially suited to the circle into which it is introduced, according to norms of culture, subculture, and situation. The acceptance or refusal of an offered account in part depends on the appropriateness of the idiom employed. Failure to employ the proper linguistic style often results in a dishonoring of the account or calls for further accounts. Sometimes the situation results in requirements of compound accounting wherein an individual, having failed to employ idiomatic propriety in his first account, is required not only to re-account for his original untoward act but also to present an account for the unacceptable language of his first account. Note that idiomatic errors on the part of a person giving an account provide an unusual opportunity for the hearer to dishonor or punish the speaker if he so wishes. Thus even if the content of the tendered account is such as to excuse or justify the act, a hearer who wishes to discredit the speaker may "trip him up" by shifting the subject away from the matter originally at hand and onto the form of the account given. Typical situations of this kind arise when persons of inferior status provide substantially acceptable accounts for their allegedly untoward behavior to their inquiring superiors but employ idiomatically unacceptable or condemnable form. Thus school children who excuse their fighting with others by not only reporting that they were acting in self-defense but also, and in the process, by using profanity may still be punished for linguistic impropriety, even if they are let off for their original defalcation.[53]

STRATEGIES FOR AVOIDING ACCOUNTS

The vulnerability of actors to questions concerning their conduct varies with the situation and the status of the actors. Where hierarchies of authority govern the social situation, the institutionalized office may eliminate the necessity of an account, or even prevent the question from arising. Military officers are thus shielded from accountability to their subordinates. Where culture distance and hierarchy are combined—as in the case of slaveholders vis-à-vis their new imported slaves—those enjoying the superior status are privileged to leave their subordinates in a perplexed and frightened state.[54]

Besides the invulnerability to giving accounts arising from the status and position of the actors are the strategies that can prevent their announcement. We may refer to these strategies as meta-accounts. Three such strategies are prominent: *mystification, referral,* and *identity switching.*[55]

When the strategy of *mystification* is employed an actor admits that he is not meeting the expectations of another, but follows this by pointing out that, although there are reasons for his unexpected actions, he cannot tell the inquirer what they are. In its simplest sense the actor says "It's a long story," and leaves it at that. Such accounts are most likely to be honored under circumstances which would normally hinder an elaborate account, as when students have a chance meeting while rushing off to scheduled classes.

More complicated versions of mystification are those that suggest that *alter* is not aware of certain facts—facts that are secret—which, if known, would explain the untoward action. Typically this is the response of the charismatic leader to his followers or the expert to his naive assistant. Thus does Jesus sometimes mystify his disciples and Sherlock Holmes his Dr. Watson. Finally, as already mentioned, certain statuses suggest mystification: in addition to charismatic leaders and experts at occult or little-understood arts are all those statuses characterized by specialized information including (but not limited to) doctors, lawyers, and spies.

Using the strategy of *referral*, the individual says, "I know I'm not meeting your expectations but if you wish to know why, please see. . . ." Typically referral is a strategy available to the sick and the subordinate. Illness, especially mental illness, allows the sick person to refer inquiries about his behavior to his doctor or psychiatrist. Subordinates may avoid giving accounts by designating superiors as the appropriate persons to be questioned. A special example of group referral is that which arises when accounts for the behavior of a whole people are

avoided by sending the interrogator to the experts. Thus juvenile delinquents can refer inquiries to social workers, Hopi Indians to anthropologists, and unwed Negro mothers to the Moynihan Report.

In *identity switching,* ego indicates to *alter* that he is not playing the role that *alter* believes he is playing. This is a way of saying to *alter,* "You do not know who I am." This technique is readily available since all individuals possess a multiplicity of identities. Consider the following example.[56] A working-class Mexican husband comes home from an evening of philandering. His wife suspects this and says, "Where were you?" He responds with: "None of your business, you're a wife." Here the husband is assuming that it is not the wife's job to pry into the affairs of her husband. She replies, "What kind of a father are you?" What the woman does here is to suggest that she is not a wife, but a mother—who is looking out for the welfare of the children. To this the husband replies: "I'm a man—and you're a woman." In other words, he is suggesting that, in this status of man, there are things that a woman just doesn't understand. We note in this example that the status of persons not only affects the honoring and nonhonoring of accounts, but also determines who can call for an account and who can avoid it. Again it should be pointed out that the normal features of such interaction depend upon the actors sharing a common set of background expectancies.

NEGOTIATING IDENTITIES AND ACCOUNTS

As our discussion of identity-switching emphasizes, accounts always occur between persons in roles—between husband and wife, doctor and patient, teacher and student, and so on. A normative structure governs the nature and types of communication between the interactants, including whether and in what manner accounts may be required and given, honored or discredited.

Accounts, as suggested, presuppose an identifiable speaker and audience. The particular identities of the interactants must often be established as part of the encounter in which the account is presented.[57] In other words, people generate role identities for one another in social situations. In an account-giving situation, to cast *alter* in a particular role is to confer upon him the privilege of honoring a particular kind of account, the kind suitable to the role identity conferred and assumed for at least the period of the account. To assume an identity is to don the mantle appropriate to the account to be offered. Identity assumption and "altercasting"[58] are prerequisites to the presentation of accounts, since the identities thus established interactionally "set" the social stage on which the drama of the account is to be played out.

The identities of speaker and audience will be negotiated as part of the encounter. Each of the interactants has a stake in the negotiations since the outcomes of the engagement will often depend on these pre-established identities. In competitive or bargaining situations[59] the interactants will each seek to maximize gains or minimize losses, and part of the strategy involved will be to assume and accept advantageous identities, refusing those roles that are disadvantageous to the situation. *Every account is a manifestation of the underlying negotiation of identities.*[60]

The most elementary form of identification is that of human and fellow human negotiated by the immediate perceptions of strangers who engage in abrupt and involuntary engagements. Thus once two objects on a street collide with one another and mutually perceive one another to be humans, an apology in the form of an excuse, or mutually paired excuses, will suffice. Those persons not privileged with full or accurate perception—the blind, myopic, or blindfolded—are not in a position to ascertain immediately whether the object with which they have collided is eligible to call for an account and to deserve an apology. In overcompensating for their inability to negotiate immediately such elementary identities, the persons so handicapped may indiscriminately offer apologies to everyone and everything with which they collide—doormen and doors, street-walkers and street signs. On the other hand, their identification errors are forgiven as soon as their handicap is recognized.

Some objects are ambiguously defined with respect to their deserving of accounts. Animals are an example. House pets, especially dogs and cats, are sometimes imputed to possess human attributes and are thus eligible for apologies and excuses when they are trodden upon by their masters. But insects and large beasts—ants and elephants, for example—do not appear to be normally eligible for accounts even when they are trodden upon by unwary (Occidental) humans.

However, there are instances wherein the anthropomorphosis of the human self is more difficult to negotiate than that of a dog. Racial minorities in caste societies often insist to no avail on the priority of their identity as "human beings" over their identification as members of a racial group.[61] Indeed the "Negro human-being" role choice dilemma is but one instance of a particular form of strategy in the negotiation of identities. The strategy involves the competition between ego and alter over particularistic versus universalistic role identities. In any encounter in which a disagreement is potential or has already occurred, or in any situation in which an account is to be offered, the particularistic or universalistic identity of the interactants might dictate the manner and outcome of the account situation. Each participant will strive for the advantageous identity. A Negro psychoanalyst with considerable experience in Europe and North Africa has shown how the form of address—either consultative or deprecatingly casual—and the tone used, are opening moves in the doctor's designation of his patient as European or Negro:[62]

Twenty European patients, one after another, came in: "Please sit down . . . Why do you wish to consult me?" Then comes a Negro or an Arab. "Sit here, boy. . . ."

And, as the psychoanalyst points out, the identity imputed to the patient might be accepted or rejected. To reject the particularistic identity in favor of a universalistic one, the Negro patient might reply, "I am in no sense your boy, Monsieur"[63] and the negotiations for identities begin again or get detoured in an argument.

In an account situation there is a further complication. Once identities have been established and an account offered, the individual has committed himself to an identity and thus seemingly assumed the assets and liabilities of that role for the duration of the encounter. If he accepts the identity as permanent and unchangeable, however, he may have limited his range of subsequent accounts. And if he wishes to shift accounts to one appropriate to another identity he may also need to account for the switch in identities.

Thus, in the face of a pejorative particularistic identity, a Negro might wish to establish his claim to a positive universalistic one devoid of the pejorative contents of the imputed one. However, once this new universalistic identity has been established, the Negro might wish to shift back to the particularistic one, if there are positive qualities to be gained thereby, qualities utterly lost by an unqualified acceptance of the universalistic identity.[64] But the switch might require an account itself.

Identity switching has retroactive dangers, since it casts doubt on the attachment the claimant had to his prior identity, and his attachment may have been a crucial element in the acceptability of his first account. On the other hand, the hearer of an account may have a vested interest in accepting the entire range of accounts and may thus accommodate or even facilitate the switch in identities. Thus the hearer may "rationalize" the prior commitment, or reinterpret its meaning so that the speaker may carry off subsequent accounts.[65] Another strategy available to a hearer is to engage in alter-casting for purposes of facilitating or frustrating an account. The fact that individuals have multiple identities makes them both capable of strategic identity change and vulnerable to involuntary identity imputations.

In ordinary life, accounts are usually "phased."[66] One account generates the question which gives rise to another; the new account requires re-negotiation of identities; the identities necessitate excuses or justifications, improvisation and alter-casting; another account is given; another question arises, and so on. The following interview between a Soviet social worker and his client, a young woman, nicely illustrates this phenomenon.[67]

A girl of about nineteen years of age enters the social worker's office and sits down sighing audibly. The interview begins on a note of *mystification* which ends abruptly when the girl establishes her identity—abandoned wife.

"What are you sighing so sadly for?" I asked. "Are you in trouble?" Lyuba raised her prim little head with a jerk, sighed pianissimo and smiled piteously.

"No . . . it's nothing much. I *was* in trouble, but it's all over now. . . ."

"All over, and you are still sighing about it?" I questioned further. Lyuba gave a little shiver and looked at me. A flame of interest had leaped into her earnest brown eyes.

"Would you like me to tell you all about it?"

"Yes, do."

"It's a long story."

"Never mind. . . ."

"My husband has left me."

The interview carries on in what must be regarded as an unsuccessful approach by the social worker. He establishes that Lyuba still loves her wayward husband, has lost faith in men, and is unwilling to take his advice to forget her first husband and remarry. The abandoned wife turns out to be an identity with which the worker has difficulty coping. He, therefore, alter-casts with telling effect in the following manner.

"Tell me, Lyuba, are your parents alive?"

"Yes, they are. Daddy and Mummy! They keep on telling me off for having got married."

"Quite right too."

"No, it's not. What's right about it?"

"Of course, they're right. You're still a child and already married and divorced."

"Well . . . what about it! What's that got to do with them?"

Aren't you living with them?"

"I have a room of my own. My husband left me and went to live with his . . . and the room is mine now. And I earn two hundred rubles. And I'm not a child! How can you call me a child?"

Note that little bits of information provide the cues for altercasting, so that Lyuba's volunteering the fact of her parents' disapproval of her first marriage, provides the grounds for the social worker's recasting her in the child role. However this new identity is rejected by Lyuba by further evidentiary assertions: she supports herself and maintains her own residence. The child role has been miscast. Even the social worker gives up his attempt at switching Lyuba out from her role as abandoned wife. He writes: "Lyuba looked at me in angry surprise and I saw that she was quite serious about this game she played in life." Thus negotiations for identities—as in financial transactions—usually end with both parties coming to an agreeable settlement.

CONCLUSION

The sociologist has been slow to take as a serious subject of investigation what is perhaps the most distinctive feature of humans—talk. Here we are suggesting a concern with one type of talk: the study of what constitutes "acceptable utterances"[68] for untoward action. The sociological study of communications has relegated linguistic utterances to linguists and has generally mapped out non-verbal behavior as its distinctive domain. We are suggesting that a greater effort is needed to formulate theory that will integrate both verbal and non-verbal behavior.[69]

Perhaps the most immediate task for research in this area is to specify the background expectations that determine the range of alternative accounts deemed culturally appropriate to a variety of recurrent situations. We want to know how the actors take bits and pieces of words and appearances and put them together to produce a perceivedly normal (or abnormal) state of affairs. This kind of inquiry crucially involves a study of background expectations.[70] On the basis of such investigations, the analyst should be able to provide a set of instructions on "how to give an account" that would be taken by other actors as "normal."[71] These instructions would specify how different categories of statuses affect the honoring of an account, and what categories of statuses can use what kinds of accounts.

Future research on accounts may fruitfully take as a unit of analysis the *speech community*.[72] This unit is composed of human aggregates in frequent and regular interaction. By dint of their association sharers of a distinct body of verbal signs are set off from other speech communities. By speech community we do not refer to language communities, distinguished by being composed of users of formally different languages. Nor do we refer simply to dialect communities, composed of persons who employ a common spoken language which is a verbal variant of a more widely used written language.

Speech communities define for their members the appropriate lingual forms to be used amongst themselves. Such communities are located in the social structure of any society. They mark off segments of society from one another, and also distinguish different kinds of activities. Thus, the everyday language of lowerclass teenage gangs differs sharply from that of the social workers who interview them, and the language by which a science teacher demonstrates to his students how to combine hydrogen and oxygen in order to produce water differs from the language employed by the same teacher to tell his inquisitive six-year-old son how babies are created. The types of accounts appropriate to each speech community differ in form and in content. The usage of particular speech norms in giving an account has consequences for the speaker depending upon the relationship between the form used and the speech community into which it is introduced.

A single individual may belong to several speech communities at the same time, or in the course of a lifetime. Some linguistic devices (such as teenage argot) are appropriate only to certain age groups and are discarded as one passes into another age grouping; others, such as the linguistic forms used by lawyers in the presence of judges, are appropriate to certain status sets and are consecutively employed and discarded as the individual moves into and out of interactions with his various status partners. Some individuals are dwellers in but a single speech community; they move in circles in which all employ the same verbal forms. The aged and enfeebled members of class or ethnic ghettos are an obvious example. Others are constant movers through differing speech communities, adeptly employing language forms suitable to the time and place they occupy. Social workers who face teenage delinquents, fellow workers, lawyers, judges, their own wives, and children, all in one day, are an example.

In concluding we may note that, since it is with respect to deviant behavior that we call for accounts, the study of deviance and the study of accounts are intrinsically related, and a clarification of accounts will constitute a clarification of deviant phenomena—to the extent that deviance is considered in an interactional framework.[73]

NOTES

1. For a now classic statement and analysis of the Hobbesian question, see the discussion by Talcott Parsons, *The Structure of Social Action*, Glencoe, Ill.: The Free Press, 1949, pp. 89-94.

2. See, for instance, William Soskin and

Vera John, "The Study of Spontaneous Talk," in *The Stream of Behavior*, edited by Roger Barker, N. Y.: Appleton-Century-Crofts, 1963, pp. 228-282. Much suggestive material and a complete bibliography can be found in Joyce O. Hertzler, *A Sociology of Language*, N. Y.: Random House, 1965.

3. An account has a family resemblance to the verbal component of a "motive" in Weber's sense of the term. Weber defined a motive as "a complex of subjective meaning which seems to the actor himself or to the observer as an adequate ground for the conduct in question." Max Weber, *Theory of Social and Economic Organization*, translated by Talcott Parsons and A. M. Henderson, Glencoe: The Free Press, 1947, pp. 98-99. Following Weber's definition and building on G. H. Mead's social psychology and the work of Kenneth Burke, C. Wright Mills was among the first to employ the notion of accounts in his much neglected essay, 'Situated Action and the Vocabulary of Motives," *American Sociological Review*, 6 (December, 1940), pp. 904-913. . . . Contemporary British philosophy, following the leads of Ludwig Wittgenstein, has (apparently) independently advanced the idea of a "vocabulary of motives." An exemplary case is R. S. Peters' *The Concept of Motivation*, London: Routledge and Kegan Paul, 1958.

4. The point is nicely illustrated by Jackson Toby in "Some Variables in Role Conflict Analysis," *Social Forces*, 30 (March, 1952), pp. 323-327.

5. Thus by an account we include also those non-vocalized but linguistic explanations that arise in an actor's "mind" when he questions his own behavior. However, our concern is with vocalized accounts and especially those that are given in face-to-face relations.

6. William J. Goode, *World Revolution and Family Patterns*, New York: The Free Press of Glencoe, 1963, pp. 254-256.

7. Moreover, common-sense understandings that violate widespread cognitive knowledge, such as are asserted in statements like "The sun rises every morning and sets every night," or avowed in perceptions that a straight stick immersed in water appears bent, are expected to be maintained. Persons who always insist on the astronomically exact statement about the earth's relation to the sun might be considered officious or didactic, while those who "see" a straight stick in a pool might be credited with faulty eyesight. For a relevant discussion of social reactions to inquiries

about taken-for-granted phenomena, see Harold Garfinkel, "Studies of the Routine Grounds of Everyday Activities," *Social Problems*, 11 (Winter, 1964), pp. 225-250, and "A Conception of and Experiments with 'Trust' as a Condition of Concerted Action," in *Motivation and Social Interaction*, edited by O. J. Harvey, New York: Ronald Press, 1963, pp. 187-238.

8. We have taken this formulation from J. L. Austin. See his *Philosophical Papers*, London: Oxford University Press, 1961, pp. 123-152.

9. *Ibid.*, p. 124.

10. These types of excuses are to be taken as illustrative rather than as an exhaustive listing.

11. Only where nothing is left to chance—as among the Azande, where particular misfortunes are accounted for by a ubiquitous witchcraft—is the excuse by accident not likely to occur. Azande do not assert witchcraft to be the sole cause of phenomena; they have a "practical" and "realistic" approach to events which would enjoy consensual support from Occidental observers. However, Azande account for what Occidentals would call "chance" or "coincidence" by reference to witchcraft. E. E. Evans-Pritchard writes: "We have no explanation of why the two chains of causation [resulting in a catastrophe] intersected at a certain time and in a certain place, for there is no interdependence between them. Azande philosophy can supply the missing link. . . . It is due to witchcraft. . . . Witchcraft explains the coincidence of these two happenings." *Witchcraft, Oracles and Magic Among the Azande*, London: Oxford University Press, 1937, p. 70.

12. Defeasibility, or the capacity of being voided, is a concept developed by H. L. A. Hart. This section leans heavily on Hart's essay, "The Ascription of Responsibility and Rights," in *Logic and Language, First Series*, edited by Anthony Flew, Oxford: Basil Blackwell, 1960, pp. 145-166.

13. For a general discussion of cultures in terms of their "fatalistic" orientations or universalist-achievement orientations, see Talcott Parsons, "A Revived Analytical Approach to the Theory of Social Stratification," in *Essays in Sociological Theory*, The Free Press of Glencoe, 1954, pp. 386-439. See also Parsons, *The Social System*, Glencoe: The Free Press, 1951.

14. Thus, in the most famous study of the psychodynamics of prejudice, one of the characteristics of the intolerant or "authoritarian" personality is "externaliza-

tion," i.e., the attribution of causality of events believed to be within the actor's power or rational comprehension to uncontrollable forces beyond his influence or understanding. See T. W. Adorno, *et al.*, *The Authoritarian Personality*, N. Y.: Harper & Row, 1950, pp. 474-475. See also Gordon W. Allport, *The Nature of Prejudice*, Garden City: Doubleday Anchor, 1958, p. 379. In a recent study an intermittently employed cab driver's insistence that there would inevitably be a revolution after which the world would be taken over by Negroes and Jews is recalled as one of several early warning cues that he is mentally ill. Marion Radke Yarrow, *et al.*, "The Psychological Meaning of Mental Illness in the Family," in Thomas J. Scheff, *Mental Illness and Social Process*, New York: Harper and Row, 1967, p. 35.

15. See Horace R. Clayton, "The Psychology of the Negro Under Discrimination," in Arnold Rose, editor, *Race Prejudice and Discrimination*, New York: Alfred Knopf, 1953, pp. 276-280; and Bertram P. Karon, *The Negro Personality*, New York: Springer, 1958, pp. 8-53, 140-160.

16. David Matza, *Delinquency and Drift*, New York: Wiley, 1964, pp. 88-90, 188-191.

17. Herbert J. Gans, *The Urban Villagers*, N. Y.: The Free Press, 1962, p. 49. According to another student of Italian-American life, slum-dwelling members of this subculture believe that "a man's health requires sexual intercourse at certain intervals." William F. Whyte, "A Slum Sex Code," *American Journal of Sociology*, 49 (July, 1943), p. 26.

18. Oscar Lewis, *The Children of Sanchez*, New York: Random House, 1961, p. 475.

19. Gordon Westwood, *A Minority*, London: Longmans, Green and Co., 1960, p. 46.

20. For an interesting study showing that criminals believe that a fellow criminal's physical attractiveness will vary with type of crime—robbers are the most attractive, murderers the least; rapists are more attractive than pedophiles, etc.—see Raymond J. Corsini, "Appearance and Criminality," *American Journal of Sociology*, 65 (July, 1959), pp. 49-51.

21. Adorno, *op. cit.*, pp. 233, 485; Allport, *op. cit.*, pp. 235-249, suggests the historicity and uniqueness of each instance of scapegoating.

22. Arturo de Hoyos and Genevieve de Hoyos, "The Amigo System and Alienation of the Wife in the Conjugal Mexican Fam-

ily," in Bernard Farber, editor, *Kinship and Family Organization*, New York: Wiley, 1966, pp. 102-115, esp., pp. 103-107.

23. Lewis, *op. cit.*, p. 143.

24. *Ibid.*, p. 202.

25. *Ibid.*, p. 86.

26. Gresham M. Sykes and David Matza, "Techniques of Neutralization," *American Sociological Review*, 22 (December, 1957), pp. 667-669.

27. One other neutralization technique mentioned by Sykes and Matza, "denial of responsibility," is subsumed in our schema under "appeal to defeasibility."

28. Note that appeal to loyalties could be an excuse if the argument runs that X did to A under the influence of Y's domination or love, or under the coercive influence of Y's injury to him were he not to act, e.g., loss of love, blackmail, etc. In other words, appeal to loyalties is an excuse if X admits it was bad to do A, but refuses to monopolize responsibility for A in himself.

29. Erving Goffman, *Asylums*, Garden City: Doubleday Anchor, 1961, pp. 150-151. The sad tale involves the most dramatic instance of the general process of reconstructing personal biography whereby—for example—a husband may account for his present divorce by reconstructing the history of earlier events in an ascending scale leading up to the final dissolution. The idea of a reconstruction of biography is a continual theme in the writings of Alfred Schutz. See his *Collected Papers*, Vol. I, edited by Maurice Natanson, The Hague: Martinus Nijhoff, 1962. A short clear summary of Schutz's contribution on the reconstruction of biography is found in Peter L. Berger, *Invitation to Sociology*, Garden City: Doubleday Anchor, 1963, pp. 54-65. Drawing on Schutz, Garfinkel details the concept of reconstruction of biography in a series of experiments on the "retrospective reading" of social action. See his "Common Sense Knowledge of Social Structures," in *Theories of the Mind*, edited by Jordon M. Scher, Glencoe: The Free Press, 1962, pp. 689-712. The empirical use of the concept of retrospective reading of action is nicely illustrated by John I. Kitsuse, "Societal Reaction to Deviant Behavior," in *The Other Side*, edited by Howard S. Becker, New York: The Free Press of Glencoe, 1964, pp. 87-102.

30. Goffman, *op. cit.*, p. 152.

31. Westwood, *op. cit.*, p. 32.

32. Tape-recorded interview, May 1967.

33. Tape-recorded interview, June 1967.

34. Erving Goffman, *Encounters*, In-

dianapolis: Bobbs-Merrill, 1961, pp. 45-48.

35. *Ibid.*, p. 51.

36. John Selden, *Table Talk*, 1696, quoted in Harry Johnson, *Sociology*, New York: Harcourt, Brace and Co., 1960, p. 552n.

37. The term is borrowed from Harold Garfinkel. Besides the footnote references to Garfinkel already cited, see his *Studies in Ethnomethodology*, Englewood Cliffs, N. J.: Prentice-Hall, 1968. For an original discussion on how the meaning of an account depends upon background expectancies and a methodology for its study, see Harvey Sacks, *The Search for Help*, unpublished doctoral dissertation, University of California, Berkeley, 1966.

38. On how background expectations are used to determine whether a person is judged criminal or sick see the neglected essay by Vilhelm Aubert and Sheldon L. Messinger, "The Criminal and the Sick," *Inquiry*, 1 (Autumn, 1958), pp. 137-160.

39. This formulation is persistently (and we believe rightly) argued in the various writings of Ernest Becker. See especially *The Revolution in Psychiatry*, N. Y.: The Free Press of Glencoe, 1964; and his essay "Mills' Social Psychology and the Great Historical Convergence on the Problem of Alienation," in *The New Sociology*, edited by Irving L. Horowitz, N. Y.: Oxford University Press, 1964, pp. 108-133.

40. In the case of schizophrenics, it has been noted that they are individuals who construct overly elaborate accounts, i.e., accounts that are perceived as being elaborately constructed. These accounts, it appears, take the form of "building up" the possibilities of a situation that others find improbable. Thus the paranoid husband accounts for his frenzied state by relating that his wife went shopping—and, to him, going shopping constitutes the most opportune occasion to rendezvous secretly with a lover. In response to the inquirer, the paranoid asks: "If you wanted to meet a lover, wouldn't you tell your spouse you're going shopping?" For a general discussion, see Becker, *The Revolution in Psychiatry*, *op. cit.*

41. Erving Goffman, *Presentation of Self in Everyday Life*, University of Edinburgh, 1956.

42. Albert J. Reiss, Jr., "The Social Integration of Queers and Peers," in *The Other Side*, *op. cit.*, pp. 181-210.

43. Marguerite Sechehaye, *Autobiography of a Schizophrenic Girl*, New York: Grune and Stratton, 1951.

44. See Thomas Scheff, *Being Mentally Ill*, Chicago: Aldine Press, 1966. See also Erving Goffman, *Asylums*, *op. cit.*

45. These terms are adapted from Erving Goffman, *Behavior in Public Places*, New York: The Free Press of Glencoe, 1963, p. 36n, and *Encounters*, *op cit.*, pp. 105 ff.

46. The theme is widely explored in the literature on formal organizations. For an early and perhaps still the clearest statement of the theme, see Robert K. Merton's widely reprinted "Bureaucratic Structure and Personality," available in *Complex Organizations*, edited by Amitai Etzioni, New York: Holt, Rinehart and Winston, 1962, pp. 48-60.

47. For a literary illustration, see the play by Peter Weiss, *The Investigation*, New York: Atheneum Books, 1967.

48. See Sherri Cavan, *Liquor License*, Chicago: Aldine Press, 1966, pp. 79-87.

49. Edward T. Hall, *The Hidden Dimension*, Garden City: Doubleday, 1966, pp. 139-144.

50. When a boy is interrupted by a call for an account in the midst of his own recounting of sexual exploits he may simply relapse into uncommunicative silence, change the subject, or withdraw from the group. To prevent any of these, and to aid in the continuity of the original story, the other members of the audience may urge the speaker to continue as before, assure him of their interest and support, and sharply reprove or perhaps ostracize from the group the person who called for the account.

51. We have adapted these styles from Martin Joos, *The Five Clocks*, New York: Harbinger Books, 1961.

52. Each of these linguistic styles is associated with distinctive physical distances between the interactants. For a discussion of this point see Hall, *op. cit.*, pp. 116-122.

53. Besides the five linguistic styles discussed, we may note that accounts may be usefully distinguished in the manner of their *delivery*. For a cogent typology see Robert E. Pittenger, *et al.*, *The First Five Minutes*, Ithaca, New York: Paul Martineau, 1960, p. 255.

54. Another kind of invulnerability arises in those situations in which physical presence is tantamount to task performance. Students in a classroom, parishioners in a church, and soldiers at a drill may be counted as "present"—their very visibility being all that is required for routine performance—although they might be

"away" in the vicarious sense of day-dreaming, musing on other matters, or relaxing into a reverie.

55. For these terms, in the context of strategies for avoiding accounts, we are indebted to Gregory Stone.

56. For this illustration we are again indebted to Gregory Stone. The illustration itself is derived from Oscar Lewis' *The Children of Sanchez, op. cit.*

57. For an excellent discussion of this point as well as an insightful analysis of the concept of identity, see Anselm L. Strauss, *Mirror and Masks*, New York: The Free Press of Glencoe, 1959.

58. The concept of "alter-casting" is developed by Eugene A. Weinstein and Paul Deutschberger, "Tasks, Bargains, and Identities in Social Interaction," *Social Forces*, V. 42 (May, 1964), pp. 451-456.

59. See the brilliant discussion by Thomas C. Schelling, *The Strategy of Conflict*, New York: Galaxy Books, 1963, pp. 21-52.

60. The terms "identities" and "roles" may be used as synonymous in that roles are identities mobilized in a specific situation; whereas role is always situationally specific, identities are trans-situational.

61. "An unconscious desire to be white, coupled with feelings of revulsion toward the Negro masses, may produce an assimilationist pattern of behavior at the purely personal level. Assimilation is in this sense a means of escape, a form of flight from 'the problem.' It involves a denial of one's racial identity which may be disguised by such sentiments as 'I'm not a Negro but a human being'—as if the two were mutually exclusive. This denial is accompanied by a contrived absence of race consciousness and a belittling of caste barriers. By minimizing the color line, the assimilationist loses touch with the realities of Negro life." Robert A. Bone, *The Negro Novel in America*, New Haven: Yale University Press, 1965, p. 4.

62. Frantz Fanon, *Black Skin, White Masks*, New York: Grove Press, 1967, p. 32.

63. *Ibid.*, p. 33.

64. Fanon, *ibid.*, provides one of the most graphic examples of this phenomenon. For a socioliterary treatment, see St. Clair Drake, "Hide My Face—On Pan-Africanism and Negritude," in Herbert Hill, editor, *Soon One Morning*, New York: Alfred Knopf, 1963, pp. 77-105.

65. Schelling, *op. cit.*, p. 34.

66. For a discussion on the "phasing" of encounters, see Strauss, *op. cit.*, p. 44 ff.

67. The following is from A. S. Makarenko, *The Collective Family*, Garden City: Doubleday Anchor, 1967, pp. 230-232.

68. The term is borrowed from Noam Chomsky, *Aspects of a Theory of Syntax*, Cambridge, Mass.: MIT Press, 1965, p. 10.

69. To our knowledge the most persuasive argument for this need is made by Kenneth L. Pike, *Language in Relation to a Unified Theory of the Structure of Human Behavior*, Glendale: Summer Institute of Linguistics, 1954. A short, clear programmatic statement is found in Dell Hymes' "The Ethnography of Speaking," in Thomas Gladwin and William C. Sturtevant, editors, *Anthropology and Human Behavior*, Washington, D. C.: Anthropological Society of Washington, 1962, pp. 72-85. For an argument that stresses the analytic separation of the content of talk from the forms of talk, see the brief but lucid statement by Erving Goffman, "The Neglected Situation," in The Ethnography of Communications, edited by John Gumperz and Dell Hymes, *American Anthropologist*, 66 (December, 1964), Part 2, pp. 133-136.

70. For the methodology of such studies sociologists may well investigate the anthropological technique of componential analysis, i.e., the study of contrast sets. The clearest statement of the method of componential analysis is that of Charles O. Frake, "The Ethnographic Study of Cognitive Systems," in *Anthropology and Human Behavior, op. cit.*, pp. 72-85. A related methodology is developed by Sacks in *The Search for Help, op. cit.*

71. See Charles O. Frake, "How to Ask for a Drink in Subanun," in The Ethnography of Communications, op. cit., pp. 127-132.

72. The idea of a "speech community" is usefully developed by John J. Gumperz in "Speech Variation and the Study of Indian Civilization," in *Language in Culture and Society*, edited by Dell Hymes, N. Y.: Harper and Row, 1964, pp. 416-423; and "Linguistic and Social Interaction in Two Communities," in *Ethnography of Communications, op. cit.*, pp. 137-153.

73. We refer to the approach to deviance clearly summarized by Howard S. Becker, *The Outsiders*, New York: The Free Press of Glencoe, 1963, esp. pp. 1-18.

16. SOCIAL STRUCTURE AND VOCABULARIES OF DISCOMFORT: WHAT HAPPENED TO FEMALE HYSTERIA?*

PAULINE BART

Reprinted from Pauline Bart, "Social Structure and Vocabularies of Discomfort: What Happened to Female Hysteria?", *Journal of Health and Social Behavior*, Vol. 9, No. 3 (Sept. 1968) pp. 188-193, with permission of the author and the *Journal of Health and Social Behavior*. Pauline Bart is an Associate Professor in the medical center at the University of Illinois, Chicago circle. She has published articles in the *Journal of Health and Social Behavior*, and has written widely on the phenomenon of depression.

Sociologists have long been aware that illness is not an "objective" fact perceived, reacted to and reported similarly by members of all sub-cultures. In 1958, Hollingshead and Redlich (244-248) pointed out that "social and cultural conditions do influence the development of various types of psychiatric disorders at different social class levels in important ways." In addition, they observed that neurotics in various classes reacted to their discomfort in different ways, so that, for example, the Class I and II neurotics expressed dissatisfaction with themselves while the Class IV neurotics ached physically (Hollingshead and Redlich, 1958:240). Zborowski (1952:16-30) showed how Irish, Italians, and Jews responded differently to pain, while Zola (1966:612-630) showed the socio-cultural determinants of perception of and reaction

to symptoms. Furthermore, Scheff, (1966:114-141) studying users and non-users of a student psychiatric clinic, found "there is a psychiatric public, whose members are oriented toward clinic-use with fewer symptoms than non-members."

Ways of expressing illness have also changed through *time*. In the nineteenth century, when Freud had just begun to develop his theories, it was fashionable for middle-class women to faint or to take to their couches or beds *a la* Elizabeth Barrett for vague interminable "illnesses." Such behavior is no longer tolerated in our more psychologically sophisticated circles. Fainting is no longer considered a sign of femininity. In some highly educated circles, *all* illnesses are suspected of being "psychosomatic"; and, rather than retiring to a couch, the individual goes to be treated on a couch. Jules Feiffer, (1960) has expressed the vocabulary of motives of this group in a cartoon monologue which reads as follows:

I woke up one morning and I couldn't breathe. So, of course, I figured it was psycho-somatic. A free flowing withdrawal from unhappy visions. After that I developed a heaviness in my chest. So, of course, I figured it was psycho-somatic. A masochistic act of self reproval toward my

*This investigation was supported in part by a pre-doctoral research training fellowship (#2-F1-MH-215-04 BEH A) from the National Institute of Mental Health of the U.S. Department of Health, Education and Welfare. Computing assistance was obtained from the Health Sciences Computing Facility, U.C.L.A.-sponsored NIH Grant FR-3. I have benefited from discussing this paper with John Horton, Ph.D., and Marvin Karno, M.D. Noelle Herzog helped in the computations. An earlier version of this paper was presented at the Pacific Sociological Association meetings, 1967.

body. Then I got this gosh awful sneeze. So, of course, I figured it was psycho-somatic. An acting out, through germs, of my latent hostility toward society. Naturally I grew worried about my emotional well-being. I went to see a psychiatrist. He told me I had a cold.

Psychoanalytic theory and technique evolved around this conversion process—that is, the process by which psychic stresses are changed into physical disabilities—since many of the patients whom Freud treated were of this type. While it has been suggested that, due to the greater psychological sophistication of the population, the conversion process as described by Freud is no longer being manifested by patients (Freud, 1963; 1948, 1936; Easser and Lesser, 1965:390-405), Szasz (1961:76) disagrees.

Those who suffer from it (the conversion process), do not as a rule consult psychiatrists or psychoanalysts. Rather they consult their family physicians or internists and are then referred to neurologists, neurosurgeons, orthopedic and general surgeons and other *medical* specialists. Rarely do medical advisors define such a patient's difficulties as psychiatric. Physicians may dread referring the patient to a psychiatrist, mainly because such a referral requires that they redefine the nature of the patient's difficulty . . .

Many researchers (Szasz, 1961:77; Miller and Swanson, 1960:397; Hollingshead and Redlich, 1958:359; Zeigler et al., 1960:901-910; Lidz: 818-836; Gurin et al., 1960:203) have stated that individuals manifesting conversion reactions are more likely to come from rural areas and tend to have a lower social class background. Hollingshead and Redlich (1958:226) pointed out that "Psychosomatic reactions . . . are related inversely to class"; Class V patients, the lowest social class, "are unable to understand that their troubles are not physical illnesses. . . . They expect 'pills and

needles' " (1958:340). Langner and Michael found that in "Midtown" the low social class respondents had more than their share of hypochondriachal and psychosomatic symptoms (1963: 407). The author of this paper suggests that—regardless of the distribution of psychosomatic illness—it is only in psychologically sophisticated circles that the psychogenic contribution to the discomfort is recognized.[1]

The intention of this study is to investigate the socio-cultural differences between (1) women who present themselves as physically ill and request admission to the Neurology Section of the U.C.L.A. Neuro-psychiatric Institute but are discharged with a psychiatric diagnoses—usually hysteria or psychophysiological reaction—and (2) those women who are willing to assume the role of the mentally ill individual[2] and apply for admission to the Psychiatry Section of the U.C.L.A. Neuro-psychiatric Institute.

HYPOTHESIS

It was hypothesized that women who entered the Neurology Service and were discharged with psychiatric diagnoses would have different socio-cultural backgrounds than women who presented themselves to the Psychiatry Service. These differences could be explained using Mills' concept of "Vocabulary of Motives". (1940) He states:

What is reason for one man is rationalization for another. The variable is the accepted vocabulary of motives, the ultimates of discourse of each man's dominant group about whose opinion he cares. . . . When they appeal to others involved in one's act, motives are strategies of action. In many social actions, others must agree, tacitly or explicitly. Thus acts often will be abandoned if no results can be found that others will accept.

In "Language, Logic and Culture" Mills remarks that language can be thought of as a system of social control with vocabularies socially canalizing thought (1939). An acceptable way of accounting for and describing pain or discontent is a type of vocabulary of motive. (As Gurin, et al., pointed out, "It is not feelings of distress alone that are important for self-referral behavior, going to a psychiatrist, physician, clergyman or other "helping professional" to discuss personal problems, but rather the ways of defining this distress." 1960:279). Therefore, it was predicted that women who entered Neurology and emerged with psychiatric diagnoses would belong to sub-cultures less likely to have psychiatric vocabularies of discomfort, and this would be reflected in the way they presented themselves, i.e., as physically rather than emotionally ill.[3]

Since groups accepting psychiatric reasons for behavior and feelings are more likely to be urban, of higher social status, have more education[4] and be Jewish, I predicted that the women entering the Neurology Service whose complaints were found to have a psychogenic origin would be of lower social status, rural, less highly educated, and not Jewish.

METHOD

As part of a larger study, (Bart, 1967) the clinical records of all women first admission[5] in-patients between the ages of 40 and 59 who entered the U.C.L.A. Neuropsychiatric Institute[6] Psychiatry Service during the years 1961 through 1964 with functional, i.e., non-organic illnesses were examined (N=63). The clinical records of women admitted to the Neurology Service for the same age group and during the same time period were also examined; that is, women who were considered by themselves, their referring physician, and the admitting physician to be suffering from an unclear but potentially specifiable organic illness such as myasthena gravis, but who were discharged with a psychiatric diagnosis (N=21). Socio-cultural data were recorded, case histories were abstracted, and percentages were obtained on the different variables.[7]

FINDINGS

The differences found between the two groups support the hypothesis. More of the women who entered the Neurology Service were housewives, and more had not worked since marriage. Therefore, they were less likely to come into contact with groups having more "sophisticated" explanations for behavior and feelings, i.e., psychiatric ones. They were more rural in both birthplaces and present residence. More were born in the South Atlantic, South Central and Mountain and Pacific states (excluding California)—the less industrialized sections of the United States, particularly when these women were growing up four decades ago. Unfortunately there is no information on their birthplace, except for native state, for 71 per cent of the women. None of the 29 per cent for whom additional information was available was born in a large city, i.e., a city that had more than a quarter of a million population in the 1920 census. Thus, one can say that they came from farms, small towns or small cities in predominantly rural states. More of them live outside Los Angeles County, generally in the small towns, such as Vista, which dot the California countryside. Fewer of the women were Jewish; and it is known that Jews as a group have the most favorable attitudes toward psychiatric treatment as a means of solving personal problems (for evidence supporting this point, see Srole et al., 1962:317; Myers and Roberts, 1948:551-559; Meadow and Vetter, 1959:198-207). Their social status was usually lower, social status being indicated by education, occupation of spouse and area of residence. Fewer of them went to college. Fewer of them had husbands who were professionals. While the median occupation for the spouses of women entering the Psychiatry Service was ranked 3.0, "administrative personnel, independent businessman or minor professional," the median occupation of the spouses of the women entering the Neurology Service was ranked 4.5, a

number falling between the occupations of clerical work and of skilled manual labor.[8] Those who did live in Los Angeles County resided more often in status areas of residence.[9]

Further evidence, albeit indirect, supporting the claim that the women entering the Neurology Service tend to somatize their difficulties may be found in their rate of hysterectomy —52 per cent compared with 21 per cent for the women in the Psychiatry Service. While one may argue that the decision to perform a hysterectomy rests with the physician, great variation exists among physicians about when this surgical procedure is necessary. For example, an M.D. (psychiatrist) I interviewed at another mental hospital suggested that *all* women over 40 have hysterectomies for

TABLE 16.1.
COMPARISON OF PSYCHIATRY AND NEUROLOGY SERVICE*
WOMEN FIRST ADMISSIONS AGED 40-59**

	Psychiatry Service		Neurology Service	
	%	(N)	%	(N)
Occupation				
Housewives	46	(63)	76	(21)
Not worked since marriage	35	(57)	71	(21)
Residence				
Out of L.A. County	19	(63)	29	(21)
Region of Birth				
Rural (less industrialized)	33	(48)	79	(19)
Religion				
Jewish	34	(56)	14	(21)
Rank of Residential Area				
Areas ranked IV, V, VI (lower)	24	(51)	40	(15)
Education				
Some college	38	(59)	20	(15)
Husbands' Occupation				
Median Rank	3		4.5	
Professional	27	(36)	14	(15)
Hysterectomy	21	(63)	52	(21)

*Those Neurology Service women discharged with psychiatric diagnoses.
**The appropriateness of x^2 is moot, since *every* case meeting the criteria for the four-year period was used; thus, this is not a *sample*. On the other hand, the four-year period can be considered a sample in *time*. For readers who take the latter position, the following differences were found to be significant: Occupation, .02; Not worked since marriage, .005; Rural, .0025; Hysterectomy, .005.

"prophylactic" purposes (to prevent cancer of the uterus). Thus it would be possible for a woman to "shop around" until she found a doctor who would perform the surgery she wanted. As the selection process was controlled for age, the differences cannot be explained in generational terms, such as might be the case if the women who entered the Psychiatry Service were younger.

At this point, three cases will be briefly examined to exemplify the differences under discussion: one who entered Neurology and then followed the staff's advice and transferred to Psychiatry; one who was a patient at Neurology and refused to transfer to Psychiatry;[10] and one who entered Psychiatry but presented many physical complaints. The first woman had characteristics of both groups—the women who entered Psychiatry and those who entered Neurology. While her background was rural and her status of origin low, she was a school teacher and a college graduate. The second woman, who refused a suggested transfer to Psychiatry, was a housewife from Arkansas and had not completed high school. While no information was available on her husband's occupation, in all likelihood she was working class, as her residential area was ranked V on a six-point scale (Meeker, 1967). The third woman, who presented herself to the Psychiatry Service with "backaches, exhaustion, and swollen glands in her neck," as well as anxiety and depression, but who accepted psychological reasons for her physical complaints according to her psychiatrist, was Jewish, was raised in Chicago, lived in Los Angeles, graduated from high school, had originally been a dancer, and now worked as a bill-collector.

ALTERNATIVE EXPLANATIONS

There are two possible alternative explanations of these data. First, higher status, better-educated hysterics may have lower visibility—that is, they may disguise the psychogenic nature of their illness so cleverly that the doctors at Neurology may not re-diagnose them. In addition, the doctors may not wish to stigmatize them with psychiatric diagnoses. Second, the rural-urban differences found may be caused by Neurology patients' from outside Los Angeles being referred to U.C.L.A., while psychiatric patients from within the area go to local psychiatric hospitals or to the psychiatric wards of local general hospitals. However, I believe that the explanation presented in this paper is more satisfactory for the following reasons: First, the doctor caring for the patient on the Neurology Service is not the patient's private physician and is, therefore, less likely to be concerned about the possible stigma of a psychiatric diagnosis. In addition, the wealth of testing equipment used to diagnose physical illness at the U.C.L.A. Neuropsychiatric Institute is so great that it would be extremely difficult to "fool" the staff. Secondly, even if the greater proportion of women coming from outside Los Angeles County can be explained by the greater likelihood of their being referred to the Neurology Service rather than being treated locally, this explanation would not tell us why there was a difference in *birthplace* among the women in the sample.[11]

CONCLUSION

It was hypothesized that women who entered a neurology service, but who were discharged with psychiatric diagnoses, would differ from women of similar age who presented themselves to the psychiatry service of the same hospital. It was predicted that the women entering the neurology service would be more likely to come from less sophisticated sub-cultures where psychiatric explanations were less prevalent. The hypotheses were supported. The women who entered Neurology were more likely to come from less sophisticated sub-cultures where psychiatric explanations were less prevalent. They were born in more rural states and were more likely to live outside Los Angeles County, were more often housewives, were less likely to have ever worked, were less likely to have gone to college, were less likely to have husbands with professional occupations, were more likely to have husbands with lower status occupations, were more likely to live in lower status areas of Los Angeles County, and were less likely to be Jewish.

NOTES

1. In this discussion, conversion is not limited to the voluntary body systems, for, as Freud put it, "We choose to designate the term 'conversion' as the transformation of psychic excitement into chronic physical symptoms, which characterized hysteria." cf. J. Breuer, and S. Freud, 1936:61. Rangell (1959:632-661) agrees with this point of view.

2. The term "assuming the role of the mentally ill person" is used because all admissions to the Psychiatry Service are "voluntary."

3. Individuals with high scores on the physical health factor are less likely to go for psychological help than people with psychological anxiety, even though the former may be an indication of psychological problems. Gurin, et al., 1960.

4. "Education operates at all three of the decision points: the higher educated more often defined problems they had experienced as mental health problems, more often translated this definition into an actual going for help, and more often chose psychiatric therapy. Thus, education represents both a more psychological orientation toward the self and the facilitating effects of a greater awareness of resources (particularly psychiatric ones) and a social climate more favorable to the use of therapy in general and in the use of psychiatric resources in particular.

Place of residence is also relevant . . . Rural people less often defined problems in mental health terms and, even within such a definition, less often go for help." Gurin, 1960:340.

5. A first admission is an individual who has had no previous admissions to a hospital for psychiatric care.

6. The U.C.L.A. Neuropsychiatric Institute is a training and research center in psychiatry and neurology.

7. The resultant N, 21, is small for purposes of analysis; however, since the U.C.L.A. NPI has been in operation only since 1961, these were *all* the cases that were available. The small N should be taken into consideration when generalizing from these data.

8. The ranking of occupations is based on the Hollingshead ranking. His occupational scale has seven categories ranging from "Higher Executives, Proprietors of Large Concerns and Major Professionals" (1) to "Unskilled Employees" (7). See Hollingshead and Redlich, 1958, Appendix Two for a more detailed description of the scale.

9. One relationship for which I have no explanation is the greater number of married, as contrasted with separated or divorced, women entering the Neurology Service. The data are, however, consistent with Gurin, et al., who found that divorced women go for psychiatric help more often than people in other groups.

10. While I did not have the necessary information telling whether other Neurology Service patients would have transferred to Psychiatry, I suspect that they wouldn't in most cases. Both Guze and Perly, in "Observations on the Natural History of Hysteria", (1963:960-965) and Zeigler et al., (1960:901-910) state that most patients with conversion reactions refuse psychotherapy. "In fact, refusal to accept a

psychiatric approach to their condition appears to be characteristic of the patients with this disorder," according to Guze and Perly.

11. There is a third theory which is not alternative but complementary. It suggests that admission to an in-patient service reflects the effect of the "helping profes-

sions" in the patient's definition of her illness. It is likely that there is an interaction between the views of one's reference groups and one's choice of doctor. Thus women without psychiatric vocabularies would reject doctors who interpreted their symptoms in psychodynamic terms.

References

Bart, Pauline B. 1967. "Depression in Middle Aged Women: Some Socio-Cultural Factors", Ph.D. Dissertation, U.C.L.A.

Breuer, J., and Sigmund Freud. 1936. "Studies in Hysteria." New York: Nervous and Mental Disease Publications.

Easser, Barbara R., and Stanley R. Lesser. 1965. "Hysterical personality: a reevaluation". The Psychoanalytic Quarterly 34 (July):390-405.

Freud, Sigmund. 1948. "The Defense

Neuro-psychoses." Collected Papers. London: Hogarth Press.

———. Dora—An Analysis of a Case of Hysteria. New York: Collier Books.

Gurin, Gerald et al. 1960. Americans View Their Mental Health. New York: Basic Books.

Guze, S. B., and Michael J. Perly. 1963. "Observations on the natural history of hysteria". American Journal of Psychiatry 119 (April):960-965.

Hollingshead, A. B., and Frederick C. Redlich. 1958. "Social Class and Mental

Illness. New York: John Wiley.

Langner, Thomas S., and T. Michael Stanley. 1963. Life Stress and Mental Health. Glencoe: Free Press.

Lidz, Theodore. "Hysteria." Encyclopedia of Mental Health III. New York: Watts.

Meadow, Arnold, and Harold J. Vetter. 1959. "Freudian theory and the Judaic value system". International Journal of Social Psychiatry 5 (Winter):198-207.

Meeker, Marchia. 1964. Background for Planning. Los Angeles: Welfare Planning Council, Los Angeles Region.

Miller, Daniel R., and Guy E. Swanson. 1960. Inner Conflict and Defense. New York: Holt, Rinehart and Winston.

Mills, C. Wright. 1939. "Language, logic and culture." American Sociological Review 4 (October).

———. 1940. "Situated actions and vocabularies of motive". American Sociological Review 5 (December).

Myers, Jerome K., and Bertram H. Roberts. 1948. "Some Relationships between Religion, Ethnic Origin, and Mental Illness." The Jews. Marshall Sklare

(ed.). Glencoe: The Free Press.

Rangell, Leo. 1959. "The nature of conversion." Journal of the American Psychoanalytic Association 7 (October):632-661.

Scheff, Thomas J. 1966. "Users and non-users of a student psychiatric clinic". Journal of Health and Human Behavior 7 (Summer):114-141.

Srole, Leo, et al. 1962. Mental Health in the Metropolis. New York: McGraw Hill.

Szasz, Thomas S. 1961. The Myth of Mental Illness. New York: Hoeber-Harper.

Times, Los Angeles. 1960. (March 6).

Zborowski, Mark. 1952. "Cultural components in response to pain". The Journal of Social Issues 8 (Fall): 16-30.

Zeigler. F. J., et al. 1960. "Contemporary conversion reactions: a clinical study". American Journal of Psychiatry 116 (April):901-910.

Zola, Irving Kenneth. 1966. "Culture and symptoms—an analysis of patients' presenting complaints". American Sociological Review 31 (October): 612-630.

V. THE NATURE OF INSTITUTED RELATIONSHIPS

Two major orientations, derived from two distinct philosophical backgrounds, have competed for the domain called social psychology. The first is a "structural" orientation, which postulates the existence of certain abstract superstructures that are seen as the locus of causation for most observable human action. The second orientation, which may be termed "process," emphasizes the ongoing nature of human action and the ways in which human beings build up the ever-changing sets of meanings around which their lives revolve. The first orientation is a kind of social psychology of boxes, the second a social psychology of streams.

Structural orientations, as Herbert Blumer[1] has suggested, generally emphasize certain "non-acting" units as the initiators of social action. These units are variously conceived as rules, norms, customs, institutions, values, or attitudes. The focus of structural analysis is on how these "non-acting" abstractions influence the responsive human organism, who is often not even aware of their existence. The usual theoretical procedure is to begin with the structural concepts and to proceed downward in an effort to understand human actions.

A dramaturgical conception of social life, as we have seen, begins with the observation that acting rather than non-acting units comprise the subject matter of social psychology. These acting units (people) are constantly engaged in a collective construction of the realities in which

1. H. Blumer, *Symbolic Interactionism: Perspective & Method.* (Englewood Cliffs: Prentice-Hall, 1969).

they live. Social order is built up through interaction rather than released out of some alleged pre-existing structure; the process of building
occurs through the twin actions of definition and interpretation. To the
extent that this process occurs more or less routinely and deals with the
same kinds of problems, we sometimes speak in the abstract of these
collective forms as "social institutions." There can be little doubt that
many of our actions occur in a context of problems that all human beings
face more or less continually. Such problems as the allocation of resources, the distribution of economic and political power, the legitimation of sexual behavior, the rearing of children, the worship of the
almighty, the confrontation with birth and death, and the control of
deviance seem to be universal. These concerns are so prevalent that
scholars sometimes forget that each of them involves a process of interpretation and definition without which their social reality would be
tenuous indeed. In addition, cross-cultural studies teach us that we
ignore this process at our own peril, for different action creates different
outcomes, even when the same types of problems are faced.[2]

The dramaturgical orientation stresses what can best be called the
relational basis of social institutions. When we speak of marriage or the
family, for example, we are ordinarily speaking of a series of relationships that are continually "instituted" or defined in more or less the
same way, in terms of a social interpretation that has wide currency in a
particular society. This interpretation, however, must, be established
and reestablished for it to be maintained, no matter how widely it is held.
Institutions, like all other forms of interactive meaning, are subject to
sequential careers of birth, life, and death.

It is the contention of the authors in the following selections that social
institutions are in fact instituted sets of behaviors that occur in continually re-established contexts. The construction of the routines establishes
the institution, not the other way around. Institutions are not reflected in
behavior nor is behavior a mere outcome of institutional "forces." If
behavior changes, the institution changes, even though the participants
may still have to deal with the same types of problems. Alternatives to
marriage, for example, still involve attempts on the part of the participants to deal with many of the same relational and social problems that
traditional marriage tries to resolve. The student ferment of the 1960s
brought into focus the idea that the behavior of acting human beings
creates the institution, and if that behavior changes even venerable
ivy-covered walls may come tumbling down.

Central to the dramaturgical conception of instituted relationships is
the matter of human responsibility. The assessment of responsibility is
one of the most routine but vital activities in which people engage. The

2. The wide variety of interpretations and concomitant social realities is explored with
great facility in the work of Carlos Castaneda; see especially his *A Separate Reality* (New
York: Pocketbooks, 1972).

outcome of the assessment process sometimes can spell the difference between whether people spend the rest of their days languishing in a jail cell or in a mental hospital. In the first selection, Thomas Scheff upsets many commonsense assumptions by arguing that whereas most persons hold an absolutist conception of responsibility, actually the entire matter is ordinarily the outcome of an interactive negotiation in which the acts of the present are reconstructing the reality of the past.

Scheff offers two illustrations of the negotiation of responsibility. The first is a psychiatric interview in which a patient's "mental illness" is being diagnosed by a psychiatrist. The patient offers her version of the problem, the psychiatrist counters with his own version, and finally the patient tells him what he wishes to hear. The other case is a fictional interview between a defense attorney and his client. In both cases we see that a drama of significant proportions is being staged, and that the institutional context is only part of the show. The stage and many of the props have been "institutionalized" in American society, but the outcomes are indeterminate in the sense that they are the result of specific moves made on the stage. The key point made by Scheff is that certain characters in a drama wield greater power to have their definitions of reality acted upon than do others. For instance, a patient in a psychiatric setting may well decide that the psychiatrist's interpretation of what he was "really doing" is accurate, or at least the most expedient interpretation, after all.

Marriage is also a negotiated reality. In the second selection, Peter Berger and Hansfried Kellner conceive of marriage as " a dramatic act in which two strangers come together and redefine themselves." Marriage, in this sense, is a transforming drama in which the acts of the partners, no matter who they were before or how long they had known each other, are essentially new. They must decide together what they are to be and how they are to live. Not surprisingly, marriage alters old realities in the process of constructing new ones. Old friends known to either spouse, or even perhaps to both of them prior to marriage, are often ignored because they suddenly do not fit the new reality being built. The couple may be attracted to others who strengthen their new definition of themselves and avoid persons who may weaken this definition. The authors argue that the sort of constructions that go on in marriage are crucial to the lives of many people and that in fact the frequency of divorce and especially of remarriage bear this out. Participants do not opt out of the drama because they don't like the play but because the play is so essential that it must be done right, even if a new cast must be found to carry it off.

One of the most important types of human relationships is instituted in the context of religious experience. Religion offers links to a sacred world that is regularly constructed by people in the course of their activities and yet, paradoxically, is regarded as independent of their constructions. Drawing on phenomenology and existentialism, Peter Berger in the next selection weaves a dialectic interpretation of society and the individual, in which human beings create their world and then see their world as creating them. According to Berger, religion is that part of the human enterprise of world building by which a sacred cosmos is established.

The final selection offers a fascinating insight into a dramaturgical world not often conceived as such. Joseph Gusfield's study of the American Temperance Movement led him to the conclusion that most theories of political action are inadequate because they do not sufficiently recognize the symbolic and dramatic elements involved in political movements. Following Kenneth Burke, Gusfield shows how political rituals function as "secular prayers" that are used to "sharpen up the pointless and blunt the too sharply pointed." Often these rituals involve two types of dramatic symbolism: gestures of cohesion and gestures of differentiation. The first serve to bring together common interests and appeal to unifying elements; coronations, inaugurals, even fireside chats are examples. In the second, politicians are confronted with the need to establish who they are by pointing to some groups they glorify and others they despise. The audience is offered a way of deciding whether the politician is "for people like us" or "against people like us." These dramatic elements of the political process point up clearly Goffman's contention that "the more the individual is concerned with the reality that is not available to perception, the more must he concentrate on appearances."[3]

3. E. Goffman, *Presentation of Self in Everyday Life* (New York: Anchor Books, 1959) p. 249.

SUGGESTED READINGS

Blumer, Herbert. "Society as Symbolic Interaction," in A. Rose, *Human Behavior and Social Processes* (Boston: Houghton-Mufflin, 1962) pp. 179-192.

Bolton, Charles. "Is Sociology A Behavioral Science?" *Pacific Sociological Review*, Vol. 6 (Spring, 1963) pp. 3-9.

Bolton, Charles. "Behavior, Experience, and Relationships: A Symbolic Interactionist Point of View," *American Journal of Sociology*, Vol. 64 (1959) pp. 45-58.

Brissett, Dennis. "Collective Behavior: The Sense of a Rubric," *American Journal of Sociology*, Vol. 74 (July, 1968) pp. 73-91.

Dreitzel, Hans Peter. *Recent Sociology No. 2* (New York: Macmillan Publishing Co., 1970).

Holtzler, Burkart. *Reality Construction in Society*, (Cambridge, Mass.: Schenkman Publishing Co., 1968).

Klapp, Orrin E. *Heroes, Villains, and Fools*, (Englewood Cliffs, N. J.: Prentice-Hall Publishing Co., 1962).

Riesman, David. *The Lonely Crowd*, (New Haven, Conn.: Yale University Press, 1950).

Stone, Gregory. "Halloween and the Mass Child," *American Quarterly*, Vol. 11 (Fall, 1959), pp. 372-379.

Wrong, Dennis. "The Oversocialized Conception of Man in Modern Sociology," *American Sociological Review*, Vol. XXVI (April, 1961) pp. 183-193.

17. NEGOTIATING REALITY: NOTES ON POWER IN THE ASSESSMENT OF RESPONSIBILITY*

THOMAS SCHEFF

Reprinted from Thomas J. Scheff, in *Social Problems,* Vol. 16, No. 1 (Summer, 1968) pp. 3-17, with permission of the author and *Social Problems.* Thomas Scheff is professor of sociology at the University of California at Santa Barbara. He was one of the first to recognize the problems associated with mental disorder as having a social and behavioral (as opposed to a medical) basis, and is the author of the well-known *Being Mentally Ill: A Sociological Theory.*

The use of interrogation to reconstruct parts of an individual's past history is a common occurrence in human affairs. Reporters, jealous lovers, and policemen on the beat are often faced with the task of determining events in another person's life, and the extent to which he was responsible for those events. The most dramatic use of interrogation to determine responsibility is in criminal trials. As in everyday life, criminal trials are concerned with both act and intent. Courts, in most cases, first determine whether the defendant performed a legally forbidden act. If it is found that he did so, the court then must decide whether he was "responsible" for the act. Reconstructive work of this type goes on less dramatically in a wide variety of other settings, as well. The social worker determining a client's eligibility for unemployment compensation, for example, seeks not only to establish that the client actually is unemployed, but that he has actively sought employment, i.e., that he himself is not responsible for being out of work.

This paper will contrast two perspectives on the process of reconstructing past events for the purpose of fixing responsibility. The first perspective stems from the common sense notion that interrogation, when it is sufficiently skillful, is essentially neutral. Responsibility for past actions can be fixed absolutely and independently of the method of reconstruction. This perspective is held by the typical member of society, engaged in his day-to-day tasks. It is also held, in varying degrees, by most professional interrogators. The basic working doctrine is one of *absolute* responsibility. This point of view actually entails the comparison of two different kinds of items: first, the fixing of actions and intentions, and secondly, comparing these actions and intentions to some pre-determined criteria of responsibility. The basic premise of the doctrine of absolute responsibility is that both actions and intentions, on the one hand, and the criteria of responsibility, on the other, are absolute, in that they can be assessed independently of social context.[1]

An alternative approach follows from the sociology of knowledge. From this point of view, the reality

*The author wishes to acknowledge the help of the following persons who criticized earlier drafts: Aaron Cicourel, Donald Cressey, Joan Emerson, Erving Goffman, Michael Katz, Lewis Kurke, Robert Levy, Sohan Lal Sharma, and Paul Weubben. The paper was written during a fellowship provided by the Social Science Research Institute, University of Hawaii.

within which members of society conduct their lives is largely of their own construction.[2] Since much of reality is a construction, there may be multiple realities, existing side by side, in harmony or in competition. It follows, if one maintains this stance, that the assessment of responsibility involves the construction of reality by members; construction both of actions and intentions, on the one hand, and of criteria of responsibility, on the other. The former process, the continuous reconstruction of the normative order, has long been the focus of sociological concern.[3] The discussion in this paper will be limited, for the most part, to the former process, the way in which actions and intentions are constructed in the act of assessing responsibility.

My purpose is to argue that responsibility is at least partly a product of social structure. The alternative to the doctrine of absolute responsibility is that of relative responsibility: the assessment of responsibility always includes a process of negotiation. In this process, responsibility is in part constructed by the negotiating parties. To illustrate this thesis, excerpts from two dialogues of negotiation will be discussed: a real psychotherapeutic interview, and an interview between a defense attorney and his client, taken from a work of fiction. Before presenting these excerpts it will be useful to review some prior discussions of negotiation, the first in courts of law, the second in medical diagnosis.[4]

The negotiation of pleas in criminal courts, sometimes referred to as "bargain justice," has been frequently noted by observers of legal processes.[5] The defense attorney, or (in many cases, apparently) the defendant himself, strikes a bargain with the prosecutor—a plea of guilty will be made, provided that the prosecutor will reduce the charge. For example, a defendant arrested on suspicion of armed robbery may arrange to plead guilty to the charge of unarmed robbery. The prosecutor obtains ease of conviction from the bargain, the defendant, leniency.

Although no explicit estimates are given, it appears from observers' reports that the great majority of criminal convictions are negotiated. Newman states:

A major characteristic of criminal justice administration, particularly in jurisdictions characterized by legislatively fixed sentences, is charge reduction to elicit pleas of guilty. Not only does the efficient functioning of criminal justice rest upon a high proportion of guilty pleas, but plea bargaining is closely linked with attempts to individualize justice, to obtain certain desirable conviction consequences, and to avoid undesirable ones such as "undeserved" mandatory sentences.[6]

It would appear that the bargaining process is accepted as routine. In the three jurisdictions Newman studied, there were certain meeting places where the defendant, his client, and a representative of the prosecutor's office routinely met to negotiate the plea. It seems clear that in virtually all but the most unusual cases, the interested parties expected to, and actually did, negotiate the plea.

From these comments on the routine acceptance of plea bargaining in the courts, one might expect that this process would be relatively open and unambiguous. Apparently, however, there is some tension between the fact of bargaining and moral expectations concerning justice. Newman refers to this tension by citing two contradictory statements: an actual judicial opinion, "Justice and liberty are not the subjects of bargaining and barter"; and an off-the-cuff statement by another judge, "All law is compromise." A clear example of this tension is provided by an excerpt from a trial and Newman's comments on it.

The following questions were asked of a defendant after he had pleaded guilty to unarmed robbery when the original charge was armed robbery. This reduction is common, and the judge was fully aware that the plea was negotiated:

Judge: You want to plead guilty to robbery unarmed?
Defendant: Yes, Sir.
Judge: Your plea of guilty is free and voluntary?
Defendant: Yes, Sir.
Judge: No one has promised you anything?
Defendant: No.
Judge: No one has induced you to plead guilty?
Defendant: No.
Judge: You're pleading guilty because you are guilty?
Defendant: Yes:
Judge: I'll accept your plea of guilty to robbery unarmed and refer it to the probation department for a report and for sentencing Dec. 28.[7]

The delicacy of the relationship between appearance and reality is apparently confusing, even for the sociologist-observer. Newman's comment on this exchange has an Alice-in-Wonderland quality:

This is a routine procedure designed to satisfy the statutory requirement and is not intended to disguise the process of charge reduction.[8]

If we put the tensions between the different realities aside for the moment, we can say that there is an explicit process of negotiation between the defendant and the prosecution which is a part of the legal determination of guilt or innocence, or in the terms used above, the assessment of responsibility.

In medical diagnosis, a similar process of negotiation occurs, but is much less self-conscious than plea bargaining. The English psychoanalyst Michael Balint refers to this process as one of "offers and responses":

Some of the people who, for some reason or other, find it difficult to cope with problems of their lives resort to becoming ill. If the doctor has the opportunity of seeing them in the first phases of their being ill, i.e. before they settle down to a definite "organized" illness, he may observe that the patients, so to speak, offer or propose various illnesses, and that they have to go on offering new illnesses until between doctor and patient an agreement can be reached resulting in the acceptance by both of them of one of the illnesses as justified.[9]

Balint gives numerous examples indicating that patients propose reasons for their coming to the doctor which are rejected, one by one, by the physician, who makes counter-proposals until an "illness" acceptable to both parties is found. If "definition of the situation" is substituted for "illness," Balint's observations become relevant to a wide variety of transactions, including the kind of interrogation discussed above. The fixing of responsibility is a process in which the client offers definitions of the situation, to which the interrogator responds. After a series of offers and responses, a definition of the situation acceptable to both the client and the interrogator is reached.

Balint has observed that the negotiation process leads physicians to influence the outcome of medical examinations, independently of the patient's condition. He refers to this process as the "apostolic function" of the doctor, arguing that the physician induces patients to have the kind of illness that the physician thinks is proper:

Apostolic mission or function means in the first place that every doctor has a vague, but almost unshakably firm, idea of how a patient ought to behave when ill. Although this idea is anything but explicit and concrete, it is immensely powerful, and influences, as we have found, practically every detail of the doctor's work with his patients. It was almost as if every doctor had revealed knowledge of what was right and what was wrong for patients to expect and to endure, and further, as if he had a sacred duty to convert to his faith all the ignorant and un-believing among his patients.[10]

Implicit in this statement is the notion that interrogator and client have un-equal power in determining the resul-tant definition of the situation. The interrogator's definition of the situa-tion plays an important part in the joint definition of the situation which is finally negotiated. Moreover, his definition is more important than the client's in determining the final out-come of the negotiation, principally because he is well trained, secure, and self-confident in his role in the trans-action, whereas the client is untu-tored, anxious, and uncertain about his role. Stated simply, the subject, because of these conditions, is likely to be susceptible to the influence of the interrogator.

Note that plea bargaining and the process of "offers and responses" in diagnosis differ in the degree of self-consciousness of the participants. In plea bargaining the process is at least partly visible to the participants them-selves. There appears to be some am-biguity about the extent to which the negotiation is morally acceptable to some of the commentators, but the par-ties to the negotiations appear to be aware that bargaining is going on, and accept the process as such. The bar-gaining process in diagnosis, how-ever, is much more subterranean. Cer-tainly neither physicians nor patients recognize the offers and responses process as being bargaining. There is no commonly accepted vocabulary for describing diagnostic bargaining, such as there is in the legal analogy, e.g. "copping out" or "copping a plea." It may be that in legal processes there is some appreciation of the dif-ferent kinds of reality, i.e. the differ-ence between the public (official, legal) reality and private reality, whereas in medicine this difference is not recognized.

The discussion so far has suggested that much of reality is arrived at by negotiation. This thesis was illustrated by materials presented on legal pro-cesses by Newman, and medical pro-cesses by Balint. These processes are similar in that they appear to represent clear instances of the negotiation of reality. The instances are different in that the legal bargaining processes ap-pear to be more open and accepted than the diagnostic process. In order to outline some of the dimensions of the negotiation process, and to establish some of the limitations of the analyses by Newman and Balint, two excerpts of cases of bargaining will be discus-sed: the first taken from an actual psychiatric "intake" interview, the second from a fictional account of a defense lawyer's first interview with his client.

THE PROCESS OF NEGOTIATION

The psychiatric interview to be dis-cussed is from the first interview in *The Initial Interview in Psychiatric Practice*.[11] The patient is a thirty-four year old nurse, who feels, as she says, "irritable, tense, depressed." She ap-pears to be saying from the very begin-ning of the interview that the external situation in which she lives is the cause of her troubles. She focuses par-ticularly on her husband's behavior. She says he is an alcoholic, is verbally abusive, and won't let her work. She feels that she is cooped up in the house all day with her two small children, but that when he is home at night (on the nights when he is at home) he will have nothing to do with her and the children. She intimates, in several ways, that he does not serve as a sexual companion. She has thought of di-vorce, but has rejected it for various reasons (for example, she is afraid she couldn't take proper care of the children, finance the baby sitters, etc.). She feels trapped.[12]

In the concluding paragraph of their description of this interview, Gill, Newman, and Redlich give this summary:

The patient, pushed by we know not what or why at the time (the children— somebody to talk to) comes for help apparently for what she thinks of as help with her external situation (her husband's behavior as she sees it). The therapist does not respond to this but seeks her role and how it is that she plays such a role. Listening to the recording it sounds as if the therapist is at first bored and disinterested and the patient defensive. He gets down to work and keeps asking, "What is it all about?" Then he becomes more interested and sympathetic and at the same time very active (participating) and demanding. *It sounds as if she keeps saying, "This is the trouble." He says, "No! Tell me the trouble." She says, "This is it!" He says, "No, tell me," until the patient finally says, "Well I'll tell you." Then the therapist says, "Good! I'll help you."*[13]

From this summary it is apparent that there is a close fit between Balint's idea of the negotiation of diagnosis through offers and responses, and what took place in this psychiatric interview. It is difficult, however, to document the details. Most of the psychiatrist's responses, rejecting the patient's offers, do not appear in the written transcript, but they are fairly obvious as one listens to the recording. Two particular features of the psychiatrist's responses especially stand out: (1) the flatness of intonation in his responses to the patient's complaints about her external circumstances; and (2) the rapidity with which he introduces new topics, through questioning, when she is talking about her husband.

Some features of the psychiatrist's coaching are verbal, however:

T. 95: Has anything happened recently that makes it . . . you feel that . . . ah . . . you're sort of coming to the end of your rope? I mean I wondered what led you . . .

P. 95: (Interrupting.) It's nothing special. It's just everything in general.

T. 96: What led you to come to a . . .

P. 96: (Interrupting.) It's just that I . . .

T. 97: . . . a psychiatrist just now? (1)

P. 97: Because I felt that the older girl was getting tense as a result of . . . of my being stewed up all the time.

T. 98: Mmmhnn.

P. 98: Not having much patience with her.

T. 99: Mmmhnn. (Short pause.) Mmm. And how had you imagined that a psychiatrist could help with this? (Short pause.) (2)

P. 99: Mmm . . . maybe I could sort of get straightened out . . . straighten things out in my mind. I'm confused. Sometimes I can't remember things that I've done, whether I've done 'em or not or whether they happened.

T. 100: What is it that you want to straighten out?

(Pause.)

P. 100: I think I seem mixed up.

T. 101: Yeah? You see that, it seems to me, is something that we really should talk about because . . . ah . . . from a certain point of view somebody might say, "Well now, it's all very simple. She's unhappy and disturbed because her husband is behaving this way, and unless something can be done about that how could she expect to feel any other way." But, instead of that, you come to the psychiatrist, and you say that you think there's something about you that needs straightening out. (3) I don't quite get it. Can you explain that to me? (Short pause.)

P. 101: I sometimes wonder if I'm emotionally grown up.

T. 102: By which you mean what?

P. 102: When you're married you should have one mate. You shouldn't go around and look at other men.

T. 103: You've been looking at other men?

P. 103: I look at them, but that's all.

T. 104: Mmmhnn. What you mean . . . you mean a grown-up person should accept the marital situation whatever it happens to be?

P. 104: That was the way I was brought up. Yes. (Sighs.)

T. 105: You think that would be a sign of emotional maturity?

P. 105: No.

T. 106: No. So?

P. 106: Well, if you rebel against the laws of society you have to take the consequences.

T. 107: Yes?

P. 107: And it's just that I . . . I'm not willing to take the consequences. I . . . don't think it's worth it.

T. *108:* Mmhnn. So in the meantime then while you're in this very difficult situation, you find yourself reacting in a way that you don't like and that you think is . . . ah . . . damaging to your children and yourself? Now what can be done about that?

P. *108:* (Sniffs; sighs.) I dunno. That's why I came to see you.

T. *109:* Yes. I was just wondering what you had in mind. Did you think a psychiatrist could . . . ah . . . help you face this kind of a situation calmly and easily and maturely? (4) Is that it?

P. *109:* More or less. I need somebody to talk to who isn't emotionally involved with the family. I have a few friends, but I don't like to bore them. I don't think they should know . . . ah . . . all the intimate details of what goes on.

T. *110:* Yeah?

P. *110:* It becomes food for gossip.

T. *111:* Mmmhnn.

P. *111:* Besides they're in . . . they're emotionally involved because they're my friends. They tell me not to stand for it, but they don't understand that if I put my foot down it'll only get stepped on.

T. *112:* Yeah.

P. *112:* That he can make it miserable for me in other ways. . . .

T. *113:* Mmm.

P. *113:* . . . which he does.

T. *114:* Mmmhnn. In other words, you find yourself in a situation and don't know how to cope with it really.

P. *114:* I don't.

T. *115:* You'd like to be able to talk that through and come to understand it better and learn how to cope with it or deal with it in some way. Is that right?

P. *115:* I'd like to know how to deal with it more effectively.

T. *116:* Yeah. Does that mean you feel convinced that the way you're dealing with it now. . . .

P. *116:* There's something wrong of course.

T. *117:* . . . something wrong with that. Mmmhnn.

P. *117:* There's something wrong with it.[14]

Note that the therapist reminds her *four times* in this short sequence that she has come to see a *psychiatrist.* Since the context of these reminders is one in which the patient is attributing her difficulties to an external situation, particularly her husband, it seems plausible to hear these reminders as subtle requests for analysis of her own contributions to her difficulties. This interpretation is supported by the therapist's subsequent remarks. When the patient once again describes external problems, the therapist tries the following tack:

T. *125:* I notice that you've used a number of psychiatric terms here and there. Were you specially interested in that in your training, or what?

P. *125:* Well, my great love is psychology.

T. *126:* Psychology?

P. *126:* Mmmhnn.

T. *127:* How much have you studied?

P. *127:* Oh (Sighs.) what you have in your nurse's training, and I've had general psych, child and adolescent psych, and the abnormal psych.

T. *128:* Mmmhnn. Well, tell me . . . ah . . . what would you say if you had to explain yourself what is the problem?

P. *128:* You don't diagnose yourself very well, at least I don't.

T. *129:* Well you can make a stab at it. (Pause.)[15]

This therapeutic thrust is rewarded: the patient gives a long account of her early life which indicates a belief that she was not "adjusted" in the past. The interview continues:

T. *135:* And what conclusions do you draw from all this about why you're not adjusting now the way you think you should?

P. *135:* Well, I wasn't adjusted then. I feel that I've come a long way, but I don't think I'm still . . . I still don't feel that I'm adjusted.

T. *136:* And you don't regard your husband as being the difficulty? You think it lies within yourself?

P. *136:* Oh he's a difficulty all right, but I figure that even . . . ah . . . had . . . if it had been other things that . . . this probably —this state—would've come on me.

T. *137:* Oh you do think so?

P. *137:* (Sighs.) I don't think he's the sole factor. No.

T. *138:* And what are the factors within. . . .

P. *138:* I mean. . . .

T. *139:* . . . yourself?

P. *139:* Oh it's probably remorse for the past, things I did.

T. 140: Like what? (Pause.) It's sumping' hard to tell, hunh? (Short pause.)[16]

After some parrying, the patient tells the therapist what he wants to hear. She feels guilty because she was pregnant by another man when her present husband proposed. She cries. The therapist tells the patient she needs, and will get psychiatric help, and the interview ends, the patient still crying. The negotiational aspects of the process are clear: After the patient has spent most of the interview blaming her current difficulties on external circumstances, she tells the therapist a deep secret about which she feels intensely guilty. The patient, and not the husband, is at fault. The therapist's tone and manner change abruptly. From being bored, distant, and rejecting, he becomes warm and solicitous. Through a process of offers and responses, the therapist and patient have, by implication, negotiated a shared definition of the situation —the patient, not the husband, is responsible.

A CONTRASTING CASE

The negotiation process can, of course, proceed on the opposite premise, namely that the client is not responsible. An ideal example would be an interrogation of a client by a skilled defense lawyer. Unfortunately, we have been unable to locate a verbatim transcript of a defense lawyer's initial interview with his client. There is available, however, a fictional portrayal of such an interview, written by a man with extensive experience as defense lawyer, prosecutor, and judge. The excerpt to follow is taken from the novel, *Anatomy of a Murder.*[17]

The defense lawyer, in his initial contact with his client, briefly questions him regarding his actions on the night of the killing. The client states that he discovered that the deceased, Barney Quill, had raped his wife; he then goes on to state that he then left his wife, found Quill and shot him.

"... How long did you remain with your wife before you went to the hotel bar?"
"I don't remember."
"I think it is important, and I suggest you try."
After a pause. "Maybe an hour."
"Maybe more?"
"Maybe."
"Maybe less?"
"Maybe."
I paused and lit a cigar. I took my time. I had reached a point where a few wrong answers to a few right questions would leave me with a client—if I took his case —whose cause was legally defenseless. Either I stopped now and begged off and let some other lawyer worry over it or I asked him the few fatal questions and let him hang himself. Or else, like any smart lawyer, I went into the Lecture. I studied my man, who sat as inscrutable as an Arab, delicately fingering his Ming holder, daintily sipping his dark mustache. He apparently did not realize how close I had him to admitting that he was guilty of first degree murder, that is, that he "feloniously, wilfully and of his malice afore-thought did kill and murder one Barney Quill." The man was a sitting duck.[18]

The lawyer here realizes that his line of questioning has come close to fixing the responsibility for the killing on his client. He therefore shifts his ground by beginning "the lecture":

The Lecture is an ancient device that lawyers use to coach their clients so that the client won't quite know he has been coached and his lawyer can still preserve the face-saving illusion that he hasn't done any coaching. For coaching clients, like robbing them, is not only frowned upon, it is downright unethical and bad, very bad. Hence the Lecture, an artful device as old as the law itself, and one used constantly by some of the nicest and most ethical lawyers in the land. "Who, me? I didn't tell him what to say," the lawyer can later comfort himself. "I merely explained the law, see." It is a good practice to scowl and shrug here and add virtuously: "That's my duty, isn't it?"

... "We will now explore the absorbing subject of legal justification or excuse," I said.

... "Well, take self-defense," I began. "That's the classic example of justifiable homicide. On the basis of what I've so far heard and read about your case I do not think we need pause too long over that. Do you?"

"Perhaps not," Lieutenant Manion conceded, "we'll pass it for now."

"Let's," I said dryly, "Then there's the defense of habitation, defense of property, and the defense of relatives or friends. Now there are more ramifications to these defenses than a dog has fleas, but we won't explore them now. I've already told you at length why I don't think you can invoke the possible defense of your wife. When you shot Quill her need for defense had passed. It's as simple as that."

"Go on," Lieutenant Manion said, frowning.

"Then there's the defense of a homicide committed to prevent a felony—say you're being robbed—; to prevent the escape of the felon—suppose he's getting away with your wallet—; or to arrest a felon—you've caught up with him and he's either trying to get away or has actually escaped." . . .

... "Go on, then; what are some of the other legal justifications or excuses?"

"Then there's the tricky and dubious defense of intoxication. Personally I've never seen it succeed. But since you were not drunk when you shot Quill we shall mercifully not dwell on that. Or were you?"

"I was cold sober. Please go on."

"Then finally there's the defense of insanity." I paused and spoke abruptly, airily: "Well, that just about winds it up." I arose as though making ready to leave.

"Tell me more."

"There is no more." I slowly paced up and down the room.

"I mean about this insanity."

"Oh, insanity," I said, elaborately surprised. It was like luring a trained seal with a herring. "Well, insanity, where proven, is a complete defense to murder. It does not legally justify the killing, like self-defense, say, but rather excuses it." The lecturer was hitting his stride. He was also on the home stretch. "Our law requires that a punishable killing—in fact, any crime—must be committed by a sapient human being, one capable, as the law insists, of distinguishing between right and wrong. If a man is insane, legally insane, the act of homicide may still be murder but the law excuses the perpetrator."

Lieutenant Manion was sitting erect now, very still and erect. "I see—and this—this perpetrator, what happens to him if he should—should be excused?"

"Under Michigan law—like that of many other states—if he is acquitted of murder on the grounds of insanity it is provided that he must be sent to a hospital for the criminally insane until he is pronounced sane." . . .

... Then he looked at me. "Maybe," he said, "maybe I was insane."

... Thoughtfully: "Hm. . . . Why do you say that?"

"Well, I can't really say," he went on slowly. "I—I guess I blacked out. I can't remember a thing after I saw him standing behind the bar that night until I got back to my trailer."

"You mean—you mean you don't remember shooting him?" I shook my head in wonderment.

"Yes, that's what I mean."

"You don't even remember driving home?"

"No."

"You don't remember threatening Barney's bartender when he followed you outside after the shooting—as the newspaper says you did?" I paused and held my breath. "You don't remember telling him, 'Do you want some, too, Buster?' ?"

The smoldering dark eyes flickered ever so little. "No, not a thing."

"My, my," I said blinking my eyes, contemplating the wonder of it all. "Maybe you've got something there."

The Lecture was over; I had told my man the law; and now he had told me things that might possibly invoke the defense of insanity. . . . [19]

The negotiation is complete. The ostensibly shared definition of the situation established by the negotiation process is that the defendant was probably not responsible for his actions.

Let us now compare the two interviews. The major similarity between them is their negotiated character: they both take the form of a series of offers and responses that continue until an offer (a definition of the situation) is reached that is acceptable to both parties. The major difference between the transactions is that one, the psychotherapeutic interview, arrives at an assessment that the client is responsible; the other, the defense attorney's interview, reaches an assessment that the client was not at fault, i.e., not responsible. How can we account for this difference in outcome?

DISCUSSION

Obviously, given any two real cases of negotiation which have different outcomes, one might construct a reasonable argument that the difference is due to the differences between the cases—the finding of responsibility in one case and lack of responsibility in the other, the only outcomes which are reasonably consonant with the facts of the respective cases. Without rejecting this argument, for the sake of discussion only, and without claiming any kind of proof or demonstration, I wish to present an alternative argument; that the difference in outcome is largely due to the differences in technique used by the interrogators. This argument will allow us to suggest some crucial dimensions of negotiation processes.

The first dimension, consciousness of the bargaining aspects of the transaction, has already been mentioned. In the psychotherapeutic interview, the negotiational nature of the transaction seems not to be articulated by either party. In the legal interview, however, certainly the lawyer, and perhaps to some extent the client as well, is aware of, and accepts the situation as one of striking a bargain, rather than as a relentless pursuit of the absolute facts of the matter.

The dimension of shared awareness that the definition of the situation is negotiable seems particularly crucial for assessments of responsibility. In both interviews, there is an agenda hidden from the client. In the

psychotherapeutic interview, it is probably the psychiatric criteria for acceptance into treatment, the criterion of "insight." The psychotherapist has probably been trained to view patients with "insight into their illness" as favorable candidates for psychotherapy, i.e., patients who accept, or can be led to accept, the problems as internal, as part of their personality, rather than seeing them as caused by external conditions.

In the legal interview, the agenda that is unknown to the client is the legal structure of defenses or justifications for killing. In both the legal and psychiatric cases, the hidden agenda is not a simple one. Both involve fitting abstract and ambiguous criteria (insight, on the one hand, legal justification, on the other) to a richly specific, concrete case. In the legal interview, the lawyer almost immediately broaches this hidden agenda; he states clearly and concisely the major legal justifications for killing. In the psychiatric interview, the hidden agenda is never revealed. The patient's offers during most of the interview are rejected or ignored. In the last part of the interview, her last offer is accepted and she is told that she will be given treatment. In no case are the reasons for these actions articulated by either party.

The degree of shared awareness is related to a second dimension which concerns the format of the conversation. The legal interview began as an interrogation, but was quickly shifted away from that format when the defense lawyer realized the direction in which the questioning was leading the client, i.e., toward a legally unambiguous admission of guilt. On the very brink of such an admission, the defense lawyer stopped asking questions and started, instead, to make statements. He listed the principle legal justifications for killing, and, in response to the client's questions, gave an explanation of each of the justifications. This shift in format put the client, rather than the lawyer, in control of the crucial aspects of the negotiation. It is the client, not the lawyer, who is allowed to pose the questions, assess the answers for their relevance to his case, and most crucially, to determine himself the most advantageous tack to take. Control of the definition of the situation, the evocation of the events and intentions relevant to the assessment of the client's responsibility for the killing, was given to the client by the lawyer. The resulting client-controlled format of negotiation gives the client a double advantage. It not only allows the client the benefit of formulating his account of actions and intentions in their most favorable light, it also allows him to select, out of a diverse and ambiguous set of normative criteria concerning killing, that criteria which is most favorable to his own case.

Contrast the format of negotiation used by the psychotherapist. The form is consistently that of interrogation. The psychotherapist poses the questions; the patient answers. The psychotherapist then has the answers at his disposal. He may approve or disapprove, accept or reject, or merely ignore them. Throughout the entire interview, the psychotherapist is in complete control of the situation. Within this framework, the tactic that the psychotherapist uses is to reject the patient's "offers" that her husband is at fault, first by ignoring them, later, and ever more insistently, by leading her to define the situation as one in which she is at fault. In effect, what the therapist does is to reject her offers, and to make his own counteroffers.

These remarks concerning the relationship between technique of interrogation and outcome suggest an approach to assessment of responsibility somewhat different than that usually followed. The common sense approach to interrogation is to ask how accurate and fair is the outcome. Both Newman's and Balint's analyses of negotiation raise this question. Both presuppose that there is an objective state of affairs that is independent of the technique of assessment. This is quite clear in Newman's discussion, as he continually refers to defendants who are "really" or "actually" guilty or innocent.[20] The situation is less clear in Balint's discussion, although occasionally he implies that certain patients are really physically healthy, but psychologically distressed.

The type of analysis suggested by this paper seeks to avoid such presuppositions. It can be argued that independently of the facts of the case, the technique of assessment plays a part in determining the outcome. In particular, one can avoid making assumptions about actual responsibility by utilizing a technique of textual criticism of a transaction. The key dimension in such work would be the relative power and authority of the participants in the situation.[21]

As an introduction to the way in which power differences between interactants shape the outcome of negotiations, let us take as an example an attorney in a trial dealing with "friendly" and "unfriendly" witnesses. A friendly witness is a person whose testimony will support the definition of the situation the attorney seeks to convey to the jury. With such a witness the attorney does not employ power, but treats him as an equal. His questions to such a witness are open, and allow the witness considerable freedom. The attorney might frame a question such as "Could you tell us about your actions on the night of _____?"

The opposing attorney, however, interested in establishing his own version of the witness' behavior on the same night, would probably approach the task quite differently. He might say: "You felt angry and offended on the night of _____, didn't you?" The witness frequently will try to evade so direct a question with an answer like: "Actually, I had started to . . . ." The attorney quickly interrupts, addressing the judge: "Will the court order the witness to respond to the question, yes or no?" That is to say, the question posed by the opposing attorney is abrupt and direct. When the witness attempts to answer indirectly, and at length, the attorney quickly invokes the power of the court to coerce the witness to answer as he wishes, directly. The witness and the attorney are not equals in power; the attorney used the coercive power of the court to force the witness to answer in the manner desired.

The attorney confronted by an "unfriendly" witness wishes to control the format of the interaction, so that he can retain control of the definition of the situation that is conveyed to the jury. It is much easier for him to neutralize the opposing definition of the situation if he retains control of the interrogation format in this manner. By allowing the unfriendly witness to respond only by yes or no to his own verbally conveyed account, he can suppress the ambient details of the opposing view that might sway the jury, and thus maintain an advantage for his definition over that of the witness.

In the psychiatric interview discussed above, the psychiatrist obviously does not invoke a third party to enforce his control of the interview. But he does use a device to impress the patient that she is not to be his equal in the interview, that is reminiscent of the attorney with an unfriendly witness. The device is to pose abrupt and direct questions to the patient's open-ended accounts, implying that the patient should answer briefly and directly; and, through that implication, the psychiatrist controls the whole transaction. Throughout most of the interview the patient seeks to give detailed accounts of her behavior and her husband's, but the psychiatrist almost invariably counters with a direct and, to the patient, seemingly unrelated question.

The first instance of this procedure occurs at T6, the psychiatrist asking the patient, "what do you do?" She replies "I'm a nurse, but my husband won't let me work." Rather than responding to the last part of her answer, which would be expected in conversion between equals, the psychiatrist asks another question, changing the subject: "How old are you?" This pattern continues throughout most of the interview. The psychiatrist appears to be trying to teach the patient to follow his lead. After some thirty or forty exchanges of this kind, the patient apparently learns her lesson; she cedes control of the transaction completely to the therapist, answering briefly and directly to direct questions, and elaborating only on cue from the therapist. The therapist thus implements his control of the interview not by direct coercion, but by subtle manipulation.

All of the discussion above, concerning shared awareness and the format of the negotiation, suggests several propositions concerning control over the definition of the situation. The professional interrogator, whether lawyer or psychotherapist, can maintain control if the client cedes control to him because of his authority as an expert, because of his manipulative skill in the transaction, or merely because the interrogator controls access to something the client wants, e.g., treatment, or a legal excuse. The propositions are:

1a. Shared awareness of the participants that the situation is one of negotiation. (The greater the shared awareness the more control the client gets over the resultant definition of the situation.)

b. Explicitness of the agenda. (The more explicit the agenda of the transaction, the more control the client gets over the resulting definition of the situation.)

2a. Organization of the format of the transaction, offers and responses. (The party to a negotiation who responds, rather than the party who makes the offers, has relatively more power in controlling the resultant shared definition of the situation.)

b. Counter-offers. (The responding party who makes counter-offers has relatively more power than the responding party who limits his response to merely accepting or rejecting the offers of the other party.)

c. Directness of questions and answers. (The more direct the questions of the interrogator, and the more direct the answers he demands and receives, the more control he has over the resultant definition of the situation.)

These concepts and hypotheses are only suggestive until such times as operational definitions can be developed. Although such terms as offers and responses seem to have an immediate applicability to most conversation, it is likely that a thorough and systematic analysis of any given conversation would show the need for clearly stated criteria of class inclusion and exclusion. Perhaps a good place for such research would be in the transactions for assessing responsibility discussed above. Since some 90 percent of all criminal convictions in the United States are based on guilty pleas, the extent to which techniques of interrogation subtly influence outcomes would have immediate policy implication. There is considerable evidence that interrogation techniques influence the outcome of psychotherapeutic interviews also.[22] Research in both of these areas would

probably have implications for both the theory and practice of assessing responsibility.

CONCLUSION: NEGOTIATION IN SOCIAL SCIENCE RESEARCH

More broadly, the application of the sociology of knowledge to the negotiation of reality has ramifications which may apply to all of social science. The interviewer in a survey, or the experimenter in a social psychological experiment, is also involved in a transaction with a client—the respondent or subject. Recent studies by Rosenthal and others strongly suggest that the findings in such studies are negotiated, and influenced by the format of the study.[23] Rosenthal's review of bias in research suggests that such bias is produced by a pervasive and subtle process of interaction between the investigator and his source of data. Those errors which arise because of the investigator's influence over the subject (the kind of influence discussed in this paper as arising out of power disparities in the process of negotiation), Rosenthal calls "expectancy effects." In order for these errors to occur, there must be direct contact between the investigator and the subject.

A second kind of bias Rosenthal refers to as "observer effects." These are errors of perception or reporting which do not require that the subject be influenced by investigation. Rosenthal's review leads one to surmise that even with techniques that are completely non-obtrusive, observer error could be quite large.[24]

The occurrence of these two kinds of bias poses an interesting dilemma for the lawyer, psychiatrist, and social scientist. The investigator of human phenomena is usually interested in more than a sequence of events, he wants to know why the events occurred. Usually this quest for an explanation leads him to deal with the motivation of the persons involved. The lawyer, clinician, social psychologist, or survey researcher try to elicit motives directly, by questioning the participants. But in the process of questioning, as suggested above, he himself becomes involved in a process of negotiation, perhaps subtly influencing the informants through expectancy effects. A historian, on the other hand, might try to use documents and records to determine motives. He would certainly avoid expectancy effects in this way, but since he would not elicit motives directly, he might find it necessary to collect and interpret various kinds of evidence which are only indirectly related, at best, to determine motives of the participants. Thus through his choice in the selection and interpretation of the indirect evidence, he may be as susceptible to error as the interrogator, survey researcher, or experimentalist—his error being due to observer effects, however, rather than expectancy effects.

The application of the ideas outlined here to social and psychological research need to be developed. The five propositions suggested above might be used, for example, to estimate the validity of surveys using varying degrees of open-endedness in their interview format. If some technique could be developed which would yield an independent assessment of validity, it might be possible to demonstrate, as Aaron Cicourel has suggested, the more reliable the technique, the less valid the results.

The influence of the assessment itself on the phenomena to be assessed appears to be an ubiquitous process in human affairs, whether in ordinary daily life, the determination of responsibility in legal or clinical interrogation, or in most types of social science research. The sociology of knowledge perspective, which suggests that people go through their lives constructing reality, offers a framework within which the negotiation of reality can be seriously and constructively studied. This paper has suggested some of the avenues of the problem that might require further study. The prevalence of the problem in most areas of human concern recommends it to our attention as a substantial field of study, rather than as an issue that can be ignored or, alternatively, be taken as the proof that rigorous knowledge of social affairs is impossible.

NOTES

1. The doctrine of absolute responsibility is clearly illustrated in psychiatric and legal discussions of the issue of "criminal responsibility," i.e., the use of mental illness as an excuse from criminal conviction. An example of the assumption of absolute criteria of responsibility is found in the following quotation, "The finding that someone is criminally responsible means to the psychiatrist that the criminal must change his behavior before he can resume his position in society. *This injunction is dictated not by morality, but, so to speak, by reality.*" See Edward J. Sachar, "Behavioral Science and Criminal Law," *Scientific American*, 209 (1963), pp. 39-45, (emphasis added).

2. *Cf.* Peter L. Berger and Thomas Luckmann, *The Social Construction of Reality: A Treatise in the Sociology of Knowledge*, New York: Doubleday, 1966.

3. The classic treatment of this issue is found in E. Durkheim, *The Elementary Forms of the Religious Life.*

4. A sociological application of the concept of negotiation, in a different context, is found in Anselm Strauss, et al., "The Hospital and its Negotiated Order," in Eliot

Freidson, editor, *The Hospital in Modern Society*, New York: Free Press, 1963, pp. 147-169.

5. Newman reports a study in this area, together with a review of earlier work, in "The Negotiated Plea," Part III of Donald J. Newman, *Conviction: The Determination of Guilt or Innocence Without Trial*, Boston: Little Brown, 1966, pp. 76-130.

6. *Ibid.*, p. 76.

7. *Ibid.*, p. 83.

8. *Idem.*

9. Michael Balint, *The Doctor, His Patient, and The Illness*, New York: International Unversities Press, 1957, p. 18. A description of the negotiations between patients in a tuberculosis sanitarium and their physicians is found in Julius A. Roth, *Timetables: Structuring the Passage of Time in Hospital Treatment and Other Careers.* Indianapolis: Bobbs-Merrill, 1963, pp. 48-59. Obviously, some cases are more susceptible to negotiation than others. Balint implies that the great majority of cases in medical practice are negotiated.

10. Balint, *op. cit.*, p. 216.

11. Merton Gill, Richard Newman, and Fredrick C. Redlich, *The Initial Interview in Psychiatric Practice*, New York: International Universities Press, 1954.

12. Since this interview is complex and subtle, the reader is invited to listen to it himself, and compare his conclusions with those discussed here. The recorded interview is available on the first L.P. record that accompanies Gill, Newman, and Redlich, *op. cit.*

13. *Ibid.*, p. 133. (Italics added.)

14. *Ibid.*, pp. 176-182. (Numbers in parenthesis added.)

15. *Ibid.*, pp. 186-187.

16. *Ibid.*, pp. 192-194.

17. Robert Traver, *Anatomy of a Murder*, New York: Dell, 1959.

18. *Ibid.*, p. 43.

19. *Ibid.*, pp. 46-47, 57, 58-59, and 60.

20. In his Foreword the editor of the series, Frank J. Remington, comments on one of the slips that occurs frequently, the "acquittal of the guilty," noting that this phrase is contradictory from the legal point of view. He goes on to say that Newman is well aware of this, but uses the phrase as a convenience. Needless to say, both Remington's comments and mine can both be correct: the phrase is used as a convenience, but it also reveals the author's presuppositions.

21. Berger and Luckmann *op. cit.*, p. 100, also emphasize the role of power, but at the societal level. "The success of particular conceptual machineries is related to the power possessed by those who operate them. The confrontation of alternative symbolic universes implies a problem of power—which of the conflicting definitions of reality will be "made to stick" in the society." Haley's discussions of control in psychotherapy are also relevant. See Jay Haley, "Control in Psychoanalytic Psychotherapy," *Progress in Psychotherapy*, 4, New York: Grune and Stratton, 1959, pp. 48-65; see also by the same author, "The Power Tactics of Jesus Christ" (in press).

22. Thomas J. Scheff, *Being Mentally Ill*, Chicago: Aldine, 1966.

23. Robert Rosenthal, *Experimenter Effects in Behavioral Research*, New York: Appleton-Century Crofts, 1966. Friedman, reporting a series of studies of expectancy effects, seeks to put the results within a broad sociological framework; Neil Friedman, *The Social Nature of Psychological Research: The Psychological Experiment as Social Interaction*, New York: Basic Books, 1967.

24. Critics of "reactive techniques" often disregard the problem of observer effects. See, for example, Eugene J. Webb, Donald T. Campbell, Richard D. Schwartz, and Lee Sechrest, *Unobtrusive Measures: Nonreactive Research in Social Science*, Chicago: Rand-McNally, 1966.

18. MARRIAGE AND THE CONSTRUCTION OF REALITY

PETER BERGER AND
HANSFRIED KELLNER

This article was originally published in Diogenes No. 46 (Summer 1964), pp. 1-24. Peter Berger is Professor of Sociology at Rutgers University and formerly taught at the New School for Social Research in New York City. Hansfried Kellner teaches at the University of Frankfurt, Germany where he works with Thomas Luckmann, the co-author of Berger's Social Construction of Reality. His specialty is socio-linguistics.

Ever since Durkheim it has been a commonplace of family sociology that marriage serves as a protection against anomie for the individual. Interesting and pragmatically useful though this insight is, it is but the negative side of a phenomenon of much broader significance. If one speaks of *anomic* states, then one ought properly to investigate also the *nomic* processes that, by their absence, lead to the aforementioned states. If, consequently, one finds a negative correlation between marriage and anomie, then one should be led to inquire into the character of marriage as a *nomos*-building instrumentality, that is, of marriage as a social arrangement that creates for the individual the sort of order in which he can experience his life as making sense. It is our intention here to discuss marriage in these terms. While this could evidently be done in a macrosociological perspective, dealing with marriage as a major social institution related to other broad structures of society, our focus will be microsociological, dealing primarily with the social processes affecting the individuals in any specific marriage, although, of course, the larger framework of these processes will have to be understood. In what sense this discussion can be described as microsociology of knowledge will hopefully become clearer in the course of it.[1]

Marriage is obviously only *one* social relationship in which this process of *nomos*-building takes place. It is, therefore, necessary to first look in more general terms at the character of this process. In doing so, we are influenced by three theoretical perspectives—the Weberian perspective on society as a network of meanings, the Meadian perspective on identity as a social phenomenon, and the phenomenological analysis of the social structuring of reality especially as given in the work of Schutz and Merleau-Ponty.[2] Not being convinced, however, that theoretical lucidity is necessarily enhanced by terminological ponderosity, we shall avoid as much as possible the use of the sort of jargon for which both sociologists and phenomenologists have acquired dubious notoriety.

The process that interests us here is the one that constructs, maintains and modifies a consistent reality that can be meaningfully experienced by individuals. In its essential forms this process is determined by the society in which it occurs. Every society has its specific way of defining and perceiving reality—its world, its universe, its overarching organization of symbols. This is already given in the language that forms the symbolic base of the society. Erected over this base, and by means of it, is a system of ready-made typifications, through which the innumerable experiences of reality come to be ordered.[3] These typifications and their order are held in common by the members of society, thus acquiring not only the character of objectivity, but being taken for granted as *the* world *tout court*, the only world that normal men can conceive of.[4] The seemingly objective and taken-for-granted character of the social definitions of reality can be seen most clearly in the case of language itself, but it is important to keep in mind that the latter forms the base and instrumentality of a much larger world-erecting process.

The socially constructed world must be continually mediated to and actualized by the individual, so that it can become and remain indeed *his* world as well. The individual is given by his society certain decisive cornerstones for his everyday experience and conduct. Most importantly, the individual is supplied with specific sets of typifications and criteria of relevance, predefined for him by the society and made available to him for the ordering of his everyday life. This ordering or (in line with our opening considerations) nomic apparatus is biographically cumulative. It begins to be formed in the individual from the earliest stages of socialization on, then keeps on being enlarged and modified by himself throughout his biography.[5] While there are individual biographical differences making for differences in the constitution of this apparatus in specific individuals, there exists in the society an overall consensus on the range of differences deemed to be tolerable. Without such consensus, indeed, society would be impossible as a going concern, since it would then lack the ordering principles by which alone experience can be shared and conduct can be mutually intelligible. This order, by which the individual comes to perceive and define his world, is thus not chosen by him, except perhaps for very small modifications. Rather, it is discovered by him as an external datum, a ready-made world that simply is *there* for him to go ahead and live in, though he modifies it continually in the process of living in it. Nevertheless, this world is in need of validation, perhaps precisely because of an everpresent glimmer of suspicion as to its social manufacture and relativity. This validation, while it must be undertaken by the individual himself, requires ongoing interaction with others who co-inhabit this same socially constructed world. In a broad sense, *all* the other co-inhabitants of this world serve a validating function. Every morning the newspaper boy validates the widest co-ordinates of my world and the mailman bears tangible validation of my own location within these co-ordinates. However, some validations are more significant than others. Every individual requires the ongoing validation of his world, including crucially the validation of his identity and place in this world, by those few who are his truly significant others.[6] Just as the individual's deprivation of relationship with his significant others will plunge him into anomie, so their continued presence will sustain for him that *nomos* by which he can feel at home in the world at least most of the time. Again in a broad sense, all the actions of the significant others and even their simple presence serve this sustaining function. In everyday life, however, the principal method employed is speech. In this sense, it is proper to view the individual's relationship with his significant others as an ongoing conversation. As the latter occurs, it validates over and over again the fundamental definitions of reality once entered into, not, of course, so much by explicit articulation, but precisely by taking the definitions silently for granted and conversing about all conceivable matters on this taken-for-granted basis.

Through the same conversation the individual is also made capable of adjusting to changing and new social contexts in his biography. In a very fundamental sense it can be said that one converses one's way through life.

If one concedes these points, one can now state a general sociological proposition: the plausibility and stability of the world, as socially defined, is dependent upon the strength and continuity of significant relationships in which conversation about this world can be continually carried on. Or, to put it a little differently: the reality of the world is sustained through conversation with significant others. This reality, of course, includes not only the imagery by which fellowmen are viewed, but also includes the way in which one views oneself. The reality-bestowing force of social relationships depends on the degree of their nearness,[7] that is, on the degree to which social relationships occur in face-to-face situations and to which they are credited with primary significance by the individual. In any empirical situation, there now emerge obvious sociological questions out of these considerations, namely, questions about the patterns of the world-building relationships, the social forms taken by the conversation with significant others. Sociologically, one must ask how these relationships are *objectively* structured and distributed, and one will also want to understand how they are *subjectively* perceived and experienced.

With these preliminary assumptions stated we can now arrive at our main thesis here. Namely, we would contend that marriage occupies a privileged status among the significant validating relationships for adults in our society. Put slightly differently: marriage is a crucial nomic instrumentality in our society. We would further argue that the essential social functionality of this institution cannot be fully understood if this fact is not perceived.

We can now proceed with an ideal-typical analysis of marriage, that is, seek to abstract the essential features involved. Marriage in our society is a *dramatic* act in which two strangers come together and redefine themselves. The drama of the act is internally anticipated and socially legitimated long before it takes place in the individual's biography, and amplified by means of a pervasive ideology, the dominant themes of which (romantic love, sexual fulfilment, self-discovery and self-realization through love and sexuality, the nuclear family as the social site for these processes) can be found distributed through all strata of the society. The actualization of these ideologically pre-defined expectations in the life of the individual occurs to the accompaniment of one of the few tranditional rites of passage that are still meaningful to almost all members of the society. It should be added that, in using the term "strangers," we do not mean, of course, that the candidates for the marriage come from widely discrepant social backgrounds—indeed, the data indicate that the contrary is the case. The strangeness rather lies in the fact that, unlike marriage candidates in many previous societies, those in ours typically come from different face-to-face contexts—in the terms used above, they come from different areas of conversation. They do not have a shared past, although their pasts have a similar structure. In other words, quite apart from prevailing patterns of ethnic, religious and class endogamy, our society is typically exogamous in terms of nomic relationships. Put concretely, in our mobile society the significant conversation of the two partners previous to the marriage took place in social circles that did not overlap. With the dramatic redefinition of the situation brought about by the marriage, however, all significant conversation for the two new partners is now centered in their relationship with each other—and, in fact, it was precisely with this intention that they entered upon their relationship.

It goes without saying that this character of marriage has its root in much broader structural configurations of our society. The most important of these, for our purposes, is the crystallization of a so-called private sphere of existence, more and more segregated from the immediate controls of the public institutions (especially the economic and political ones), and yet defined and utilized as the main social area for the individual's self-realization.[8] It cannot be our purpose here to inquire into the historical forces that brought forth this phenomenon, beyond making the observation that these are closely connected with the industrial revolution and its institutional consequences. The public institutions now confront the individual as an immensely powerful and alien world, incomprehensible in its inner workings, anonymous in its human character. If only through his work in some nook of the economic machinery, the individual must find a way of living in this alien world, come to terms with its power over him, be satisfied with a few conceptual rules of thumb to guide him through a vast reality that otherwise remains opaque to his understanding, and modify its anonymity by whatever *human relations* he can work out in his involvement with it. It ought to be emphasized, against some critics of 'mass society,' that this does not inevitably leave the individual with a sense of profound unhappiness and lostness. It would rather seem that large numbers of people in our society are quite content with a situation in which their public involvements have little subjective importance, regarding work as a not too bad necessity and politics as at best a spectator sport. It is usually only intellectuals with ethical and political commitments who assume that such people must be terribly desperate. The point, however, is that the individual in this situation, no matter whether he is happy or not, will turn elsewhere for the experiences of self-realization that do have importance for him. The private sphere, this interstitial area created (we would think) more or less haphazardly as a by-product of the social metamorphosis of industrialism, is mainly where he will turn. It is here that the individual will seek power, intelligibility and, quite literally, a name—the apparent power to fashion a world, however Lilliputian, that will reflect his own being: a world that, seemingly having been shaped by himself and thus unlike those other worlds that insist on shaping him, is translucently intelligible to him (or so he thinks); a world in which, consequently, he is *somebody*—perhaps even, within its charmed circle, a lord and master. What is more, to a considerable extent these expectations are not unrealistic. The public institutions have no need to control the individual's adventures in the private sphere, as long as they really stay within the latter's circumscribed limits. The private sphere is perceived, not without justification, as an area of individual choice and even autonomy. This fact has important consequences for the shaping of identity in modern society that cannot be pursued here. All that ought to be clear here is the peculiar location of the private sphere within and between the other social structures. In sum, it is above all and, as a rule, only in the private sphere that the individual can take a slice of reality and fashion it into his world. If one is aware of the decisive significance of this capacity and even necessity of men to externalize themselves in reality and to produce for themselves a world in which they can feel at home, then one will hardly be surprised at the great importance which the private sphere has come to have in modern society.[9]

The private sphere includes a variety of social relationships. Among these, however, the relationships of the family occupy a central position and, in fact, serve as a focus for most of the other relationships (such as those with friends, neighbors, fellow-members of religious and other voluntary associations). Since, as the ethnologists keep reminding us, the family in our society is of the conjugal type, the central relationship in this whole area is the marital one. It is on the basis of marriage that, for most adults in our society, existence in the private sphere is built up. It will be clear that this is not at all a universal or even cross culturally wide function of marriage. Rather has marriage in our society taken on a very peculiar character and functionality. It has been pointed out that marriage in contemporary society has lost some of its older functions and taken on new ones instead.[10] This is certainly correct, but we would prefer to state the matter a little differently. Marriage and the family used to be firmly embedded in a matrix of wider community relationships, serving as extensions and particularizations of the latter's social controls. There were few separating barriers between the world of the individual family and the wider community, a fact even to be seen in the physical conditions under which the family lived before the industrial revo-

lution.[11] The same social life pulsated through the house, the street and the community. In our terms, the family and within it the marital relationship were part and parcel of a considerably larger area of conversation. In our contemporary society, by contrast, each family constitutes its own segregated sub-world, with its own controls and its own closed conversation.

This fact requires a much greater effort on the part of the marriage partners. Unlike an earlier situation in which the establishment of the new marriage simply added to the differentiation and complexity of an already existing social world, the marriage partners now are embarked on the often difficult task of constructing for themselves the little world in which they will live. To be sure, the larger society provides them with certain standard instructions as to how they should go about this task, but this does not change the fact that considerable effort of their own is required for its realization. The monogamous character of marriage enforces both the dramatic and the precarious nature of this undertaking. Success or failure hinges on the present idiosyncrasies and the fairly unpredictable future development of these idiosyncrasies of only two individuals (who, moreover, do not have a shared past)—as Simmel has shown, the most unstable of all possible social relationships.[12] Not surprisingly, the decision to embark on this undertaking has a critical, even cataclysmic connotation in the popular imagination, which is underlined as well as psychologically assuaged by the ceremonialism that surrounds the event.

Every social relationship requires objectivation, that is, requires a process by which subjectively experienced meanings become objective to the individual and, in interaction with others, become common property and thereby massively objective.[13] The degree of objectivation will depend on the number and the intensity of the social relationships that are its carriers. A relationship that consists of only two individuals called upon to sustain, by their own efforts, an ongoing social world will have to make up in intensity for the numerical poverty of the arrangement. This, in turn, accentuates the drama and the precariousness. The later addition of children will add to the, as it were, density of objectivation taking place within the nuclear family, thus rendering the latter a good deal less precarious. It remains true that the establishment and maintenance of such a social world make extremely high demands on the principal participants.

The attempt can now be made to outline the ideal-typical process that takes place as marriage functions as an instrumentality for the social construction of reality. The chief protagonists of the drama are two individuals, each with a biographically accumulated and available stock of experience.[14] As members of a highly mobile society, these individuals have already internalized a degree of readiness to redefine themselves and to modify their stock of experience, thus bringing with them considerable psychological capacity for entering new relationships with others.[15] Also, coming from broadly similar sectors of the larger society (in terms of region, class, ethnic and religious affiliations), the two individuals will have organized their stock of experience in similar fashion. In other words, the two individuals have internalized the same overall world, including the general definitions and expectations of the marriage relationship itself. Their society has provided them with a taken-for-granted image of marriage and has socialized them into an anticipation of stepping into the taken-for-granted roles of marriage. All the same, these relatively empty projections now have to be actualized, lived through and filled with experiential content by the protagonists. This will require a dramatic change in their definitions of reality and of themselves.

As of the marriage, most of each partner's actions must now be projected in conjunction with those of the other. Each partner's definitions of reality must be continually correlated with the definitions of the other. The other is present in nearly all horizons of everyday conduct. Furthermore, the identity of each now takes on a new character, having to be constantly matched with that of the other, indeed being typically perceived by people at large as being symbiotically conjoined with the identity of the other. In each partner's psychological economy of significant others, the marriage partner becomes the other *par excellence,* the nearest and most decisive co-inhabitant of the world. Indeed, all other significant relationships have to be almost automatically re-perceived and re-grouped in accordance with this drastic shift.

In other words, from the beginning of the marriage each partner has new modes in his meaningful experience of the world in general, of other people and of himself. By definition, then, marriage constitutes a nomic rupture. In terms of each partner's biography, the event of marriage initiates a new nomic process. Now, the full implications of this fact are rarely apprehended by the protagonists with any degree of clarity. There rather is to be found the notion that one's world, one's other-relationships and, above all, oneself have remained what they were before—only, of course, that world, others and self will now be shared with the marriage partner. It should be clear by now that this notion is a grave misapprehension. Just because of this fact, marriage now propels the individual into an unintended and unarticulated development, in the course of which the nomic transformation takes place. What typically *is* apprehended are certain objective and concrete problems arising out of the marriage—such as tensions with in-laws, or with former friends, or religious differences between the partners, as well as immediate tensions between them. These are apprehended as external, situational and practical difficulties. What is *not* apprehended is the subjective side of these difficulties, namely, the transformation of *nomos* and identity that has occurred and that continues to go on, so that all problems and relationships are experienced in a quite new way, that is, experienced within a new and ever-changing reality.

Take a simple and frequent illustration—the male partner's relationships with male friends before and after the marriage. It is a common observation that such relationships, especially if the extra-marital partners are single, rarely survive the marriage, or, if they do, are drastically re-defined after it. This is typically the result of neither a deliberate decision by the husband nor deliberate sabotage by the wife. What rather happens, very simply, is a slow process in which the husband's image of his friend is transformed as he keeps talking about this friend with his wife. Even if no actual talking goes on, the mere presence of the wife forces him to see his friend differently. This need not mean that he adopts a negative image held by the wife. Regardless of what image she holds or is believed by him to hold, it will be different from that held by the husband. This difference will enter into the joint image that now must needs be fabricated in the course of the ongoing conversation between the marriage partners—and, in due course, must act powerfully on the image previously held by the husband. Again, typically, this process is rarely apprehended with any degree of lucidity. The old friend is more likely to fade out of the picture by slow degrees, as new kinds of friends take his place. The process, if commented upon at all within the marital conversation, can always be explained by socially available formulas about "people changing," "friends disappearing" or oneself "having become more mature." This process of conversational liquidation is especially powerful because it is onesided—the husband typically talks with his wife about his friend, but *not* with his friend about his wife. Thus the friend is deprived of the defense of, as it were, counter-defining the relationship. This dominance of the marital conversation over all others, is one of its most important characteristics. It may be mitigated by a certain amount of protective segregation of some non-marital relationships (say, "Tuesday night out with the boys," or "Saturday lunch with mother"), but even then there are powerful emotional barriers against the sort of conversation (conversation *about* the marital relationship, that is) that would serve by way of counter-definition.

Marriage thus posits a new reality. The individual's relationship with this new reality, however, is a dialectical one—he acts upon it, in collusion with the marriage partner, and it acts back upon both him and the partner, welding together their reality. Since, as we have argued before, the objectivation that constitutes this reality is precarious, the groups with which the couple associates are called upon to assist in co-defining the new reality. The couple is pushed towards groups that strengthen their new definition of themselves and the world, avoids those that weaken this definition. This in turn releases the commonly known pressures of group association, again acting upon the marriage partners to change their definitions of the world and of themselves. Thus the new reality is not posited once and for all, but goes on being redefined not only in the marital interaction itself but also in the various maritally based group relationships into which the couple enters.

In the individual's biography marriage, then, brings about a decisive phase of socialization that can be compared with the phases of childhood and adolescence. This phase has a rather different structure from the earlier ones. There the individual was in the main socialized into already existing patterns. Here he actively collaborates rather than passively accommodates himself. Also, in the previous phases of socialization, there was an apprehension of entering into a new world and being changed in the course of this. In marriage there is little apprehension of such a process, but rather the notion that the world has remained the same, with only its emotional and pragmatic connotatons having changed. This notion, as we have tried to show, is illusionary.

The re-construction of the world in marriage occurs principally in the course of conversation, as we have suggested. The implicit problem of this conversation is how to match two individual definitions of reality. By the very logic of the relationship, a common overall definition must be arrived at—otherwise the conversation will become impossible and, *ipso facto*, the relationship will be endangered. Now, this conversation may

be understood as the working away of an ordering and typifying apparatus —if one prefers, an objectivating apparatus. Each partner ongoingly contributes his conceptions of reality, which are then "talked through," usually not once but many times, and in the process become objectivated by the conversational apparatus. The longer this conversation goes on, the more massively real do the objectivations become to the partners. In the marital conversation a world is not only built, but it is also kept in a state of repair and ongoingly refurnished. The subjective reality of this world for the two partners is sustained by the same conversation. The nomic instrumentality of marriage is concretized over and over again, from bed to breakfast table, as the partners carry on the endless conversation that feeds on nearly all they individually or jointly experience. Indeed, it may happen eventually that no experience is fully real unless and until it has been thus "talked through."

This process has a very important result—namely, a hardening or stabilization of the common objectivated reality. It should be easy to see now how this comes about. The objectivations ongoingly performed and internalized by the marriage partners become ever more massively real, as they are confirmed and reconfirmed in the marital conversation. The world that is made up of these objectivations at the same time gains in stability. For example, the images of other people, which before or in the earlier stages of the marital conversation may have been rather ambiguous and shifting in the minds of the two partners, now become hardened into definite and stable characterizations. A casual acquaintance, say, may sometimes have appeared as lots of fun and sometimes as quite a bore to the wife before her marriage. Under the influence of the marital conversation, in which this other person is frequently "discussed," she will now come down more firmly on one or the other of the two characterizations, or on a reasonable compromise between the two. In any of these three options, though, she will have concocted with her husband a much more stable image of the person in question than she is likely to have had before her marriage, when there may have been no conversational pressure to make a definite option at all. The same process of stabilization may be observed with regard to self-definitions as well. In this way, the wife in our example will not only be pressured to assign stable characterizations to others but also to herself. Previously uninterested politically, she now identifies herself as a liberal. Previously alternating between dimly articulated religious positions, she now declares herself an agnostic. Previously confused and uncertain about her sexual emotions, she now understands herself as an unabashed hedonist in this area. And so on and so forth, with the same reality—and identity—stabilizing process at work on the husband. Both world and self thus take on a firmer, more reliable character for both partners.

Furthermore, it is not only the ongoing experience of the two partners that is constantly shared and passed through the conversational apparatus. The same sharing extends into the past. The two distinct biographies, as subjectively apprehended by the two individuals who have lived through them, are overruled and re-interpreted in the course of their conversation. Sooner or later, they will "tell all"—or, more correctly, they will tell it in such a way that it fits into the self-definitions objectivated in the marital relationship. The couple thus construct not only present reality but reconstruct past reality as well, fabricating a common memory that integrates the recollections of the two individual pasts.[16] The comic fulfilment of this process may be seen in those cases when one partner "remembers" more clearly what happened in the other's past than the other does—and corrects him accordingly. Similarly, there occurs a sharing of future horizons, which leads not only to stabilization, but inevitably to a narrowing of the future projections of each partner. Before marriage the individual typically plays with quite discrepant daydreams in which his future self is projected.[17] Having now considerably stabilized his self-image, the married individual will have to project the future in accordance with this maritally defined identity. This narrowing of future horizons begins with the obvious external limitations that marriage entails, as for example, with regard to vocational and career plans. However, it extends also to the more general possibilities of the individual's biography. To return to a previous illustration, the wife, having "found herself" as a liberal, an agnostic and a "sexually healthy" person, *ipso facto* liquidates the possibilities of becoming an anarchist, a Catholic or a Lesbian. At least until further notice she has decided upon who she is—and, by the same token, upon who she will be. The stabilization brought about by marriage thus affects the total reality in which the partners exist. In the most far-reaching sense of the word, the married individual "settles down"—and must do so, if the marriage is to be viable, in accordance with its contemporary institutional definition.

It cannot be sufficiently strongly emphasized that this process is typically unapprehended, almost automatic in character. The protagonists of the marriage drama do not set out de-liberately to re-create their world. Each continues to live in a world that is taken for granted—and keeps its taken-for-granted character even as it is metamorphosed. The new world that the married partners, Prometh-eus-like, have called into being is per-ceived by them as the normal world in which they have lived before. Re-constructed present and re-interpreted past are perceived as a continuum, ex-tending forwards into a commonly projected future. The dramatic change that has occurred remains, in bulk, un-apprehended and unarticulated. And where it forces itself upon the individual's attention, it is retrojected into the past, explained as having al-ways been there, though perhaps in a hidden way. Typically, the reality that has been "invented" within the mari-tal conversation is subjectively per-ceived as a "discovery." Thus the partners "discover" themselves and the world, "who they really are," "what they really believe," "how they really feel, and always have felt, about so-and-so." This retrojection of the world being produced all the time by themselves serves to enhance the sta-bility of this world and at the same time to assuage the "existential anxi-ety" that, probably inevitably, accom-panies the perception that nothing but one's own narrow shoulders supports the universe in which one has chosen to live. If one may put it like this, it is psychologically more tolerable to be Columbus than to be Prometheus.

The use of the term "stabilization" should not detract from the insight into the difficulty and precariousness of this world-building enterprise. Often enough, the new universe col-lapses in statu nascendi. Many more times it continues over a period, sway-ing perilously back and forth as the two partners try to hold it up, finally to be abandoned as an impossible under-taking. If one conceives of the marital conversation as the principal drama and the two partners as the principal protagonists of the drama, then one can look upon the other individuals involved as the supporting chorus for the central dramatic action. Children, friends, relatives and casual acquain-tances all have their part in reinforcing the tenuous structure of the new real-ity. It goes without saying that the children form the most important part of this supporting chorus. Their very existence is predicated on the mari-tally established world. The marital partners themselves are in charge of their socialization into this world, which to them has a preexistent and self-evident character. They are taught from the beginning to speak precisely those lines that lend themselves to a supporting chorus, from their first in-vocations of "Daddy" and "Mummy" on to their adoption of the parents' or-dering and typifying apparatus that now defines their world as well. The marital conversation is now in the pro-cess of becoming a family symposium, with the necessary consequence that its objectivations rapidly gain in den-sity, plausibility and durability.

In sum: the process that we have been inquiring into is, ideal-typically, one in which reality is crystallized, narrowed and stabilized. Ambiva-lences are converted into certainties. Typifications of self and of others be-come settled. Most generally, pos-sibilities become facticities. What is more, this process of transformation remains, most of the time, unap-prehended by those who are both its authors and its objects.[18]

We have analyzed in some detail the process that, we contend, entitles us to describe marriage as a nomic instru-mentality. It may now be well to turn back once more to the macrosocial context in which this process takes place—a process that, to repeat, is peculiar to our society as far as the institution of marriage is concerned, although it obviously expresses much more general human facts. The narrowing and stabilization of identity is functional in a society that, in its major public institutions, must insist on rigid controls over the individual's conduct. At the same time, the narrow enclave of the nuclear family serves as a macrosocially innocuous "play area," in which the individual can safely exercise his world-building proclivities without upsetting any of the important social, economic and political applecarts. Barred from expanding himself into the area occupied by these major institutions, he is given plently of leeway to "discover himself" in his marriage and his family, and, in view of the difficulty of this undertaking, is provided with a number of auxiliary agencies that stand ready to assist him (such as counseling, psychotherapeutic and religious agencies). The marital adventure can be relied upon to absorb a large amount of energy that might otherwise be expended more dangerously. The ideological themes of familism, romantic love, sexual expression, maturity and social adjustment, with the pervasive psychologistic anthropology that underlies them all, function to legitimate this enterprise. Also, the narrowing and stabilization of the individual's principal area of conversation within the nuclear family is functional in a society that requires high degrees of both geographical and social mobility. The segregated little world of the family can be easily detached from one milieu and transposed into another without appreciably interfering with the central processes going on in it. Needless to say, we are not suggesting that these functions are deliberately planned or even apprehended by some mythical ruling directorate of the society. Like most social phenomena, whether they be macro- or microscopic, these functions are typically unintended and unarticulated. What is more, the functionality would be impaired if it were too widely apprehended.

We believe that the above theoretical considerations serve to give a new perspective on various empirical facts studied by family sociologists. As we have emphasized a number of times, our considerations are idealtypical in intention. We have been interested in marriage at a normal age in urban, middle-class, western societies. We cannot discuss here such special problems as marriages or remarriages at a more advanced age, marriage in the remaining rural subcultures, or in ethnic or lower-class minority groups. We feel quite justified in this limitation of scope, however, by the empirical findings that tend towards the view that a global marriage type is emerging in the central strata of modern industrial societies.[19] This type, commonly referred to as the nuclear family, has been analyzed in terms of a shift from the so-called family of orientation to the so-called family of procreation as the most important reference for the individual.[20] In addition to the well-known socioeconomic reasons for this shift, most of them rooted in the development of industrialism, we would argue that important macrosocial functions pertain to the nomic process within the nuclear family, as we have analyzed it. This functionality of the nuclear family must, furthermore, be seen in conjunction with the familistic ideology that both reflects and reinforces it. A few specific empirical points may suffice to indicate the applicability of our theoretical perspective. To make these we shall use selected American data.

The trend towards marriage at an earlier age has been noted.[21] This has been correctly related to such factors as urban freedom, sexual emancipation and equalitarian values. We would add the important fact that a child raised in the circumscribed world of the nuclear family is stamped by it in terms of his psychological needs and social expectations. Having to live in the larger society from which the nuclear family is segregated, the adolescent soon feels the need for a "little world" of his own, having been socialized in such a way that only by having such a world to withdraw into can he successfully cope with the anonymous "big world" that confronts him as soon as he steps outside his parental home. In other words, to be "at home" in society entails, per definitionem, the construction of a maritally based sub-world. The parental home itself facilitates such an early jump into marriage precisely because its controls are very narrow in scope and leave the adolescent to his own nomic devices at an early age. As has been studied in considerable detail, the adolescent peer group functions as a transitional nomos between the two family worlds in the individual's biography.[22]

The equalization in the age of the marriage partners has also been noted.[23] This is certainly also to be related to equalitarian values and, concomitantly, to the decline in the "double standard" of sexual morality. Also, however, this fact is very conducive to the common reality-constructing enterprise that we have analyzed. One of the features of the latter, as we have pointed out, is the re-construction of the two biographies in terms of a cohesive and mutually correlated common memory. This task is evidently facilitated if the two partners are of roughly equal age. Another empirical finding to which our considerations are relevant is the choice of marriage partners within similar socio-economic backgrounds.[24] Apart from the obvious

practical pressures towards such limitations of choice, the latter also ensure sufficient similarity in the biographically accumulated stocks of experience to facilitate the described reality-constructing process. This would also offer additional explanation to the observed tendency to narrow the limitations of marital choice even further, for example in terms of religious background.[25]

There now exists a considerable body of data on the adoption and mutual adjustment of marital roles.[26] Nothing in our consideration detracts from the analyses made of these data by sociologists interested primarily in the processes of group interaction. We would only argue that something more fundamental is involved in this role-taking—namely, the individual's relationship to reality as such. Each role in the marital situation carries with it a universe of discourse, broadly given by cultural definition, but continually re-actualized in the ongoing conversation between the marriage partners. Put simply: marriage involves not only stepping into new roles, but, beyond this, stepping into a new world. The mutuality of adjustment may again be related to the rise of marital equalitarianism, in which comparable effort is demanded of both partners.

Most directly related to our considerations are data that pertain to the greater stability of married as against unmarried individuals.[27] Though frequently presented in misleading psychological terms (such as "greater emotional stability," "greater maturity," and so on), these data are sufficiently validated to be used not only by marriage counselors but in the risk calculations of insurance companies. We would contend that our theoretical perspective places these data into a much more intelligible sociological frame of reference, which also happens to be free of the particular value bias with which the psychological terms are loaded. It is, of course, quite true that married people are more stable emotionally (i.e. operating within a more controlled scope of emotional expression), more mature in their views (i.e. inhabiting a firmer and narrower world in conformity with the expectations of society), and more sure of themselves (i.e. having objectivated a more stable and fixated self-definition). Therefore they are more liable to be psychologically balanced (i.e. having sealed off much of their "anxiety," and reduced ambivalence as well as openness towards new possibilities of self-definition) and socially predictable (i.e. keeping their conduct well within the socially established safety rules). All of these phenomena are concomitants of the overall fact of having "settled down"—cognitively, emotionally, in terms of self-identification. To speak of these phenomena as indicators of "mental health," let alone of "adjustment to reality," overlooks the decisive fact that reality is socially constructed and that psychological conditions of all sorts are grounded in a social matrix.

We would say, very simply, that the married individual comes to live in a more stable world, from which fact certain psychological consequences can be readily deduced. To bestow some sort of higher ontological status upon these psychological consequences is *ipso facto* a symptom of the mis-or non-apprehension of the social process that has produced them. Furthermore, the compulsion to legitimate the stabilized marital world, be it in psychologistic or in traditional religious terms, is another expression of the precariousness of its construction.[28] This is not the place to pursue any further the ideological processes involved in this. Suffice it to say that contemporary psychology

functions to sustain this precarious world by assigning to it the status of "normalcy," a legitimating operation that increasingly links up with the older religious assignment of the status of "sacredness." Both legitimating agencies have established their own rites of passage, validating myths and rituals, and individualized repair services for crisis situations. Whether one legitimates one's maritally constructed reality in terms of "mental health" or of the "sacrament of marriage" is today largely left to free consumer preference, but it is indicative of the crystallization of a new overall universe of discourse that it is increasingly possible to do both at the same time.

Finally, we would point here to the empirical data on divorce.[29] The prevalence and, indeed, increasing prevalence of divorce might at first appear as a counter-argument to our theoretical considerations. We would contend that the very opposite is the case, as the data themselves bear out. Typically, individuals in our society do not divorce because marriage has become unimportant to them, but because it has become so important that they have no tolerance for the less than completely successful marital arrangement they have contracted with the particular individual in question. This is more fully understood when one has grasped the crucial need for the sort of world that only marriage can produce in our society, a world without which the individual is powerfully threatened with anomie in the fullest sense of the word. Also, the frequency of divorce simply reflects the difficulty and demanding character of the whole undertaking. The empirical fact that the great majority of divorced individuals plan to remarry and a good majority of them actually do, at least in America, fully bears out this contention.[30]

NOTES

1. The present article has come out of a larger project on which the authors have been engaged in collaboration with three colleagues in sociology and philosophy. The project is to produce a systematic treatise that will integrate a number of now separate theoretical strands in the sociology of knowledge.

2. Cf. especially Max Weber, *Wirtschaft und Gesellschaft* (Tuebingen: Mohr 1956), and *Gesammelte Aufsaetze zur Wissenschaftslehre* (Tuebingen: Mohr 1951); George H. Mead, *Mind, Self and Society* (University of Chicago Press 1934); Alfred Schutz, *Der sinnhafte Aufbau der sozialen Welt* (Vienna: Springer, 2nd ed. 1960) and Collected Papers, I (The Hague: Nijhoff 1962); Maurice Merleau-Ponty, *Phénoménologie de la perception* (Paris: Gallimard 1945) and *La structure du comportement* (Paris: Presses universitaires de France 1953).

3. Cf. Schutz, *Aufbau*, 202-20 and *Collected Papers*, I, 3-27, 283-6.

4. Cf. Schutz, *Collected Papers*, I, 207-28.

5. Cf. especially Jean Piaget, *The Child's Construction of Reality* (Routledge & Kegan Paul 1955).

6. Cf. Mead, op. cit., 135-226.

7. Cf. Schutz, *Aufbau*, 181-95.

8. Cf. Arnold Gehlen, *Die Seele im technischen Zeitalter* (Hamburg: Rowohlt 1957), 57-69 and *Anthropologische Forschung* (Hamburg: Rowohlt 1961), 69-77, 127-40; Helmut Schelsky, *Soziologie der Sexualitaet* (Hamburg: Rowohlt 1955), 102-33. Also cf. Thomas Luckmann, "On religion in modern society," *Journal for the Scientific Study of Religion* (Spring 1963), 147-62.

9. In these considerations we have been influenced by certain presuppositions of Marxian anthropology, as well as by the anthropological work of Max Scheler, Helmuth Plessner and Arnold Gehlen. We are indebted to Thomas Luckmann for the clarification of the social-psychological significance of the private sphere.

10. Cf. Talcott Parsons and Robert Bales, *Family: Socialization and Interaction Process* (Routledge & Kegan Paul 1956), 3-34, 353-96.

11. Cf. Philippe Ariès, *Centuries of Childhood* (New York: Knopf 1962), 339-410.

12. Cf. Georg Simmel (Kurt Wolff ed.), *The Sociology of Georg Simmel* (Collier-Macmillan 1950), 118-44.

13. Cf. Schutz, *Aufbau*, 29-36, 149-53.

14. Cf. Schutz, *Aufbau*, 186-92, 202-10.

15. David Riesman's well-known concept of 'other-direction' would also be applicable here.

16. Cf. Maurice Halbwachs, *Les Cadres sociaux de la mémoire* (Paris: Presses universitares de France 1952), especially 146-77; also cf. Peter Berger, *Invitation to Sociology- A Humanistic Perspective* (Garden City, N. Y.: Doubleday-Anchor 1963), 54-65 (available in Penguin).

17. Cf. Schutz, *Collected Papers*, I, 72-3, 79-82.

18. The phenomena here discussed could also be formulated effectively in terms of the Marxian categories of reification and false consciousness. Jean-Paul Sartre's recent work, especially *Critique de la raison dialectique*, seeks to integrate these categories within a phenomenological analysis of human conduct. Also cf. Henri Lefebvre, *Critique de la vie quotidienne* (Paris: l'Arche 1958-61).

19. Cf. Renate Mayntz, *Die moderne Familie* (Stuttgart: Enke 1955); Helmut Schelsky, *Wandlungen der deutschen Familie in der Gegenwart* (Stuttgart: Enke 1955); Maximilien Sorre (ed.), *Sociologie comparée de la famille contemporaine* (Paris: Centre National de la Recherche Scientifique 1955); Ruth Anshen (ed.), *The Family—Its Function and Destiny* (New York: Harper 1959); Norman Bell and Ezra Vogel, *A Modern Introduction to the Family* (Routledge & Kegan Paul 1961).

20. Cf. Talcott Parsons, *Essays in Sociological Theory* (Collier-Macmillan 1949), 233-50.

21. In these as well as the following references to empirical studies we naturally make no attempt at comprehensiveness. References are given as representative of a much larger body of materials. Cf. Paul Glick, *American Families* (New York: Wiley 1957), 54. Also cf. his "The family cycle," *American Sociological Review* (April 1947), 164-74. Also cf. Bureau of the Census, *Statistical Abstracts of the United States* 1956 and 1958; *Current Population Reports*, Series P-20, no. 96 (Nov. 1959).

22. Cf. David Riesman, *The Lonely Crowd* (New Haven: Yale University Press 1953), 29-40; Frederick Elkin, *The Child and Society* (New York: Random House 1960), passim.

23. Cf. references given above note 21.

24. Cf. W. Lloyd Warner and Paul Lunt, *The Social Life of a Modern Community*

(New Haven: Yale University Press 1941),
436-40; August Hollingshead, "Cultural
factors in the selection of marriage mates,"
American Sociological Review (October
1950), 619-27. Also cf. Ernest Burgess and
Paul Wallin, "Homogamy in social
characteristics," *American Journal of Sociology* (September 1943), 109-24.

25. Cf. Gerhard Lenski, *The Religious
Factor* (Garden City, N. Y.: Doubleday
1961), 48-50.

26. Cf. Leonard Cottrell, "Roles in marital adjustment," *Publications of the American Sociological Society* (1933), 27, 107-15;
Willard Waller and Reuben Hill, *The
Family–A Dynamic Interpretation* (New
York: Dryden 1951), 253-71; Morris Zelditch, "Role differentiation in the nuclear
family," in Parsons and Bales, op. cit.,

307-52. For a general discussion of role interaction in small groups, cf. especially
George Homans, *The Human Group* (Routledge & Kegan Paul 1951).

27. Cf. Waller and Hill, op. cit., 253-71,
for an excellent summation of such data.

28. Cf. Dennison Nash and Peter Berger,
"The family, the child and the religious
revival in suburbia," *Journal for the Scientific Study of Religion* (Fall 1962), 85-93.

29. Cf. Bureau of the Census, op. cit.

30. Cf. Talcott Parsons, "Age and Sex in
the Social Structure of the United States,"
American Sociological Review (December
1942), 604-16; Paul Glick, "First marriages
and remarriages," *American Sociological
Review* (December 1949), 726-34; William
Goode, *After Divorce* (Chicago: Free Press
1956), 269-85.

19. RELIGION AND WORLD CONSTRUCTION

PETER BERGER

Reprinted from "Religion and World Construction," copyright© 1967 by Peter L. Berger from *The Sacred Canopy*. Reprinted by permission of Doubleday & Company, Inc. This article is drawn from a small portion of Berger's extensive writings in the sociology of religion. In addition to *The Sacred Canopy*, Berger has written *The Precarious Vision, The Noise of Solemn Assemblies*, and *A Rumor of Angels*.

Every human society is an enterprise of world-building. Religion occupies a distinctive place in this enterprise. Our main purpose here is to make some general statements about the relationship between human religion and human world-building. Before this can be done intelligibly, however, the above statement about the world-building efficacy of society must be explicated. For this explication it will be important to understand society in dialectic terms[1].

Society is a dialectic phenomenon in that it is a human product, and nothing but a human product, that yet continuously acts back upon its producer. Society is a product of man. It has no other being except that which is bestowed upon it by human activity and consciousness. There can be no social reality apart from man. Yet it may also be stated that man is a product of society. Every individual biography is an episode within the history of society, which both precedes and survives it. Society was there before the individual was born and it will be there after he has died. What is more, it is within society, and as a result of social processes, that the individual becomes a person, that he attains and holds onto an identity, and that he carries out the various projects that constitute his life. Man cannot exist apart from society. The two statements, that society is the product of man and that man is the product of society, are not contradictory. They rather reflect the inherently dialectic character of the societal phenomenon. Only if this character is recognized will society be understood in terms that are adequate to its empirical reality[2].

The fundamental dialectic process of society consists of three moments, or steps. These are externalization, objectivation, and internalization. Only if these three moments are understood together can an empirically adequate view of society be maintained. Externalization is the ongoing outpouring of human being into the world, both in the physical and the mental activity of men. Objectivation is the attainment by the products of this activity (again both physical and mental) of a reality that confronts its original producers as a facticity external to and other than themselves. Internalization is the re-appropriation by men of this same reality, transforming it once again from structures of the objective world into structures of the subjective consciousness. It is through externalization that society is a human product. It is through objectivation that society becomes a reality *sui generis*. It is through internalization that man is a product of society[3].

Externalization is an anthropological necessity. Man, as we know him empirically, cannot be conceived of apart from the continuous outpouring of himself into the world in which he finds himself. Human being cannot be understood as somehow resting within itself, in some closed sphere of interiority, and *then* setting out to express itself in the surrounding world. Human being is externalizing in its essence and from the beginning[4]. This anthropological root fact is very probably grounded in the biological constitution of man[5]. *Homo sapiens* occupies a peculiar position in the animal kingdom. This peculiarity manifests itself in man's relationship both to his own body and to the world. Unlike the other higher mammals, who are born with an essentially completed organism, man is curiously "unfinished" at birth[6]. Essential steps in the process of "finishing" man's development, which have already taken place in the foetal period for the other higher mammals, occur in the first year after birth in the case of man. That is, the biological process of "becoming man" occurs at a time when the human infant is in interaction with an extra-organismic environment, which includes both the physical and the human world of the infant. There is thus a biological foundation to the process of "becoming man" in the sense of developing personality and appropriating culture. The latter developments are not somehow superimposed as alien mutations upon the biological development of man, but they are grounded in it.

The "unfinished" character of the human organism at birth is closely related to the relatively unspecialized character of its instinctual structure. The non-human animal enters the world with highly specialized and firmly directed drives. As a result, it lives in a world that is more or less completely determined by its instinctual structure. This world is closed in terms of its possibilities, programmed,

as it were, by the animal's own constitution. Consequently, each animal lives in an environment that is specific to its particular species. There is a mouse-world, a dog-world, a horse-world, and so forth. By contrast, man's instinctual structure at birth is both underspecialized and undirected toward a species-specific environment. There is no man-world in the above sense. Man's world is imperfectly programmed by his own constitution. It is an open world. That is, it is a world that must be fashioned by man's own activity. Compared with the other higher mammals, man thus has a double relationship to the world. Like the other mammals, man is *in* a world that antedates his appearance. But unlike the other mammals, this world is not simply given, prefabricated for him. Man must *make* a world for himself. The world-building activity of man, therefore, is not a biologically extraneous phenomenon, but the direct consequence of man's biological constitution.

The condition of the human organism in the world is thus characterized by a built-in instability. Man does not have a given relationship to the world. He must ongoingly establish a relationship with it. The same instability marks man's relationship to his own body[7]. In a curious way, man is "out of balance" with himself. He cannot rest within himself, but must continuously come to terms with himself by expressing himself in activity. Human existence is an ongoing "balancing act" between man and his body, man and his world. One may put this differently by saying that man is constantly in the process of "catching up with himself." It is in this process that man produces a world. Only in such a world produced by himself can he locate himself and realize his life. But the same process that builds his world also "finishes" his own being. In other words, man not only produces a world, but he also produces himself. More precisely, he produces himself in a world. . . .

It may now be understandable if the proposition is made that the socially constructed world is, above all, an ordering of experience. A meaningful order, or nomos, is imposed upon the discrete experiences and meanings of individuals[8]. To say that society is a world-building enterprise is to say that it is ordering, or nomizing, activity. The presupposition for this is given, as has been indicated before, in the biological constitution of *homo sapiens*. Man, biologically denied the ordering mechanisms with which the other animals are endowed, is compelled to impose his own order upon experience. Man's sociality presupposes the collective character of this ordering activity. The ordering of experience is endemic to any kind of social interaction. Every social action implies that individual meaning is directed toward others and ongoing social interaction implies that the several meanings of the actors are integrated into an order of common meaning[9]. It would be wrong to assume that this nomizing consequence of social interaction must, from the beginning, produce a nomos that embraces *all* the discrete experiences and meanings of the participant individuals. If one can imagine a society in its first origins (something,. of course, that is empirically unavailable), one may assume that the range of the common nomos expands as social interaction comes to include ever broader areas of common meaning. It makes no sense to imagine that this nomos will ever include the totality of individual meanings. Just as there can be no totally socialized individual, so there will always be individual meanings that remain outside

of or marginal to the common nomos. Indeed, as will be seen a little later, the marginal experiences of the individual are of considerable importance for an understanding of social existence. All the same, there is an inherent logic that impels every nomos to expand into wider areas of meaning. If the ordering activity of society never attains to totality, it may yet be described as totalizing[10].

The social world constitutes a nomos both objectively and subjectively. The objective nomos is given in the process of objectivation as such. The fact of language, even if taken by itself, can readily be seen as the imposition of order upon experience. Language nomizes by imposing differentiation and structure upon the ongoing flux of experience. As an item of experience is named, it is *ipso facto*, taken out of this flux and given stability *as* the entity so named. Language further provides a fundamental order of relationships by the addition of syntax and grammar to vocabulary. It is impossible to use language without participating in its order. Every empirical language may be said to constitute a nomos in the making, or, with equal validity, as the historical consequence of the nomizing activity of generations of men. The original nomizing act is to say that an item is *this*, and thus *not that*. As this original incorporation of the item into an order that includes other items is followed by sharper linguistic designations (the item is male and not female, singular and not plural, a noun and not a verb, and so forth), the nomizing act intends a comprehensive order of *all* items that may be linguistically objectivated, that is, intends a totalizing nomos.

On the foundation of language, and by means of it, is built up the cognitive and normative edifice that passes for "knowledge" in a society. In what it "knows," every society imposes a common order of interpretation upon experience that becomes "objective knowledge" by means of the process of objectivation discussed before. Only a relatively small part of this edifice is constituted by theories of one kind or another, though theoretical "knowledge" is particularly important because it usually contains the body of "official" interpretations of reality. Most socially objectivated "knowledge" is pretheoretical. It consists of interpretative schemas, moral maxims and collections of traditional wisdom that the man in the street frequently shares with the theoreticians. Societies vary in the degree of differentiation in their bodies of "knowledge." Whatever these variations, every society provides for its members an objectively available body of "knowledge." To participate in the society is to share its "knowledge," that is, to co-inhabit its nomos.

The objective nomos is internalized in the couse of socialization. It is thus appropriated by the individual to become his own subjective ordering of experience. It is by virtue of this appropriation that the individual can come to "make sense" of his own biography. The discrepant elements of his past life are ordered in terms of what he "knows objectively" about his own and others' condition. His ongoing experience is integrated into the same order, though the latter may have to be modified to allow for this integration. The future attains a meaningful shape by virtue of the same order being projected into it. In other words, to live in the social world is to live an ordered and meaningful life. Society is the guardian of order and meaning not only objectively, in its institutional structures, but subjectively as well, in its structuring of individual consciousness.

It is for this reason that radical separation from the social world, or anomy, constitutes such a powerful threat to the individual[11]. It is not only that the individual loses emotionally satisfying ties in such cases. He loses his orientation in experience. In extreme cases, he loses his sense of reality and identity. He becomes anomic in the sense of becoming worldless. Just as an individual's nomos is constructed and sustained in conversation with significant others, so is the individual plunged toward anomy when such conversation is radically interrupted. The circumstances of such nomic disruption may, of course, vary. They might involve large collective forces, such as the loss of status of the entire social group to which the individual belongs. They might be more narrowly biographical, such as the loss of significant others by death, divorce, or physical separation. It is thus possible to speak of collective as well as of individual states of anomy. In both cases, the fundamental order in terms of which the individual can "make sense" of his life and recognize his own identity will be in process of disintegration. Not only will the individual then begin to lose his moral bearings, with disastrous psychological consequences, but he will become uncertain about his cognitive bearings as well. The world begins to shake in the very instant that its sustaining conversation begins to falter.

The socially established nomos may thus be understood, perhaps in its most important aspect, as a shield against terror. Put differently, the most important function of society is nomization. The anthropological presupposition for this is a human craving for meaning that appears to have the force of instinct. Men are congenitally compelled to impose a meaningful order upon reality. This order, however, presupposes the social enterprise of ordering world-construction. To be separated from society exposes the individual to a multiplicity of dangers with which he is unable to cope by himself, in the extreme case to the danger of imminent extinction. Separation from society also inflicts unbearable psychological tensions upon the individual, tensions that are grounded in the root anthropological fact of sociality. The ultimate danger of such separation, however, is the danger of meaninglessness. This danger is the nightmare *par excellence*, in which the individual is submerged in a world of disorder, senselessness and madness. Reality and identity are malignantly transformed into meaningless figures of horror. To be in society is to be "sane" precisely in the sense of being shielded from the ultimate "insanity" of such anomic terror. Anomy is unbearable to the point where the individual may seek death in preference to it. Conversely, existence within a nomic world may be sought at the cost of all sorts of sacrifice and suffering—and even at the cost of life itself, if the individual believes that this ultimate sacrifice has nomic significance[12].

The sheltering quality of social order becomes especially evident if one looks at the marginal situations in the life of the individual, that is, at situations in which he is driven close to or beyond the boundaries of the order that determines his routine, everyday existence[13]. Such marginal situations commonly occur in dreams and fantasy. They may appear on the horizon of consciousness as haunting suspicions that the world may have another aspect than its "normal" one, that is, that the previously accepted definitions of reality may be fragile or even fraudulent[14]. Such suspicions extend to the identity of both self and others, positing the possibility of shattering metamorphoses. When these suspicions invade the central areas of consciousness they take on, of course, the constellations that modern psychiatry would call neurotic or psychotic. Whatever the epistemological status of these constellations (usually decided upon much too sanguinely by psychiatry, precisely because it is firmly rooted in the everyday, "official," social definitions of reality), their profound terror for the individual lies in the threat they constitute to his previously operative nomos. The marginal situation *par excellence*, however, is death[15]. Witnessing the death of others (notably, of course, of significant others) and anticipating his own death, the individual is strongly propelled to question the *ad hoc* cognitive and normative operating procedures of his "normal" life in society. Death presents society with a formidable problem not only because of its obvious threat to the continuity of human relationships, but because it threatens the basic assumptions of order on which society rests.

In other words, the marginal situations of human existence reveal the innate precariousness of all social worlds. Every socially defined reality remains threatened by lurking "irrealities." Every socially constructed nomos must face the constant possibility of its collapse into anomy. Seen in the perspective of society, every nomos is an area of meaning carved out of a vast mass of meaninglessness, a small clearing of lucidity in a formless, dark, always ominous jungle. Seen in the perspective of the individual, every nomos represents the bright "dayside" of life, tenuously held onto against the sinister shadows of the "night." In both perspectives, every nomos is an edifice erected in the face of the potent and alien forces of chaos. This chaos must be kept at bay at all cost. To ensure this, every society develops procedures that assist its members to remain "reality-oriented" (that is, to remain within the reality as "officially" defined) and to "return to reality" (that is to return from the marginal spheres of "irreality" to the socially established nomos). . . .

The social world intends, as far as possible, to be taken for granted[16]. Socialization achieves success to the degree that this taken-for-granted quality is internalized. It is not enough that the individual look upon the key meanings of the social order as useful, desirable, or right. It is much better (better, that is, in terms of social stability) if he looks upon them as inevitable, as part and parcel of the universal "nature of things." If that can be achieved, the individual who strays seriously from the socially defined programs can be considered not only a fool or a knave, but a madman. Subjectively, then, serious deviance provokes not only moral guilt but the terror of madness. For example, the sexual program of a society is taken for granted not simply as a utilitarian or morally correct arrangement, but as an inevitable expression of "human nature." The so-called "homosexual panic" may serve as an excellent illustration of the terror unleashed by the denial of the program. This is not to deny that this terror is also fed by practical apprehensions and qualms of conscience, but its fundamental motorics is the terror of being thrust into an outer darkness that separates one from the "normal" order of men. In other words, institutional programs are endowed with an ontological status to the point where to deny them is to deny being itself—the being of the universal order of things and, consequently, one's own being in this order.

Whenever the socially established nomos attains the quality of being taken for granted, there occurs a merging of its meanings with what are considered to be the fundamental meanings inherent in the universe. Nomos and cosmos appear to be co-extensive. In archaic societies, nomos appears as a microcosmic reflection, the world of men as expressing meanings inherent in the universe as such. In contemporary society, this archaic cosmization of the social world is likely to take the form of "scientific" propositions about the nature of men rather than the nature of the universe[17]. Whatever the historical variations, the tendency is for the meanings of the humanly constructed order to be projected into the universe as such[18]. It may readily be seen how this projection tends to stabilize the tenuous nomic constructions, though the mode of this stabilization will have to be investigated further. In any case, when the nomos is taken for granted as appertaining to the "nature of things," understood cosmologically or anthropologically, it is endowed with a stability deriving from more powerful sources than the historical efforts of human beings. It is at this point that religion enters significantly into our argument.

Religion is the human enterprise by which a sacred cosmos is established[19]. Put differently, religion is cosmization in a sacred mode. By sacred is meant here a quality of mysterious and awesome power, other than man and yet related to him, which is believed to reside in certain objects of experience[20]. This quality may be attributed to natural or artificial objects, to animals, or to men, or to the objectivations of human culture. There are sacred rocks, sacred tools, sacred cows. The chieftain may be sacred, as may be a particular custom or institution. Space and time may be assigned the same quality, as in sacred localities and sacred seasons. The quality may finally be embodied in sacred beings, from highly localized spirits to the great cosmic divinities. The latter, in turn, may be transformed into ultimate forces or principles ruling the cosmos, no longer conceived of in personal terms but still endowed with the status of sacredness. The historical manifestations of the sacred vary widely, though there are certain uniformities to be observed cross-culturally (no matter here whether these are to be interpreted as resulting from cultural diffusion or from an inner logic of man's religious imagination). The sacred is apprehended as "sticking out" from the normal routines of everyday life, as something extraordinary and potentially dangerous, though its dangers can be domesticated and its potency harnessed to the needs of everyday life. Although the sacred is apprehended as other than man, yet it refers to man, relating to him in a way in which other non-human phenomena (specifically, the phenomena of non-sacred nature) do not. The cosmos posited by religion thus both transcends and includes man. The sacred cosmos is confronted by man as an immensely powerful reality other than himself. Yet this reality addresses itself to him and locates his life in an ultimately meaningful order.

On one level, the antonym to the sacred is the profane, to be defined simply as the absence of sacred status. All phenomena are profane that do not "stick out" as sacred. The routines of everyday life are profane unless, so to speak, proven otherwise, in which latter case they are conceived of as being infused in one way or another with sacred power (as in sacred work, for instance). Even in such cases, however, the sacred quality attributed to the ordinary events of life *itself* retains its extraordinary character, a character that is typically reaffirmed through a variety of rituals and the loss of which is tantamount to secularization, that is, to a conception of the events in question as *nothing but* profane. The dichotomization of reality into sacred and profane spheres, however related, is intrinsic to the religious enterprise. As such, it is obviously important for any analysis of the religious phenomenon.

On a deeper level, however, the sacred has another opposed category, that of chaos.[21] The sacred cosmos emerges out of chaos and continues to confront the latter as its terrible contrary. This opposition of cosmos and chaos is frequently expressed in a variety of cosmogonic myths. The sacred cosmos, which transcends and includes man in its ordering of reality, thus provides man's ultimate shield against the terror of anomy. To be in a "right" relationship with the sacred cosmos is to be protected against the nightmare threats of chaos. To fall out of such a "right" relationship is to be abandoned on the edge of the abyss of meaninglessness. It is not irrelevant to observe here that the English "chaos" derives from a Greek word meaning "yawning" and "religion" from a Latin one meaning "to be careful." To be sure, what the religious man is "careful" about is above all the dangerous power inherent in the manifestations of the sacred themselves. But behind this danger is the other, much more horrible one, namely that one may lose all connection with the sacred and be swallowed up by chaos. All the nomic constructions, as we have seen, are designed to keep this terror at bay. In the sacred cosmos, however, these constructions achieve their ultimate culmination—literally, their apotheosis.

Human existence is essentially and inevitably externalizing activity. In the course of externalization men pour out meaning into reality. Every human society is an edifice of externalized and objectivated meanings, always intending a meaningful totality. Every society is engaged in the never completed enterprise of building a humanly meaningful world. Cosmization implies the identification of this humanly meaningful world with the world as such, the former now being grounded in the latter, reflecting it or being derived from it in its fundamental structures. Such a cosmos, as the ultimate ground and validation of human nomoi, need not necessarily be sacred. Particularly in modern times there have been thoroughly secular attempts at cosmization, among which modern science is by far the most important. It is safe to say, however, that originally *all* cosmization had a sacred character. This remained true through most of human history, and not only through the millennia of human existence on earth preceding what we now call civilization. Viewed historically, most of man's worlds have been sacred worlds. Indeed, it appears likely that only by way of the sacred was it possible for man to conceive of a cosmos in the first place.[22]

It can thus be said that religion has played a strategic part in the human enterprise of world-building. Religion implies the farthest reach of man's self-externalization, of his infusion of reality with his own meanings. Religion implies that human order is projected into the totality of being. Put differently, religion is the audacious attempt to conceive of the entire universe as being humanly significant.

NOTES

1. The term "world" is here understood in a phenomenological sense, that is, with the question of its ultimate ontological status remaining in brackets. For the anthropological application of the term, *cf.* Max Scheler, *Die Stellung des Menschen im Kosmos* (Munich, Nymphenburger Verlagshandlung, 1947). For the application of the term to the sociology of knowledge, *cf.* Max Scheler, *Die Wissensformsn und die Gesellschaft* (Bern, Francke, 1960); Alfred Schutz, *Der sinnhafte Aufbau der sozialen Welt* (Vienna, Springer, 1960), and *Collected Papers*, Vols. I-II (The Hague, Nijhoff, 1962-64). The term "dialectic" as applied to society is here understood in an essential Marxian sense, particularly as the latter was developed in the *Economic and Philosophical Manuscripts of 1844*.

2. We would contend that this dialectic understanding of man and society as mutual products makes possible a theoretical synthesis of the Weberian and Durkheimian approaches to sociology without losing the fundamental intention of either (such a loss having occurred, in our opinion, in the Parsonian synthesis). Weber's understanding of social reality as ongoingly constituted by human signification and Durkheim's of the same as having the character of *choseité* as against the individual are *both* correct. They intend, respectively, the subjective foundation and the objective facticity of the societal phenomenon, *ipso facto* pointing toward the dialectic relationship of subjectivity and its objects. By the same token, the two understandings are only correct *together*. A quasi-Weberian emphasis on subjectivity *only* leads to an idealistic distortion of the societal phenomenon. A quasi-Durkheimian emphasis on objectivity *only* leads to sociological reification, the more disastrous distortion toward which much of contemporary American sociology has tended. It should be stressed that we are not implying here that such a dialectic synthesis would have been agreeable to these two authors themselves. Our interest is systematic rather than exegetical, an interest that permits an eclectic attitude toward previous theoretical constructions. When we say, then, that the latter "intend" such a synthesis, we mean this in the sense of intrinsic theoretical logic rather than of the historical intentions of these authors.

3. The terms "externalization" and "objectivation" are derived from Hegel (*Entaeusserung* and *Versachlichung*), are understood here essentially as they were applied to collective phenomena by Marx. The term "internalization" is understood as

commonly used in American social psychology. The theoretical foundation of the latter is above all the work of George Herbert Mead, for which cf. his *Mind, Self and Society* (Chicago, University of Chicago Press, 1934); Anselm Strauss (ed.), *George Herbert Mead on Social Psychology* (Chicago, University of Chicago Press, 1956). The term "reality sui generis," as applied to society, is developed by Durkheim in his *Rules of Sociological Method* (Glencoe, Ill., Free Press, 1950).

4. The anthropological necessity of externalization was developed by Hegel and Marx. For more contemporary developments of this understanding, in addition to the work of Scheler, cf. Helmut Plessner, *Die Stuffen des Organischen und der Mensch* (1928), and Arnold Gehlen, *Der Mensch* (1940).

5. For the biological foundation of this argument, cf. F. J. J. Buytendijk, *Mensch und Tier* (Hamburg, Rowohlt, 1958); Adolf Portmann, *Zoologie und das neue Bild des Menschen* (Hamburg, Rowohlt, 1956). The most important application of these biological perspectives to sociological problems is to be found in the work of Gehlen.

6. This has been succinctly put in the opening sentence of a recent anthropological work written from an essentially Marxian viewpoint: "L'homme naît inachevé" (Georges Lapassade, *L'entrée dans la vie* [Paris, Editions de Minuit, 1963], p. 17).

7. Plessner has coined the term "eccentricity" to refer to this innate instability in man's relationship to his own body. Cf. op. cit.

8. The term "nomos" is indirectly derived from Durkheim by, as it were, turning around his concept of *anomie*. The latter was first developed in his *Suicide* (Glencoe, Ill., Free Press, 1951); cf. especially pp. 241 ff.

9. The definition of social action in terms of meaning derives from Weber. The implications of this definition in terms of the social "world" were especially developed by Schutz.

10. The term "totalization" is derived from Jean-Paul Sartre. Cf. his *Critique de la raison dialectique*, Vol. I (Paris, Gallimard, 1960).

11. "Anomy" is an Anglicization of Durkheim's *anomie* favored by several American sociologists, though not by Robert Merton (who sought to integrate the concept within his structural-functionalist theory, retaining the French spelling). We have adopted the Anglicized spelling for stylistic reasons only.

12. This suggests that there are nomic as well as anomic suicides, a point alluded to but not developed by Durkheim in his discussion of "altruistic suicide" (*Suicide*, pp. 217 ff.).

13. The concept of "marginal situations" (*Grenzsituationen*) derives from Karl Jaspers. Cf. especially his *Philosophie* (1932).

14. The notion of the "other aspect" of reality has been developed by Robert Musil in his great unfinished novel, *Der Mann ohne Eigenschaften*, in which it is a major theme. For a critical discussion, cf. Ernst Kaiser and Eithne Wilkins, *Robert Musil* (Stuttgart, Kohlhammer, 1962).

15. The concept of death as the most important marginal situation is derived from Martin Heidegger. Cf. especially his *Sein und Zeit* (1929).

16. The concept of the world-taken-for-granted is derived from Schutz. Cf. especially his *Collected Papers*, Vol. I, pp. 207 ff.

17. The term "cosmization" is derived from Mircea Eliade. Cf. his *Cosmos and History* (New York, Harper, 1959), pp. 10 f.

18. The concept of projection was first developed by Ludwig Feuerbach. Both Marx and Nietzsche derived it from the latter. It was the Nietzschean derivation that became important for Freud.

19. This definition is derived from Rudolf Otto and Mircea Eliade.... Religion is defined here as a human enterprise because this is how it manifests itself as an empirical phenomenon. Within this definition the question as to whether religion may also be something more than that remains bracketed, as, of course, it must be in any attempt at scientific understanding.

20. For a clarification of the concept of the sacred, cf. Rudolf Otto, *Das Heilige* (Munich, Beck, 1963); Gerardus van der Leeuw, *Religion in Essence and Manifestation* (London, George Allen & Unwin, 1938); Mircea Eliade, *Das Heilige und das Profane* (Hamburg, Rowohlt, 1957). The dichotomy of the sacred and the profane is used by Durkheim in his *The Elementary Forms of the Religious Life* (New York, Collier Books, 1961).

21. Cf. Eliade, *Cosmos and History*, *passim*.

22. Cf. Eliade, *Das Heilige und das Profane*, p. 38: "Die Welt laesst sich als 'Welt', als 'Kosmos' insofern fassen, als sie sich als heilige Welt offenbart."

20.   A DRAMATISTIC THEORY OF STATUS POLITICS

JOSEPH R. GUSFIELD

Reprinted from Joseph R. Gusfield, *Symbolic Crusade* (Chicago: University of Illinois Press, 1963) pp. 166-183, with permission of University of Illinois Press and the author. Joseph R. Gusfield is Professor of Sociology at the University of California, San Diego. He has contributed extensively to the literature on political and social change, comparative sociology, and the sociology of higher education.

Political action has a meaning inherent in what it signifies about the structure of the society as well as in what such action actually achieves. . . . Prohibition and Temperance have operated as symbolic rather than as instrumental goals in American politics. The passage of legislation or the act of public approval of Temperance has been as significant to the activities of the Temperance movement as has the instrumental achievement of an abstinent society. The agitation and struggle of the Temperance adherents has been directed toward the establishment of their norms as marks of social and political superiority.

The distinction between political action as significant per se and political action as means to an end is the source of the theory underlying our analysis of the Temperance movement. We refer to it as a dramatistic theory because, like drama, it represents an action which is make-believe but which moves its audience. It is in keeping with Kenneth Burke's meaning of dramatism, "since it invites one to consider the matter of motives in a perspective that, being developed from the analysis of drama, treats language and thought primarily as modes of action."[1] It is make-believe in that the action need have no relation to its ostensible goal. The effect upon the audience comes from the significance which they find in the action as it represents events or figures outside of the drama.

. . . Our theory is further dramatistic in its perspective on political action as symbolic action, as action in which "the object referred to has a range of meaning beyond itself."[2] . . . [T]his is the literary sense of the symbol as distinguished from the linguistic. It is in this sense that we refer to the flag as a symbol of national glory, to the cross as a symbol of Christianity, or the albatross as a symbol of charity in *The Rime of the Ancient Mariner*.

The dramatistic approach has important implications for the study of political institutions. . . . Governments affect the distribution of values through symbolic acts, as well as through the force of instrumental ones. The struggle to control the symbolic actions of government is often as bitter and as fateful as the struggle to control its tangible effects. Much of our response to political events is in terms of their dramatic, symbolic meaning.

This is especially the case where elements of the status order are at issue. The distribution of prestige is partially regulated by symbolic acts of public and political figures. Such persons "act out" the drama in which one status group is degraded and another is given deference. In seeking to effect their honor and prestige in the society, a group makes demands upon governing agents to act in ways which serve

243

to symbolize deference or to degrade the opposition whose status they challenge or who challenge theirs. . . .

SYMBOLIC ISSUES IN POLITICS

THE STATE AND THE PUBLIC

Following Max Weber, it has become customary for sociologists to define the state as the legitimate monopolizer of force.[3] A major defect of this view, however, is that it minimizes the extent to which governments function as representatives of the total society. Other organizations or institutions claim to represent the values and interests of one group, subculture, or collectivity within the total social organization. Government is the only agency which claims to act for the entire society. It seeks its legitimation through the claim that it is effected with a "public interest" rather than with a special, limited set of goals. Much of the effective acceptance of government as legitimate rests upon the supposition that it is representative of the total society, that it has the moral responsibility "to commit the group to action or to perform coordinated acts for its general welfare."[4]

The public and visible nature of governmental acts provides them with wider consequences for other institutions than is true of any other area of social life. The actions of government can affect the tangible resources of citizens but they can also affect the attitudes, opinions, and judgments which people make about each other.

It is readily apparent that governments affect the distribution of resources and, in this fashion, promote or deter the interest of economic classes. The passage of a minimum wage law does affect the incomes of millions of laborers and the profits of thousands of owners of capital. The Wagner Labor Relations Act and the Taft-Hartley Act have changed the conditions of collective bargaining during the past 26 years. Tariff laws do influence the prices of products. While these legislative actions may not direct and control behavior as much as was contemplated in their passage, they nevertheless find their *raison d'être* as instruments which have affected behavior to the delight of some and the dismay of others. They are instruments to achieve a goal or end through their use.

That governmental acts have symbolic significance is not so readily appreciated, although it has always been recognized. We see the act of recall of an ambassador as an expression of anger between one government and another. We recognize in the standardized pattern of inaugural addresses the gesture toward consensus after the strain of electoral conflict. These acts, of ambassadorial recall and of presidential oratory, are not taken at face value but as devices to induce response in their audiences, as symbolic of anger or of appeal for consensus.

Not only ritual and ceremony are included in symbolic action. Law contains a great deal which has little direct effect upon behavior. The moral reform legislation embodying Temperance ideals has largely been of this nature, as have other reforms, such as those directed against gambling, birth control, and prostitution. The impact of legislation on such problems as civil rights, economic monopoly, or patriotic loyalties is certainly dubious. While we do not maintain that Temperance legislation, and the other legislation cited, has had no effect on behavior, we do find its instrumental effects are slight compared to the response which it entails as a symbol, irrespective of its utility as a means to a tangible end.

NATURE OF THE SYMBOL

In distinguishing symbolic from instrumental action we need to specify the way in which a symbol stands for something else. It is customary in linguistic analysis to distinguish between "sign" and "symbol."[5] The former points to and indicates objects or experiences to our senses. The latter represents objects and events apart from any sensory contacts. Thus the ringing of the doorbell is a sign that someone is at the front door. The word "doorbell" is a symbol, as is the concept of "democracy." Our usage is not linguistic in this sense,[6] but literary. We are concerned with the multiplicity of meanings which the same object or act can have for the observer and which, in a society, are often fixed, shared, and standardized. The artist and the writer have developed language and visual art with the use of symbols as major tools of communication. Religious institutions have developed a rich culture around the use of objects whose meanings are symbolic. The wine and wafer of the Mass are but one example of objects which embody a multiple set of meanings for the same person at the same time.

This distinction between instrumental and symbolic action is, in many ways, similar to the difference between denotative and connotative discourse. In denotation, our eyes are on the referent which, in clear language, is the same for all who use the term. Instrumental action is similar in being oriented as a means to a fixed end. Connotative references are more ambiguous, less fixed. The symbol is connotative in that "it has acquired a meaning which is added to its immediate intrinsic significance."[7]

It is useful to think of symbolic acts as forms of rhetoric, functioning to organize the perceptions, attitudes, and feelings of observers. Symbolic acts "invite consideration rather than overt action."[8] They are persuasive devices which alter the observer's view of the objects. Kenneth Burke, perhaps the greatest analyst of political symbolism, has given a clear illustration of how a political speech can function rhetorically by the use of language to build a picture contradicting the instrumental effects of political action. For example, if action is proposed or performed which will offend the businessman, language is produced in speeches which glorify the businessman. In this context, language functions to persuade the "victim" that government is not really against him. It allays the fears and "softens the blow." Burke refers to this technique as "secular prayer." It is the normal way in which prayer is used, "to sharpen up the pointless and blunt the too sharply pointed."[9]

It is not only language which is utilized in symbolic fashion by political agents. Any act of government can be imbued with symbolic import when it becomes associated with noninstrumental identifications, when it serves to glorify or demean the character of one group or another. Ceremony and ritual can become affected with great significance as actions in which the political agent, as representative of the society, symbolizes the societal attitude, the public norm, toward some person, object, or social group. Law, language, and behavior can all function ceremonially. They persuade men to a form of thought or behavior rather than force them to it. "The officer who doubts the obedience of his men may meet the situation by raising his voice, adopting a truculent tone, and putting on a pugnacious swagger."[10] This, too, is a form of rhetoric, of persuasive art.

TYPES OF POLITICAL SYMBOLISM

We find it useful to distinguish between two forms of political symbolism: *gestures of cohesion* and *gestures of differentiation.* The first type, gestures of cohesion, serve to fix the common and consensual aspects of the society as sources of governmental support. They appeal to the unifying elements in the society and the grounds for the legitimacy of the political institution, irrespective of its specific officeholders and particular laws. They seek to mobilize the loyalties to government which may exist above and across the political conflict of parties, interest groups, and factions. National holidays, inaugural addresses, and the protocols of address and behavior are ways in which the President of the United States attempts this function in his actions and words. The coronation of the monarch in Great Britain represents a highly ritualized method of symbolizing legitimacy.[11]

Gestures of differentiation point to the glorification or degradation of one group in opposition to others within the society. They suggest that some people have a legitimate claim to greater respect, importance, or worth in the society than have some others. In such gestures, governments take sides in social conflicts and place the power and prestige of the public, operating through the political institution, on one side or the other. The inauguration ceremonies of two presidents can be used as illustrations. In his 1953 inaugural, Dwight Eisenhower prefaced his address with a short, personally written prayer. Commenting on this freely, a WCTU officer remarked approvingly, "Imagine that prayer written in the morning in an offhand way! It's the finest thing we've had in years from a president's lips." This gesture placed government on the side of the traditionalist and the devout and separated it from identification with the secularist and freethinker. In the inau-gural of John F. Kennedy, the appearance of the poet Robert Frost was greeted as a symbol of respect and admiration for art, conferring prestige upon the poets by granting them places of honor in public ceremonies.

Such gestures of differentiation are often crucial to the support or opposition of a government because they state the character of an administration in moralistic terms. They indicate the kinds of persons, the tastes, the moralities, and the general life styles toward which government is sympathetic or censorious.[12] They indicate whether or not a set of officials are "for people like us" or "against people like us." It is through this mechanism of symbolic character that a government affects the status order.

STATUS AS A PUBLIC ISSUE

DEFERENCE CONFERRAL

In what sense can the prestige of a status group be a matter at issue? Conflicts about the appropriate deference to be shown can, and do, exist. Currently the relations between whites and Negroes in the United States are examples of a status system undergoing intensive conflict. An issue, however, is a proposal that people can be for or against. A public issue has status implications insofar as its public outcome is interpretable as conferrring prestige upon or withdrawing it from a status group.

Desegregation is a status issue par excellence. Its symbolic characteristics lie in the deference which the norm of integration implies. The acceptance of token integration, which is what has occurred in the North, is itself prestige-conferring because it establishes the public chracter of the norm supporting integration. It indicates what side is publicly legitimate and dominant. Without understanding this symbolic quality of the desegregation issue, the fierceness of the struggle would appear absurd. Since so little actual change in concrete behavior ensues, the question would be moot if it were not for this character as an act of deference toward Negroes and of degradation toward whites.

Unlike the desegregation question, many public issues are confrontations between opposed systems of moralities, cultures, and styles of life. Examples of these are issues of civil liberties, international organizations, vivisection, Sunday "blue laws," and the definition and treatment of domestic Communism. Probably the clearest of such issues in American public life has been the . . . issue of restrictive or permissive norms governing drinking. Status issues indicate, by their resolution, the group, culture, or style of life to which government and society are publicly committed. They answer the question: On behalf of which ethnic, religious, or other cultural group is this government and this society being carried out? We label these as *status issues* precisely because what is at issue is the position of the relevant groups in the status order of the society. Such issues polarize the society along lines of status group differentiation, posing conflicts between divergent styles of life. They are contrasted with *class issues*, which polarize the society along lines of economic interests.[13]

Status issues function as vehicles through which a noneconomic group has deference conferred upon it or degradation imposed upon it. Victory in issues of status is the symbolic conferral of respect upon the norms of the victor and disrespect upon the norms of the vanquished. The political institution or public is thus capable of confirming or disconfirming the individual's conception of his place in the social order.[14] Such actions serve to reconstitute the group as a social object by heaping shame or honor upon it through the support or rejection displayed toward its tastes, values, and customs. When the indignation of the abstinent toward the drinker is publicly confirmed by prohibitory legislation it is, in Harold Garfinkel's analysis of degradation ceremonies, an act of public denunciation: "We publicly deliver the curse: 'I call upon all men to bear witness that he is not as he appears but is otherwise and *in essence* of a lower species.' "[15]

Symbolic properties of deference and degradation can be involved in a wide range of issues and events. They may be implicated as a major theme in some issues or as a peripheral element in other issues, where the groups and themes are more directly those of specific economic interests. David Riesman and Ruel Denney have given us an excellent analysis of American football as a carrier of symbols which served to heighten the prestige of some social groups at the expense of the degradation of others.[16] The victories of Knute Rockne and Notre Dame over the previously championship teams of the Ivy League symbolized the growing social and educational equality of the non-Protestant middle-class Midwest vis-à-vis the Protestant upper-class East. Fans could identify themselves with football teams as carriers of their prestige, whether or not they were college graduates themselves. Knute Rockne was football's equivalent of Al Smith in politics.

STATUS INTERESTS

Precisely because prestige is far from stable in a changing society, specific issues can become structured as tests of status when they are construed as symbols of group moralities and life styles. A civil liberties issue, such as domestic Communism, takes much of its affect and meaning from the clashes between traditionalized and modernist groups in American culture. Elements of educational sophistication, religious secularism, or political liberalism may appear as alien, foreign, and in direct contradiction to the localistic ways of life of the traditional oriented culture. Issues of civil liberties become fields on which such cultural and educational groups fight to establish their claims to public recognition and prestige.

In his analysis of McCarthyism, Peter Vierick has referred to just this kind of process in characterizing the attack on officials in the State Department. Vierick placed one source of this attack in the feeling of degradation which the Midwestern, agricultural, middle class felt at political domination by the aristocracy of the Eastern seaboard, educated at Ivy League schools and so prominent in State Department affairs. They symbolized the State Department personnel as "striped-pants diplomats" and "cookie-pushers." "Against the latter (the Foreign Service—ed.) the old Populist and La Follette weapon against diplomats of 'you internationalist Anglophile snob' was replaced by 'you egghead security risk.' "[17]

In the struggle between groups for prestige and social position, the demands for deference and the protection from degradation are channeled into government and into such institutions of cultural formation as schools, churches, and media of communication. Because these institutions have power to affect public recognition, they are arenas of conflict between opposing status groups. Their ceremonial, ritual, and policy are matters of interest for status groups as well as for economic classes.

It is in this sense that status politics is a form of interest-oriented politics. The enhancement or defense of a position in the status order is as much an interest as the protection or expansion of income or economic power. The activities of government, as the most public institutions, confer respect upon a given style of life or directly upon a specific group. For this reason questions of institutional support of tastes, morals, and other aspects of life styles have consequences for the prestige of persons. Where status anxieties exist, they are then likely to be represented in the form of symbolic issues through which they are resolved.

To see that government, as do other institutions, is a prestige-granting agency is to recognize that status politics is neither extraordinary nor an irrational force in American history. Seymour Lipset appears to be quite mistaken when he writes, "Where there are status anxieties, there is little or nothing which a government can do."[18] Governments constantly affect the status order. During the 1930's the Democratic Party won many votes by increasing the number of Jews and Catholics appointed to state and federal judgeships. Such jobs did little to increase the total number of jobs open to these ethnic and religious groups. They did constitute a greater representation and through this a greater recognition of the worth of these groups. In this sense they were rituals of prestige enhancements, just as Andrew Jackson's inauguration symbolized the advent of the "common man" to power and prestige by the fact that rough men in boots strode across the floors of the White House.

. . . We have been interested in the efforts of Temperance people to reform the habits of others. While such efforts have indeed been motivated by the desire to perfect others in accordance with the reformer's vision of perfection, they have also become enmeshed in consequences affecting the distribution of prestige. Temperance issues have served as symbols around which groups of divergent morals and values have opposed each other.[19] On the side of Temperance there has been the rural, orthodox Protestant, agricultural, native American. On the side of drinking there has been the immigrant, the Catholic, the industrial worker, and the secularized upper class. In more recent years the clash has pitted the modernist and the urbanized cosmopolitans against the traditionalists and the localites, the new middle classes against the old.

When Temperance forces were culturally dominant, the confrontation was that of the social superior. He sought to convert the weaker members of the society through persuasion backed by his dominance of the major institutions. Where dominance of the society is in doubt, then the need for positive governmental and institutional action is greater. The need for symbolic vindication and deference is channeled into political action. What is at stake is not so much the action of men, whether or not they drink, but their ideals, the moralities to which they owe their public allegiance.

POLITICAL MODELS AND STATUS POLITICS[20]

Our analysis of symbolic acts has implications for traditional theories of American politics. In attempting to understand political processes and movements sociologists, political scientists, and psychologists have operated with two major models of politi-

cal motivation. One model has been drawn from economic action and reflects the struggle for economic interests. This model we have designated *class politics*. The other model has been drawn from clinical psychology and reflects a view of politics as an arena into which "irrational" impulses are projected. The latter model, which we have called *psychological expressivism*, has been utilized by others to describe movements of status politics. Our use of a model of symbolic action has been intended to distinguish movements of status politics from both economic interest on the one hand, and psychological expressivism on the other. This section . . . indicates the implications of our analysis for theoretical political sociology.

CLASS POLITICS AND THE PLURALISTIC MODEL

The view of the political process as a balance of economic forces organized as classes has led to a compromise model of political actions. The pluralistic model assumes a multiple number of specific interest groups whose demands conflict with and contradict each other. Farmers, bankers, skilled workers, unskilled workers, and professionals are represented through pressure groups and occupational associations. Political decisions are resultants of the compromises mediated between the various groups in accordance with the distribution of political power. Each group tries to get as much as they can but accepts partial losses in return for partial gains.

Compromise and the model of the political arena as one of mutually cooperating yet antagonistic groups presupposes a "political culture" in which victory and defeat are only end points on a continuum. An expediential attitude of calculation and exchange must govern the trading and bargaining. The language and imagery of compromise is drawn to a considerable extent from the marketplace, where monetary transactions enable interaction to be expressed in measurable quantities and mutual advantages. We "meet people halfway," develop political programs that are "deals," and operate through political parties talked about as "brokers of interests."

The "rules of the game" governing pluralistic politics are sharply antithetical to the "poor loser," the "sorehead," the intolerant ideologue who considers himself morally right and all others morally evil. He cannot accept the legitimacy of an institution in which even partial defeat occurs. For him politics is not a search for benefits in his work and life but a battleground between forces of good and evil. He reacts with passion in ways which contradict the rules of pluralistic politics. He rejects the presupposition that everybody in the political arena has a legitimate right to get something and nobody has a legitimate right to get everything. He typifies the moralizer in politics, described by Riesman. . . .

PSYCHOLOGICAL EXPRESSIVISM AS A
MODEL OF STATUS POLITICS

The analytical scheme of pluralistic politics is most applicable to movements of class politics and instrumental action. Movements such as Prohibition, civil rights, religious differences, and educational change are puzzles to the sociologist and political scientist precisely because they cannot be analyzed in instrumental terms. Their goals and major images appear "irrational" and unrelated to the content of their aims. Being puzzles, a resort is often made to schemes which stress the impulsive, uncontrolled elements of spontaneous and unconscious behavior. Thus Lipset writes of status discontents as one source of rightist extremism: "It is not surprising therefore that political movements which have successfully appealed to status resentments have been irrational in character and have sought scapegoats which conveniently serve to symbolize the status threat."[21]

The essential idea in psychological expressivism is that the adherence to the movement is explainable as an expression of the adherent's personality. "Thus the mass man is vulnerable to the appeal of mass movements which offer him a way of overcoming the pain of self-alienation by shifting attention away from himself and by focusing it on the movement."[22] Unlike instrumental action, which is about conflicts of interest, the substance of political struggles in expressive politics is not about anything because it is not a vehicle of conflict but a vehicle of catharsis—a purging of emotions through expression. The analysis of politics as expressive takes on the attributes of magic, as in Malinowski's classic defintion: "Man, engaged in a series of practical activities, comes to a gap . . . passive inaction, the only thing dictated by reason, is the last thing in which he can acquiesce. His nervous system and his whole organism drive him to some substitute activity."[23]

If we utilize only the two models of instrumental actions and psychological expressivism we tend to divide political and social movements into two categories—the rational and the irrational. Status politics, as we have seen in both Lipset and Hofstadter, gets readily classified as "irrational": "Therefore, it is the tendency of status politics to be expressed more in vindictiveness, in sour memories, in the search for scapegoats, than in realistic proposals for concrete action."[24] Between instrumental and expressive politics there is no bin into which the symbolic goals of status movements can be analytically placed. Our usage of symbolic politics is an effort to provide such a bin.

SYMBOLIC POLITICS AND STATUS INTERESTS

The consequences of interpreting status movements in the language of psychological expressivism is that the analyst ignores the reality of the status conflict. Expressive politics cannot be referred back to any social conflict which is resolved by the action taken. It is not a vehicle through which conflicts are mediated or settled. We have tried to show, in the instance of the Temperance movement, that the attempt to utilize political action was not only expressive but was a way of winning a concrete and very real struggle over the distribution of prestige in American society.

Discontents that arise from the status order are often as sharp and as powerful as those that emerge in the struggles over income and employment. In a society of diverse cultures and of rapid change, it is quite clear that systems of culture are as open to downward and upward mobility as are occupations or persons. Yesterday's moral virtue is today's ridiculed fanaticism. As the cultural fortunes of one group go up and those of another group go down, expectations of prestige are repulsed and the ingredients of social conflict are produced.

The dramatistic approach we have used in this study includes language but is by no means only a linguistic analysis. It is applicable to acts of legislation, such as Prohibition or fluoridation, to court decisions, and to official ceremony. Arguments about symbolic action are real in the sense that men's regard for respect, honor, and prestige is real. We do live in a forest of symbols, and within that forest there is disagreement, conflict, and disorder.

We are not maintaining a symbolic approach to politics as an alternative to instrumental or expressive models. We conceive of it as an addition to methods of analysis but an addition which can best help us understand the implications of status conflicts for political actions and, vice versa, the ways in which political acts affect the distribution of prestige. Most movements, and most political acts, contain a mixture of instrumental, expressive, and symbolic elements. The issues of style, which have troubled many social scientists in recent years, have not lent themselves well to political analysis. Those issues which have appeared as "matters of principle" now appear to us to be related to status conflicts and understandable in symbolic terms.

An example of what we have in mind can be seen in the political issues presented by controversies over school curricula in American municipalities. During the 1950's there has been much agitation to force American schools and universities to require more American history or courses on Communism as ways to establish patriotic loyalties among students and oppose Communist doctrine. Observers of American life are likely to deride these actions as pathetic attempts to control a situation with ineffective weapons or denounce such actions as coercion over the content of education. Beneath these programs, however, is the assumption that the school personnel are not succeeding in transmitting some value which the pressure groups feel important. The symbols of "Communism" are related to the cultural conflicts between fundamentalist and modernizing forces in American life, as well as the foreign policy conflicts between Russia and the United States. Cultural conflicts become easily centered upon school curricula because the content of education depends upon cultural assumptions. As our schools are increasingly manned by professionalized, college-trained personnel they come to represent modern, cosmopolitan values against which fundamentalists struggle.[25] Whose values shall the school system enunciate? Whose values shall be legitimized and made dominant by being the content of education? The manifest intent of such curricular changes may be inducement of patriotic feeling, but the latent, symbolic issue is not so directly educational. Psychologists may show that the pledge of allegiance every morning has no discernible effect upon patriotic feeling, but this is not the issue as status elements are involved. What such curricular changes "bear witness" to is the domination of one cultural group and the subordination of another. As most educators know, schools are run for adults, not for children. There is more than expression of feeling in such demands. There is an effort to dominate the rituals by which status is discerned.

A political model that ignores symbolic action in politics would exclude an important category of governmental action. It is a major way in which conflicts in the social order are institutionalized as political issues. Groups form around such issues, symbols are given specific meaning, and opposing forces have some arena in which to test their power and bring about compromise and accommodation, if possible. This is precisely what the issues of Prohibition and Temper-

ance have enabled the status groups involved as Wets and Drys to accomplish. Turning status conflicts into political conflicts is precisely what Lasswell seems to have meant when he described politics as "the process by which the irrational bases of society are brought out into the open."[26]

Our approach also differs somewhat from that of Murray Edelman, who has been the most salient political scientist to recognize the role of symbolic action in legislative acts. He has pointed out that groups frequently seem satisfied by the passage of legislation, even though the execution of the acts often contradicts the intent of the legislation. This has been true in cases such as antitrust laws, the work of the Federal Communications Commission and other regulatory commissions, and in much civil rights legislation. "The most intensive dissemination of symbols commonly attends the enactment of legislation which is most meaningless in its effects upon resource allocation."[27] Edelman's analysis assumes, however, that this discrepancy is a result of the "psychological reassurance" given to such groups that their interests are being protected. We suggest that while this is a credible theory, especially in economic issues, there are some real interests at stake as well.

These can be specified as two different types of ways in which status interests enter into political issues. First, any governmental action can be an act of deference because it confers power on one group and limits some other group. It bolsters or diminishes the claims of a group to differential treatment. Second, the specific status order, as distinct from the constellation of classes, is affected by actions which bear upon styles of life. The issues of Temperance and Prohibition have had particular relevance to the prestige of old and new middle-class ways of life.

We live in a human environment in which ₊symbolic gestures have great relevance to our sense of pride, mortification, and honor. Social conflicts and tensions are manifested in a disarray of the symbolic order as well as in other areas of action. Dismissing these reactions as "irrational" clouds analysis and ignores the events which have significance for people. Kenneth Burke has pointed out the pejorative implications which emerge when noninstrumental usages are described as "magical." He distinguishes be-

tween poetic language, which is action for its own sake, scientific language, which is a preparation for action, and rhetorical language, which is inducement to action or attitude. If you think of acts as either magical or scientific there is no place to classify symbolic acts of the kind we have been considering, where an interest conflict is resolved but in noninstrumental symbolic terms. Consequently, a great deal of political activity is dismissed as ritual, magic, or irrational waste when "it should be handled in its own terms as an aspect of what it really is: Rhetoric."[28]

NOTES

1. Kenneth Burke, *A Grammar of Motives* (New York: Prentice-Hall, 1945), p. xxii.

2. M. H. Abrams, quoted in Maurice Beebe (ed.), *Literary Symbolism* (San Francisco: Wadsworth Publishing Co., 1960), p. 18.

3. Max Weber, *Theory of Social and Economic Organization*, tr. A. M. Henderson and Talcott Parsons (New York: Oxford University Press, 1947), p. 156. "The claim of the modern state to monopolize the use of force is as essential to it as its character of compulsory jurisdiction and of continuous organization." This definition is open both to the objection discussed above and to the inadequacy of singling out "force" as a major method of compulsion. Other institutions compel behavior by effective means other than violence, such as the ecclesiastical controls of a priesthood or the employment powers of management. The phenomena of "private governments" is not included in Weber's definition but the only ground of exclusion which is sociologically significant is the public character of governing bodies.

4. Frances X. Sutton, "Representation and the Nature of Political Systems," Comparative Studies in Society and History, 2 (October, 1959), 1-10, at 6. Sutton points out that in primitive societies the political officers are often only representatives to other tribes rather than agents to enforce law.

5. See the discussion of signs and sym-

bols in Susanne K. Langer, *Philosophy in a New Key* (Baltimore, Md.: Penguin Books, 1948), pp. 45-50.

6. Neither is our usage to be equated with the discussion of symbolic behavior used in the writings of the symbolic interaction school of social psychology, best represented by the works of George H. Mead. The idea of symbolic behavior in that context emphasizes the linguistic and imaginative processes as implicated in behavior. It is by no means contrary to our usage of symbols but the context is not specifically literary. The symbolic interactionists call attention to the fact that objects are given meanings by the systems of concept formation. We emphasize one aspect of this process.

7. Talcott Parsons, *The Social System* (Glencoe, Ill.: The Free Press, 1954), p. 286.

8. Phillip Wheelwright, *The Burning Fountain* (Bloomington: Indiana University Press, 1954), p. 23.

9. Burke, *op. cit.*, p. 393. My debt to Burke's writings is very great. He has supplied the major conceptual and theoretical tools for bridging literary and political analysis. In addition to *A Grammar of Motives*, see his *Attitudes Toward History* (Los Altos, Calif.: Hermes Publications, 1959), and *Permanence and Change* (New York: New Republic, Inc., 1935). Two sociologists, heavily influenced by Burke, have been extremely useful in developing attention to symbolic behavior in the sense used here. They are Erving Goffman, whose

works are cited throughout this study, and Hugh D. Duncan, *Language and Literature in Society* (Chicago: University of Chicago Press, 1953).

10. Harold Lasswell, "Language of Politics," in Ruth Anshen (ed.), *Language* (New York: Harper and Bros., 1957), pp. 270-284, at 281.

11. Edward Shils and Michael Young have studied the consensual effects of the coronation ceremony in England. See their "The Meaning of the Coronation," *Sociological Review*, 1, n.s. (December, 1953), 63-81. The use of ritual and ceremony to establish cohesion and social control through historical pagents and holidays in modern society is studied empirically in W. Lloyd Warner, *The Living and the Dead* (New Haven, Conn.: Yale University Press, 1959), esp. Pts. I and II. These aspects of "political religion" have received comparatively little attention from students of modern societies although most recognize the importance of such rituals and would agree with Hugh Duncan that "Any institution can 'describe' the way it wants people to act but only as it develops rites, ceremonies and symbols for communication through rite in which people can act does it rise to power." Duncan, *op. cit.*, p. 18.

12. Another example of this symbolic process in political issues can be found in the conflicts over city manager plans. Development of city manager government is usually supported by middle-class voters and opposed by the lower socioeconomic groups. The impersonal, moralistic, and bureaucratized "good government" is much closer to standards of conduct typical in middle classes. The machine politician is closer to the open, personalized, and flexible government that represents the lower-class systems of social control. The issue of the city manager poses the two subcultures against each other. One study of the advent of city manager government reported that the first thing the new council did was to take away jobs from Catholic employees and, under merit employment, give them to Protestants. The city manager people celebrated their political victory with a banquet at the Masonic hall. See the discussion in Martin Meyerson and Edward Banfield, *Politics, Planning and the Public Interest* (Glencoe, Ill.: The Free Press, 1955), pp. 290-291.

13. Essentially the same distinction is made by students of the voting process. Berelson, Lazarsfeld, and McPhee distinguish between issues of style ("ideal" is-

sues) and issues of position ("material" issues). Bernard Berelson, Paul Lazarsfeld, and William McPhee, *Voting* (Chicago: University of Chicago Press, 1959), p. 184.

14. "... the individual must rely on others to complete the picture of him ... each individual is responsible for the demeanour image of himself and deference image of others, so that for a complete man to be expressed, individuals must hold hands in a chain of ceremony, each giving deferentially with proper demeanor to the one on the right what will be received deferentially from the one on the left." Erving Goffman, "The Nature of Deference and Demeanor," *American Antropologist*, 58 (June, 1956), 473-502, at 493. Goffman's writings constitute an important discussion of deference and degradation ceremonies in interpersonal interaction. In addition to the article cited above see *The Presentation of Self in Everyday Life* (New York: Doubleday Anchor Books, 1959), and *Encounters* (Indianapolis, Ind.: Bobbs-Merrill, 1961).

15. Harold Garfinkel, "Conditions of Successful Degradation Ceremonies," *American Journal of Sociology*, 61 (March, 1956), 420-424, at 421.

16. David Riesman and Ruel Denney, "Football in America," *The American Quarterly*, 3 (Winter, 1951), 309-325.

17. Peter Vierick, "The Revolt Against the Elite," in Daniel Bell (ed.), *The New American Right* (New York: Criterion Books, 1955), pp. 91-116, at 103.

18. Seymour Lipset, "The Sources of the Radical Right," in *ibid.*, pp. 166-234, at 168.

19. This is evident in Lee Benson, *The Concept of Jacksonian Democracy* (Princeton, N. J.: Princeton University Press, 1961), esp. Ch. 9. Benson's work ... provides valuable evidence for the role of moral issues, and especially Temperance, in developing party loyalties in New York state in the 1840's. Using the concept of negative reference groups. Benson shows that economic interests played less of a role than did religious, cultural, and moral differences as influences on voting. Voters tended to see the two major parties as linked to one or another ethnocultural group.

20. Some of the matters discussed in this section are treated in greater detail in my "Mass Society and Extremist Politics," *American Sociological Review*, 27 (February, 1962), 19-30.

21. Lipset, *op. cit.*, p. 168.

22. William Kornhauser, *The Politics of*

Mass Society (Glencoe, Ill.: The Free Press, 1959), p. 112.

23. Bronislaw Malinowski, *Magic, Science and Religion* (New York: Doubleday Anchor Books, 1954; orig. pub., 1925), p. 79.

24. Richard Hofstadter, "The Pseudo-Conservative Revolt," in Bell (ed.), *op. cit.*, pp. 33-55, at 44.

25. For an analysis of one such school controversy in which "Communism," "human relations," "progressive education," and UNESCO were symbols of a feared cosmopolitanism see National Education Association of the United States, *The Pasadena Story* (Washington, D. C.: National Education Association, 1951). This same use of these symbols is linked to group conflict in many of the speeches and pamphlets of the extreme right wing in the 1950's and early 1960's. They underline the cultural values which are the center of the struggle. One example is the following from a reprinted speech: "Our most dangerous enemies are the thousands and thousands of disguised vermin who crawl all around us and, in obedience to orders from their superiors in the conspiracy, poison the minds of those about them with glib talk about 'social justice,' 'progressive education,' 'civil rights,' 'the social gospel,' 'one world' and 'peaceful coexistence.' You will find them everywhere: in your clubs, in your schools, in your churches, in your courts." R. P. Oliver, "Communist Influence in the Federal Government," speech to the fifth annual convention of We, the People! Chicago, September, 1959.

26. Harold Lasswell, *Psychopathology and Politics* (Chicago: University of Chicago Press, 1930), p. 184.

27. Murray Edelman, "Symbols and Political Quiescence," *American Political Science Review*, 54 (September, 1960), 695-704, at 697.

28. Kenneth Burke, *A Rhetoric of Motives* (New York: Prentice-Hall, 1950), p. 42.

VI. THE NATURE OF DEVIANCE AND MENTAL DISORDER

As a developing perspective still in its early stages, the dramaturgical model has been applied in patchwork fashion to relatively few areas of social life. One of the places where it has received an increasing audience, however, is in social psychological discussions of deviance and mental disorder. Here its emphasis on the essentially *moral* nature of the human enterprise illuminates a number of issues that are obscured by those points of view that treat deviance as an absolute set of meanings that are automatically invoked when rules are broken.

For centuries, deviance of all sorts has been construed as a matter of fact. There were two rather rigidly conceived worlds—deviant and respectable—separate and unequal, and the only question was how to account for why some persons deviated and others did not. From this commonsense framework came a host of explanations by various scholars. Biologists constructed elaborate paradigms that explained social deviance in terms of such body characteristics as bumps on and shapes of the head, muscular structure, fragmented or extra chromosomes, and even genital pathologies and the number of tooth cavities. Psychologists offered other causal explanations, usually couched in terms of psychological aberrations: "maladjusted" personalities, psychopathic and sociopathic "tendencies," "emotional disturbances," and so on. Those with psychoanalytic leanings saw deviance as a weak superego being taken over by a chaotic id.[1] Sociologists offered explana-

1. Steven Box, *Deviance, Reality and Society*, (New York: Holt, Rinehart & Winston, 1971).

tions in structural terms, emphasizing social disorganization, "anomie," deteriorating environments, and other points of wear in the social machine.

The questions raised by these perspectives revolved around the motivations of the deviant, and the answer was sought in terms of factors that allegedly moved the passive human organism to deviant action. Such explanations conflict sharply with a dramaturgical understanding. First, most of them smack of tautology, or circular reasoning. No matter how sophisticated they are, their main point is usually that a set of observations is to be explained in terms of some structure, and the structure is itself inferred from the observations. As J. L. Simmons[2] suggests, this is tantamount to asking:

> Why does Johnny deviate? Because he's disturbed. How do you know he's disturbed? Well, just look at his deviant behavior.

Second, these points of view tend to equate deviance with rule-breaking, but the data on which they are based include only those people already identified or *labeled* as deviant. Thus they miss the process by which the rule-breakers come to be labeled in the first place, a process that is potent in its consequences, irrespective of whether or not the person actually violated some normative code. Also, when we look closely at the process by which miscreants are labeled, we discover that a key factor is the presence or absence of a dramaturgical ritual that makes the rule-breaker visible to an audience that acts toward him in morally negative terms.

Dramaturgical analysis, then, moves the study of deviance from a concentration on given acts of rule-breaking to the problematic question of how moral meanings are socially constructed. In the first selection, Jack Douglas reworks the concepts of deviance and respectability by showing the interdependence of moral opposites. He thereby places the entire question of deviance squarely in the human (as opposed to the infrahuman or suprahuman) arena. Few ministers thank God on Sunday morning for the existence of sin, but one implication of Douglas' argument is that they very well might, for without it their positive moral exhortations would be meaningless. Every time we dramatize evil in what Harold Garfinkel[3] has called a "degradation ceremony," we likewise establish the goodness of the rest of us. And ages of saints turn out to be ages of demons, for one could hardly exist without the reference point provided by the other.

Moral meanings are continually being built up in social life, particularly on those occasions when we choose up sides. The usual scientific terms in which such issues are discussed, claims Douglas, are really inadequate to their phenomenological character. For as Kenneth Burke points out, every drama is essentially a morality play, and the social

2. J. L. Simmons, *Deviants* (San Francisco: Glendessary Press, 1969) p. 9.
3. Harold Garfinkel, "Conditions of Successful Degradation Ceremonies," *American Journal of Sociology*, Volume 61, March 1956, pp. 420-424.

psychologist ignores morality at the cost of substituting his own reality for that of his subjects.

The next selection is from John Lofland's *Deviance and Identity*. It offers a conceptual scheme for a dramaturgical analysis of deviant behavior. Lofland indicates that there is often a separating process in assuming a deviant identity. The interactions of actor and audience give an increasingly deviant twist to the actor's behavior. This involves (1) a redefinition of current acts in which morally negative interpretations replace either neutral or morally positive ones, and (2) a reconstruction of the actor's entire biography, in which one's past life is reinterpreted to show that the new deviant label put on the person really stems from an aberrant character that existed all along.

Lofland also is concerned with those characteristics of a scene that give rise to an imputation of deviance. Not only are actors morally labeled but also places. Indeed, one's mere presence in deviant places, whether formal institutions like mental hospitals and prisons or less formal places like "dives" and houses of "ill repute," is often sufficient to label the individual as a deviant.

As we saw in Sheldon Messinger's article in Section I, one of the earliest applications of dramaturgical thinking was in the sociology of mental disorder. Ernest Becker's selection is part of a growing tendency to depart from the conventional medical view that mental illness is a disease entity, whose symptoms are manifested in the patient's deviant social behavior. To reduce a piece of social conduct in all its meaningful complexity to a mere "symptom" is seen by most dramaturgists as a social and political move in medical guise. Stone and Farberman[4] have stated the case well:

> Most [behavioral] extremism may be construed as based on an alien moral alternative. Such extremism implies willfulness, responsibility, and choice, and therefore is dangerous politically to those in power. One unobtrusive and fairly routine technique for rendering such moral opposition politically harmless is to assert that it is not rooted in a moral alternative at all, but rather in a medical pathology. When extremism is construed as being grounded in pathology rather than morality, it is relieved of responsibility and dutifully placed under medical surveillance.

Nevertheless, the problems of living encountered by those enmeshed in the drama of mental illness are quite real. Becker locates the roots of many psychiatric problems in a socialization process that inadequately equips people for the roles they are called upon to enact. The self is built out of words and therefore can be destroyed by words. To be able to perform properly, the actor must learn to create contexts of action for others, for society is built on a precarious but meaningful fiction sus-

4. Stone and Farberman, *Social Psychology Through Symbolic Interaction*, p. 621. For a brilliant fictional illustration of this process, see the example of Randall Patrick McMurphy in Ken Kesey's *One Flew Over The Cuckoo's Nest*, (New York: Signet Paperbacks, 1962).

tained by such rituals as demeanor (coming off) and deference (protecting the coming off of others). "Let us all protect each other by sincere demeanor and convincing presentations, so that we can carry on the business of living" seems to be the major creed. Given the essentially symbolic and fictional basis of social dramas, it is not surprising that some people stumble. Nor is it the least bit astonishing that we reserve our most devastating labels of deviance for those who are unwilling to play at all—those who, in Goffman's[5] words, "are least ready to project a sustainable self."

For those readers who are more hard-headed in their evaluation of these assertions, Rosenhan's empirical study, conducted in several mental hospitals, offers considerable support for the notion that "mental illness" is a set of socially constructed labels. These labels correspond not to an aberrant subworld of behavior but to the logic and language through which the behavior of the mental patient is viewed. Psychiatry appears to operate on the cherished assumption that normality and abnormality, sanity and insanity, exist substantively and can be distinguished by those who are properly trained. However, Rosenhan's study casts considerable doubt on this, for it seems that in mental hospitals one can't tell who the players are without a playbill.

5. E. Goffman, "The Nature of Deference and Demeanor," *American Anthropologist* Vol. LVIII (No. 3), 1956, p. 497.

SUGGESTED READINGS

Becker, Ernest. *The Revolution in Psychiatry* (Glencoe: The Free Press, 1964).

Becker, Howard S. *The Other Side* (Glencoe: The Free Press, 1963).

Becker, Howard S. *Outsiders: Studies in the Sociology of Deviance* (New York: The Free Press, 1963).

Douglas, Jack. *The Social Meanings of Suicide* (Princeton, N. J.: Princeton University Press, 1967).

Glasser, William, *Reality Therapy* (New York: Harper & Row, 1965).

Goffman, Erving. *Asylums*, (New York: Anchor Paperbacks, 1961).

Halleck, Seymour. *The Politics of Therapy* (New York: Harper & Row, 1972).

Leifer, Ronald. *In The Name of Mental Health* (New York: Science House, 1969).

Jacobs, Jerry. *Deviance: Field Studies and Self Disclosure* (Palo Alto: Cal.: National Press Books, 1973).

MacAndrew, Craig and Robert Edgerton. *Drunken Comportment* (Chicago: Aldine Publishing Co., 1969).

Matza, David. *Becoming Deviant.* (Englewood Cliffs, N. J.: Prentice-Hall, 1969).

Scheff, Thomas. *Being Mentally Ill: A Sociological Theory,* (Chicago: Aldine Publishing Co., 1966).

Simmons, J. L. *Deviants*, (Berkeley: The Glendessary Press, 1969).

Szasz, Thomas S. *The Myth of Mental Illness*, (New York: Dell Publishing Co., 1961).

21. DEVIANCE AND RESPECTABILITY: THE SOCIAL CONSTRUCTION OF MORAL MEANINGS

JACK DOUGLAS

Reprinted from Chapter 1. "Deviance and Respectability: The Social Construction of Moral Meanings" by Jack D. Douglas, in *Deviance and Respectability: The Social Construction of Moral Meanings*, Edited by Jack D. Douglas, © 1970 by Basic Books, Inc., Publishers, New York. Jack Douglas is a leader in what has come to be known as ethnomethodology, a point of view in sociology that has many affinities to the dramaturgical framework. He is Professor of Sociology at the University of California at San Diego, and has published a variety of books and articles on sociological theory, deviant behavior, and social problems.

Deviance and respectability are necessarily linked together: each necessarily implies the other; each is a necessary condition for the existence of the other. This is by no means simply a matter of abstract and arbitrary definitions given to the terms by sociologists. Deviance and respectability are necessarily linked together in the social meanings of the terms as used by the members of our society in their everyday lives: when we observe and analyze the moral communications in our everyday lives we find that the social meanings of either deviance (immorality) or respectability (morality) can be adequately understood only if reference, whether implicit or explicit, is made to the other, its opposite.

As some Christian theologians have argued over the centuries, without evil there would be no good, without Satan no God. The existence of Satan and his evil has not only been as necessary to Western man's way of thinking as God and his good but has at the same time been a necessary condition for adequately understanding the nature of God and his good. (This necessary relationship was, in fact, commonly expressed by the popular definition of evil as the absence of good or of good as the absence of evil.) To Western man being, certainly its moral aspect, is dualistic,[1] and many of the problems of his existence are concerned with working out the relations between this dual and oppositional nature of reality.

In the same way, in our everyday lives morality and immorality, respectability and disreputability, the otherworldly and the this-worldly, the sacred and the secular—each term necessarily implies the existence of its opposite and, consequently, depends on its opposite for its own meaning and, above all, for much of the force it exerts on our lives. Why should there be this necessary dependency between moral opposites?

For one thing, it seems likely that Plato was right in arguing that there are certain fundamental categories of existence that necessarily imply their opposites; or, rather, he would have been right at least in arguing that this is a basic premise of Western thought. As he saw, for Western man life necessarily implies death; death necessarily implies life; and each is wholly meaningful only because of the existence of its opposite. In the same way, he argued that truth and falsehood necessarily imply each other.

While it may be valuable for some purposes to try to explain the existence of this necessary and oppositional dualism, for our purposes here it is sufficient merely to note its existence, its taken-for-granted character in everyday moral communications, and then to proceed to analyze it and its consequences.

The most general consequence of this necessary linkage in social meanings between good and evil is that we will always have evil at the same time that—and precisely because—we have good. Going further, we should even expect that the more intense the belief in good, or the striving for it, the more intense will be the belief in evil, or the attacks on good. An age of saints, then, will also necessarily be an age of satans or demons, and vice versa. An individual striving for goodness will to the same degree be striving against evil, and vice versa.

We can see, then, just why it is that we always have "deviants" and "criminals" with us, why it is that immorality and crime seem such necessary parts of society. Durkheim was certainly right in arguing that immorality and crime are a necessary part of society, but he failed to see how fundamental this necessity is.[2] While it is certainly true, as John Adams and many other men who have helped to construct governments have long argued, that the (official) dramatization of evil-doing and its punishment serve to strengthen "good" behavior, it is far more important to see that the "good" behavior cannot exist unless there is also its opposite, the "evil" behavior. It is for this reason that immorality in its many forms is a necessary and inevitable part of our social reality. As long as our basic categories, our fundamental criteria for evaluating existence, are relativistic in this way, we will have evil, immorality, disreputability, and crime. And there is no indication at all that our basic categories are getting less relativistic. If we do eradicate our present evils, we will simply construct new ones. What really happens is that

we eradicate some of our presently worse evils and then we readapt our comparisons: what used to be lesser evils are now the worse evils. (Anyone who objectively observes the current anguish in American society over our "terrible" social problems and immorality could hardly doubt the obvious truth of this statement: what used to be the lesser social problems are now the worse social problems.)

In addition, the comparisons or contrasts between good and evil are not simply linear comparisons—comparisons between better and worse. While it is true that there are social categories to designate many degrees of good and evil, and any comparison can be made in terms of better or worse, it is also true that any comparison between good and evil is at the same time a categorical or absolute comparison. That is, anything that is immoral is subject to the categorical distinction between good and evil. It is this categorical distinction which lies behind the dichotomizing of the social world into morally disjunct categories—right side of the tracks versus wrong side of the tracks, criminal versus noncriminal, stigmatized versus nonstigmatized, respectable versus disreputable, evil versus good, black versus white, and so on. The necessary opposition makes the deviant and criminal necessary, and the categorical contrast makes him into a necessarily different type of being. And, at the same time that good necessarily implies its opposite of evil (and vice versa), good necessarily implies a categorical contrast; if there is a good type, there must be an evil type. . . .

THE NATURE OF MORALITY AND RESPONSIBILITY

Sociologists have generally preferred not to deal directly with morality and immorality or with the many related phenomena of everyday life —good and evil, respectability and disreputability, innocence and guilt, wicked, tarnished, angelic, and the like. Instead, they have followed the positivist practice of substituting phenomena of their own construction for those of common-sense, everyday life and then studying their own ad hoc phenomena as if these constituted "reality." They have done this in part to avoid the complexities and "biases" of common-sense terms, but the study of their ad hoc reality has simply created another level of complexity: since they have still wanted their studies to be ultimately related to everyday life, they have had to shift back and forth between their ad hoc phenomena and the everyday phenomena, constructing post hoc systems of translating devices and other devices.

The sociologists have generally substituted "values" for the common-sense term of "morality." They have then proceeded to construct many hundreds of confusing and sterile ad hoc definitions of values. In the process they have made things ever more complex and have proved unable to tell us much of value about the important matters of morality and immorality or the many related phenomena.

Philosophers, theologians, moralists, and many others have been more directly concerned with analyzing the everyday phenomena of morality for several thousand years. But they have normally been primarily concerned with discovering what is "really" moral and immoral, rather than with the scientific task of analyzing the properties of the everyday phenomena of morality and immorality. However, in the past fifty years or so the philosophers, and the others in turn, have become increasingly concerned

with analyzing the language of morality. These linguistic philosophers, especially those who have taken seriously Wittgenstein's edict that the meaning of language is provided by its use, have had an increasing effect on sociologists' analyses of rules and meanings in general, as can be seen in Blum's analysis of the social meanings of "insanity."[3] Sociologists are now beginning to do the vast amount of research that will be required to determine, through the study of social usage, the meanings of morality—and rules in general—in everyday life. Until we have systematic participant-observer studies of moral meanings (in use), we shall be forced to make use of our current strategy, that is, making extensive use of our own common-sense experience to analyze everyday moral meanings, but tempering this by the use of whatever good participant-observer information we can obtain.

The basic problem with the ordinary approaches to the analysis of the meanings of morality is that they concentrate almost exclusively on disembodied moral statements, assuming that it will be possible eventually to produce a set of rules which can be used to generate all acceptable moral statements which members of society might make and that this kind of analysis provides the meanings of morality. But this kind of covert behaviorism violates the most basic principle of any analysis of social meanings and actions, the principle of the contextual determination of meaning: the concrete meaning of anything (rule, statement, and so forth) is adequately given to members only when its concrete or situated context is provided.[4] The linguist does, indeed, give careful consideration to the contextual effects to be found in conversations themselves. As Moermann has said, "One prominent feature of conversations is that their participants orient to the sequential placement of the utterances which compose them. The situated intelligibility which an utterance has for participants frequently depends upon the particular ways in which they tie that utterance to particular preceding ones."[5] But this approach still treats language as disembodied both from the rest of subjective or phenomenal experience and from the social situation in which the conversation occurs. Because these contexts are even very generally the determinants, for the members, of both what is said and the meanings of what is said, as we can see in such analyses (as Penzin's analysis of intimate relations[6]), this linguistic approach will not provide an adequate analysis of social meanings and actions in everyday life. (They are, however, a necessary part of such analyses of everyday life.)

Maurice Mandelbaum's phenomenological analysis of morals has gone somewhat beyond the strictly linguistic approach by analyzing the fundamental meanings of morals in the everyday experience of members of society,[7] though he has remained at the philosophical level, rather than making use of systematic observations and descriptions of moral arguments. As Mandelbaum sees it, there have been three crucial dimensions of meaning involved in moral communications. First of all, moral experience has been seen by members of society as *external* to themselves, as *given* to them, rather than created by them. Morality, then; is independent of the will of man and has, indeed, normally been seen as given by God (or by nature) to man. Second, morality has been seen as necessary, so that there is no escaping it by denying it or hiding from it. Even if one were sincerely astounded to discover that he had done

something immoral, he would still be immoral for having done it—and would suffer divine punishment for it. These first two dimensions are actually general properties of the absolutist world view which has almost completely dominated Western thought until recently. This absolutist world view sees social meanings in general (beliefs, ideas, truth, values, and so on) as part of some necessary being that is timeless, eternal, external, and independent of man and to which man is necessarily subject.[8] Third, and most distinctively, moral experience involves a feeling of "appropriateness."

There are a number of basic problems involved in this analysis of moral experience. The most important problem is the seeming circularity of the feeling of appropriateness. What meaning can one give to appropriateness that is not already apparent in morality so that appropriateness provides a better understanding of morality? Appropriateness appears to be simply a more general term of which morality is one form or type of appropriateness, so that morality may help us to better understand appropriateness, but it is very hard to see how the opposite can be true. The attempt to better understand morality in terms of appropriateness is actually an indication of how basic and irreducible the experience of morality is. It is so basic that it can hardly be defined in terms of other, more basic terms. Rather, it must be the basis for defining other terms and must remain largely undefinable except by the ostensive definition of pointing out to a fellow member of society that one means by moral experience the kind of feeling he has in such and such a situation (such as the contemplation of incest).

Another basic problem with this approach, and one which is intimately related to the first, is that it focuses on intrasubjective experience; that is, it deals with the experience of morality in the abstract or independently of concrete situations in which morals are used. Rather than being independent of social situations, a point of view which was fostered by the absolutist world view, concrete moral experience is necessarily intersubjective. That is, any concrete experience of morality necessarily involves the idea of actual or potential social response of approval or disapproval. (This is the idea behind the insight that calling something good, right, moral, or the like, simply means that one approves.) Even the saint in the desert struggling to purge his soul of evil is implicitly treating morality as an experience necessarily involving social response: to him something is moral or immoral because God has decreed it (it is good because God has decreed it, rather than God decreeing it because it is good), and he seeks to be moral by submitting to that decree. (It should be noted, however, that the ideas of God and of the good have been so interlocked that Western theologians have argued for centuries over whether God decrees the good because it is good or it is good because God decrees it, while agreeing that God is the good and so on. Because of the relationship of identity, or near identity, it seemed plausible to argue it either way; yet the combatants, like most combatants, could rarely take such a theoretic stance.)

We must, then, shift the focus of our analyses of moral experience. Rather than attempting to analyze moral experience in the abstract, or independently of its social context, we must always focus on the everyday uses of morality, both through linguistic statements and by other forms of communication, found in social interaction. When we shift our focus in this way we become concerned with

somewhat different questions than those which have been of primary moment to Mandelbaum and other phenomenologists concerned with intrasubjective experience. Most importantly, we become concerned primarily with the conditions under which the members of society consider any concrete thing to be moral or immoral (approvable or disapprovable).

Sociologists first turned to this approach in considering the labeling processes[9] or categorization processes by which members of society imputed categories of morality and immorality to individuals. This early approach was a crucial break with the traditional structural approach, which took for granted the common-sense assumption that certain things are necessarily (homogeneously, unchangingly, and nonproblematically) considered immoral by the members of society.[10] Labeling theory argued, on the contrary, that the categorization of something or someone is an independent variable, so that it is problematic. The initial emphasis of the labeling theorists was on the effects of different labels on people, but it was a short jump to considering the social determinants of labeling processes.

But labeling theorists never came to see the problems involved in the application of categories. Most importantly, they never saw the need to determine the conditions under which one category would be applied rather than another. What Blum has argued about mental illness holds equally for meaningful categories in general: " 'Labelling theorists' . . . do not describe the labelling process, but rather, affirm that the process exists and use this as grounds for attacking traditional conceptions of mental illness."[11] What is needed to begin with is the microscopic analysis of the social uses of the categories to determine the general properties of such uses. Blum's analysis of the social uses of the categories of mental illness is one of the few attempts to do this and clearly shows the fundamental importance of the situational (social) contextual determination of the meanings of such categories for the members of society.

When we then analyze the specific conditions under which members of society consider someone (or his actions) to be moral or immoral, as Peter McHugh does . . .[12]) we find that the fundamental problem is that of determining the conditions of responsibility: under what conditions is an individual considered by members of our society to be (morally) responsible or (morally) unresponsible for a given event? We find in concrete situations that an individual is considered to be responsible for his actions if and only if (1) he has intended to commit those actions and knows the rules relevant to them (They have what McHugh calls theoreticity.) and (2) he chose to commit those actions freely, without external restraint (they have conventionality). Actions can be considered to be moral or immoral, then, only to the degree that they are seen to be other than they might have been and done with the knowledge that they are moral or immoral.

The most important conclusion from this argument is that situational determinations of morality and immorality in our society are necessarily problematic. Since it is a necessary condition of morality and immorality that the actions performed might have been otherwise, there are necessarily grounds for argument with oneself and with others over the question of morality: if the actions had to be performed, if he had no arguable choice to make, then he could not possibly be (morally) responsible. As McHugh has put it, "Moral rules not only permit but create

and require the possibility of argument, denial, and disconfirmation."[13] This is true as well because intention (and, to a lesser extent, all internal or subjective states) is necessarily problematic. This is true primarily because our common-sense epistemology (or theory of knowledge) considers all events not immediately sense-perceivable to be less certain (and less real).[14]

Given this necessarily problematic nature of moral meanings in our society, we must also conclude that there will necessarily be situational conflicts within and/or between individuals concerning any moral question. We are led, then, to conclude that, contrary to the assumptions of structural-functional and systems theories of society, conflicts over morality and immorality will necessarily occur even when individuals do share the same morals.

But it must also be apparent that social order is possible only if there are means either to resolve such necessary conflicts on other than moral grounds or to bridge them (contain their effects). In our society we find that many devices have been created and used to do both. We find that intention (and other internal states) is objectified by various rule-of-thumb procedures by which we agree to act as if we had objective knowledge of intention. We find, especially, that certain external, antecedent states are treated as if they stand for (are identical with) the internal states, so we have only to observe the external situation to "know" what was intended, what motives were operative, and so on. (In a very important way our positivistic behavioral sciences have simply sought to meet this common-sense need for nonsubjective or objective knowledge about people.)

Even more importantly, this necessary gap makes the use of power essential to the maintenance of social order in our society. The traditional (structural) idea of sociologists has been that there is some level of sharedness of morals sufficient to produce reciprocal (or "doubly contingent") patternings of action in such a way that social order will be created and maintained (if not constituted by that patterning). In this view "authority" (or power exercised in accord with the shared values) is sometimes considered to be necessary (or most efficient) in "maintaining" the actions patterned by the shared morality (that is, to limit "deviance"). If, however, situated moral experience is necessarily problematic, then, regardless of the degree of sharedness of morals, there will always be moral disagreement and there will always be imputations of "deviance" (or immorality). We are led, then, to a totally different conclusion concerning the use of power: the use of power, independently of the necessarily different and conflicting moral experiences of the individuals involved, is necessary to maintain social order in our society.[15]

There is, of course, at least one commonly understood alternative to such use of power, though it really seems to be merely a major strategy of such a-moral exercise of power. This is *mystification*. Men of power normally use various strategies of mystification to construct the appearance of common moral experience to bridge the necessary gap. This is especially apparent in the realm of legal and judicial decision making, in which power and mystification are combined in complex ways to provide a general sense of justice in spite of the fact that some of the participants inevitably feel a sense of injustice. God, tradition, reason, democracy, nationalism, and symbols of power and justice of many kinds (black robes, showing deference to the judges, scales, gavels, flags, and

the rest) are interposed to bridge the inevitable gap: the inevitable sense of injustice is checked by trust that God and other higher powers will enforce a greater right, by the belief that wrongs in this immediate situation are outweighed by rights in the greater social context, and by the fears of one's own impotence in the face of the awe-inspiring symbols of power.

The management of such devices of mystification in order to construct social order in a concrete situation is merely one instance of the general social use of moral meanings to help in constructing social order. . . .

SITUATED CONSTRUCTIONS OF MORAL MEANINGS

In a society in which there is a dominant conception of morality as absolute and as the only appropriate determinant of action, there will inevitably be a fundamental difference between public morality and private morality.[16] And, as a result of this necessary difference between public and private morality, the situated constructions of moral meanings (that is, the concrete interpretations of abstract morals) will be treated by the members maintaining that situated actions as if they are identical (or "indexical"[17]) with the abstract moral meanings.

Life is immensely too complex, too uncertain, too conflictful, and too changing for any set of abstract and predetermined rules to specify activities that will have results seen as adequate by the individual actors. Life itself would soon end if one tried to live in that way. Any rules actually to be applied to life must, therefore, be changeable and adaptable to meet the contingencies of living. Yet this is completely contrary to the absolutist conception of morality and its relation to living. The absolutist insists on subjugating life to the absolute rules.

For whatever reason, it is clear that the Western societies became firmly committed to an absolutist world view, and certainly an absolutist conception of morality, many centuries ago. While this absolutism has waxed and waned, it has always remained dominant and has been very strong in certain societies since its great resurgence in the Protestant Reformation. There are now very serious challenges to this absolutism, and there is clear evidence of changes taking place in the social conceptions of morality (see below), but the absolutist conception remains dominant. As long as this is true, any overt disagreement or challenge of the absolute morality will be seen as immoral by most members of society.

In addition, because most members of our society see this absolute morality as a homogeneous unit in which each part is necessary to all others, and because they believe that this absolute morality is the fundamental determinant of whatever happens in society, they firmly believe that immorality causes social disorder (or disintegration) and, indeed, that for many purposes immorality can be treated as merely an instance of (or identical with) social disorder. (The sociological theories of disorganization and deviance, especially those of the Durkheimian school and the Chicago ecological school, were firmly grounded in this common-sense theory and show the same confusion over whether there is a causal or an identity relation between factors of disorganization and immorality. Factors of disorganization, anomie, and the like, are both defined in terms of immorality and used to explain this immorality.) As long as these beliefs exist, a disagreement or

challenge to any part of the absolute morality—and certainly a challenge to the absolutism of morality itself—will be seen as a threat to social order and, thence, to the very existence of society. A challenge to the absolute morality, then, is seen not only as immoral but as legitimate reason for the greatest anxiety.

Both of these factors, the social responses of anxiety-induced repression and charges of immorality, make it very unwise for members of our society to challenge the absolute morality. Today there is a third factor that makes it even more costly to challenge the official morality. In the past one hundred years American society, like other Western societies, has increasingly become an officially controlled society.[18] The control of thought and behavior seen as immoral, abnormal, and threatening has been increasingly turned over to numerous kinds of official experts of control. The official organizations of control and the laws governing them were largely founded at a time when the absolute morality was even more dominant than it is today, and they were unequivocally entrusted with enforcing that absolute morality and legally given wide discretion to do so. These official organizations have objectified the absolute morality for the whole society: they have become a largely independent force external to the great majority of individuals in society and exercising power over them in matters of morality, normalcy, and social order. (If Durkheim had seen that it is in this sense that morality is external and thinglike to individuals, as well as in the sense that they think of it as absolute, hence external to themselves, he would not have fallen into the fallacy of concretizing "society" and, thereby, perpetrating so much nonsense about society's being a level of existence separate from that of individuals.) These official organizations of control then transmit the absolute morality from one generation of officials to another through their training practices and by promoting those most zealous in upholding the absolute morality. The officials then become the protectors of the absolute (official) morality, even to the extent of educating (or propagandizing) the public about the needs for the absolute morality and, thereby, advancing their own interests.[19]

An individual who is seen as not acting in accord with the absolute morality—or, even more, one seen to be challenging that absolute morality and, therefore, threatening the foundations of social order—becomes subject both to condemnation by any segment of the public that wants to attack him (for whatever reason) and, more importantly, to (public) stigmatization by official control agents. We have a situation, then, in which any challenge to the absolute morality can lead to official stigmatization, including arrest and imprisonment (or commitment), regardless of the amount of private support one might actually have among the general public. Even if a majority of the population agrees (privately) with the challenge—or rejection—of the absolute morality, it will normally be impossible for an individual to show this to be the case, since anyone who (publicly) challenges that absolute morality will be subject to the same stigmatization. It is for this reason that we get the public obeisance to and celebration of the absolute morality. When we remember as well that life, especially the complex, rapidly changing lives in our pluralistic and international technological society, cannot actually be lived in terms of that (abstract) absolute morality, we see that there will necessarily develop a split between one's professed (public) reasons for doing something and one's actual (private) reasons for doing it, but that this difference between public and private justifications will in almost all cases be denied and hidden by rhetorical interpretations of the absolute morality for the situation at hand intended to make the interpretation appear to others to fit the (abstract) absolute morality. This is to say that there are, indeed, conflicts (as defined by the members involved) between the absolute morality and the situated interpretations and that the situated interpretations are in significant part (purposeful) rhetorical constructions intended either to prevent moral attacks or to win any moral attacks that might occur. These rhetorical constructions of moral meanings, then, are a crucial element in what Goffman and others analyze as self-presentation (and group presentation).

As the split between the public morality and private morality becomes greater, due, presumably, to greater changes and complexities of living adequately, we get the highly purposeful form of self-presentation known as public relations, and, in a very real sense, everyone, or everyone who sees how to be successful, becomes his own public-relations man. In a society in which the changes in living are making this split ever greater and more recognizable, such as in Machiavelli's Renaissance Italy and our own society, there is a proliferation of common-sense thought concerning the strategies of self-management (for example, how to win friends and influence people). At the same time, in a society such as ours, in which there are such great dangers from disclosure of the truth, resulting from the enforcement activity of the official control agencies, this growing recognition of the split between the (public) fronts and what individuals can be seen to say and do in private leads to a growing sense of hypocrisy and attacks on dishonesty from those who are committed to the absolute morality or wish to profit by appearing to be so committed. In American society it is mainly the young and the isolated rural communities who have lived almost entirely in simple societies, such as the family, in which there is more of a feeling of fit between the public and private who become so alienated from and angry at the hypocritical modern world.

While it should be apparent that this social constructionist theory of morality and social actions constitutes an immensely more complex view of their relations and of the nature of social order in our society than that proposed by the traditional structural theories, which assumed the absolutist perspective, it should not be concluded that anything goes, that all talk of morality is merely sham, and so on. Certainly we must consider this to be a serious possibility, but the evidence does not yet seem to indicate this to be true. At the same time, while it now seems clear that the situatedness of moral meanings . . . makes it far more possible to "get away with anything" than has traditionally been assumed by the simplistic structural theories, the evidence from this argument does not yet support the conclusion that "anything goes."

First of all, the necessary involvement of social response (or of anticipated social response) in any moral experience . . . does not mean that moral experience and social response or social use are identical in all situations in our society. This might appear to be a legitimate conclusion from carrying the social response theories, such as C. Wright Mills's argument concerning the "situated vocabulary of motives," to their logical conclusion.[20] Mills's argument was essentially that the anticipation of acceptance or rejection by others was a, if not the, basic determinant of the morally meaningful motives an individual would give to his actions, and the possibilities of constructing plausible imputations of this sort, then, became basic determinants of what one would do. Mills's whole argument actually rests on the implicit assumption that at some point there are shared morals which determine social response, simply because it is the existence of such shared morals which is, presumably, determining the acceptability or nonacceptability of the morally meaningful motives imputed to one's actions. If there were no such ultimately shared morals, or something to serve the same function (which is an important consideration), social response would be indeterminant (if not random), so one might as well impute any motive he wished, and actions would be disordered.

The shared abstract moral meanings do appear to set some very broad social limits on what can be justified in any situation in several important ways. First of all, they are socially defined as a necessary part of the symbolic resources that must be used in constructing any justification or any account[21] of one's activities. Most importantly, there are included in this the morally sanctioned rules of reasoning (and of normalcy) which one must be seen to be acting in accord with in constructing any account of one's actions. It is these rules, whether consciously used (foreground) or implicitly assumed (background), which, for example, determine the process of analogizing involved in the moral reasoning by which one moves to a social construction of the moral meanings of a new situation, and it is this that is so crucial in preventing any random leap to a totally new (utopian) definition.

What does appear to happen, however, is that individuals and groups move through progressive situated interpretations of moral meanings. Since all of us live in rapidly changing environments, we all frequently face what we see as new problems and new situations with new meanings for us and demanding new solutions. Through a progressive sequence of such situated interpretations the difference between the public and private morality will grow greater (unless the society in general is moving in the same direction), but the degree to which the individuals involved recognize any such difference must depend on their degree of involvement with an openness to observation by the outside (public). The more private or intimate relations are within the situation, the more they are cut off or secret from public observation, the greater the difference that will develop and the greater their tolerance for this difference. Indeed, in highly intimate relations these differences from the recognized (and accepted for public purposes) public morality may be highly prized and celebrated—and breaches of public morality may be used to demonstrate and increase the feeling of intimacy. This, for example, is what Norman Denzin has found in the highly intimate or private relations of the family,[22] and self-revelations of one's private morality and deviations from the public morality are very generally used to help construct the ethos of intimacy which has been analyzed by Alexander Blumenstiel.[23]

Individuals and groups who, for any reason, have developed what is potentially seen in terms of the absolute morality as a highly immoral form of behavior will tend to make their behavior situated in two ways. First of all, they will seek to justify their behavior by presenting it as an appropriate interpretation of the absolute morality for their situation. Second, they will seek to cut it off—situate it —from the rest of social experience, especially from public experience; and success in keeping it a secret may actually be a fundamental justification for allowing it to continue: it's all right as long as it is not subject to view by the public, the innocent strangers who might be tempted by it were they to know of it and thereby endanger the dominance of the public morality, which would in turn endanger the very foundations of social order. We can, in fact, see this whole process at work in Weinberg's analysis of nudism.[24]

Over long periods of time various groups have succeeded in situating the abstract morality with respect to their own activities so that they are allowed to do what would normally (or under *any* other conditions) be considered to be violations of the abstract morality. These activities are of the nature of moral exceptions (and are direct analogues to the exceptions found so essential centuries ago to making Roman law work adequately in non-Roman Europe). But, even as exceptions, they have always been justified in terms of the absolute morality by arguing that they are actually in the service of the absolute morality—they are only apparent or surface violations. But the appearances have always been of crucial importance (since all appearances are also "real"), so these moral exceptions are always situated as well by hiding or isolating them from public view, thereby making them partially a form of private morality made accountable to the public (absolute) morality.

Professional groups are especially likely to develop such moral exceptions. The way in which the medical profession has over centuries developed the profound exceptions to the sacredness of the body and the privacy of the sex organs is especially informative. But other groups have succeeded as well in constructing such situated moral exceptions. Silvers' study of the construction of an amoral definition of themselves by artists, justified in terms of its necessity for artistic creativity, which is highly valued in society, is an excellent example of this.[25]

As Western society, and American society above all, has become ever more complex in the last century, it has come increasingly to be made up of such groups with their own highly situated (private) moralities to whom the absolute morality has increasingly been seen as an external force which one must simply manage effectively in constructing moral appearances that will be acceptable for public purposes. As I have previously argued,[26] this is one important way in which American society has become increasingly pluralistic, so that we have moved ever further from the simple state of a social system, if, indeed, it makes any sense to argue that American society ever was in such a state. This society is now far more of the nature of a social conglomerate made up of largely independent groups which are tied together by certain generally shared, abstract goals (health, prosperity, and security). In this social conglomerate the traditional absolute morality has increasingly become used only for public purposes, as already noted, and has a decreasing effect on what the powerful groups do in private. In the public arena this absolute morality now serves mainly as a public celebration of community (we are all Americans, all Christians—or Judeo-Christians, and so on) and as a primary means of maintaining the myth of the social system (that is, the myth of the dominant absolute morality), by which there probably is an important slowing of the recognition that the absolute morality is no longer a primary determinant (presumably through individual consciences) of what people do in private. And, as I have also argued, even this effect in public situations has continued only because of the power of the official organizations of control.

TOWARD A NEW ETHICS

Yet even the power of the officials has not been sufficient to prevent the spreading recognition that there is no longer an absolute morality to which we can all turn for solutions to any moral questions that might arise in our everyday lives, confidently taking it for granted that all others must do so as well (because all consciences are predetermined by the one universal moral good—God) and will necessarily arrive (in their hearts, at least) at the one necessary answer—an answer which will be enforced with infinite power for all time—and beyond, to the unimaginable unlimits of eternity. In this very important sense, while it would certainly be false to say with the radical theologians that "God is dead," it seems very true to say that God is dying. There is a spreading recognition that morality is not absolute, but situational; not obvious, but problematic; and not unchanging, but changing very rapidly. There is, as well, a growing feeling that moral experience is not what it once was, so that the very term *morality* hardly communicates the right meaning and must be replaced with some new term, perhaps *ethics*.[27]

The failure of the officials to prevent

this growing awareness, and their having to be content (or discontent) with merely slowing (or controlling) it, has probably been due more to the growth of free speech than anything else. Free speech has, of course, traditionally been subject to control work by officials just like most other spheres of everyday life, especially public life. But the ancient pluralism of Anglo-Saxon society, which long ago produced the ethos of individual freedoms "guaranteed" by government officials, and the American emphasis on the free speech guarantee, have been important in keeping speech relatively freer from official control than actions. (The distinction between mere talk and deeds has been of crucial importance in this whole process.) The growing importance of science in our society, with its fundamental emphasis on free enquiry and free communication, has increased the demands for free speech. Most importantly, the growth of the psychological and social sciences has led to increasing revelations of secret (often supposedly unconscious) thoughts and deeds. The effects of this, especially of the so-called Freudian revolution, have been profound. Today it is easy for (non-fundamentalist) people to talk publicly about private matters which involve profound challenges to the absolute morality—matters which were probably very difficult to talk about in greatest privacy two generations ago. While it is still potentially very costly to admit private violations of the absolute morality through such talks, the effects of this growing free speech on our social conceptions of morality have been profound.

Most importantly, it has become increasingly clear to individuals that they are not alone in their thoughts and actions and that other individuals and groups have very different private moral feelings from their own. This has produced a growing recognition of the insincerity of public moral pronouncements, coupled with the rage for authenticity or sincerity in personal relations (getting behind what are now seen as fronts) and of the actually problematic nature of moral experience. Increasingly it is recognized that moral decisions are not, and cannot be, taken for granted, but rather must be purposefully constructed by the individuals for the purposes at hand. Increasingly it is recognized that moral experience is not imposed on man from outside, but rather is created by man out of his experience in everyday life (his existence) for use in his situations. Increasingly it is recognized that this situational nature of morality (or ethics: rules of interaction) and of action means that individuals are never solely responsible for their own actions, but rather that responsibility must be seen as interactional, as partly individual and partly social. And, last, it is increasingly recognized that this understanding of the existential (or problematic and situational) nature of moral experience and action poses profound problems for social order.

It is not at all clear to members of our society, including the social scientists, where these growing changes are taking us or whether it will be possible for us to maintain social order, while maintaining and building our individual freedoms, in a society in which most of the members do not think of the social rules as absolutes founded in the very nature of being. Whether these new understandings of the human condition will serve to free us from ancient bonds, or will drive us to create a new tyranny to suppress a war of all against all resulting from a sense of libertinage, of freedom from personal responsibility and accountability, will be determined only by the creative efforts that lie ahead. But surely the understandings of moral experience and social order provided by sociologists will be of crucial importance in deciding the success or failure of those creative efforts.

NOTES

1. This necessary dualism has very likely been the basis for the continual appeal of Manichaeism in the Western societies.

2. See E. Durkheim, *Rules of Sociological Method*, ed. G. Catlin (Glencoe: The Free Press, 1950), especially pp. 65-73.

3. See Alan F. Blum, "The Sociology of Mental Illness," in J. Douglas, *Deviance and Respectability* (New York: Basic Books, 1970), Chapter 2.

4. For a treatment of the principle of the (situated) contextual determination of meanings, see Jack D. Douglas, *The Social Meanings of Suicide* (Princeton: Princeton University Press, 1967), pp. 235-254.

5. M. Moermann, "Analysis of Lue Conversation: Providing Accounts, Finding Breaches and Taking Sides," Working Paper No. 12 (Berkeley, Calif.: Language-Behavior Laboratory, 1968), p. 13.

6. See Norman K. Denzin, "Rules of Conduct and the Study of Deviant Behavior," in J. Djuglas, *Deviance and Respectability* (New York: Basic Books, 1970), Chapter 5.

7. See Maurice Mandelbaum, *The Phenomenology of Moral Experience* (New York: The Free Press, 1955).

8. For a discussion of absolutism, see my essay on, "The Impact of the Social Sciences," in Jack D. Douglas, ed., *The Impact of the Social Sciences* (New York: Appleton-Century-Crofts, 1969).

9. See especially Edwin M. Lemert, *Human Deviance, Social Problems, and Social Control* (Englewood Cliffs: Prentice-Hall, 1967); and Howard S. Becker, *Outsiders: Studies in the Sociology of Deviance* (New York: The Free Press, 1963).

10. For a detailed criticism of the structural theories of deviance, see Douglas, "Deviance in a Pluralistic Society."

11. See Blum, *op. cit.*

12. Peter McHugh, "A Common-Sense Conception of Deviance," in J. Douglas, *Deviance and Respectability* (New York: Basic Books, 1970), Chapter 3.

13. *Ibid.*

14. For discussions of this, see Jack D. Douglas, "The Relevance of Sociology," in Jack D. Douglas, ed., *The Relevance of Sociology* (New York: Appleton-Century-Crofts, 1969); and Jack D. Douglas, "Crime and Justice in American Society," in Jack D. Douglas, ed., *Crime and Justice in American Society* (New York: Bobbs-Merrill, 1970).

15. See Jack D. Douglas, "Deviance in a Pluralistic Society," in E. A. Tiryakian and John McKinney, eds., *Perspectives on Sociological Theory* (New York: Appleton-Century-Crofts, 1969).

16. See the discussion of public versus private in Douglas, "Deviance in a Pluralistic Society"; and in Jack D. Douglas, *Deviance and Social Order* (New York: The Free Press, 1970).

17. On "indexicality," see Harold Garfinkel, *Studies in Ethnomethodology* (Englewood Cliffs: Prentice-Hall, 1967).

18. See Douglas, "Crime and Justice in American Society."

19. See the treatment of the origins of the Marijuana Stamp Tax Act in Becker, *op. cit.*

20. C. Wright Mills, "Situated Actions and Vocabularies of Motive," *American Sociological Review*, V (1940), 904-913.

21. See Marvin B. Scott and Stanford M. Lyman, "Accounts, Deviance, and Social Order," in Jack Douglas, *Deviance and Respectability* (New York: Basic Books, 1970), Chapter 4.

22. See Denzin, *op. cit.*

23. See Alexander David Blumenstiel, "An Ethos of Intimacy: Constructing and Using a Situational Morality," in J. Douglas, *Deviance and Respectability* (New York: Basic Books, 1970), Chapter 14.

24. See Martin S. Weinberg, "The Nudist Management of Respectability: Strategy for, and Consequences of, the Construction of a Situated Morality," in Jack Douglas, *Deviance and Respectability* (New York: Basic Books, 1970), Chapter 12.

25. See Ronald J. Silvers, "The Modern Artist's Associability: Constructing a Situated Moral Revolution," in Jack Douglas, *Deviance and Respectability* (New

York: Basic Books, 1970), Chapter 13.

26. See Douglas, "Deviance in a Pluralistic Society."

27. For a discussion of the "new ethics," see Douglas, "Crime and Justice in American Society." For an example of this, see Joseph Fletcher, *Situation Ethics: The New Morality* (Philadelphia: Westminster, 1966).

22. DEVIANCE AND IDENTITY

JOHN LOFLAND WITH THE
ASSISTANCE OF LYN LOFLAND

Excerpted from John Lofland, *Deviance and Identity* (Englewood Cliffs, N. J.: Prentice-Hall, Inc. 1969), with permission of the authors and Prentice-Hall, Inc. John Lofland is Associate Professor of Sociology at the University of California, Davis. He received his Ph.D. from the University of California at Berkeley in 1964.

ESCALATION AND INTERACTION

There are many types of . . . interaction processes, but we are here concerned only with *spiraling* or *escalation* processes. Many interaction processes involve only well-known routines wherein an initiated sequence runs a predictable and expected course, arriving at an expected and unremarkable terminus, with the status quo quite undisturbed. Each party to the interaction is able to anticipate and, in a relatively unreflective way, take account of the other party's action. Such processes may be said to be in stable equilibrium. They maintain and confirm preexisting arrangements and identities (Goffman, 1956). On the other hand, parties may become involved in interaction in which they feel and are perceived as feeling that the Other's response is of such a character that previously exercised responses are not sufficient. The present response must be, in some way, stronger, more firm or more drastic. If both parties come to feel and act this way about each other's actions, there exists a spiraling or escalation process.[1]

This latter type of interaction process appears to be prominently involved in the building of personal identification with many categories of identity, including deviant ones.[2] As an inherently unstable process, escalation cannot continue indefinitely. One way in which equilibrium is eventually achieved is through Actor's accepting the identity embodied in the escalating actions of Others. This acceptance of the proffered identity is, of course, only one among many ways in which escalation can terminate. Others include one or both parties physically destroying the other or one or both parties leaving the field (including, literally, running away).

At this time very little of a detailed character is known about the dynamics of the escalation process per se. We have some knowledge of what to feed into the black box to get out a deviant identification of self, but we have meager knowledge of its contents. That is, we are in a position similar to that of the little old lady who knows what to feed into her automobile to get out movement but has only a vague conception of what is under the hood. Although I will explicate something of what we know about the contents of the black box—and make some additional guesses—the primary focus will be on elements that may be fed in.[3]

ESCALATION AND DEVIANT IDENTITY

If the escalation process has the *formal* structure detailed above, what might be its more specific and substantive features? Although Actor and Other are enmeshed in a process of mutual contingency, some general features of their respective lines of action appear to be of the following kind.

OTHERS

During escalation, Others experience both increasing doubts that Actor can reasonably be imputed a normal pivotal identity and increasing faith in the imputation of his pivotal deviance. Initiated imputation can be a fragile, tentative or even reluctant act. As an identity possibility, it can be important in the sense that Others take strong account of it, but, like a hypothesis, it awaits confirmation. However, the identity hypotheses of everyday life structure the degree to which Others act in a self-protective manner. Even though the imputation as deviant may be tentative, the very fact that suspicion has been aroused is likely to conduce action which takes account of that suspicion and attempts to protect Others against the worst that Actor might do.

Such subtle and tentative shifting of the ground of perception begins a process whereby Others double-code Actor's emissions, scrutinizing him for indications of pivotal normality and pivotal deviance. And, because of certain features of human activity which I will discuss momentarily, confirmation of the tentative imputation is likely to begin to occur, leading to increasing certainty on the part of Others that Actor should definitely be coded as an instance of a deviant type. Such growing confirmation may attain a critical mass of informational input, precipitating a gestalt switch in the perception of Actor. In discussing the escalation process in paranoia, Lemert puts it this way:

At some point in the chain of interactions, a new configuration takes place in the perceptions others have of the individual, with shifts in figureground relations. The individual, as we have already indicated, is an ambiguous figure, comparable to textbook figures of stairs or outlined cubes which reverse themselves when studied intently. From a normal variant, the person becomes "unreliable," "untrustworthy," "dangerous" or someone with whom others "do not wish to be involved." (Lemert, 1962:8.)

Throughout escalation, there can occur some general perceptual processes which have the character of feeding upon themselves as well as feeding upon the possibly changing emissions of Actor. These processes involve the shedding of new light on (1) Actor's current acts and (2) his biography.

Redefinition of Current Acts. First, a wide range of Actor's current activity that was previously not defined as indicative might now be so defined. Although Actor may be emitting the same acts, they can take on different meanings. Instead of having imagination, he may now be a wild visionary. Instead of being optimistic, he may now be gullible. Instead of having a philosophy of life, he may now be blindly following dogma. Instead of engaging in a debate or spat, he may now be prone to quarrels and fights. Instead of failing by oversight, he may now fail by negligence. Instead of being stoic or stolid, he may now be apathetic. Instead of having naughty sexual interest, he is now interested in pornography and is perverted. Instead of engaging in escapades or indiscretions, he may now have tawdry affairs. Instead of giving due consideration, he may now be stalling. Instead of being enterprising, he may now be opportunistic. Instead of voicing a legitimate complaint, he may now be a chronic malcontent. Instead of being merely determined, he may now be pigheaded. Instead of being prudent, he may be timid. Instead of dressing casually, he may be seen as sloppy.

Instead of showing a good deal of hopefulness, he may now be seen as living in a fool's paradise. Instead of being diplomatic, he is now two-faced. Instead of having engaged in a harmless prank, he has now perpetrated vandalism. Instead of being shy, he is aloof and a loner. Instead of displaying irony, he is now sarcastic and nasty. Instead of being trusting, he is naïve. Rather than being circumspect, he is now suspicious and distrusting.[4]

Because of the threatening image that is therein created, such redefinition serves to magnify the visibility of Actor, making it all the more likely that ever more qualities will additionally be noticed. In escalation to what is labeled paranoia, this redefinition is concomitant with magnification of acts, and even of Actor's physical qualities. There can occur

distortions of his image, most pronounced in the inner coterie of exclusionists. His size, physical strength, cunning and anecdotes of his outrages are exaggerated, with a central thematic emphasis on the fact that he is dangerous. Some individuals give cause for such beliefs in that previously they have engaged in violence or threats; others do not. One encounters characteristic contradictions in interviews on this point, such as: "No, he has never struck anyone around here—just fought with the policeman at the State Capitol," or, "No, I am not afraid of him, but one of these days he will explode." (Lemert, 1962:13.)

This is not to say that such redefinition of Actor's emissions, bringing them in harmony with already suspected deviance, violates the empirical facts of Actor's conduct in any important way. It is quite easy to engage in this sort of recoding because the acts and character of persons are in fact ambiguous. People and their acts do not have "unequivocally stable meanings," to quote Egon Bittner (1963). As a long tradition of social psychological experimentation suggests, ambiguous situations are open to the imputation of meaning. Once imputation as a deviant begins, the inherent ambiguity of action makes possible redefinition of a wide range of Actor's conduct. This redefinition involves little or no empirical contradiction, since the empirical materials provided by persons are almost never very clear.

Reconstruction of Biography. Second, there can begin a process of biographical reconstruction. Whatever may have been the preexisting selection of facts from the Actor's life line that supported a view by Others of him as a pivotal normal, there now begins a reexamination of that life line to discover if these selected biographical events are consistent with the prospective reclassification. Efforts are made to render the known facts consistent, either through discounting (or redefining the significance of) what is known or through undertaking to discover additional facts that support the new imputation.

It is in such biographical reconstructions that we see most clearly the social need of Others to render Actors as consistent objects. As mentioned previously, one of the most broadly and deeply held of human beliefs in recent Western societies is that an Actor must have some consistent and special history that explains the current social object that he is seen as being. It is believed that a person's acts must arise from or be a manifestation of an imputed social character. Personal history cannot simply involve the universal experience of being human and being subjected to human society; there must be a *special* history that *specially* explains current imputed identity. Relative to deviance, the *present evil* of current character must be related to *past evil* that can be discovered in biography.

These premises are most clearly played out by specialists in biographical reconstruction, most prominently by those involved in the "professions" of psychology and psychiatry. Their work is, however, merely a more elaborate and detailed version (as one might expect from persons who do it for a living) of a well-nigh universal practice. Acts in his past that were once viewed in a certain way are reinterpreted. Other acts, which had gone unnoticed or had seemed irrelevant, are brought forth and considered central, for they help Others to understand that Actor was that way all along.

This biographical reconstruction is also clearly seen at the public level, in the efforts that newspapers make relative to persons who commit widely publicized crimes. In July, 1966, eight student nurses were murdered in a Chicago apartment, and some days later one Richard Speck was apprehended and charged with these acts. Wire services and local newspapers went into a frenzy of research to find out about Richard Speck. The initial material published on his biography seemed unsatisfactory (at least to the *Detroit Free Press*, in which I followed the story), for interviews with people who liked and defined Speck as an intelligent, gentle and sensitive young man were buried in the back pages. However, four days after his apprehension enough appropriate material was available to credibly present the "right" biography on the front page. Under the headline "Richard Speck's Twisted Path," the rite of consistency could begin:

Charged with the brutal slaying of eight student nurses, Richard Speck was trapped by the tattoo that bore his credo: Born to Raise Hell. Here is a special report on the man accused of mass murder, a report on the twisted path that led to tragedy. (*Detroit Free Press*, July 24, 1966:1.)

And, of course, the facts presented were consistent. He was a "murder suspect" in another case who "had been hating for a long time," and "had been arrested 36 times." In his youth he was already "a reckless tough . . . with the leather jacket crowd" who "would drink anything." "A high school dropout" who was "divorced," he had served three years for burglary and was "woman crazy."

This consistent biographical construction was considerably easier to accomplish than that required when another well-publicized set of acts occurred in August of the same year. Charles Whitman's shooting of fourteen people from atop a tower at the University of Texas required rather more strenuous efforts, because the most public facts of his biography were less amenable to reconstruction than were Speck's. Whitman's Eagle Scout boyhood in Texas, unexceptional service in the Marines, and superior grades in college were first defined as a puzzle in connection with his act and finally seen as unrelated. Other events had to be discovered, and it took the newspapers an entire week to produce the first version of a biography supportive of a mad murderer identity. Buried in the third section of the *Detroit Free Press*, a *New York Times* story headlined: "Friends and the Record Dispute Sniper's All-American Image."

Charles J. Whitman . . . has been described as an all-American boy. But according to his friends, he has gambled with criminals, poached deer, written bad checks, kept illegal guns and tried to sell pornography. (*Detroit Free Press*, August 19, 1966.)

Interestingly enough, the concrete acts that are then spelled out in the story seem less malevolent than the abstract characterization of them given above. This is perhaps why the *Detroit Free Press* felt the story merited only page three of section three for that day. The problems posed in the effort to reconstruct consistently Whitman's biography possibly explains the later popularity of attributing his acts to an alleged brain tumor. When social and psychological explanations fail, one can always try biological or physiological ones. Regardless of the character of the account, Actor must be accounted for.

Note that Whitman's all-American image had to be *disputed,* but one could as well suggest that his acts were very much related to his all-American properties. As some wags have observed, being a Texan, a Boy Scout and a Marine would seem to be ideal training for a disposition toward and skills in the use of violence.

Perhaps more commonly, exactly the opposite kind of biographical rendering also occurs at the public level. Almost daily the mass media, as well as private persons, carry stories of meritorious promotion or transfer, stories which also contain a rehearsal of biographical events that in some sense support the current change and lend credence to the consistency and orderly character of persons (Scheff, 1963:445). Employment forms demand such consistency, too, even to the point of inquiring for arrests and mental disorders, the clear implication being that, if one wants to be hired, these lines should be left blank.

Paralleling the ambiguity of current action permitting coding as a deviant type, the concrete events of biography are also ambiguous, permitting the same items to be variously defined. More important, it is likely the case that the life lines of almost all Actors contain enough events of a discrediting kind to support a wide variety of deviant identities. When people can relate their biographies with assured anonymity, one finds that discrediting episodes are reported with enormous frequency.[5] Since existing studies of

the evil episodes populating the biographies of normals have focused on only a few delimited aspects of a sample's life line, one wonders if a *full* census of deviant episodes for almost any individual might not yield up more than enough evidence to convince others that the individual was, indeed, really the sort of person to have done this—almost regardless of how heinous the "this" in question. (One can, of course, also show for most individuals enough good biographical events to make him good enough to have been able to do something wonderful, heroic or exceptionally meritorious.)

No actual biographical rendering of an individual is exhaustive. What is called biography is of necessity an extremely short and highly *selective* list of events drawn from the totality of an individual's past. This must be so if for no other reason than that a *total* rendering would require the same amount of time in rendition as the individual has already existed, doubling the Actor's biography-to-be-told in the very process of working on a total telling of it. The fact of enormous selectivity, without benefit of a sampling frame or random selection procedures, means that the biographies available on Actors are likely to be highly distorted (in the probability sense), for what is known is unlikely to depict accurately the essential features of the vast amount that is unknown.[6] The reported biography of an Actor will, then, be very much a function of how much control he has over concealing his past, of the access that Others have to it and of what they are attuned to detect and report.

These forms of evidential coding are accompanied by an increasing intensity in the actual treatment of Actor as a deviant person. Actor may become increasingly implicated in surveillance, concern, patronization, put-downs and other abuses which communicate to him the nature of his true character. In addition, deviants of his imputed kind may begin to treat him with increasing solicitude. The following kinds of cumulating differential treatments are reported by Lemert as characterizing the process of escalation to an identity clinically labeled "paranoid."

In an office research team . . . staff members huddled around a water cooler to discuss the unwanted associate. They also used office telephones to arrange coffee breaks without him and employed symbolic cues in his presence, such as humming the *Dragnet* theme song when he approached the group. An office rule against extraneous conversation was introduced with the collusion of supervisors, ostensibly for everyone, actually to restrict the behavior of the isolated worker. In another case an interview schedule designed by a researcher was changed at a conference arranged without him. When he sought an explanation at a subsequent conference, his associates pretended to have no knowledge of the changes.

*   *   *

Concern about secrecy in . . . groups [excluding the imputed person] is revealed by such things as carefully closing doors and lowering of voices when ego is brought under discussion. Meeting places and times may be varied from normal procedures; documents may be filed in unusual places and certain telephones may not be used during a paranoid crisis.

The visibility of the individual's behavior is greatly magnified during this period; often he is the main topic of conversation among the exclusionists, while rumors of the difficulties spread to other groups, which in some cases may be drawn into the controversy. At a certain juncture steps taken to keep the members of the ingroup continually informed of the individual's movements and, if possible, of his plans. In effect, if not in form, this amounts to spying. Members of one embattled group, for example, hired an outside person unknown to their accuser to take notes on a speech he delivered to enlist a community organization on his side. In another case, a person having an office

opening onto that of a department head was persuaded to act as an informant for the nucleus of persons working to depose the head from his position of authority. This group also seriously debated placing an all-night watch in front of their perceived malefactor's house. (Lemert, 1962:12-13.)

ACTOR

Actor is unlikely to be oblivious to the beginning and subsequent development of this new coding, and he finds himself confronting a rather perplexing range of alternative responses. He can act as if nothing were amiss; that is, he can strive to act normally. But by doing so, since he then takes no overt action explicitly to deny what is suspected, his behavior may be taken as indicating insensitivity, evasiveness or even assent to what is suspected. He can seek to counter the suspicions through denials and counterdefinitions of himself, but such a response is easily read as protesting too much or being too defensive and as confirmation of Others' doubts about his normalcy. Or, he can act in compliance with the identity imputed to him. The irony is, of course, that, once begun, the practices of Others toward Actor operate to confirm what is suspected, almost irrespective of what Actor does. This is especially true if the imputations arouse in Actor a new level of anxiety and concern over what seems to be believed about him, thereby altering his orientation to the situation. . . .

None of this should be taken as necessarily implying that Actor dislikes the deviant identity tentatively proffered to him. He may well wish to reinforce the imputed identity or, at least, not be wholly adverse to the possibility of his pivotal deviance. For example, after spending eighteen months in a federal prison for refusing the Vietnam draft, a young man could feel that the experience was "worth it because it defined the kind of person I am, it defined my beliefs for me" (cf. Lorber, 1967). Nor is it necessarily the case that Actor and Others are agreed as to the concrete sort of deviant of which he is an instance. For successful escalation it need only be agreed that Actor is *deviant*. Within this agreement there may be continuing negotiation over the specific type. In the paranoia cases quoted above, some of the Actors apparently saw themselves as embattled social reformers, a self-identity nicely compatible, at the practical level of treatment, with the label of paranoia eventually applied to them. The treatment accorded people who come to believe they are Jesus Christ or some other such figure is not strongly imcompatible with the way in which Jesus Christ *et al.* might expect to be treated in the modern world (Rokeach, 1964). . . .

DEVIANT PLACES

PLACE IMPUTATION

Places themselves vary in the definitions accorded them by the public at large. Just as human bodies are the kinds of objects to which deviant and normal imputations can be made, so too are physical territories or places. Thus human beings speak of "good places" and "bad places," "nice places" and "crummy places," "clean places" and "dirty places." Human beings can impute to territories, somewhat independently of people, a character or identity. In this sense, pieces of land and people are much the same kinds of objects.

Imputations to places imply some conception of an appropriate (even if immoral clientele felt typically to inhabit or to frequent them. Nice places are frequented by that kind of people;

crummy places are frequented by their kind of people. And, some places come to be defined in public consciousness as the kinds of physical territories in which one finds one or another kind of deviant person. Mental hospitals, jails, prisons, psychiatric clinics, welfare offices and crowded, unkempt parts of a city have attributed to them a populace of suspect personal character. These are to be contrasted with places whose populaces are not presumptively suspect, such as most work settings, homes, churches, schools, business organizations, stores and manufacturing plants. The places into which humans have divided the world, then, are distinguishable in terms of their presumptive *habitation* or *frequence by deviants or normals*.

Those places presumably inhabited by deviants are in turn distinguishable in terms of whether this presumption is *formal* or *informal*. Some are formally so designated even to the extent of being written into the budget of a government under titles such as "State Prison," "State Mental Hospital" and "Boys' Reformatory." Signs may be erected on public frontage declaring to the passerby that these are places for deviants. (Of course, the ironic cuphemisms adopted of late serve only to amuse the public without changing the definition, e.g., a boys' prison being called a "conservation camp" or a private mental hospital being called a "rest home.") Entire sections of cities may even be formally declared as occupied by deviants, although the euphemistic treatment of these formal efforts under the rubric of "urban renewal" slightly obscures the definition. Many other places presumptively occupied by deviants may not have had their use so formally acknowledged, but the definition may still be a matter of more or less common knowledge. These *informal* places include criminal and homosexual bars or entire sets of service institutions catering to deviant clienteles. Bars and other such informally designated sites become known, especially to taxi drivers and tourists and to locals who often derive an evening's entertainment from moving among them.[11]

FORMAL DEVIANT PLACES

Assuming that the strongest conditions enumerated thus far exist for Actor, it can be suggested that escalation is additionally facilitated if all places in the Actor's round are *formally* defined as occupied by *deviants*. Formal definition of Actor's places as territories for deviants serves to impress upon him, in a quite literal fashion, his "place" in the world. He derives his very character from the territory within which he resides. Part of his essential nature is generated by the territory he occupies. Character can be embodied in the very architecture and in the physical arrangements which bear the stamp: deviants live here. The following description of a mental hospital ward for the elderly provides some sense of facilitative ways in which places for deviants can be designed.

The patient sleeps in a dormitory with 40 elderly persons, eats in the dining room with a like number and sits with them in an enormous day room. Privacy or a place for belongings is hard to come by. Most of the single and double rooms are already occupied by the tractable long-stay patients who comprise the working force of the hospital.

* * *

The newly admitted patient . . . has probably never lived in such a large area or been so close to so many people. (Sommer, 1959:589.)

Referring to a state mental hospital, a reporter provides a further sense of how places for deviants might by their very features facilitate communication of Actor's special character:

A prison-like atmosphere permeates most of the wards—where there are locks on the elevators, bars on the windows, bolts on the doors and even locks on the light switches.

There is one shower to serve a ward of 70 men. (McDonald, 1965.)

Traditional prisons are, of course, the most explicit and straightforward regarding the chracter of their clientele.

Mechanical security measures . . . includ[e] . . . the building of high walls or fences around prisons, construction of gun towers, the searching of inmates as they pass through certain checkpoints, pass systems to account for inmate movement and counts at regular intervals. (President's Commission, . . . *Corrections*, 1967:46.)

At the level of immediate social interaction within a place *formally defined* for *deviants*, a number of practices on the part of normals also promote escalation. Of primary importance, and resting upon the normal's presumption of deviant character, is the practice of *role distance denial*. By "role distance" is meant the "margin of face-saving reactive expression —sullenness, failure to offer usual signs of deference, *sotto voce* profaning asides or fugitive expressions of contempt, irony and derision"— that an individual engages in when he "must accept circumstances and commands that affront his conception of self" (Goffman, 1961a:36). Life among normals in civil society abounds in small expressions by persons of their incomplete acceptance of the arrangements in which they are enmeshed. Role distance is normal in the sense that those who engage in it and those who observe it take it as a typical and to-be-expected reaction under a variety of even mildly vexing circumstances. Indulged in with sufficient moderation and selectivity, expressions of role distance seem even to be obligatory if witnessing Others are to feel that a witnessed Actor is a good guy. Persons who seem to embrace the vexations of circumstance too happily are themselves slightly suspect.

However, in places formally defined as populated by deviants, a different kind of interaction game is played. The normal caretakers of these places typically define expressions of role distance by those defined as deviant not as normal griping but as revealingly symptomatic of deviant character. Deviants in total institutions formally defined as being for them may find that they have considerably less freedom to act normally in this regard than they would have had in normal places. Much more is likely to be made of their expressions of dislike of the place itself and of the staff who runs it than, let us say, similar expressions in a total institution such as the U. S. Army, where those who do not express role distance may be objects of suspicion. There is a tendency, then, to deny to participants a measure of normal role distance. It is made, rather, an object of concern and is defined as a manifestation of deviant character and/or as a type of expression best suppressed through punishment. Ironically, there is a significant sense in which those with the worst lot are expected to be most accepting of it.

ATTENUATED SITUATIONS

Although the place round situation of an Actor participating only in *formally* designated *deviant* places appears to be the strongest condition,[12] escalation can also occur (usually with less frequency and effectiveness) under more attenuated circumstances. Participation in a place round of *informally* designated *deviant* places is one such attenuated situation. Underlying or highly correlated with the formal-informal distinction is the dimension of the degree to which the Others have the *power* to force candidate Actor to sustain his participation. Others who manage places formally designated for deviants typically have the police powers of some political unit at their disposal. The Others of informal places must, in contrast, rely upon persuasion and the evocation of attractiveness to Actor. Since his presence there is more or less voluntary, Actor may simply go away or fail to come back. Even under circumstances of united Others in an integrated round, escalation in informal worlds (such as deviant religious milieux, homosexual undergrounds or hippy culture) is a very tenuous affair. Escalation becomes even more problematic when the degree of integration of the place round is also decreased. When unanimity of imputation and the proportion of even informally defined deviant places in Actor's place round are also attenuated, it is a wonder that any new personnel are taken on at all—and worlds characterized by these conditions do indeed have personnel problems.

It is for these sorts of reasons that normative, emotional ties to Others who already wear the deviant label become particularly important in place rounds made up of at least some informal deviant places. . . . The institution and success of escalation seem sometimes to rest heavily upon the availability of informal sites that make possible rather powerful emotive attractions and attachments in a relatively short amount of time. It may be, for example, that the particular and peculiar characteristics of homosexual bars as a *type of place* are instrumental in the success of the homosexual milieu in populating its places. Hooker reports that such

bars also serve as induction and training and integration centers for the community.

These functions are difficult to separate. The young man who may have had a few isolated homosexual experiences in adolescence, or indeed none at all, and who is taken to a "gay" bar by a group of friends whose homosexuality is only vaguely suspected or unknown to him, may find the excitement and opportunities for sexual gratification appealing and thus begin active participation in the community life. Very often, the debut, referred to by homosexuals as "coming out," of a person who believes himself to be homosexual but who has struggled against it, will occur in a bar when he, for the first time, identifies himself publicly as a homosexual in the presence of other homosexuals by his appearance in the situation. If he has thought of himself as unique, or has thought of homosexuals as a strange and unusual lot, he may be agreeably astonished to discover large numbers of men who are physically attractive, personable and "masculine" appearing, so that his hesitancy in identifying himself as a homosexual is greatly reduced. Since he may meet a complete cross-section of occupational and socioeconomic levels in the bar, he becomes convinced that far from being a small minority, the "gay" population is very extensive indeed. (Hooker, 1961:52.)

Informal deviant milieux whose participants feel that they have a recruitment problem might well benefit from adopting the practices of the homosexual milieu, at least as it is organized in Los Angeles, the setting of the above description.

Another attenuated situation, that of a place round composed exclusively of sites formally and/or informally designated for normals, seems not to preclude escalation but to be marginally facilitative. Of more interest are place rounds composed of a mixed variety of sites, some defined (formally or informally) as for deviants and some defined as territories for normals. Within or across such a mixture of sites, normal and deviant Others may be divided on their imputations of Actor, and in addition the Actor himself may move in a relatively segregated round. This is one of the more complicated of

possible place rounds, and it is probably among the empirically most common. In it, escalation is problematic. The Actor who regularly frequents his social work agency, his outpatient clinic, his parole office, his Students for Democratic Society headquarters or his homosexual bar but is at other times in sites where very different kinds of imputations will be made of him will less easily come to embrace (and maintain) any deviant identity. Although Others in these places surely engage in the denial of role distance, the moralization of minutiae, the reconstruction of current activity and of biography and all the rest, their location in such a complex and varied place round weakens their ability to prosecute their inclinations vis-à-vis Actor. Not only can their definitions be contradicted, but the time and effort they can devote to their efforts are severely limited.[13]

The assumption of a personal identity, deviant or otherwise, is facilitated not only by particular arrangements of Others and places but also by certain manipulations of hardware and by certain states of our central figure himself, Actor. . . .

CHARACTER AND COMPONENTS OF HARDWARE

What humans believe themselves and others to be rests, in part, upon the physical items surrounding and structuring the representations they can make to one another. There is a significant sense in which clothes, most generally construed, not only *make* the man but *are* the man. The props on the stages of social life provide the physical underpinnings which help make possible the belief among humans that they are really and certainly what they believe themselves to be.

Sufficiently large and weighty supplies of such props, imbued with a degree of positive emotional value, serve quite literally to hold down their human possessors. Should humans come to doubt that they are really what their physical artifacts construe them to be, anticipation of the effort required to dispose of these artifacts may give such doubters second thoughts and conduce a return to that identity communicated by their hardware.[14]

The term "hardware" is intended to denote both those physical objects that can be attached or affixed to the body of an Actor and those that can be picked up or manipulated. The term is limited to items which can be moved with relative ease by one or, at most, a few Actors. Hardware may be as light as false eyelashes or as heavy or heavier than an automobile. To retrieve this term from the submerged background of common-sense, unproblematic affairs, let me briefly explicate some of its main categories, thereby enabling us to see some of the ways in which available hardware can vary and to note the identity implications of such variance.

There are, first, items of physical attire, typically, although far from exclusively, constructed of cloth. Second, there may be a stock of apparel-maintenance devices, such as shoeshine equipment, washing machines, irons, coat hangers and the like. Third, Actors may possess a range of body-grooming equipment composed of such simple items as combs, deodorants and soaps and of somewhat more elaborate devices such as hairdriers, electric razors and various cosmetics. Fourth, Actors are likely to have feeding and sleeping equipment (excluding the actual site where such equipment is stored), including eating utensils, food, pots, pans, beds, lamps, etc. Fifth, affluent Actors can embroider their existence with elaborate place furnishings. Sixth, some Actors are to be found possessing occupational equipment (used here in the narrow sense of items employed directly in the task of making some sort of living). Seventh—and of some prominence in suburban America—is a range of recreational equipment, sometimes including special types of motorized vehicles but more typically involving television sets, radio receivers, outdoor grills and the like. Finally, there are the ideological artifacts (used here in the limited sense of physical embodiments defined by Actors as expressions either of the most general principles by which they live or of the most significant events of their lives). Among these there may be special books (such as Bibles and scrapbooks), mementos, trophies, diplomas or accouterments thought of as art. The Actors of the world, of course, differ enormously in the number, variety, quality, state of repair and stylishness of the items within and across these categories which they possess. Some Actors may have a large number in all of these and in other categories; others may possess none or very few items in every category.

NORMAL HARDWARE WITHDRAWN, DEVIANT HARDWARE SUPPLIED

Holding constant the number and variety of items possessed, we may consider two general principles applicable to the manipulation of hardware for purposes of facilitating escalation. First, in order to precipitate and escalate doubt on the part of Actor (and Others) that he is an instance of some normal category, all hardware conventionally associated with a normal identity should be *withdrawn* from his possession. Reciprocally, in order to facilitate Actor's personal identification (and to facilitate Others' continued imputations of him), hardware conventionally identified with a given deviant category should be *supplied*.

Withdrawal of normal hardware decreases the possibility of Actor's thinking of himself as that kind of person. At the level of concrete arrangements, total institutions of many kinds perform this withdrawal in a prototypically facilitative way. Entry into some prisons and mental hospitals (and convents and military institutions) is often accompanied by a shearing off of almost all the hardware enumerated in the above list and conventionally associated with living under the label, normal. Actors are even stripped of their "identity kits," to use Goffman's phrase; that is, their grooming equipment and maintenance devices are confiscated. (Goffman, 1961a.) Of entry into a reform school, a young man can thus relate:

I was still attired in a good suit and would not have looked out of place at a high school prom as we stepped inside [the juvenile "reform" school]. Twenty minutes later I had stripped, taken a shower and been marched through a tray of smelly disinfectant. I was issued one of the rough uniforms and, as a final indignity, my head was shaved. I was a reform school inmate. (Sands, 1964:23.)

The same person's account of hardware stripping upon entry into San Quentin is considerably more graphic and appreciative of the identity implications of dress.

Then came the grey—my prison uniform. Across the back pockets of grey pants, over the left breast pocket of grey shirt, across the back of the shirt, on the back and the inside of the grey prison jacket was a number: 66836.

I was 66836. There was no longer an entity called Wilber Power Sewell or Bill or Sewell. I was to answer as "six-six-eight-three-six." That was "who" I was. Shaved

head, grey uniform, a number. (Sands, 1964:36.)

To the degree that more modern institutions abolish this practice, as some are now doing, destruction of existing identification as some kind of normal is inhibited.

Correspondingly, escalation is facilitated by providing Actor with a wide range of new hardware that is publicly defined as the physical expression of the deviant category in question. Again, many total institutions for deviants perform this with some effectiveness, as suggested in the above quote, by providing uniforms, handbooks of rules and other paraphernalia applicable to the deviant category. It should be noted, however, that the range and variety of hardware provided in public total institutions are rather meager when one considers the range and variety that are possible. Although inmates of prisons and mental hospitals may have available to them (but do not own) a few items in each of the enumerated categories, their total supply tends to be rather sparse and spartan. Perhaps for budgetary reasons, keepers of such institutions have not exploited the rich possibilities for providing hardware specially identified with the categories of convict and mental patient.

Humans already living under a deviant label, who are actively interested in recruiting additional Actors, sometimes seem more aggressive in sponsoring a rich repertoire of hardware particular to their category. Thus organizations such as the American Nazi Party, the Ku Klux Klan or the Hell's Angels, or loose worlds such as the current hippy milieu, seem to display a broader and richer range of distinctive physical artifacts, including formal or informal uniforms and feeding, sleeping, occupational and recreational equipment. However, organizations and milieux of these sorts do not have the coercive power to strip the Actor of his existing hardware or to enforce the use of a new set. Unlike state-sponsored institutions, these more voluntary affiliations are likely to find escalation more tenuous and subject to breakdown partly because of their rather low control over hardware. In addition, meagerness of resources with which to assemble distinctive hardware is also likely to be a feature of deviant groups at large in civil society. Many categories of deviants are unlikely to have the funds necessary to work up a truly distinctive complement of physical artifacts. Often they are forced to accord this matter rather low priority in their hierarchy of ways in which resources should be expended. This is most poignantly the case for deviant categories whose occupants are drawn from low-income sectors of the population. In cults and other bizarre religions, for example, we find that some small lapel pin or headpiece (as is largely the case in the Black Muslims) may be as far as a category will feel it can go.

That is, I am suggesting that, in contemporary America, even those deviants operating outside state institutions who are proud of their deviant identification seem not to have exploited possibilities for distinctive hardware nearly to the extent that deviants have in other times and other places. Even so aggressively self-righteous a category as the Black Muslims content themselves, in large measure, with the distinctiveness of white middle-class hardware. There is a sense in which the utopian communities of the 19th century were more nearly on the right track in elaborating the entire range of hardware, even to the point of growing their own special varieties of foods and of manufacturing distinctive sleeping, eating and occupational equipment (Kanter, 1967). It may be that the hippy movement and the Hell's Angels organizations of the late sixties have been the objects of particular note by normal Others primarily because of their utilization of distinctive hardware—especially distinctive when compared with the pallid outfitting characteristic of many, if not most, deviant categories.

It can be suggested, then, that escalation is facilitated when candidate-identifiers with a deviant category are provided with a full supply of hardware items distinctive to that category.

NOTES

1. Participation in escalating interaction may or may not be a routine matter for Others. There are, of course, professional escalators.

2. Escalating interaction is, of course, not confined to matters of personal identity. The term, as is evident, is drawn from the modern analysis of war and conflict.

3. Speculation in addition to that which follows, some of which informs the present statement, may be found in Parsons, 1951:Chap. 7; Cohen, 1955 and 1959; and, most important, Lemert, 1951:Chap. 4, especially pp. 76-78, and 1967a:Chap. 3. See also the empirical materials in Werthman, 1967; Schafer and Polk, 1967; and

the principles of "covert communication" in interaction summarized by Abrahamson, 1966:Chaps. 3 and 16; Halmos, 1966:90-105.

4. Kudos to columnist Sidney Harris (1965, 1966, 1967) for his apprehension of the ambiguity of human action from which I have here borrowed. See further Strauss, 1959:Chap. 4; Kitsuse, 1962; Ward and Kassebaum, 1965:85-88; Erikson, 1966; Lindesmith, 1968:188-89. By way of preview, empirical demonstration of the relation between negative imputation and the self (at least among male sixth-grade children imputed by teachers to be headed for contact with legal officials) is presented in

Reckless, Dinitz and Kay, 1957; Dinitiz, Scarpetti and Reckless, 1962. See also the D. B. Harris (1968) and Toby (1968) interpretation of how a delinquency prevention program increased, under some conditions, the number of youth officially imputed as delinquent by legal authorities. The moral valence of such imputations can, of course, operate in the opposite direction, as, for instance, in Rosenthal and Jacobson's (1966) demonstration of the relation between teachers' beliefs and pupils' IQ gains.

5. See Leighton et al., 1963; Srole et al., 1962; Wheeler, 1960; Short and Nye, 1958; Kinsey, Pomeroy and Martin, 1953; Porterfield, 1949; Wallerstein and Wyle, 1947; Murphy, Shirley and Witmer, 1946; Cohen, 1966:25-29.

6. Indeed, biographies composed of a true random sampling of events might be so contradictory that it would be very difficult for persons to impute identities to one another. If humans were fully informed about one another, they might, as Gerald Suttles has suggested, hesitate forever in a pit of ambivalence (Suttles, personal communication.)

7. In its own way, such slumming by normals is the functional equivalent of the tours through loony bins taken for amusement by aristocrats of a former era.

8. Cf. McKay, 1967:113: "The greater the participation of the young person in the institutions for treatment of the juvenile offender [in Chicago, Cook County and the State of Illinois], the greater is his probability of acquiring a record of adult criminality."

9. Although I will not pursue them here, each of the foregoing (and subsequent)

maximally facilitative states have, in turn, their respective social organizational sources. The varying strengths that any given element can assume may themselves be made the objects of analysis. Thus, for example, one can ask under what conditions there will (or will not) arise in a society places formally defined as specific resorts for people believed to be deviant sorts of persons. (Cf. Eaton and Weil's report [1955:Chap. 11] of a case where they have not arisen.) Under what conditions will such places, once occurring, manifest a distinctively impugning design and physical facilities far less comfortable than those prevailing in the culture at large? Such third level questions ... direct our attention again to the encompassing social order, to its history, to the current interests of, and conflicts among, the major institutions and to the dominant groups' conceptions of what is proper and practical. Relative to the occurrence (and persistence) of distinctively impugning formal deviant places, for example, there can arise particular interest in how state and federal legislators come to make decisions to support such places and to support them at a given financial level. (A provisional answer to this specific question is provided in Grob's [1966] excellent historical analysis of the Worcester State Hospital in Massachusetts, 1830-1920. See also Nelson, 1967.)

10. About a million Americans a year are reported, however, still to find it possible to skip out on their assembly of hardware (largely because they owe a great deal of money on it) and to take up residence under some different category in some other place. See "Vanishing Americans," *Newsweek*, February 24, 1964.

REFERENCES

Abrahamson, M., *Interpersonal Accommodation*. Princeton, N. J.: D. Van Nostrand Company, Inc., 1966.

Bittner, E., "Radicalism and the Organization of Radical Movements." *American Sociological Review*, 28:928-40 (December, 1963).

Cohen, A. K., *Delinquent Boys*. Glencoe, Ill.: The Free Press, 1955.

———, "The Study of Social Disorganization and Deviant Behavior," in R. K. Merton, L. Broom and L. S. Cottrell, editors, *Sociology Today*. New York: Basic Books, Inc., 1959, pp. 461-84.

———, *Deviance and Control*. Englewood Cliffs, N. J.: Prentice-Hall, Inc., 1966.

Dinitz, S., F. R. Scarpitti and W. C. Reckless, "Delinquency Vulnerability: A Cross Group and Longitudinal Analysis." *American Sociological Review*, 27:515-17 (August, 1962).

Eaton, J. W., in collaboration with R. J. Weil, *Culture and Mental Disorders: A Comparative Study of Hutterites and Other Populations*. Glencoe, Ill.: The Free Press, 1955.

Erikson, K. T., *Wayward Puritans: A Study in the Sociology of Deviance*. New York: John Wiley & Sons, Inc., 1966.

Goffman, E., "The Nature of Deference and Demeanor." *American Anthropologist*, 58:473-502 (June, 1956).

———, *Asylums*. New York: Doubleday & Company, Inc., 1961.

Grob, G. N., The State and the Mentally Ill: A History of the Worcester State Hospital in Massachusetts, 1830-1920. Chapel Hill, N. C.: University of North Carolina Press, 1966.

Halmos, P., *The Faith of the Counsellors: A Study in the Theory and Practice of Social Case Work and Psychotherapy*. New York: Schocken Books, 1966.

Harris, D. B., "On Differential Stigmatization for Predelinquents." *Social Problems*, 15:507-8 (Spring, 1968).

Harris, Sidney. *Columns, Detroit Free Press*, April 6, May 4, June 8, December 13, 1965; March 29, June 21, October 11, 1966; March 13, 1967.

Hooker, E., "The Homosexual Community." *Proceedings of the XIV International Congress of Applied Psychology*. Copenhagen: Munksgaard, 1961, pp. 40-59.

Kanter, R. M., "Utopia: A Study in Comparative Organization." Unpublished Ph.D. dissertation, Department of Sociology, The University of Michigan, 1967.

Kinsey, A. C., W. B. Pomeroy and C. C. Martin, *Sexual Behavior in the Human Male*. Philadelphia: W. B. Saunders Company, 1953.

Kitsuse, J. I., "Societal Reaction to Deviant Behavior: Problems of Theory and Method." *Social Problems*, 9:247-56 (Winter, 1962).

Leighton, D. C., et al., *The Character of Danger*. New York: Basic Books, Inc., Publishers, 1963.

Lemert, E. M., *Social Pathology*. New York: McGraw-Hill Book Company, 1951.

———, "Paranoia and the Dynamics of Exclusion." *Sociometry*, 25:2-20 (March, 1962).

Lindesmith, A. R., *Addiction and Opiates*. Chicago: Aldine Publishing Company, 1968.

Lorber, J., "Deviance as Performance: The Case of Illness." *Social Problems*, 14:302-10 (Winter, 1967).

McDonald, H. J., Series on Mental Hospitals in Michigan, *Ann Arbor News*, May 3-6, 1965.

McKay, H. D., "Report on the Criminal Careers of Male Delinquents in Chicago," in President's Commission on Law Enforcement and Administration of Justice, *Task Force Report: Juvenile Delinquency and Youth Crime*. Washington, D. C.: U. S. Government Printing Office, 1967, Appendix F, pp. 107-13.

Murphy, F. J., M. M. Shirley and H. Witmer, "The Incidence of Hidden Delinquency." *American Journal of Orthopsychiatry*, 16:686-96 (October, 1946).

Nelson, S. E., "History Repeats Itself." *Contemporary Psychology*, 12:516 (October, 1967).

Parsons, T., *The Social System*. Glencoe, Ill.: The Free Press, 1951.

Porterfield, A. L., *Youth In Trouble*. Fort Worth, Texas: Leo Potishman Foundation, 1949.

President's Commission on Law Enforcement and Administration of Justice, *Task Force Report: Corrections*. Washington, D. C.: U. S. Government Printing Office, 1967.

Reckless, W. C., S. Dinitz and B. Kay, "The Self Concept in Potential Delinquency and Potential Nondelinquency." *American Sociological Review*, 22:566-70 (October, 1957).

Rokeach, M., *The Three Christs of Ypsilanti*. New York: Alfred A. Knopf, Inc., 1964.

Rosenthal, R., and L. Jacobson, "Teachers' Expectancies: Determinants of Pupils' IQ Gains." *Psychological Reports*, 19:115-18 (1966).

Sands, B., *My Shadow Ran Fast*. New York: Signet, 1964.

Schafer, W. E., and K. Polk, "Delinquency and the Schools," in President's Commission on Law Enforcement and Administration of Justice, *Task Force Report: Juvenile Delinquency and Youth Crime*. Washington, D. C.: U. S. Government Printing Office, 1967, Appendix M, pp. 222-77.

Scheff, T. J., "The Role of the Mentally Ill and the Dynamics of Mental Disorder: A Research Framework." *Sociometry* 26:436-53 (December, 1963).

Short, J. F., and F. I. Nye, "Extent of Unrecorded Delinquency." *Journal of Criminal Law, Criminology and Police Science*, 49:296-302 (December, 1958).

Sommer, R., "Patients Who Grow Old in a Mental Hospital." *Geriatrics*, 14:581-90 (September, 1959).

Srole, L. T., et al., *Mental Health in the Metropolis*. New York: McGraw-Hill Book Company, 1962.

Strauss, A. L., *Mirrors and Masks: The Search for Identity*. Glencoe, Ill.: The Free Press, 1959.

Toby, J., "A Reply to Harris." *Social Problems*, 15:508-9 (Spring, 1968).

Wallerstein, J. S., and C. J. Wyle, "Our Law-Abiding Law-breakers." *Probation*, 25:107-12 (April, 1947).

Ward, D. A., and G. Kassebaum,

"Homosexuality: A Mode of Adaptation in a Prison for Women." *Social Problems,* 12:159-77 (Fall, 1964).

Werthman, C., and I. Pilliavin, "Gang Members and the Police," in D. Bordua, editor, *The Police: Six Sociology Essays.* New York: John Wiley & Sons, Inc. 1967, pp. 56-98.

Wheeler, S., "Sex Offenses: A Sociological Critique." *Law and Contemporary Problems,* 25:258-78 (Spring, 1960).

23. SOCIALIZATION, COMMAND OF PERFORMANCE, AND MENTAL ILLNESS

ERNEST BECKER

Reprinted from Ernest Becker, "Socialization, Command of Performance, and Mental Illness," *American Journal of Sociology*, Vol. 67 (March, 1962) pp. 494-501, with permission of the author and the *American Journal of Sociology*. Ernest Becker was one of the first to depart from the medical view of mental disorder, and to root its problems in the social psychology of performances. In addition to his writings on the social psychiatry in *The Birth and Death of Meaning* and *The Revolution in Psychiatry*, Becker has written a definitive piece on paranoia in his *Angel in Armor*.

The essentials for a sociological understanding of behavioral malfunction presented here underline a crucial but simple consideration which has not been sufficiently stressed in discussions of mental illness.[1] It is clear that whatever the origin of malfunction —in biological substrata or in conventional social definition of desirable norm—there are individuals who will not meet the behavioral requirements of their fellows. But in addition to this consideration, there is a less obvious one, namely, that to a self-reflexive, symbol-using animal, the *purely symbolic, social definition of normative behavior is as crucial to action* as is instinctive patterning to any lower organism. The basis for this conclusion is common knowledge to the clinician. However, recapitulation of several crucial features of man's uniqueness in the animal kingdom is warranted in the present context inasmuch as these features become, as we shall review below, the central problem in negotiating social action.

THE PECULIARITY OF HUMAN ACTION

Freud's genius has been credited with many discoveries, notably the dynamic unconscious and the importance of infantile sexuality, with the multifarious effects of these on human behavior. But it is becoming increasingly obvious—or should be—that a comprehensive theory of human behavior will draw upon those discoveries of Freud which figure less prominently in clinical matters and which are of more general import. I am referring specifically to the genesis of the self and the ego, and to the fact of the Oedipal transition—a transition from biological proximal relationship to a succoring figure, to a distanced, symbolic relationship to the internalized values of that figure. These two general, universal developmental trends are crucial in the humanization of Homo sapiens. It is important to underscore that they are based upon one continuous thread: the change from a stimulus-response reaction to primitive anxiety, to an ego-controlled reaction.[2] The latter interposes a series of complex mechanisms between anxiety and the organism, which we have come to know as the self-system.[3] The bootstraps, so to speak, by which man lifts himself above the other animals are those which enable him to handle primitive animal annihilation-anxiety with a durative defense. The self-system is an anxiety-buffering motor that is always idling.

Now it is well known that this unique development in the animal kingdom is possible for only one reason: the development of language, which permits a self-referential existence. As the infant learns "mine-me-I" in that order, he fixes himself in a spacetime world populated by named, identifiable objects. Sullivan referred to the self-system as largely a series of linguistic tricks by which the human conciliates his environment —allays his anxiety, that is. Thus, self-reflexivity and anxiety avoidance are two sides of the same coin. They create symbolic action possibilities by making the world safe for a symbolic, self-reflexive animal.

THE SOCIOLOGICAL VIEW

Sociologists have tended to focus their attention, not on the individual, intrapsychic aspects of the defensive operations of this animal, but rather on the fact that a symbolic animal must be fashioned from the symbols inculcated by other animals. Society co-operates in its instrumental dominance over the natural environment by a joint allegiance to a shared symbolic system of meaning. If the behavioral world of the self-reflexive animal is based on a pronominal "I," then the "I" must be separated from the "not-I." In other words, the motivational goals, and the proper actions for reaching those goals, must be jointly defined as more desirable than other alternatives.[4] The animal must have, in brief, a feeling of primary value in a world of meaningful objects. Culture, in this sense, is a symbolic fiction without which the psychological animal could not act. The basis of this fiction is a pattern of values which gives vital meaning and permits action.

The problem of human behavior in social terms is nothing short of prodigious: How to bring the acutely anxiety-sensitive animals to act together, without endangering the fragile self-system of each. How, in other words, to confront a multitude of individuals with each other, and still permit them all the conviction (the fiction) that each is an object of primary value in a world of meaningful objects. In the social encounter, the indispensable internal sentiment of warm self-value that serves as an anxiety buffer is exposed to possible undermining by the very same sentiments of all others. We miss the point completely when we consider "face" an idle preoccupation of a decrepit Chinese culture. The apt term "face" refers to the turning outward for public view, and possible mishandling, of the anxiety-buffering self-esteem, so laboriously fashioned in the process of humanization. Social interaction, in other words, is a potential anarchy of psychological destruction.

When we say that an individual is properly socialized, we mean simply that the process of formation of the self-system has been secure enough to enable him to sustain interaction with someone other than the agents of his immediate socialization. If he can do this, society provides him with a conventional code of rules for interaction, by which to sustain his own face and to protect the face of others. The intricacies of this code have been masterfully detailed by Erving Goffman, in a series of landmarking writings.[5] With his two central concepts of deference and demeanor, he has shown how society provides for and even maximizes the primary sense of self-value that the individual brings with him to social encounters.

DEFENSIVE NEEDS VERSUS REQUIREMENTS OF SOCIAL ACTION

The problem, from a social point of view, is to respect the privacy and integrity of the individual and, at the very same time, to include him in social interaction. Society does this by a series of conventions which Goffman includes under two main headings: deferential rituals of avoidance and deferential rituals of presentation. The body privacy, separateness, and the integral self of the individual must be accorded a degree of avoidance behavior. Avoidance implies that everyone has the right to keep others at a certain distance and recognizes that the self is personal. Presentation, on the other hand, implies that everyone has the right to engage others, *if it is done properly*; the self is recognized as social. Thus, all the conventions of salutation, farewell, quick formal smiles of acknowledgment, facile compliments, brief adjustments of another's tie or brushing his clothing, and so on, are presentation rituals which engage his self in social intercourse.[6]

When we are slighted by a "snub" we are simply protesting that someone did not acknowledge the social existence of our self. The "Hi" makes "electric" contact and fuses two discrete selves into a social unity. The problem of deference is an extremely touchy one, precisely because self-esteem is at stake. We must exercise a social claim on each other and yet not seem to manipulate. The simple act of engaging someone by offering him a seat is fraught with possibilities of bungling. Rituals of farewell are delicately sensitive, because here the self is being released from a social situation. The release must be gentle, and not an ejection into isolation. An Italian watching his friends pull away in a train will remain on the platform waving a handkerchief in farewell until they are well out of sight—one must not coarsely break off the social fusion of selves; the magic melding must be sustained until it becomes a

thinnest thread. The members of a group long accustomed to being together develop subtle cues for taking leave and will melt apart at a slight signal, perhaps undetectable to an observer.

The further problem is that the gestures of presentation which engage the individuals in social intercourse must not encroach too much on their private selves; "a peculiar tension must be maintained"[7] between avoidance and presentation rituals. The individual, in sum, must be assured that if he intrusts his fallible face to society, it will take good care of it for him: "A social relationship . . . can be seen as a way in which the person is more than ordinarily forced to trust his self-image and face to the tact and good conduct of others."[8] If this all seems axiomatic, its simplicity is deceptive. It is only when we consider the complement to deference, the phenomenon of demeanor, that the fictional fabric of social life becomes transparently clear. Demeanor refers to the problem of social action from the point of view of the individual. Demeanor means proper deportment, dress, bearing—in a word, self-regard. The individual is tasked to respect and maintain a sense of self. For an individual to have a sense of self—and this is of fundamental importance—means sustaining a named, identifiable locus of symbolic causality, which can be counted on to communicate within the social conventions. Demeanor is the *obligation to have a self*, so that there is *something socially transactable*. But the self-contained locus of communication must behave in an expected manner, so that his inclusion within the larger plot is a matter of facility. Otherwise, people would endanger themselves in undertaking interaction with someone who does not present a socially viable self. They would expose their fragile self-esteem to an entirely capricious monstrosity.

Crucial to our understanding of the delicately staged plot of social actors within a social fiction of learned meanings, goals, and values is this: An individual who engages us by manifesting the proper deference must have an equally appropriate sense of demeanor to make the deference socially meaningful—he must present a credible stage personality. If our interlocutor does not have proper self-regard, he threatens us at the very core of our artificial action. It is fundamental to the implicit rules of social life that there must be no hint or revelation of the *unbelievably flimsy basis* for our impassioned life-and-death actions: the revelation that the self is merely an attitude of self-regard and a learned set of arbitrary conventions designed to facilitate symbolic action. The hopeful enjoinder that upholds the social fiction is: "Let us all protect each other by sincere demeanor and convincing presentations, so that we can carry on the business of living." The self-esteem of plural numbers of anxiety-prone animals must be protected so that symbolic action can continue. Not only must it be protected, it must in fact be enhanced by an intricate web of rituals for delicate handling of the self. Man must make provision for the utmost sensitivity in social intercourse. This fine social sensitivity is, as Goffman observes, largely what we mean when we speak of "universal human nature." That marvelous performer, Goethe, who even in his old age radiated an aura of indomitable selfhood, said that there was a "courtesy of the heart which is akin to love." The courtesy is the delicate handling of other selves. The love is the control of one's self so that social life can go on.

The culture protects social action in two ways. By providing a strict code of social ritual, it makes available an adaptational device designed to prevent the contamination of social intercourse with private data. The more or less "proper" thing to say in each situation is provided. At the same time, it protects the on-going action situation by ablating the irrelevancies of private data. The socially awkward person is one who is not "successfully" socialized from roughly two points of view: (1) His reaction-sensitivity prevents effective communication, and the forward motion of social action in a situation. (2) He has not learned to use with facility the social ritual rules for interaction. We can ask of an individual in this context: "How much 'reaction-sensitivity' is present in his social presentation of face (of his positive-self valuation)?" "To what extent do his needs and susceptibilities risk contaminating the smooth flow of face-saving ritual that the culture needs in order to function?"[9]

THE LINGUISTIC BASIS OF POWER

It is perhaps in the manipulation of the conversational gambits of politeness that we see best the importance to the individual of learning to use the ritual rules for interaction. It is not widely enough recognized that easy handling of the verbal context of action gives the possibility *of direct exercise of power over others.* The individual who uses with facility "I'm *terribly sorry," Good show!" "Good* to see you!" and so on, *creates the context of action* for his interlocutor, by his confident manipulation of the conventional ritual verbiage. The parent's enjoinder "Say 'thank you' to the man" is not an inculcation of obsequiousness so much as it is a training in control. It is now up to "the man" to frame an appropriate response, or to end the social situation gracefully. The proper formula delivered defines the situation for the other and is the most direct means of power. The newly liberated slave's reluctance to relinquish his lifelong pattern of obsequious formulas of deference does not derive from his "degenerate character." Rather, the formulas are his only tools for confident manipulation of the interpersonal situation—proven methods of control for which substitutes are not easily learned. Furthermore, as mentioned above, by verbally setting the tone for action by the proper ritual formula, we permit complementary action by our interlocutor. Not only do we permit it, we compel it, if mutual face is to be sustained. Thus, the subordinate not only calls the tune for his superior, but by doing his part in permitting action to continue, he infuses the situation with meaning. Finally, since action within shared meaning provides the only framework for the continual social validation of the actors, we can understand that deference is the means we have of enhancing one another.[10] The ability to use its formulas with facility actually means the power to manipulate others by providing the symbolic context for their action.[11]

Conversely, this power has a central role in the creation of the self. The simplest definition of identity is the experience of one's self as the subject and agent of one's powers.[12] Thus, the person who has not been able to exercise his powers has little experience of self, therefore, little identity. Now, using the deference-demeanor model, we can see how identity and self-experience are socially created: only by exercising demeanor and experiencing deference does the person fashion and renew himself by purposeful action in meaningful contexts.

Thus, loneliness is not only a suspension in self-acquaintance, it is a suspension in the very fashioning of identity, because, cut off from one's fellows, one cannot exercise demeanor or experience deference. Therefore, he cannot experience his own powers and come to know himself as agent of them. In this sense, identity is simply the measure of power and participation of the individual in the joint cultural staging of self-enhancing ceremony. One might say that everyone should be a talented *metteur en scène* to get along in social life. But he who is so need-disposition sensitive that he fails to learn to manipulate the ritual rules in his early peer contacts is seriously handicapped in building a strong identity: he never feeds his own power and self-acquaintance with the proper staging of demeanor, as well as with the fuel of deference from his fellows.

It is important to realize that the delicate balance of avoidance and presentation rituals is not an easy one to manipulate. And, in order to have any skill at it at all, one needs a clear definition of the situation. It is precisely this that is obscured by poor socialization. A clear definition of the situation demands an apprehension of one's private self, a sensitivity to needs and expectancies in the interaction, and last but not least, a sure cognizance of self-other discreteness. Thus, in simplest terms, we might say that the basis for social ineptitude is the failure to form an adequate phenomenological self. A feeling of primary value, separation, and de-identification of self from the succoring figure, sure possession of one's body—these have all to be under the individual's control if he is at all to get started in the complicated game of role-playing. Otherwise, we have the familiar gaucheries of an overdoing of avoidance ritual, as, for example, by not allowing oneself to be touched when it is quite in order; or overdoing of presentation ritual by overpersonal manipulations and attentions. (Cf. manic kissing and overly intimate compliments, and so on, so upsetting to his interlocutors. "Oh, there's the doctor who was *so* nice to me! Look everyone, there's the most wonderful doctor in the world; Oh I love him, I do love him, he is so super-wonderful. Here let me straighten your glasses, so you can look as handsome as you are wonderful.")

The notorious attribution to children of "cruelty" is simply a recognition that they have not yet learned to use the face-preserving and mutually enhancing social conventions. When a child first steps out into the peer group, the selves of others are not yet recognized except as something to be overcome rather than used. ("Cripple!" "fatty!" "four-eyes!") One still basks in the parental omnipotence and has no need as yet to be socially sustained and created. Actually, the early peer group contacts are crucial in learning the social rituals. One result of role-taking practice is sensitivity in sustaining a constant presentation of self against a variably responsive background. Thus, the child learns to sustain his own sense of value even in the face of negative responses. He learns whose evaluation to discount, who is overly private; he sees others making improperly personal gambits in the social situation. We all remember, hopefully, at least one such person with whom we could compare ourselves favorably in early peer interaction, and feel "properly social" at a very early age. For example, there was always one "sore loser" who filled us with a sense of social righteousness. Furthermore, in early peer contacts, the child may learn that he is justified in refusing a negative response as

emanating solely from another's private evaluation, not from his own *improperly presented self*: "Wasn't I right?" is a plea for reassurance that one is sustaining the social fiction with proper demeanor. By thus mastering early unjust evaluations in the early peer group, the child learns to sustain a steady self-valuation, without resorting to bolstering paranoid responses. He learns a realistic appraisal of the other's unwarranted privatization of the social context.

In the last analysis, power over others consists in presenting an infallible self and in commanding dexterous performance of deference. The power of the "natural leader" resides perhaps in such fortunate socialization that a convincing self is invariably put forth, with sharp separation of personal and reality needs. By putting forth a convincing self, the actor obliges others to a more careful deference. The strong self forces others to make an effort at performance that may often be beyond their means. Thus, the aura of his infallibility is enforced as their performance stumbles or becomes painfully effortful. In this sense, everyone is a potential *metteur en scène* who fashions the plot and provides the cues for proper performance by others.[13] Some are more fortunately endowed to set implicitly the tone for the performance by presenting a model self and an unshakable command of the script.[14]

SOCIALIZATION AS TRAINING IN COMMAND OF PERFORMANCE

Socialization, then, is a preparation for *social performance* of the individual actor. Using this scheme (deference-demeanor) we might ask two key sociological questions of this individual preparation, questions familiar to the clinician:

"With what behavioral style has the individual *learned* to get his self-rights respected?" How, in other words, has the child obtained appreciation from significant adults of his discrete social self? The manner of obtaining respect for self would be his basic method of comportment, or demeanor. The other important question has to do with determining his basic pattern of orientation to deference: "How has he learned to react to the hierarchialized status of others?" In other words, what kind of cognizance does he have of the plot, the fiction of social action in which he will be expected to perform? These two sets of questions are separated for conceptual purposes; actually they are part of the same judgment: *How has the actor been trained as a performer?* The social judgment of the individual can be phrased in stark terms of his rule-following ability.

Transference, understood sociologically, is simply rule-following ability as it is constricted within a narrow stylistic range. The artificial crystallization of this stylistic range is what takes place in psychoanalytic therapy. By analyzing it, the analyst hopes to permit performance over a broader range: he presents the patient "with the possibility of a greater number of choices."[15]

The individual we term schizophrenic may well be one who has never learned the simple bases for the possession of real power over his fellows by aptly wielding the verbal armament of social ritual. In Bateson's double-bind theory of schizophrenia, the individual is prevented, by ambiguities and inconsistencies of the environment, from forming a firmly oriented and consistently recognized self. From the outset, therefore, he does not have the wherewithal to play the ritual game on social terms. He has nothing that he can consistently present to confront the potential threats and uncertainties of the environment (except perhaps a certain "unanchored" symbolic dexterity to be satisfied in library halls; or, if illiterate, in shamanistic fantasies). The young schizophrenic may often provide the best example of failure to handle even the simple greeting. With a self-esteem brittle to the core, the threat of an encounter can be overwhelming. One schizophrenic at the beginning of his army career quickly signaled his "queerness" to other soldiers. He learned that a simple greeting used by all never failed to elicit a friendly response. He followed others around, even to the latrine, repeating the greeting again and again. Another learned, perhaps for the first time, a sure ritual of presentation, a reliable way to engage another in social intercourse, without eliciting a hostile response: one had only to offer a cigarette. But even this act has its appropriateness, and the others quickly became embarrassed by his incessant offerings of handfuls of cigarettes, often at inappropriate times.

One cannot overemphasize the fact that the basic pattern of deference-demeanor in a society is the necessary social nutrient for the continuing creation of the personal significance of the social actors—a sort of public mana in which everyone is rejuvenated and supplied. There is a continuing affirmation of meaning in deference-demeanor social transactions which, although purely on a fictional-symbolic level of discourse, seems vital to the very organization of the self. This symbolic sustenance, in other words, seems a *sine qua non* for creating and maintaining an integral symbolic animal. This idea in itself is certainly not new, but its consequences have still not been followed through broadly enough in psychiatry, nor with the requisite theoretical relentlessness: that we cogitate this whole problem on the organism's purely symbolic level of functioning.

Using his idea of deference and demeanor within the framework of a socially self-sustaining fiction, Goffman makes a bold attack upon the label "mental illness." It would refer, simply, to those individuals "who are the least ready to project a sustainable self."[16] Those, in other words, who most directly undermine the mutually sustaining fiction of social ceremonial and who thus prevent the peculiar type of self-justifying action necessary to the continual anxiety-buffering needs of the human animal. It is these individuals who frustrate, by their ineptitude, the best efforts of the other *metteurs en scène* to make the show go on. "One of the bases upon which mental hospitals throughout the world segregate their patients is degree of easily apparent 'mental illness.' By and large this means that patients are graded according to the degree to which they violate ceremonial rules of social intercourse."[17] However, it would be wrong to be misled by words like "cermonial" into thinking that failure to perform is anything but a vitally serious matter to a symbolic animal. Whether we use the word "fictional" to describe the anxiety-buffering self-system that is created by artificial linguistic symbols, or "ceremonial" to subsume the social means of protecting this fragile self-system, it is plain that we are not talking about inconsequential matters. These fictions are not superfluous creations that could be "put aside" so that the "more serious" business of life could continue. The flesh-and-blood action of lower animals is no more infused with seriousness than is the ethereal,

shadowy, symbolic conduct with which man organizes his dominion over nature. We may deal with flimsier coin, but like the abstractness of high finance, the business is perhaps even the more serious for it.

CONCLUSION

The view that social life is a symbolic, fictional nutrient for a self-reflexive, symbolic animal represents one direct, theoretical approach to the problems of behavioral malfunction. Seen from the individual point of view, this problem presents itself in terms of the individual's ability to sustain a self of positive value in a world of meaning and to act according to the social conventions for sustaining and reinforcing that meaning by mutual support. when we realize that the action world of a symbolic animal is fictional and continually fabricated, nourished, and validated, this does not diminish the importance of the world to the behavior of Homo sapiens. There remains the problem of individuals who *cannot follow* the social ritual rules. Questions to which behavioral specialists should be sensitized are: "In what ways is the manner in which this individual has learned to handle anxiety a hindrance in his performance of the ceremonial that permits sustenance of the social fiction of shared meaning?" "What are the rules for performance which society itself projects?" Alertness to questions such as these would lead to a more sensitive understanding of the variations in performance ability of the individual actors, and (as in existing research) the reasons for that variation. Finally, and not least important, it would contribute to a greater flexibility of appraisal of the conditions for social becoming in an open democratic society.[18]

NOTES

1. See, e.g., D. P. Ausubel, "Personality Disorder Is Disease," *American Psychologist*, XVI, No. 2 (February, 1961), 69-74; O. H. Mowrer, 'Sin,' the Lesser of Two Evils," *American Psychologist*, XV (1960), 301-4; T. S. Szasz, "The Myth of Mental Illness," *American Psychologist*, XV (1960), 113-18, and his *The Myth of Mental Illness: Foundations of a Theory of Personal Conduct* (New York: Paul B. Hoeber Inc., 1961). See also my forthcoming *The Birth and Death of Meaning: A Perspective in Psychiatric Anthropology* (New York: Free Press of Glencoe).

2. S. Freud, *The Problem of Anxiety* (New York: W. W. Norton & Co., 1936).

3. H. S. Sullivan, *The Interpersonal Theory of Psychiatry* (New York: W. W. Norton & Co., 1953).

4. A. I. Hallowell, *Culture and Experience* (Philadelphia: University of Pennsylvania Press, 1955).

5. "On Face-Work, an Analysis of Ritual Elements in Social Interaction," *Psychiatry*, XVIII (1955), 213-31; "The Nature of Deference and Demeanor," *American Anthropologist*, LVIII, No. 3 (1956), 473-502; and *The Presentation of Self in Everyday Life* ("Doubleday Anchor Book" [Garden City, N. Y.: Doubleday & Co., 1959]).

6. The details of these rituals are infinite, and nowhere better conceptualized than by Goffman. Each society, of course, has its own conventions for laying social claim to the personal self. In traditional Japan, for example, the self had to be available to society at almost all times—to close one's door during the day was a community offense.

7. Goffman, "The Nature of Deference and Demeanor," *op. cit.*, p. 488.

8. Goffman, "On Face-Work, an Analysis of Ritual Elements in Social Interaction," *op. cit.*, p. 227.

9. For example, a schizophrenic may be overperceptive, unable to shut out irrelevant definitions of the interaction situation. Thus, by his inordinate sensitivity to his interlocutor's genitals, for example, he upsets a comfortably singly defined situation with his own private data.

10. Goffman, "The Nature of Deference and Demeanor," *op. cit.*, p. 493.

11. The manic seems to make a frantic bid for this power. But his exaggerated manipulations of the verbal properties are shown to be unnatural by the discomfort they create—in place of the comfort they are supposed to create. Only the manic himself is bemusedly comfortable; and in a social context this discrepancy defines his deviance.

12. E. Fromm, *The Sane Society* (New York: Rinehart & Co., 1955).

13. Witness man's enormous expenditure of time in self-torture over having failed to say just the right thing at a particular point in conversation: "If only I had said *that!*" "If *only* I had said that." The implication in this galling preoccupation is that it was at *that* point that one could have exercised majesic control over the interaction.

14. To follow along with the film analogy: One explanation for "involutional" depression lies simply in the fact that an individual can realistically appraise his life as having fallen far short of hoped-for goals, and give up in the face of a bad job (cf. E. Bibring, "The Mechanism of Depression," in P. Greenacre [ed.], *Affective Disorders* [New York: International Universities Press, 1953]). If a sixty-year span can be calculated imaginatively as a fictional saga of sixty minutes, one can imagine the depressed *metteur en scène* who after forty minutes (forty years) of plot sees the whole thing as botched. He simply cannot pin a happy ending within twenty minutes on a forty-minute background which does not support the ending with any credulity. Therefore, the fictional meaning of the whole plot is undermined, and he can give it up as an insurmountable assignment by depressive withdrawal.

15. In this context, it is worth mentioning the usual fascination of youth for the theater. Goethe, it will be remembered, thought of acting as an indispensable preparation for adult life (Wilhelm Meister). Theatrical acting is a vicarious freedom of acting *control* of a situation. Especially noteworthy of our attention here is that this control is gained merely *by properly saying the right things*. Perfect acting is a unique exercise in omnipotence; by infallible wielding of deference and demeanor, the actor is at one and the same time indisputed director. Those of us who have never performed theatrically have perhaps experienced the sheer power-control aspects of language in learning a foreign tongue. Facility in speaking a foreign language partakes somewhat of a kindred experience in psychotherapy: the individual may find that he is capable of utterances which usher others into appropriate complementary action; but which utterances, because they are new (and in a foreign tongue) he at first experiences as unreal and somewhat ego-

alien. It is then that he can best "watch himself perform" and see in action the power aspects of language. When the utterances are finally reduced to habit, the self-critical and the acting individual becomes more fused. One's first sojourn abroad may be a quasi-psychotherapeutic exercise in freedom and power.

16. E. Goffman, "The Nature of Deference and Demeanor," *op. cit.*, p. 497.

17. *Ibid.*

18. E. Becker, "The Relevance to Psychiatry of Recent Research in Anthropology," *American Journal of Psychotherapy*, Spring, 1962.

24. ON BEING SANE IN INSANE PLACES

D. L. ROSENHAN

Reprinted from *Science*, Vol. 179, pp. 250-258, 19 January 1973. Copyright 1973 by the American Association for the Advancement of Science. The author is Professor of Psychology and Law at Stanford University, Stanford, California. Portions of Prof. Rosenhan's study were presented to colloquiums of the Psychology departments at the University of California at Berkeley and Santa Barbara, the University of Arizona, and Harvard University.

If sanity and insanity exist, how shall we know them?

The question is neither capricious nor itself insane. However much we may be personally convinced that we can tell the normal from the abnormal, the evidence is simply not compelling. It is commonplace, for example, to read about murder trials wherein eminent psychiatrists for the defense are contradicted by equally eminent psychiatrists for the prosecution on the matter of the defendant's sanity. More generally, there are a great deal of conflicting data on the reliability, utility, and meaning of such terms as "sanity," "insanity," "mental illness," and "schizophrenia"[1]. Finally, as early as 1934, Benedict suggested that normality and abnormality are not universal[2]. What is viewed as normal in one culture may be seen as quite aberrant in another. Thus, notions of normality and abnormality may not be quite as accurate as people believe they are.

To raise questions regarding normality and abnormality is in no way to question the fact that some behaviors are deviant or odd. Murder is deviant. So, too, are hallucinations. Nor does raising such questions deny the existence of the personal anguish that is often associated with "mental illness." Anxiety and depression exist. Psychological suffering exists. But normality and abnormality, sanity and insanity, and the diagnoses that flow from them may be less substantive than many believe them to be.

At its heart, the question of whether the sane can be distinguished from the insane (and whether degrees of insanity can be distinguished from each other) is a simple matter: do the salient characteristics that lead to diagnoses reside in the patients themselves or in the environments and contexts in which observers find them? From Bleuler, through Kretchmer, through the formulators of the recently revised *Diagnostic and Statistical Manual* of the American Psychiatric Association, the belief has been strong that patients present symptoms, that those symptoms can be categorized, and, implicitly, that the sane are distinguishable from the insane. More recently, however, this belief has been questioned. Based in part on theoretical and anthropological considerations, but also on philosophical, legal, and therapeutic ones, the view has grown that psychological categorization of mental illness is useless at best and downright harmful, misleading, and pejorative at worst. Psychiatric diagnoses, in this view, are in the minds of the observers and are not valid summaries of characteristics displayed by the observed[3-5].

Gains can be made in deciding which of these is more nearly accurate by getting normal people (that is, people who do not have, and have never suffered, symptoms of serious psychiatric disorders) admitted to psychiatric hospitals and then determining whether they were discovered to be sane and, if so, how. If the sanity of such pseudo-patients were always detected, there would be prima facie evidence that a sane individual can be distinguished from the insane context in which he is found. Normality (and presumably abnormality) is distinct enough that it can be recognized wherever it occurs, for it is carried within the person. If, on the other hand, the sanity of the pseudopatients were never discovered, serious difficulties would arise for those who support traditional modes of psychiatric diagnosis. Given that the hospital staff was not incompetent, that the pseudopatient had been behaving as sanely as he had been outside of the hospital, and that it had never been previously suggested that he belonged in a psychiatric hospital, such an unlikely outcome would support the view that psychiatric diagnosis betrays little about the patient but much about the environment in which an observer finds him.

This article describes such an experiment. Eight sane people gained secret admission to 12 different hospitals[6]. Their diagnostic experiences constitute the data of the first part of this article; the remainder is devoted to a description of their experiences in psychiatric institutions. Too few psychiatrists and psychologists, even those who have worked in such hospitals, know what the experience is like. They rarely talk about it with former patients, perhaps because they distrust information coming from the previously insane. Those who have worked in psychiatric hospitals are likely to have adapted so thoroughly to the settings that they are insensitive to the impact of that experience. And while there have been occasional reports of researchers who submitted themselves to psychiatric hospitalization[7], these researchers have commonly remained in the hospitals for short periods of

time, often with the knowledge of the hospital staff. It is difficult to know the extent to which they were treated like patients or like research colleagues. Nevertheless, their reports about the inside of the psychiatric hospital have been valuable. This article extends those efforts.

PSEUDOPATIENTS AND THEIR SETTINGS

The eight pseudopatients were a varied group. One was a psychology graduate student in his 20's. The remaining seven were older and "established." Among them were three psychologists, a pediatrician, a psychiatrist, a painter, and a housewife. Three pseudopatients were women, five were men. All of them employed pseudonyms, lest their alleged diagnoses embarrass them later. Those who were in mental health professions alleged another occupation in order to avoid the special attentions that might be accorded by staff, as a matter of courtesy or caution, to ailing colleagues[8]. With the exception of myself (I was the first pseudopatient and my presence was known to the hospital administrator and chief psychologist and, so far as I can tell, to them alone), the presence of pseudopatients and the nature of the research program was not known to the hospital staffs[9].

The settings were similarly varied. In order to generalize the findings, admission into a variety of hospitals was sought. The 12 hospitals in the sample were located in five different states on the East and West coasts. Some were old and shabby, some were quite new. Some were research-oriented, others not. Some had good staff-patient ratios, others were quite understaffed. Only one was a strictly private hospital. All of the others were supported by state or federal funds or, in one instance, by university funds.

After calling the hospital for an appointment, the pseudopatient arrived at the admissions office complaining that he had been hearing voices. Asked what the voices said, he replied that they were often unclear, but as far as he could tell they said "empty," "hollow," and "thud." The voices were unfamiliar and were of the same sex as the pseudopatient. The choice of these symptoms was occasioned by their apparent similarity to existential symptoms. Such symptoms are alleged to arise from painful concerns about the perceived meaninglessness of one's life. It is as if the hallucinating person were saying, "My life is empty and hollow." The choice of these symptoms was also determined by the *absence* of a single report of existential psychoses in the literature.

Beyond alleging the symptoms and falsifying name, vocation, and employment, no further alterations of person, history, or circumstances were made. The significant events of the pseudopatient's life history were presented as they had actually occurred. Relationships with parents and siblings, with spouse and children, with people at work and in school, consistent with the aforementioned exceptions, were described as they were or had been. Frustrations and upsets were described along with joys and satisfactions. These facts are important to remember. If anything, they strongly biased the subsequent results in favor of detecting sanity, since none of their histories or current behaviors were seriously pathological in any way.

Immediately upon admission to the psychiatric ward, the pseudopatient ceased simulating *any* symptoms of abnormality. In some cases, there was a brief period of mild nervousness and anxiety, since none of the pseudopatients really believed that they would be admitted so easily. Indeed, their shared fear was that they would be immediately exposed as frauds and greatly embarrassed. Moreover, many of them had never visited a psychiatric ward; even those who had, nevertheless had some genuine fears about what might happen to them. Their nervousness, then, was quite appropriate to the novelty of the hospital setting, and it abated rapidly.

Apart from that short-lived nervousness, the pseudopatient behaved on the ward as he "normally" behaved. The pseudopatient spoke to patients and staff as he might ordinarily. Because there is uncommonly little to do on a psychiatric ward, he attempted to engage others in conversation. When asked by staff how he was feeling, he indicated that he was fine, that he no longer experienced symptoms. He responded to instructions from attendants, to calls for medication (which was not swallowed), and to dining-hall instructions. Beyond such activities as were available to him on the admissions ward, he spent his time writing down his observations about the ward, its patients, and the staff. Initially these notes were written "secretly," but as it soon became clear that no one much cared, they were subsequently written on standard tablets of paper in such public places as the dayroom. No secret was made of these activities.

The pseudopatient, very much as a true psychiatric patient, entered a hospital with no foreknowledge of when he would be discharged. Each was told that he would have to get out by his own devices, essentially by convincing the staff that he was sane. The psychological stresses associated with hospitalization were considerable, and all but one of the pseudopatients desired to be discharged almost immediately after being admitted. They were, therefore, motivated not only to behave sanely, but to be paragons of cooperation. That their behavior was in no way disruptive is confirmed by nursing reports, which have been obtained on most of the patients. These reports uniformly indicate that the patients were "friendly," "cooperative," and "exhibited no abnormal indications."

THE NORMAL ARE NOT DETECTABLY SANE

Despite their public "show" of sanity, the pseudopatients were never detected. Admitted, except in one case, with a diagnosis of schizophrenia[10], each was discharged with a diagnosis of schizophrenia "in remission." The label "in remission" should in no way be dismissed as a formality, for at no time during any hospitalization had any question been raised about any pseudopatient's simulation. Nor are there any indications in the hospital records that the pseudopatient's status was suspect. Rather, the evidence is strong that, once labeled schizophrenic, the pseudopatient was stuck with that label. If the pseudopatient was to be discharged, he must naturally be "in remission"; but he was not sane, nor, in the institution's view, had he ever been sane.

The uniform failure to recognize sanity cannot be attributed to the quality of the hospitals, for, although there were considerable variations among them, several are considered excellent. Nor can it be alleged that there was simply not enough time to observe the pseudopatients. Length of hospitalization ranged from 7 to 52 days, with an average of 19 days. The pseudopatients were not, in fact, carefully observed, but this failure clearly speaks more to traditions within psychiatric hospitals than to lack of opportunity.

Finally, it cannot be said that the failure to recognize the pseudopatients' sanity was due to the fact that they were not behaving sanely. While there was clearly some tension present in all of them, their daily visitors could detect no serious behavioral consequences—nor, indeed, could other patients. It was quite common for the patients to "detect" the pseudopatients' sanity. During the first three hospitalizations, when accurate counts were kept, 35 of a total of 118 patients on the admissions ward voiced their suspicions, some vigorously. "You're not crazy. You're a journalist, or a professor [referring to the continual note-taking]. You're checking up on the hospital." While most of the patients were reassured by the pseudopatient's insistence that he had been sick before he came in but was fine now, some continued to believe that the pseudopatient was sane throughout his hospitalization[11]. The fact that the patients often recognized normality when staff did not raises important questions.

Failure to detect sanity during the course of hospitalization may be due to the fact that physicians operate with a strong bias toward what statisticians call the type 2 error[5]. This is to say that physicians are more inclined to call a healthy person sick (a false positive, type 2) than a sick person healthy (a false negative, type 1). The reasons for this are not hard to find: it is clearly more dangerous to misdiagnose illness than health. Better to err on the side of caution, to suspect illness even among the healthy.

But what holds for medicine does not hold equally well for psychiatry. Medical illnesses, while unfortunate, are not commonly pejorative. Psychiatric diagnoses, on the contrary, carry with them personal, legal, and social stigmas[12]. It was therefore important to see whether the tendency toward diagnosing the sane insane could be reversed. The following experiment was arranged at a research and teaching hospital whose staff had heard these findings but doubted that such an error could occur in their hospital. The staff was informed that at some time during the following 3 months, one or more pseudopatients would attempt to be admitted into the psychiatric hospital. Each staff member was asked to rate each patient who presented himself at admissions or on the ward according to the likelihood that the patient was a pseudopatient. A 10-point scale was used, with a 1 and 2 reflecting high confidence that the patient was a pseudopatient.

Judgments were obtained on 193 patients who were admitted for psychiatric treatment. All staff who had had sustained contact with or primary responsibility for the patient—attendants, nurses, psychiatrists, physicians, and psychologists—were asked to make judgments. Forty-one patients were alleged, with high confidence, to be pseudopatients by at least one member of the staff. Twenty-three were considered suspect by at least one psychiatrist. Nineteen were suspected by one psychiatrist and one other staff member. Actually, no genuine pseudopatient (at least from my group) presented himself during this period.

The experiment is instructive. It indicates that the tendency to designate sane people as insane can be reversed when the stakes (in this case, prestige and diagnostic acumen) are high. But what can be said of the 19 people who were suspected by being "sane" by one psychiatrist and another staff member? Were these people truly "sane,"

or was it rather the case that in the course of avoiding the type 2 error the staff tended to make more errors of the first sort—calling the crazy "sane"? There is no way of knowing. But one thing is certain: any diagnostic process that lends itself so readily to massive errors of this sort cannot be a very reliable one.

THE STICKINESS OF PSYCHODIAGNOSTIC LABELS

Beyond the tendency to call the healthy sick—a tendency that accounts better for diagnostic behavior on admission than it does for such behavior after a lengthy period of exposure—the data speak to the massive role of labeling in psychiatric assessment. Having once been labeled schizophrenic, there is nothing the pseudopatient can do to overcome the tag. The tag profoundly colors others' perceptions of him and his behavior.

From one viewpoint, these data are hardly surprising, for it has long been known that elements are given meaning by the context in which they occur. Gestalt psychology made this point vigorously, and Asch[13] demonstrated that there are "central" personality traits (such as "warm" versus "cold") which are so powerful that they markedly color the meaning of other information in forming an impression of a given personality.[14] "Insane," "schizophrenic," "manic-depressive," and "crazy" are probably among the most powerful of such central traits. Once a person is designated abnormal, all of his other behaviors and characteristics are colored by that label. Indeed, that label is so powerful that many of the pseudopatients' normal behaviors were overlooked entirely or profoundly misinterpreted. Some examples may clarify this issue.

Earlier I indicated that there were no changes in the pseudopatient's personal history and current status beyond those of name, employment, and, where necessary, vocation. Otherwise, a veridical description of personal history and circumstances was offered. Those circumstances were not psychotic. How were they made consonant with the diagnosis of psychosis? Or were those diagnoses modified in such a way as to bring them into accord with the circumstances of the pseudopatient's life, as described by him?

As far as I can determine, diagnoses were in no way affected by the relative health of the circumstances of a pseudopatient's life. Rather, the reverse occurred: the perception of his circumstances was shaped entirely by the diagnosis. A clear example of such translation is found in the case of a pseudopatient who had had a close relationship with his mother but was rather remote from his father during his early childhood. During adolescence and beyond, however, his father became a close friend, while his relationship with his mother cooled. His present relationship with his wife was characteristically close and warm. Apart from occasional angry exchanges, friction was minimal. The children had rarely been spanked. Surely there is nothing especially pathological about such a history. Indeed, many readers may see a similar pattern in their own experiences, with no markedly deleterious consequences. Observe, however, how such a history was translated in the psychopathological context, this from the case summary prepared after the patient was discharged.

This white 39-year-old male . . . manifests a long history of considerable ambivalence in close relationships, which begins in early childhood. A warm relationship with his

mother cools during his adolescence. A distant relationship to his father is described as becoming very intense. Affective stability is absent. His attempts to control emotionality with his wife and children are punctuated by angry outbursts and, in the case of the children, spankings. And while he says that he has several good friends, one senses considerable ambivalence embedded in those relationships also. . . .

The facts of the case were unintentionally distorted by the staff to achieve consistency with a popular theory of the dynamics of a schizophrenic reaction.[15] Nothing of an ambivalent nature had been described in relations with parents, spouse, or friends. To the extent that ambivalence could be inferred, it was probably not greater than is found in all human relationships. It is true the pseudopatient's relationships with his parents changed over time, but in the ordinary context that would hardly be remarkable—indeed, it might very well be expected. Clearly, the meaning ascribed to his verbalizations (that is, ambivalence, affective instability) was determined by the diagnosis: schizophrenia. An entirely different meaning would have been ascribed if it were known that the man was "normal."

All pseudopatients took extensive notes publicly. Under ordinary circumstances, such behavior would have raised questions in the minds of observers, as, in fact, it did among patients. Indeed, it seemed so certain that the notes would elicit suspicion that elaborate precautions were taken to remove them from the ward each day. But the precautions proved needless. The closest any staff member came to questioning these notes occurred when one pseudopatient asked his physician what kind of medication he was receiving and began to write down the response. "You needn't write it," he was told gently. "If you have trouble remembering, just ask me again."

If no questions were asked of the pseudopatients, how was their writing interpreted? Nursing records for three patients indicate that the writing was seen as an aspect of their pathological behavior. "Patient engages in writing behavior" was the daily nursing comment on one of the pseudopatients who was never questioned about his writing. Given that the patient is in the hospital, he must be psychologically disturbed. And given that he is disturbed, continuous writing must be a behavioral manifestation of that disturbance, perhaps a subset of the compulsive behaviors that are sometimes correlated with schizophrenia.

One tacit characteristic of psychiatric diagnosis is that it locates the sources of aberration within the individual and only rarely within the complex of stimuli that surrounds him. Consequently, behaviors that are stimulated by the environment are commonly misattributed to the patient's disorder. For example, one kindly nuuse found a pseudopatient pacing the long hospital corridors. "Nervous, Mr. X?" she asked. "No, bored," he said.

The notes kept by pseudopatients are full of patient behaviors that were misinterpreted by well-intentioned staff. Often enough, a patient would go "berserk" because he had, wittingly or unwittingly, been mistreated by, say, an attendant. A nurse coming upon the scene would rarely inquire even cursorily into the environmental stimuli of the patient's behavior. Rather, she assumed that his upset derived from his pathology, not from his present interactions with other staff members. Occasionally, the staff might assume that the patient's family (especially when they had recently visited) or other patients had stimulated the outburst. But never were the staff found to assume that one of themselves or the structure of the hospital had anything to do with a patient's behavior. One psychiatrist pointed to a group of patients who were sitting outside the cafeteria entrance half an hour before lunchtime. To a group of young residents he indicated that such behavior was characteristic of the oral-acquisitive nature of the syndrome. It seemed not to occur to him that there were very few things to anticipate in a psychiatric hospital besides eating.

A psychiatric label has a life and an influence of its own. Once the impression has been formed that the patient is schizophrenic, the expectation is that he will continue to be schizophrenic. When a sufficient amount of time has passed, during which the patient has done nothing bizarre, he is considered to be in remission and available for discharge. But the label endures beyond discharge, with the unconfirmed expectation that he will behave as a schizophrenic again. Such labels, conferred by mental health professionals, are as influential on the patient as they are on his relatives and friends, and it should not surprise anyone that the diagnosis acts on all of them as a self-fulfilling prophecy. Eventually, the patient himself accepts the diagnosis, with all of its surplus meanings and expectations, and behaves accordingly.[5]

The inferences to be made from these matters are quite simple. Much as Zigler and Phillips have demonstrated that there is enormous overlap in the symptoms presented by patients who have been variously diagnosed,[16] so there is enormous overlap in the behaviors of the sane and the insane. The sane are not "sane" all of the time. We lose our tempers "for no good reason." We are occasionally depressed or anxious, again for no good reason. And we may find it difficult to get along with one or another person—again for no reason that we can specify. Similarly, the insane are not always insane. Indeed, it was the impression of the pseudopatients while living with them that they were sane for long periods of time—that the bizarre behaviors upon which their diagnoses were allegedly predicated constituted only a small fraction of their total behavior. If it makes no sense to label ourselves permanently depressed on the basis of an occasional depression, then it takes better evidence than is presently available to label all patients insane or schizophrenic on the basis of bizarre behaviors or cognitions. It seems more useful, as Mischel[17] has pointed out, to limit our discussions to *behaviors*, the stimuli that provoke them, and their correlates.

It is not known why powerful impressions of personality traits, such as "crazy" or "insane," arise. Conceivably, when the origins of and stimuli that give rise to a behavior are remote or unknown, or when the behavior strikes us as immutable, trait labels regarding the *behaver* arise. When, on the other hand, the origins and stimuli áre known and available, discourse is limited to the behavior itself. Thus, I may hallucinate becauue I am sleeping, or I may hallucinate because I have ingested a peculiar drug. These are termed sleep-induced hallucinations, or dreams, and drug-induced hallucinations, respectively. But when the stimuli to my hallucinations are unknown, that is called craziness, or schizophrenia—as if that inference were somehow as illuminating as the others. . . .

THE CONSEQUENCES OF LABELING AND DEPERSONALIZATION

Whenever the ratio of what is known to what needs to be known approaches zero, we tend to invent "knowledge" and assume that we understand more than we actually do. We seem unable to acknowledge that we simply don't know. The needs for diagnosis and remediation of behavioral and emotional problems are enormous. But rather than acknowledge that we are just embarking on understanding, we continue to label patients "schizophrenic," "manic-depressive," and "insane," as if in those words we had captured the essence of understanding. The facts of the matter are that we have known for a long time that diagnoses are often not useful or reliable, but we have nevertheless continued to use them. We now know that we cannot distinguish insanity from sanity. It is depressing to consider how that information will be used.

Not merely depressing, but frightening. How many people, one wonders, are sane but not recognized as such in our psychiatric institutions? How many have been needlessly stripped of their privileges of citizenship, from the right to vote and drive to that of handling their own accounts? How many have feigned insanity in order to avoid the criminal consequences of their behavior, and, conversely, how many would rather stand trial than live interminably in a psychiatric hospital—but are wrongly thought to be mentally ill? How many have been stigmatized by well-intentioned, but nevertheless erroneous, diagnoses? On the last point, recall again that a "type 2 error" in psychiatric diagnosis does not have the same consequences it does in medical diagnosis. A diagnosis of cancer that has been found to be in error is cause for celebration. But psychiatric diagnoses are rarely found to be in error. The label sticks, a mark of inadequacy forever.

NOTES

1. P. Ash, *J. Abnorm. Soc. Psychol.* 44, 272 (1949); A. T. Beck, Amer. J. Psychiat. 119, 210 (1962); A. T. Boisen, *Psychiatry* 2, 233 (1938); N. Kreitman, *J. Ment. Sci.* 107, 876 (1961); N. Kreitman, P. Sainsbury, J. Morrisey, J. Towers, J. Scrivener, *ibid.*, p. 887; H. O. Schmitt and C. P. Fonda, *J. Abnorm. Soc. Psychol.* 52, 262 (1956); W. Seeman, *J. Nerv. Ment. Dis.* 118, 541 (1953). For an analysis of these artifacts and summaries of the disputes, see J. Zubin, *Annu. Rev. Psychol.* 18, 373 (1967); L. Phillips and J. G. Draguns, *ibid.* 22, 447 (1971).

2. R. Benedict, *J. Gen. Psychol.* 10, 59 (1934).

3. See in this regard H. Becker, *Outsiders: Studies in the Sociology of Deviance* (Free Press, New York, 1963); B. M. Braginsky, D. D. Braginsky, K. Ring, *Methods of Madness: The Mental Hospital as a Last Resort* (Holt, Rinehart & Winston, New York, 1969); G. M. Crocetti and P. V. Lemkau, *Amer. Sociol. Rev.* 30, 577 (1965); E. Goffman, *Behavior in Public Places* (Free Press, New York, 1964); R. D. Laing, *The Divided Self: A Study of Sanity and Madness* (Quadrangle, Chicago, 1960); D. L. Phillips, *Amer. Sociol. Rev.* 28, 963 (1963); T. R. Sarbin, *Psychol. Today* 6, 18 (1972); E. Schur, *Amer. J. Sociol.* 75, 309 (1969); T. Szasz, *Law, Liberty and Psychiatry* (Macmillan, New York, 1963); *The Myth of Mental Illness: Foundations of a Theory of Mental Illness* (Hoeber Harper, New York, 1963). For a critique of some of these views, see W. R. Gove. *Amer. Sociol. Rev.* 35, 873 (1970).

4. E. Goffman, *Asylums* (Doubleday, Garden City, N.Y., 1961).

5. T. J. Scheff, *Being Mentally Ill: A Sociological Theory* (Aldine, Chicago, 1966).

6. Data from a ninth pseudopatient are not incorporated in this report because, although his sanity went undetected, he falsified aspects of his personal history, including his marital status and parental relationships. His experimental behaviors therefore were not identical to those of the other pseudopatients.

7. A. Barry, *Bellevue Is a State of Mind* (Harcourt Brace Jovanovich, New York, 1971); I. Belknap, *Human Problems of a State Mental Hospital* (McGraw Hill, New York, 1956); W. Caudill, F. C. Redlich, H. R. Gilmore, E. B. Brody, *Amer. J. Orthopsychiat.* 22, 314 (1952); A. R. Goldman, R. H. Bohr, T. A. Steinberg, *Prof. Psychol.* 1,

427 (1970); unauthored, *Roche Report* 1 (No. 13), 8 (1971).

8. Beyond the personal difficulties that the pseudopatient is likely to experience in the hospital, there are legal and social ones that, combined, require considerable attention before entry. For example, once admitted to a psychiatric institution, it is difficult, if not impossible, to be discharged on short notice, state law to the contrary notwithstanding. I was not sensitive to these difficulties at the outset of the project, nor to the personal and situational emergencies that can arise, but later a writ of habeas corpus was prepared for each of the entering pseudopatients and an attorney was kept "on call" during every hospitalization. I am grateful to John Kaplan and Robert Bartels for legal advice and assistance in these matters.

9. However distasteful such concealment is, it was a necessary first step to examining these questions. Without concealment, there would have been no way to know how valid these experiences were; nor was there any way of knowing whether whatever detections occurred were a tribute to the diagnostic acumen of the staff or to the hospital's rumor network. Obviously, since my concerns are general ones that cut across individual hospitals and staffs, I have respected their anonymity and have eliminated clues that might lead to their identification.

10. Interestingly, of the 12 admissions, 11 were diagnosed as schizophrenic and one, with the identical symptomatology, as manic-depressive psychosis. This diagnosis has a more favorable prognosis, and it was given by the only private hospital in our sample. On the relations between social class and psychiatric diagnosis, see A. deB. Hollingshead and F. C. Redlich, *Social Class and Mental Illness: A Community Study* (Wiley, New York, 1958).

11. It is possible, of course, that patients have quite broad latitudes in diagnosis and therefore are inclined to call many people sane, even those whose behavior is patently aberrant. However, although we have no hard data on this matter, it was our distinct impression that this was not the case. In many instances, patients not only singled us out for attention, but came to imitate our behaviors and styles.

12. J. Cumming and E. Cumming, *Community Ment. Health* 1, 135 (1965); A. Farina and K. Ring, *J. Abnorm. Psychol.* 70,

47 (1965); H. E. Freeman and O. G. Simmons, *The Mental Patient Comes Home* (Wiley, New York, 1963); W. J. Johannsen, *Ment. Hygiene* 53, 218 (1969); A. S. Linsky, *Soc. Psychiat.* 5, 166 (1970).

13. S. E. Asch, *J. Abnorm. Soc. Psychol.* 41, 258 (1946); *Social Psychology* (Prentice-Hall, New York, 1952).

14. See also I. N. Mensh and J. Wishner, *J. Personality* 16, 188 (1947); J. Wishner, *Psychol. Rev.* 67, 96 (1960); J. S. Bruner and R. Tagiuri, in *Handbook of Social Psychology*, G. Lindzey, Ed. (Addison-Wesley, Cambridge, Mass., 1954), vol. 2, pp. 634-654; J. S. Bruner, D. Shapiro. R. Tagiuri, in *Person Perception and Interpersonal Behavior*, R. Tagiuri and L. Petrullo, Eds. (Stanford Univ. Press, Stanford, Calif., 1958), pp. 277-288.

15. For an example of a similar self-fulfilling prophecy, in this instance dealing with the "central" trait of intelligence, see R. Rosenthal and L. Jacobson, *Pygmalion in the Classroom* (Holt, Rinehart & Winston, New York, 1968).

16. E. Zigler and L. Phillips, *J. Abnorm. Soc. Psychol.* 63, 69 (1961). See also R. K. Freudenberg and J. P. Robertson, *A.M.A. Arch. Neurol. Psychiatr.* 76, 14 (1956).

17. W. Mischel, *Personality and Assessment* (Wiley, New York, 1968).

VII. THE NATURE OF PHYSICAL DISORDER AND DEATH

When Thomas Szasz first published his analysis of the "myth" of mental illness,[1] he was soundly denounced by most of the professionals in the field of social psychiatry. This was understandable, for Szasz was actually attacking the central assumption upon which most of social psychiatry had been operating, that mental illness was a disease entity whose distribution and social etiology could (and should) be analyzed in the same fashion as physical illness. Szasz was asking for a fundamental change of thinking regarding the subject matter of one medical specialty, psychiatry. He considered a social and not a medical definition of this subject matter essential for the adequate understanding and amelioration of "psychiatric problems." No longer was the task of social psychiatry solely to document the etiological factors producing or contributing to the medically designated disease state. Rather, the task became one of examining the whole set of interpersonal interactions that are involved in the process of being labeled and treated as a "mentally ill" person.

What Szasz argued regarding the subject matter and focus of psychiatry has slowly begun to make inroads into the social psychological analysis of other areas of medicine. Although it has long been argued that physical illness contains social and psychological components, it has only recently been attested that many of the same interactional processes that characterize becoming mentally ill typify becoming physically ill as well. The idea of a "sociology in medicine" is beginning to stand beside the traditional "sociology of medicine"[2] as a motif in medical sociology. It is presently felt by many medical sociologists that the proper understanding of human illness demands an intensive

1. Thomas A. Szasz, "The Myth Of Mental Illness," *American Psychologist* XV (February, 1960) pp. 113-118.
2. Robert Strauss, "The Nature and Status of Medical Sociology," *American Sociological Review*, Volume 22 (1957) pp. 200-204.

analysis of the social meanings that are built up around illness. This view "stresses the way in which men shape and organize the knowledge, perception, and experience of illness, and much of the substance of illness behavior, its management and treatment."[3] Human beings are biological organisms, but they respond to themselves and others in terms of the social meanings they build up in relation to the physical and biological world.

This change in thinking regarding the nature of physical illness has been most forcefully presented by Eliot Freidson. In the first article in this section, Freidson indeed argues that illness can best be understood if viewed as a social concept rather than a medical fact. He views illness as essentially one type of social deviance. The social-psychological processes involved in becoming ill differ little from the processes involved in becoming a criminal; depending on the social imputations of responsibility or non-responsibility and degree of seriousness, a deviant consults either his doctor or his lawyer. Using as his context differences in social reaction to deviance, Freidson develops an expanded classification of illness, one described in social psychological rather than medical terms.

In the second selection, Joan Emerson shows how the reality of at least one type of patient-physician relationship is embodied in social routines and reaffirmed in social interaction. Utilizing the theoretical concepts of precariousness, multiple contradictory definitions of reality, and implicit communication, she describes and documents the precarious drama of gynecological examination. In this situation, sustaining the "proper" definition of the situation involves a tremendous amount of interactive work. Among other matters, one's tone of voice, one's conversational style, and even the focus of one's eyes must be carefully managed in order that a clearly sexual contact not become an erotic one. Most gynecological examinations proceed smoothly and, consequently, the definition of the situation is established and maintained without much difficulty by the participants. However, physician and patient occasionally find themselves engaged in a definitional struggle during the encounter. In fact, neutralizing those events that threaten the "proper" reality sometimes becomes the main involvement of the relationship.

With the growing realization that illness and illness behavior are in a fundamental sense social psychological as well as physiological problems, it is not at all surprising that the phenomena of death and dying are also being analyzed in social as well as medical terms. The last two selections in this section are excerpted from some of the finest work in this relatively new area of research. The major assertion is that dying is a form of behavior. Death and dying are not identical; death is the end of life for the patient (although it may be only one incident in the career of

3. Foreword to Eliot Freidson and Judith Lorber, *Medical Men And Their Work* (Chicago: Aldine-Atherton, Inc., 1972).

those who attended the patient), while dying is a form of life that is subject to the same kinds of analysis we would apply to other episodes of conduct. The person who is dying is engaged, of course, in a type of living, and a dramaturgical social psychologist is interested in how the dying patient's life is meaningfully transformed.

David Sudnow's work is based on extensive field observations at two hospitals, one public and one private. In the selection that follows, Sudnow first establishes the fact of dying as a highly problematic social concern as opposed to a relatively straightforward medical one. While it may be said in the abstract that everyone is dying from the moment of birth, in hospitals as well as in everyday discourse the phrase "he is dying" marks off a specially labeled career on which the dying person is now embarked, one that inevitably changes both the way he looks at himself and the way others view him.

Hospitals are organized to handle death, and Sudnow distinguishes between "clinical death," or the appearance of death signs on physical examination, "biological death," or the cessation of cellular activity, and "social death," or the "point at which a patient is treated essentially as a corpse, though perhaps still clinically and biologically alive." When a person is labeled dead by others, the nature of their actions toward the dead one must change. The consequences of being labeled socially (as opposed to clinically) dead are nowhere as poignant as in the last paragraph of Sudnow's essay.

The final piece is taken from a larger set of works by Glaser and Strauss on death and dying in hospital settings. While Sudnow's work concentrates on the organizational features of the hospital itself, Glaser and Strauss' major concern is with describing the interactions between the dying patient, the hospital staff, and certain other persons. The authors' research indicates that one of the most important elements in the career of the dying patient is *awareness*.

A patient who is brought to the hospital irrevocably comatose and diagnosed as dying presents very different and many fewer problems than the patient who is conscious. With patients who die over a relatively long period of time, a decision must be reached as to whether they should be informed of their condition. Three awareness contexts are possible: (1) closed awareness, where the doctor and often other members of the staff and even the patient's family know the patient is dying but keep this information to themselves; (2) open awareness, where the patients are told they are going to die and the interaction moves on that assumption; and (3) suspicion awareness, where patients suspect they are dying and try to confirm their suspicions by seeking information from those they believe have it.

In closed awareness, the task is to manage information in such a way that the patients do not find out they are dying. Teams must be formed, dramaturgical loyalty must be elicited, and a convincing performance must be sustained whenever those who know are in the presence of the patient who does not. While closed awareness is initially easy to accomplish, it tends to break down, especially as the patient's physical condition deteriorates. Closed awareness tends to change to suspicion awareness, which eventually may become open awareness. Furthermore, the hospital is organized as a kind of information sieve, where the doctor is regarded as the only legitimate authority on such matters, as the following parable shows:

> Once upon a time a patient died and went to heaven, but was not certain where he was. Puzzled, he asked a nurse who was standing nearby: 'Nurse, am I dead?' The answer she gave him was, 'Have you asked your doctor?'[4]

Glaser and Strauss focus on a situation that contains elements of both closed and open awareness. The ritual drama of mutual pretense pertains to those situations where the patient and the staff both know the patient is dying but pretend otherwise. Their behavior denies what they both know to be true. The interaction is very subtle; either player begins the pretense game and the other must pick it up and play it properly; realistic or nonfictional action may destroy the game, and eventually the pretense ends. Both sides avoid issues that could destroy the pretense; they talk only about "safe" topics, and those things that could destroy the fiction are either ignored or managed in some way. Glaser and Strauss liken this interaction to a masquerade party in which the interactants perform carefully for each other only as long as they are together. The upshot of it all is really one of the ironies of the *American* attitude toward dying. Because *Americans* have few opportunities to engage in rehearsals for their own or others' dying performances, pretense seems easier to carry off than openness.

4. Glaser and Strauss, *Awareness of Dying* (Chicago: Aldine Publishing Co., 1965) p. VII

SUGGESTED READINGS

Becker, Ernest. *The Denial of Death*, (New York: The Free Press, 1973).

Birenbaum, A., "On Managing A Courtesy Stigma," *Journal of Health and Social Behavior*, Vol. 11 (June, 1970), pp. 196-206.

Brim, Orville, *et al.*, (eds.) *The Dying Patient*, (New York: Russell Sage Foundation, 1970).

Dreitzel, Hans Peter. *Recent Sociology No. 3: The Social Organization of Health* (New York: Macmillan, 1973).

Feifel, Herman (ed.) *The Meaning of Death*, (New York: McGraw-Hill Book Company, 1959).

Freidson, Eliot, *Professional Dominance*, (New York: Atherton Press, 1970).

Fulton, Robert (ed.). *Death and Identity*, (New York: John Wiley and Sons, 1965).

Glaser, Barney and Anselm Strauss. *Time For Dying*, (Chicago: Aldine Publishing Co., 1968).

Goffman, Erving. *Stigma*, (Englewood Cliffs, N. J.: Prentice-Hall, 1963).

Kubler-Ross, Elisabeth. *On Death and Dying*, (New York: Macmillan and Co., 1969).

Skipper, James K., and Robert C. Leonard. *Social Interaction and Patient Care*, (New York: Lippincott, 1965).

Voysey, Margaret. "Impression Management by Parents with Disabled Children," *Journal of Health and Social Behavior*, Vol. 13, No. 1 (March, 1972) pp. 80-89.

25. THE SOCIAL MEANINGS OF ILLNESS

ELIOT FREIDSON

Reprinted by permission of Dodd, Mead & Company, Inc. from *Profession o Medicine* by Eliot Freidson. Copyright© 1970 by Dodd, Mead & Company, Inc. Eliot Freidson is on the faculty at New York University. He was one of the first to recognize and write about the sociological nature of the medical enterprise. He is the author of *Profession of Medicine* and co-author of *Medical Men and Their Work*.

THE SOCIAL MEANINGS OF ILLNESS

. . . . Let us begin with the meaning of illness. As Parsons has pointed out,[1] in our time the term "illness," when used to give meaning to perceived deviance, implies that what is thought to be deviant does not arise through the deliberate, knowing choice of the actor and that it is essentially beyond his own control—that is, it is unmotivated. Furthermore, it implies that what is wrong with him is determinable by rational knowledge, and is likely to be known to and manageable by a special class of practitioners holding such knowledge. One does not therefore "judge" a sick person, for he is not to be held responsible for himself. Rather, he should put himself, or be put, into the hands of one of a number of specialists who have the knowledge and skill to help him return to as normal a state as possible. The help of those specialists usually takes the form of education and training or treatment and manipulation: economic or physical punishment is not considered to be an effective or moral method of management.

In his discussion of the social meaning of illness, Parsons goes on to delineate "the sick role." Four particular aspects of the role of the sick person are specified as follows: (1) the individual's incapacity is thought to be beyond the exercise of his own choice, and so he is *not held responsible* for it. Some curative process apart from his own motivation is necessary for recovery. (2) His incapacity is grounds for his *exemption from normal obligations.* (3) Being ill is thus to be able to *deviate legitimately,* but legitimation is conditional on the sufferer's recognition that to be ill is undesirable, something one assumes the obligation to overcome. (4) Insofar as he cannot get well by himself, the sufferer is therefore expected to *seek competent help* for his illness and to *cooperate* with attempts to get him well.

It is clear that as Parsons has defined it, the sick role requires that the incumbent seek competent help and therefore that he adopt the *patient* role. The sick role functions to put the deviant into the doctor's hands. It is composed of a set of conditions that move the sick person into the doctor's care: it thus enables the doctor to bring his competence to bear on the sick person. The physician's role in turn makes acceptable to the patient the things the physician must do in order to perform his function.

The sick role is analytically significant because it constitutes a form of deviance that is caught up in a process of social control that at once seals the deviant off from nondeviants and prevents him from becoming permanently alienated. It insulates the sick person from the well, depriving the former of unconditional legitimacy and reinforcing the latter's motivation *not* to fall ill, while at the same time pushing the former into professional institutions where he becomes dependent on those who are not sick. "The sick role is . . . a mechanism which . . . channels deviance so that the two most dangerous potentialities, namely, group formation and successful establishment of the claim to legitimacy, are avoided. The sick are tied up, not with other deviants to form a 'subculture' of the sick, but each with a group of non-sick, his personal circle and, above all, physicians. The sick thus become a statistical status class and are deprived of the possibility of forming a solidary collectivity. Furthermore, to be sick is by definition to be in an undesirable state, so that it simply does not 'make sense' to assert a claim that the way to deal with the frustrating aspects of the social system is 'for everybody to get sick.' "[2]

IMPUTING RESPONSIBILITY AND SERIOUSNESS

Parsons' notion of the sick role has stimulated a number of people in the field.[3] And with good reason, for it is a penetrating and apt analysis of sickness from a distinctly sociological point of view. However, a number of problems are raised by Parsons' formulation which must be resolved if the notion of the sick role is to have some useful relation to social reality. Let me take up the problems one by one.

First, one must note that Parson's discussion of the patient-doctor roles is intended to be relevant mainly to modern industrial society, not to all human societies. In this sense, much of what he says about such roles has no necessary relationship to his characterization of the sick role as such except in the context of Western societies.[4] Nonetheless, we may expect to find attributes of the sick role even where modern scientific medicine does not exist. What is

generically critical to the sick role is a series of social imputations and expectations, *a specific societal reaction*, not modern medicine as such. There is no logical reason why absolution from blame need rest on a medical foundation, for it can also rest on a supernatural foundation or even a foundation of chance or luck. The point is that there is absolution from blame, no matter what the rationale for it, and that where such absolution exists, the deviant is managed permissively rather than punitively. The first characteristic of the sick role—not holding the deviant responsible[5] for his deviance —thus specifies a meaning assigned to deviance that has significant implications for the way others respond to the deviant whether or not the premises of modern Western medicine are adopted.

The second aspect of the sick role —exemption from normal obligations —cannot be accepted at general, face value because variation in the degree and quality of exemption is closely related to whether or not the sufferer will be encouraged to seek treatment and even to whether exemption will be conditional or not. The degree of exemption defines whether one can adopt a specific sick role or not. In instances of what is considered minor illness, exemption is only from some of the obligations connected with an everyday role, allowing one to perform it in a somewhat variant way "because" of indisposition. In what is considered major illness, one is exempted from everyday role obligations entirely and is allowed to adopt a specific sick role instead.[6] In extreme cases—as in the "magical fright," whereby a person who believes that powerful black magic has been invoked against him obliges the magician by dying,[7] and in the self-confirming Siriono response to an individual's inability to eat by assuming he is a hopeless case and abandoning him on the trail to starve and be eaten[8]—"exemption" from ordinary obligations is so thoroughgoing that death is the consequence. Underlying and explaining the degree of exemption, then, is an imputation of a degree of seriousness to the deviance. Exemption is a *consequence* of the seriousness imputed to the deviance. By the same token, the conditional legitimation given to the behavior of the person thought to be sick, as well as the requirement that he seek competent help for the alleviation of his incapacity, are consequences of the core meanings of illness. The assignment of nonresponsibility to the person labeled deviant legitimizes his behavior so that it is conditionally acceptable to others, who "manage" or "control" him by exempting him from ordinary obligations but nonetheless requiring him to cooperate with treatment.

I believe that it is possible to use the variables stated or implied by Parsons' analysis of the sick role to serve as the foundation for a system of classifying not only illness but also other forms of deviance. The two prime variables suggested by my discussion are (1) the imputation of responsibility to the person being labeled (with all that responsibility implies for imputed motivation) and (2) the degree of seriousness imputed to his offense (with all that it implies for adopting a new role). These may be treated as independent variables from which flow variations in what is expected of the deviant, how people will behave toward him, and therefore how he will act. Whether or not a person is believed to be responsible for his perceived offenses bears closely on his moral identity and on the obligations others may feel toward him, for when a man is believed to be responsible for his misbehavior, pun-

ishment is likely to be involved in its management and moral condemnation is attached to him.[9] When he is not held responsible for it, even though the behavior itself is not what people expect of him and therefore requires some sort of control, management is likely to involve instruction, treatment, or at most permissive constraint.

The imputation of responsibility as a "ground" for behavior[10] is important precisely because it allows us to predict some of the more critical ways in which the deviant will be responded to—the content of the societal reaction. The imputation of seriousness predicts the quantity and quality of management. For example, the medical distinction between a mild upper respiratory infection and a life-threatening cardiac arrest, like the legal distinction between the offenses of jaywalking and of murder, distinguishes differences of intensity that reflect differences in quality of response. Beyond a certain point, the strength of the societal reaction in itself forces primary deviation to become secondary. Even if the societal reaction does not contain within it prescriptions for the degradation ceremony that may formally create secondary deviation,[11] we should expect that, when responded to strongly enough by others, the individual will himself organize a specifically defensive or offensive role. Thus, not mere degree or quantity of response in and of itself is what is important here. What is analytically of prime importance is the assumption that at a certain point the strength of the imputation of deviance leads to the assignment by self or others of a special deviant role to the individual. It is the strength of the societal reaction, measured by the seriousness it imputes to deviance, that may be used to predict whether primary or secondary deviation will result.

A TRIAL CLASSIFICATION OF DEVIANCE

Let us use these two dimensions to create a trial classification of deviance so that we can perceive better how it might work and what it may lack. Table 1 represents such a tentative trial with, as illustration in each cell, a label appropriate to the societal reaction of the contemporary middle class.

deviant organizing his behavior into a new role, with a sharp change in obligations and privileges.

The first thing to note about the table's representation of societal reactions which distinguish between the individual's responsibility and lack of responsibility is that it reflects two of the major social control institutions of our time—law and medicine. It does not reflect directly the professional

TABLE 25.1.

TYPES OF DEVIANCE, BY QUALITY AND QUANTITY OF THE SOCIETAL REACTION
(Contemporary American Middle-Class Reaction)

Imputation of Seriousness	Imputation of Responsibility	
	Individual Held Responsible	*Individual Not Held Responsible*
Minor Deviation	"Parking violation" Slight addition to normal obligations; minor suspension of a few ordinary privileges.	"A Cold" Partial suspension of a few ordinary obligations; slight enhancement of ordinary privileges. Obligation to get well.
Serious Deviation	"Murder" Replacement of ordinary obligations by new ones; loss of ordinary privileges.	"Heart Attack" Release from most ordinary obligations; addition to ordinary privileges. Obligation to seek help and cooperate with treatment.

. . . [T]he use of such labels (and the attributes and behaviors to which they are attached) varies by time, place, and perspective, so that any particular label may be placed in one specific cell only by adopting a given historical, cultural, professional, or other social viewpoint. What I hypothesize to be stable and independent of time, place, and perspective is not the label but the way the deviance is managed once responsibility or its lack is assigned —the obligations and privileges allowed deviants by those labeling them. So far as the deviant's own behavior goes, in both cases of the imputation of seriousness to his deviance

secondary deviation is produced, the point of view of those institutions . . .—but rather the way those institutions are embodied selectively in American middle-class reactions to deviation. Superficially, and accurately in only the most qualifiedly general way, "crimes" are those deviant acts or attributes for which people are held responsible or accountable, and "illnesses" are those for which they are not. The reactive consequence of imputing the former is punishment, whether by fine or imprisonment; the consequence of the latter is permissiveness conditional on treatment.

The other axis of classification—imputed seriousness—distinguishes the magnitude of the societal reaction, the consequences of which are either to leave the offender in his "normal" role, somewhat tempered and qualified by now-deviant attributes (that is, primary deviation, in Lemert's terms) or to push him into a new, specifically deviant role (i.e., secondary deviation). This is to say, one does not become a criminal upon being convicted of a petty offense any more than one is rushed to the hospital and put on the critical list upon being thought to have a cold.

In the case of illness the table makes a prime distinction between illness or impairment that is not organized into a special role and that which is. In the former case, exemplified by "a cold," a great many recognized illnesses and impairments fall as temporary or permanent, acute or chronic attributes of the individual that can be accommodated to while performing the roles of everyday life. No single biological "cause" or "system" joins them all together, for among them will be found what a physician may diagnose as virus or bacterial infections, trauma, and malformations, all of most diverse apparent origin, related to diverse organs, members, and systems. Furthermore, we will find there what physicians might call very serious or even inevitably fatal illness: they will fall there before they are so diagnosed and can remain there indefinitely so long as they do not impose severe material limits on performance. By and large, it is the societal reaction that establishes the homogeneity of the items falling into the category, nothing else. The same, of course, can be said for illnesses which become organized into a special role, exemplified by "heart attack": what joins them together is their identification as serious or severe and their being stripped of ordinary obligations. Such identification places the person in a new role. The biological qualities of the illness are tangential except in the context of a specific social situation involving a specific set of agents with a given diagnostic bias.

Furthermore, I might point out that some of what are *medically* labeled as illness fall into the column in which the individual is held responsible for the deviance imputed to him—that is, they become like crimes. In our present-day society, for example, lay and professional reactions toward venereal diseases tend to reflect preoccupation with the way the infection was obtained—a way for which they hold the sufferer responsible.[12] Such preoccupation is not found in the case of infections more innocently arrived at (as from the legendary toilet seat). In another context, it was observed that medical personnel withheld respect, and even care from people who attempted suicide, or were victims of brawls, or of accidents thought to occur by reason of drunkenness or carelessness.[13] While these reactions may not be prominent in the modern middle-class world, they are probably more common than we think, particularly where the sufferer has already been warned and so was expected to know better than to become sick. In any event, it must be emphasized that what might be an illness medically, sometimes in our culture and often in others, *can* fall into the left-hand column of my table as a "crime" and will be managed accordingly by those who impute to the individual responsibility for it. This *social* taxonomy is independent of a *biophysical* or medical taxonomy, though it can accommodate its content.

LEGITIMACY, STIGMA, AND PERMANENCE

The trial scheme seems to distinguish some major differences in societal reaction, yielding a typology of deviance that contains within itself both important social meanings involved in labeling and the outcomes of labeling in the form of obligations and privileges allowed to or required from the deviant. But it is nonetheless too simple a scheme to differentiate empirically significant variations in the form that socially organized illness behavior may take. It must be expanded enough to encompass those variations, but not so much as to lose the esthetic and practical virtues of simplicity.

In order to discern some of the inadequacies of the trial scheme, let us reconsider the third aspect of Parson's sick role: the conditional legitimacy assigned to the deviance.[14] To the degree that recovery is believed possible, the sick person's exemption is temporary and its legitimacy conditional on trying to get well, as Parsons indicates. But this temporary exemption is proper only for what are considered acute illnesses. It is quite inappropriate for many kinds of aberrations, including those called chronic disease and disability or impairment.[15] In such cases, legitimacy is not conditional on trying to get well, for it is believed impossible to do so. The legitimacy of the exemption is in fact absolute and invariant so long as "incurability" is imputed to the aberration. It is true that *acceptance* by others hinges on maintaining properly undisturbed social relations with them[16] and that, in our society, legitimacy is, in the case of impairment, conditional on improving oneself even though one is incurable in an absolute sense. A chronically ill or permanently impaired person who "expects too much" or "makes too many demands" is likely to be rejected by others. In that case, legitimacy is not conditional on seeking help as it is for illness believed to be acute and curable. Rather, legitimacy is conditional on limiting demands for privileges to what others consider appropriate (to what others believe one cannot be held responsible for).[17] In such an instance, then, the legitimacy of deviant behavior is *unconditional*, the variable being the limits on the amount and type of deviant behavior. I suspect that in our time more varied types of behavior and a greater amount of deviant behavior are likely to be considered legitimate, even if conditionally, for the person believed to have an acute, curable illness, than for one believed to have a chronic, "incurable" impairment.

Another special situation in which the concept of legitimacy seems to be involved is that occurring when stigma is attached to an attribute or act. If we follow Goffman's discussion of stigma, we see it as a societal reaction that "spoils" normal identity. It is a reaction that, if it does not require the performance of a normal role, at least requires that the normal role be performed incompletely, be itself deformed, and that everyday interaction be in some sense strained. What is analytically peculiar about the assignment of stigma is the fact that while a stigmatized person need not be held responsible for what is imputed to him, nonetheless, somewhat like those to whom responsibility is imputed, he is denied the ordinary privileges of social life. As the term itself implies, the societal reaction, although ambiguously, attributes moral deficiency to the stigmatized. Furthermore, unlike other imputed qualities, stigma is by definition ineradicable and irreversible: it is so closely connected with identity that even after the cause of the imputation of stigma has been removed and the societal reaction has been ostensibly redirected, identity is formed by the fact of *having* been in a stigmatized role: the cured mental patient is not just another person, but an ex-mental patient; the rehabilitated criminal gone straight is an ex-convict. One's identity is permanently spoiled. We do not similarly label people ex-traffic offenders, or ex-asthmatics—cases in which stigma is not attached to the deviation.[18]

Essentially, I believe it can be said that while many of those stigmatized by others are not held responsible for their deviance, the assignment of stigma in essence withholds legitimacy from the privileges they seek and imposes special obligations on them. In this it resembles crime more than illness. As I have already noted in referring to Goffman's analysis, the stigmatized person's *identity*, if not health, is incurably spoiled, in that having been a stigmatized deviant remains a part of his identity even though the physically visible or institutional stigmata have been removed. A stigma, furthermore, interferes with normal interaction, for while people need not hold the deviant responsible for his stigma, they are nonetheless embarrassed, upset, or even revolted by it. The "good" stigmatized deviant is therefore expected to take special pains to organize his behavior and his life in such a way as to save others from embarrassment. For "normal" illness, many normal obligations are suspended; only the obligation to seek help is incurred. But in the case of the stigmatized, a complex variety of new obligations is incurred. Whereas in the former instance the burden of adjustment (through permissiveness and support) lies on the

"normals" around the sick person, the burden in the latter lies on the stigmatized person when he is around "normals."

Finally, and obviously, in the light of what has already been said, I may note that Parsons' fourth component of the sick role—the obligations to seek competent help and to cooperate in treatment—is relevant to acute curable illness, but relevant to others only in a quite variable way. Some attributes defined as illness, impairment, or deficiency remain merely that—an idiosyncrasy of the person, adjusted to by others without any special problem or expectation that he seek treatment. The slightly hard-of-hearing person, the "sickly" woman, and those with "rose fever" and "lumbago" all establish the legitimacy of their foibles without incurring the obligation to seek help, perhaps because, or as long as, their claim to privilege is rather modest. Even if their "illnesses" are "curable" or "improvable," so long as they are the basis for only minor claims, others seem to apply little pressure to them to seek treatment. At the other extreme are those which have been explicitly defined as chronic, hopeless, or incurable. These two do not maintain legitimacy by seeking competent help: they gain legitimacy by having been defined as chronic.

AN EXPANDED CLASSIFICATION OF ILLNESS

Close examination of the four elements of the sick role postulated by Parsons leads inevitably to the conclusion that we cannot rest content with the trial classification, which merely distinguishes "crime" from "illness," and minor crime or illness from crime or illness organized into a criminal or sick role. Foregoing concern with "crime," which is not the focus of interest here, it is patent that "illness" as a form of deviance must be classified in a more complicated way to mirror the implications of words like "chronicity" and "stigma." This is the task I shall undertake now.

The key to ordering the classifying of the societal reaction elicited by such labels as "acute," "chronic," and "stigma" is, I believe, the notion of legitimacy. In Parsons' analysis one may remember that the notion of legitimacy is important in distinguishing the criminal from the sick. In the case of the sick role in particular, however, it is a special kind of legitimacy that is operative—conditional and temporary legitimacy. In Parsons' analysis, it is precisely the conditional character of the legitimacy that motivates the sick to seek care and/or return to normal. But where imputed illness is thought to be incurable or chronic, its legitimacy can no longer be conditional; the legitimacy of being considered deviant is in effect unconditional. And when a stigmatized illness is imputed, one may say that the illness is actually illegitimate; it is not an acceptable kind of deviance even though it may be thought to be an illness. In sum, one may distinguish three kinds of legitimacy: (1) *conditional legitimacy*, the deviant being temporarily exempted from normal obligations and gaining some extra privileges on the condition that he seek the help necessary to rid himself of his deviance; (2) *unconditional legitimacy*, the deviant being exempted permanently from normal obligations and obtaining additional privileges in view of the hopeless character imputed to his deviance; and (3) *illegitimacy*, the deviant being exempted from some normal obligations by virtue of deviance for which he is not held technically responsible, but

gaining few if any privileges and taking on some especially handicapping new obligations.

This third dimension of classification is present in Table 2, along with examples of the "illnesses" likely to be assigned to each of the categories by the middle class of our time. In evaluating the examples, one must remember that other social groups or cultures in this and other times and places would assign deviance differently and use different labels. Most important to remember is that the ideology (if not the actual behavior) of contemporary professionals in the health field asserts that to the professional all is legitimate, that there is no illegitimate illness. There may be illegitimate ways of *acting* sick, but not of *being* sick. Should we create a table for the professional societal reaction, and should we choose to mirror the professional ideology, we would have to leave the "illegitimate" column empty. We would, however, have to think carefully about the social nature of such medical labels as "hypochondriasis" and "malingering."[19]

The first distinction to be noted in the table is that between the rows, "minor" and "serious." These differences in reaction to and imputation of deviance are significant here because they recognize the empirical fact of the strength of response to an attribute. They are also important because they imply the analytical distinction between deviance that is allowed to remain an individual attribute (an idiosyncratic mode of performing everyday roles), and deviance that becomes organized into a special role (distinct from one's other roles and even on occasion central to one's identity, dominating all other roles). It is only in the latter case, along the second row, that special deviant roles may be said to exist. In cell 1, stigma somewhat spoils one's regular identity, but does not replace it. In cells 2 and 3, "illness" or "impairment" qualifies but does not replace regular roles, the qualification being temporary in cell 2 and permanent in cell 3. The *sick role*, as Parsons defines it, is only to be found in cell 5 of the table. *Stigmatized roles* are to be found in cell 4, and, insofar as nothing more can be done for them by experts, *chronic sick or dying roles* are to be found in cell 6.[20]

By means of my classification I have identified six analytically distinct varieties of deviance that might all ordinarily have been called "illness." Each implies quite different consequences for the individual and for the social system in which he is to be found, consequences for personal identity on the one hand, and for the formation of deviant strata in society on the other. Each is managed or treated differently

by those around the deviant. The deviant must therefore behave differently in turn.

ILLNESS AS PROCESS

The analytical categories to be found in Table 2 are, naturally, static and fixed by the nature of the taxonomic method. However, neither the physician's view of disease nor the sociologist's view of deviance can afford to confuse static taxonomic categories with reality. Organically, diseases have onsets, climaxes, and outcomes that, during any single course, pass through identifiable stages marked by stable configurations of signs and symptoms. This movement is also to be observed in human efforts at finding meaning in experience. In medicine, the physician's diagnostic

TABLE 25.2.

TYPES OF DEVIANCE FOR WHICH THE INDIVIDUAL IS NOT HELD RESPONSIBLE, BY IMPUTED LEGITIMACY AND SERIOUSNESS

(Contemporary American Middle Class Societal Reaction)

Imputed Seriousness	Illegitimate (Stigmatized)	Conditionally Legitimate	Unconditionally Legitimate
Minor Deviation	Cell 1. "Stammer" Partial suspension of some ordinary obligations; few or no new privileges; adoption of a few new obligations.	Cell 2. "A Cold" Temporary suspension of few ordinary obligations; temporary enhancement of ordinary privileges. Obligation to get well.	Cell 3. "Pockmarks" No special change in obligations or privileges.
Serious Deviation	Cell 4. "Epilepsy" Suspension of some ordinary obligations; adoption of new obligations; few or no new privileges.	Cell 5. "Pneumonia" Temporary release from ordinary obligations; addition to ordinary privileges. Obligation to cooperate and seek help in treatment.	Cell 6. "Cancer" Permanent suspension of many ordinary obligations; marked addition to privileges.

(or labeling) behavior may also be seen to have a course, moving from one diagnosis (or imputation of deviance) to another in the process of trying to find a consequential method of management: some diagnoses are imputed only after all others have yielded negative results. And so it is with the lay middle-class societal reaction of our time—that the first response to perceived illness is likely to be found in cell 2, and end there. If, however, the perception of deviance persists and responses to it intensify, responses may move to any one of the other cells, though they are most likely to move to cell 5—the sick role—first, and only then move to other possibilities.[21]

One way to see these sequential relationships is to take the set of possibilities commonly surrounding poliomyelitis a decade ago in the United States and arrange them according to my classification.[22] This is tentatively done in Table 3. The first perception tends to be of a cold (Cell 2), but then the individual is moved into a sick role and diagnosed as having poliomyelitis (Cell 5). If no ill effect is thought to follow, recovery is said to occur and the person is returned to normal, for it is in the nature of the sick role to be temporary.[23] But following illness a number of other things can and do

happen. Matters may progress to the point where recovery, even survival is thought to be impossible, leading into a chronic sick or dying role (Cell 6). Or as a consequence of infection, severe paralysis may follow such that the individual needs braces and supports to move about and must learn to play the stigmatized role of the cripple (Cell 4). Or he may recover sufficiently to be left with only a slight, visible limp, which is a mildly stigmatized part of his normal roles (Cell 1). Or finally, he may be left with some relatively easily concealed, minimal muscular impairment that merely marks his personal manner of performing everyday roles—labeled scholarly or unathletic, without stigmatizing him (Cell 3). Generally, I suspect that most movements through these categories are irreversible in any single course of illness, through miraculous recoveries have been known to occur, as have remissions.

This course of movement through the various categories of deviance is not unusual. Rather, it is normal and everyday procedure for one to assume that he has a cold that will go away by itself before he assumes he has pneumonia, to assume a sprain before a fracture, eyestrain before glaucoma, nervousness before psychosis. It is also

TABLE 25.3.
SYMPTOMS AND SEQUELAE OF POLIOMYELITIC BY TYPE OF DEVIANCE
(Lower-Middle Class Americans, 1955) *

Imputation of Seriousness	Illegitimate	Conditionally Legitimate	Unconditionally Legitimate
Minor	"Limp" Cell 1	"Cold" Cell 2	"Weak" Cell 3
Serious	"Cripple" Cell 4	"Polio victim" Cell 5	"Iron lung case" Cell 6

*Cf. Fred Davis, *Passage Through Crisis, Polio Victims and Their Families* (Indianapolis: The Bobbs-Merrill Co., 1963).

obvious that seeking help and cooperating in treatment do not always end the matter: it may lead to assignment to a stigmatized form of deviance, or it may have after-effects in the form of impairment. Since movement or reassignment is quite common, and since the points of movement can be labeled and therefore conventionalized, their meaning common for all engaged in the movement, it is appropriate to call the movement a career—a conventionally patterned sequence of social events through which people pass. And thus we may impose form on change, pointing to the orderly social processes experienced by the deviant by the use of the concept of career.[24] We can define the points of the sequence by the roles or imputations that the individual experiences in the course of his movement through various agencies of social control, medical or otherwise.

The concept of career does more than merely arrange the various types of deviance like beads on a string of time. It also provides a conceptual mechanism that links individuals and their experience to the community, lay and professional, for in his movement from one position to another, the individual typically has experience with different agents and agencies of social control.[25] On the most ordinary level of primary deviation he is largely in contact with his intimates, familial or otherwise. But, by Parsons' definition, when he moves into the sick role in the United States, he is obliged to move into the purview of a professional, usually the physician. Similarly, when he moves across to one of the other roles connected with illness and disability, he is likely to move into the purview of other agents—a medical specialist, to take the most common contingency. Thus, the shape of his career of illness can be constructed out of the sequence of agents and agencies he passes through, much as the shape of an occupational career is often constructed out of the sequence of jobs and employers a man holds during his working life.

NOTES

1. The following discussion is based on Talcott Parsons, *The Social System* (New York: The Free Press of Glencoe, 1951), pp. 428-447.

2. *Ibid.*, p. 477.

3. See, for example, Gerald Gordon, *Role Theory and Illness* (New Haven, Connecticut: College and University Press, 1966).

4. Cf. Parsons, *op. cit.*, pp. 475-476.

5. The idea of personal responsibility is a critical foundation for Western society, if not all societies. Its importance may not be overemphasized even though I cannot dwell on it at any length here. For some important distinctions among types of responsibility in a medical setting, see Thomas S. Szasz, *Law, Liberty and Psychiatry* (New York: The Macmillan Co., 1963), pp. 124-125. For an empirical study of its importance, see C. Richard Fletcher, "Attributing Responsibility to the Deviant: A Factor in Psychiatric Referrals by the General Public," *Journal of Health and Social Behavior*, VIII (1967), 185-196.

6. For an empirical exploration, see Andrew C. Twaddle, "Health Decisions and Sick Role Variations: An Exploration," *Journal of Health and Social Behavior*, X (1969), 105-115.

7. See W. B. Cannon, "Voodoo Death," *American Anthropologist*, XLIV (1942), 169-181; John Gillin, "Magical Fright," *Psychiatry*, I (1948), 387-400; W. Lloyd Warner, *A Black Civilization* (New York: Harper, 1936), pp. 240-243.

8. Alan Holmberg, "Nomads of the Long Bow: The Siriono of Eastern Bolivia," *Smithsonian Institution Publication* No. 10 (1950), pp. 86-87.

9. See the extensive and sophisticated discussion of Villhelm Aubert and Sheldon Messinger, "The Criminal and the Sick," *Inquiry*, I (1958), 137-160.

10. See Harold Garfinkel, "Conditions of

Successful Degradation Ceremonies," *American Journal of Sociology*, LXI (1956), 420-424.

11. *Ibid.*

12. See, for example, the description in Howard S. Becker *et al.*, *Boys in White* (Chicago: University of Chicago Press, 1961), pp. 323-327.

13. Barney G. Glaser and Anselm L. Strauss, *Awareness of Dying* (Chicago: Aldine Publishing Co., 1965), p. 83.

14. For an empirical exploration, see Frank A. Petroni, "The Influence of Age, Sex and Chronicity in Perceived Legitimacy to the Sick Role," *Sociology and Social Research*, LIII (1969), 180-193.

15. For a review of a great deal of material bearing on impairment and disabling illness, see Roger Barker *et al.*, "Adjustment to Physical Handicap and Illness: A Survey of the Social Psychology of Physique and Disability," *Social Science Research Council Bulletin*, 55 (revised 1953); and Beatrice A. Wright, *Physical Disability, a Psychological Approach* (New York: Harper and Row, 1960). For an attempt to make sense of these problems sociologically see Eliot Freidson, "Disability as Social Deviance," in M. B. Sussman, ed., *Sociology and Rehabilitation* (Washington, D. C.: American Sociological Association, 1966), pp. 71-99.

16. See Erving Goffman, *Stigma: Notes on the Management of Spoiled Identity* (Englewood Cliffs, New Jersey: Spectrum Books, 1963).

17. See the discussion in Edwin J. Thomas, "Problems of Disability from the Perspective of Role Theory," *Journal of Health and Human Behavior*, VII (1966), 2-13.

18. See the discussion of Thomas J. Scheff, *Being Mentally Ill: A Sociological Theory* (Chicago: Aldine Publishing Co., 1966), pp. 55-101.

19. See Thomas S. Szasz, "Malingering: 'Diagnosis' or Social Condemnation," *AMA Archives of Neurology and Psychiatry*, LXXVI (1956), 438-440.

20. See Aaron Lipman and Richard S. Sterne, "Aging in the United States: Ascription of a Terminal Sick Role," *Sociology and Social Research*, LIII (1969), 194-203.

21. We must not forget that people also anticipate the occurrence of deviance. Some seek to prevent it by special precautions. Others, like those descending from the unhappy Long Island couple from whom Huntington's chorea is traced, may anticipate only death at an early middle age. I am indebted to Paul J. Sanazaro for this reminder.

22. Here I rely on Fred Davis, *Passage Through Crisis, Polio Victims and Their Families* (Indianapolis: Bobbs-Merrill Co., 1963).

23. The cyclical character of the movement from normal to sick and back to normal is stressed in Bernard Goldstein and Paul Dommermuth, "The Sick Role Cycle: An Approach to Medical Sociology," *Sociology and Social Research*, XLVII (1961), 1-12.

24. See the remarks on the use of the idea of career for understanding the etiology of social deviance in Howard S. Becker, *Outsiders, Studies in the Sociology of Deviance* (New York: The Free Press of Glencoe, 1963), pp. 19-39.

25. See Elaine Cumming, *Systems of Social Regulation* (New York: Atherton Press, 1968).

26. BEHAVIOR IN PRIVATE PLACES: SUSTAINING DEFINITIONS OF REALITY IN GYNECOLOGICAL EXAMINATIONS

JOAN EMERSON

Reprinted from Hans Peter Dreitzel, *Recent Sociology No. 2* (New York: Macmillan, 1970), pp. 74-97, with permission of the author and Macmillan. Joan Emerson completed her Ph.D. at the University of California at Berkeley. Her dissertation dealt with the social functions of humor. Dr. Emerson has taught at the State University of New York at Buffalo.

I. INTRODUCTION*

In *The Social Construction of Reality*, Berger and Luckmann discuss how people construct social order and yet construe the reality of everyday life to exist independently of themselves.[1] Berger and Luckmann's work succeeds in synthesizing some existing answers with new insights. Many sociologists have pointed to the importance of social consensus in what people believe; if everyone else seems to believe in something, a person tends to accept the common belief without question. Other sociologists have discussed the concept of legitimacy, an acknowledgment that what exists has the right to exist, and delineated various lines of argument which can be taken to justify a state of affairs. Berger

* Arlene K. Daniels has applied her talent for editing and organizing to several drafts of this paper. Robert M. Emerson, Roger Pritchard, and Thomas J. Scheff have also commented on the material. The investigation was supported in part by a predoctoral fellowship from the National Institute of Mental Health (Fellowship Number MPM—18,239) and by Behavioral Sciences Training Grant MH—8104 from the National Institute of Mental Health, as well as General Research Support Grant I—SOI—FR—05441 from the National Institutes of Health, U.S. Department of Health, Education, and Welfare to the School of Public Health, University of California, Berkeley.

and Luckmann emphasize three additional processes that provide persons with evidence that things have an objective existence apart from themselves. Perhaps most important is the experience that reality seems to be out there before we arrive on the scene. This notion is fostered by the nature of language, which contains an all-inclusive scheme of categories, is shared by a community, and must be learned laboriously by each new member. Further, definitions of reality are continuously validated by apparently trivial features of the social scene, such as details of the setting, persons' appearance and demeanor, and "inconsequential" talk. Finally, each part of a systematic world view serves as evidence for all the other parts, so that reality is solidified by a process of intervalidation of supposedly independent events.

Because Berger and Luckmann's contribution is theoretical, their units of analysis are abstract processes. But they take those processes to be grounded in social encounters. Thus, Berger and Luckmann's theory provides a framework for making sense of social interaction. In this paper observations of a concrete situation will be interpreted to show how reality is embodied in routines and reaffirmed in social interaction.

Situations differ in how much effort

it takes to sustain the current definition of the situation. Some situations are relatively stable; others are precarious.[2] Stability depends on the likelihood of three types of disconforming events. Intrusions on the scene may threaten definitions of reality, as when people smell smoke in a theater or when a third person joins a couple and calls one member by a name the second member does not recognize. Participants may deliberately decline to validate the current reality, like Quakers who refused to take off their hats to the king. Sometimes participants are unable to produce the gestures which would validate the current reality. Perhaps a person is ignorant of the relevant vocabulary of gestures. Or a person, understanding how he should behave, may have limited social skills so that he cannot carry off the performance he would like to. For those who insist on "sincerity," a performance becomes especially taxing if they lack conviction about the trueness of the reality they are attempting to project.

A reality can hardly seem self-evident if a person is simultaneously aware of a counterreality. Berger and Luckmann write as though definitions of reality were internally congruent. However, the ordinary reality may contain not only a dominant definition, but in addition counterthemes opposing or qualifying the dominant definition. Thus, several contradictory definitions must be sustained at the same time. Because each element tends to challenge the other elements, such composite definitions of reality are inherently precarious even if the probability of disconfirming events is low.

A situation where the definition of reality is relatively precarious has advantages for the analysis proposed here, for processes of sustaining reality should be more obvious where that reality is problematic. The situation chosen, the gynecological examination,[3] is precarious for both reasons discussed above. First, it is an excellent example of multiple contradictory definitions of reality, as described in the next section. Second, while intrusive and deliberate threats are not important, there is a substantial threat from participants' incapacity to perform.

Dramaturgical abilities are taxed in gynecological examinations because the less convincing reality internalized by secondary socialization is unusually discrepant with rival perspectives taken for granted in primary socialization.[4] Gynecological examinations share similar problems of reality-maintenance with any medical procedure, but the issues are more prominent because the site of the medical task is a woman's genitals. Because touching usually connotes personal intimacy, persons may have to work at accepting the physician's privileged access to the patient's genitals.[5] Participants are not entirely convinced that modesty is out of place. Since a woman's genitals are commonly accessible only in a sexual context, sexual connotations come readily to mind. Although most people realize that sexual responses are inappropriate, they may be unable to dismiss the sexual reaction privately and it may interfere with the conviction with which they undertake their impersonal performance. The structure of a gynecological examination highlights the very features which the participants are supposed to disattend. So the more attentive the participants are to the social situation, the more the unmentionable is forced on their attention.

The next section will characterize the complex composition of the definition of reality routinely sustained in gynecological examinations. Then some of the routine arrangements and interactional maneuvers which embody and express this definition will be described. A later section will discuss threats to the definition which arise in the course of the encounter. Measures that serve to neutralize the threats and reaffirm the definition will be analyzed. The concluding section will turn to the theoretical issues of precariousness, multiple contradictory definitions of reality, and implicit communication.

II. THE MEDICAL DEFINITION AND ITS COUNTERTHEMES

Sometimes people are in each other's presence in what they take to be a "gynecological examination." What happens in a gynecological examination is part of the common stock of knowledge. Most people know that a gynecological examination is when a doctor examines a woman's genitals in a medical setting. Women who have undergone this experience know that the examination takes place in a special examining room where the patient lies with her buttocks down to the edge of the table and her feet in stirrups, that usually a nurse is present as a chaperone, that the actual examining lasts only a few minutes, and so forth. Besides knowing what equipment to provide for the doctor, the nurse has in mind a typology of responses patients have to this situation, and a typology of doctors' styles of performance. The doctor has technical knowledge about the examining procedures, what observations may be taken to indicate, ways of getting patients to relax, and so on.

Immersed in the medical world where the scene constitutes a routine, the staff assume the responsibility for a credible performance. The staff take part in gynecological examinations many times a day, while the patient is a fleeting visitor. More deeply convinced of the reality themselves, the staff are willing to convince skeptical patients. The physician guides the patient through the precarious scene in a contained manner: taking the initiative, controlling the encounter, keeping the patient in line, defining the situation by his reaction, and giving cues that "this is done" and "other people go through this all the time."

Not only must people continue to believe that "this is a gynecological examination," but also that "this is a gynecological examination going right." The major definition to be sustained for this purpose is "this is a medical situation" (not a party, sexual assault, psychological experiment, or anything else). If it is a medical situation, then it follows that "no one is embarrassed"[6] and "no one is thinking in sexual terms."[7] Anyone who indicates the contrary must be swayed by some nonmedical definition.

The medical definition calls for a matter-of-fact stance. One of the most striking observations about a gynecological examination is the marked implication underlying the staff's demeanor toward the patient: "Of course, you take this as matter-of-factly as we do." The staff implicitly contend: "In the medical world the pelvic area is like any other part of the body; its private and sexual connotations are left behind when you enter the hospital." The staff want it understood that their gazes take in only medically pertinent facts, so they are not concerned with an aesthetic inspection of a patient's body. Their nonchalant pose attempts to put a gynecological examination in the same light as an internal examination of the ear.

Another implication of the medical

definition is that the patient is a technical object to the staff. It is as if the staff work on an assembly line for repairing bodies; similar body parts continually roll by and the staff have a particular job to do on them. The staff are concerned with the typical features of the body part and its pathology rather than with the unique features used to define a person's identity. The staff disattend the connection between a part of the body and some intangible self that is supposed to inhabit that body.

The scene is credible precisely because the staff act as if they have every right to do what they are doing. Any hint of doubt from the staff would compromise the medical definition. Since the patient's nonchalance merely serves to validate the staff's right, it may be dispensed with without the same threat. Furthermore, the staff claim to be merely agents of the medical system, which is intent on providing good health care to patients. This medical system imposes procedures and standards which the staff are merely following in this particular instance. That is, what the staff do derives from external coercion—"We have to do it this way"—rather than from personal choices which they would be free to revise in order to accommodate the patient.

The medical definition grants the staff the right to carry out their task. If not for the medical definition the staff's routine activities could be defined as unconscionable assaults on the dignity of individuals. The topics of talk, particularly inquiries about bodily functioning, sexual experience, and death of relatives might be taken as offenses against propriety. As for exposure and manipulation of the patient's body, it would be a shocking and degrading invasion of privacy were the patient not defined as a technical object. The infliction of pain

would be mere cruelty. The medical definition justifies the request that a presumably competent adult give up most of his autonomy to persons often subordinate in age, sex, and social class. The patient needs the medical definition to minimize the threat to his dignity; the staff need it in order to inveigle the patient into cooperating.

Yet definitions that appear to contradict the medical definition are routinely expressed in the course of gynecological examinations. Some gestures acknowledge the pelvic area as special; other gestures acknowledge the patient as a person. These counterdefinitions are as essential to the encounter as the medical definition. We have already discussed how an actor's lack of conviction may interfere with his performance. Implicit acknowledgments of the special meaning of the pelvic area help those players hampered by lack of conviction to perform adequately. If a player's sense of "how things really are" is implicitly acknowledged, he often finds it easier to adhere outwardly to a contrary definition.

A physician may gain a patient's cooperation by acknowledging her as a person. The physician wants the patient to acknowledge the medical definition, cooperate with the procedures of the examination, and acknowledge his professional competence. The physician is in a position to bargain with the patient in order to obtain this cooperation. He can offer her attention and acknowledgment as a person. At times he does so.

Although defining a person as a technical object is necessary in order for medical activities to proceed, it constitutes an indignity in itself. This indignity can be canceled or at least qualified by simultaneously acknowledging the patient as a person.

The medical world contains special

activities and special perspectives. Yet the inhabitants of the medical world travel back and forth to the general community where modesty, death, and other medically relevant matters are regarded quite differently. It is not so easy to dismiss general community meanings for the time one finds oneself in a medical setting. The counterthemes that the pelvic area is special and that patients are persons provide an opportunity to show deference to general community meanings at the same time that one is disregarding them.

Sustaining the reality of a gynecological examination does not mean sustaining the medical definition, then. What is to be sustained is a shifting balance between medical definition and counterthemes.[8] Too much emphasis on the medical definition alone would indermine the reality, as would a flamboyant manifestation of the counterthemes apart from the medical definition. The next three sections will suggest how this balance is achieved.

III. SUSTAINING THE REALITY

The appropriate balance between medical definition and counterthemes has to be created anew at every moment. However, some routinized procedures and demeanor are available to participants in gynecological examinations. Persons recognize that if certain limits are exceeded, the situation would be irremediably shattered. Some arrangements have been found useful because they simultaneously express medical definition and countertheme. Routine ways of meeting the task requirements and also dealing with "normal trouble" are available. This section will describe how themes and counterthemes are embodied in routinized procedures and demeanor.

The prevasiveness of the medical definition is expressed by indicators that the scene is enacted under medical auspices.[9] The action is located in "medical space" (hospital or doctor's office). Features of the setting such as divisions of space, decor, and equipment are constant reminders that it is indeed "medical space." Even background details such as the loudspeaker calling, "Dr. Morris. Dr. Armand Morris" serve as evidence for medical reality (suppose the loudspeaker were to announce instead, "Five minutes until post time"). The staff wear medical uniforms, don medical gloves, use medical instruments. The exclusion of lay persons, particularly visitors of the patient who may be accustomed to the patient's nudity at home, helps to preclude confusion between the contact of medicine and the contact of intimacy.[10]

Some routine practices simultaneously acknowledge the medical definition and qualify it by making special provision for the pelvic area. For instance, rituals of respect express dignity for the patient. The patient's body is draped so as to expose only that part which is to receive the technical attention of the doctor. The presence of a nurse acting as "chaperone" cancels any residual suggestiveness of male and female alone in a room.[11].

Medical talk stands for and continually expresses allegiance to the medical definition. Yet certain features of medical talk acknowledge a nonmedical delicacy. Despite the fact that persons present on a gynecological ward must attend to many topics connected with the pelvic area and various bodily functions, these topics are generally not discussed. Strict conventions dictate what unmentionables are to be acknowledged under what circumstances. However, persons are exceptionally free to refer to the genitals and related matters on the obstetrics-gynecology service. If technical matters in regard to the pelvic area come up, they are to be discussed nonchalantly.

The special language found in staff-patient contacts contributes to depersonalization and desexualization of the encounter. Scientific-sounding medical terms facilitate such communication. Substituting dictionary terms for everyday words adds formality. The definite article replaces the pronoun adjective in reference to body parts, so that for example, the doctor refers to "the vagina" and never "your vagina." Instructions to the patient in the course of the examination are couched in language which bypasses sexual imagery; the vulgar connotation of "spread your legs" is generally metamorphosed into the innocuous "let your knees fall apart."

While among themselves the staff generally use explicit technical terms, explicit terminology is often avoided in staff-patient contacts.[12] The reference to the pelvic area may be merely understood, as when a patient says: "I feel so uncomfortable there right now" or "They didn't go near to this area, so why did they have to shave it?" In speaking with patients the staff frequently uses euphemisms. A doctor asks: "When did you first notice difficulty down below?" and a nurse inquires: "Did you wash between your legs?" Persons characteristically refer to pelvic examinations euphemistically in staff-patient encounters. "The doctors want to take a peek at you," a nurse tells a patient. Or "Dr. Ryan wants to see you in the examining room."

In the pelvic examination there was a striking contrast between the language of staff and patient. The patient was graphic; she used action words connoting physical contact to refer to the examination procedure: feeling, poking, touching, and punching. Yet she never located this action in regard to her body, always omitting to state where the physical contact occurred. The staff used impersonal medical language and euphemisms: "I'm going to examine you"; "I'm just cleaning out some blood clots"; "He's just trying to fix you up a bit."

Sometimes the staff introduce explicit terminology to clarify a patient's remark. A patient tells the doctor, "It's bleeding now" and the doctor answers, "You? From the vagina?" Such a response indicates the appropriate vocabulary, the degree of freedom permitted in technically oriented conversation, and the proper detachment. Yet the common avoidance of explicit terminology in staff-patient contacts suggests that despite all the precautions to assure that the medical definition prevails, many patients remain somewhat embarrassed by the whole subject. To avoid provoking this embarrassment, euphemisms and understood references are used when possible.

Highly specific requirements for everybody's behavior during a gynecological examination curtail the leeway for the introduction of discordant notes. Routine technical procedures organize the event from beginning to end, indicating what action each person should take at each moment. Verbal exchanges are also constrained by the technical task, in that the doctor uses routine phrases of direction and reassurance to the patient. There is little margin for ad-libbing during a gynecological examination.

The specifications for demeanor are elaborate. Foremost is that both staff and patient should be nonchalant about what is happening. According to the staff, the exemplary patient should be "in play": showing she is attentive to the situation by her bodily tautness, facial expression, direction of glance, tone of voice, tempo of speech and bodily movements, timing and appropriateness of responses. The patient's voice should be controlled, mildly pleasant, self-confident, and impersonal. Her facial expression should be attentive and neutral, leaning toward the mildly pleasant and friendly side, as if she were talking to the doctor in his office, fully dressed and seated in a chair. The patient is to have an attentive glance upward, at the ceiling or at other persons in the room, eyes open, not dreamy or "away," but ready at a second's notice to revert to the doctor's face for a specific verbal exchange. Except for such a verbal exchange, however, the patient is supposed to avoid looking into the doctor's eyes during the actual examination because direct eye contact between the two at this time is provocative. Her role calls for passivity and self-effacement. The patient should show willingness to relinquish control to the doctor. She should refrain from speaking at length and from making inquiries which would require the doctor to reply at length. So as not to point up her undignified position, she should not project her personality profusely. The self must be eclipsed in order to sustain the definition that the doctor is working on a technical object and not a person.

The physician's demeanor is highly stylized. He intersperses his examination with remarks to the patient in a soothing tone of voice: "Now relax as much as you can"; "I'll be as gentle as I can"; "Is that tender right there?" Most of the phrases with which he encourages the patient to relax are routine even though his delivery may suggest a unique relationship. He demonstrates that he is the detached professional and the patient demonstrates that it never enters her mind

that he could be anything except detached. Since intimacy can be introduced into instrumental physical contact by a "loving" demeanor (lingering, caressing motions and contact beyond what the task requires), a doctor must take special pains to insure that his demeanor remains a brisk, no-nonsense show of efficiency.[13]

Once I witnessed a gynecological examination of a forty-year-old woman who played the charming and scatterbrained Southern belle. The attending physician stood near the patient's head and carried on a flippant conversation with her while a resident and medical student actually performed the examination. The patient completely ignored the examination, except for brief answers to the examining doctor's inquiries. Under these somewhat trying circumstances she attempted to carry off a gay, attractive pose and the attending physician cooperated with her by making a series of bantering remarks.

Most physicians are not so lucky as to have a colleague conversing in cocktail-hour style with the patient while they are probing her vagina. Ordinarily the physician must play both parts at once, treating the patient as an object with his hands while simultaneously acknowledging her as a person with his voice. In this incident, where two physicians simultaneously deal with the patient in two distinct ways, the dual approach to the patient usually maintained by the examining physician becomes more obvious.[14]

The doctor needs to communicate with the patient as a person for technical reasons. Should he want to know when the patient feels pain in the course of examination or information about other medical matters, he must address her as a person. Also the doctor may want to instruct the patient on how to facilitate the examination. The most reiterated instruction refers to re-laxation. Most patients are not suffi-ciently relaxed when the doctor is ready to begin. He then reverts to a primitive level of communication and treats the patient almost like a young child. He speaks in a soft, soothing voice, probably calling the patient by her first name, and it is not so much the words as his manner which is signifi-cant. This caressing voice is routinely used by hospital staff members to pa-tients in critical situations, as when the patient is overtly frightened or dis-oriented. By using it here the doctor heightens his interpersonal relation with the patient, trying to reassure her as a person in order to get her to relax.

Moreover even during a gynecologi-cal examination, failing to acknowl-edge another as a person is an insult. It is insulting to be entirely instrumental about instrumental contacts. Some acknowledgment of the intimate con-notations of touching must occur. Therefore, a measure of "loving" de-meanor is subtly injected. A doctor cannot employ the full gamut of loving insinuations that a lover might infuse into instrumental touching. So he in-directly implies a hint of intimacy which is intended to counter the insult and make the procedure acceptable to the woman. The doctor conveys this loving demeanor not by lingering or superfluous contact, but by radiating concern in his general manner, offer-ing extra assistance, and occasionally by sacrificing the task requirements to "gentleness."

In short, the doctor must convey an optimal combination of impersonality and hints of intimacy that simultane-ously avoid the insult of sexual famil-iarity and the insult of unacknowl-edged identity. The doctor must man-age this even though the behavior emanating from each definition is con-tradictory. If the doctor can achieve this feat, it will contribute to keeping the patient in line. In the next section, we will see how the patient may threaten this precarious balance.

IV. PRECARIOUSNESS IN GYNECOLOGICAL EXAMINATIONS

Threats to the reality of a gynecolog-ical examination may occur if the bal-ance of opposing definitions is not maintained as described above. Real-ity in gynecological examinations is challenged mainly by patients. Occa-sionally a medical student, who might be considerably more of a novice than an experienced patient, seemed un-comfortable in the scene.[15] Experi-enced staff members were rarely ob-served to undermine the reality.

Certain threatening events which could occur in any staff-patient en-counter bring an added dimension of precariousness to a gynecological ex-amination because the medical aegis screens so much more audacity at that time. In general, staff expect patients to remain poised and in play like a friendly office receptionist; any show of emotion except in a controlled fash-ion is objectionable. Patients should not focus on identities of themselves or the staff outside those relevant to the medical exchange. Intractable patients may complain about the pain, dis-comfort, and indignities of submitting to medical treatment and care. Patients may go so far as to show they are re-luctant to comply with the staff. Even if they are complying, they may indi-rectly challenge the expert status of the staff, as by "asking too many questions."

Failure to maintain a poised perfor-mance is a possible threat in any social situation. Subtle failures of tone are common, as when a performer seems to lack assurance. Performers may fumble for their lines: hesitate, begin a line again, or correct themselves. A show of embarrassment, such as blushing, has special relevance in gynecological examinations. On rare occasions when a person shows signs of sexual response, he or she really has something to blush about. A more subtle threat is an indication that the actor is putting an effort into the task of maintaining nonchalant demeanor; if it requires such an effort, perhaps it is not a "natural" response.

Such effort may be indicated, for example, in regard to the direction of glance. Most situations have a common visual focus of attention, but in a gynecological examination the logical focus, the patient's internal organs, is not accessible, and none of the alternatives, such as staring at the patient's face, locking glances with others, or looking out the window are feasible. The unavailability of an acceptable place to rest the eyes is more evident when the presence of several medical students creates a "crowd" atmosphere in the small cubicle. The lack of a visual focus of attention and the necessity to shift the eyes from object to object requires the participants to remain vaguely aware of their directions of glance. Normally the resting place of the eyes is a background matter automatically managed without conscious attention. Attentiveness to this background detail is a constant reminder of how awkward the situation is.

Certain lapses in patient's demeanor are so common as hardly to be threatening. When patients express pain it can be overlooked if the patient is giving other signs of trying to behave well, because it can be taken that the patient is temporarily overwhelmed by a physiological state. The demonstrated presence of pain recalls the illness framework and counters

sexual connotations. Crying can be accredited to pain and dismissed in a similar way. Withdrawing attention from the scene, so that one is not ready with an immediate comeback when called upon, is also relatively innocuous because it is close to the required passive but in play demeanor.

Some threats derive from the patient's ignorance of how to strike an acceptable balance between medical and non-medical definitions, despite her willingness to do so. In two areas in particular, patients stumble over the subtleties of what is expected: physical decorum (proprieties of sights, sounds, and smells of the body) and modesty. While the staff is largely concerned with behavioral decorum and not about lapses in physical decorum, patients are more concerned about the latter, whether due to their medical condition or the procedure. Patients sometimes even let behavioral decorum lapse in order to express their concern about unappealing conditions of their bodies, particularly discharges and odors. This concern is a vestige of a nonmedical definition of the situation, for an attractive body is relevant only in a personal situation and not in a medical one.

Some patients fail to know when to display their private parts unashamedly to others and when to conceal them like anyone else. A patient may make an "inappropriate" show of modesty, thus not granting the staff the right to view what medical personnel have the right to view and others do not. But if patients act as though they literally accept the medical definition this also constitutes a threat. If a patient insists on acting as if the exposure of her breasts, buttocks, and pelvic area are no different from exposure of her arm or leg, she is "immodest." The medical definition is supposed to be in force only as necessary to facilitate specific medical tasks. If a patient becomes nonchalant enough to allow herself to remain uncovered for much longer than is technically necessary she becomes a threat. This also holds for verbal remarks about personal matters. Patients who misinterpret the license by exceeding its limits unwittingly challenge the definition of reality.[16]

V. NEUTRALIZING THREATENING EVENTS

Most gynecological examinations proceed smoothly and the definition of reality is sustained without conscious attention.[17] Sometimes subtle threats to the definition arise, and occasionally staff and patient struggle covertly over the definition throughout the encounter.[18] The staff take more preventive measures where they anticipate the most trouble: young, unmarried girls; persons known to be temporarily upset; and persons with reputations as uncooperative. In such cases the doctor may explain the technical details of the procedure more carefully and offer direct reassurance. Perhaps he will take extra time to establish personal rapport, as by medically related inquiries ("how are you feeling?" "do you have as much pain today?"), personal inquiries ("where do you live?"), addressing the patient by her first name, expressing direct sympathy, praising the patient for her behavior in this difficult situation, speaking in a caressing voice, and affectionate gestures. Doctors also attempt to reinforce rapport as a response to threatening events.

The foremost technique in neutralizing threatening events is to sustain a nonchalant demeanor even if the patient is blushing with embarrassment, blanching from fear, or moaning in pain. The patient's inappropriate gestures may be ignored as the staff convey, "We're waiting until you are ready to play along." Working to bring the scene off, the staff may claim that this is routine, or happens to patients in general; invoke the "for your own good" clause; counterclaim that something is less important than the patient indicates; assert that the unpleasant medical procedure is almost over; and contend that the staff do not like to cause pain or trouble to patients (as by saying, "I'm sorry" when they appear to be causing pain). The staff may verbally contradict a patient, give an evasive answer to a question, or try to distract the patient. By giving a technical explanation or rephrasing in the appropriate hospital language something the patient has referred to in a nonmedical way, the staff member reinstates the medical definition.

Redefinition is another tactic available to the staff. Signs of embarrassment and sexual arousal in patients may be redefined as "fear of pain." Sometimes sexual arousal will be labeled "ticklishness." After one examination the doctor thanked the patient, presumably for her cooperation, thus typifying the patient's behavior as cooperative and so omitting a series of uncooperative acts which he had previously acknowledged.

Humor may be used to discount the line the patient is taking. At the same time, humor provides a safety valve for all parties whereby the sexual connotations and general concern about gynecological examinations may be expressed by indirection. Without taking the responsibility that a serious form of the message would entail, the participants may communicate with each other about the events at hand. They may discount the derogatory implications of what would be an invasion of privacy in another setting by dismissing the procedure with a laugh. If a person can joke on a topic, he demonstrates to others that he possesses a laudatory degree of detachment.

For example, in one encounter a patient vehemently protests, "Oh, Dr. Raleigh, what are you doing?" Dr. Raleigh, exaggerating his southern accent, answers, "Nothin'." His levity conveys: "However much you may dislike this, we have to go on with it for your own good. Since you know that perfectly well, your protest could not be calling for a serious answer." Dr. Raleigh also plays the seducer claiming innocence, thus obliquely referring to the sexual connotations of where his hand is at the moment. In another incident Doctor Ryan is attempting to remove some gauze which has been placed in the vagina to stop the bleeding. He flippantly announces that the remaining piece of gauze has disappeared inside the patient. After a thorough search Doctor Ryan holds up a piece of gauze on the instrument triumphantly: "Well, here it is. Do you want to take it home and put it in your scrapbook?" By this remark Doctor Ryan ridicules the degree of involvement in one's own medical condition which would induce a patient to save this kind of memento. Later in the same examination Dr. Ryan announces he will do a rectal examination and the (elderly) patient protests, "Oh, honey, don't bother." Dr. Ryan assures her jokingly, "It's no bother, really." The indirect message of all three jokes is that one should take gynecological procedures casually. Yet simultaneously an undercurrent of each joke acknowledges a perspective contrary to the medical definition.

While in most encounters the nurse remains quietly in the background, she comes forward to deal actively with the patient if the definition of reality is threatened. In fact, one of the main functions of her presence is to provide a team member for the doctor in those occasional instances where the patient threatens to get out of line. Team members can create a more convincing reality than one person alone. Doctor and nurse may collude against an uncooperative patient, as by giving each other significant looks. If things reach the point of staff collusion, however, it may mean that only by excluding the patient can the definition of reality be reaffirmed. A more drastic form of solidifying the definition by excluding recalcitrant participants is to cast the patient into the role of an "emotionally disturbed person." Whatever an "emotionally disturbed person" may think or do does not count against the reality the rest of us acknowledge.

Perhaps the major safeguard of reality is that challenge is channeled outside the examination. Comments about the unpleasantness of the procedure and unaesthetic features of the patient's body occur mainly between women, two patients or a nurse and a patient. Such comments are most frequent while the patient gets ready for the examination and waits for the doctor or after the doctor leaves. The patient may establish a momentary "fellow-woman aura" as she quietly voices her distaste for the procedure to the nurse. "What we women have to go through" the patient may say. Or, "I wish all gynecologists were women." Why? "They understand because they've been through it themselves." The patient's confiding manner implies: "I have no right to say this, or even feel it, and yet I do." This phenomenon suggests that patients actually have strong negative reactions to gynecological examinations which belie their acquiescence in the actual situation. Yet patients' doubts are expressed in an innocuous way which does not undermine the definition of reality when it is most needed.

To construct the scene convincingly, participants constantly monitor their own behavior and that of others. The tremendous work of producing the scene is contained in subtle maneuvers in regard to details which may appear inconsequential to the layman. Since awareness may interfere with a convincing performance, the participants may have an investment in being as unself-conscious as possible. But the sociologist is free to recognize the significance of "inconsequential details" in constructing reality.

VI. CONCLUSION

In a gynecological examination the reality sustained is not the medical definition alone, but a dissonance of themes and counterthemes. What is done to acknowledge one theme undermines the others. No theme can be taken for granted because its opposite is always in mind. That is why the reality of a gynecological examination can never be routinized, but always remains precarious.

The gynecological examination should not be dismissed as an anomaly. The phenomenon is revealed more clearly in this case because it is an extreme example. But the gynecological examination merely exaggerates the internally contradictory nature of definitions of reality found in most situations. Many situations where the dominant definition is occupational or technical have a secondary theme of sociality which must be implicitly acknowledged (as in buttering up the secretary, small talk with sales clerks, or the undertaker's show of concern for the bereaved family). In "business entertaining" and conventions of professional associations a composite definition of work and pleasure is sustained. Under many circumstances a composite definition of action as both deviant and unproblematic prevails. For example, while Donald Ball stresses the claim of respectability in his description of an abortion clinic, his material illustrates the interplay of the dominant theme of respectability and a countertheme wherein the illicitness of the situation is acknowledged.[19] Internally inconsistent definitions also are sustained in many settings on who persons are and what their relation is to each other.

Sustaining a sense of the solidness of a reality composed of multiple contradictory definitions takes unremitting effort. The required balance among the various definitions fluctuates from moment to moment. The appropriate balance depends on what the participants are trying to do at that moment. As soon as one matter is dealt with, something else comes into focus, calling for a different balance. Sometimes even before one issue is completed, another may impose itself as taking priority. Further, each balance contains the seeds of its own demise, in that a temporary emphasis on one theme may disturb the long-run balance unless subsequent emphasis on the countertheme negates it. Because the most effective balance depends on many unpredictable factors, it is difficult to routinize the balance into formulas that prescribe a specific balance for given conditions. Routinization is also impractical because the particular forms by which the themes are expressed are opportunistic. That is, persons seize opportunities for expression according to what would be a suitable move at each unique moment of an encounter. Therefore, a person constantly must attend to how to express the balance of themes via the currently available means.

Multiple contradictory realities are expressed on various levels of explicitness and implicitness. Sustaining a sense of solidness of reality depends on the right balance of explicit and implicit expressions of each theme through a series of points in time. The most effective gestures express a multitude of themes on different levels. The advantages of multiple themes in the same gesture are simultaneous qualification of one theme by another, hedging (the gesture lacks one definite meaning), and economy of gestures.

Rational choices of explicit and implicit levels would take the following into account. The explicit level carries the most weight, unless countered by deliberate effort. Things made explicit are hard to dismiss or discount compared to what is left implicit. In fact, if the solidification of explication is judged to be nonreversible, use of the explicit level may not be worth the risk. On the other hand, when participants sense that the implicit level is greatly in use, their whole edifice of belief may become shaken. "I sense that a lot is going on underneath" makes a person wonder about the reality he is accepting. There must be a lot he does not know, some of which might be evidence which would undermine what he currently accepts. The invalidation of one theme by the concurrent expression of its countertheme must be avoided by various maneuvers. The guiding principle is that participants must prevent a definition that a contradiction exists between theme and countertheme from emerging. Certain measures routinely contribute to this purpose. Persons must try to hedge on both theme and countertheme by expressing them tentatively rather than definitely and simultaneously alluding to and discounting each theme. Theme and countertheme should not be presented simultaneously or contiguously on the explicit level unless it is possible to discount their contradictory features. Finally, each actor must work to keep the implicit level out of awareness for the other participants.

The technique of constructing reality depends on good judgment about when to make things explicit and when to leave them implicit, how to use the implicit level to reinforce and qualify the explicit level, distributing themes among explicit and implicit levels at any one moment, and seizing opportunities to embody messages. To pursue further these tentative suggestions on how important explicit and implicit levels are for sustaining reality, implicit levels of communication must be explored more systematically.

NOTES

1. Peter Berger and Thomas Luckmann, *The Social Construction of Reality* (Garden City, N. Y.: Doubleday & Company, Inc., 1966).

2. The precarious nature of social interaction is discussed throughout the work of Erving Goffman.

3. The data in this article are based on observations of approximately 75 gynecological examinations conducted by male physicians on an obstetrics-gynecology ward and some observations from a medical ward for comparison. For a full account of this study, see Joan P. Emerson, "Social Functions of Humor in a Hospital Setting," unpublished doctoral dissertation, University of California at Berkeley, 1963. For a sociological discussion of a similar setting, see William P. Rosengren and Spencer DeVault, "The Sociology of Time and Space in an Obstetrical Hospital" in *The Hospital in Modern Society*, Eliot Freidson, ed. (New York: The Free Press of Glencoe, 1963), pp. 266-292.

4. It takes severe biographical shocks to disintegrate the massive reality internalized in early childhood; much less to destroy the realities internalized later.

Beyond this, it is relatively easy to set aside the reality of the secondary internalizations." Berger and Luckmann, *op. cit.*, p. 142.

5. As stated by Lief and Fox: "The amounts and occasions of bodily contact are carefully regulated in all societies, and very much so in ours. Thus, the kind of access to the body of the patient that a physician in our society has is a uniquely privileged one. Even in the course of a so-called routine physical examination, the physician is permitted to handle the patient's body in ways otherwise permitted only to special intimates, and in the case of procedures such as rectal and vaginal examinations in ways normally not even permitted to a sexual partner." Harold I. Lief and Renee C. Fox, "Training for 'Detached Concern' in Medical Students" in Harold I. Lief, *et al.*, (eds.), *The Psychological Basis of Medical Practice* (New York: Harper & Row, Inc., 1963), p. 32. As Edward Hall remarks, North Americans have an inarticulated convention that discourages touching except in moments of intimacy. Edward T. Hall, *The Silent Language* (Garden City, N. Y.: Doubleday & Company, 1959), p. 149.

6. For comments on embarrassment in the doctor-patient relation, see Michael Balint, *The Doctor, His Patient, and the Illness* (New York: International Universities Press, Inc., 1957), p. 57.

7. Physicians are aware of the possibility that their routine technical behavior may be interpreted as sexual by the patient. The following quotation states a view held by some physicians: "It is not unusual for a suspicious hysterical woman with fantasies of being seduced to misinterpret an ordinary movement in the physical examination as an amorous advance." E. Weiss and O. S. English, *Psychosomatic Medicine* (Philadelphia: W. B. Saunders Co., 1949). Quoted in Marc Hollender, *The Psychology of Medical Practice* (Philadelphia: W. B. Saunders Co., 1958), p. 22. An extreme case suggests that pelvic examinations are not without their hazards for physicians, particularly during training: "A third-year student who had prided himself on his excellent adjustment to the stresses of medical school developed acute anxiety when about to perform, for the first time, a pelvic examination on a gynecological patient. Prominent in his fantasies were memories of a punishing father who would unquestionably forbid any such explicitly sexual behavior." Samuel Bojar, "Psychiatric

Problems of Medical Students" *Emotional Problems of the Student* in Graham B. Glaine, Jr., *et al.* (eds.) (Garden City, N. Y.: Doubleday & Company, 1961), p. 248.

8. Many other claims and assumptions are being negotiated or sustained in addition to this basic definition of the situation. Efforts in regard to some of these other claims and assumptions have important consequences for the fate of the basic definition. That is, in the actual situation any one gesture usually has relevance for a number of realities, so that the fates of the various realities are intertwined with each other. For example, each participant is putting forth a version of himself which he wants validated. A doctor's jockeying about claims about competence may reinforce the medical definition and so may a patient's interest in appearing poised. But a patient's ambition to "understand what is really happening" may lead to undermining of the medical definition. Understanding that sustaining the basic definition of the situation is intertwined with numerous other projects, however, we will proceed to focus on that reality alone.

9. Compare Donald Ball's account of how the medical definition is conveyed in an abortion clinic, where it serves to counter the definition of the situation as deviant. Donald W. Ball, "An Abortion Clinic Ethnography," *Social Problems*, 14: pp. 293-301, Winter, 1967.

10. Glaser and Strauss discuss the hospital prohibition against examinations and exposure of the body in the presence of intimates of the patient. Barney Glaser and Anselm Strauss, *Awareness of Dying* (Chicago: Aldine Publishing Co., 1965), p. 162.

11. Sudnow reports that at the county hospital he studied, male physicians routinely did pelvic examinations without nurses being present, except in the emergency ward. David Sudnow, *Passing On: The Social Organization of Dying* (Englewood Cliffs, N. J.: Prentice-Hall, Inc. 1967), p. 78.

12. The following quotation suggests that euphemisms and understood references may be used because the staff often has the choice of using "lewd words" or not being understood. "Our popular vocabulary for describing sexual behavior has been compounded of about equal parts of euphemism and obscenity, and popular attitude and sentiment have followed the same duality. Among both his male and female subjects, the interviewers found

many who knew only the lewd words for features of their own anatomy and physiology." Nelson N. Foote, "Sex as Play" in Jerome Himelhock and Sylvia F. Fava, *Sexual Behavior in American Society* (New York: W. W. Norton and Co., Inc., 1955), p. 239.

13. The doctor's demeanor typically varies with his experience. In his early contacts with patients the young medical student may use an extreme degree of impersonality generated by his own discomfort in his role. By the time he has become accustomed to doctor-patient encounters, the fourth-year student and intern may use a newcomer's gentleness, treating the scene almost as an intimate situation by relying on elements of the "loving" demeanor previously learned in non-professional situations. By the time he is a resident and focusing primarily on the technical details of the medical task, the physician may be substituting a competent impersonality, although he never reverts to the extreme impersonality of the very beginning. The senior doctor, having mastered not only the technical details but an attitude of detached concern as well, reintroduces a mild gentleness, without the involved intimacy of the intern.

14. The management of closeness and detachment in professional-client relations is discussed in Charles Kadushin, "Social Distance between Client and Professional," *American Journal of Sociology*, 67: pp. 517-531, March 1962. Wilensky and Lebeaux discuss how intimacy with strangers in the social worker-client relation is handled by accenting the technical aspects of the situation, limiting the relationship to the task at hand, and observing the norms of emotional neutrality, impartiality and altruistic service. Harold L. Wilensky and Charles N. Lebeaux, *Industrial Society and Social Welfare* (New York: Russell Sage Foundation, 1958), pp. 299-303.

15. For a discussion of the socialization of medical students toward a generally detached attitude, see Lief and Fox, *op. cit.*, pp. 12-35. See also Morris J. Daniels, "Af-

fect and its Control in the Medical Intern," *American Journal of Sociology*, 66: pp. 259-267, November 1960.

16. The following incident illustrates how a patient may exceed the limits. Mrs. Lane, a young married woman, was considered by the physicians a "seductive patient," although her technique was subtle and her behavior never improper. After examining Mrs. Lane, an intern privately called my attention to a point in the examination when he was pressing on the patient's ovaries and she remarked to the nurse: "I have this pain in intercourse until my insides are about to come out." The intern told me that Mrs. Lane said that to the nurse, but she wanted him to hear. He didn't want to know that, he said; it wasn't necessary for her to say that. The intern evidently felt that Mrs. Lane's remark had exceeded the bounds of decorum. A specific medical necessity makes the imparting of private information acceptable, the doctor's reaction suggests, and not merely the definition of the situation as medical.

17. There is reason to think that those patients who would have most difficulty in maintaining their poise generally avoid the situation altogether. Evidence that some uncool women avoid pelvic examinations is found in respondents' remarks quoted by Rainwater: "I have thought of going to a clinic for a diaphragm, but I'm real backward about doing that. I don't even go to the doctor to be examined when I'm pregnant. I never go until about a month before I have the baby." "I tell you frankly, I'd like a diaphragm but I'm just too embarrassed to go get one." Lee Rainwater, *And the Poor Get Children* (Chicago: Quadrangle Books, 1960), pp. 10, 31.

18. An example of such a struggle is analyzed in Joan P. Emerson, "Nothing Unusual is Happening" in Tamotsu Shibutani, editor, *Human Nature and Collective Behavior: Papers in Honor of Herbert Blumer* Englewood Cliffs, N. J.: Prentice-Hall, Inc., 1970).

19. Donald Ball, *op. cit.*

27. DEATH AND DYING AS SOCIAL STATES OF AFFAIRS

DAVID SUDNOW

Reprinted from David Sudnow, *Passing On: The Social Organization of Dying.* © 1967, pp. 61-77. Reprinted by permission of Prentice-Hall, Inc., Englewood Cliffs, New Jersey. David Sudnow is presently on the sociology faculty at the University of Massachusetts. He has been instrumental in developing the ethnomethodological approach, and in addition to writing *Passing On: The Social Organization of Dying*, is the editor of *Studies in Social Interaction*.

"DYING" AS A SOCIAL FACT

That a person is "dying" is not an altogether straightforward notion, given the possibility that in a manner of speaking it can properly be said of all persons that, from the moment of birth onward, they move closer to death each day and are, in that sense, continually and forever dying. This recognition is, of course, at the same time both a major resource and dilemma of existential philosophy and literature.

Despite the awareness of continual "dying-from-birth," considered by some as the most profound awareness of man, people in Western society, at least, ordinarily employ "dying" with respect to a rather delimited class of states and persons, and in so doing, seem to confront no great philosophical conflict in saying of that one: "he is dying," yet not admitting the same fact of themselves. It is the more mundane, ordinary use of the characterization the analysis of which is of direct relevance to my concerns. While perhaps philosophically admissible as a description of anyone, the notion "dying" has a strictly circumscribed domain of proper use in the hospital setting. I should like to propose an empirical description of this use, as well as the assessment "he is dead," it too being a somewhat problematic notion.[1]

It is to be noted from the outset that the characterizations "he is dead" and "he is dying" (as well as their chief lexical variants in the hospital setting: "he is deceased" and "he is terminally ill"), are the products of assessment procedures, i.e., constitute the outcomes of investigative inquiries of more or less detail, undertaken by persons more or less practically involved in the consequences that discovery of those outcomes foreseeably have. To be "dead" or "dying" is, from our sociological perspective, to be so regarded by those who routinely and rightfully engage in assessing those states and premising courses of action, both for themselves and others, on the basis of these assessments. An interest we take in these phenomena is directed towards explicating how these assessments are made and reported upon within the organizational milieu of the hospital social system. I shall begin by considering "dying" and then move to treat "death." . . .

It is perhaps not altogether impossible to conceive of the circumstance where "dying" was not a matter which persons attended to, where persons simply died, for varieties of reasons, and where, at the time of the death it would be regarded as strange to be asked to retrospectively locate that point at which "dying" could be said to have begun, e.g., "he started last year." The philosophic recognition

344

that "dying" begins when life does might seem to make such a location attempt quite arbitrary, if not meaningless.

Yet deaths occur in a social order. The thoughts, concerns, activities, projects, prospects, and fate of others are more or less linked to the one who dies and the fact of his death. The character of this linkage is partially given by the location of the person in a variety of social structures, e.g., the family, the hospital, the occupationally structured careers of the society, the age-graded system generally, etc., and it provides, in turn, for the varying degrees of relevance of anticipating death and programming courses of action on the basis of such an anticipation. Death occurs in an organizationally based medical order as well. The programming of courses of treatment, the activities of diagnosis and prognosis, the appropriation of time, interest, and money—these are among the practical and sanctionable concerns of the medical professionals, and the anticipation of persons' deaths figures prominently into the way such concerns are concretely organized.[2]

"Dying" comes to be noticed at certain points and not others in the course of a life, despite the existential proposition of dying-from-birth, and whatever the medical basis of its proper recognition (and that perhaps is problematic), there are many respects in which the most criterial features of the notion's use have to do with explicitly social considerations. It is these I propose to explore.

The medical, or biological, or physiochemical basis for regarding a person as "dying" are not entirely clear. Noticing "dying" seems to be a quite different order of conceptual activity from noticing bleeding, or fibrillating, or employing a disease category to organize some set of symptoms and findings. As a "medical category,"

"dying" seems clearly distinguished from disease categories on one hand and bio-chemico-physical states and processes on the other. "Dying" does not, in the American system of medicine at least, stand as an appropriate answer to questions on the order of "what's wrong with me, doctor?"—which questions seem partially definitive of "diseases." Disease categories can be said to consist of those linguistic items that can properly be taken to stand as answers to questions taking the form "what's wrong with me?" or "what have I got?" "Dying" does not properly stand as such an answer.[3]

The question "what's wrong with me (or him, etc.)?" does not always elicit a disease category as an answer but does, on occasion, elicit an enumeration of some set of symptoms or purported happenings or conditions. So the question "what's wrong with him?" may elicit, as proper responses, "he has X," "he complains of X," "he is X-ing," and, of course, variations on "I don't know." The elements of enumerations, when they are given, may or may not be organizable into some disease category or categories. "Dying" however, is not an appropriate description term in such enumerations as they occur in our society generally and in the medical world specifically.

"Dying" seems to be an essentially predictive term. It appears to be the case that when nurses in the hospital say "you can tell that someone is dying just by looking at them," what they are pointing to is the fact that given some set of observable happenings, or known about happenings, or assumed happenings, death is likely to occur in such and such a period of time. Seeing "dying" is seeing the likelihood of death within some temporal perspective; it is not like seeing a cancer, or seeing shock, or seeing bleeding. In the medical world one learns to see dying when, in the course of his experience with critically ill persons, he can learn to detect signs which warrant a particular order of time-specific death predictions.

What the existential proposition of "dying-from-birth" may perhaps provide is an extended temporal perspective based on the recognition of man's mortality; the actuarial table provides a more specified age-graded system of temporal reference brackets in terms of which "death" can be statistically predicted; disease categories, symptoms, and biochemical happenings —the data and conceptual apparatus of medicine—provide a still more specified temporal perspective. So the existentialist can, in his philosophical moments, regard the newborn baby (or yet-to-be-born fetus) as "dying"; and the insurance salesman, in his calculation of premium rates (the likelihood of "deaths" within varying specifiable times), predict death with varying degrees of accuracy; and the physician or nurse, or person otherwise knowledgeable in matters of illness, the likelihood of "death" given X and Y symptoms, or happenings, or diseases.

What the medical perspective on life provides, via the use of diseases and biological events generally as prognosticators, is another among a variety of possible timetables in terms of which predictions of "death" or talk of "dying" are framed. In our society, at least, medical people seem to have obtained a franchise on the notion of "dying," despite the philosopher's existential recognition and the insurance man's predictive tables. If one seeks to know if he is "dying" he consults his physician, not his insurance broker. There appears to be some special power to the notion of "fatal illness," such that the philosopher's description of "life as a fatal illness" does not

constitute a threat but the doctor's discovery of a cancer does. Wherein that special power lies is a matter of some interest; first, the notion of the "fatal illness" requires comment.

To say of a person that he "died from cancer" is, in some circles, e.g., that of medical pathologists, a somewhat strange way of talking.[4] The actual occurrence of a death involves the operation of a rather specific set of mechanisms, none of which is currently understood in great detail, and none of which is specifically included under the general rubric *cancer*, neither as its definitive features, nor as cancer's specific inevitable consequences. To "die," some say, the heart must cease beating, and that can occur as a direct result of one or more of a series of quite specific bio-chemico-physical occurrences, e.g., the heart can burst open in certain kinds of trauma, the nerve tissue which provides the heart with its electrical stimulation can be damaged, or weakened through a loss of blood supply, etc. Yet cessation of the heart is currently considered by some to be merely a "sign" of death, and not definitive of it. In certain medical circles there is considerable disagreement over the precise biological meaning of death; some argue that the cessation of cellular activity constitutes death, others insist upon a more specific attention to properties of cellular multiplication; all generally agree that the definition of "death" that will be most satisfactory will be one based on an understanding of life's specific mechanisms and not "disease categories," which can be regarded as only "predisposing conditions." As predisposing conditions they constitute, or some of them—the so-called "fatal illnesses"—constitute good predictors of death, i.e., their located presence warrants making a prediction of death within limits that could not be specified without their location.

Some persons argue that "dying" is a thing which becomes recognizable once such a deadly disease is located, i.e., that "dying" is a state wherein a person suffers from a disease which is nonreversible and is known to "produce death." For purposes of setting up my argument, let me examine this position from a somewhat critical perspective. An argument with lay conceptions is not intended. My concern in regarding them critically is eventually to focus on their definitive features.

On one count, location of a "death-causing disease" does not warrant talk of "dying," namely that talk occurs· when a disease of this character cannot be located, i.e., when certain symptoms, biological events, or conditions are noticed but where the organization of those matters into a disease category cannot, for a variety of reasons, be successfully achieved. The patient who arrives in the Emergency Ward of County in a state of deep "shock" may be considered "dying," even though no disease has been cited as a description or causal account of his condition. The disease may be discovered retrospectively, at an autopsy, or there may be no disease whatever, the death being described as due to some traumatic occurrence, e.g., the ingestion of a barbiturate, a gunshot wound, etc.

On another count, the location of a "death-causing disease" does not warrant talk of "dying"—namely, that the present set of diseases does not, in any strict sense, stand as an adequate causal account of death. On still a third count, the location of a "death-causing disease" does not exclusively warrant talk and treatment of a person as "dying," for persons with such "diseases" are not always so regarded. In

the hospital, an 85-year-old man with advanced arteriosclerosis will not always, on the basis of the disease itself, be regarded as a "dying man."

In nearly every hospital in the U. S. there is a book one will find at nurses' stations, on doctors' desks, and in the hospital morgue, that contains a lengthy list of items headed "causes of death," any one of which can properly be entered in the legal death certificate where the "cause of death" is asked for.[5] In addition to disease categories, like "carcinoma of the stomach," "myocardial infarction," and the rest, are certain physical occurrences that are considered "nonnatural," like "poisoning," "drowning," "natural amputation," etc. These "causes of death" consist of those diseases, physical occurrences, and the like that are legally taken as sufficient explanations of the death, i.e., they stand as legitimate, adequate answers to the question: "Why did he die?"; they are answers for recording on the death certificate, for telling members of the deceased's family why he died, for satisfying insurance requirements for a "natural death," etc. Their adequacy as accounts is a legal and socially given adequacy and not a biochemically descriptive adequacy.

The collection of diseases, including the so-called "fatal illnesses," which medicine, at any point in its development, employs in organizing treatment, teaching its students, filling out death certificates, und the like, is a product of the current state of medical knowledge. As that knowledge changes, the culturally defined collection of disease categories becomes more elaborate; diseases that were previously considered independent of one another come to be recognized, under the auspices of new principles of organizing biochemical facts, as related in formerly unrecognized ways;

diseases that were earlier thought to be varieties of some more generic diseases come to be regarded as worthy of independent status as distinctive entities; new diseases are discovered; etc.[6] That *cancer*, for example, is now regarded as a "fatal illness" and a prevalent "cause of death" is a function of the direction which medical inquiry currently takes. It is conceivable (and indeed a goal of researchers in this field) that as cancer's mechanisms are better understood, the antecedents of cancer will become more precisely locatable, so that one may detect this "fatal illness" in its presymptomatic stages, perhaps to the extent that a new order of phenomenon, having to do with the multiplying propensities of certain cellular structures, becomes designated as the "fatal illness." In some important senses, it can be said that the goal of medical research is to locate the fatal illnesses we all contain within us—a principled medical description of "life as a fatal illness."

The point of the above paragraphs is to suggest that currently available and employed categories of diseases, as sanctionably used "causes of death" are culturally constituted entities, and that death is an "outcome" of "diseases" in a socially sanctioned manner of speaking, but not in any strict biochemical sense.[7] What seems to set off the cancer patients from the "well," or at least some cancer patients, is not simply that they have a "fatal disease which will kill them," for it can be said of all of us that we have "fatal diseases in progress" which will kill us and which could be located (and perhaps will be) were it not for the particular diagnostic direction medical inquiry currently takes and the current state of medical knowledge. A partially distinguishing fact about the cancer patient is the degree of accuracy with which predictions of his death within some specifiable time period can be

made by virtue of the detected presence of a cancerous growth; and that predictive accuracy is the outcome, in turn, of the fact that medical people spend a great deal of time developing prognostic indicators and fatality tables for the disease *cancer*. It is to be noted, of course, that actuarial tables provide a reasonably accurate basis for temporally specifying predictions of death. So that, for example, the 80-year-old with no locatable disease of a so-called "fatal" character, can statistically be predicted to die within a short time period and with as much predictive accuracy as the person with a newly developed cancer.

Yet such an 80-year-old will not, in our society, always be conceived as "dying," nor in the hospital as a "terminal patient." If predictive accuracy in foreseeing death within specifiable time periods and the location of a so-called "fatal illness" are not, in themselves, sufficient conditions for conceiving of a person as "dying"—and given the way that notion is used they appear not to be—then what is? The 80-year-old who develops carcinoma of the stomach will not always be regarded as "dying," yet the 20-year-old who develops Hodgkins Disease often will be.

It can be suggested that the answer seems to lie in the way temporal specification of a prediction of forthcoming death is linked 1. to the person's location along the temporal dimensions of a variety of social structures and 2. the way temporal specifications of predictions of death involve those who make them in a variety of organizational, interactional, and professional problems. I shall consider each of these forms of linkage in turn and argue that an understanding of them is required to grasp adequately what the notion of "dying" means within the hospital context.

That a 20-year-old is expected to die

in 10 years is, in our society, an apparently more relevant fact than that a 75-year-old may have a similar length of time to live before his death, and that relevance has to do, it seems, with the respective place of each in a variety of social structures. "Dying" becomes an important, noticeable "process" insofar as it serves to provide others, as well as the patient, with a way to orient to the future, to organize activities around the expectability of death, to "prepare for it." The notion of "dying" appears to be a distinctly social one, for its central relevance is provided for by the fact that it establishes a way of attending a person. Physicians and nurses don't treat "dying" but diseases and symptoms and happenings, yet they seem to have a special way of regarding and caring for persons once they come to conceive of them as "dying." In the hospital, as elsewhere, what the notion of "dying" does, as a predictive characterization, is place a frame of interpretation around a person. What that frame entails in the way of concrete social activities shall be the topic of the remaining sections. . . .

In the County hospital setting, the greatest proportion of patients, over 75 per cent, are over 60 years of age. The mere location of a "fatal illness" does not, for hospital personnel, warrant employing "dying," or "terminality," with any special sense. Many of County's patients have locatable "fatal illnesses," i.e., illnesses which, should the person die, could appropriately be entered on a death certificate as "causes of death." The patient population includes many persons with advanced carcinomas, arteriosclerotic heart disease, severe liver and kidney malfunctioning, etc.

Generally and ideally, for persons so located in the age structure of the society, the fact of their eventual and perhaps shortly upcoming deaths is attended by family members; the social

structures in which they are involved are oriented to the fact of their forthcoming death; their families have become increasingly independent of them; the scope of references to the "future" has progressively narrowed; their careers are regarded retrospectively and not prospectively.[8] It is considered proper to treat the "fact" of their "dying" as of considerably less consequence for others, e.g., it is not felt to be a matter requiring drastic revision of others' life plans, as does the "fact" that a young adult is "dying."

Physicians, in treating and attending their elderly patients, do not regard the fact of "death within ten years" as warranting any special consideration (though that fact is a very basic one as regards the way the whole structure of medical practice with the elderly is organized). In dealing with elderly patients, there need be no conscious avoidance of future references, as is characteristically the case in conversing with the young adult who is expected to die within an abnormally short time period. Such references are, in our society, systematically and "naturally" dropped from conversation with the aged. A most noticeable fact about interaction between medical personnel and young "dying" patients is the careful avoidance of long-term future references. A nurse reported about her trouble in talking to a young teenager who was "dying" of Hodgkins Disease and knew her life span was expectably short: the greatest problem she experienced was to keep from talking about plans for school, a marriage, a career, etc. In conversing with the elderly, in our society, the future becomes attended as the days and the weeks to follow and "dying," the older the patient, comes to mean for hospital personnel *dying on this admission to the hospital*. That the patient may die within the year or the month becomes, within the hospital context at least, a manageable possibility so long as the patient is old, i.e., a possibility that requires no special daily interactional contortions, no planned avoidance of death and the future as conversational topics.

With the young person, noticing "dying" is a crucial matter as regards certain interactional problems. A young teenager at County had moderately advanced leukemia, a disease that often does not seriously debilitate its victim until its very late stages. This girl was in the ambulatory section of the female medical ward and spent most of her days in the hospital walking up and down the corridors (she came to County during the critical phases of her illness; in the course of several years she was purportedly in and out of the hospital dozens of times, a characteristic hospital career pattern for patients with this disease). A new member of the nursing staff engaged her in conversation on the first day of a new admission, and, in the course of talking about those things which one talks with teenage girls about, e.g., "do you have a boyfriend," "when do you want to get married?" etc., the girl, who was said to be "very mature" in her attitude toward her illness, interrupted the nurse with the announcement: "I'm going to die in a few years and have learned not to think about such things." The nurse was visibly upset by the fact that she had unwittingly led the conversation in such directions; other nurses apologized for not having told her about the facts of the case.

Few such cases are available from my data at County, where the average age of the patient population is well over 50.[9] In the local area there are several specialized children's hospitals and teaching hospitals which accept "charity cases," so that County treats very few young "dying" patients. Of the some 250 deaths on which my observations are based only a handful involved persons under 40 years old.

With the average County patients, the danger of unwittingly entering conversation inappropriate with a "dying" patient is relatively nonexistent, for on one hand few of the hospital's patients are in any condition for sociable interaction, and conversation with the "dying"—in County the elderly—need not be specially modified insofar as the things one normally discusses with them are not premised on, or take their meaning from, any understanding of a long-term future. At County, "dying" shifts in importance from a fact the notice of which is of great relevance as a basis for attending the younger person within a long-term temporal perspective, e.g., in terms of a career, family, etc., to a fact the relevance of which, with the elderly, is great only if death is considered an imminent possibility. For hospital personnel, the domain of relevant considerations is the hospital organization and the activities that go on within it, and "dying" takes its central sense against the background of these activities. The older the patient, the more readily hospital personnel can attend the expectation of death within years, and restrict the sense of "dying" to "dying this time."

There are, of course, exceptions to the general tendency for "dying" to become increasingly restricted in temporal reference and significance with age; the most notable instances are those where the person whose death is contemplated occupies some special place in the wider social structure. That an elder statesman is expected to die within the term of his office, can become a quite relevant matter; and "dying" in the case of an elderly man can be of utmost import to, for example, an heir-to-be awaiting his inheritance, or those members of the family whose daily activities may be severely restricted by the care they give their aging relative. Where the social consequences of death are taken to be of greater import we find reference to the fact of "dying" made within more extended temporal schema of anticipation.

In the hospital setting, however, "dying" takes on its central significance insofar as death is considered likely on the current admission, for it is then that the hospital, its personnel, and its activities are directly involved in the affair of the death. That all very old patients are, in some more general sense of the term, "dying" is an irrelevant issue, not because of the absence or presence of "fatal diseases" but because the consequences of regarding them in that way are both immaterial from the standpoint of the hospital's activities, and, it could be argued, quite detrimental to the ideological organization of medical practice with the elderly. For physicians to assume an existential posture toward death, or operate under the auspices of an actuarial calculus, would seem to undercut the central notion that the doctor's job is to "prevent death." That the greatest proportion of very ill patients in our society are elderly, provides for the essential importance of restricting the temporal confines of predictions of death and action based upon an assessment of inevitable demise. In orienting his daily treatment activities with the elderly, the physician must develop the ability to disattend the possibility of death, unless it is quite imminent. Pessimism about life and actions based on that pessimism seem warranted, in the medical world at least, only when death becomes contemplated within the temporal confines of the hospi-

tal-doctor-patient-relative contractual relationship, and that temporally bounded contract, at County Hospital, extends little beyond the boundaries of any given hospital admission. The case of the private physician, with a different kind of contractual involvement in the affairs of his patient, within a more extended temporal matrix, is presumably quite different. Dying takes on a more extended temporal significance to the degree that the physician is more implicated into the social worlds of his patients and their families, and when his patients are recurrently his patients.

The "dying" patients at County are those who are expected to die within the course of their present hospital admission. As a short term, acute treatment institution, this course seldom exceeds 10 or 15 days. Let me now turn to examine some of the activities that recognition of "dying" seems to entail in the treatment of patients during the expected final week of life. Later, I shall consider some of the ways in which that recognition of likely death is achieved, pointing to certain central structural constraints that set the conditions under which the recognition is properly employed as a basis for treatment. . . .

"SOCIAL DEATH"[10]

When, in the course of a patient's illness his condition is considered such that he is "dying" or "terminally ill," his name is "posted" on the "critical patients' list." Once "posted" a patient has the theoretical right to receive visitors throughout the day and night and not merely at the appointed visiting hours. Posting also serves as an internally relevant message, notifying certain key hospital personnel that a death may be forthcoming and that appropriate preparations for that possibility are tentatively warranted. In the hospital morgue, scheduling is an important requirement. Rough first drafts of the week's expected work load are made, with the number of possible autopsies being a matter which, if possible, is to be anticipated and planned for. In making such estimates the morgue attendant consults "posted lists" from which he makes a guess as to the work load of the coming week. The "posted list" is also consulted by various medical personnel who have some special interest in various anatomical regions. County's morgue attendant made it a practice to alert the ward physician that Doctor S. wanted to get all the eyes he could (Doctor S. was a research ophthalmologist). To provide Dr. S. with the needed eyes, the morgue attendant habitually checked the "posted list" and tried, in informal talk with the nurses about the patient's family, to assess his chances of getting the family's permission to relinquish the eyes of the patient for research. Apparently, when he felt he had located a likely candidate, a patient whose family could be expected to give permission at the time of death, he thus informed the pathologist, who made an effort, via the resident physician, to have special attention given to the request for an eye donation. (At several places in the hospital: on the admission nurse's desk, in the morgue, in doctors' lounges, and elsewhere, there were periodically placed signs that read "Dr. S. needs eyes," "Dr. Y. needs kidneys," etc.)

At County there is a Catholic chaplain whose main responsibility, it seems, is administering last rites. Each morning he makes "rounds" through the various wards of the hospital. At each ward, he consults a master schedule, which is an index file containing patients' names, religions, sex, and diagnoses. All patients who have been posted are identified with a red plastic border which is placed on their cards. The chaplain goes through this file daily and writes down the names of all known Catholic patients who have been posted, whereupon he enters these patients' rooms and administers extreme unction. After completing his round on each ward, he stamps the index card of the patient with a rubber stamp which reads:

Last Rites Administered
Date_____
Clergyman_____

Each day he consults the files anew to see if new patients have been admitted to the wards and/or put on the critical list. His stamp serves to prevent him from performing the rites twice on the same patient.

In fact, many "posted patients" do not die, for "posting" is often done well before obvious impending death is noted. Quite a few people therefore leave County alive, yet formally relieved of their earthly sins. The priest reported that such cleansing is not permanent, however, and that upon readmission to the hospital one must, before he dies, receive last rites again; the first administration is no longer operative.

It is significant that some seriously ill "posted patients" can be properly regarded as prospective candidates for autopsies before their deaths, a conception not entertained at Cohen Hospital. Indicative of the general stance taken toward some dying patients at County is the following conversation that occurred between two resident physicians at the bedside of a "terminally ill patient" in the first stages of a coma from uremic poisoning:

A: Do you think, really, that both kidneys are as bad?

B: I know they're both bad because the output is so damned low. Let's put it this way, neither one is good.

A: Well, we'll find out for sure at autopsy.

B: Right.

To discuss a patient's forthcoming autopsy, while that patient is still a patient, would be severely sanctioned at Cohen, without respect for the fact that the patient might be considered "comatose" and not aware of conversation in his presence. At County, there is a decided phasingout of attention given to "dying" patients, such that the possibility of death within the period of a given work shift itself is taken to warrant instituting certain forms of postdeath treatment.

A tentative distinction can be made between "clinical death": the appearance of "death signs" upon physical examination; "biological death": the cessation of cellular activity; and a third category, "social death" which, within the hospital setting, is marked by that point at which a patient is treated essentially as a corpse, though perhaps still "clinically" and "biologically" alive. The following example is illustrative of what is intended by the term "social death": A nurse on duty with a woman who she explained was "dying," was observed to spend some two or three minutes trying to close the woman's eyelids. This involved slowly but somewhat forcefully pushing the two lids together to get them to adhere in a closed position. After several unsuccessful moments she managed to get them to stay shut and said, with a sigh of accomplishment, "Now they're right." When questioned about what she had been doing, she reported that a patient's eyelids are always closed after death, so that the body will resemble a sleeping person. After

death, however, she reported, it was more difficult to accomplish a complete lid closure, especially after the body muscles have begun to tighten; the eyelids become less pliable, more resistant, and have a tendency to move apart; she always tried, she reported, to close them before death; while the eyes are still elastic they are more easily manipulated. This allowed ward personnel to more quickly wrap the body upon death (if death indeed occurred), without having to attend to cosmetic matters, and was considerate, she pointed out, of those who preferred to handle dead bodies as little as possible.

"Social death" can be said to be marked by that point at which socially relevant attributes of the patient begin permanently to cease to be operative as conditions for treating him, and when he is, essentially, regarded as already dead. "Social death" thus consists of a set of practices and can be seen to define some features of what "dying" means within the hospital context. These practices are to be distinguished from such activities as conversation in the presence of an anesthetized patient, for example, unless such conversation involves reference to the person as essentially a corpse, i.e., where the reference terms, activities discussed, and the like are those which are typically and properly discussed only with respect to persons actually dead.

It is perhaps analytically tempting to conceive of social "death" as any instance of radically asocial treatment of a person, but such a usage would be, at the same time, analytically ambiguous, permitting such things as desertion by one's family, "nonperson treatment," and the like, to be so conceived. In keeping with the literal sense of "death," I intend a more delimited sense of "dead," i.e., where death is the warrantable basis for doing such things as planning an autopsy, disposing of personal effects, contracting mortuary institutions, putting a body in the morgue, informing insurance companies, remarrying, grieving, announcing the contents of a will, preparing obituary notices, transferring properties to another name, and, generally, engaging in those organizational, ceremonial, and economic activities associated with death, those matters which mark the end of social existence. Treatments or activities which often accompany the death of a person, or his "dying," but which accompany other kinds of states as well, are not specifically instances of "social death treatment," in my terminology. So the tapering off of visits on the part of relatives becomes an instance of "treatment as dead" when those activities which are substituted for visiting are ones that would occur only after the patient had died. The distinction is not entirely without ambiguity, but within the hospital setting at least, a specific set of activities and treatments can usually be clearly located. When such activities occur, "social death" or "dying as a form of treatment" is said to occur, and whether that takes place before, concurrent with, or well after actual "biological" or "clinical" death is a matter for analysis.

A clear instance is seen in the circumstance where autopsy permits are filled out prior to death. For an autopsy to be performed, permission of the closest surviving relative must be obtained.[11] Two forms of permission constitute legally actionable documents: 1. a signature on a prepared "autopsy permission form"[12] and 2. a telegram from the surviving relative to the hospital, authorizing an autopsy. Obtaining an autopsy permit is regarded as a very important administra-

tive necessity at the time of death. In order to qualify for AMA accreditation as a "teaching hospital," and thus to be able to offer internships and residencies, a hospital must have an autopsy rate exceeding 25 per cent, i.e., autopsies must be performed on 25 per cent or more of the hospital's deceased patients. The minimum rate is not considered sufficient and most hospitals strive for as high a rate as is possible. It is an apparently relevant question for a prospective resident to ask of the hospital: "What is your autopsy rate?" and for him partially to base his decision on where to do a residency on the basis of these rates.[13]

County's doctors are concerned to obtain autopsy permission whenever possible, in part because they can be negatively sanctioned for acting indifferently in this regard. When they expect that they will lose contact with a relative, they will, on those occasions where doing an autopsy is considered quite important (say, for example, on a particularly interesting or diagnostically troublesome case), sometimes approach the relative of a patient who is considered to be "dying" and tactfully request that, "given the circumstances," a form be signed at the present time. At County this practice was employed only in cases where an autopsy was especially desired and then only if the relative had been previously been made well aware that the patient was expected to die shortly.[14] There is the feeling, moreover, that one can risk the possible sanctioning that a proposal might incur only with either the very uneducated relative or the very sophisticated and emotionally cool one.

A typical instance of "social death" involved a male patient who was admitted to the Emergency Unit with a sudden perforation of a duodenal ulcer. He was operated upon, and, for a period of six days, remained in quite critical condition. His wife was informed that his chances of survival were poor, whereupon she stopped her visits to the hospital. After two weeks, the man's condition improved markedly and he was discharged in ambulatory condition. The next day he was readmitted to the hospital with a severe coronary. Before he died, he recounted his experience upon returning home. His wife had removed all of his clothing and personal effects from the house, had made preliminary arrangements for his burial with the mortuary establishment (she had written a letter which he discovered on his bureau, requesting a brochure on their rates), she no longer wore his wedding ring, and was found with another man, no doubt quite shocked at her husband's return. He reported that he left the house, began to drink heavily, and had a heart attack.

NOTES

1. By conceiving of these categories as "problematic" I do not intend at all to suggest that their use is problematic for either professional or lay persons, but rather that, from the sociologist's standpoint, they must be so conceived if the proper analytic attitude toward them is to be maintained. I intend the term "problematic" in accord with Harold Garfinkel's usage, as for example in his "Studies in the Routine Grounds of Everyday Activities," *Social Problems*, 11, No. 3 (Winter, 1964), 235-250.

2. Of relevance to this analysis is Glaser and Strauss and their "Awareness Contexts and Social Interaction," *American Sociological Review*, 29 (October, 1964), 669-678. See also their book, *Awareness of Dying* (Chicago: Aldine Publishing Co., 1965). A key difference between my approach and theirs is that in their analysis, what "dying" consists of is not treated as a problematic phenomenon. Their central interest, of considerable social-psychological importance, is the management of information in interaction; their central issue is "awareness of dying" and for their purposes what "dying" is has not been accorded central attention. I have found it necessary, being less concerned with interaction between staff and patient and more concerned with the organization of ward activities, to regard the very phenomenon of "dying" as troublesome, an understanding of its sense requiring location of those practices which its use warrants.

Generally, I have not considered the "patient's knowledge" of the likelihood of his own forthcoming death, a topic of considerable interest and one which Glaser and Strauss treat in detail. Only infrequently in my observations at County did I encounter conversations between staff and patients about forthcoming death, or among staff about patients' awarenesses. The deaths I witnessed seldom involved a patient whose condition was such that interaction with him was likely. It is my feeling that a considerable number of deaths involve the circumstance where awareness of "dying" is irrelevant, from an organizational perspective, with a chief exception being cancer, where both patients and staff members are involved in daily social interaction. Deaths of patients suffering from other diseases, e.g., heart disease, kidney disease, CVA's (strokes), and liver diseases, have a course such that at that point when "dying" becomes noticeable, during the patient's "last admission" to the hospital, the patient is, so to speak, out of the picture. The greatest "cause of death," heart disease, typically "produces" death in the course of a short-term hospital admission, eventuating from an "attack" and is not preceded by that lengthy period of consciousness which is the fate of the cancer victim.

For other discussions of "awareness" see S. Standard and H. Nathan, *Should the Patient Know the Truth?* (New York: Springer Publishing Co., Inc., 1955); W. D. Kelly and S. R. Friesen, "Do Cancer Patients Want to Be Told?" *Surgery*, 27 (1950), 822; M. Field, *Patients Are People* (New York: Columbia University Press, 1953), pp. 72-76.

3. This conception of "disease categories" is taken from the excellent paper by Charles Frake, "The Diagnosis of Disease Among the Subanun of Mindanao," *American Anthropologist*, 63 (1961), 113-132.

4. See R. Pearl, *The Biology of Death*

(Philadelphia: J. B. Lippincott Co., 1922), particularly pp. 102-110, and W. Riese, *The Conception of Disease* (New York: Philosophical Library, Inc., 1953). When pathologists give reports on the cause of death in the course of hospital "death rounds" their descriptions generally make no mention of a "disease," but rather, a detailed tracing of lesions and a sequential account of the progressive destruction of cellular tissue are provided.

5. American Medical Association, *Standard Nomenclature of Diseases and Operations*, 4th edition, (Philadelphia: Blakiston, 1952).

6. For discussions of the changing character of disease categories see R. Dubos, *Mirage of Health* (Garden City, N. Y.: Doubleday & Company, Inc., 1961), especially Chapters IV and VI; H. E. Sigarest, *A History of Medicine*, 2 volumes (New York: Oxford University Press, Inc., 1951); and Sir James Spence, "The Methodology of the Clinical Sciences," in *Lectures on the Scientific Basis of Medicine* (London: Athlono Press, 1952-53), Volume II, pp. 1-14.

A listing of "causes of death" in 1736 in London included "apoplexy," "old age," "lunacy," and "jaundice." "Old age" was the largest "killer." See *The Gentleman's Magazine and the London Bill of Mortality, 1731-1778* (New Jersey: Ross Paxton, 1963), p. 24.

7. The juxtaposition of "biochemical" and "social" is here intended merely for the sake of my argument, which is, in fact, that such distinctions are not necessarily viable. As in the case with the concepts "death" and "dying" so it is expectably the case with other hard-and-fast natural dichotomies, namely, that they are through and through socially constituted. The very biologic determination of death as a judgmental activity performed by actors in an organizational environment, can be seen as itself a socially prescribed activity. For a brilliant analysis of sexual status which treats the issue of "natural" facts of life in detail, see H. Garfinkel, "Passing and the Management of Achieved Sexual Status in an Intersexed Person," U.C.L.A., mimeographed.

8. For a general discussion of the disengagement of the elderly from ongoing social life, see E. Cummings and W. Henry, *Growing Old* (New York: Basic Books, 1961), especially Chapter XII. For an extended treatment of the place of the elderly in non-Western societies, see L. Simmons, *The Role of the Aged in Primitive Societies*

(New Haven: Yale University Press, 1945).

9. Glaser and Strauss, "Awareness Contexts and Social Interaction," *op. cit.*, pp. 55-56, locate the control of future references in the degree of awareness staff have of the patients' conditions. While that is certainly an important determinant, as is seen in the example cited above, my argument is that a considerable amount of "natural control" is provided for by the general way in which older persons are treated within limited temporal perspectives. "Awareness" is most relevant only with patients with whom, were staff not aware, matters like the future would relevantly be discussed, i.e., the nonelderly.

10. During the course of observations in a mental institution, Erving Goffman observed predeath treatments of patients. It was he who first directed my attention to the notion of "social death." My restricted usage of the notion does not necessarily coincide with his intended interest in it.

11. This is apparently not true in all sections of the country. In some jurisdictions physicians can perform "limited autopsies," exploring only those areas of the body which are believed to be directly associated with the death, without obtaining permission from the family. See, for example, S. R. Cutolo, *Bellevue Is My Home* (Garden City: Doubleday & Company, Inc., 1956), p. 155. In those cases in which the coroner's office is involved in a death, no autopsy permission need be obtained.

12. The autopsy permit reads:

I _____ bearing the relation of _____ to _____, a patient recently deceased in County Hospital, authorize the proper authorities to examine the body and head of said deceased patient and to remove organs and to retain such portions as may be considered necessary for further study to ascertain the correct cause of death.
Signed _____

Nearest Relative

13. The autopsy percentage of hospital deaths reflects the degree of excellence of the medical staff. Institutions which conduct intern and resident programs should obtain an autopsy rate of 25 per cent as a minimum. The average good general hospital should aim for a minimum of 50 per cent, although some outstanding institutions obtain percentages of 70 or higher.

J. K. Owen, *Modern Concepts of Hospital Administration* (Philadelphia: W. B. Saunders Co., 1962), p. 304. Physicians have a vested interest in the over-all death rate. A hospital where few patients die is less suitable for training, whatever the percentage of autopsies. It is a high percentage of a large number of cases, providing many autopsy possibilities, that is desired. With every death, it is claimed, more experience is gained.

14. In some hospitals, however, obtaining autopsy permits before death is openly encouraged, as for example at Cook County:

One of the most important characteristics of a well regulated hospital is that it obtains as many autopsies as possible. For this the hospital depends to the largest degree on the residents and interns of the ward. They must recognize cases in which death is imminent or likely, and must make an immediate effort to advise the nearest of kin of the seriousness of the case, and to request written permit of autopsy. They must use their ingenuity in acquainting the relative with the importance of the autopsy. . . . Often in hopeless cases, the intern can succeed in obtaining a permit for a limited autopsy if he can show that it is not more than an operation.

A. Bernstein, *Intern's Manual (Cook County Hospital)* (Chicago: Year Book Medical Publishers, Inc., 1959), p. 190.

28. THE RITUAL DRAMA OF MUTUAL PRETENSE

BARNEY GLASER AND ANSELM STRAUSS

Reprinted from *Awareness of Dying*, Copyright© 1965 by Barney G. Glaser and Anselm L. Strauss, with permission from Aldine Publishing Company. Barney Glaser and Anselm Strauss have collaborated on a number of research and writing projects. *Awareness of Dying* and a companion volume entitled *Time for Dying* were part of a series of four works emerging from a six-year research project financed by the National Institutes of Health. An additional theoretical effort by the authors entitled *The Discovery of Grounded Theory* also came from these studies. Glaser and Strauss are both senior members of the faculty of the University of California Medical Center at San Francisco.

When patient and staff both know that the patient is dying but pretend otherwise—when both agree to act as if he were going to live—then a context of mutual pretense exists. Either party can initiate his share of the context; it ends when one side cannot, or will not, sustain the pretense any longer. . . .

Once we visited a small Catholic hospital where medical and nursing care for the many dying patients was efficiently organized. The staff members were supported in their difficult work by a powerful philosophy—that they were doing everything possible for the patient's comfort—but generally did not talk with patients about death. This setting brought about frequent mutual pretense. This awareness context is also predominant in such settings as county hospitals, where elderly patients of low socioeconomic status are sent to die; patient and staff are well aware of imminent death but each tends to go silently about his own business.[1] Yet, as we shall see, sometimes the mutual pretense context is neither silent nor unnegotiated.

The same kind of ritual pretense is enacted in many situations apart from illness. A charming example occurs when a child announces that he is now a storekeeper, and that his mother should buy something at his store. To carry out his fiction, delicately coop-erative action is required. The mother must play seriously, and when the episode has run its natural course, the child will often close it himself with a rounding-off gesture, or it may be concluded by an intruding outside event or by the mother. Quick analysis of this little game of pretense suggests that either player can begin; that the other must then play properly; that realistic (nonfictional) action will destroy the illusion and end the game; that the specific action of the game must develop during interaction; and that eventually the make-believe ends or is ended. Little familial games or dramas of this kind tend to be continual, though each episode may be brief.

For contrast, here is another example that pertains to both children and adults. At the circus, when a clown appears, all but the youngest children know that the clown is not real. But both he and his audience must participate, if only symbolically, in the pretense that he is a clown. The onlookers need do no more than appreciate the clown's act, but if they remove themselves too far, by examining the clown's technique too closely, let us say, then the illusion will be shattered. The clown must also do his best to sustain the illusion by clever acting, by not playing too far "out of character." Ordinarily nobody addresses him as if he were other than the character he is pretending to be. That is, everybody takes him seriously, at face value. And unless particular members return to see the circus again, the clown's performance occurs only once, beginning and ending according to a prearranged schedule.

Our two simple examples of pretense suggest some important features of the particular awareness context.... The make-believe in which patient and hospital staff engage resembles the child's game much more than the clown's act. It has no institutionalized beginning and ending comparable to the entry and departure of the clown; either the patient or the staff must signal the beginning of their joint pretense. Both parties must act properly if the pretense is to be maintained, because, as in the child's game, the illusion created is fragile, and easily shattered by incongruous "realistic" acts. But if either party slips slightly, the other may pretend to ignore the slip.[2] Each episode between the patient and a staff member tends to be brief, but the mutual pretense is done with terrible seriousness, for the stakes are very high.[3]

INITIATING THE PRETENSE

This particular awareness context cannot exist, of course, unless both the patient and staff are aware that he is dying. . . . In addition, at least one interactant must indicate a desire to pretend that the patient is not dying and the other must agree to the pretense, acting accordingly.

A prime structural condition in the existence and maintenance of mutual pretense is that unless the patient initiates conversation about his impending death, no staff member is required to talk about it with him. As typical Americans, they are unlikely to initiate such a conversation; and as professionals they have no rules commanding them to talk about death with the patient, unless he desires it. In turn, he may wish to initiate such conversation, but surely neither hospital rules nor common convention urges it upon him. Consequently, unless either the aware patient or the staff members breaks the silence by words or gestures, a mutual pretense . . . will exist; as, for example, when the physician does not care to talk about death, and the patient does not press the issue though he clearly does recognize his terminality.

The patient, of course, is more likely than the staff members to refer openly to his death, thereby inviting them, explicitly or implicitly, to respond in kind. If they seem unwilling, he may decide they do not wish to confront openly the fact of his death, and then he may, out of tact or genuine empathy for their embarrassment or distress, keep his silence. He may misinterpret their responses, of course, but . . . he probably has correctly read their reluctance to refer openly to his impending death.

Staff members, in turn, may give him opportunities to speak of his death, if they deem it wise, without their directly or obviously referring to the topic. But if he does not care to act or talk as if he were dying, then they will support his pretense. In doing so, they have, in effect, accepted a complementary assignment of status— they will act with pretense toward his pretense. (If they have misinterpreted his reluctance to act openly, then they have assigned, rather than accepted, a complementary status.)

Two related professional rationales permit them to engage in the pretense. One is that if the patient wishes to pretend, it may well be best for his health, and if and when the pretense finally fails him, all concerned can act more realistically. A secondary rationale is that perhaps they can give him better medical and nursing care if they do not have to face him so openly. In addition, as noted earlier, they can rely on common tact to justify their part in the pretense. Ordinarily, Americans believe that any individual may live— and die—as he chooses, so long as he does not interfere with others' activities, or, in this case, so long as proper care can be given him.

To illustrate the way these silent bargains are initiated and maintained, we quote from an interview with a special nurse. She had been assigned to a patient before he became terminal, and she was more apt than most personnel to encourage his talking openly, because as a graduate student in a nursing class that emphasized psychological care, she had more time to spend with her patient than a regular floor nurse. Here is the exchange between interviewer and nurse:

Interviewer: Did he talk about his cancer or his dying?
Nurse: Well, no, he never talked about it. I never heard him use the word cancer. . . .
Interviewer: Did he indicate that he knew he was dying?
Nurse: Well, I got that impression, yes. . . . It wasn't really openly, but I think the day that his roommate said he should get up and start walking, I felt that he was a little bit antagonistic. He said what his condition was, that he felt very, very, very ill that moment.
Interviewer: He never talked about leaving the hospital?
Nurse: Never.
Interviewer: Did he talk about his future at all?
Nurse: Not a thing. I never heard a word. . . .
Interviewer: You said yesterday that he was more or less isolated, because the nurses felt that he was hostile. But they have dealt with patients like this many many times. You said they stayed away from him?
Nurse: Well, I think at the very end. You see, this is what I meant by isolation . . . we don't communicate with them. I didn't, ex-

cept when I did things for him. I think you expect somebody to respond to, and if they're very ill we don't . . . I talked it over with my instructor, mentioning things that I could probably have done; for instance, this isolation, I should have communicated with him . . .
Interviewer: You think that since you knew he was going to die, and you half suspected that he knew it too, or more than half; do you think that this understanding grew between you in any way?
Nurse: I believe so . . . I think it's kind of hard to say but when I came in the room, even when he was very ill, he'd rather look at me and try to give me a smile, and gave me the impression that he accepted . . . I think this is one reason why I feel I should have communicated with him . . . and this is why I feel he was rather isolated. . . .

From the nurse's account, it is difficult to tell whether the patient wished to talk openly about his death, but was rebuffed; or whether he initiated the pretense and the nurse accepted his decision. But it is remarkable how a patient can flash cues to the staff about his own dread knowledge, inviting the staff to talk about his destiny, while the nurses and physicians decide that it is better not to talk too openly with him about his condition lest he "go to pieces." The patient . . . picks up these signals of unwillingness, and the mutual pretense context has been initiated. A specific and obvious instance is this: an elderly patient, who had lived a full and satisfying life, wished to round it off by talking about his impending death. The nurses retreated before this prospect, as did his wife, reproving him, saying he should not think or talk about such morbid matters. A hospital chaplain finally intervened, first by listening to the patient himself, then by inducing the nurses and the wife to do likewise, or at least to acknowledge more openly that the man was dying. He was not successful with all the nurses.

The staff members are more likely to sanction a patient's pretense, than his family's. The implicit rule is that though the patient need not be forced to speak of his dying, or to act as if he were dying, his kin should face facts. After all, they will have to live with the facts after his death. Besides, staff members usually find it less difficult to talk about dying with the family. Family members are not inevitably drawn into open discussion, but the likelihood is high, particularly since they themselves are likely to initiate discussion or at least to make gestures of awareness.

Sometimes, however, pretense protects the family member temporarily against too much grief, and the staff members against too immediate a scene. This may occur when a relative has just learned about the impending death and the nurse controls the enusing scene by initiating temporary pretense. The reverse situation also occurs: a newly arrived nurse discovers the patient's terminality, and the relative smooths over the nurse's distress by temporary pretense.

THE PRETENSE INTERACTION

An intern whom we observed during our field work suspected that the patient he was examining had cancer, but he could not discover where it was located. The patient previously had been told that she probably had cancer, and she was now at this teaching hospital for that reason. The intern's examination went on for some time. Yet neither he nor she spoke about what he was searching for, nor in any way suggested that she might be dying. We mention this episode to contrast it with ... more extended interactions. ... These have an episodic quality —personnel enter and leave the patient's room, or he occasionally emerges and encounters them—but their extended duration means that

special effort is required to prevent their breaking down, and that the interactants must work hard to construct and maintain their mutual pretense. By contrast, in a formally staged play, although the actors have to construct and maintain a performance, making it credible to their audience, they are not required to write the script themselves. The situation that involves a terminal patient is much more like a masquerade party, where one masked actor plays carefully to another as long as they are together, and the total drama actually emerges from their joint creative effort.

A masquerade, however, has more extensive resources to sustain it than those the hospital situation provides. Masqueraders wear masks, hiding their facial expressions; even if they "break up" with silent laughter (as a staff member may "break down" with sympathy), this fact is concealed. Also, according to the rules ordinarily governing masquerades, each actor chooses his own status, his "character," and this makes his role in the constructed drama somewhat easier to play. He may even have played similar parts before. But terminal patients usually have had no previous experience with their pretended status, and not all personnel have had much experience. In a masquerade, when the drama fails it can be broken off, each actor moving along to another partner; but in the hospital the pretenders (especially the patient) have few comparable opportunities.

Both situations share one feature —the extensive use of props for sustaining the crucial illusion. In the masquerade, the props include not only masks but clothes and other costuming, as well as the setting where the masquerade takes place. In the hospital interaction, props also abound. Patients dress for the part of not-dying patient, including careful attention to grooming, and to hair and makeup by female patients. The terminal patient may also fix up his room so that it looks and feels "just like home," an activity that supports his enactment of normalcy. Nurses may respond to these props with explicit appreciation—"how lovely your hair looks this morning"—or even help to establish them, as by doing the patient's hair. We remember one elaborate pretense ritual involving a husband and wife who had won the nurses' sympathy. The husband simply would not recognize that his already comatose wife was approaching death, so each morning the nurses carefully prepared her for his visit, dressing her for the occasion and making certain that she looked as beautiful as possible.

The staff, of course, has its own props to support its ritual prediction that the patient is going to get well: thermometers, baths, fresh sheets, and meals on time! Each party utilizes these props as he sees fit, thereby helping to create the pretense anew. But when a patient wishes to demonstrate that he is finished with life, he may drive the nurses wild by refusing to cooperate in the daily routines of hospital life—that is, he refuses to allow the nurses to use their props. Conversely, when the personnel wish to indicate how things are with him, they may begin to omit some of those routines.

During the pretense episodes, both sides play according to the rules implicit in the interaction. Although neither the staff nor patient may recognize these rules as such, certain tactics are fashioned around them, and the action is partly constrained by them. One rule is that dangerous topics should generally be avoided. The most obviously dangerous topic is the patient's death; another is events that

will happen afterwards. Of course, both parties to the pretense are supposed to follow the avoidance rule.

There is, however, a qualifying rule: Talk about dangerous topics is permissible as long as neither party breaks down. Thus, a patient refers to the distant future, as if it were his to talk about. He talks about his plans for his family, as if he would be there to share their consummation. He and the nurses discuss today's events—such as his treatments—as if they had implications for a real future, when he will have recovered from his illness. And some of his brave or foolhardy activities may signify a brave show of pretense, as when he bathes himself or insists on tottering to the toilet by himself. The staff in turn permits his activity. (Two days before he returned to the hospital to die, one patient insisted that his wife allow him to travel downtown to keep a speaking engagement, and to the last he kept up a lively conversation with a close friend about a book they were planning to write together.)

A third rule, complementing the first two, is that each actor should focus determinedly on appropriately safe topics. It is customary to talk about the daily routines—eating (the food was especially good or bad), and sleeping (whether one slept well or poorly last night). Complaints and their management help pass the time. So do minor personal confidences, and chatter about events on the ward. Talk about physical symptoms is safe enough if confined to the symptoms themselves, with no implied references to death. A terminal patient and a staff member may safely talk, and at length, about his disease so long as they skirt its fatal significance. And there are many genuinely safe topics having to do with movies and movie stars, politics, fashions—with everything, in short, that signifies that life is going on "as usual."

A fourth interactional rule is that when something happens, or is said, that tends to expose the fiction that both parties are attempting to sustain, then each must pretend that nothing has gone awry. Just as each has carefully avoided calling attention to the true situation, each now must avert his gaze from the unfortunate intrusion. Thus, a nurse may take special pains to announce herself before entering a patient's room so as not to surprise him at his crying. If she finds him crying, she may ignore it or convert it into an innocuous event with a skillful comment or gesture—much like the tactful gentleman who, having stumbled upon a woman in his bathtub, is said to have casually closed the bathroom door, murmuring "Pardon me, *sir*." The mutuality of the pretense is illustrated by the way a patient who cannot control a sudden expression of great pain will verbally discount its significance, while the nurse in turn goes along with his pretense. Or she may brush aside or totally ignore a major error in his portrayal, as when he refers

spontaneously to his death. If he is tempted to admit impulsively his terminality, she may, again, ignore his impulsive remarks or obviously misinterpret them. Thus, pretense is piled upon pretense to conceal or minimize interactional slips.

Clearly then, each party to the ritual pretense shares responsibility for maintaining it. The major responsibility may be transferred back and forth, but each party must support the other's temporary dominance in his own action. This is true even when conversation is absolutely minimal, as in some hospitals where patients take no particular pains to signal awareness of their terminality, and the staff makes no special gestures to convey its own awareness. The pretense interaction in this case is greatly simplified, but it is still discernible. Whenever a staff member is so indelicate, or so straightforward, as to act openly as if a terminal patient were dying, or if the patient does so himself, then the pretense vanishes. If neither wishes to destroy the fiction, however, then each must strive to keep the situation "normal."[4]

NOTES

1. Robert Kastenbaum has reported that at Cushing Hospital, "a Public Medical Institution for the care and custody of the elderly" in Framingham, Massachusetts, "patient and staff members frequently have an implicit mutual understanding with regard to death . . . institutional dynamics tend to operate against making death 'visible' and a subject of open communication. . . . Elderly patients often behave as though they appreciated the unspoken feelings of the staff members and were attempting to make their demise as acceptable and unthreatening as possible." This observation is noted in Robert Kastenbaum, "The Interpersonal Context of Death in a Geriatric Institution," abstract of paper presented at the Seventeenth Annual Scientific Meet-

ing, Gerontological Society (Minneapolis: October 29-31, 1964).
2. I. Bensman and I. Garver, "Crime and Punishment in the Factory," in A. Gouldner and H. Gouldner (eds.), *Modern Society* (New York: Harcourt, Brace and World, 1963), pp. 593-96.
3. A German communist, Alexander Weissberg, accused of spying during the great period of Soviet spy trials, has written a fascinating account of how he and many other accused persons collaborated with the Soviet government in an elaborate pretense, carried on for the benefit of the outside world. The stakes were high for the accused (their lives) as well as for the Soviet. Weissberg's narrative also illustrated how uninitiated interactants must be

coached into their roles and how they must be cued into the existence of the pretense context where they do not recognize it. See Alexander Weissberg, *The Accused* (New York: Simon and Schuster, 1951).

4. A close reading of John Gunther's poignant account of his young son's last months shows that the boy maintained a sustained and delicately balanced mutual pretense with his parents, physicians and nurses. John Gunther, *Death Be Not Proud* (New York: Harper and Bros., 1949). Also see Bensman and Gerver, *op. cit.*

APPENDIX

If dramaturgical social psychology can be said to have a founding father, it is Kenneth Burke. However, Burke was a literary critic and his concerns are not centrally social psychological, nor is his writing style of the linear, sequential type usually encountered in the social sciences. Consequently, his writings are often unintelligible to many social psychologists. It should be borne in mind that in the following selections Burke is simply explaining his own dramatistic method of literary criticism. He is not attempting to formulate a social psychology in the conventional manner.

In the opening selection, Burke insists that a dramatistic understanding of human conduct should (1) entail a persistent orientation to action or behavior and (2) stress the symbol-using nature of human beings. In other words, humans are construed as active creatures, as doers, who characteristically manipulate symbols in the course of their behavior. Any useful understanding of people must be consistent with this nature.

Burke goes on to indicate the role symbols play in the construction of social worlds. The characteristic nature of a human being as a symbol-using creature transcends a generic nature as a biological organism and in the process gives rise to such artifacts as property rights and obligations. Large-scale social concerns, such as classes, order, and authority, are viewed as outcomes of symbolic manipulation by human beings. The social order is said to be permeated by mystery, a condition that, while promoting a kind of social cohesion, often places the very existence of that cohesion in jeopardy.

The second selection by Burke more explicitly enunciates the method of dramatism. The basic theme is human motivation. In keeping with his emphasis on symbolic action, Burke views motives not as biological, psychological, or social forces, but rather as the basic forms of thought by which human beings experience their world. It is here that Burke articulates what he considers to be the five key terms of dramatism: agent, act, scene, agency, and purpose.[1] He then places the whole question of human motivation into three broad categories: the *Grammar of Motives*, which has to do with the types of motivational terms themselves; the *Symbolic of Motives*, which principally concerns the modes of expression in the fine arts; and the *Rhetoric of Motives*, which involves the basic strategies that individuals employ in their manipulation of one another.[2]

The selection also includes Burke's unique thinking on the prevalence and importance of ambiguity in the social world. Rather than have human understanding "dispose of" or resolve this ambiguity, Burke points to the necessity of confronting and clarifying its resources.

1. In the transformation of dramatism into dramaturgical social psychology, Burke's ideas regarding "the forms of thought which one understands behavior" have been applied directly to behavior itself. In this sense, Burke's work can be seen as an analysis of the forms of human understanding. When his analysis was given behavioral substance, it emerged in social psychology as an analysis of the forms of human behavior. In this emergence, a sixth element (the audience) was added and, in fact, became the key term.

2. It is the Rhetoric of Motives that has been most emphasized in social psychology. In fact, the Symbolic has been neglected almost totally, and the Grammar only recently is being explored, primarily in the work of ethnomethodologists.

29. ON HUMAN BEHAVIOR CONSIDERED "DRAMATISTICALLY"

KENNETH BURKE

Reprinted from Kenneth Burke, *Permanence and Change* (Chicago: the Bobbs Merrill Co., 1965) pp. 274-278, by permission of Bobbs Merrill Co. and the author.

Human conduct, being in the realm of action and end (as contrasted with the physicist's realm of motion and position) is most directly discussible in dramatistic terms. By "dramatistic" terms are meant those that begin in theories of *action* rather than in theories of *knowledge*. Terminologies grounded in the observing of sensory perception would be classed as theories of Knowledge.[1] In the same classification would fall all theories of *conditioning* (which is the lowest form of learning). We do not mean to imply that "scientist" approaches (in terms of knowledge or learning), do not yield good results. On the contrary, such perspectives can contribute many important *modifiers* to the *essential nouns* of human relationship. Also, it often happens that "scientist" perspectives end by adding coordinates which while not strictly deducible from the basic experiment upon which they are presumably based, do contrive, by a kind of "leap," or *non-sequitur*, to use an experiment of narrower circumference as specious justification for an interpretation of wider circumference.

Man being specifically a symbol-using animal, we take it that a terminology for the discussion of his social behavior must stress symbolism as a motive, if maximum scope and relevancy is required of the terminology.

However, man being generically a biological organism, the ideal terminology must present his symbolic behavior as grounded in biological conditions. (This statement is *not* the same as saying that symbolism is *reducible* to biology. *On the contrary.*)

In this purely biological sense, property is a necessity. (The science of "ecology" has to do with the kinds of balance that prevail among biological organisms, considered as members of a sub-verbal, extra-verbal, or non-verbal community. The members of such a community are so interrelated that assimilation, or appropriation, is mutual, as with animals that fertilize the vegetation they feed on.)

Though man as a biological organism requires property in the sheerly biological sense, by reason of his nature as a characteristically symbol-using species he can conceptualize a symbolic analogue. We have particularly in mind his terms for "rights" and "obligations." Biologically, the rudimentary properties of living, such as food and shelter, are not "rights," but "necessities." *Symbolically,* there can be property to which one has, or claims, a "right," though the possessing of it may not be biologically necessary.

The notion of "rights" in nature is a quasi-naturalistic, metaphysical subterfuge for sanctioning in apparently biological terms a state of affairs that is properly discussed in terms specifically suited to the treatment of symbolism as motive. Jeremy Bentham's juristic critique of language was particularly sharp in helping us to realize that "rights" are not in "nature"; rather, like "obligations," they are a result of man-made laws, which depend upon the resources of language for their form.

The function of words is obvious, in the inventing, perfecting, and handing-on of instruments and methods. (Think of a factory or a laboratory planned and managed without the guidance of terms!) But the full rôle of symbols in shaping men's views of such property, or "capital," is not obvious. For once the division of labor and the handing-down of property (with its attendant "rights" and "obligations") have given rise to classes, there must be some "order" among these classes.[2]

Such "order" is not just "regularity." It also involves a distribution of *authority*. And such mutuality of rule and service, with its uncertain dividing-line between loyalty and servitude, takes roughly a pyramidal or hierarchal form (or, at least, it is like a ladder with "up" and "down").

Thus the purely *operational* motives binding a society become inspirited by a corresponding condition of *Mystery*. (Owing to their different modes of living and livelihood, classes of people become "mysteries" to one another.) This condition of Mystery is revealed most perfectly in primitive priestcraft, which serves in part to promote cohesion among disparate classes, and in part to perpetuate ways that, while favoring some at the expense of others, may at times thereby endanger the prosperity of the tribe as a whole.

But in a society so complicated as ours, the normal priestly function, of partly upholding and partly transcending the Mysteries of class, is distributed among many kinds of symbol-users (particularly educators, legislators, journalists, advertising men, and artists).

The priestly stress upon Mystery (which attains its grandest expression in the vision of a celestial hierarchy loosely imagined after the analogy of a human social order) becomes secularized and distributed among these rôles, each of which treats the social Mystery after its fashion. Thus, the educator has his testimonials of academic rank; the legislator has ways of identifying respect for himself with respect for the august body of which he is a member; the artist helps surround a system of social values with "glamor," as he finds tricks that transform the austere religious passion into a corresponding romantic, erotic passion; journalists and advertising men make a good team, since the one group keeps us abreast of the world's miseries, and the other keeps us agog with promises of extreme comfort, the two combining to provide a crude, secular analogue of the distinction between Christus Crucifixus and Christus Triumphans.

In part, the new modes of Mystery are needed because the many new instruments have given the world a strongly secular cast. In part they are needed because the traditionalists of religion come in time to rely upon images surviving from an earlier social order. And while these have their appeal precisely by reason of their remoteness, they must be supplemented by images more in tune with the times.

Though we would stress the element of Mystery arising from the social hierarchy, we must recognize that there are other mysteries, other orders. There are the mysteries of dream, of creation, of death, of life's stages, of thought (its arising, its remembering, its diseases). There are the mysteries of adventure and love. (As property is part natural, part doctrinal, so love is part natural, part courtesy.) We mention such other sources of mystery to guard against the assumption that we are reducing mystery in general to the social mystery in particular. On the contrary, we are saying: The social mystery gains in depth, persuasiveness, allusiveness and illusiveness precisely by reason of the fact that it becomes inextricably interwoven with mysteries of these other sorts, quite as these other mysteries must in part be perceived through the fog of the social mystery.[3]

NOTES

1. [We might now describe *P & C* dialectics-wise as an individual's approach to motives in terms of the collectivity. Asking what new but related item we might append to the present edition by way of indicating later developments in this same direction, we append the somewhat reworked version of a paper that was originally presented in a symposium on "Organizational Behavior," held at Princeton University in 1951, under the auspices of the Ford Foundation. The conference concerned the problem of ideal "models" that might guide the social scientist in his attempts to discuss human conduct, as it is affected by specific organizations.

Several of the papers approached the problem in mathematical or technological ways (as with the theory of "stochastic processes," or with the "Cybernetics" approach to such problems). But the present paper was among those that favored the retaining of an ethical or psychological terminology. It is based on the assumption that, human behavior being in the realm of morals, the kind of certainty best obtainable here is "moral certainty." Abandoning hopes of "scientific prediction," it believes rather in the "scientifically documented admonition." That is, it looks upon historiography purely as a kind of parable or Æsop's fable, as a mere *warning* backed by data, as a reminder that "We should take such-and-such into account, or else. . ."

However, in contrast with a sheerly pluralistic emphasis that might look upon each situation as unique, the attempt here is to consider what should be the over-all terms for naming relationships and developments that, *mulatis mutandis,* are likely to figure in all human association. To this end, the stress is placed upon the motives of Guilt, Redemption, Hierarchy, and Victimage that supplement and modify men's purely natural or biological inclinations. Such social, linguistically grounded motives can be said to "perfect" nature, in a purely *technical* sense.]

2. Though other animals may manifest the rudiments of language or of tool-using, man's distinctive genius is in his capacity for doing things at one remove, as when he uses words about words and makes tools for making tools.

3. The attempt to treat *social* "rights" as though they were "natural rights" would be a case in point. The social rights were first *ascribed* to nature, and then "derived" from it. Such a mode of sanction could seem persuasive only because "nature" itself was being perceived through a terministic fog that took form by analogy with sociopolitical principles then current.

30. THE FIVE KEY TERMS OF DRAMATISM

KENNETH BURKE

Reprinted from Kenneth Burke, *A Grammar of Motives and A Rhetoric of Motives* (New York: The World Publishing Co., 1962) pp. XVII-XXV, by permission of World Publishing Co. and the author.

What is involved, when we say what people are doing and why they are doing it? An answer to that question is . . . concerned with the basic forms of thought which, in accordance with the nature of the world as all men necessarily experience it, are exemplified in the attributing of motives. . . . These forms of thought can be embodied profoundly or trivially, truthfully or falsely. They are equally present in systematically elaborated metaphysical structures, in legal judgments, in poetry and fiction, in political and scientific works, in news and in bits of gossip offered at random.

We shall use five terms as generating principle (sic) of our investigation. They are: Act, Scene, Agent, Agency, Purpose. In a rounded statement about motives, you must have some word that names the *act* (names what took place, in thought or deed), and another that names the *scene* (the background of the act, the situation in which it occurred); also, you must indicate what person or kind of person (*agent*) performed the act, what means or instruments he used (*agency*) and the purpose. Men may violently disagree about the purposes behind a given act, or about the character of the person who did it, or how he did it, or in what kind of situation he acted; or they may even insist upon totally different words to name the act itself. But be that as it may, any complete statement about motives will offer *some kind* of answers to these five questions: what was done (act), when or where it was done (scene), who did it (agent), how he did it (agency), and why (purpose).

Act, Scene, Agent, Agency, Purpose. Although, over the centuries, men have shown great enterprise and inventiveness in pondering matters of human motivation, one can simplify the subject by this pentad of key terms, which are understandable almost at a glance. They need never to be abandoned, since all statements that assign motives can be shown to arise out of them and to terminate in them. By examining them quizzically, we can range far; yet the terms are always there for us to reclaim, in their everyday simplicity, their almost miraculous easiness, thus enabling us constantly to begin afresh. When they might become difficult, when we can hardly see them, through having stared at them too intensely, we can of a sudden relax, to look at them as we always have, lightly, glancingly. And having reassured ourselves, we can start out again, once more daring to let them look strange and difficult for a time.

In an exhibit of photographic murals (*Road to Victory*) at the Museum of Modern Art, there was an aerial photograph of two launches, proceeding side by side on a tranquil sea. Their wakes crossed and recrossed each other in almost an infinity of lines. Yet despite the intricateness of this tracery, the picture gave an impression of great simplicity, because one could quickly perceive the generating principle of its design. Such, ideally, is the case with our pentad of terms, used as generating principle. It should provide us with a kind of simplicity that can be developed into considerable complexity, and yet can be discovered beneath its elaborations.

We want to inquire into the purely internal relationships which the five terms bear to one another, considering their possibilities of transformation, their range of permutations and combinations—and then to see how these various resources figure in actual statements about human motives. Strictly speaking, we mean by a Grammar of motives a concern with the terms alone, without reference to the ways in which their potentialities have been or can be utilized in actual statements about motives. Speaking broadly we could designate as "philosophies" any statements in which these grammatical resources are specifically utilized. Random or unsystematic statements about motives could be considered as fragments of a philosophy.

One could think of the Grammatical resources as *principles*, and of the various philosophies as *casuistries* which apply these principles to temporal situations. For instance, we may examine the term Scene simply as a blanket term for the concept of background or setting *in general*, a name for *any* situation in which acts or agents are placed. In our usage, this concern would be "grammatical." And we move into matters of "philosophy" when we note that one thinker uses "God" as his term for the ultimate ground or scene of human action, another uses "nature," a third uses "environment," or "history," or "means of production," etc. And whereas a statement about the grammatical principles of motivation might lay claim to a universal validity, or complete certainty, the choice of any

one philosophic idiom embodying these principles is much more open to question. Even before we know what act is to be discussed, we can say with confidence that a rounded discussion of its motives must contain a reference to *some kind of* background. But since each philosophic idiom will characterize this background differently, there will remain the question as to which characterization is "right" or "more nearly right."

It is even likely that, whereas one philosophic idiom offers the best calculus for one case, another case answers best to a totally different calculus. However, we should not think of "cases" in too restricted a sense. Although, from the standpoint of the grammatical principles inherent in the internal relationships prevailing among our five terms, any given philosophy is to be considered as a casuistry, even a cultural situation extending over centuries is a "case," and would probably require a much different philosophic idiom as its temporizing calculus of motives than would be required in the case of other cultural situations.

In our original plans for this project, we had no notion of writing a "Grammar" at all. We began with a theory of comedy, applied to a treatise on human relations. Feeling that competitive ambition is a drastically over-developed motive in the modern world, we thought this motive might be transcended if men devoted themselves not so much to "excoriating" it as to "appreciating" it. Accordingly, we began taking notes on the foibles and antics of what we tended to think of as "the Human Barnyard."

We sought to formulate the basic stratagems which people employ, in endless variations, and consciously or unconsciously, for the outwitting or cajoling of one another. Since all these devices had a "you and me" quality about them, being "addressed" to some person or to some advantage, we classed them broadly under the heading of a Rhetoric. There were other notes, concerned with modes of expression and appeal in the fine arts, and with purely psychological or psychoanalytic matters. These we classed under the heading of Symbolic.

We had made still further observations, which we at first strove uneasily to class under one or the other of these two heads, but which we were eventually able to distinguish as the makings of a Grammar. For we found in the course of writing that our project needed a grounding in formal considerations logically prior to both the rhetorical and the psychological. And as we proceeded with this introductory groundwork, it kept extending its claims until it had spun itself from an intended few hundred words into nearly 200,000, of which the present book is revision and abridgement.

Theological, metaphysical, and juridical doctrines offer the best illustration of the concerns we place under the heading of Grammar; the forms and methods of art best illustrate the concerns of Symbolic; and the ideal material to reveal the nature of Rhetoric comprises observations on parliamentary and diplomatic devices, editorial bias, sales methods and incidents of social sparring. However, the three fields overlap considerably. And we shall note, in passing, how the Rhetoric and the Symbolic hover about the edges of our central theme, the Grammar.

A perfectionist might seek to evolve terms free of ambiguity and inconsistency (as with the terministic ideals of symbolic logic and logical positivism). But we have a different purpose in view, one that probably retains traces of its "comic" origin. We take it for

granted that, insofar as men cannot themselves create the universe, there must remain something essentially enigmatic about the problem of motives, and that this underlying enigma will manifest itself in inevitable ambiguities and inconsistencies among the terms for motives. Accordingly, what we want is *not terms that avoid ambiguity, but terms that clearly reveal the strategic spots at which ambiguities necessarily arise.*

Occasionally, you will encounter a writer who seems to get great exaltation out of proving, with an air of much relentlessness, that some philosophic term or other has been used to cover a variety of meanings, and who would smash and abolish this idol. As a general rule, when a term is singled out for such harsh treatment, if you look closer you will find that it happens to be associated with some cultural or political trend from which the writer would dissociate himself; hence there is a certain notable ambiguity in this very charge of ambiguity, since he presumably feels purged and strengthened by bringing to bear upon this particular term a kind of attack that could, with as much justice, be brought to bear upon any other term (or "title") in philosophy, including of course the alternative term, or "title," that the writer would swear by. Since no two things or acts or situations are exactly alike, you cannot apply the same term to both of them without thereby introducing a certain margin of ambiguity, an ambiguity as great as the difference between the two subjects that are given the identical title. And all the more may you expect to find ambiguity in terms so "titular" as to become the marks of a philosophic school, or even several philosophic schools. Hence, instead of considering it our task to "dispose of" any ambiguity by merely disclosing the fact that it is an ambiguity, we rather consider it our task to study and clarify the *resources of ambiguity*. For in the course of this work, we shall deal with many kinds of *transformation*—and it is in the areas of ambiguity that transformations take place; in fact, without such areas, transformation would be impossible. Distinctions, we might say, arise out of a great central moltenness, where all is merged. They have been thrown from a liquid center to the surface, where they have congealed. Let one of these crusted distinctions return to its source, and in this alchemic center it may be remade, again becoming molten liquid, and may enter into new combinations, whereat it may be again thrown forth as a new crust, a different distinction. So that A may become non-A. But not merely by a leap from one state to the other. Rather, we must take A back into the ground of its existence, the logical substance that is its causal ancestor, and on to a point where it is consubstantial with non-A; then we may return, this time emerging with non-A instead.

And so with our five terms: certain formal interrelationships prevail among these terms, by reason of their role as attributes of a common ground or substance. Their participation in a common ground makes for transformability. At every point where the field covered by any one of these terms overlaps upon the field covered by any other, there is an alchemic opportunity, whereby we can put one philosophy or doctrine of motivation into the alembic, make the appropriate passes, and take out another. From the central moltenness, where all the elements are fused into one togetherness, there are thrown forth, in separate crusts, such distinctions as those between freedom and necessity, activity and passiveness, coöperation and competition, cause and effect, mechanism and teleology.

Our term, "Agent," for instance, is a general heading that might, in a given case, require further subdivision, as an agent might have his act modified (hence partly motivated) by friends (co-agents) or enemies (counter-agents). Again, under "Agent" one could place any personal properties that are assigned a motivational value, such as "ideas," "the will," "fear," "malice," "intuition," "the creative imagination." A portrait painter may treat the body as a property of the agent (an expression of personality), whereas materialistic medicine would treat it as "scenic," a purely "objective material"; and from another point of view it could be classed as an agency, a means by which one gets reports of the world at large. Machines are obviously instruments (that is, Agencies); yet in their vast accumulation they constitute the industrial scene, with its own peculiar set of motivational properties. War may be treated as an Agency, insofar as it is a means to an end; as a collective Act, subdivisible into many individual acts; as a Purpose, in schemes proclaiming a cult of war. For the man inducted into the army, war is a Scene, a situation that motivates the nature of his training; and in mythologies war is an Agent, or perhaps better a super-agent, in the figure of the war god. We may think of voting as an act, and of the voter as an agent; yet votes and voters both are hardly other than a politician's medium or agency; or from another point of view, they are a part of his scene. And insofar as a vote is cast without adequate knowledge of its consequences, one might even question whether it should be classed as an activity at all; one might rather call it passive, or perhaps sheer motion (what the behaviorists would call a Response to a Stimulus).

Or imagine that one were to manipulate the terms, for the imputing of motives, in such a case as this: The hero (agent) with the help of a friend (co-agent) outwits the villain (counter-agent) by using a file (agency) that enables him to break his bonds (act) in order to escape (purpose) from the room where he has been confined (scene). In selecting a casuistry here, we might locate the motive in the agent, as were we to credit his escape to some trait integral to his personality, such as "love of freedom." Or we might stress the motivational force of the scene, since nothing is surer to awaken thoughts of escape in a man than a condition of imprisonment. Or we might note the essential part played by the co-agent, in assisting our hero to escape—and, with such thoughts as our point of departure, we might conclude that the motivations of this act should be reduced to social origins.

Or if one were given to the brand of speculative enterprise exemplified by certain Christian heretics (for instance, those who worshipped Judas as a saint, on the grounds that his betrayal of Christ, in leading to the Crucifixion, so brought about the opportunity for mankind's redemption) one might locate the necessary motivational origin of the act in the counter-agent. For the. hero would not have been prodded to escape if there had been no villain to imprison him. Inasmuch as the escape could be called a "good" act, we might find in such motivational reduction to the counter-agent a compensatory transformation whereby a bitter fountain may give forth sweet waters. . . .

Pragmatists would probably have referred the motivation back to a source in agency. They would have noted that our hero escaped by using an instrument, the file by which he severed his bonds; then in this same line of thought, they would have observed that the hand holding the file was also an instrument; and by the same token the brain that guided the hand would

be an instrument, and so likewise the educational system that taught the methods and shaped the values involved in the incident.

True, if you reduce the terms to any one of them, you will find them branching out again; for no one of them is enough. Thus, Mead called his pragmatism a philosophy of the act. And though Dewey stresses the value of "intelligence" as an instrument (agency, embodied in "scientific method"), the other key terms in his casuistry, "experience" and "nature," would be the equivalents of act and scene respectively. We must add, however, that Dewey is given to stressing the overlap of these two terms, rather than the respects in which they are distinct, as he proposes to "replace the traditional separation of nature and experience with the idea of continuity." (The quotation is from Intelligence and the Modern World.)

As we shall see later, it is by reason of the pliancy among our terms that philosophic systems can pull one way and another. The margins of overlap provide opportunities whereby a thinker can go without a leap from any one of the terms to any of its fellows. (We have also likened the terms to the fingers, which in their extremities are distinct from one another, but merge in the palm of the hand. If you would go from one finger to another without a leap, you need but trace the tendon down into the palm of the hand, and then trace a new course along another tendon.) Hence, no great dialectical enterprise is necessary if you would merge the terms, reducing them even to as few as one; and then, treating this as the "essential" term, the "causal ancestor" of the lot, you can proceed in the reverse direction across the margins of overlap, "deducing" the other terms from it as its logical descendants.

This is the method, explicitly and in

the grand style, of metaphysics which brings its doctrines to a head in some over-all title, a word for being in general, or action in general, or motion in general, or development in general, or experience in general, etc., with all its other terms distributed about this titular term in positions leading up to it and away from it. There is also an implicit kind of metaphysics, that often goes by the name of No Metaphysics, and aims at reduction not to an over-all title but to some presumably underlying atomic constituent. Its vulgar variant is to be found in techniques of "unmasking," which would make for progress and emancipation by applying materialistic terms to immaterial subjects (the pattern here being, "X is nothing but Y," where X designates a higher value and Y a lower one, the higher value being thereby reduced to the lower one).

The titular word for our own method is "dramatism," since it invites one to consider the matter of motives in a perspective that, being developed from the analysis of drama, treats language and thought primarily as modes of action. The method is synoptic, though not in the historical sense. A purely historical survey would require no less than a universal history of human culture; for every judgment, exhortation, or admonition, every view of natural or supernatural reality, every intention or expectation involves assumptions about motive, or cause. Our work must be synoptic in a different sense: in the sense that it offers a system of placement, and should enable us, by the systematic manipulation of the terms, to "generate," or "anticipate" the various classes of motivational theory. And a treatment in these terms, we hope to show, reduces the subject synoptically while still permitting us to appreciate its scope and complexity.

NAME INDEX

SUBJECT INDEX

Accounts, 153, 171-187
  and background expectations, 177-180, 190
  and linguistic styles, 171, 180-182
  excuses, 172-177
  justifications, 172-177
  negotiating, 183-186
  strategies for avoiding, 182-183
  types of, 172-177
Act, 24, 366
Action
  human, 27, 201
  instrumental, 243, 245, 250
  meaningful, 62, 64
  political, 204, 243
  symbolic, 243, 245, 249, 366, 367
Activity
  as system, 129
  situational, 5
Actor, 2, 28, 32, 33, 40, 64, 97, 111, 164, 276, 277-278, 280, 281-282, 283
Agency, 24, 26, 366, 370-375
Agenda
  hidden, 213
Agent, 24, 366, 370-375
Alternation, 14, 91-100, 103
Ambiguity, 1, 48, 107, 278, 280, 353, 366, 372
Anomie, 74, 219, 237, 238, 242
Appraisals
  reflected, 81
Appearance, 5, 80, 178, 207, 329
  and meaning, 78-80

  and performance, 35, 38, 39
  and self, 57, 78-88
"Apostolic" function, 207
Appreciation, 84
Attachment, 179
Attitude, 28, 57, 89, 116
  as activation of identity, 86
  as incipient action, 59, 86
  anticipation of, 81
Audience, 34, 35, 40, 76, 133, 134, 152, 184, 361
Authenticity
  and inauthenticity, 19-20, 21, 51, 53
Autonomy, 222
Awareness
  closed contexts, 314-315
  open contexts, 314-315
  shared, 213, 215, 216, 315
  suspicion contexts, 315

Bad Faith, 18, 19
Behavior
  meaningful, 2, 78-80
  non-verbal, 5, 186
  verbal, 5, 186
Biologese, 23

Career, 327
Causality, 4, 43, 44, 201
  and motivation, 157-159
  linguistic, 58
  symbolic, 294
Chaos, 239, 240

383